The Palgrave Handbook of Interactive Marketing

Cheng Lu Wang
Editor

The Palgrave Handbook of Interactive Marketing

Volume 1

palgrave
macmillan

Editor
Cheng Lu Wang
University of New Haven
West Haven, CT, USA

ISBN 978-3-031-14960-3   ISBN 978-3-031-14961-0 (eBook)
https://doi.org/10.1007/978-3-031-14961-0

© The Editor(s) (if applicable) and The Author(s), under exclusive license to Springer Nature Switzerland AG 2023, corrected publication 2023, 2024
Chapter 41 is licensed under the terms of the Creative Commons Attribution 4.0 International License (http://creativecommons.org/licenses/by/4.0/). For further details see license information in the chapter.
This work is subject to copyright. All rights are solely and exclusively licensed by the Publisher, whether the whole or part of the material is concerned, specifically the rights of translation, reprinting, reuse of illustrations, recitation, broadcasting, reproduction on microfilms or in any other physical way, and transmission or information storage and retrieval, electronic adaptation, computer software, or by similar or dissimilar methodology now known or hereafter developed.
The use of general descriptive names, registered names, trademarks, service marks, etc. in this publication does not imply, even in the absence of a specific statement, that such names are exempt from the relevant protective laws and regulations and therefore free for general use.
The publisher, the authors, and the editors are safe to assume that the advice and information in this book are believed to be true and accurate at the date of publication. Neither the publisher nor the authors or the editors give a warranty, expressed or implied, with respect to the material contained herein or for any errors or omissions that may have been made. The publisher remains neutral with regard to jurisdictional claims in published maps and institutional affiliations.

Cover credit: © oxygen/Getty images

This Palgrave Macmillan imprint is published by the registered company Springer Nature Switzerland AG
The registered company address is: Gewerbestrasse 11, 6330 Cham, Switzerland

Foreword

I do not like to use Latin words, preferring to write with shorter, blunter English words whose roots are in Anglo-Saxon or Norse. So it is odd that we chose the word "interactive" over 30 years ago to sum up a claim about the future of marketing, that the back-and-forth between marketers and consumers would define a coming "age of addressability."[1] And there was a price to pay for the choice. It gave us an excuse not to think too graphically about the many ways that the consumer side of market transactions would talk back to the concentrated power of marketers. I would like in this foreword to make amends.

But before the atonement, let us acknowledge that this clumsy word, a melding of Latin's "inter" and "activus," has lasted remarkably well. In fact, it is fair to describe it, as Charles Wang does, as still defining one of marketing's fastest growing academic fields. It has led Professor Wang to invite me to write a foreword to this book. The breadth of this book's contents amply justifies the claim that the interactivity theme in marketing is still growing, and indeed at an accelerating pace. Interactivity is at the core of many frontier market-making issues, the internet of things, the metaverse, platform business models, and live streaming, to name just four of the book's feast of themes.

So in trying to redress the abstractness of the interaction label, I shall respond to Professor Wang's kind invitation not with more abstract theorizing on the frontier issues of interactivity in marketing, but instead by pointing to some concrete interaction phenomena, believing as I do that theorizing should proceed from phenomena (imperfectly understood and slightly puzzling patterns of fact in the world) to theory.

Consider the phenomenon of the Johnny Depp versus Amber Heard libel trial. It gave us just such a pattern of fact to puzzle over when legacy media's coverage of the trial was beaten by the coverage of "influencers." The trial was

---

[1] Blattberg, Robert C. and John Deighton (1991), "Interactive Marketing: Exploiting the Age of Addressability," *Sloan Management Review*, 33 (Fall), 5–14.

live streamed on cable networks, which should have given them an unbeatable market share advantage. The cable format of live sessions and breakaways to commentaries had dominated the marketing of media products such as the OJ Simpson and Kyle Rittenhouse trials. Refined over decades of broadcasting, it should have been the way to do trial-as-media-product. And yet it was not. A relatively new form of packaging, commentary by specialist influencers, won out. Emily D. Baker, a former Los Angeles County deputy district attorney who started her online career by unboxing an iPhone, led the assault with 500,000 weekly views. Her podcast, "The Emily Show," rose to first place on Apple Podcasts for US entertainment news during the trial, but she was just one of several direct-to-consumer law pundits who covered the trial. What advantages did these solo media stars have over legacy media? Beyond their legal credentials, they were interactive. To simple chat they could add, for a fee, Super Chat, a feature offered by the YouTube Partner program. It let viewers win immediate prominence for their questions. They could also add, for another fee, Super Stickers to decorate their chat stream entries. The money to be made by selling these premium chat features was nothing compared to ad revenue (Emily Baker reportedly made $109,000 monthly during the Depp/Heard trial) but the chance to interact helped build the audience that advertisers bought. A Los Angeles Times reporter said that at one moment in the proceedings Baker had about 128,000 live viewers, compared to 72,000 for LiveNOW, the Fox cable channel's streaming service and 86,000 for the cable channel ET.[2]

Twitch is a closely related case in point. Is the bond among esports stars, commentators, and followers more intense than the bonds found in legacy media because the chat stream, the real-time responses to the show, became part of the show?

Physical store retailing is interactive, in a limited sense because stores offer goods, shoppers respond, and stores respond to the responses. But it fails a basic test of interactivity over time in that the shopper is anonymous until after the transaction is over, and not even then if they pay with cash. Shopkick and Ibotta are platforms that let store retailing become as interactive as online retailing. Their apps run on the phones carried by shoppers, and let brands and retailers manage two-way conversations with identified shoppers. The merchants give points, known as kicks, for walking into stores, inspecting products on shelves, and making purchases. Shoppers react by doing what the apps suggest. The puzzle to be solved is that this kind of offline interaction has been slower to be accepted than online. Compared to passive loyalty programs, shoppers are reluctant to take part in the active interaction required to make the Shopkick and Ibotta apps partners in conversation.

---

[2] Sakoui, Anousha. (2022). "The Amber Heard-Johnny Depp trial has turned this ex-L.A. prosecutor into a YouTube star", Los Angeles Times, May 26, 2022. https://www.latimes.com/entertainment-arts/business/story/2022-05-26/johnny-depp-amber-heard-trial-youtube-emily-baker.

Shein, the leading fast fashion brand in the USA, takes interaction in a new direction. Shein operates as a front end to about 6000 Chinese clothing factories, promoting their goods to customers in the USA on Tik Tok, Instagram, and email. Where is the interaction? It is in a three-way conversation between the brand, consumers, and the factories. Shein scours the internet for clothing ideas, often finding them in the ideas of fashion influencers. It invites factories to supply small quantities based on these ideas, and if an idea is a success, invites factories to fill larger orders. Where Zara might ask factories to fill minimum orders of 2000 items in 30 days, Shein's first ask may be for 100 products in 10 days. The conversation is conducted not in the medium of language, but in orders, deliveries, and sales.

Like Shein, Tik Tok itself is interactive in behavior, not messaging. The platform offers a short video to an anonymous viewer. Depending on reaction, the next video will be similar or different. After several rounds of this interaction, Tik Tok's algorithm will have begun to converge on the taste profile of the viewer with more precision than many algorithms can do by using personal data to profile the consumer. Of course, Tik Tok viewers may share a persistent identifier such as an email address with Tik Tok, so that new visits can start with a known profile, but viewers who prefer to be anonymous are at very little disadvantage.

I promised no theory, but I cannot resist drawing an inductive generalization from these concrete cases. It amounts to a definition of interactivity. An action and a reaction fall short of being an interaction. To be interactive, three steps are needed. First there is an action, typically by the marketer on the consumer. It can be a message or a non-verbal provocation like a coupon or in Shein's case an invitation to do business. Second there is a reaction. The second actor, typically the consumer, responds, or fails to respond. Third, the first actor acts again, in a way that takes account of the second actor's response or lack of response. Round three of an interaction is not just a repetition of round one. The first actor learns. Persistent identity is vital to interactivity unless, as in Tik Tok, the second actor stays in the relationship. Those cases aside, a vital characteristic of the topic of this book is the ability of the parties to recognize each other on subsequent encounters.

Boston, USA   John A. Deighton

John A. Deighton is the Harold M. Brierley Professor of Business Administration Emeritus at Harvard Business School. He specializes in data-driven marketing. His recent published research includes "The Economic Impact of the Market-Making Internet," IAB, 2021 "The Socioeconomic Impact of Internet Tracking," IAB, 2020, and "Learning to Become a Taste Expert" (with Katherine LaTour), *Journal of Consumer Research*, 2019. His Twitter feed is @HBSmktg.

He is a past editor of the *Journal of Consumer Research* and the *Journal of Interactive Marketing*, was Executive Director of the Marketing Science Institute, and was a Director of the Berkman-Klein Center for Internet and Society at Harvard University.

The original version of the front matter was revised: List of contributors were updated. The correction to this chapter is available at https://doi.org/10.1007/978-3-031-14961-0_43

Acknowledgements

I would like to extend my sincere gratitude to all authors who contribute to this handbook meanwhile taking the role as peer reviewers for other chapters. Their collective efforts and commitments make this book possible. I also appreciate the assistance from Miss Jia Qi Cao, a graduate student from Asia-Europe Business School at East China Normal University, who provided tremendous help to communicate with authors and reviewers and to check the format of each chapter.

My special thanks also go to additional reviewers who provide peer review service to at least one chapter. Their valuable comments and constructive suggestions to chapter authors significantly enhance the quality of each chapter during the iterative revision process. The names of reviewers below are listed alphabetically.

Dr. Victor A. Barger, University of Wisconsin-Whitewater, USA
Dr. Ana Margarida Barreto, Universidade NOVA de Lisboa—ICNOVA, Portugal
Dr. Nicky Chang Bi, University of Nebraska at Omaha, USA
Dr. Ricardo Godinho Bilro, ISCTE—Lisbon University Institute, Portugal
Dr. Andrew J. Dahl, University of Wisconsin-Whitewater, USA
Dr. Thi Cam Tu Dinh, Yeungnam University, South Korea
Dr. Antonia Estrella-Ramón, University of Almería, Spain
Dr. Yang Feng, San Diego State University, USA
Dr. Youjiang Gao, Zhejiang University of Finance & Economics, China
Professor Sumeet Gupta, Indian Institute of Management Raipur, India
Dr. Nieves García de Frutos, University of Almería, Spain
Professor Sejin Ha, University of Tennessee, USA
Dr. Muhammad Iskandar Hamzah, Universiti Teknologi MARA, Malaysia
Dr. Tyler Hancock, University of Toledo, USA
Professor Ai-Zhong He, Hunan University, China

Mr. Daniel Alejandro Mora Hernandez, Johannes Kepler University Linz, Austria
Associate professor Hei-Fong Ho, Chang Jung Christian University, Taiwan
Professor Jacob Hornik, Tel Aviv University, Israel
Dr. Sara H. Hsieh, Tunghai University, Taiwan
Dr. Peng Hu, Anhui Agricultural University, China
Professor Minxue Huang, Wuhan University, China
Ms. Xiao Huang, Auburn University, USA
Dr. Fahad Ibrahim, Swansea University, UK
Dr. Krishnan Jeesha, Indian Institute of Management Lucknow, India
Dr. Chunli Ji, Macao Polytechnic University, China
Dr. Ying Jiang, Ontario Tech University, Canada
Dr. Eunsin Joo, Waseda University, Japan
Dr. Do Yuon Kim, Auburn University, USA
Dr. Jung-Hwan Kim, University of South Carolina, USA
Assist. Prof. Dr. Ines Kožuh, University of Maribor, Slovenia
Dr. Soyeon Kwon, Korea University, South Korea
Dr. Yoonjae Lee, Yeungnam University, South Korea
Dr. Crystal T. Lee, Shantou University, China
Professor Gang Li, North China University of Water Resources and Electric Power, China
Associate Professor Junyun Liao, Jinan University, China
Professor Weng Marc Lim, Swinburne University of Technology, Australia and Malaysia
Professor Wumei Liu, Lanzhou University, China
Associate Professor Laura Lucia-Palacios, University of Zaragoza, Spain
Dr. Rania B. Mostafa, Al Ain University, UAE
Dr. Kaustav Mukherjee, Coal India Limited, India
Mr. Jani Pavlič, University of Maribor, Slovenia
Dr. Elizabeth Manser Payne, University of South Dakota, USA
Professor Keyoor Purani, Indian Institute of Management Kozhikode, India
Dr. Tareq Rasul, Australian Institute of Business (AIB), Australia
Mr. Mohsin Abdur Rehman, University of Oulu, Finland
Professor Jin Sun, University of International Business and Economics, China
Dr. Kemal Cem Söylemez, Market Development Specialist in Yarin DNS, Turkey
Dr. Patricia R. Todd, Western Kentucky University, USA
Dr. Tina Tomažič, University of Maribor, Slovenia
Dr. Ahmet Tuğrul Tuğer, Piri Reis University, Turkey
Dr. Kiseol Yang, University of North Texas, USA
Dr. Hye Jin Yoon, University of Georgia, USA
Dr. Ruonan Zhang, Auburn University at Montgomery, USA

Mr. Robert Zimmermann, University of Applied Sciences Upper Austria, Austria

Cheng Lu Wang, Ph.D., Editor

CONTENTS

Foreword   v
John A. Deighton

1   Interactive Marketing is the New Normal   1
     Cheng Lu Wang

Part I   Advancement of Interactive Marketing: An Overview

2   Evolution of Research in Interactive Marketing:
     A Bibliometric and Thematic Review   15
     Deepak Verma, Satish Kumar, and Divesh Kumar

3   From Direct Marketing Toward Interactive Marketing:
     The Evolving Interactive Marketing Tools   43
     Anne Moes, Marieke L. Fransen, Tibert Verhagen,
     and Bob Fennis

4   Bridging the Theory and Practice of Digital Marketing
     from Interactive Marketing Perspective: A Historical Review   65
     Ayşegül Sağkaya Güngör and Tuğçe Ozansoy Çadırcı

5   Interactive Digital Marketing Mechanisms: The
     Significance in Digital Transformation   93
     Mona Rashidirad and Hamidreza Shahbaznezhad

6   Empowering Consumers in Interactive Marketing:
     Examining the Role of Perceived Control   117
     Xiaohan Hu

7   How Brands Drive Electronic Word-of-Mouth
     in an Interactive Marketing Environment: An Overview
     and Future Research Directions   149
     Ya You and Yi He

Part II Technology Development and Interactive Marketing

8 Technological Innovations in Interactive Marketing: Enhancing Customer Experience at the New Retail Age 183
Sahil Singh Jasrotia

9 The Role of Artificial Intelligence in Interactive Marketing: Improving Customer-Brand Relationship 199
Wajeeha Aslam and Kashif Farhat

10 How Internet of Things Is Shaping Consumer Behavior? The Interactive Experience Between Customer and Smart Object 219
Ching-Jui Keng, Hsin-Ying Liu, and Yu-Hsin Chen

11 The Physical Presence and Relationship Distance for Efficient Consumer–AI-Business Interactions and Marketing 239
Corina Pelau, Dan-Cristian Dabija, and Daniela Serban

12 Humanizing Chatbots for Interactive Marketing 255
Wan-Hsiu Sunny Tsai and Ching-Hua Chuan

13 Affective Interaction with Technology: The Role of Virtual Assistants in Interactive Marketing 275
Guillermo Calahorra Candao, Carolina Herrando, and María José Martín-De Hoyos

Part III Interactivity in the Virtual World

14 Augmented Reality in Interactive Marketing: The State-Of-The-Art and Emerging Trends 301
Marc Riar, Jakob J. Korbel, Nannan Xi, Sophia Meywirth, Rüdiger Zarnekow, and Juho Hamari

15 Interactive Marketing with Virtual Commerce Tools: Purchasing Right Size and Fitted Garment in Fashion Metaverse 329
Sadia Idrees, Gianpaolo Vignali, and Simeon Gill

16 Virtual Influencer as a Brand Avatar in Interactive Marketing 353
Alice Audrezet and Bernadett Koles

17 Sentimental Interaction with Virtual Celebrities: An Assessment from Customer-Generated Content 377
Bình Nghiêm-Phú and Jillian Rae Suter

18 The Conceptualization of "Presence" in Interactive Marketing: A Systematic Review of 30 Years of Literature 397
Chen Chen, Xiaohan Hu, and Jacob T. Fisher

Part IV Platform Revolution and Customer Participation

19 The Platform Revolution in Interactive Marketing: Increasing Customer-Brand Engagement on Social Media Platforms   433
Zheng Shen

20 When in Rome, Do as the Romans Do: Differences of Interactive Behaviors Across Social Media Networks   451
Qingjiang Yao

21 Enhancing Customer–Brand Interaction: Customer Engagement on Brand Pages of Social Networking Sites   475
Zalfa Laili Hamzah and Azean Johari

22 Live Streaming as an Interactive Marketing Media: Examining Douyin and Its Constructed Value and Cultural Preference of Consumption in E-commerce   499
Boris L. F. Pun and Anthony Y. H. Fung

23 Interactive Experience of Collaborative Online Shopping: Real-Time Interaction and Communication   519
Mohammad Rahim Esfidani and Behnam Izadi

Part V E-WOM and Influencer Marketing in the Interactive Era

24 Reconceptualizing eWOM Communication: An Interactive Perspective   547
Hongfei Liu and Chanaka Jayawardhena

25 Complaint Handling and Channel Selection in the Interactive Marketing Era   571
Mariola Palazón and Inés López-López

26 What Do We Know About Influencers on Social Media? Toward a New Conceptualization and Classification of Influencers   593
María Sicilia and Manuela López

27 Influencer Marketing: A Triadically Interactive Relationship Between Influencers, Followers, and Brands   623
Delphine Caruelle

28 Optimising the Effect of Influencer Marketing: Exploring Consumers' Interaction with Different Influencer Types on Instagram   641
Daniella Ryding, Rosy Boardman, and Rafaella Konstantinou

Part VI Predictive Analytics and Personalized Targeting

29 Applying Predictive Analytics in Interactive Marketing: How It Influences Customer Perception and Reaction? 667
Maggie Wenjing Liu, Qichao Zhu, Yige Yuan, and Sihan Wu

30 AI-Based Recommendation Systems: The Ultimate Solution for Market Prediction and Targeting 683
Sandra Habil, Sara El-Deeb, and Noha El-Bassiouny

31 Deep Learning Applications for Interactive Marketing in the Contemporary Digital Age 705
Billy Yu

32 Personalized Recommendation During Customer Shopping Journey 729
Shobhana Chandra and Sanjeev Verma

33 Location-Based Proximity Marketing: An Interactive Marketing Perspective 753
Aida Loussaief, Edward Ying-Lun Cheng, Marta Yuan-Chen Lin, and Julian Ming-Sung Cheng

Part VII Practical Implications of Interactive Marketing

34 Customer Interactive Experience in Luxury Retailing: The Application of AI-Enabled Chatbots in the Interactive Marketing 785
Ni Zeng, Liru Jiang, Gianpaolo Vignali, and Daniella Ryding

35 Engaging and Entertaining Customers: Gamification in Interactive Marketing 807
Devika Vashisht

36 Interactive Experience of Physical Servicescape and Online Servicescape: A Review and Future Research 837
Zalfa Laili Hamzah and Muhammad Waqas

37 The Role of Touch, Touchscreens, and Haptic Technology in Interactive Marketing: Evolution from Physical Touch to Digital Touch 867
Ying Zhu

38 It's Fun to Play: Emoji Usage in Interactive Marketing Communication 893
Ruijuan Wu

Part VIII A Necessary Evil? Unintended Consequences of Interactive Marketing

39 Consumer Incivility in Virtual Spaces: Implications for Interactive Marketing Research and Practice   917
Denitsa Dineva

40 The Dark Side of Gamification in Interactive Marketing   939
Chitrakshi Bhutani and Abhishek Behl

41 Ethical Considerations in Gamified Interactive Marketing Praxis   963
Samaan Al-Msallam, Nannan Xi, and Juho Hamari

42 Value Co-creation or Value Co-destruction? the Role of Negative Emotions in Consumer-Firm Interaction in the Social Media Platform   987
Moreno Frau, Luca Frigau, Francesca Cabiddu, and Francesco Mola

Correction to: The Palgrave Handbook of Interactive Marketing   C1
Cheng Lu Wang

Correction to: Ethical Considerations in Gamified Interactive Marketing Praxis   C3
Samaan Al-Msallam, Nannan Xi, and Juho Hamari

Glossary   1013

Index   1037

Notes on Contributors

Dr. Samaan Al-Msallam is Postdoctoral Fellow in the Gamification Group at the Faculty of Information Technology and Communication Sciences at Tampere University. Before joining Tampere University, he worked as Postdoctoral Researcher at the University of St. Gallen, Switzerland. Dr. Al-Msallam's research focuses on studying gamification from the perspective of marketing and ethics. His research has been published in journals and conferences such as The European Marketing Academy Conference (EMAC) and *Journal of Marketing and Consumer Research*. In his prior work, he has investigated many new marketing phenomena from perspectives of consumer experience and psychology, for example, aberrant consumer behavior, customer engagement, and brand loyalty in social media, as well as tourism marketing. Dr. Al-Msallam taught several courses in Marketing.

Wajeeha Aslam is Lecturer in the Business Administration Department of IQRA University, Karachi, Pakistan. She is pursuing her doctorate studies in Marketing from the University of Karachi, Pakistan. She received her M.Phil. in Marketing from IQRA University and M.Sc. in Mathematics from the University of Karachi. She has published several research papers in reputed journals such as in *Journal of Interactive Advertising*, *TQM Journal*, *Technology in Society*, *Kybernetes*, *International Journal of Green Energy*, and *Journal of Internet Commerce*. Her research interest includes consumer behavior, technology adoption, electronic word-of-mouth, and switching behavior.

Dr. Alice Audrezet is Professor of Marketing at Institut Français de la Mode, France. With a background in social sciences and humanities (B.Sc. in both psychology and sociology), she holds an M.Sc. in marketing and a Ph.D. in management sciences from Paris-Dauphine University. Her research focuses on social media in society and fashion studies. She published in top international journals including *Journal of Retailing and Consumer Services* and

Journal of Business Research. She currently co-guests editing a special issue on virtual influencers on the *Journal of Business Research.* In an effort of science dissemination, the results of her research are also available in Harvard Business Review and various French media sites. She teaches courses related to her research interests to Bachelor's and Master's students and to professional executives.

Abhishek Behl is Assistant Professor at Management Development Institute, Gurgaon, India in the area of information technology and analytics. He has earned his second Ph.D. from the Indian Institute of Technology, Bombay where his research is in the area of crowdfunding and gamification. Dr. Behl is a winner of the prestigious "Naik and Rastogi award for excellence in Ph.D." from IIT Bombay. He holds a rich experience in teaching, research, and consultancy. He has taught subjects like Business Analytics; Marketing Analytics; Digital Marketing; Marketing Research. He has also served as a Senior Manager—Research at Centre for Innovation Incubation and Entrepreneurship, IIM Ahmedabad. His research is in the area of business analytics and decision sciences with a focus on gamification, stakeholder engagement, sustainability, and e-commerce startups. He is Associate Editor of the *Journal of Global Information Management* (ABDC:A) *Journal of Cases on Information Technology* (ABDC: C) and an area editor (South Asia) of the *International Journal of Emergency Services* (ABDC:C). He features on the editorial board of many journals like *Journal of Global Marketing* (ABDC: B); *Journal of Electronic Commerce in Organization* (ABDC:B); *Young Consumers* (ABDC:B).

Chitrakshi Bhutani is a research scholar, pursuing FPM in marketing at Fortune Institute of International Business, Delhi, India. She has over 2.5 years of experience, including 1.5 years as a management associate in the industry. During her corporate stint, she has been invited as a guest speaker at business schools in India. In academia, she is developing her skills to write research that creates impact on academics, industry, and society. Her areas of research include consumer-brand relationships, new-age technologies, digital platforms, and gamification in marketing. She is currently serving as the peer reviewer for reputed journals like *Journal of Global Information Management (JGIM)*, and *Information Resources Management Journal (IRMJ)*.

Dr. Rosy Boardman is Senior Lecturer in Fashion Business at the Department of Materials, University of Manchester. Rosy's research focuses on digital strategy and innovation in the fashion retail industry. In particular, her research specializes in e-commerce, digital marketing, and social media marketing, using eye tracking technology and qualitative research methods. Her interest is in exploring fashion retail's current and future developments, focusing on the digital economy and consumer behavior as well as how technology can be used to solve issues related to both social and environmental sustainability. Rosy has published several peer-reviewed academic papers in world-leading journals as well as books, including *Social Commerce: Consumer Behaviour in Online Environments* (Springer, 2019) and *Fashion Buying and Merchandising in a Digital Society* (Routledge, 2020).

Francesca Cabiddu is Full Professor at the Department of Economics and Business, University of Cagliari (Italy). Her research has appeared in *Annals of Tourism Research*, *Business Horizons*, *The Service Industries Journal*, *Industrial Marketing Management*, *Journal of Service Research*, *Tourism Management*, and other academic and applied journals.

Tuğçe Ozansoy Çadırcı has a Ph.D. degree in marketing. She is working as Assistant Professor of marketing at Yıldız Technical University (YTU), Turkey. Her main research areas include consumer behavior, digital consumption, and fashion marketing. Currently, she is lecturing on consumption theory, e-commerce, digital marketing, consumer behavior, and marketing research at YTU.

Guillermo Calahorra Candao, M.Sc. is a Ph.D. student in Business Administration (Marketing) at the University of Zaragoza (Spain) and he coordinates and produces post-production virtual reality projects within the Horizon 2020 EU Research and Innovation Programme. His research interests are in the field of emotions, social media, and online consumer behavior. Particularly, he is focused on the categorization of emotions through different ways of communication within the Internet.

Dr. Delphine Caruelle is Associate Professor in Marketing at Kristiania University College (Oslo, Norway). She holds a Ph.D. in Marketing from BI Norwegian Business School (Oslo, Norway). Dr. Caruelle has presented her research at international academic conferences such as AMA Winter Academic Conference, Frontiers in Service, EMAC Doctoral Colloquium, and QUIS Symposium. Her work has been published in *Journal of Business Research*. She won the Liam Glynn Research Scholarship Award in 2018 and was selected as a finalist for the SERVSIG Best Dissertation Award in 2020.

Ms. Shobhana Chandra is currently a doctoral student in Nitie (National Institute of Industrial Engg., Mumbai). She has worked for eminent organizations like ICICI Bank, 3M India Ltd, SP Jain Institute of Management and Research in Marketing & Sales and Administration. In recent past she had participated in the 8th UN PRME held in 2018. She has published two articles "Big Data and Sustainable Consumption: A Review and Research Agenda" and "Personalization in Personalized Marketing: Trends and Ways forward."

Chen Chen (ORCID: 0000-0003-1013-6932) is a Ph.D. student with interests focusing on how an immersive environment modulates individuals' information processing and consequently influences their cognitive performance and decision-making. It turns into three interrelated areas: (1) Identifying the underlying mechanisms of an immersive experience; (2) Understanding these mechanisms' cognitive and persuasion outcomes; (3) Exploring how the characteristics of the immersive environment modify these processes.

Edward Ying-Lun Cheng is currently studying in the Department of Electronic and Electrical Engineering, University College London, UK. His current research interests are speech emotional recognition, location detection through GPS, and architecture and landscape design with integrated engineering. His research has been published in journals such as *Journal of Business Research*, among others.

Julian Ming-Sung Cheng is Professor of Marketing in the Business Administration Department, National Central University, Taiwan. Dr. Cheng is also Professor in the College of Business, University of Economics Ho-Chi-Minh City, Vietnam. His research interests include marketing channels, martech, branding, glocal marketing, sustainability marketing, AI and marketing, and meta-analysis. His research has been published in various marketing journals such as *Journal of the Academy of Marketing Science, Journal of International Marketing, Industrial Marketing Management, International Journal of Operations and Production Management, Journal of Business Research, Journal of Advertising Research*, and *European Journal of Marketing*, among others.

Dr. Yu-Hsin Chen is currently Assistant Professor in the Department of International Business, Shih Chien University, Taipei, Taiwan. His research focuses on Internet marketing, customer behavior, and social network services.

Dr. Ching-Hua Chuan is currently Assistant Professor in Interactive Media at the School of Communication, University of Miami, USA. Dr. Chuan is a computer scientist who conducts research on human-centered computing and computational communication. Her research interests include artificial intelligence, machine learning, music information retrieval, audio signal processing, data inclusion, and AI literacy.

Dan-Cristian Dabija is Full Professor and Ph.D. Supervisor at the Department of Marketing, Babeș-Bolyai University, Romania. Dr. Dabija successfully supervised one Ph.D. student who recently graduated and has led research projects on sustainability and the COVID-19 Resilience in Retail. He published more than 100 papers in international ranked journals, participated in numerous prestigious conferences, and serves as an associate or guest editor for *Amfiteatru Economic, Kybernetes, Journal of International Management*. His teaching disciplines are Retailing, International Marketing, Sales Promotion, and Strategic Marketing. He was awarded the first book prize of the Romanian Association of Economic Faculties (2017), the "Victor Slăvescu" Prize (2019) of the Romanian Academy of Science, the Publons "Excellent Reviewers" and the "Top Reviewers in Economics and Business" Awards (2018), the "2020 MDPI Top Reviewer Award."

Denitsa Dineva (Ph.D.) is Assistant Professor (Lecturer) in Marketing and Strategy at Cardiff Business School, Cardiff University, UK. Her research area revolves around the dark side of social media and particularly around the different forms and moderation of uncivil consumer behaviors (e.g., trolling, conflicts) on social media networks. Denitsa's work has been published in inter-disciplinary outlets including marketing, information technology, and social psychology.

Prof. Noha El-Bassiouny is Vice Dean for Academic Affairs and Professor and Head of Marketing at the Faculty of Management Technology, the German University in Cairo (GUC), Egypt. She also acts as the lead academic coordinator of the Business and Society research group which aims at bridging the interface between business and society in the modern world in terms of research, teaching, and community outreach. Her research interests lie in the domains of consumer psychology, Islamic marketing, ethical marketing, corporate social responsibility, and sustainability. She has wide international exposure and has published her works in reputable journals including the *Journal of Business Research*, the *International Journal of Consumer Studies*, the *Journal of Consumer Marketing*, the *Social Responsibility Journal*, the *Journal of Islamic Marketing*, the *International Journal of Bank Marketing*, the *International Journal of Pharmaceutical and Healthcare Marketing*, *Journal of Cleaner Production* as well as *Young Consumers*. She is currently the Editor-in-Chief of *Management & Sustainability: An Arab Review (MSAR)* as well as Associate Editor of the *Journal of Islamic Marketing*. She has also received many international awards including the prestigious Abdul Hameed Shoman Arab Researchers Award (2019) on the level of the whole Arab world as well as several Emerald Outstanding Reviewer Awards and Highly Commended Paper awards.

Dr. Sara El-Deeb is a marketing scholar in the Faculty of Management Technology at the German University in Cairo (GUC), Egypt. She teaches a wide range of topics in Digital Marketing and Media Psychology in GUC Egypt and in GIU Berlin. She is particularly interested in cross-cultural studies, digital marketing, consumer behavior, and media psychology. She is a researcher, practitioner, and advisor in which she delivered corporate training and audits for startups and for multinational firms. She is also an expert in quantitative techniques including structural equation modelling and in various use of quantitative software programs. She is a reviewer for several journals including International Journal of Sociology and Social Policy and International Journal of Internet Marketing and Advertising.

Mohammad Rahim Esfidani is Assistant Professor at the faculty of management, university of Tehran, Iran. He holds a B.A., an M.S. in management, and a Ph.D. in marketing management from the University of Tehran. His research interests are consumer behavior, business-to-business marketing, and ethical marketing. His work has been published in various journals, including the *International Journal of Retail & Distribution Management*, *Journal of*

Research in Interactive Marketing, *Journal of Electronic Commerce Research*, and the *International Journal of Contemporary Hospitality Management*.

Kashif Farhat is Senior Lecturer in Management Sciences department of Muhammad Ali Jinnah University, Karachi, Pakistan. He did Doctorate of Philosophy in Marketing from Universiti Utara Malaysia. His research interest includes consumer engagement behavior, technology adoption, and switching behavior. He has published several research papers in reputed journals such as *Journal of Interactive Advertising*, the *TQM Journal*, and *Journal of Internet Commerce*.

Bob Fennis (Ph.D.) is Professor of Consumer Behavior at the University of Groningen. He has published extensively on the psychology of persuasion and social influence, and the role of consumer self-regulation in these processes.

Jacob T. Fisher is Assistant Professor in the College of Media at the University of Illinois Urbana-Champaign. His research leverages brain imaging, computational methods, and behavioral experiments to investigate how we pay attention and make decisions in digital worlds and how the design of digital technologies influences our attention and self-control. His work aims to develop recommendations for developing digital messages and environments that help us direct our attention in more effective ways.

Marieke L. Fransen (Ph.D.) is Professor of Positive Communication Science at Radboud University. Her research focuses on communication, consumer resistance, and consumer empowerment. She studies these topics from different perspectives and publishes in communication, advertising, marketing, and consumer-related journals.

Moreno Frau is Research Fellow at the Marketing Management Department, Corvinus University of Budapest (Hungary). He holds a Ph.D. in Business and Economics taken at the University of Cagliari (Italy) with honours and the additional label of Doctor Europaeus, thanks to a period of research spent at the BI Norwegian Business School. His research interests focus on marketing, digital transformation, sustainability, and interactive value formation. He is holding a Marie Curie research project called FooDization about the impact of digital transformation on sustainable food production. His research has appeared in peer-reviewed journals such as the *Journal of Service Research*, *TQM Journal*, *International Journal of Marketing Studies*, and other academic and applied journals.

Luca Frigau is Assistant Professor in Statistics and Market Analysis at the Department of Economics and Business Science of the University of Cagliari. He was elected member of the ISBIS Executive as Vice-President for y-BIS and Chair of the y-BIS Committee, as well as being a member of the International Statistical Institute (ISI), International Society for Business and Industrial Statistics (ISBIS), the International Federation of Classification Societies (IFCS), and the Italian Statistical Society (SIS). His main research interests are Computational Statistics, Machine Learning, Statistical Classification, Image Analysis, Shape Analysis, Big Data, Tree-based models, Regularization, Text Mining, and Topic Modelling.

Anthony Y. H. Fung is Professor in the School of Journalism and Communication at the Chinese University of Hong Kong as well as a Professor in the School of Art and Communication at Beijing Normal University at Beijing. His research interests and teaching focus on popular culture and cultural studies, popular music, gender and youth identity, cultural industries and policy, and digital media studies. He has published widely in international journals, and he has authored and edited more than 20 Chinese and English books. His recent books are *Youth Cultures in China* (Polity Press, 2016) (co-authored with de Kloet), *Global Game Industries and Cultural Policy* (Palgrave Macmillan, 2016), *Hong Kong Game Industry, Cultural Policy and East Asian Rivalry* (Rowman & Littlefield, 2018), and *Made in Hong Kong: Studies in Popular Music* (Routledge, 2020).

Simeon Gill is Senior Lecturer in Fashion Technology, with the Department of Materials, Faculty of Science and Engineering, Sackville Street Building M13WE, University of Manchester, UK. Dr. Gill is a specialist in body scanning and the application of body measurements in product development and a core member of the Apparel Design Engineering (ADE) group at the University of Manchester. His research seeks to build clear links between individual bodies and pattern shape requirements to address product fit and performance. Developing body to pattern theory helps enable more sustainable bespoke production methods as well as engage with better theory to support mass production more inclusively.

Ayşegül Sağkaya Güngör has a Ph.D. degree in marketing. She is working as Associate Professor of marketing at İstanbul Medeniyet University (IMU). Her main research area is digital marketing and its impact on consumer behavior. Currently, she is lecturing on digital marketing, marketing management, strategic marketing, and e-commerce at IMU.

Ms. Sandra Habil is Marketing Assistant Lecturer and Ph.D. Candidate in the Faculty of Management Technology at the German University in Cairo (GUC), Egypt. She teaches various courses in Consumer Behavior, Integrated Marketing Communications and International Marketing in GUC Egypt. She is interested in certain research domains including artificial intelligence, augmented reality, online consumer experience, digital marketing, and consumer behavior. She has sufficient knowledge in quantitative data analysis software (i.e., SPSS and AMOS). She also completed multiple certification in artificial intelligence, emerging technologies, and digital marketing diploma. She participated lately in American Marketing Association (AMA) winter conference, 2022 and presented her work titled "Generation Covid: Augmented Reality and the New Digital Consumer."

Dr. Juho Hamari is Professor of gamification and the leader of the Gamification Group at the Faculty of Information Technology and Communication Sciences at Tampere University. Professor Hamari is leading research on gamification under the Academy of Finland Flagship, Profiling, and Center of Excellence programs. His and his group's research covers several forms of information technologies such as games, motivational information systems, new media (social networking services, eSports), peer-to-peer economies (sharing economy, crowdsourcing), and virtual economies. Dr. Hamari has authored several seminal empirical, theoretical, and meta-analytical scholarly articles on these topics from perspectives of consumer behavior, human-computer interaction, game studies, and information systems science.

Dr. Zalfa Laili Hamzah is currently serving as Senior Lecturer at the Faculty of Business and Economics, Universiti Malaya, Malaysia. Majority of her research is directed toward an understanding of customer and brand experience of corporate, product, service, and social media branding. Her research works are published in *Journal of Business Research, Journal of Brand Management, Journal of Interactive Marketing, Journal of Research in Interactive Marketing, Online Information Review, International Journal of Bank Marketing, Journal of Consumer Marketing, Management Review Quarterly* and *International Journal of Internet Marketing and Advertising*. Her research interests are mainly in the area of branding and consumer psychology/behavior.

Dr. Yi He is the Chair and Professor of Marketing in the College of Business and Economics at California State University, East Bay. She completed her Ph.D. in International Marketing at the University of Hawaii at Manoa. She received her Master's degree from University of Cincinnati. Her current research interests include branding and brand portfolio management, social media marketing, consumer psychology, and advertising effectiveness. Her studies have appeared in journals such as *Journal of Academy of Marketing Science, Journal of Advertising, Marketing Letters, Journal of Interactive Marketing, Journal of Business Research, Journal of International Marketing, International Marketing Review* and *International Journal of Advertising*.

Dr. Carolina Herrando is currently Assistant Professor at the University of Zaragoza, Spain. Herrando's research interests are in the fields of customer experience and digital marketing. Her work has been published in journals such as *Journal of Business Research, Internet Research,* International *Journal of Information Management, Electronic Commerce Research, Online Information Review,* or *Frontiers in Psychology*.

Dr. María José Martín-De Hoyos holds a Ph.D. in Business Administration and is Associate Professor in the Department of Marketing and Market

Research at the University of Zaragoza in Spain. Her research interests include issues in e-commerce and consumer behavior, acceptance of new technologies, and marketing management systems. Her work has been published in several journals such as *Industrial Marketing Management*, *Technovation*, *Journal of Business Research*, *Interacting with Computers*, *Internet Research* or *Journal of Research* and *Consumer Services*.

Xiaohan Hu is a Ph.D. Candidate in the Institute of Communications Research (ICR) at University of Illinois at Urbana-Champaign. She earned her M.S. in Advertising at University of Illinois at Urbana-Champaign and B.A. in Advertising at Wuhan University in Wuhan, China. Her research interests include interactive and digital advertising, consumer psychology, and consumer behavior. Her current research projects investigate the role of user control in affecting digital advertising and marketing effectiveness.

Sadia Idrees is a Ph.D. researcher and a textile designer. She has worked with different fashion brands and renowned designers in Pakistan as a textile designer. She has almost 7 years of teaching experience in Pakistan as a lecturer and in the UK as a teaching assistant at the University of Manchester, UK. She is also certified as an associate fellow of the higher education academy (UK). Moreover, she has worked as a paper setter and examiner for PBTE (Punjab Board of Technical Education) TEVTA Lahore, and the University of the Punjab. She completed her education (Bachelor's to M.Phil.) in textile and fashion design from the College of Home Economics (University of the Punjab), Lahore, Pakistan. Now she is doing a Ph.D. Textile design Fashion and Management (Department of Materials, Faculty of Science and Engineering) from the University of Manchester, UK. During her Ph.D., she presented her research work at various international conferences. Additionally, she received the best presentation award, on the topic "Technological advancement in fashion online retailing: A comparative study of Pakistan and UK fashion e-commerce" presented at ICATT 2020: International Conference on Applications of Textile Technology in Amsterdam.

Behnam Izadi holds a Ph.D. in Marketing Management at the University of Tehran. He holds an M.S. in Marketing Management from the University of Tehran and a B.A. in Industrial Engineering from Kar University. His research interests are in the areas of Social Commerce and Consumer Behavior. His recent work has been published in the *Journal of Electronic Commerce Research*.

Dr. Sahil Singh Jasrotia is Assistant Professor in the Area of Marketing at Jaipuria Institute of Management, Indore, Madhya Pradesh, India. His research interests include Consumer Behaviour, Retailing, Tourism Management, and Marketing Education. His research has been published in journals including *International Journal of Retail and Distribution Management*, *Journal of the Knowledge Economy*, *Journal of Education*, and *Journal of Public Affairs*.

Chanaka Jayawardhena is Professor of Marketing at Surrey Business School, University of Surrey, Head of Department of Marketing and Retailing, and Visiting Professor at University of Hull and University of Jyväskylä, Finland. Research interests include customer relationships, particularly in virtual and service marketplaces and how organizations use technology in attracting, developing, and maintaining customer relationships; how consumers evaluate services, influence of social media and word-of-mouth on consumer decision-making in consumption of services. Chanaka has over 100 articles published in specialist journals and proceedings, including *Industrial Marketing Management*, *Journal of Business Research*, *European Journal of Marketing*, *Journal of Marketing Management*.

Liru Jiang is a Ph.D. student at Department of Material, University of Manchester, Written works: "What makes consumers have neutral or negative responses to celebrity endorsement on social media? A mixed methods study based on Chinese luxury fashion market since Covid-19" (accepted by 28th International Conference on Recent Advances in Retailing and Consumer Science); joined EuroMed conference and MMU DFI conference in 2021; associate Fellowship awarded during her being a teaching assistant in University of Manchester.

Azean Johari is a graduate from Universiti Malaya who studied in Master of Management in Graduate School of Business, Faculty of Business and Economics, Universiti Malaya, Kuala Lumpur, Malaysia. She has applied the knowledge in her business in fabric handicrafts in Malaysia.

Dr. Ching-Jui Keng is currently Professor in the Department of Business Management, National Taipei University of Technology. He completed his Ph.D. at National Chengchi University. Professor Keng's research interests include consumer behavior, e-commerce, Internet marketing, and social network services. He has published papers in Computers in *Human Behavior*, *Information Research*, *Journal of Applied Social Psychology*, *Contemporary Management Research*, *Electronic Commerce Research*, *International Journal of Service Industry Management*, and *Cyberpsychology & Behavior*.

Dr. Bernadett Koles is Associate Professor of Marketing and Consumer Behaviour, and the Academic Director for the Bachelor of International Business program at IÉSEG School of Management in Paris, France. She holds a Doctorate (Ph.D.) in Marketing and Consumer Behaviour from Durham University Business School (UK) and a Doctorate (Ed.D.) in Psychology from Harvard University (USA). Bernadett's research covers a range of areas reflecting upon her multidisciplinary background and expertise. She has devoted many years to studying the role of innovative technologies (e.g., Social Media, virtual environments, Virtual Reality, Artificial Intelligence) on individuals, consumers, and organizations, and currently pursues projects that focus on various aspects of digital user behavior (human and virtual influencers, streamers, gamers and consumers) on online gaming and social media platforms. Bernadett has further expertise in a range of consumer behavioral topics (e.g., compensatory consumption, consumer compromise, brand love) which she applies to understand human actions in digital and offline settings. Prior to joining IÉSEG, she held professorial positions in the USA, Portugal, Hungary, the UK, and France. Bernadett serves on the Editorial Board of the *International Journal of Consumer Studies* as an Associate Editor and has published widely in international peer-reviewed journals. She also has experience in managing Special Issues at different high-quality outlets, including *Journal of Business Research*, *Psychology & Marketing*, and *International Journal of Consumer Studies*.

Ms. Rafaella Konstantinou completed her Master's by Research Degree in Fashion Marketing & Management at the Department of Materials, University of Manchester and she now works as a practitioner in the field.

Jakob J. Korbel received the B.Sc. degree in industrial engineering and management from the Friedrich-Alexander-University, Erlangen-Nuremberg, Germany, in 2014, and the M.Sc. degree in industrial engineering and management from the Technical University of Berlin, Germany, in 2017 where he is currently employed as a research associate at the Chair for Information and Communication Management. In recent projects, he participated in the examination and implementation of a virtual reality application for the treatment of psychological disorders and an augmented reality application for retail. His research focuses on 3D models in the form of virtual goods and products in the manufacturing and gaming industry from a developer and user (innovation) perspective as well as on data analysis of e-commerce platforms and online communities.

Dr. Divesh Kumar is Assistant Professor in Department of Management Studies, Malaviya National Institute of Technology (MNIT) Jaipur. He has also taught at FORE School of Management, New Delhi and ICFAI Academy Hyderabad prior to joining MNIT. He did Ph.D. from Department of Management Studies, Indian Institute of Technology (IIT) Roorkee in 2015 and M.B.A. from Madan Mohan Malviya University of Technology, Gorakhpur in 2008.

His research work is published in reputed international publishers like Emerald, Taylor and Francis, and ScienceDirect. He has also a forthcoming book in the area of Integrated Marketing Communication from a leading international publisher. He actively participated in various national and international conferences. He regularly reviews for research submissions at Emerald publishing, Springer, Taylor and Francis, and Inderscience journals.

Dr. Kumar has won highly commended award "South Asian Management Research Fund Award 2013" for the project "Problems and prospects of compost marketing in Uttarakhand, India." His research interest includes

Sustainable consumption behavior, sustainable supply chain, and sustainability marketing strategies.

Dr. Satish Kumar is Associate Professor (Finance Area), Department of Management Studies at Malaviya National Institute of Technology (MNIT) Jaipur and Adjunct Associate Professor at Swinburne University of Technology, Malaysia Campus. He has over eighteen years of teaching and research experience at management institutes of repute in India and abroad. Dr. Kumar has obtained his doctorate from the Indian Institute of Technology (IIT) Roorkee in 2011. He also qualified Junior Research Fellowship (JRF) in 2007. His research interest includes corporate finance small business finance, corporate governance, consumer economics, systematic literature review, and bibliometric analysis.

He has over 140 research publications in his credit with work appearing in journals such as FT 50, A*, A category of ABDC journal ranking and high impact factor journals like Contemporary Accounting Research, Journal of Corporate Finance, and Journal of Service Research among others. His research work has received google scholar citations of 4120 (as on March 26, 2022) with h-index and i-index index of 31 and 70, respectively. Dr. Kumar is Associate Editor of leading journals including *Journal of Business Research, Electronic Commerce Research, Research in International Business and Finance, Qualitative Research in Financial Markets*, and *Journal of Asia Business Studies*.

Manuela López (Ph.D. from the University of Murcia, Spain) is Assistant professor of Marketing at the University of Murcia. She has been a visiting scholar at the School of Communication Research at the University of Amsterdam (The Netherlands) and assistant professor at Universidad Católica del Norte (Chile). Her research interests are focused on the influence of eWOM in consumer behavior, WOM marketing, and social media. She has published articles in journals such as the *Electronic Commerce Research and Applications, European Journal of Marketing, Internet Research, Journal of Research in Interactive Marketing, Online Information Review, Journal of Product and Brand Management, Journal of Theoretical and Applied Electronic Commerce Research* and *Journal of Simulation*.

Inés López-López is Associate Professor at the University of Murcia, Spain. She received her Ph.D. Degree in Marketing from the same institution. Her current research interests include social networks, consumption-related emotions, service failure and recovery, and corporate social responsibility. Her papers have been published in journals such as *Journal of Service Research, Journal of Research in Interactive Marketing, Ecological Economics, Internet Research, Marketing Letters, Electronic Commerce Research & Applications, Online information Review*, and *Service Science*, among others. She has attended and presented her research in international conferences such as those organized by the Society for Consumer Psychology, Association for Consumer

Research, European Marketing Academy and the Spanish Association for Marketers and Marketing Scholars.

Marta Yuan-Chen Lin is Researcher at Science and Technology International Strategy Center, Industrial Technology Research Institute, Taiwan. Her current research interest primarily concerns Martech. Her research has been published in journals such as *Journal of Business Research*, *Journal of Research in Interactive Marketing*, and *Asian Pacific Journal of Marketing and Logistics*, among others.

Hongfei Liu is Associate Professor in Marketing at Southampton Business School, University of Southampton, UK. Hongfei's research interests primarily lie in digital marketing and social media. His research focuses on the impact of digitalization and technologization on individuals, businesses, and societies. His work has been published in highly regarded journals, including *Journal of Business Research*, *Journal of Business Ethics*, *European Journal of Marketing*, *Industrial Marketing Management*, *Tourism Management* and *Journal of Travel Research*, among others. Hongfei serves as an Associate Editor for *Journal of Research in Interactive Marketing* and as a guest editor for *Journal of Business Research*.

Hsin-Ying Liu graduated from the Department of Business Management, National Taipei University of Technology.

Dr. Maggie Wenjing Liu is Associate Professor of Marketing at the School of Economics and Management, Tsinghua University, China. She has published at journals such as *Production and Operations Management*, *International Journal of Research in Marketing*, *Journal of Consumer Psychology*, *INFORMS Journal on Computing*, *Journal of International Marketing*, and *Marketing Letters*. She has authored book chapters in *Handbook of Consumer Psychology*, *International Handbook of Consumer Psychology*, and *Customer-Brand Relationships: Theory and Practice*, with the former two books used as textbooks in many Ph.D. programs across the world.

Aida Loussaief is Assistant Professor in the Economics and Management Department, Time University, Tunisia. Her research interests focus on Islamic marketing and Islamic finance. Her research has been published in journals such as *International Journal of Ethics and Systems* and *International Tourism and Hospitality Journal*, among others.

Sophia Meywirth received a B.Sc. in Information Systems Management from the Technical University of Berlin, where she is currently writing her Master's thesis regarding the technology acceptance of augmented reality applications in e-commerce and stationary retail. Her previous research focused on the use of virtual reality applications for the treatment of anxiety disorders and was published in the proceedings of the ECIS 2021.

Anne Moes is a Ph.D. Candidate at the University of Groningen and serves as a researcher and lecturer at the Amsterdam University of Applied Sciences. Her research focuses on impulsive consumer behavior, consumer empowerment and persuasion. She publishes in both scientific journals and trade journals for marketing and advertising professionals.

Francesco Mola is Full Professor of Statistics at the Department of Economics and Business Science of the University of Cagliari since 2008 and Rector of the University of Cagliari since 2021. He was elected member of the Council of the European (Regional) Board of the Council of the International Association for Statistical Computing (IASC) and is a member of the International Statistical Institute (ISI), International Society for Business and Industrial Statistics (ISBIS), the International Federation of Classification Societies (IFCS), and the Italian Statistical Society (SIS). He has published more than seventy papers on international journals, encyclopedias, conference proceedings, and revised monographs, acts as a referee of many international journals, and contributed to numerous international conferences. His main topics include Partitioning Algorithms and Decision Trees for Classification and Regression, non and semiparametric Regression Modeling, Data Editing, Image Segmentation and Causal Inference.

Dr. Bình Nghiêm-Phú is currently Associate Professor at the School of Economics and Management, University of Hyogo, Japan. The majority of his research are directed toward the understanding of consumers' perceptions and evaluations of the characteristics or images of products, services, organizations, and places. He adopts the approaches of applied psychology theories to the implementation of marketing and management activities.

Mariola Palazón is Associate Professor of Marketing at the University of Murcia (Spain). Her current research interests include communication on social networks, consumer behavior, marketing communication and corporate social responsibility. Her papers have appeared in *Psychology and Marketing*, the *International Journal of Market Research*, the *European Journal of Marketing*, *Journal of Retailing and Consumer Services*, the *Journal of Product and Brand Management*, *Journal of Consumer Behavior*, *Online Information Review*, and *Electronic Commerce Research and Applications*. She has attended and presented her research in international conferences such as American Marketing Association, European Marketing Academy and the Spanish Association for Marketers and Marketing Scholars.

Corina Pelau is Full Professor and Ph.D. Supervisor at the Bucharest University of Economic Studies, Romania, UNESCO Department for Business Administration. Her research has been published by indexed journals such as *Computers in Human Behavior*, *Energy Policy*, *Amfiteatru Economic*, and others. Her main research interest is consumer behavior with focus on the relation with artificial intelligence. Since 2021 she has been a member of the Executive Committee of the European Marketing Academy (EMAC) as National Representative for Romania.

Boris L. F. Pun is Postdoctoral Fellow affiliated with the Hong Kong Institute of Asia-Pacific Studies, the Chinese University of Hong Kong. His research interests mainly relate to popular culture and subcultural studies, especially in fandom of Animation, Comic and Game (ACG). He is also interested in the issues of youth culture, cultural industries and policy, and globalization and transculturation. His current research target is TikTok and its global cultural influence on youth. His previous works about fandom economy have been included in *The Handbook of Research on the Impact of Fandom in Society and Consumerism* and *Exploring the Rise of Fandom in Contemporary Consumer Culture*.

Dr. Mona Rashidirad is Lecturer in Strategy and Marketing at University of Sussex Business School. She holds her Ph.D. in Management from University of Kent, Canterbury, UK. Dr. Rashidirad is a fellow in Higher Education Academy (HEA) following her completion of Postgraduate Certificate in Higher Education (PGCHE), awarded by the University of Kent in 2012. Also, she is a Certified Management and Business Educator (CMBE) from Chartered Association of Business Schools (CABS) in the UK. Dr. Rashidirad has been an active researcher since 2010, which has resulted in publishing several peer-reviewed journal papers, a number of book chapters, and several conference presentations. Her research focuses on "social Media Marketing," which is one of the key strands of Interactive Marketing. Dr. Rashidirad takes a special interest in research that embraces social media user engagement and the way companies can improve their users' participation on their social media platforms.

Marc Riar is a doctoral candidate at Technical University of Berlin and an associated researcher at Gamification Group, Tampere University. His research lies at the intersection of behavioral sciences and information systems, with special focus on motivational design, the use of gamification to motivate cooperation and the adoption of augmented reality in E-Business. He holds an M.Sc. in Business Informatics from the University of Mannheim and a B.Sc. in Information Systems Management from Karlsruhe University of Applied Sciences. In addition to his scientific endeavors, Mr. Riar has worked at various companies, including Lufthansa German Airlines in New York, SAP in Walldorf, Systec & Services GmbH as well as Fiducia IT AG in Karlsruhe, Germany.

Dr. Daniella Ryding is Senior Lecturer in Fashion Marketing in the Department of Materials at the University of Manchester, and the Academic Lead for the New Academics Programme in the Faculty of Science and Engineering. Daniella has a keen commitment and interest in educational research and has supervised doctoral work within this remit. In addition, she is an active researcher within her subject specialism with over 50 published articles, and several textbook contributions, and she sits on the editorial board for a number of academic business journals. Daniella is a member of the scientific committee and abstract coordinator for CIRCLE International (Centre for international Research on Consumers in their Locations and Environments), which hosts an annual conference with over 88 University members. The author's main discipline-specific research centers on complex cognition, further exploring the psychological and behavioral mechanisms which impact on consumer decision-making within the field of contemporary retail marketing. She is actively involved with a number of research projects which involve studies, surrounding Environmental Sustainability, Social Sustainability, and Social Media Marketing.

Daniela Serban is Full Professor in the Department of Statistics and Econometrics at the Bucharest University of Economic Studies, Romania. Her research has been published by indexed journals such as Economic Research-Ekonomska Istraživanja, Economic Computation and Economic Cybernetics Studies and Research, Amfiteatru Economic, and others. She has been a director of two European Projects within FP7 and a member in eight research grants. Her research work has been awarded an Excellency Diploma by the National Institute of Statistics and the Romanian Society of Statistics for outstanding research results and the teaching activity.

Dr. Hamidreza Shahbaznezhad is a digital transformation lead in NZ Post. He attained his Ph.D. from the Information Systems and Operations Research (ISOM) Department of the University Auckland in New Zealand. He is an active researcher in digital marketing, knowledge transfer, data science, and cybersecurity. He has published a significant number of journal articles and conference papers, including a most recent one on "The Role of Social Media Content Format and Platform in Users' Engagement Behavior," published at *Journal of Interactive Marketing* in 2021.

Dr. Zheng Shen is currently Associate Professor at the Shi Liangcai School of Journalism and Communication, Zhejiang Sci-Tech University. The majority of her research is directed by the understanding of customer engagement in social media marketing. She adopts data mining techniques to implement marketing and management communication on social media.

María Sicilia (Ph.D. from the University of Murcia, Spain) is Associate Professor of Marketing at the University of Murcia (Spain). She has been a visiting scholar at Columbia Business School (New York) and at King's College Business School (London). She is currently lecturing in advertising, digital consumer behavior, and market research. Her research interests are focused on social media, advertising, and consumer behavior. She has published articles in the *Journal of Interactive Marketing*, *Journal of Advertising*, *Journal of Business Research*, *Electronic Commerce Research and Applications*, *Internet Research* and *Journal of Research in Interactive Marketing*.

Dr. Jillian Rae Suter is currently Assistant Professor at the Faculty of Informatics, Shizuoka University, Japan. Her research is directed by the social marketing theories. She is implementing research on consumer culture, notably the impact of the rise and fall in popularity of "Cool Japan" on both the national economy and society and the global market.

Dr. Wan-Hsiu Sunny Tsai is currently Professor in Strategic Communication at the School of Communication, University of Miami, USA. Her research examines the influence of advertising and marketing communication as a powerful cultural institution. Specifically, she has investigated topics such as minority consumers' response to multicultural advertising, glocalization of brand meanings, social media engagement, and recently, AI and emerging technologies like chatbot and augmented reality in advertising.

Dr. Devika Vashisht is presently working as Assistant Professor at Indian Institute of Management Sirmaur, Paonta Sahib, Himachal Pradesh, India. She is a Ph.D. in management from IBS Hyderabad, IFHE University, India and was a visiting research scholar at Fogelman College of Business & Economics, The University of Memphis, TN, USA. Her areas of interest are Marketing Management, Brand Management, Advertising, Branded Entertainment, Persuasion, Brand Placements, Advergames, Tourism Marketing and Marketing Research. She bagged the Best Teacher Award for her excellence in teaching in 2019. She has presented several research papers in international conferences and published various research articles in international peer-reviewed journals, such as *European Journal of Marketing, Computers in Human Behaviour, Internet Research, Journal of Product and Brand Management, Marketing Intelligence & Planning, Asia Pacific Journal of Marketing and Logistics, Young Consumers, Journal of Indian Business Research, Journal of Asia Business Studies, International Journal of Internet Marketing and Advertising, Journal of Research in Interactive Marketing, Management Research Review, Arts and the Market, Spanish Journal of Marketing, Journal of Management and Economic Studies* and *Business Sciences International Research Journal (IMRF Journals)*. In her research line, she has won three Best Paper Awards: one at International Marketing Conference held at IIM-Lucknow, India in the year 2017, another at "Globalizing Brand India: Opportunities and Challenges" International Marketing Conference conducted by IIM-Kashipur, India in the year 2015 and also at "2015 Society for Marketing Advances Conference" held at San Antonio, Texas, USA.

Tibert Verhagen (Ph.D.) is Professor at the Centre for Market Insights of the Amsterdam University of Applied Sciences. His research interests include emerging digital technology, information systems, and retail innovation. His research has been published in information systems, e-commerce, media and marketing journals.

Dr. Deepak Verma is Assistant Professor in Department of Management Studies, Malaviya National Institute of Technology (MNIT) Jaipur since 2013. A doctorate in Online Marketing and postgraduate in Management (MBA) with dual specialization in Marketing and Information Technology, Dr. Verma has over 22 years of cross-functional postgraduate teaching and industry (business development) experience. Dr. Verma has organized more than three dozen workshops for management graduates, academicians, and professionals. He has a book published on computer networks and internet applications in business, apart from having developed courses and study material for many universities/academic institutions. He has been part of consulting projects totalling over US$ 1.7 million.

His teaching interests revolve around statistical decision-making, marketing/business analytics, and research methods. His research area relates to understanding behavioral issues in digital/online environments and issues in technology adoption.

Dr. Sanjeev Verma is Associate Professor in Nitie (National Institute of Industrial Engg., Mumbai) with above 18 years of experience in Academics. His area of expertise is Consumer Engagement and Experience, Services Marketing and Marketing Research. He has published more than 30 articles in various journals. The most recent publication is "Past, Present and Future of Electronic Word of Mouth (EWOM)" in *Journal of Interactive Marketing* September 2020.

Gianpaolo Vignali is Senior Lecturer in Fashion Business and Academic Lead for the Manchester Engineering Campus Development (MECD), with the Department of Materials, Sackville Street Building M13WE, University of Manchester, UK. Gianpaolo is a graduate from UMIST with his first degree in Mathematics. Furthermore, He did Master's in strategic management and initiated his career as a part-time Lecturer and Researcher at Manchester Metropolitan University before joining a full-time employment in the department of Retail at Leeds Metropolitan University. He then became the program leader for Fashion Buying & Merchandising at Manchester Metropolitan University until he achieved his Ph.D. and moved to Manchester University working in the School of Materials where he delivers on both undergraduate and postgraduate programs. He presented at various international conferences and has written more than 40 papers and books in the Marketing and Management field.

Dr. Cheng Lu Wang is Professor of marketing at the University of New Haven. Dr. Wang's research is mainly in consumer behavior and interactive marketing. Dr. Wang has over one hundred scholarly publications at *Journal of Consumer Psychology, Journal of Business Ethics, Journal of World Business, Industrial Marketing Management,* and *Journal of Business Research,* among others. His work has been widely cited and he has been named in the world's top 2% of Scientists List by a researcher team from Stanford University.

Dr. Wang is the editor-in-chief of the *Journal of Research in Interactive Marketing*. He has also served as the managing guest editor for over a dozen of SSCI (ABDC-A ranking) journals, including *Journal of Business Research, Industrial Marketing Management, European Journal of Marketing, International Marketing Review*, etc. Dr. Wang has served as the chair or co-chair for over ten international conferences or symposiums in several countries and regions. In addition, he published and/or edited books, including *Interpersonal Psychology* (Shanghai People's Publishing House, 1987), *Contemporary Marketing in China: Theories and Practices* (Nova Science Publishers, Inc., New York. USA 2011), *Brand Management in Emerging Markets: Theories and Practices* (IGI Global, PA. USA, 2014), *Exploring the Rising Fandom in Contemporary Consumer Culture* (IGI Global, PA. USA, 2017), and *Handbook of Research on the Impact of Fandom in Society and Consumerism* (IGI Global, PA. USA, 2019).

Dr. Muhammad Waqas is Assistant Professor at NUST Business School, National University of Sciences and Technology, Islamabad, Pakistan. His research interests include customer experience in social media, customer engagement in social media, and social media advertising. He has published in the *Journal of Brand Management, Journal of Interactive Marketing, Journal of Research in Interactive Marketing* and has presented papers in international conferences.

Ruijuan Wu is Professor at Tianjin University of Technology. Dr. Wu's research is primarily on consumer behavior. Her work has appeared in the *Journal of Business Research, European Journal of Marketing, Electronic Commerce Research and Applications, Computers in Human Behavior, Asia Pacific Journal of Marketing and Logistics, Online Information Review, International Journal of Consumer Studies, Journal of Cleaner Production*, as well as a number of peer-reviewed journals.

Sihan Wu is a Ph.D. Candidate in Marketing at the School of Economics and Management, Tsinghua University, China. She is interested in public policy and digital marketing, mainly on how green policy impacts consumer behavior.

Dr. Nannan Xi is Assistant Professor (tenure track) in the Unit of Information and Knowledge Management, at Faculty of Management and Business, Tampere University. Her research is mainly focused on game-based approaches (gamification, XR/AR/VR, multimodality, wearable technology) in information systems, management, consumer psychology, and organization studies toward responsible consumption, sustainable decision-making, harmonious organizations, and digital business transformation. Dr. Xi's research has been published in a variety of prestigious journals, such as *Journal of Business Research, International Journal of Human-Computer Studies, International Journal of Information Management, Information Systems Frontiers,* and *Industrial Management & Data Systems*.

Dr. Qingjiang Yao is Associate Professor of Communication and Media at Lamar University (Texas), obtained his Master's degree from Beijing Normal University and Ph.D. from the University of South Carolina. He has taught at the University of Iowa, Fort Hays State University (Kansas), and LU in the areas of strategic communications. His research interest lies in examining the persuasive effects of the mass, digital, and social media, publishing in such journals as Asian *Journal of Communication, China Advertising, Environment Systems and Decisions, Journal of International Crisis and Risk Communication Research, Journal of Internet Law, Journal of Marketing for Higher Education, Journal of Media and Religion, Journal of Research in Interactive Marketing, Public Relations Review, Science Communication,* and *Telematics and Informatics.*

Dr. Ya You is Associate Professor of Marketing in the College of Business and Economics at California State University, East Bay. She received her Ph.D. in Marketing from University of Central Florida. Her research interests include online word-of-mouth, social media, advertising, and marketing strategies. Her research has been published in *Journal of Marketing, Journal of the Academy of Marketing Science, Journal of Advertising, Information & Management, Journal of Business Research* and has been covered in several media outlets, including Science Daily and Phys.org. She is the recipient of the 2015 Marketing Science Institute H. Paul Root Award and the 2021 Swiss Academy of Marketing Science Rigor & Relevance Research Award (Honorable Mention). She is also the finalist for the 2020 Sheth Foundation/Journal of Marketing Award and the 2020 JAMS Sheth Foundation Best Paper Award.

Dr. Billy Yu is currently Associate Professor in the Faculty of Business, Macao Polytechnic University, Macau SAR. He is particularly keen on using advanced analysis techniques and diverse data types to gain insight into marketing and management practices. Many of his students are qualified professionals in SAS@ Certified Predictive Modeler, a recognized qualification in data mining for analytical customer relationship management (aCRM). He administered and provided consultancy services on multiple government-funded and commercial research projects. He also lectured and delivered keynote speeches to practitioners in industries. His researches focus on investigating shared patterns and causal factors in novel hypotheses. He published over a dozen articles in scholarly journals indexed in the Web of Science. His publications mostly take a customer-centric view for organizational or marketing performance. Recently, he works on deep learning applications for emerging topics in electronic commerce and Fintech. Dr. Billy Yu seeks new data to inform how human behaviors could be manipulated, controlling for objective circumstances.

Yige Yuan is a Ph.D. Candidate in Marketing at the School of Economics and Management, Tsinghua University, China. She has published several papers at journals such as *Journal of Business Research* and *International Journal of Advertising*.

Dr. Rüdiger Zarnekow holds the Chair of Information and Communication Management at Technical University of Berlin. His research focuses on the areas of IT management and digital business models. He has led numerous research projects on IT service management, digital health services, Gamification and Internet business models. From 2001 through 2006 he was an Assistant Professor and Researcher at the Institute of Information Management at the University of St. Gallen, Switzerland, where he led the competence center "Industrialization of Information Management." As an author Prof. Zarnekow has published various books and research articles in leading national and international journals and conferences. He holds a Ph.D. from University of Freiberg, a Master of Science in Advance Software Technologies from the University of Wolverhampton and studied Computer Science and Business Administration at the European Business School, Oestrich-Winkel.

Ni Zeng is a Ph.D. student at Department of Material, University of Manchester, UK. She focuses on the effect of interactive technologies on customer responses and customer engagement area. Written works: "The Influence of the Digital In-Store Experience on Customer Engagement in the Luxury Sector" (accepted by 28th International Conference on Recent Advances in Retailing and Consumer Science). Joined EuroMed conference in 2021.

Qichao Zhu is a Ph.D. Candidate in Marketing at the School of Economics and Management, Tsinghua University, China. He has published several papers at journals such as *Marketing Letters and Frontiers in Psychology*.

Dr. Ying Zhu is an Assistant Professor of Marketing in the Faculty of Management at the University of British Columbia-Okanagan campus. She received her Ph.D. in Marketing from the Mays Business School at Texas A&M University. Her research interests include digital marketing, consumer behavior, business analytics, branding, and social networks. Her recent research focuses on investigating the impact of technology on consumers. Her research has been published in the *European Journal of Marketing*, *Psychology & Marketing*, *Journal of Retailing and Consumer Service*, *Journal of Brand Management*, and *Internet Research*, among others.

List of Figures

Chapter 2

Fig. 1	CiteScore trends	18
Fig. 2	Source-wise growth of publications	22
Fig. 3	Top 10 sources of local citations	23
Fig. 4	Most relevant affiliations (top 10)	23
Fig. 5	Country-specific production	24
Fig. 6	Corresponding author country	25
Fig. 7	Three-field analysis for author-country-affiliation	25
Fig. 8	Word cloud (top 50 author keywords)	29
Fig. 9	Top 10 author keywords	30
Fig. 10	Keyword dynamics (top 10 author keywords)	31
Fig. 11	Document coupling using author keywords	31
Fig. 12	Strategic diagram of the four clusters	33
Fig. 13	Thematic evolution of interactive marketing literature	34
Fig. 14	Strategic diagram of themes for period 1997–2012	36
Fig. 15	Strategic diagram for the period 2013–2017	37
Fig. 16	Strategic diagram for the period 2018–2022	37

Chapter 4

Fig. 1	Research workflow	69
Fig. 2	The conceptual evolution of digital marketing	72
Fig. 3	The evolution of digital marketing themes (1990–2020)	73

Chapter 5

Fig. 1	The position of IDM in relation to interactive and digital marketing strategies	98
Fig. 2	Six categories of IDM mechanisms	101

Chapter 6

| Fig. 1 | Theoretical framework for examining perceived control in interactive marketing | 119 |

Chapter 7

| Fig. 1 | Conceptual model | 151 |

Chapter 9

| Fig. 1 | Chatbot service quality | 203 |
| Fig. 2 | Conceptual model | 206 |

Chapter 10

| Fig. 1 | Concepts of the customer-smart object interaction experience | 221 |

Chapter 11

| Fig. 1 | Classification of AI based on physical presence and relationship distance to the consumers | 242 |

Chapter 13

Fig. 1	Circumplex model representing valence and arousal. Own elaboration from (Russell, 1980)	280
Fig. 2	Valence-arousal-dominance emotional space	280
Fig. 3	Communication tools in interactive marketing	281
Fig. 4	How a virtual assistant works. Own elaboration	285

Chapter 14

| Fig. 1 | Framework for consumer response in interactive AR marketing based on S–O-R theory | 304 |
| Fig. 2 | Unified overview of interactive AR marketing | 307 |

Chapter 16

Fig. 1	*Kizuna AI*, a Japanese cartoon-like virtual singer, gamer and VTuber (credit: Kizuna AI Wikipedia page)	359
Fig. 2	Brud's activity timeline (*Source* Adapted from commons.wikimedia.org)	362
Fig. 3	Key stages of developmental trajectory to approximate the evolution of influencers	363

Chapter 17

| Fig. 1 | Hatsune Miku (*Source* Taken by the second author) | 378 |

Chapter 18

| Fig. 1 | Document acquisition and selection process | 402 |

Chapter 19

| Fig. 1 | Hashtags and caption words most used | 443 |

Chapter 21

| Fig. 1 | Structural Model | 490 |

Chapter 23

Fig. 1	Separate navigation with location cue (Yue et al., 2014)	527
Fig. 2	Shared navigation (Wei et al., 2017)	528
Fig. 3	Split screen navigation (Yue, 2014)	528
Fig. 4	Interactive experience of collaborative online shopping (*Source* Proposed by the authors)	529

Chapter 25

| Fig. 1 | Interactive channels for complaining | 574 |
| Fig. 2 | Theoretical framework for complaint handling | 585 |

Chapter 26

Fig. 1	Main factors that determine influencers' impact on their followers	603
Fig. 2	Sponsored content (permanent post) created by the influencer Justin Tse about a new product on Instagram	610
Fig. 3	Sponsored content (permanent post) created by the influencer Canoopsy about a new product on Instagram	611
Fig. 4	Sponsored content on Instagram by Amanda Holtzer about tosh snacks	613

Chapter 27

| Fig. 1 | The influencer phenomenon as a triadic relationship | 625 |

Chapter 28

Fig. 1	Social media influencer types based on Campbell and Farrell (2020)	647
Fig. 2	Independent constructs—Ohanian (1991) model of source credibility	649
Fig. 3	The influencer types that the participants followed on Instagram	652

Chapter 29

| Fig. 1 | Theoretical framework for the effects of predictive analytics on customer engagement | 671 |

Chapter 31

Fig. 1	Micro-level customer purchasing prediction	710
Fig. 2	Autoencoder	711
Fig. 3	Reinforcement learning	712
Fig. 4	Federated learning	714
Fig. 5	Illustration of word embedding	715
Fig. 6	Generative adversarial network	716

Chapter 32

Fig. 1	Recommender system interaction process	731
Fig. 2	Conceptual model role of system-generated personalized recommendations (PR) on consumer shopping journey	745

Chapter 33

Fig. 1	Conceptual model of antecedents and consequences of proximity technologies	770

Chapter 36

Fig. 1	PRISMA article search process	841
Fig. 2	Model of antecedents and consequences of physical interactive experience of servicescape	850
Fig. 3	Conceptual model of the antecedents and consequences of online interactive experience	854
Fig. 4	Conceptual model of antecedents and consequences of phygital interactive experience of servicescape	857

Chapter 37

Fig. 1	Conceptual Framework of Touch Research in Interactive marketing	870

Chapter 39

Fig. 1	Incivility excerpt	918
Fig. 2	A Framework of Consumer Incivility on SMNs	921

Chapter 40

Fig. 1	Critical dimensions of the dark side of gamification in online marketing (*Source* Developed by authors)	947
Fig. 2	Framework on challenges in the implementation of gamified marketing solutions (*Source* Developed by authors)	954

Chapter 42

Fig. 1   The empirical fluctuation process is expressed in relative terms. The continuous line exceeding the boundaries (dashed lines) identifies the significant negative comments peaks   995

Fig. 2   The negative comments distribution. The solid black line is the relative cubic smoothing spline. The polygons indicate the four periods characterized by statistically significant ($p < 0.05$) structural changes from a flat trend   996

List of Tables

Chapter 2

Table 1	Summary of selected sources	18
Table 2	Search results—main information	20
Table 3	Articles published, mean citations per year and per article	21
Table 4	Top 10 authors and their impact	22
Table 5	Most cited countries	26
Table 6	Most globally cited articles (top 10)	27
Table 7	Most local cited articles (top 10)	28
Table 8	Clustering by author keywords—keywords, frequency, centrality and impact	32

Chapter 3

Table 1	Overview of the ten discussed interactive marketing tools	56

Chapter 4

Table 1	Performance analysis (1990–1999)	74
Table 2	Performance analysis (2000–2004)	75
Table 3	Performance analysis (2005–2009)	77
Table 4	Performance analysis (2010–2014)	80
Table 5	Performance analysis (2015–2020)	85

Chapter 5

Table 1	An analysis of the IDM mechanisms	104

Chapter 6

Table 1	Summary of literature in perceived control and interactive marketing research	133

Chapter 7

Table 1	Summary of selected studies of how brands drive WOM	157
Table 2	Summary of elements of interactive marketing environment	169

Chapter 9

Table 1	Dimensions of customer-brand relationship	204
Table 2	Chatbot service quality dimensions	206

Chapter 10

Table 1	Summary of manipulation check results	231
Table 2	Convergent validity, reliability, and discriminant validity	232
Table 3	Results of the main effect	232
Table 4	Results of the moderating effects of user types and parasocial interaction	233

Chapter 13

Table 1	Databases that integrate emotions and stimuli (text-image-sound)	279
Table 2	Most popular virtual assistants and their keyword to wake up. Own elaboration	284
Table 3	Examples of anthropomorphic theories and their application in VPA studies. Own elaboration	287
Table 4	Dimensions of the interactive relationships between consumers and virtual assistants. Own elaboration	289

Chapter 14

Table 1	Overview of the conducted interviews	306

Chapter 15

Table 1	AIDA Marketing framework with assessment Of VR, AR, MR, and 3D Mobile app scanners for interactive marketing	345

Chapter 16

Table 1	Identification and key attributes of notable virtual influencers	361

Chapter 17

Table 1	Sentiments toward product and product attributes	388

Chapter 18

Table 1	Presence Search Strings	401
Table 2	Definition table of presence that has been cited in interactive marketing	404

Chapter 19

Table 1	Comparison with recent relevant studies	439
Table 2	Brand descriptions	440
Table 3	Customer-brand engagement rates of brands	441

Chapter 20

Table 1	User Demographics of the Representative Social Media	454

Chapter 21

Table 1	Measurement Items for All Constructs	487
Table 2	Internal Consistency Reliability and Convergent Validity Test	488
Table 3	Discriminant Validity—Fornell and Larcker	489
Table 4	HTMT Discriminant Validity	489
Table 5	Results of Structural Model	490

Chapter 22

Table 1	Users' satisfaction ratings for the Douyin platform	508

Chapter 24

Table 1	Typology of eWOM media	551

Chapter 26

Table 1	Previous definitions of influencers	598
Table 2	Classifications of influencers based on their number of followers	600
Table 3	New classification of influencers based on potential reach	601
Table 4	Research agenda	615

Chapter 32

Table 1	Review procedure under SPAR-4-SLR procedure (Paul et al., 2021)	734
Table 2	Customer shopping journey	738

Chapter 33

Table 1	Various types of technologies applied for proximity marketing and their applications in practice	761
Table 2	Applied theories in proximity marketing	766

Chapter 34

Table 1	The application of chatbots in luxury retail	792
Table 2	The research gap and further research directions	800

Chapter 38

Table 1	Summary of studies	896
Table 2	Emoji functions	899
Table 3	The effects of emojis	904

Chapter 39

| Table 1 | Uncivil consumer behaviors and examples | 922 |

Chapter 40

| Table 1 | A review of literature on the dark side of gamification through the TCCM framework (Singh & Dhir, 2019) (*Source* Developed by authors) | 946 |

Chapter 42

Table 1	Visual model for the mixed methods explanatory sequential design study	993
Table 2	The number of comments (%) and emotions percentage distribution of the three topics identified in the first period (from June 23, 2013, to August 11, 2013)	997
Table 3	Summary of the first peak of problematic interaction	998
Table 4	The number of comments (%) and emotions percentage distribution of the three topics identified in the second period (from October 23, 2015, to November 17, 2015)	999
Table 5	Summary of the second peak of problematic interaction	1000
Table 6	The number of comments (%) and emotions percentage distribution of the three topics identified in the third period (from August 30, 2016, to September 23, 2016)	1000
Table 7	Summary of the third peak of problematic interaction	1002
Table 8	The number of comments (%) and emotions percentage distribution of the three topics identified in the fourth period (from December 26, 2016, to January 30, 2017)	1003
Table 9	Summary of the fourth peak of problematic interaction	1005

CHAPTER 1

Interactive Marketing is the New Normal

Cheng Lu Wang

Interactive marketing, as one of the fastest growing academic fields in contemporary business world, is the multi-directional value creation and mutual-influence marketing process through active customer connection, engagement, participation and interaction (Wang, 2021). Such a definition reflects the nature of interactive marketing as bilateral communication that emphasizes consumer active participation in the marketing process. Interactive marketing, which emerged with the digital edge and wide application of e-commerce (Deighton, 1996), has dramatically expanded its scale and scope thanks to the newly developed technologies.

Indeed, contemporary interactive marketing has moved beyond the scope of direct marketing or digital marketing, as the market is becoming a forum for conversations and interactions among connected actors or participants in platform ecosystems (Lim et al., 2022; Wang, 2021). The advancement of mobile technology with interactive content and personalized experience makes interactive marketing the new normal in the business world. The increasing use of artificial intelligence, mobile device and social media further facilitate marketers to deliver convenience and personalized content with immersive experiences that allow customers to dive in and enjoy the seamless interactive shopping journey via omnichannels on a deeper level.

C. L. Wang (✉)
University of New Haven, West Haven, CT, USA
e-mail: cwang@newhaven.edu

© The Author(s), under exclusive license to Springer Nature Switzerland AG 2023
C. L. Wang (ed.), *The Palgrave Handbook of Interactive Marketing*,
https://doi.org/10.1007/978-3-031-14961-0_1

Marketing activities in the connected world at various social media networks take an "organic" form that integrates shopping with daily live events through generating, disseminating and sharing news, new personal stories, creative works, photos and ideas. As social media content is merging with online shopping and consumers are persistently browsing, exploring, sharing and engaging with different forms of content, users read news, share photos, express opinions, surf websites, play games and meanwhile participate in organic marketing by sharing and recommending a product/brand.

Despite such dramatic changes in marketplaces, theoretical advancement or academic inquiry of the mechanisms of interactive marketing strategies has largely lagged behind industry innovation and market practices. This handbook aims at theoretical advancement with managerial relevance that shed insights on interactive marketing in the digitalization era. In particular, as a collection of cutting-edge research, both in conceptual development and empirical evidence, this handbook reflects a contemporary landscape of interactive marketing, from historical overview, current theoretical and practical advancement to emerging trends of interactive marketing.

1 What Are the Unique Features of This Handbook?

- This is one of a kind of the handbook in the fast-growing interactive marketing field that provides most updated knowledge and cutting-edge research findings.
- This is the most comprehensive interactive marketing book, with 41 chapters covering all aspects of contemporary interactive marketing real, including social media and influencer marketing, big data and machine learning in predictive analytics, mobile marketing and proximity marketing, interactive digital marketing and Omnichannel marketing, AI, VR and AR in business applications.
- With a focal point on interactive marketing, this handbook takes a multi-discipline perspective, from new technology innovations, social media and platform application, economic and cultural impacts, social and psychological analysis, and management and information system.
- As a collective work written by over 100 authors from more than 20 countries across all continents of the world, this book is indeed "global" and reflects a collaborative work across cultural backgrounds.

2 Who Will Benefit from Reading This Book?

- It provides a timely and comprehensive textbook companion and/or course project resource for college educators and students used for variety of graduate and undergraduate marketing courses, such as Digital

Marketing, Internet Marketing, Social Media Marketing, New Media Communication, Marketing Analytics and Marketing Management, etc.
- It offers valuable references for academic researchers who are interested in conducting and publishing in interactive marketing research. The state-of-art review and emerging new trends presented in the book are particularly useful for research idea generation and conceptual development.
- It puts forward insightful guidelines and practical tools for business management in the application of new interactive marketing strategies and applications in the real-world practices.

3 Organization of the Book

The book contains 42 chapters that are organized into 8 sections, each consisting of 4–6 chapters. A brief description of each section and each chapter follows.

3.1 Part 1: Advancement of Interactive Marketing: An Overview

Since interactive marketing as a field evolved from traditional form of direct marketing and e-commerce around three-decade ago, it has grown dramatically to be the fastest developed business discipline with a particular focus on interactivity and consumer participation. The market is becoming a forum for conversations and interactions among connected actors or participants through digital and mobile marketing activities. This section provides an overview of the historical advancement of interactive marketing discipline.

Chapter 2 offers an author-keyword-based bibliometric analysis of the research published in the domain of interactive marketing to develop and present the thematic evolution of various research subthemes in the area. The analysis presents the performance analysis of scholarly research in interactive marketing and identifies the most influential authors, affiliations and countries in the domain. Authors have identified major subthemes comprising the research scholarship and how these subthemes have evolved over time.

Chapter 3 discusses the transformation from the traditional direct marketing to the contemporary interactive marketing field in terms of the ten evolving interactive marketing tools. The authors assess these tools in terms of the three dimensions of interactivity (active control, two-way communication and synchronicity) and the potential positive (e.g., cognition) and negative (privacy concerns and intrusiveness) outcomes in marketing practices.

Chapter 4 gives an historical overview of the advancement of digital marketing in the past 30 years, laying out the digital marketing domain as a subset of interactive marketing with a focus on interactivity. The authors conclude that interactive digital marketing has evolved from business-oriented toward consumer-oriented and gradually closed the gap between industry practices and theoretical advancement.

Chapter 5 closely looks at the interactive digital marketing (IDM) concept, which reflects a focus on interactivity in digital marketing. The chapter discusses six IDM mechanisms, including mobile marketing, online PR, social media marketing, interactive display advertising, online partnership and email marketing. The authors discuss how these IDM mechanisms are applied though digital transformation based on a case study of a New Zealand company.

Chapter 6 addresses the changing role of consumers in the interactive marketing process from reactive to proactive and the underlying mechanism of consumer empowerment. The author proposes a theoretical framework that examines perceived control and related psychological processes in the interactive marketing context. The chapter further discusses the relationship between interactivity and perceived control as well as the effect of perceived control on consumers' affective, cognitive and behavioral responses.

Chapter 7 presents a "Five As" (awareness, associations, attitude, attachment and activity) model to synthesize the impact of branding factors on Word-of-Mouth communication in the interactive marketing environment. The authors deliberate evolving interactive marketing environment elements, such as new technologies, platform revolution and participatory culture, that moderate the relationship between various branding factors and electronic WOM.

3.2 Part 2: Technology Development and Interactive Marketing

The booming of interactive marketing echoes the rapid development and innovations of new technologies and Internet of Things, which fuels the growth of interactive marketing with powerful tools. The wide application of artificial intelligence, virtual reality, machine learning, chatbots and voice assistance has greatly changed the retailing and communication landscape, enhancing customer shopping experience and direct interaction with the firm or brand.

Chapter 8 discusses some recent technological innovations in the retailing industry, such as smart mirrors, checkout-free stores, chatbots, facial recognition, etc. Recognizing the growing competition and increased customer awareness that have forced retailers to innovate and bring in new technologies, the authors suggest that such interactive technologies enhance consumer interactive experience at the new retail age.

Chapter 9 examines the role of AI-powered chatbot's service quality in developing customer-brand relationship and their impact on electronic word-of-mouth in improving interactive marketing. The authors contend that understanding the dimensions of chatbot's service quality can help marketers enhance user experience, build customer-brand relationship and encourage customers to involve in positive eWOM.

Chapter 10 evaluates the impact of Internet of Things on consumer behavior in terms of the interactive experience with smart devices. The authors explore the optimal scenario of synergistic experience between customers and AI-based smart objects by integrating interpersonal orientation, objects' orientation and social orientation.

Chapter 11 compares two kinds of AI devices in terms of physical or virtual presence. The personal AI assistants are involved in consumer daily life whereas the external voice assistants or service robots are the devices that interact with consumers during the product or service acquisition. Accordingly, the physical presence and the friendliness of the voice assistant may impact the interactivity in different ways.

Chapter 12 takes a unique perspective to look at text-based, anthropomorphic social chatbots in various digital platforms. The authors synthesize the literature on computer-mediated communication and human–computer interaction, with a focus on humanizing chatbots for interactive marketing. The chapter probes into the various anthropomorphic cues used in chatbot design and messaging, including human identity cues, verbal and non-verbal cues, along with related concepts including social presence, parasocial interaction and the role of emotion in consumer-chatbot interactions.

Chapter 13 further explores the issue of affective interaction with technologies, focusing on virtual assistants such as chatbots or service robots. The authors discuss interactive marketing experiences through text, sound and image in assessing the role of transferring emotions based on anthropomorphic characteristics of the virtual assistants.

3.3 Part 3: Interactivity in the Virtual World

The advert of Metaverse signals our life becoming a mix of physical and virtual worlds in socialization, play and work. The development of technologies, such as cloud computing techniques, blockchain and 5G/6G wireless communication networks along with virtual reality and augmented reality devices, dramatically changed retailing activities and shopping experience. Consumers can either experience the product in the digital landscape by virtual fitting room or bring digital world to physical store where shoppers can experience every facet of the brand through immersive multimedia content.

Chapter 14 evaluates the application of augmented reality in interactive marketing. From the consumer perspective, AR gives rise to diverse cognitive, affective and social-psychological outcomes, which can translate into behavioral consequences including purchase intentions, word-of-mouth intentions and brand engagement. From the marketer's perspective, the advancement toward an easy integration of AR within existing IT infrastructures and efficient ways to create virtual product replicas are crucial for the adoption of AR by small retailers.

Chapter 15 inspects how e-commerce marketing migrates to the interactive v-commerce metaverse environment. The chapter outlines the recent v-commerce tools including mobile 3D body scanning for interactive marketing in fashion metaverse. The authors indicate that the practicability of v-commerce tools (mobile body scanners, VR, AR and MR) with four main elements such as immersive technology, interactivity, attractiveness, and accuracy have a potential to enhance the virtual interactive experience.

Chapter 16 looks over the emerging virtual influencers in interactive marketing. The authors indicate that virtual influencers as computer-generated characters or avatars designed and maintained by experts and digital agencies help brands appeal and reach desirable target groups effectively through their digital personalities. The chapter provides recommendations for marketers to incorporate virtual into interactive branding strategy based on literature review and exploratory interviews with young consumers.

Chapter 17 delves into the effect of virtual celebrity on product endorsement with a comparison with human endorsers. Based on two empirical studies, the author finds that viewers' sentiments toward a virtual celebrity and the parasocial interaction with a virtual celebrity vary, depending on the virtual celebrity types (artificial figure and dead human figure), the markets where the products are sold and the life cycles of the products.

Chapter 18 scrutinizes the conceptualization of "presence" concept in the interactive marketing literature. The authors argue that consumers' feelings of being "there" in a mediated environment increase the effectiveness of the immersive experience, making the concept of "presence" a central process of interest to researchers and practitioners in interactive marketing. Based on a systematic review of the literature, the chapter develops a theoretical framework that identifies the technological antecedents (e.g., sensory breadth), associated subdimensions (e.g., ecological validity) and cognitive processes (e.g., self-location and action possibilities).

3.4 *Part 4: Platform Revolution and Customer Participation*

Platform revolution is forming a new business ecosystem for customer connections and interactivities (Parker et al., 2016). Platform-orchestrated multi-sided network interactions reshaping the retail industry by prioritizing consumers' needs and source sharing through data-driven matchmaking. The process of value creation is rapidly shifting from the product- and firm-centric view to personalized and interactive customer experience. Social network platforms are particularly effective to enable people to work collaboratively, generating, disseminating and sharing news, personal stories, ideas and creative works through livestreaming.

Chapter 19 assesses the effectiveness of customer-brand engagement across social media platforms, including Twitter, Instagram and TikTok through data mining. The author finds that TikTok has higher customer-brand engagement than Twitter and Instagram, despite the latter being larger platforms and widely used by brands. The author suggests that the choice of brand content format can increase customer-brand engagement in interactive marketing.

Chapter 20 proposes five categories of social media networks, including social networking, content sharing, social knowledge and news, shopping reviewing and rating, and virtual world. The authors further identify five types of major interactive marketing functions of social media, including organic content, influencer marketing and social word-of-mouth, social ads, social event planning and social care. The chapter also examines social media analytics, measurements and ethical issues in interactive marketing and explores how social media can function more effectively in interactive marketing with the advancement of the new technologies.

Chapter 21 investigates the effect of customer-brand interaction on brand pages of social networking sites, such as Facebook, WhatsApp, Instagram, Twitter, etc. In particular, the authors analyze the role of customer involvement, practical benefits and social benefits of the fabric handicraft page that could influence customer engagement, trust and purchase intention.

Chapter 22 uses Douyin as a case of interactive livestreaming media to illustrate the constructed value and cultural preference of consumption in e-commerce. The chapter shows the mechanism of Douyin in interactive marketing could be operated and sustained even without the expected economic gain. The authors draw strategic implications for the e-commerce livestreaming industry.

Chapter 23 elaborates the emerging business practice, termed collaborative online shopping (COS), which creates interactive experiences through specific touchpoints in the joint customer journey. The chapter elaborates two forms of real-time interaction and communication during collaborative online shopping: the interpersonal interactions and interactions with the COS platforms. The authors conclude that the shoppers experience during COS can be enhanced by improving the interactive touchpoints of COSPs and enhancing the interpersonal interactions between shoppers and their companions through the social presence and flow.

3.5 Part 5: EWOM and Influencer Marketing in the Interactive Era

Participatory culture (Jenkins et al., 2006), enabled by web technology, provides individuals new forms of expression, increasing consumer engagement in public discourse, user-generated content, electronic WOM Communication and influencer marketing. Fan culture and fandom behavior, in particular, have changed the consumer-brand relationship as such that consumers are acting roles like enthusiasts, hobbyists, reviewers, bloggers live streamers and influencers in various digital platforms (Wang, 2020). Such real-life influencers from grassroots not only have a significant following but a higher number of buying conversations and conversions.

Chapter 24 offers a new conceptualization of eWOM through the theoretical lens of interactive marketing. Focusing on the interactivity of eWOM, this chapter develops a new typology of eWOM media based on their functionality, information types and interactivity. Beyond the customer-to-customer communication in eWOM, this chapter takes a managerial perspective to categorize and evaluate proactive and reactive eWOM strategies.

Chapter 25 talks over the common issues of complaint handling and channel selection in the interactive marketing era. The authors contend that consumers are turning to new interactive tools to raise their voice against companies because of the wide array of private (i.e., WhatsApp) and public channels (i.e., review platforms) available to them, raising challenges to marketers in brand building with integral complaint handling strategy.

Chapter 26 attempts to reconceptualize influencers on social media considering the dynamic nature of the influencer phenomenon. While influencer types are often classified based on the number of followers, the authors propose an improved classification based on influencers' potential reach, such as mega-reach, macro-reach, medium-reach and mini-reach influencers.

Chapter 27 examines interactive relationship among influencer-follower, influencer-brand and follower-brand involved in this triadic interplay. The authors discuss the way that three parties interact with each other in a digitally mediated dialogue using interactive tools such as likes, comments, tags, etc. in social media. The interactive nature of the influencer phenomenon has the potential to trigger brand-related conversations and instant sales via using shoppable posts and livestream shopping sessions revolving around the content that influencers create and share with their followers.

Chapter 28 focuses on understanding what makes one influencer type more credible than another does in their social media marketing campaigns for fashion brands. The authors find that while celebrity influencers have high follower counts and have been influential in traditional marketing advertising campaigns, their lack of online interaction with their followers lowers engagement rates among consumers and consequently becomes less impactful compared to some influencers of lessor followers.

3.6 Part 6: Predictive Analytics and Personalized Targeting

Big data and marketing automation via artificial intelligence and machine learning have enhanced the interactive marketing research to measure user experience metrics and increase more accurate and personalized prediction and targeting. Therefore, application of predictive analytics and smart recommendations help marketing to conduct AI-driven targeting, Interactive advertising and Ad optimization, content creation and generation, dynamic pricing, customized design and customer design experience. Interactive marketing has indeed achieved personalization and customization of marketing without soaring costs.

Chapter 29 provides a theoretical framework to understand customer engagement in predictive analytics, which is the process of using current and/or historical data with a combination of statistical techniques to assess the likelihood of a certain event happening in the future. The authors propose that predictive analytics positively influences customer engagement through need for meaningful affiliation, which is moderated by self-construal. Meanwhile, the authors suggest that predictive analytics may negatively influence customer engagement through sense of control, which is moderated by data use transparency and trust.

Chapter 30 explores the role of AI-driven systems in creating value for consumers and retailers through the lens of personalized recommendation systems and retargeted ads. Authors conducted a case study on the pioneer e-commerce platform Amazon to showcase how consumers and businesses relationship can be enhanced by AI-driven systems outcomes. The chapter suggests that the AI-based recommendation system provides informative, relevant and accurate content to consumers, and meanwhile, helps retailers to enhance consumers' loyalty, satisfaction and develop new products by predicting consumers' behaviors.

Chapter 31 seeks to guide how to leverage deep learning in interactive marketing. It characterizes eleven typical issues that marketers have to deal with. They include the curse of dimensionality, complex data processing, language-image nexus and customer privacy. Correspondingly, the chapter elucidates some solution techniques to address the issues, like generative adversarial networks, transfer learning and federated learning.

Chapter 32 surveys the interactive marketing literature on application of personalized recommendation. The authors suggest that Recommender Agents tend to assist customers by decreasing the information overload and presenting focused and curated content. The chapter identifies the role of recommender agents in purchase and post-purchase stages of customer shopping journey, including technology acceptance, persuasion, attitude formation human recommender interaction, consumer response and decision-making.

Chapter 33 aims to clarify the concept of an emerging interactive marketing strategy, i.e., location-based proximity marketing. The chapter discusses how technological breakthrough has facilitated customer and marketer interaction through continuous live location information collection and transmission via mobile devices. The authors examine the emergence of proximity marketing, which is based on pre-programmed marketing actions that deliver relevant information to potential customers at the right time and in the right place.

3.7 Part 7: Practical Implications of Interactive Marketing

Spearheaded by industry-wide marketing practices and strategic applications under various interactive innovations, the advent of interactive marketing has witnessed the declining impacts of passive broadcast advertising and one-way persuasive communication. Interactivity has become an integral part of contemporary marketing practices from retailing, service marketing to recently growing gamification in mobile marketing. With location identification technology, firms engage with the customer at the right place and time through proximity marketing via interactive wireless transmitter. Built-in interactive features of social media and mobile apps have enhanced seamless online surfing/shopping experience with the synchronization of digital and physical worlds through omnichannel marketing.

Chapter 34 explicates the practical application of artificial intelligent-enabled chatbot technology to enhance customer engagement and customer experience in the luxury retail. The authors suggest that chatbots in luxury retail need to have low cost, quick response, attractiveness, personalized service, intelligence and interactive features.

Chapter 35 demonstrates the role of incorporating the appropriately designed gamified content for a brand to establish itself in the competitive market. The author argues that gamification can be an effective interactive marketing strategy that aids brands cut the advertising clutter, standing out and escaping mediocrity. The chapter outlines the need to gamify and different ways of gamified interactive marketing.

Chapter 36 assesses the interactive experience in servicescape from both physical environment and online interaction perspectives. The authors indicate that an understanding of this interactive experience for physical and online contexts is important to practitioners to respond to a consumer's preferences, expectations and demands in a timely and appropriate manner.

Chapter 37 analyzes the role of touch in consumers' experiences in both physical and digital realms. Because consumers use their sense of touch to interact with products and salespeople in direct marketing, they use touch-screen devices to interact with products and others on e-commerce and mobile commerce platforms. The author outlines how touchscreen devices (e.g., smartphones, tablets) and haptic technology (smart wearables) influence consumers' experiences in the digital world.

Chapter 38 assesses the usage of emojis in interactive marketing in terms of emotional (e.g., expressing sentiment) and semantic functions (e.g., substituting textual messaging). The chapter examines the effects of emojis (the presence of emojis, the position of emojis, the repetition of emojis, the meanings of emojis and the type of emojis) in interactive marketing communication. The author concludes that emojis greatly influence interaction between the brand and consumers, and connections among active consumers.

3.8   Part 8: A Necessary Evil? Unintended Consequences of Interactive Marketing

The rapid development and application of powerful AI tools and mobile technologies greatly increased consumer connectivity and meanwhile intruded deeply into consumer lives, bringing various unanticipated consensus (Deighton & Kornfeld, 2009). Interactive marketing creates both opportunities and challenges for business and it is important to identify the potential dark side of applying interactive and personalized technologies. The potential risks and ethical considerations include consumer vulnerability, privacy and information security when interactive devices, big data and advanced AI technologies are used in interactive marketing activities.

Chapter 39 provides an overview of a dark side of interactive marketing about customer incivility or a set of undesirable behaviors in virtual space. Drawing on research across several disciplines, the chapter outlines emerging distinct forms of incivility in a consumerism context and discusses their distinguishing characteristics. The author puts forward strategic implications suitable for managing consumer incivility on social media networks.

Chapter 40 attempts to cast attention on the dark side of using gamification in interactive marketing, or incorporating game mechanics in non-gaming contexts like social media marketing, email marketing, customer relationship management, e-commerce and mobile marketing. The authors elaborate the dark side surrounding three key themes: design-based challenges in gamification, adopting gamified marketing solutions and user-based issues leading to lesser or no impact of gamification in online marketing.

Chapter 41 looks at the effect of gamification on customers' psychological status, raising potential challenges on ethical concerns, such as manipulation, exploitation, psychological harm, and conflict with cultural norms. The authors identify special ethical implications related to using gamification as an interactive tool and assess how consumer shape their ethical judgment toward gamification. The chapter concludes with strategic implications for marketers, designers and policymakers to minimize the unethical consequences of gamification and ensure that companies will use gamification to compete ethically and responsibly.

Chapter 42 investigates how customers' negative emotions can destroy value in online brand communities. The chapter pinpoints customers' negative emotions (anger, dissatisfaction, disgust, fear and sadness) and detects their value co-destructing effects in the customer-firm interaction. According to the authors, value co-destruction in the social media context can be understood as an exchange of negative comments in which customers' mix of emotions and the firm's responses determine the magnitude of value destruction.

References

Deighton, J. (1996, November–December). The future of interactive marketing. *Harvard Business Review*, 74(6), 151–60.

Deighton, J., & Kornfeld, L. (2009, Winter). Interactivity's unanticipated consequences for marketers and marketing. *Journal of Interactive Marketing*, 23(1), 4–10.

Jenkins, H., Clinton, K., Puroshotma, R., Robinson, A., & Weigel, M. (2006). *Confronting the challenges of participatory culture: Media education for the 21st century*. The MacArthur Foundation.

Lim, W. M., Kumar, S., Pandey, N., Rasul, T., & Gaur, V. (2022). From direct marketing to interactive marketing: A retrospective review of the Journal of Research in Interactive Marketing. *Journal of Research in Interactive Marketing*, In print. https://doi.org/10.1108/JRIM-11-2021-0276

Parker, G. G., Van Alstyne, M. W., & Choudary, S. P. (2016). *Platform revolution: How networked markets are transforming the economy—And how to make them work for you*. W. W. Norton.

Wang, C. L. (2020). Contemporary perspectives on fandom research: An introduction. In C. L. Wang (Ed.), *Handbook of research on the impact of fandom in society and consumerism*. IGI Global Inc.

Wang, C. L. (2021). New frontiers and future directions in interactive marketing: Inaugural editorial. *Journal of Research in Interactive Marketing, 15*(1), 1–9.

Advancement of Interactive Marketing: An Overview

CHAPTER 2

Evolution of Research in Interactive Marketing: A Bibliometric and Thematic Review

Deepak Verma, Satish Kumar, and Divesh Kumar

1   INTRODUCTION

Information and communication technologies (ICT) have revolutionized almost all spheres of our lives and the way businesses are conceived, managed and conducted. With the availability of technologies for communicating highly interactive messages using rich media and ubiquitous access to the Internet, the passive broadcast of marketing messages has become a thing of history. Wang (2021) defines interactive marketing as a bi-directional value creation and mutual-influence marketing process through active customer connection, engagement, participation and interaction. Communication and interaction between marketers and their customers are thus essential to interactive marketing. In the past, the role of communicating with the customer was more or less designated to advertising and later, to a certain extent, to direct marketing. In the current context of hypercompetitive markets and highly savvy customers, relying only on mass advertising and direct marketing may prove fruitless. The speed at which interactions take place between customers

D. Verma (✉) · S. Kumar · D. Kumar
Malaviya National Institute of Technology Jaipur, Jaipur, India
e-mail: dverma.dms@mnit.ac.in

S. Kumar
e-mail: skumar.dms@mnit.ac.in

D. Kumar
e-mail: divesh.dms@mnit.ac.in

© The Author(s), under exclusive license to Springer Nature Switzerland AG 2023
C. L. Wang (ed.), *The Palgrave Handbook of Interactive Marketing*,
https://doi.org/10.1007/978-3-031-14961-0_2

and the richness and interactivity that modern information and communication technologies offer has made it mandatory for marketers to improve their strategies and keep up to date with the latest trends relating to how their customers interact. It is not just web sites and online forums that affect how customers think and act. The consumer psyche is now being influenced more than ever by platforms like YouTube, Facebook, Twitter and so on. With recent developments in technologies such as virtual reality (VR) and augmented reality (AR), there is now only a thin veil between the real world and the digital one. Such confluences can result in multiple applications which can cause a manifold increase in the quality of customer interactions and experiences with brands and marketers. Marketers have also tried to keep in pace with these technological developments. There is a significant improvement in the way marketers are now treating their interactions with customers. They are no longer confined to the fringes of business strategy, but now assuming more of a central stage with a strategic focus.

The contemporary landscape of engagement and communication between businesses and their customers has undergone a systematic change in comparison to the days of one-way mass communication primarily driven by advertising. The nature of communication is now more bi-directional in nature. The content, speed and variety have all evolved. This has also resulted in the evolution of interactive marketing over time to keep up with these changes. There have, however, been only a few attempts made to retrospectively review the research scholarship in this domain and the subthemes addressed. This chapter makes an attempt to employ bibliometric methods to retrospectively study the research scholarship in the domain of interactive marketing. Specifically, it focuses on answering the following three questions:

1. Which are the most influential studies and who are the most important authors and their affiliations in the domain of interactive marketing?
2. What are the major themes in the domain of interactive marketing, and how do they interact?
3. What are the major themes of research in the domain of interactive marketing, and how have these themes evolved?

In order to answer these questions, a bibliometric analysis approach was taken. The first question was answered using a performance analysis of bibliometric data focusing on publication patterns. The second was answered using document coupling based on author-supplied keywords. Finally, thematic mapping and strategic diagrams were developed on the basis of the co-word analysis of the author keywords performed to answer the third.

The remainder of the chapter is broadly divided as follows: the second section relates to the method used to analysis the bibliometric data. Section 3 presents the results of the performance analysis, demonstrates the outcomes of the document coupling based on author keywords, and the thematic evolution of the subthemes in the domain of interactive marketing and finally, Sect. 4 concludes the chapter while including the key takeaways and future research directions.

2 Method

In order to achieve the stated objectives of this chapter, a bibliometric analysis approach was used. A bibliometric approach is considered suitable for handling large amount of quantitative bibliographic data (Donthu et al., 2021) as in this case. The methodology has been widely used in multiple domains of research scholarship to analyse and visualize knowledge networks and intellectual structures (Donthu et al., 2022; Kumar et al., 2022). There are vast amounts of knowledge inherent to the scholastic documents produced in any field, which, if harnessed, analysed and visualized properly, can provide valuable insights into the knowledge networks and intellectual structures of a research domain. Using bibliographic data, such networks can be analysed and visualized at various levels, including documents, authors, affiliations, countries and keywords.

One of the earliest proponents of bibliographic coupling was Kessler (1963) and now, with the availability of computing resources and the abundance of documents in digital forms, it is gaining popularity in many fields of research. Such analysis can provide valuable insights not only into the intellectual structures and subthemes being explored, but also in relation to how these are evolving (Zhao & Strotmann, 2014). Bibliographic coupling may be defined as two or more documents sharing certain items in their references, implying common research themes (Yang et al., 2016). Such an understanding can be extended to include other document components such as author keywords, as frequently used ones may imply common, specific research themes (Morris & Yen, 2004). The analysis in the current chapter uses author keywords as the common base for analysing and visualizing the underlying intellectual structures and subthemes in the area.

For the purpose of this chapter, bibliographic data for the two most prominent journals in the domain of interactive marketing—the *Journal of Interactive Marketing* and the *Journal of Research in Interactive Marketing*—were extracted from SCOPUS. The *Journal of Interactive Marketing* (JIM), published by Elsevier, is inarguably the most impactful source in the domain of interactive marketing focusing on both online and offline topics related to the analysis, targeting and service of individual customers. The journal has an impact factor of 6.258. The *Journal of Research in Interactive Marketing* (JIRM), originally started as *Direct Marketing: An International Journal*, is another internationally acclaimed and referred journal. It changed its name in 2010 to expand its scope to interactive marketing, which is an extension of direct marketing (or the use of direct media technologies) into new media technologies that allow for multi-way communication between buyers and sellers. JIRM has an impact factor of 4.509. Both of these are highly respected journals in the field of marketing in general and represent the epitome of impactful research specifically in the domain of interactive marketing, as evidenced by their wide acceptance and impressive impact metrics and indexing.

A summary of the various impact measures of JIM and JIRM based on their 2022 ranking by SCOPUS (CiteScore, 2020/2022) is presented in Table 1 and Fig. 1.

The initial search resulted in the extraction of 942 documents from the two journals, 615 from the *Journal of Interactive Marketing* (JIM) and 327 from the *Journal of Research in Interactive Marketing* (JIRM). For the purpose of this chapter, only articles (873), editorials (41) and review papers (17)

Table 1 Summary of selected sources

	Journal of Interactive Marketing	*Journal of Research in Interactive Marketing*
Coverage in SCOPUS	1997–present	2010–present
Total publications	581	290
Total citations	52,754	6,833
h-index	117	43
g-index	213	67
m-index	4.5	3.31
CiteScore 2020	11.4	6.2
SJR 2021	3.62	1.56
SJR quartile 2021	Q1	Q1
SNIP 2020	2.880	1.419
CiteScore tracker (as on 6 April 2022)	**12.7**	**9.1**
CiteScore rank (marketing)	7/185 (96th percentile)	32/185 (82nd percentile)

*2021 CiteScore as on 6 April 2022

Fig. 1 CiteScore trends

were retained. A summary of the main information extracted from the initial search results and the final selected documents for the analysis are presented in Table 2.

The analysis of the documents was divided into two parts: a bibliometric performance analysis of the documents extracted and the analysis and visualization of major subthemes and their intellectual structures.

The first part of analysis, the bibliometric performance analysis, included metrics such as the total documents produced, average citations per year and per article, most cited sources, most impactful authors, top relevant institutional affiliations, production of articles by country and so on. This section also incorporated the identification of the top author-supplied keywords. This is supplemented by the keyword dynamics of the top keywords and the trending topics in the domain for the last five years.

The second part of the analysis focuses on major subthemes and their evolution using author-supplied keywords. In order to map the thematic evolution in the area, this chapter adopts the general approach proposed by Garfield (1994) by building maps from bibliometric information. Although there are multiple forms of scientific mapping that can be performed using bibliometric information (Small, 2006), two of the most common approaches are by using co-word analysis (Small, 1973), which is primarily used to map the structure of a scientific research space, and co-citation analysis, which mainly outlines the conceptual structures (Cobo et al., 2011; Mora-Valentín et al., 2018).

3 Results

In the first stage of the study, a performance analysis was completed to compile the publication trends among articles in the domain. Table 3 presents the year-wise summary of the number of documents published, as well as the average number of citations per article, and per year, and the total citable years. This is supplemented with Fig. 2, which presents the year-wise breakdown of the growth in the number of documents published in the two selected sources. It can be seen that there is a steady increase in the number of documents published in the field over time.

Table 4 presents the 10 most impactful authors. While Shankar, V. is the most productive author with 21 publications to his name, the most impactful author in terms of total citations is Malthouse, E.C., with a total of 1,602 citations. Dholakia, U.M. has the most citations per publication (221.5), having received 1,329 citations for six publications. The top two most productive authors, Shankar, V. and Malthouse, E.C., are also the authors with highest h-index (12). The highest m-index (21) and g-index (0.600) among the most productive authors belongs to Shankar, V. making him the most influential and impactful author with the highest number of publications, second-highest total citation count and top place in all indices.

Figure 3 presents the top 10 locally cited sources. The *Journal of Interactive Marketing* occupies the top slot with 2,275 citations, followed by the

Table 2 Search results—main information

	Initial search results			Final selected
	Journal of Interactive Marketing	Journal of Research in Interactive Marketing	Total	
Timespan	1997:2021	2010:2022	1997:2022	1997:2022
Sources (journals, books, etc.)	1	1	2	2
Documents	615	327	942	931
Average years from publication	11.9	4.99	9.52	9.49
Average citations per documents	85.64	20.61	63.06	63.78
Average citations per year per doc	6.927	3.368	5.692	5.754
References	26,196	19,267	43,625	43,577
Document types				
Article	566	306	872	873
Conference paper	5		5	
Editorial	34	7	41	41
Erratum	4		4	
Note	1	1	3	
Retracted	1		1	
Review	4	13	17	17
Document contents				
Author keywords (DE)	1,302	871	1,981	1,979
Authors				
Authors	1,196	686	1,812	1,810
Author appearances	1,623	821	2,444	2,419
Authors of single-authored documents	73	43	116	115
Authors of multi-authored documents	1,123	643	1,696	1,695
Author collaboration				
Single-authored documents	92	54	146	140
Documents per author	0.514	0.477	0.52	0.514
Authors per document	1.94	2.1	1.92	1.94
Co-authors per documents	2.64	2.51	2.59	2.6

(continued)

Table 2 (continued)

	Initial search results			Final selected
	Journal of Interactive Marketing	Journal of Research in Interactive Marketing	Total	
Collaboration index	2.15	2.36	2.13	2.14

Table 3 Articles published, mean citations per year and per article

Year	N	Mean TC per art	Mean TC per year	Citable years
1997	33	28.18	1.13	25
1998	15	60.80	2.53	24
1999	12	109.17	4.75	23
2000	15	53.60	2.44	22
2001	21	121.62	5.79	21
2002	24	131.79	6.59	20
2003	21	94.62	4.98	19
2004	27	306.15	17.01	18
2005	21	158.29	9.31	17
2006	18	55.11	3.44	16
2007	20	201.45	13.43	15
2008	17	59.82	4.27	14
2009	35	126.43	9.73	13
2010	46	62.00	5.17	12
2011	41	47.44	4.31	11
2012	45	98.56	9.86	10
2013	45	78.80	8.76	9
2014	37	87.54	10.94	8
2015	36	41.00	5.86	7
2016	48	40.35	6.73	6
2017	54	38.39	7.68	5
2018	59	25.46	6.36	4
2019	62	20.40	6.80	3
2020	56	19.39	9.70	2
2021	103	4.83	4.83	1
2022	20	1		0
Average annual growth rate (until 2021) (%)	9.61	20.08	34.03	

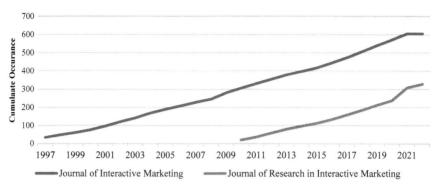

Fig. 2 Source-wise growth of publications

Table 4 Top 10 authors and their impact

Author	NP	TC	TC/NP	h-index	g-index	m-index	PY_start
Shankar V	21	1,582	75.34	12	21	0.600	2003
Malthouse EC	15	1,609	107.27	12	15	0.500	1999
Peltier JW	12	603	50.25	11	12	0.423	1997
Verhoef PC	10	618	61.8	9	10	0.500	2005
Hofacker CF	9	706	78.45	8	9	0.348	2000
Milne GR	8	951	118.87	7	8	0.292	1999
De Ruyter K	8	674	84.25	8	8	0.364	2001
Kim J	7	1,124	160.57	7	7	0.350	2003
Dholakia UM	6	1,329	221.5	6	6	0.286	2002
Kim H	6	317	52.84	6	6	0.429	2009

Note NP = number of publications; TC = total citations; TC/NP = citations per publication; h = h-index (n articles getting at least n citations); g = g-index (n articles getting at least n^2 citations); m = m-index (h-index divided by number of years author has been active); PY_Start = year of first publication

Journal of Marketing with 2300 citations. The *Journal of Consumer Research* (2,140 citations) and *Journal of Marketing Research* (1,968 citations) are other notable sources of local citations.

Figure 4 presents the most relevant affiliations in terms of the number of publications produced. Northwestern University tops the list with 41 publications, followed by Texas A&M University with 28. The third spot is occupied by the University of Groningen (The Netherlands) with 17. Institutions from the USA dominate the list, as seven out of the top 10 institutions are based in the USA. Apart from the University of Groningen (The Netherlands) in the third position, the other two non-USA institutions are the University of Amsterdam (The Netherlands) and Ghent University (Belgium).

Figure 5a presents the spread of geographic affiliations. It can be noted that the research production in the domain of interactive marketing is

Fig. 3 Top 10 sources of local citations

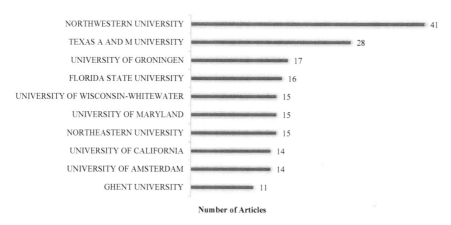

Fig. 4 Most relevant affiliations (top 10)

primarily concentrated in North America, Europe, Australia and Oceania, and South Asia (primarily India) and Southeast Asia (including China). Figure 5b presents the top 10 countries with the highest numbers of publications. The USA, with a total of 1,008 publications, leads the list with quite a margin, followed by Germany with 100 to its credit. Apart from Germany, three more countries—The Netherlands (in the third position), the UK (fifth) and Spain (ninth) are featured from the European region. Three Asian countries, China, South Korea and India, feature on the list at the fourth, seventh and eighth positions, respectively. Canada is the other North American country, occupying the 10th position, whereas Australia is sixth. There were no countries in the top 10 from South America or Africa.

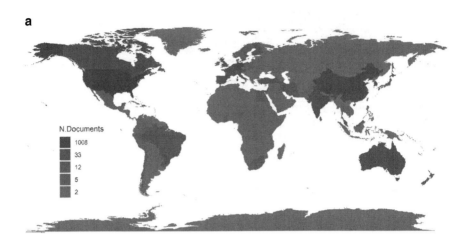

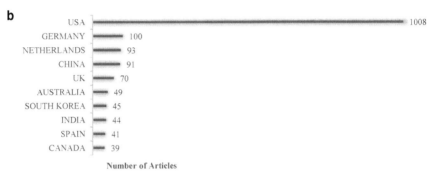

Fig. 5 Country-specific production

An analysis was conducted to identify the corresponding author's country affiliations. Figure 6 presents the results. The USA naturally tops the list by huge margins, both in terms of single country publications (SCP) and multiple country publications (MCP). Germany and China closely followed each other in the second and third positions. Interestingly, it can be seen from the figure that India is the only country in the list with all SCP and no MCP. This implies a lack of international collaborations in the area from India, though it may be emerging as a source of scholarship.

Lastly, a three-field analysis for author-country-affiliation was performed to identify the linkages between the most influential authors, countries and affiliations. Figure 7 exhibits the linkages in the form of a Sankey diagram. It can be seen the USA is the most influential country as all of the top 10 authors as well as the top 10 institutional affiliations are linked to it. The second most influential country in terms of linkages is The Netherlands, whereas Northwestern University and Texas A&M University are the most linked affiliations. The University of Groningen and the University of Amsterdam, both belonging

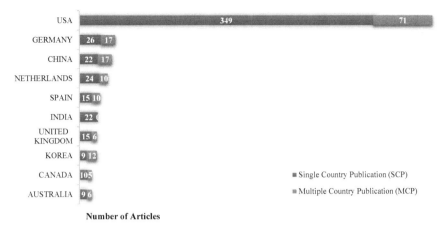

Fig. 6 Corresponding author country

to The Netherlands, and Ghent University (Belgium) are the only non-USA universities in the top 10 list.

Table 5 presents the 10 most cited countries in the domain. It comes as no surprise that the list is again dominated by the USA, with a total of 30,520

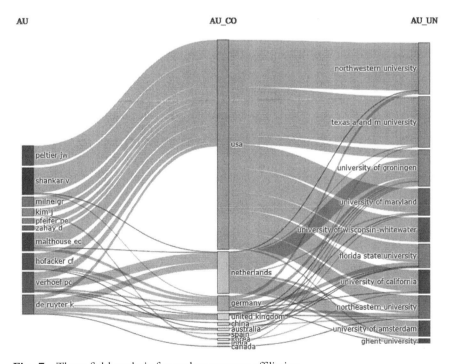

Fig. 7 Three-field analysis for author-country-affiliation

citations. The Netherlands and Germany occupy the second and third positions on the list with 3,247 and 2,487 citations, respectively. In total, there are five countries from the European region on the list—The Netherlands, Germany, the UK, Spain and Italy, two countries each from North America (the USA and Canada) and Asia (South Korea and China). This indicates that although there might be a relative increase in the number of publications coming out of large emerging markets, like India, the area is still dominated by the scholarship from the developed markets, especially North America and Europe.

Table 6 presents the most globally cited articles. The most cited article is Prahalad and Ramaswamy (2004), which is cited 2,989 times and focuses on the dynamics of interactions between a firm and its customers and how it leads to the creation of value. The second and third places on the list are occupied by Hennig-Thurau et al. (2004) and Hollebeek et al. (2014), respectively. While the former focuses on the development of a typology for the motives of online consumer articulation, the latter attempts to conceptualize, develop and validate a scale for consumer brand engagement in the context of social media. Interestingly, five of the top 10 most cited articles relate to word-of-mouth communication or customer reviews. Customer engagement and value creation are the other dominant themes. It can also be noted that all of the top 10 globally cited documents are published in the *Journal of Interactive Marketing*.

Table 7 presents the list of the top 10 most locally cited articles. The most locally cited article is Wang (2021), the inaugural editorial for the *Journal of Research in Interactive Marketing*, which focuses on the major driving forces of research in interactive marketing and how the research landscapes are changing in the domain.

Figure 8 presents a word cloud based on the top 50 author keywords extracted from the selected articles. It can be seen that the social media and social networking sites themselves are the dominant themes. Some

Table 5 Most cited countries

Country	Total citations	Average article citations
USA	30,520	72.7
The Netherlands	3,247	95.5
Germany	2,487	57.8
UK	1,550	73.8
Korea	1,490	71.0
New Zealand	1,291	322.8
China	1,250	32.1
Canada	1,037	69.1
Spain	793	31.7
Italy	707	78.6

Table 6 Most globally cited articles (top 10)

Authors	Year	Title	TC	TC_Yr	Norm_TC
Prahalad CK & Ramaswamy V	2004	Co-creation experiences: The next practice in value creation	2,989	157.32	9.76
Hennig-Thurau T, Gwinner KP, Walsh G & Gremler DD	2004	Electronic word-of-mouth via consumer-opinion platforms: What motivates consumers to articulate themselves on the Internet?	2,847	149.84	9.30
Hollebeek LD, Glynn MS & Brodie RJ	2014	Consumer brand engagement in social media: Conceptualization, scale development and validation	1,176	130.67	13.43
Bickart B & Schindler RM	2001	Internet forums as influential sources of consumer information	1,007	45.77	8.28
de Vries L, Gensler S & Leeflang PSH	2012	Popularity of brand posts on brand fan pages: An investigation of the effects of social media marketing	1,005	91.36	10.20
Brown J, Broderick AJ & Lee N	2007	Word of mouth communication within online communities: Conceptualizing the online social network	958	59.88	4.76
Dellarocas C, Zhang X & Awad NF	2007	Exploring the value of online product reviews in forecasting sales: The case of motion pictures	899	56.19	4.46
Bagozzi RP & Dholakia UM	2002	Intentional social action in virtual communities	857	40.81	6.50
Sawhney M, Verona G & Prandelli E	2005	Collaborating to create: The Internet as a platform for customer engagement in product innovation	853	47.39	5.39
Sen S & Lerman D	2007	Why are you telling me this? An examination into negative consumer reviews on the Web	687	42.94	3.41

Note TC = total citations; TC_Yr = total citations per year; Norm_TC = normalized total citations

other prominent themes relate to e-commerce, marketing communication, consumer behaviour and Internet marketing.

For a further analysis, the top 10 author keywords were extracted. Figure 9 presents a tree map of the top 10 author keywords. The most dominant theme that can be identified from the tree map relates to social media,

Table 7 Most local cited articles (top 10)

Author	Year	Title	LC	GC	LC/GC (%)	Norm LC	Norm GC
Wang CL	2021	New frontiers and future directions in interactive marketing: Inaugural editorial	60	87	68.97	43.52	17.99
Hennig-Thurau T, Gwinner KP, Walsh G & Gremler DD	2004	Electronic word-of-mouth via consumer-opinion platforms: What motivates consumers to articulate themselves on the Internet?	56	2,847	1.97	8.35	9.3
Hollebeek LD, Glynn MS & Brodie RJ	2014	Consumer brand engagement in social media: Conceptualization, scale development and validation	38	1,176	3.23	8.27	13.43
Calder BJ, Malthouse, EC & Schaedel, U	2009	An experimental study of the relationship between online engagement and advertising effectiveness	37	547	6.76	3.39	4.33
de Vries L, Gensler S & Leeflang PSH	2012	Popularity of brand posts on brand fan pages: An investigation of the effects of social media marketing	34	1,005	3.38	7.05	10.2
Shankar V & Balasubramanian S	2009	Mobile marketing: A synthesis and prognosis	34	252	13.49	3.12	1.99
Brown J, Broderick AJ & Lee N	2007	Word of mouth communication within online communities: Conceptualizing the online social network	32	958	3.34	3.5	4.76

(continued)

Table 7 (continued)

Author	Year	Title	LC	GC	LC/GC (%)	Norm LC	Norm GC
Hoffman DL & Novak TP	2009	Flow online: Lessons learned and future prospects	30	487	6.16	2.75	3.85
King RA, Racherla P & Bush VD	2014	What we know and don't know about online word-of-mouth: A review and synthesis of the literature	29	551	5.26	6.31	6.29
Shankar V, Venkatesh A, Hofacker C & Naik P	2010	Mobile marketing in the retailing environment: Current insights and future research avenues	29	344	8.43	6.84	5.55

Note LC = local citations; GC = global citations; LC/GC(%) = ratio of local citations to global citations; Norm_LC = normalized local citations; Norm_GC = normalized global citations

Fig. 8 Word cloud (top 50 author keywords)

with 42% occurrences if the four keywords social media (15%), social media marketing (13%), social networking sites (6%) and Facebook (8%) are considered together. The other dominant theme related to consumer behaviour with 27% occurrences, if the two keywords consumer behaviour (17%) and online consumer behaviour (10%) are considered together. E-Commerce (11%), advertising (8%), marketing communications (7%) and Internet marketing (6%) were other keywords in the list of the top 10 author keywords.

Figure 10 presents the cumulative occurrences of the top 10 author keywords for the period 2009–2022. It can be seen that consumer behaviour

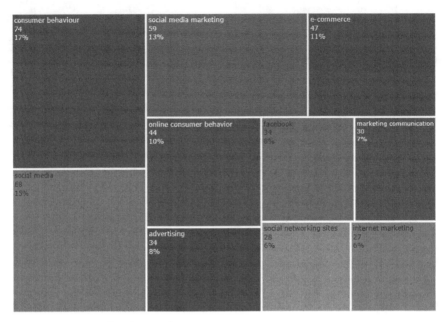

Fig. 9 Top 10 author keywords

remains the most popular keyword from 2010 onwards. Social media and social media marketing, which rose a little late, around 2012 and 2016, respectively, currently occupy the second and third positions in 2022. E-commerce, which was at the top of the list in 2009, is placed in the fourth position in 2022. The top five list is completed by online consumer behaviour, which has been steadily gaining numbers and emerging as one of the most popular author keywords, especially after 2016.

Next, document coupling was performed by using author keywords as coupling measures and global citation scores as impact measures. The visual representation of the clusters is presented in Fig. 11 and the cluster-wise major keywords, cluster frequency and their centrality and impact are presented in Table 8. Four major clusters were identified.

Cluster 1 was identified by the keywords *social media, Facebook, social media marketing, consumer engagement* and *digital marketing*, indicating that social media and customer engagements are the major themes of the cluster. The top articles included in the cluster are Hollebeek et al. (2014), de Vries et al. (2012) and King et al. (2014).

Cluster 2 was defined by the keywords *e-commerce, online advertising, Internet marketing, mobile marketing* and *online marketing*, indicating marketing using the digital and electronic medium as the core theme. The top articles included in this cluster are Calder et al. (2009), Hoffman and Novak (2009) and Shankar and Yadav (2010).

2 EVOLUTION OF RESEARCH IN INTERACTIVE ... 31

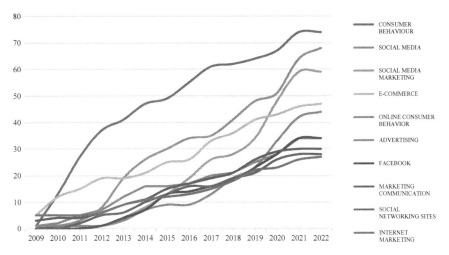

Fig. 10 Keyword dynamics (top 10 author keywords)

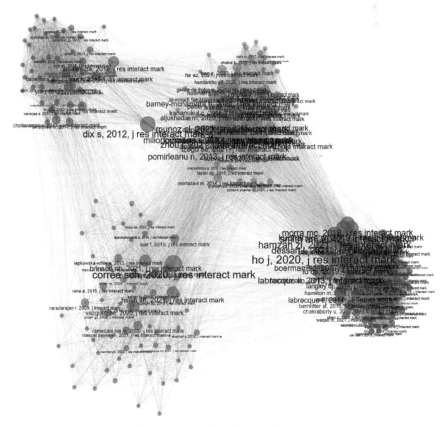

Fig. 11 Document coupling using author keywords

Table 8 Clustering by author keywords—keywords, frequency, centrality and impact

Cluster	Top keywords	Frequency	Centrality	Impact
1	Social media Facebook Social media marketing Consumer engagement Digital marketing	67	0.436	3.379
2	E-commerce Online advertising Internet marketing Mobile marketing Online marketing	65	0.310	2.836
3	Social media marketing Facebook Social networking sites Marketing communications Consumer behaviour	71	0.450	1.918
4	Consumer behaviour United States of America Internet Electronic commerce Web sites	47	0.394	1.703

Cluster 3, the largest of the four clusters, comprised keywords such as *social media marketing, Facebook, social networking sites, marketing communications* and *consumer behaviour*, indicating marketing communication and consumer behaviour in the context of social media as the core theme of the cluster. The top articles in the cluster included Barger et al. (2016), Kabadayi and Price (2014), Wang and Kim (2017), Swani et al. (2013) and Schivinski and Dabrowski (2015).

Lastly, Cluster 4, the smallest of the clusters, was based on the keywords *consumer behaviour, United States of America, Internet, electronic commerce* and *web sites*. The top articles included in the cluster are Kim and Lennon (2013), Rodrigues Pinho and Soares (2011), Dix (2012), Lin et al. (2012) and Limbu et al. (2012).

A strategic diagram (as presented in Fig. 12) of the four clusters was drawn based on their centrality and impact in order to clarify the maturity and cohesion represented by these clusters. It can be seen that Cluster 1 has both high centrality and impact, implying that these articles and keywords have strong external linkages and have matured enough to serve as the motor themes for the domain. Cluster 2 has high impact but low centrality, meaning that though the themes in the cluster have high impact in terms of citations, they are not much linked with the other subthemes in the domain. Such themes are usually labelled niche themes. Cluster 3 has a high centrality score but low impact scores, implying that although these subthemes do not have very high global citations, they have strong external linkages with other subthemes in the domain. Such themes are usually labelled as basic themes. Lastly, Cluster 4 has low scores on both the centrality and impact measures. This implies that either these are declining themes that are losing currency with the researchers in the domain or are new emerging themes that are yet to forge linkages with other subthemes in the domain and create impact in terms of citations.

The next step was to map the evolution of various subthemes in interactive marketing literature. For the purpose of charting the thematic evolution, three timespans are considered, 1997–2012, 2013–2017 and 2018–2022. The difference in the number of years in the first period and the latter two can primarily be attributed to the significant increase in the number of publications in recent years. The results are presented in Fig. 13.

For the first period (1997–2012), the predominant subthemes in the interactive marketing literature were driven by research related to *social media*. Other dominant subthemes included *advertising*, *consumer behaviour* and *interactive marketing*. The third rung of important subthemes during this period were related to *online marketing*, *e-commerce* and *customer relationship management*. Additionally, there was also some research related to marketing strategy.

As is common in most emerging areas of research scholarship, the subthemes from the initial period consolidated themselves into various related subthemes or were split into further subthemes in the next period

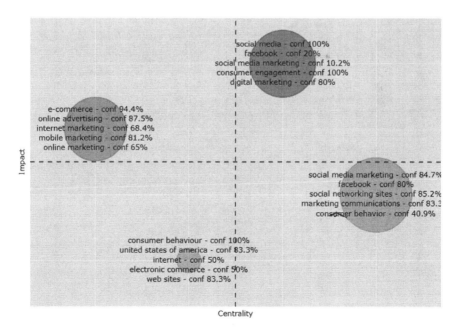

Fig. 12 Strategic diagram of the four clusters

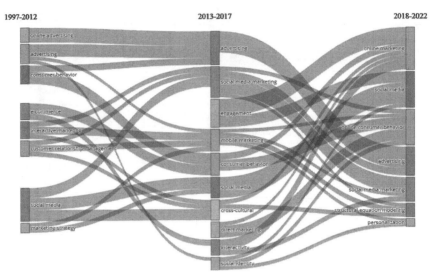

Fig. 13 Thematic evolution of interactive marketing literature

(2013–2017). During this period *advertising* emerged as one of the largest subthemes, consolidating its evolution from the *online advertising*, *advertising* and *consumer behaviour* subthemes of the previous period. *Social media marketing* emerged as another major influential subtheme evolving from the subthemes *interactive marketing*, *customer relationship management* and *social media* from the previous timespan. The subtheme mobile marketing emerged as a consolidation of research in subthemes *advertising*, *interactive marketing* and *marketing strategy*. The subtheme consumer behaviour from the previous period evolved further in this one by drawing from the e-commerce subtheme of the prior timespan. Another significant subtheme emerging during this period was *cross-cultural*, indicating an expansion of the initial research scholarship to include cross-cultural implications. This subtheme primarily evolved from *customer relationship management*, *interactive marketing* and *social media* subthemes from the previous period. Some other themes that emerged independently of the subthemes of the preceding years were *engagement*, a very influential subtheme during this period, and *direct marketing*. Other notable subthemes that can be identified for the timespan are *interactivity* and *social identity*, which evolved from the *e-commerce* and *advertising* subthemes, respectively, of the previous period.

The more recent time period 2018–2022 represents a further consolidation of the subthemes. The top three subthemes that emerged during this period are *online marketing*, *social media* and *online consumer behaviour*. The new version of the subtheme *online marketing* consolidated research from the previous subtheme of *engagement*, *interactivity*, *consumer behaviour*, *cross-culture* and *direct marketing*. The newer version of *social media* extended the subtheme of the previous period to include research in the subthemes of *engagement* and *social identity*. Similarly, the advertising subtheme from the previous period evolved further by including inputs from the social media marketing subtheme. Two new subthemes evolved during the latest period—*structure equation modelling* and *personalization*. While the former predominantly borrows from *social media marketing*, *mobile marketing* and *cross-cultural* themes, it also indicates the emerging importance and adoption of complex statistical modelling to understand the underlying relationships in the domain.

Lastly, thematic landscapes were analysed for each of the selected periods using strategic diagrams. A two-dimensional strategic diagram can be obtained from the two parameters of the keyword network or theme—centrality, which represents the degree of interaction of a network with other networks, and density, which is the measure of the internal strength of the network (Callon et al., 1991). While centrality can be thought of in terms of the strength of external ties of a network, density can be thought of in terms of the strength of internal ties. Based on these two dimensions, the identified themes based on co-keyword analysis can be placed into the four quadrants of a strategic diagram (Callon et al., 1991; Muñoz-Leiva et al., 2012). The first quadrant represents the themes that are both high in centrality and density. This means that the themes in this quadrant have strong external linkages with other themes as well as strong internal cohesion. Such themes are well developed and provide structure to the research in the field and are labelled *motor themes*. The second quadrant contains themes which have high centrality but are low in density. These themes usually represent the categories which are *basic themes* in nature and are more useful in creating underlying linkages and interactions between other subthemes. This means that these subthemes are more traversal. Those in the third quadrant are low in centrality but high in density, indicating that these themes do not interact much with other themes, but have strong internal linkages. Such themes represent specialized subthemes in the area, and are also sometimes labelled *niche themes*. The last and fourth quadrant represents themes which are neither high on centrality nor on density. This essentially means that these themes are low on maturity and linkages with other themes. Usually, this quadrant represents themes that have either declined and lost relevance or have only recently emerged.

Figure 14 presents the strategic diagram for the first period of analysis, i.e. 1997–2012. It can be noted that *consumer behaviour* was the most influential theme for the period. Although it has high centrality, indicating strong linkages with other themes, it has moderate density, placing it at the border of the first and second quadrants. Another significant theme that exhibited similar characteristics was *interactive marketing*. It can also be seen that *digital technology* and *advertising* were the motor themes for the period, which could serve the purpose of creating underlying linkages for other themes. *Customer relationship management* and *e-commerce* indisputably served as the

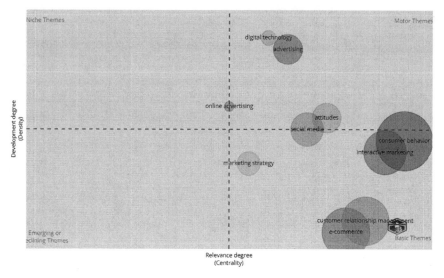

Fig. 14 Strategic diagram of themes for period 1997–2012

basic themes. No niche or declining/emerging themes were identified for this period.

Figure 15 presents the strategic diagram for the period 2013–2017. It can be observed that *advertising* and, to some extent, *direct marketing* served as the motor themes for the period. Most of the influential themes, *social media marketing*, *consumer behaviour*, *interactivity*, *mobile marketing* and social identity, were all in the second quadrant and thus served as the basic themes. This may denote that although these themes had high centrality indicating their importance, they needed to further mature and develop as research themes. It can also be observed that the period marks the emergence of some niche subthemes in the *recall*, *engagement* and *viral video advertising*. An emerging subtheme, *cross-cultural*, can also be identified.

Figure 16 presents the strategic diagram of the major themes for the current period spanning 2018–2022. It can be noted that the *social media* serves as the major influencing motor theme for the period. Another new subtheme, *structural equation modelling*, seems to have moderate to high centrality as well as density, indicating that this subtheme might be emerging as a major influential subtheme in the future. Increasing centrality indicates that it has strong external linkages with other themes and an increasing density suggests increasing maturity. Given that structural equation modelling relates to a quantitative modelling of complex relationships, it does present a strong potential for serving as the underlying framework to link various subthemes creating linkages between them. It can also be inferred from the strategic diagram for the period that the subthemes—*social media marketing*, *online marketing*, *online consumer behaviour* and *advertising* serve as the basic

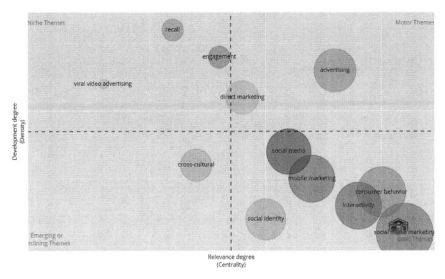

Fig. 15 Strategic diagram for the period 2013–2017

themes for the period. It can also be observed that subthemes of scholarly research in interactive marketing *mobile commerce* and *consumer attitudes* are located between quadrants three and four. This may indicate the potential of these themes to develop into niche themes in the future.

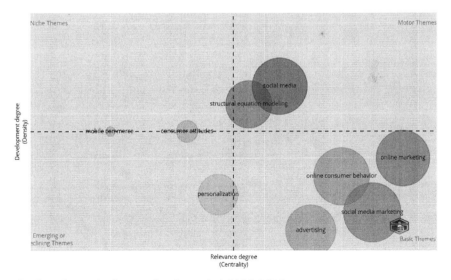

Fig. 16 Strategic diagram for the period 2018–2022

4 Conclusion

4.1 Key Takeaways

This chapter uses bibliographic data to analyse and visualize the intellectual structures of the research scholarship in the domain of interactive marketing. In doing so it retrospectively analysed the bibliographic data from research published in two of the leading journals in the area—the *Journal of Interactive Marketing* and the *Journal of Research in Interactive Marketing*. Three major objectives were identified for the review of the bibliometric data. A summary of the results is presented below.

For the first objective of identifying the patterns in publications and the most influential contributors in the domain, a performance analysis of the research publications was carried out. The analysis showed a continuous and steady increase in the number of documents published over time. Shankar, V. was found to be most influential author with the highest number of publications and second-highest number of citations (Malthouse, E.C. has the highest number of citations), joint highest h-index (with Malthouse, E.C.), highest g-index and highest m-index among all the contributors in the research domain. The *Journal of Interactive Marketing* was found to be the most locally cited source, followed by the *Journal of Marketing and Journal of Consumer Research*. Among the institutional affiliations, Northwestern University and Texas A&M University were the top contributors. The list of top contributing affiliations was dominated by the institutions located in the USA, with seven of the top 10 universities belonging to the USA. The remaining three universities were from Europe (two from The Netherlands and one from Belgium). It was observed that the USA dominated the research landscape by huge margins compared to any other country. Most of the countries that significantly influence the research domain are matured and developed economies, leaving a huge gap for emerging and developing economies. Among all the significant contributing countries, multiple country publications were found to form a significant proportion, with the exception of India. This essentially means that, barring India, authors are collaborating internationally in order to execute their research studies. The list, obviously, is dominated by the USA both in terms of single country publications and multiple country publications. An attempt was also made to identify the most influential research in the domain. Prahalad and Ramaswamy (2004), Hennig-Thurau et al. (2004) and Hollebeek et al. (2014) were found to be most globally cited articles. Similarly, Wang (2021), Hennig-Thurau et al. (2004) and Hollebeek et al. (2014) were found to be the most locally cited documents.

In order to identify the major subthemes in the research domain, an analysis of author keywords was also undertaken. The top five keywords used by the authors in the domain were found to be consumer behaviour, social media, social media marketing, e-commerce and online consumer behaviour. This indicates that the research involving social and digital media, and e-commerce, are the driving influences in the field of interactive marketing. Furthermore, an analysis of the keyword dynamics over last 13 years indicated that the above listed five keywords are the fastest growing author keywords in the research domain.

Next, a bibliographic coupling of the articles was performed using author keywords as coupling measures and global citation scores as impact measures. A total of four clusters were obtained. Cluster 1 comprised 67 articles with the major keywords—social media, Facebook, social media marketing, consumer engagement and digital marketing. The cluster has both high centrality and impact, making it the cluster representing the motor themes in the domain. Cluster 2 contained 65 articles with major keywords—e-commerce, online advertising, Internet marketing, mobile marketing and online marketing. Cluster 3 included 71 articles with major keywords such as social media marketing, Facebook, social networking sites, marketing communications and consumer behaviour. This cluster has high centrality but low impact, implying that these themes are mature enough to provide linkages to other subthemes in the domain, but do not have high impact on their own. The last, and the smallest, Cluster 4 incorporated 47 articles with major keywords, such as consumer behaviour, United States of America, Internet, electronic commerce and web sites. This cluster is both low on centrality and impact. Usually, such clusters represent themes which are declining and are no longer popular with researchers. Such centrality and impact scores may also represent emerging themes which have not yet matured enough to provide external linkages to other subthemes in the domain, or evolved enough to have a high impact of their own.

The chapter also included an analysis of evolution of major subthemes in the domain of interactive marketing since 1997. For this purpose, three periods were identified as 1997–2012, 2013–2017 and 2018–2022. The analysis revealed that the subthemes have consolidated and interacted with each other to evolve into a complex lot which are interlinked and borrow from each other. Such interactions and linkages are a sign of increasing maturity in the research domain. The analysis indicated that the contemporary subthemes in interactive marketing are driven by social media and online technologies, and focus more on (online) consumer behaviour. This is natural, as interactive marketing is based on the basic premise of bi-directional communication between the marketers and customers Wang (2021), and online media, especially the social media, has emerged as the biggest and most prominent channel driving community-style conversation in the contemporary markets.

4.2 Future Directions

Moving forward, interactive marketing can be considered one of the most interesting and impactful domains of research in marketing. It should be noted that with the advent and evolution of ubiquitous communication technologies and rich interactive media, the fundamental nature in which customers interact among themselves and with businesses and marketers have changed. Such fast-evolving dynamics are bound to present new challenges to marketers, who need to align their strategies and communication channels with their customers in light of these developments. As noted by Wang (2021) in his inaugural editorial for JIRM, the interactions between customers and marketers are evolving from unidirectional mass communication to bi-directional value creation and mutual influencing marketing processes. Technologies such as virtual reality (VR), augmented reality (AR) and artificial intelligence, as well as the proliferation of mobile networks and its access, coupled with increasingly savvy customers in ever-connected virtual communities, are promoting a dynamic and ever-evolving communication landscape. Such dynamics, although increasing the complexities for marketing managers, also provide huge opportunities for them to create strong mutually beneficial and value-creating bonds with customers.

Marketers can leverage social networks and media to drive community-style conversations, promoting customer-driven content generation that creates higher values for customers. Such customer-driven value co-creation may not only help in forging closer relationships with the customer, but can also help in creating a more loyal and sticky customer base. However, this dilution of control over content created for brands has its own perils and complications. Marketers should be wary of the control over the narrative of their brands over social media and need to monitor this proactively. In addition, fake identities and news over social media create their own peculiar complexities. Future research related to understanding and development of such dynamics can help the development of a strong community within the target customers, benefitting both customers as well as businesses.

References

Barger, V., Peltier, J. W., & Schultz, D. E. (2016). Social media and consumer engagement: A review and research agenda. *Journal of Research in Interactive Marketing, 10*(4), 268–287. https://doi.org/10.1108/JRIM-06-2016-0065

Calder, B. J., Malthouse, E. C., & Schaedel, U. (2009). An experimental study of the relationship between online engagement and advertising effectiveness. *Journal of Interactive Marketing, 23*(4), 321–331. https://doi.org/10.1016/j.intmar.2009.07.002

Callon, M., Courtial, J. P., & Laville, F. (1991). Co-word analysis as a tool for describing the network of interactions between basic and technological research: The case of polymer chemistry. *Scientometrics, 22*(1), 155–205. https://doi.org/10.1007/BF02019280

Cobo, M. J., López-Herrera, A. G., Herrera-Viedma, E., & Herrera, F. (2011). An approach for detecting, quantifying, and visualizing the evolution of a research field: A practical application to the Fuzzy Sets Theory field. *Journal of Informetrics, 5*(1), 146–166. https://doi.org/10.1016/J.JOI.2010.10.002

de Vries, L., Gensler, S., & Leeflang, P. S. H. (2012). Popularity of brand posts on brand fan pages: An investigation of the effects of social media marketing. *Journal *of Interactive Marketing, 26*(2), 83–91. https://doi.org/10.1016/j.intmar.2012.01.003

Dix, S. (2012). Introduction to the special issue on social media and mobile marketing. *Journal of Research in Interactive Marketing, 6*(3), 17–20. https://doi.org/10.1108/jrim.2012.32506caa.001

Donthu, N., Kumar, S., Mukherjee, D., Pandey, N., & Lim, W. M. (2021). How to conduct a bibliometric analysis: An overview and guidelines. *Journal of Business Research, 133*, 285–296. https://doi.org/10.1016/j.jbusres.2021.04.070

Donthu, N., Kumar, S., Sahoo, S., Lim, W. M., & Joshi, Y. (2022). Thirty years of product and brand management research: A retrospective review of the Journal of Product and Brand Management using bibliometric analysis. *Journal of Product & Brand Management*, ahead-of-print. https://doi.org/10.1108/JPBM-02-2022-3878

Garfield, E. (1994). Scientography: Mapping the tracks of science. *Current Contents: Social & Behavioural Sciences, 7*(45), 5–10.

Hennig-Thurau, T., Gwinner, K. P., Walsh, G., & Gremler, D. D. (2004). Electronic word-of-mouth via consumer-opinion platforms: What motivates consumers to articulate themselves on the Internet? *Journal of Interactive Marketing, 18*(1), 38–52. https://doi.org/10.1002/dir.10073

Hoffman, D. L., & Novak, T. P. (2009). Flow online: Lessons learned and future prospects. *Journal of Interactive Marketing, 23*(1), 23–34. https://doi.org/10.1016/j.intmar.2008.10.003

Hollebeek, L. D., Glynn, M. S., & Brodie, R. J. (2014). Consumer brand engagement in social media: Conceptualization, scale development and validation. *Journal of Interactive Marketing, 28*(2), 149–165. https://doi.org/10.1016/j.intmar.2013.12.002

Kabadayi, S., & Price, K. (2014). Consumer—Brand engagement on Facebook: Liking and commenting behaviors. *Journal of Research in Interactive Marketing, 8*(3), 203–223. https://doi.org/10.1108/JRIM-12-2013-0081

Kessler, M. M. (1963). Bibliographic coupling between scientific papers. *American Documentation, 14*(1), 10–25. https://doi.org/10.1002/ASI.5090140103

Kim, J., & Lennon, S. J. (2013). Effects of reputation and website quality on online consumers' emotion, perceived risk and purchase intention: Based on the stimulus-organism-response model. *Journal of Research in Interactive Marketing, 7*(1), 33–56. https://doi.org/10.1108/17505931311316734

King, R. A., Racherla, P., & Bush, V. D. (2014). What we know and don't know about online word-of-mouth: A review and synthesis of the literature. *Journal of Interactive Marketing, 28*(3), 167–183. https://doi.org/10.1016/j.intmar.2014.02.001

Kumar, S., Sharma, D., Rao, S., Lim, W. M., & Mangla, S. K. (2022). Past, present, and future of sustainable finance: Insights from big data analytics through machine learning of scholarly research. *Annals of Operations Research*, 1–44. https://doi.org/10.1007/s10479-021-04410-8

Limbu, Y. B., Wolf, M., & Lunsford, D. (2012). Perceived ethics of online retailers and consumer behavioral intentions: The mediating roles of trust and attitude. *Journal of Research in Interactive Marketing, 6*(2), 133–154. https://doi.org/10.1108/17505931211265435

Lin, T. M. Y., Lu, K.-Y., & Wu, J.-J. (2012). The effects of visual information in eWOM communication. *Journal of Research in Interactive Marketing, 6*(1), 7–26. https://doi.org/10.1108/17505931211241341

Mora-Valentín, E. M., Ortiz-de-Urbina-Criado, M., & Nájera-Sánchez, J. J. (2018). Mapping the conceptual structure of science and technology parks. *Journal of Technology Transfer, 43*(5), 1410–1435. https://doi.org/10.1007/S10961-018-9654-8/TABLES/11

Morris, S. A., & Yen, G. G. (2004). Crossmaps: Visualization of overlapping relationships in collections of journal papers. *Proceedings of the National Academy of Sciences, 101*(Suppl. 1), 5291–5296. https://doi.org/10.1073/pnas.0307604100

Muñoz-Leiva, F., Viedma-del-Jesús, M. I., Sánchez-Fernández, J., & López-Herrera, A. G. (2012). An application of co-word analysis and bibliometric maps for detecting the most highlighting themes in the consumer behaviour research from a longitudinal perspective. *Quality & Quantity, 46*(4), 1077–1095. https://doi.org/10.1007/s11135-011-9565-3

Prahalad, C. K., & Ramaswamy, V. (2004). Co-creation experiences: The next practice in value creation. *Journal of Interactive Marketing, 18*(3), 5–14. https://doi.org/10.1002/dir.20015

Rodrigues Pinho, J. C. M., & Soares, A. M. (2011). Examining the technology acceptance model in the adoption of social networks. *Journal of Research in Interactive Marketing, 5*, 116–129. https://doi.org/10.1108/17505931111187767

Schivinski, B., & Dabrowski, D. (2015). The impact of brand communication on brand equity through Facebook. *Journal of Research in Interactive Marketing, 9*(1), 31–53. https://doi.org/10.1108/JRIM-02-2014-0007

Shankar, V., & Yadav, M. S. (2010). Emerging perspectives on marketing in a multichannel and multimedia retailing environment. *Journal of Interactive Marketing, 24*(2), 55–57. https://doi.org/10.1016/j.intmar.2010.02.003

Small, H. (1973). Co-citation in the scientific literature: A new measure of the relationship between two documents. *Journal of the American Society for Information Science, 24*(4), 265–269. https://doi.org/10.1002/ASI.4630240406

Small, H. (2006). Tracking and predicting growth areas in science. *Scientometrics, 68*(3), 595–610. https://doi.org/10.1007/S11192-006-0132-Y

Swani, K., Milne, G., & Brown, B. P. (2013). Spreading the word through likes on Facebook: Evaluating the message strategy effectiveness of Fortune 500 companies. *Journal of Research in Interactive Marketing, 7*(4), 269–294. https://doi.org/10.1108/JRIM-05-2013-0026

Wang, C. L. (2021). New frontiers and future directions in interactive marketing: Inaugural editorial. *Journal of Research in Interactive Marketing, 15*(1), 1–9. https://doi.org/10.1108/JRIM-03-2021-270

Wang, Z., & Kim, H. G. (2017). Can social media marketing improve customer relationship capabilities and firm performance? Dynamic capability perspective. *Journal of Interactive Marketing, 39*, 15–26. https://doi.org/10.1016/j.intmar.2017.02.004

Yang, S., Han, R., Wolfram, D., & Zhao, Y. (2016). Visualizing the intellectual structure of information science (2006–2015): Introducing author keyword coupling analysis. *Journal of Informetrics, 10*(1), 132–150. https://doi.org/10.1016/J.JOI.2015.12.003

Zhao, D., & Strotmann, A. (2014). The knowledge base and research front of information science 2006–2010: An author cocitation and bibliographic coupling analysis. *Journal of the Association for Information Science and Technology, 65*(5), 995–1006. https://doi.org/10.1002/asi.23027

CHAPTER 3

From Direct Marketing Toward Interactive Marketing: The Evolving Interactive Marketing Tools

Anne Moes, Marieke L. Fransen, Tibert Verhagen, and Bob Fennis

1 INTRODUCTION

'Without interaction, nothing new happens. Without interaction no meaning is generated. Without interaction no experience is created' (Ascott, 1997, p. 338). This quote nicely illustrates why interactivity between companies and customers has become a crucial element of marketing (Lee, 2005). This chapter presents an overview of empirical studies on interactivity in the context of interactive marketing tools to provide insight in both the promising and troubling effects that interactivity may elicit.

Interactivity is defined as *'The degree to which two or more communication parties can act on each other, on the communication medium, and on the messages and the degree to which such influences are synchronized'* (Liu &

A. Moes (✉) · B. Fennis
University of Groningen, Groningen, The Netherlands
e-mail: a.moes@hva.nl

B. Fennis
e-mail: b.m.fennis@rug.nl

A. Moes · T. Verhagen
Amsterdam University of Applied Sciences, Amsterdam, The Netherlands
e-mail: t.verhagen@hva.nl

M. L. Fransen
Radboud University, Nijmegen, The Netherlands
e-mail: marieke.fransen@ru.nl

© The Author(s), under exclusive license to Springer Nature Switzerland AG 2023
C. L. Wang (ed.), *The Palgrave Handbook of Interactive Marketing*,
https://doi.org/10.1007/978-3-031-14961-0_3

Shrum, 2002, p. 54). Interactivity comprises three dimensions: (1) active control, which refers to experiencing feelings of control during an interaction and is measured with items such as 'I can browse on my own pace'; (2) two-way communication, which refers to the ability of two parties sending information to *and* receiving information from each other. Two-way communication is often measured with items such as 'I had the opportunity to talk back'; and (3) synchronicity, referring to the speed in which someone is responded to and is measured with items such as 'I felt I was getting an instantaneous response' (Liu & Shrum, 2002, see also Moes et al., 2021). These dimensions of interactivity cannot be simplified to dualistic constructs where active control, two-way communication, and synchronicity are either present or not. Rather, the dimensions exist on a gradual scale (Liu & Shrum, 2002). This also means that not all three dimensions have to be equally present in an interactive marketing tool, for this tool to be recognized as interactive. The definition of interactive marketing, in its turn, combines dimensions of interactivity, such as two-way communication, with marketers' intended effects of using interactive tools. Wang (2021) brings these concepts together in the following definition of interactive marketing: '*the bi-directional value creation and mutual-influence marketing process through active customer connection, engagement, participation and interaction*' (p. 1).

Since the rise of the digital age, one-way mass media communication had to make room for more interactive ways of communication, and traditional direct marketing had to make room for contemporary interactive marketing (Wang, 2021). Accordingly, marketing tools have evolved tremendously in the past thirty years, which also affected the focus of scientific research. In the 1990s, when the internet was introduced, web browsers and search engines had a huge influence on marketing, and, in the second half of the 1990s, online marketing also received much academic attention (Ratchford, 2020). Research on total engagement (flow) with online tasks arose (Hoffman & Novak, 1996), the viability of online marketing for different products and services was studied (Peterson et al., 1997), and the effects of internet shopping on consumers and marketers were discovered (e.g., Alba et al., 1997; Lal & Sarvary, 1999; see Ratchford, 2020 for a full overview). However, the internet really increased in popularity when WiFi was adapted widely in the first decade of 2000. Companies started to create websites and web shops en masse, and increasingly improved their interactive functions (Kucuk, 2016). These functionalities allowed companies, for example, to enhance shopping experiences (Wang, 2021) and to serve their customers 24/7, instead of the eight hours per day that was common before the start of the digital age (Barwise & Farley, 2005; Wang, 2021). Also, social networks (2005) and smartphones (2007) were introduced, and later (2009) were commonly used (Ratchford, 2020). The number of internet-related studies in marketing literature grew exponentially in this decade. Topics included online advertising (Chen et al., 2009), online customization (Ansari & Mela, 2003), and motives for posting on social media (Schau & Gilly, 2003; see Ratchford, 2020 for a full overview). In the

2010s interactive marketing again took a flight. Tools that were once, not so long ago, seen as futuristic, such as virtual assistants, smart home devices, and location tracking, were becoming more and more common (Ratchford, 2020). Research started to study the implications of using contemporary techniques as marketing tools. These tools included, but were not limited to, virtual reality (Moes & Van Vliet, 2017), chatbots (Liebrecht & Hooijdonk, 2019), personalized ads and news items (Krafft et al., 2017), and augmented reality (Butt et al., 2021).

It can be concluded that early marketing tools were mainly focused on one-way communication and limited in their functionalities. However, marketing tools are getting increasingly interactive, and two-way contemporary interactive marketing tools bring countless opportunities for companies to reshape and strengthen relationships with consumers (Lim et al., 2022; Wang, 2021). Additionally, the past thirty years demonstrated that interactive marketing tools contributed to build a participatory culture for customers, meaning that contemporary customers can actively contribute to their own shopping experiences, or even to (co-)produce products. They are no longer the passive consumers that they once were (Wang, 2021). Hence, interactive marketing applications can be beneficial for both customers and companies in many ways. However, not all research on interactivity shows beneficial effects. Interactive marketing tools can also be perceived as intrusive (e.g., Krafft et al., 2017) or they can backfire and have negative effects on, for example, buying urges (Moes et al., 2021).

In the past thirty years we have witnessed an accelerated development within the scope of interactive marketing tools (Wang, 2021). This chapter presents an extensive, however not exhaustive, overview of important studies on such tools. It discusses ten of the most pioneering tools used in interactive marketing, ranging from relatively older, classical tools, such as websites and banners to more contemporary and innovative interactive marketing tools, such as virtual reality (VR) and interactive advertising screens.

2   Literature Overview

This part of the chapter discusses ten types of interactive marketing tools. For each tool it is first demonstrated how it relates to the three dimensions of interactivity (active control, two-way communication, synchronicity; Liu & Shrum, 2002). In doing so, this chapter also provides insights in what dimensions are the driving forces behind the discussed interactive marketing tools. Second, this chapter will highlight the most important, sometimes contradicting, effects that each tool has on its users. Both positive and negative effects will be discussed. Third, and final, this chapter also provides practical guidelines for each tool that marketers should keep in mind when developing an interactive marketing strategy.

The ten tools that will be discussed here are either commonly used by companies or increasingly used by companies: (1) websites, (2) branded apps,

(3) banners, (4) email, (5) social media, (6) online chatbots, (7) virtual reality (VR), (8) augmented reality (AR), (9) location-based messaging, and (10) interactive advertising screens (e.g., Barwise & Farley, 2005; Farías, 2018; Hartemo, 2016; Kaczorowska-Spychalska, 2019; Moes et al., 2021; Moes & Van Vliet, 2017; Moriuchi et al., 2021; Sreejesh et al., 2020; Van Noort & Van Reijmersdal, 2019; Verhagen et al., 2021). Innovative, contemporary, tools in interactive marketing are less extensively researched than their older counterparts, due to the fact that they are relatively new. In this literature review we provide valuable knowledge on both the more classical tools that are already researched for over thirty years, and on the more contemporary tools that are only studied relatively recently.

2.1 Websites

One of the most widely adopted interactive marketing applications is websites (Barwise & Farley, 2005; Main, 2021). The extent to which active control is possible in websites depends on the site's features. However, generally, websites can be classified as featuring high active control because users can control their own pace and navigation within the digital environments. Compared to active control, the presence of two-way communication on a website can be considered less self-evident. The most basic form of two-way communication found on websites is the opportunity for its users to click on something (e.g., a tab), where the website responds to. However, looking at more advanced websites, users are increasingly asked to 'talk back' by liking, reviewing, or commenting on products or services. In these cases, a website would score higher on the two-way communication dimension. Finally, the synchronicity level of websites mostly depends on external factors such as a user's internet speed (see Liu & Shrum, 2002). However, it is also important for companies to optimize their website on a regular basis to make it load quicker, since 40% of website users will stop engaging with it when they experience it as too slow (> 2 seconds loading time; Main, 2021). Hence, websites do have the potential to score high on synchronicity.

Most companies nowadays have a website (e.g., Main, 2021). Customers use websites to gain information, ask specific questions, or buy products. Research shows that high interactive websites, compared to low interactive websites, lead to a higher favorability toward the website and the exposed products (Sicilia et al., 2005). In line with these outcomes, interacting with product images on retailers' websites has been found to benefit experimental and instrumental value (Fiore et al., 2005). A meta-analysis shows that website interactivity positively affects enjoyment of using the website, attitude toward websites and products, and behavioral intentions such as recommendation and purchase intention (Yang & Shen, 2018). Additionally, Huang (2016) found a positive relationship between browsing on a website and impulse buying behavior. However, there is some debate on the effectiveness of interactivity on cognitive responses. While Sicilia et al. (2005), found a positive effect of website interactivity on information processing, Kim and Stout (2010) did not find any effect of interactivity on such cognitive responses, and Sundar and Constantin (2004) even found a negative effect. A possible explanation for these different results can be found in the level of interactivity. Moderated interactivity seems to be beneficial, however, too much interactivity is possibly perceived as overwhelming and cognitively distracting and may therefore backfire (Liu & Shrum, 2002; Yang & Shen, 2018). Marketers are therefore advised to keep in mind that more interactivity is not always for the better, and to actively test what level of interactivity in their website functionalities works best for their customers. Moreover, it is important to consider that actual interactivity can differ from perceived interactivity. This means that adding more interactive website functionalities does not necessarily lead to a stronger perception of interactivity (and vice versa, Voorveld et al., 2011).

2.2 Branded Apps

Due to consumers' fast adaption of smartphones, more than 50% of website traffic happens through mobile devices (HubSpot, 2021). Driven by this fact, brands also increasingly make use of branded mobile apps as an interactive marketing tool (Van Noort & Van Reijmersdal, 2019), and consumers seem willing to use them. Nowadays, on average, consumers spend over 4 hours a day on apps on their mobile phones (Annie, 2021) and almost 40% of all smartphone users prefer to shop on a brand's app over a website, since they find this easier or faster (HubSpot, 2021). Similar to websites, branded apps score high on active control since users determine the pace and navigation. Depending on its features, apps also have the potential to score high on two-way communication. There are basic apps, where users can, for example, only view content, and more elaborate apps, where an app's functionalities allow users to interact with at least one other party. Concerning synchronicity, a marketer only has a limited amount of influence on the synchronicity level of this tool. Marketers can, for example, offer chat functionalities within the app-environment with which they can directly respond to customers. However, also here a consumer's internet speed can affect this dimension tremendously, which makes it difficult for marketers to fully control this third dimension of interactivity (see Liu & Shrum, 2002).

Branded apps are a very promising interactive marketing tool (Wang et al., 2016), since they are voluntarily downloaded and used by consumers who find them entertaining and/or functional (Bellman et al., 2011). Other advertising formats, on the contrary, may come with resistance since consumers may perceive unsolicited persuasive messages as a threat to freedom (Fransen et al., 2015). Arguably, using branded apps as an interactive marketing tool can therefore result into positive outcomes. However, results on the effectiveness of branded apps are mixed. For example, where Van Noort and Van Reijmersdal (2019) reported a positive effect of branded app usage on brand attitude, Hoogendoorn (2013) did not find an effect. Also, the effects of branded apps on cognitive responses are not conclusive (Seitz & Aldebasi, 2016). A possible explanation for these observed differences is the type of branded app. For example, entertaining branded apps may mainly evoke affective brand responses, such as a positive attitude toward the brand and the feeling of having a close relationship with the brand. Informational branded apps, on the other hand, may generally only evoke cognitive brand responses, such as brand recall, brand beliefs, and brand recognition (Van Noort & Van Reijmersdal, 2019). Therefore, it seems important for marketers to consciously decide on the goals they aim to achieve with the branded app. Moreover, it should be considered that 80% of the consumers only download an app from a trustworthy and familiar company (HubSpot, 2021), which makes it difficult for new companies to deploy branded apps as consumers may not yet be familiar with these companies. Moreover, many consumers (72%) are concerned about their privacy when using apps (HubSpot, 2021). Therefore, a clear privacy statement, accessible to consumers, could probably benefit brands.

2.3   Banners

A third interactive marketing tool that is frequently used is banners (Barwise & Farley, 2005). Banners, in the USA, are the third largest advertising investment online (Farías, 2018) which makes it a popular tool to use. As opposed to websites and apps, banners are difficult to control actively by its users since they cannot determine when and where the banners should (or should not) pop up. Banners, therefore, score low on active control. Also on two-way communication, banners show little potential. However, banners allow a very basic form of communicating with its user, which makes the literature consider the tool as interactive. Namely, a user can click on a banner, in which the banner responds by, for example, opening a new tab. Generally, this response is immediate, which makes this tool scores high on synchronicity. However, due to the very little interactive features of banners, the synchronicity level largely depends on external factors such as internet speed (see Liu & Shrum, 2002).

Research shows that banners do not frequently lead to clicks (only in about 1% of the time, see e.g., Cho, 2003), and thus often fail to evoke interaction. An explanation for this low click-rate is that banner advertisements are often perceived as misleading and untrustworthy when it comes to data security. Especially men, compared to women, seem to be impatient to deal with banners (Krushali et al., 2018) and are therefore possibly more likely to install pop-up blockers. Moreover, banners are also perceived as intrusive (Krammer, 2008). Nevertheless, banners can still elicit positive effects. They can be effective in improving one's brand recall, attitudes toward the advertised brand, and purchase intention (e.g., Chiu et al., 2017). However, as most consumers experience banners as invaluable distractions, banners are increasingly being ignored by customers. This 'banner blindness' can prevent possible positive effects (Resnick & Albert, 2014). Marketers are therefore recommended to design creative banners that stand out with visual saliency, and are, at the same time, congruent with the webpage where the banner is meant to pop up (Yang et al., 2021). Although banners technically are an interactive marketing tool, marketers are advised not to use them for this purpose. Yet, banner ads are very useful for improving recall and in this way strengthening a company's marketing position (Yang et al., 2021).

2.4 Email

Another form of frequently used online interactive marketing is email marketing (Hartemo, 2016). Email is one of the most cost-effective marketing channels and can be used to empower consumers (Hartemo, 2016). In terms of interactivity, email can be classified as high active control, since users can control their own pace and navigation. Moreover, email has the potential to score very high on two-way communication, since this tool allows someone to start a dialogue with someone else and (at least) two parties can respond endlessly to each other. However, companies increasingly use so-called do-not-reply email-addresses. Such email use can be categorized as one-way communication because these email accounts can only send emails, and not receive them. Additionally, emails do not always score high on synchronicity, the third dimension of interactivity (see Liu & Shrum, 2002). Although emails can be responded to immediately, practice shows that emails from customers to companies are seldomly answered directly (TimetoReply, 2020).

Email marketing appears to positively affect purchase intention, both on the short term and on the long term (Wu et al., 2018). For marketers, it is particularly beneficial to email customers who did not purchase something recently, since research shows that especially those customers are sensitive to email promotions (Wu et al., 2018). Email is therefore still considered a profitable communication channel. Although email marketing can have positive effects, it can also be experienced as annoying, untrustworthy, and boring (Mahmoud et al., 2019). Consequently, sending too many emails can cost marketers customers. According to research, the optimal number of emails that a company should send each month to a single customer is seven. However, this number is depended on how likely it is that a customer will buy a product. The lower a customer's purchase-state is, as estimated by marketers, the more emails a company should send (and vice versa, Zhang et al., 2017). Therefore, marketers are recommended to segment their customers into groups that reflect their purchase-state and adjust the number of emails they send per group.

2.5 Social Media

Another interactive marketing tool that this chapter discusses here is social media. A substantial amount of the B2C companies have at least one social media account (Sreejesh et al., 2020). Social media can be viewed as highly interactive. Besides that social media users can control the pace in which they watch or post content (active control), social media are also interactive marketing tools that pre-eminently score high on two-way communication. They are designed to interact and connect with another party by, for example, chatting, liking, or posting (Obar & Wildman, 2015). Furthermore, social media messages are often quickly responded to and therefore also score high on synchronicity (see Liu & Shrum, 2002). Nevertheless, it is still possible to distinguish different levels of interactivity in social media, depending on how a social media account is managed by the marketer.

Research shows that the level of message interactivity on social media positively affects perceived informativeness, which, subsequently, has a positive effect on ad effectiveness (Ott et al., 2016). Additionally, interactivity in social media positively affects brand attitude, brand loyalty, and purchase intention (Kim & Lee, 2019). Consistent with these findings, Colliander et al. (2015) show that companies that enter a dialogue with their followers on Twitter, versus companies that follow a one-way communication strategy, enhance brand attitudes and purchase intentions among their followers. However, these findings do not mean that more interactivity on social media is always better. A study by Sreejesh et al. (2020), show that very highly interactive social media accounts, compared to less interactive accounts, lead to low ad attentions and low recall. The authors explain these negative effects with cognitive absorption, which entails that when a user is preoccupied with a main activity (such as interacting), it limits other cognitive functions (such as memory). In other words, interactivity seems to have a, yet to discover, sweet spot. Based on the literature, marketers are recommended to interact with their customers through social media. However, if a company wants to elicit cognitive responses with their customers, interaction levels must be moderate.

2.6   *Online Chatbots*

Online chatbots are increasingly used in marketing (Kaczorowska-Spychalska, 2019). Online chatbots score, in general, relatively high on active control. A chatbot is an artificial intelligent computer program that communicates with users in a natural language, often in the form of text messages. Such bots are programmed to understand and respond to users, in a way that fits the communication style of the organization that uses the bots (Kaczorowska-Spychalska, 2019). Although some chatbots start a conversation unasked, when visiting a website for example, users can decide if, when, and how they respond. Users are therefore actively in control of the conversation, at least of the pace and content at which they respond to the chatbot. Moreover, online chatbots are developed to pursue an actual two-way conversation in a natural language with their users. Chatbots, therefore, also score high on two-way communication. Under the assumption that external factors, such as internet speed, are sufficient, chatbots score high on synchronicity as well (see Liu &

Shrum, 2002). After all, most chatbots can respond quicker to a question than humans can (Nawaz & Gomes, 2019).

Chatbots can help companies to answer customers' questions about offered products and services (Kaczorowska-Spychalska, 2019). Customers value the information-providing feature of chatbots, especially when it comes to simple, to-the-point information (Arsenijevic & Jovic, 2019). Perhaps not surprising, chatbots can therefore elicit numerous positive effects (Hoyer et al., 2020). For example, Chung et al. (2020) show that online chatbots can help luxury retail brands to build positive customer relationships. The perceived dialogue, between customers and bots, also enhances interaction satisfaction and brand likeability (Tsai et al., 2021). Furthermore, chatbots can reduce hesitation to purchase (Hoyer, et al., 2020). However, mixed results are found when it comes to using chatbots as an engaging technology. Some find them to increase user engagement (Tsai et al., 2021), while others state that engagement cannot be pursued with the use of chatbots (Moriuchi et al., 2021). Overall, the literature seems to agree that chatbots are a great communication tool for consumers who have unambiguous questions (Moriuchi et al., 2021). Nonetheless, chatbots are only beneficial to companies if customers decide to use them. Research shows that when people are concerned about their privacy, this negatively moderates the effect of their attitude toward bots and their intention to use them (de Cosmo et al., 2021). For companies who consider using chatbots, it could therefore be recommended to use human-like chatbots (opposed to machine-like chatbots). Human-like chatbots are found to decrease privacy concerns (Ischen et al., 2019). Consequently, people are not only more eager to use bots (de Cosmo et al., 2021), but also disclose more information to the bots, and are more willing to follow the bots' recommendations (Ischen et al., 2019).

2.7   Augmented Reality

Similar as with chatbots, AR applications are increasingly popular in the marketing domain. AR offers its users a live image of reality, accompanied by a virtual, computer-simulated, layer (TotalReality, n.d.). AR, therefore, offers a range of possibilities; from making it possible to show in 3D how a (virtual) couch fits in a user's living room (e.g., Mens, 2017), to showing how (virtual) sunglasses look on a potential buyer (e.g., CharlieTemple, n.d.). AR scores high on active control, since users decide where and when to click and in which direction they look. Users can also communicate with each other, and with the company offering the AR application, while experiencing AR (TotalReality, n.d.). However, two-way communication does not necessarily mean that there must be a conversation between two parties. It can also be about exchanging information (Liu & Shrum, 2002) between a user and a virtual environment for example, which makes that AR has a great potential to score high on two-way communication. Lastly, AR also scores high on synchronicity. In fact, the synchronic and instantaneous connection between virtual and real content is an important feature of AR (Liang & Roast, 2014; also see Liu & Shrum, 2002).

AR has been found being able to create positive customer experiences, especially the more interactive AR-tools have the potential of achieving this. High interactive AR can, probably because of its ability to create an experience, also create a deep level of engagement between a brand and their customers (Moriuchi et al., 2021). Companies who aim to establish an engaging relationship with their customers, without having to be physically together per se, could therefore benefit from AR applications. Moreover, AR applications can also inspire their users, which positively affects customers' brand attitudes (Rauschnabel et al., 2019). However, it is important for AR applications to be developed professionally, since poorly developed apps can lead to negative customer experiences and consequently result in negative brand effects (Rauschnabel et al., 2019). Nevertheless, the literature is mostly positive about using AR as a marketing tool. Research even shows that high interactive AR can affect revisiting intentions to an online store, shopping intention (Moriuchi et al., 2021), and purchase intention (Sung, 2021). The positive effect of AR on purchase intentions can be explained by perceived informativeness and enjoyment (Smink et al., 2019). If the means are available for companies to do it in a professional manner, they are advised to develop highly interactive AR applications that offer their customers an experience.

2.8 *Virtual Reality*

VR is a computer-simulated environment, which places the user in a virtual experience. VR thus differs from AR, since VR only shows a virtual world and completely shuts of reality from its users (TotalReality, n.d.). VR and AR *are* similar when it comes to the degree of interactivity they offer. As with AR, VR scores high on active control since users determine how quick, or slow, they move within the virtual environment. VR also scores high on two-way communication since the environment and user within that environment respond to each other. For example, with VR users can walk around a company's latest launched product. The environment will show a different image depending on where users are standing and the direction of their eyes. Not rarely people can communicate with others while using VR (TotalReality, n.d.). Finally, also VR cannot function accurately if it would score low on synchronicity. VR therefore (should) also score high on this third dimension of interactivity (see Liu & Shrum, 2002).

In line with the results of Moes and Van Vliet (2017) showing that VR stimulates visit and purchase intentions, Yung et al. (2021) show that VR has a stronger effect on visiting and recommendation intentions than traditional media. Correspondingly, Kim et al. (2022) found that exploring a physical store in VR (versus on a website) enhances users' visit intentions. The positive effects of VR are explained by flow state (Kim et al., 2022), novelty of the medium, enjoyment (Moes & Van Vliet, 2017), and presence (Yung et al., 2021). Although many positive effects of VR are found, there is still much uncertainty about the exact consequences of using VR as an interactive marketing tool. Regarding recall, for example, some studies argue that being immersed in an environment (which is often the case with VR) benefits users' recall (Chowdhury et al., 2017). Others, however, do not find effects of VR on recall (Moes & Van Vliet, 2017). Therefore, more research is needed on the effects of VR in marketing (Xi & Hamari, 2021). In addition, it should be considered that VR asks for a device, such as an Oculus rift of Google cardboard, for customers to experience it. Research shows that most consumers are unwilling to buy their own Google cardboard to use branded VR applications, despite being very affordable. Hence, marketers should consider distributing such tools for free or only target those people who already possess VR glasses (Moes & Van Vliet, 2017).

2.9 Location-Based Messages

Location-based messages, as opposed to most other interactive marketing tools, cannot be actively controlled by the receiver. Location-based messaging software uses customers' geographic data and automatically sends messages to customers when they are physically close to a company, such as a store. It thus allows environmental monitoring of customers and permits marketers to address customers at the exact right place. Location-based messaging is therefore a form of proximity marketing (Flavián et al., 2019; Wang, 2021). The messages can, for example, contain special offers for customers if they immediately visit the store (Verhagen et al., 2021). After users' consent, they can receive (sometimes unlimited) messages from companies, based on their geographic location. Users often cannot determine on what moment they will receive the messages, nor do they have influence on how quickly they receive messages in succession. This interactive marketing tool, therefore, scores low on active control. Location-based messages also score low on two-way communication. The software responds to the place where a customer is located, by sending the customer a message. Customers who want to respond to the message can do this, for example, by visiting the company. However, in general it is not possible to respond to the location-based text messages by sending a text message back. Location-based messages *do* score high on synchronicity (see Liu & Shrum, 2002). In fact, it is crucial that this marketing tool contains a high level of synchronicity. After all, the software must respond directly to where a user is located at that exact moment, for the message to be location relevant (Verhagen et al., 2021).

Concerning the effectiveness of location-based messaging, Meents et al. (2020) show that these messages can enhance store visit intention, especially when they contain a scarcity message. However, location-based messages can also be perceived as intrusive (Verhagen et al., 2021). The more intrusive the message, the less positive a recipient's attitude toward the message is. Arguably, this explains why customers still seem to prefer a static poster over location-based messages (Gazley et al., 2015). When a company decides to send location-based messages, it is therefore important to make them as relevant as possible for the recipient. This means, firstly, that the messages should be congruent with the place where consumers are located. Research shows that location congruency is the most important construct for location-based messaging to be perceived as valuable by the recipient (Verhagen et al., 2021). Secondly, companies can make location-based messages more relevant for their recipients by customizing its content to their interests. By doing so, customers' attitudes toward the messages improve (Gazley et al., 2015).

2.10   Interactive Advertising Screens

Lastly, this chapter discusses interactive advertising screens. Interactive advertising screens are digital screens, placed in a shopping street for example, with commercial content meant for consumers to interact with (Moes et al., 2021). Consumers can actively control the pace in which they interact with the screen, which makes this tool score high on active control. Also, interactive screens have the potential to communicate in a two-way direction. With features such as asking for users' opinions or responding to given likes, these screens can achieve experienced two-way communication with users (Moes et al., 2021). For the screens to be perceived as more interactive, it is necessary that the screen immediately responds to the actions of the users. Interactive screens are able to do this and therefore potentially also score high on synchronicity (Moes et al., 2021; also see Liu & Shrum, 2002).

We know that interacting with a screen, such as a tablet, can come with positive effects (Sicilia et al., 2005). However, offline customers differ from online customers on many levels. The latter, for example, more often value variety (e.g., Donthu & Garcia, 1999) and convenience (Monsuwé et al., 2004). Nevertheless, Moes et al. (2021) found similar positive effects for interacting with an interactive advertising screen in a physical shopping environment, as others found for interacting with a screen while shopping from home. Results of this study show that the level of interactivity (low versus high) on interactive advertising screens (in a physical shopping surrounding) has a positive effect on self-agency, which, subsequently, benefits impulse store visit urges and impulse buying urges. In other words, interacting with an advertising screen in a shopping street enhances customers' feelings of 'being in charge of the situation', which translates to higher urges to visit the store and to buy something unplanned. However, the same study also shows a negative residual effect, when self-agency was taken into account, of interactivity on impulse visits and impulse buying. This means that there is a negative effect of interactivity as well. In the previous paragraphs we have learned that interactivity can also be too high. Too much interactivity could possibly be perceived as overwhelming, which could translate into negative effects (Liu & Shrum, 2002; Yang & Shen, 2018). Possibly this also explains the negative residual effect found in the study on interactive advertising screens. Perhaps users felt, simultaneously, overwhelmed by the interaction and being in charge of the situation (self-agency), which both led to a conflicting outcome. Hence, when a company decides to use interactive advertising screens, they are advised to select those screens that have the ability to elicit feelings of self-agency with users, without being overwhelming. This means that the user should completely be in charge of the interaction and, probably, that the interaction contains little surprise to the ones that use the screen.

Table 1 provides an overview of the ten discussed interactive marketing tools and (1) their level of interactivity and (2) the most important effects they can elicit.

3 Discussion and Insights for Future Directions in Interactive Marketing

3.1 Conclusion

This chapter provided an overview of significant empirical literature on interactivity in the context of interactive marketing. Overall, three conclusions can be drawn. First, although the literature considers all ten discussed tools as interactive, they score differently on the three dimensions of interactivity. With a few exceptions, it appears that the newer a tool is, the higher it scores on the interactivity dimensions. Second, the two tools that score low on active control *and* two-way communication (banners and location-based messaging) are both potentially experienced as intrusive. It would be interesting to study whether active control and two-way communication, which both emphasize participation of the user, indeed affect experienced intrusiveness (see Table 1). Third, research on the ten interactive marketing tools generally shows positive effects on diverse outcome variables. These include affective outcomes, such as attitude and enjoyment, and behavioral outcomes, such as visit intention and buying intention (see Table 1). Also, positive effects of interactive tools on cognitive outcome variables were found, such as on recall and recognition. However, the literature seems indecisive on these effects since some studies failed to find similar results or even found negative effects of interactive marketing tools on cognitive outcomes. This may be explained by, among other things, cognitive absorption when interactivity levels are too high.

3.2 Implications for Practice

This chapter also provided some practical guidelines that marketers should keep in mind when developing an interactive marketing strategy. For at least websites, social media, and interactive screens hold that higher levels of interactivity are not always better. Especially when aiming for cognitive responses, such as brand or ad recall, interactivity levels must be moderate. Furthermore, marketers were advised to anticipate on possible negative perceptions of interactive marketing tools. Email, for example, could be perceived as annoying,

Table 1 Overview of the ten discussed interactive marketing tools

Tool	Interactivity level[a]	Positive outcomes[b]	Negative outcomes[c]
Websites	AC: high TC: low S: high	Attitude toward website and products Experimental value website Instrumental value website Enjoyment Information processing Recommendation Purchase intention Impulse buying behavior	Cognitive responses, such as information processing, recall, and recognition
Branded apps	AC: high TC: high S: high	Experimental value Instrumental value Brand attitude Attitude toward the brand Feeling of having a close relationship with the brand Brand recall Brand beliefs Brand recognition	Cognitive responses, such as information processing, recall, and recognition Privacy
Banners	AC: low TC: low S: high	Brand recall Purchase intention	Misleading Untrustworthy Invaluable distractions Banner blindness Intrusiveness
Email	AC: high TC: high S: low	Short term purchase intention Long term purchase intention	Annoying Untrustworthy Boring
Social media	AC: high TC: high S: high	Perceived informativeness Ad effectiveness Brand loyalty Purchase intention Brand attitudes	Ad attentions Recall
Online chatbots	AC: high TC: high S: high	Positive customer relationships Interaction satisfaction Brand likeability Reduce hesitation User engagement	Engagement Privacy Attitude toward bots Intention to use them

(continued)

Table 1 (continued)

Tool	Interactivity level[a]	Positive outcomes[b]	Negative outcomes[c]
Augmented reality	AC: high TC: high S: high	Customer experience Engagement Inspiration Brand attitude Revisiting intention Shopping intention Purchase intention Perceived informativeness Enjoyment	Customer experiences (with poorly developed apps) Brand effects (with poorly developed apps)
Virtual reality	AC: high TC: high S: high	Visit intention Purchase intention Recommendation intention Flow Enjoyment Presence Recall	Consumers are unwilling to buy their own device to use branded VR applications
Location-based messages	AC: low TC: low S: high	Visit intention Attitude toward the message (when e.g., congruent)	Intrusiveness Attitude toward the message (when e.g., intrusive) Customers prefer a static poster over location-based messages
Interactive advertising screens	AC: high TC: high S: high	Self-agency Impulse visit urges Impulse buying urges	Impulse visit urges (depending on what psychological process is activated) Impulse buying urges (depending on what psychological process is activated)

[a] Potential score on Liu and Shrum's dimensions of interactivity (2002). AC = active control; TC = two-way communication; S = synchronicity. NB: Synchronicity levels also depend on external factors such as internet speed
[b] Found positive effects of, or opinions about, (interactivity within) the tool
[c] Found negative effects of, or opinions about, (interactivity within) the tool
[b,c]: In some cases, conflicting outcomes were found, which resulted in listing that variable in both the positive outcome column and negative outcome column

but not if the number of emails is tailored to the recipient's needs. Location-based messages can be experienced as intrusive, but can also be valued when the messages are congruent with the location and interests of the consumer. Banners are often experienced as invaluable distractions, but can elicit positive effects when they are visual salient and congruent to the banner-page. And, finally, branded apps and chatbots can raise privacy concerns, which can be anticipated on by using, respectively, clear privacy statements and human-like chatbots. Hence, *how* an interactive tool is designed and implemented influences its effects tremendously. Lastly, it was recommended to develop interactive marketing tools in a professional and accessible manner. Poorly developed AR, for example, can result into unwanted effects, and VR is not accessible for people without VR glasses which makes it difficult to reach the full target group. An important caveat to all these results, however, is that research on the effects of interactivity, especially on cognitive outcomes, is not yet totally clear. We still do not completely understand when and why interactive marketing tools have positive effects, negative effects, or no effects at all. Therefore, guidelines for practitioners in interactive marketing may change over time when new insights come to light. Moreover, technological developments are moving fast, providing practitioners with endless possibilities to use innovative interactive marketing tools. Generally, it can be stated that the newer a tool is, the less research on the effectivity of these tools exists. Implementation of such tools should therefore go hand in hand with continuously monitoring the effects they elicit.

3.3 Future Research

Based on the results, this chapter suggests several recommendations for future research. First, it is suggested that more attention in studies on interactive marketing tools should go to the role of the three dimensions of interactivity. Insights in these characteristics of interactivity tools could help researchers to better understand what interactivity dimension contributes the most to certain outcomes, both positive and negative. For example, if low levels of active control and two-way communication indeed lead to feelings of intrusiveness with the customer, this would be valuable to know. Furthermore, this chapter recommends future research to keep focusing on the effects of innovative, contemporary marketing tools on important outcomes such as enjoyment, attitudes, cognition, and behavior. This is necessary to reinforce findings and clarify the observed contradictions in the literature. In this focus on contemporary tools, attention should go to technology adaptation as well. Studying technology adaptation is not only important to gain insights in how contemporary tools are perceived and used by customers, but also to predict what other new technologies would fit interactive marketing purposes (Lim et al., 2022).

A strong focus on innovative, contemporary tools in future research should, however, not mean that the focus on commonly used interactive tools should fade. On the contrary, these tools are also still rapidly developing, and it is recommended that their effects are continuously studied. Social media, for example, was once about Twitter and Facebook, but nowadays contains TikTok and influencer-marketing as well. It is necessary to continue mapping such developments within each interactive marketing tool on a micro-level and to keep studying their effects on brand-customer interactions (Lim et al., 2022; Wang, 2021). Likewise, for other commonly used tools, such as websites, email, and banners, it is encouraged to closely monitor their (possible) developments and how these contribute to interactive marketing purposes. For example, it would be interesting to study the increasing degree of gamification and entertainment on brand websites and how this affects interactive marketing (Wang, 2021). This chapter encourages (future) marketers and researchers to stay curious and join powers. It is of importance that they contribute to both practice-oriented research and scientific research, on all types of interactive marketing tools since literature on interactive marketing is far from saturated.

Acknowledgements This work is supported by The Netherlands Organization for Scientific Research (NWO) [grant number: 023.011.008]

References

Alba, J., Lynch, J., Weitz, B., Janiszewski, C., Lutz, R., Sawyer, A., & Wood, S. (1997). Interactive home shopping: Consumer, retailer, and manufacturer incentives to participate in electronic marketplaces. *Journal of Marketing, 61*(3), 38–53.

Annie. (2021). Retrieved on 14 December 2021, from https://www.appannie.com/en/insights/market-data/q1-2021-market-index

Ansari, A., & Mela, C. F. (2003). E-customization. *Journal of Marketing Research, 40*(2), 131–145.

Arsenijevic, U., & Jovic, M. (2019). *Artificial intelligence marketing: Chatbots*. 2019 International Conference on Artificial Intelligence: Applications and Innovations (IC-AIAI), pp. 19–193. IEEE.

Ascott, R. (1997). Cultivando o hipercórtex. In D. Domingues (Org.), *A arte no século XXI: a humanização das tecnologias* (336–344). São Paulo: Fundação Ed. da UNESP.

Barwise, P., & Farley, J. U. (2005). The state of interactive marketing in seven countries: Interactive marketing comes of age. *Journal of Interactive Marketing, 19*(3), 67–80.

Bellman, S., Potter, R. F., Treleaven-Hassard, S., Robinson, J. A., & Varan, D. (2011). The effectiveness of branded mobile phone apps. *Journal of Interactive Marketing, 25*(4), 191–200.

Butt, A., Ahmad, H., Muzaffar, A., Ali, F., & Shafique, N. (2021). WOW, the make-up AR app is impressive: A comparative study between China and South Korea. *Journal of Services Marketing, 36*(1), 73–88.

CharlieTemple. (n.d.). *Bril passen*. Retrieved on 15 February 2022, from https://www.charlietemple.com/nl-nl/klantenservice/bril-passen

Chen, J. Q., Liu, D., & Whinston, A. B. (2009). Auctioning keywords in online search. *Journal of Marketing, 73*(4), 125–141.

Chiu, Y. P., Los, S. K., & Hsieh, A. Y. (2017). How colour similarity can make banner advertising effective: Insights from Gestalt Theory. *Behaviour & Information Technology, 36*(6), 606–619.

Cho, C. H. (2003). Factors in influencing clicking of banner ads. *Cyber Psychology & Behavior, 6*(2), 201–215.

Chowdhury, T. I., Costa, R., & Quarles, J. (2017, September). Information recall in a mobile VR disability simulation. 2017 9th International conference on virtual worlds and games for serious applications (VS-games), pp. 125–128. IEEE.

Chung, M., Ko, E., Joung, H., & Kim, S. J. (2020). Chatbot e-service and customer satisfaction regarding luxury brands. *Journal of Business Research, 117*, 587–595.

Colliander, J., Dahlén, M., & Modig, E. (2015). Twitter for two: Investigating the effects of dialogue with customers in social media. *International Journal of Advertising, 34*(2), 181–194.

de Cosmo, L. M., Piper, L., & Di Vittorio, A. (2021). The role of attitude toward chatbots and privacy concern on the relationship between attitude toward mobile advertising and behavioral intent to use chatbots. *Italian Journal of Marketing, 2021*(1), 83–102.

Donthu, N., & Garcia, A. (1999). The internet shopper. *Journal of Advertising Research, 39*(3), 53–62.

Farías, P. (2018). The effect of advergames, banners and user type on the attitude to brand and intention to purchase. *Revista Brasileira de Gestão de Negócios, 20*, 194–209.

Fiore, A. M., Kim, J., & Lee, H. H. (2005). Effect of image interactivity technology on consumer responses toward the online retailer. *Journal of Interactive Marketing, 19*(3), 38–53.

Flavián, C., Ibáñez-Sánchez, S., & Orús, C. (2019). The impact of virtual, augmented and mixed reality technologies on the customer experience. *Journal of Business Research, 100*, 547–560.

Fransen, M. L., Smit, E. G., & Verlegh, P. W. (2015). Strategies and motives for resistance to persuasion: An integrative framework. *Frontiers in Psychology, 6*, 1201.

Gazley, A., Hunt, A., & McLaren, L. (2015). The effects of location-based-services on consumer purchase intention at point of purchase. *European Journal of Marketing, 49*(9/10), 1686–1708.

Hartemo, M. (2016). Email marketing in the era of the empowered consumer. *Journal of Research in Interactive Marketing, 10*(3), 212–230.

Hoffman, D. L., & Novak, T. P. (1996). Marketing in hypermedia computer-mediated environments: Conceptual foundations. *Journal of Marketing, 60*(3), 50–68.

Hoogendoorn, S. (2013). *Branded mobile phone apps: A research on the effect of entertainment and informational branded smartphone apps on consumer' brand equity* (Doctoral dissertation). Graduate School of Communication Master's Programme on Persuasive Communication, University of Amsterdam. dare.uva.nl/cgi/arno/show.cgi

Hoyer, W. D., Kroschke, M., Schmitt, B., Kraume, K., & Shankar, V. (2020). Transforming the customer experience through new technologies. *Journal of Interactive Marketing, 51*, 57–71.

Huang, L. T. (2016). Flow and social capital theory in online impulse buying. *Journal of Business Research, 69*(6), 2277–2283.

HubSpot. (2021). Retrieved on 14 December 2021, from https://www.hubspot.com/marketing-statistics

Ischen, C., Araujo, T., Voorveld, H., van Noort, G., & Smit, E. (2019). *Privacy concerns in chatbot interactions*. International Workshop on Chatbot Research and Design, pp. 34–48. Springer, Cham.

Kaczorowska-Spychalska, D. (2019). Chatbots in marketing. *Management, 23*(1), 251–270.

Kim, G., Jin, B., & Shin, D. C. (2022). Virtual reality as a promotion tool for small independent stores. *Journal of Retailing and Consumer Services, 64*, 102822.

Kim, H., & Stout, P. A. (2010). The effects of interactivity on information processing and atti-tude change: Implications for mental health stigma. *Health Communication, 25*, 142–154.

Kim, J., & Lee, K. H. (2019). Influence of integration on interactivity in social media luxury brand communities. *Journal of Business Research, 99*, 422–429.

Krafft, M., Arden, C. M., & Verhoef, P. C. (2017). Permission marketing and privacy concerns: Why do customers (not) grant permissions? *Journal of Interactive Marketing, 39*, 39–54.

Krammer, V. (2008). *An effective defense against intrusive web advertising*. 2008 Sixth Annual Conference on Privacy, Security and Trust, pp. 3–14. IEEE.

Krushali, S., Jojo, N., & Manivannan, A. S. (2018). Cognitive marketing and purchase decision with reference to pop up and banner advertisements. *The Journal of Social Sciences Research, 4*(12), 718–735.

Kucuk, S. U. (2016). Consumerism in the digital age. *Journal of Consumer Affairs, 50*(3), 515–538.

Lal, R., & Sarvary, M. (1999). When and how is the internet likely to decrease price competition? *Marketing Science, 18*(4), 485–503.

Liebrecht, C., & Hooijdonk, C. V. (2019, November). *Creating humanlike chatbots: What chatbot developers could learn from webcare employees in adopting a conversational human voice*. International Workshop on Chatbot Research and Design, pp. 51–64. Springer, Cham.

Lee, T. (2005). The impact of perceptions of interactivity on customer trust and transaction intentions in mobile commerce. *Journal of Electronic Commerce Research, 6*(3), 165.

Liang, S., & Roast, C. (2014, June). *Five features for modeling Augmented reality*. International Conference on Human-Computer Interaction, pp. 607–612. Springer, Cham.

Lim, W. M., Kumar, S., Pandey, N., Rasul, T., & Gaur, V. (2022, forthcoming). From direct marketing to interactive marketing: A retrospective review of the Journal of Research in Interactive Marketing. *Journal of Research in Interactive Marketing* (in press). https://doi.org/10.1108/JRIM-11-2021-0276

Liu, Y., & Shrum, L. J. (2002). What is interactivity and is it always such a good thing? Implications of definition, person, and situation for the influence of interactivity on advertising effectiveness. *Journal of Advertising, 31*(4), 53–64.

Mahmoud, A. B., Grigoriou, N., Fuxman, L., Hack-Polay, D., Mahmoud, F. B., Yafi, E., & Tehseen, S. (2019). Email is evil! Behavioural responses towards permission-based direct email marketing and gender differences. *Journal of Research in Interactive Marketing, 13*(2), 227–248.

Main, K. (2021). *19 useful website statistics every business should know*. Retrieved on 18 February 2022, from https://fitsmallbusiness.com/website-statistics/

Meents, S., Verhagen, T., Merikivi, J., & Weltevreden, J. (2020). Persuasive location-based messaging to increase store visits: An exploratory study of fashion shoppers. *Journal of Retailing and Consumer Services, 57*, 102174.

Mens, R. (2017). *Ikea Place: praktische augmented reality-app nu beschikbaar*. Retrieved on 15 February 2022, from https://www.onemorething.nl/2017/09/ikea-place-augmented-reality-beschikbaar/

Moes, A., Fransen, M., Fennis, B., Verhagen, T., & van Vliet, H. (2021). In-store interactive advertising screens: The effect of interactivity on impulse buying explained by self-agency. *Journal of Research in Interactive Marketing*, ahead of print.

Moes, A., & van Vliet, H. (2017). The online appeal of the physical shop: How a physical store can benefit from a virtual representation. *Heliyon, 3*(6), e00336.

Monsuwé, T. P. Y., Benedict, G. C., & Ko de Ruyter, D. (2004). What drives consumers to shop internet? A literature review. *International Journal of Service Industry Management, 15*(1), 102–121.

Moriuchi, E., Landers, V. M., Colton, D., & Hair, N. (2021). Engagement with chatbots versus augmented reality interactive technology in e-commerce. *Journal of Strategic Marketing, 29*(5), 375–389.

Nawaz, N., & Gomes, A. M. (2019). Artificial intelligence chatbots are new recruiters. *International Journal of Advanced Computer Science and Applications, 10*(9), 1–5.

Obar, J. A., & Wildman, S. S. (2015). Social media definition and the governance challenge: An introduction to the special issue. *Telecommunications Policy, 39*(9), 745–750.

Ott, H. K., Vafeiadis, M., Kumble, S., & Waddell, T. F. (2016). Effect of message interactivity on product attitudes and purchase intentions. *Journal of Promotion Management, 22*(1), 89–106.

Peterson, R. A., Balasubramanian, S., & Bronnenberg, B. J. (1997). Exploring the implications of the internet for consumer marketing. *Journal of the Academy of Marketing Science, 25*(4), 329–346.

Rauschnabel, P. A., Felix, R., & Hinsch, C. (2019). Augmented reality marketing: How mobile AR-apps can improve brands through inspiration. *Journal of Retailing and Consumer Services, 49*, 43–53.

Ratchford, B. T. (2020). The history of academic research in marketing and its implications for the future. *Spanish Journal of Marketing-ESIC, 24*(1), 3–36.

Resnick, M., & Albert, W. (2014). The impact of advertising location and user task on the emergence of banner ad blindness: An eye-tracking study. *International Journal of Human-Computer Interaction, 30*(3), 206–219.

Schau, H. J., & Gilly, M. C. (2003). We are what we post? Self-presentation in personal web space. *Journal of Consumer Research, 30*(3), 385–404.

Seitz, V. A., & Aldebasi, N. M. (2016). The effectiveness of branded mobile apps on user's brand attitudes and purchase intentions. *Review of Economic and Business Studies, 9*(1), 141–154.

Sicilia, M., Ruiz, S., & Munuera, J. L. (2005). Effects of interactivity in a web site: The moderating effect of need for cognition. *Journal of Advertising, 34*(3), 31–44.

Smink, A. R., Frowijn, S., van Reijmersdal, E. A., van Noort, G., & Neijens, P. C. (2019). Try online before you buy: How does shopping with augmented reality affect brand responses and personal data disclosure. *Electronic Commerce Research and Applications, 35*, 100854.

Sreejesh, S., Paul, J., Strong, C., & Pius, J. (2020). Consumer response towards social media advertising: Effect of media interactivity, its conditions and the underlying mechanism. *International Journal of Information Management, 54*, 102–155.

Sundar, S. S., & Constantin, C. (2004, May 27). *Does interacting with media enhance news memory? Automatic vs. controlled processing of interactive news features.* Paper presented at the Annual Conference of International Communication Association, New Orleans, LA. http://www.allacademic.com/meta/p113221_index.html

Sung, E. C. (2021). The effects of augmented reality mobile app advertising: Viral marketing via shared social experience. *Journal of Business Research, 122*, 75–87.

TimetoReply. (2020). Retrieved on 18 February 2022, from https://timetoreply.com/blog/what-is-a-standard-email-response-time-policy-and-why-do-you-need-one/

TotalReality. (n.d.). Retrieved on 31 January 2022, from https://www.totalreality.nl/technologies/.

Tsai, W. H. S., Liu, Y., & Chuan, C. H. (2021). How chatbots' social presence communication enhances consumer engagement: The mediating role of parasocial interaction and dialogue. *Journal of Research in Interactive Marketing, 15*(3), 460–482.

Van Noort, G., & Van Reijmersdal, E. A. (2019). Branded apps: Explaining effects of brands' mobile phone applications on brand responses. *Journal of Interactive Marketing, 45*, 16–26.

Verhagen, T., Meents, S., Merikivi, J., Moes, A., & Weltevreden, J. (2021). How location-based messages influence customers' store visit attitudes: an integrative model of message value. *International Journal of Retail & Distribution Management*, ahead of print.

Voorveld, H. A., Neijens, P. C., & Smit, E. G. (2011). The relation between actual and perceived interactivity. *Journal of Advertising, 40*(2), 77–92.

Wang, B., Kim, S., & Malthouse, E. C. (2016). Branded apps and mobile platforms as new tools for advertising. *The New Advertising: Branding, Content, and Consumer Relationships in the Data-Driven Social Media Era, 2*, 123–156.

Wang, C. L. (2021). New frontiers and future directions in interactive marketing: Inaugural Editorial. *Journal of Research in Interactive Marketing, 15*(1), 1–9.

Wu, J., Li, K. J., & Liu, J. S. (2018). Bayesian inference for assessing effects of email marketing campaigns. *Journal of Business & Economic Statistics, 36*(2), 253–266.

Xi, N., & Hamari, J. (2021). Shopping in virtual reality: A literature review and future agenda. *Journal of Business Research, 134*, 37–58.

Yang, F., & Shen, F. (2018). Effects of web interactivity: A meta-analysis. *Communication Research, 45*(5), 635–658.

Yang, Q., Zhou, Y., Jiang, Y., & Huo, J. (2021). How to overcome online banner blindness? A study on the effects of creativity. *Journal of Research in Interactive Marketing, 15*(2).

Yung, R., Khoo-Lattimore, C., & Potter, L. E. (2021). VR the world: Experimenting with emotion and presence for tourism marketing. *Journal of Hospitality and Tourism Management, 46*, 160–171.

Zhang, X., Kumar, V., & Cosguner, K. (2017). Dynamically managing a profitable email marketing program. *Journal of Marketing Research, 54*(6), 851–866.

CHAPTER 4

Bridging the Theory and Practice of Digital Marketing from Interactive Marketing Perspective: A Historical Review

Ayşegül Sağkaya Güngör and Tuğçe Ozansoy Çadırcı

1 Introduction

The adoption of the Internet by the masses is the biggest and the most critical event that has affected marketing theoretically and practically over the last three decades. The growth of digital has transformed marketing to a personalized phenomenon (Erdem et al., 2016). The digital revolution has been reflected in how companies and consumers embrace interactive technologies and how the new technologies facilitate experiences, interactions, and, most importantly, behaviors.

Interactive marketing includes many operational and strategic decisions that are only successful with a thorough understanding of the consumer. As a result, with the undeniable impact of the Internet and the introduction of new channels to conduct marketing activities, interactive marketing has become one of the most studied subjects in academic journals.

Marketing interactivity can be defined as "a person-to-person or person-to-technology exchange designed to effect a change in the knowledge or behavior of at least one person" (Haeckel, 1998). This definition highlights the impact of technology on interactive marketing. Digitalization of marketing activities since the beginning of the 90s created strong connections between

A. S. Güngör (✉)
Istanbul Medeniyet University, Istanbul, Turkey
e-mail: agngor@yahoo.com

T. O. Çadırcı
Yıldız Technical University, Istanbul, Turkey

interactive marketing and digital marketing (DM) literature. Over the years, interactive marketing has been divided into specialized and focused areas, one being the DM. In the domain of contemporary interactive marketing, DM is a remarkable area with its specific focus on interactivity.

Defining the conceptual evolution of DM research for the last 30 years can help us to deeply understand the domain and create the potential to adopt a forward-looking approach. Building on the existing literature, the main objective of this chapter is threefold: By taking the DM domain, a subset of interactive marketing, we aim to: (1) identify the dominant themes within DM research; (2) provide insights into the longitudinal change in these themes over time with the use of science mapping and bibliometrics; (3) compare and contrast the change within the practice and the research perspectives over time.

2 Literature Review and Background

Before the widespread use of information and communication technologies (ICT) in marketing, the communication form used by marketers was the traditional form of direct marketing (Zahay, 2021). As the Internet and networking became prevalent in the customers' lives, the marketing turned into a dialog between the customers and the companies, thus, becoming interactive. As of definition, interactive marketing emphasizes interactivity, characterized by two-way communication, personalization, value co-creation, participation, interaction, and engagement (Wang, 2021; Zahay, 2021). In the literature, interactive marketing is defined with three central constructs: communication in the form of dialog, responses, and proactive behaviors to create value, and engagement to modify and control the environment (Steuer, 1992; Wang, 2021).

Digital media and marketing have spawned the most significant influence on the evolution of interactive marketing. The interrelationships between interactivity and digital channels can be analyzed through many aspects, including e-wom (Çadırcı & Güngör, 2016; Güngör & Çadırcı, 2013; López et al., 2021); search engines (Barwise & Farley, 2005; Shankar & Malthouse, 2007); personalization (Kaya & Güngör, 2012; Wang, 2021); e-services (Elsharnouby & Mahrous, 2015; Finn et al., 2009); customer reviews and recommendations (Güngör & Özgen, 2020; Malthouse & Hofacker, 2010; Wang, 2021); co-creation (Payne et al., 2021; Wang, 2021); virtual communities and environments (Malthouse & Shankar, 2009; Park & Feinberg, 2010; Wang, 2021); e-auctions (Malthouse & Hofacker, 2010) and many others. As can be observed in the research subjects, interactive marketing is a term that includes DM but also has unique characteristics that are beyond DM (Wang, 2021). In nature, DM is a form of interactive marketing and is highly related to the interactive domain (Wang, 2021). The domains are so intertwined that they are even referred to as interactive digital marketing (IDM) (See Krishen et al., 2021).

As digital channels mainly dominate interactive media, defining and forecasting the possible changes within DM research can provide deeper insights into the evolution of interactive marketing. There have been attempts to understand, forecast, and classify the DM domain from different aspects. For example, Vanhala et al. (2020) studied a corpus of 495 articles (2000–2018) to investigate online consumer behavior. Leung et al. (2017) relied on bibliometrics, co-citation, and co-word analyses in their attempt to define the social media research domain. They analyzed 406 papers from 16 journals published between 2007 and 2016. Another stream of research focused on future research opportunities. In their effort to develop a framework, Kannan and Li (2017) researched the extant literature on DM. They highlighted the digital technologies which are prevailing and will have a significant effect on marketing strategies. They came up with the agenda for future research. Likewise, Lamberton and Stephen (2016) analyzed the changes in digital, social media, and mobile marketing themes. They worked on five premier marketing journals and focused on 15 years (2000–2015). Again, the study resulted in suggestions for future research. By pursuing a multi-disciplinary approach and using data extracted from the Scopus database, Krishen et al. (2021) have defined the main research topics and their evolution in IDM research. They were able to identify five different stages: the start-up, customer satisfaction and analysis, social networking and review, co-creation and customer engagement, and lastly, machine intelligence and IoT-based virtual reality.

Taking a different approach from the previous studies, this chapter covers the whole realm of DM. The data was extracted from the WoS database, not specific to any journal but specific to the keywords (detailed in the methodology section). To the best of our knowledge, this chapter is the first to apply science mapping to DM research which sets the present chapter apart from previous works. Third, this chapter presents the theoretical evolution of DM followed by practical changes and developments in the domain. This presentation enables us to show the alignment between the subjects of academia and practical applications of digital marketers while enabling a better understanding of the evolution of interactive marketing.

Relying on collective wisdom, we divided the 30 years into 5-year intervals to examine the themes in detail (only 1990–1999 was a ten-year interval since there were a very small number of publications on DM yet). As stated by Lamberton and Stephen (2016), interesting changes appear at approximately 5-year intervals in the domain of digital. We observed that most of the time, the practical evolution has its reflections in theory in the next period. And sometimes, the foundations of a concept are built theoretically first, and it comes to life in practice in the following period.

3 Methodology

Analyzing scientific texts is a good way of understanding the evolution and the performance of a research domain. In the current study, a complete bibliometric analysis was used to analyze the evolution of DM as a research domain. A typical bibliometric analysis produces two evaluations: performance analysis and science mapping (Cobo et al., 2011). Performance analysis is based on the publications (articles), and it produces information on the outputs of these publications that are based on documents, authors, and citations (Noyons et al., 1999a). The most significant sources and articles can be derived through the performance analysis, information on the author, and country productivity. Also, the impact can be obtained using performance analysis, information on source, and article.

Science mapping provides information on the cognitive structure of a research domain with the inclusion of its evolution over time (Noyons et al., 1999b). To understand the cognitive structure through science mapping, mostly semantic maps created with co-word analysis are used (Börner et al., 2003). Co-word analysis creates clusters of keywords used within a corpus that are semantically or conceptually related (Lopez-Herrera et al., 2010) based on their co-occurrences within the documents in the corpus. Co-word analysis can be attributed as a form of content analysis that operates with the association strength between words (Callon et al., 1983). In other words, co-word analysis works with the assumption that the content of multiple documents can be derived from the co-occurrence of keywords associated with the document (Callon et al., 1991). Maps created with co-word analysis can be used to understand the existence of keyword clusters within a period and their evolution through consecutive periods (Cobo et al., 2011).

A longitudinal science mapping analysis has a set of steps (Börner et al., 2003; Callon et al., 1991; Van Eck et al., 2006): (1) Collection of data; (2) Selection of the unit of measurement; (3) Information extraction; (4) Detection of research themes with the calculation of similarities and the use of a clustering algorithm; (5) Building strategic diagrams and thematic maps; and (6) Conducting a performance analysis of the themes. Figure 1 exhibits the research workflow of the study.

(1) *Collection of Data*. The data was extracted from Web of Science™ (ISI WoS) Core Collection (e.g., Social Sciences Citation Index) to analyze and visualize the current situation of DM literature. In data extraction, certain keywords (e.g., digital marketing, internet marketing, electronic marketing, etc.) were searched in the title, keywords, and abstracts of the papers.

Papers without keywords and content, like book reviews and editorials, were excluded from the data, and only articles belonging to the subject category of "business" were included in the analysis. The final data included document titles, source title, author names (8,816 authors), the author-assigned (11,683), and WoS-assigned (5,262) keywords, cited references, times cited,

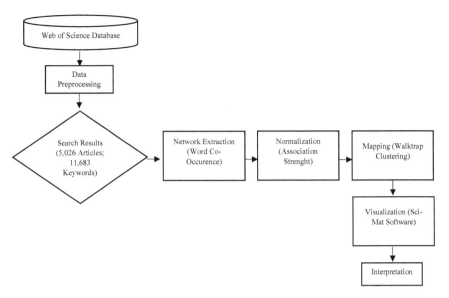

Fig. 1 Research workflow

and publication date of 5,026 articles. The average citation per document was 34.9, and the number of authors per document was 2.64.

(2) *Selection of the unit of measurement and information extraction.* As the data was extracted from ISI WoS, each document had two groups of keywords. The first group included author-assigned keywords, and the second group was WoS-assigned keywords. The author-assigned keywords were selected since WoS-assigned keywords were more generic, and the use of author keywords was expected to be more reflective of the studies.

(3) *Detection of Research Themes.* Using the frequency of keyword co-occurrences, similarities between articles can be calculated. Association strength, also known as proximity index, is a measure that provides a fair comparison between high volume and low volume word co-occurrences (Van Eck & Waltman, 2007, 2009). The association strength measure was used in the normalization process of co-occurrences. In plain words, articles sharing similar keywords are grouped together to form a research theme. The researcher should locate the subgroups of keywords that exhibit a strong association during this step. The network map that presents the subgroups can only be created with the use of a clustering algorithm. Although there are multiple clustering algorithms that can be used in science mapping studies, we used the Walktrap clustering algorithm to cluster the extracted keywords. Pons and Latapy (2005) proposed that the walk trap algorithm relies highly on the distance between word clusters. The general assumption of the algorithm is that as the nodes within a graph are highly associated (in the same cluster), the distance between these nodes should be short (Lee et al., 2020).

(4) *Mapping of the Research Themes.* The detected themes are positioned on the thematic map based on centrality and density (Callon et al., 1991).

- Centrality is the measure of the external strength of a network, and it presents the interaction of a network of words with other word networks.

$$c = 10 * \sum e_{k,h};$$

where, k: keyword belonging to the theme; and h: keyword belonging to other themes.

- Density is the measure of the internal strength of the network, and it presents the interaction of words within the same network.

$$d = 100 * \sum \frac{e_{i,j}}{w}$$

where, i and j: keywords belonging to the same theme; and w: number of keywords in the same theme.

The themes are positioned on a two-dimensional map, and their positions are determined based on their centrality and density ranks (López-Herrera et al., 2010; Muñoz-Leiva et al., 2013). They are calculated as $c_r = \text{rank}_i^c / N$; and $d_r = \text{rank}_i^d / N$. In these equations, rank_i^c and rank_i^d represent the position of the theme in the list of themes in ascending order of centrality and density, respectively. N represents the total number of themes and is used for normalization purposes. Following the calculations of centrality and density rankings, a map is produced with four separate quadrants representing four different groups of themes: "*a) motor themes; b) basic or transversal themes, c) emerging or declining themes, d) specialized and isolated themes*" (Callon et al., 1991). Each research theme in each quadrant is represented with a sphere, and the size of each sphere is proportional to the number of documents in each theme (Cobo et al., 2011).

a. Upper-right quadrant (Motor Themes): Themes in this position present a high level of centrality and density. Each theme positioned in this quadrant is highly developed and they have strong external and internal strength.
b. Lower-right quadrant (Transversal and Basic Themes): The themes in this quadrant have a high level of internal strength, but they are not as highly developed as themes in the upper-right quadrant. They mostly represent general and basic themes.

c. Lower-left quadrant (Declining or Emerging Themes): The themes positioned in this quadrant are weakly developed, lacking internal and external strengths. Due to their low centrality and density measures, they are expected to disappear or emerge in the research domain.
d. Upper-left quadrant (Specialized and Isolated themes): Themes in this quadrant have a high level of centrality but a low level of density. These themes exhibit a peripheral character and have a high level of internal strength.

(5) *Performance Analysis*. The last phase of science mapping includes performance analysis. The rationale behind performance analysis is to determine the themes with the highest impact. Each theme's productivity is determined by the number of documents and average citations generated by each theme and their h-index. The common way of understanding bibliometric evaluation is using different indexes like the h-index (Hirsch, 2007), and g-index (Egghe, 2006). h-index is a micro-level evaluation of a single scientist's achievement over time. According to Hirsch (2005, p. 16,569), "a scientist has index h if his or her papers have at least h citations each, and the other (n−h) papers have ≤ h citations each." In time, the h-index gained more extensive use as an assessment of scientific productivity (Martínez et al., 2014; Rousseau, 2006).

4   Results and Discussion

To present the conceptual structure of DM, we created maps based on scientific production and analyzed and discussed the evolution of DM—both practically and theoretically—in 5 consecutive periods with the use of SciMAT software. The results of the thematic analysis are summarized in five thematic maps (Fig. 2) and an evolution map (Fig. 3).

4.1   1990–1999: The Dawn of New Beginnings

The Practical Landscape (1990–1999). The early 90s were the first decade of the Internet, known as Web 1.0. With the launch of the mass-market browser Netscape, in 1994, the World Wide Web project became public. As a response to the increasing number of Web users, search engines Yahoo! (1994) and Google (1997), e-commerce sites Amazon (1994), eBay (1995), and e-mail service provider Hotmail (1997) were commercialized. The first e-commerce-oriented websites acted as digital brochures with limited marketing and customer engagement possibilities. There was only traditional one-way communication at any Web site without any interaction. DM was still in the proximity of interactive marketing in that era, not fully capitalized yet. The 90s were the era when consumers and companies realized the opportunities and threats of being online.

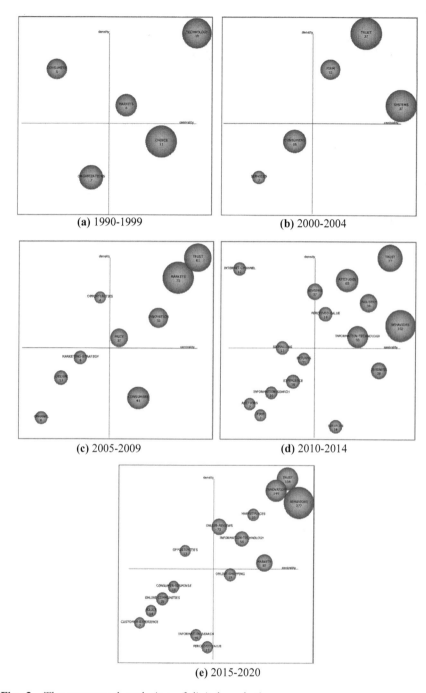

Fig. 2 The conceptual evolution of digital marketing

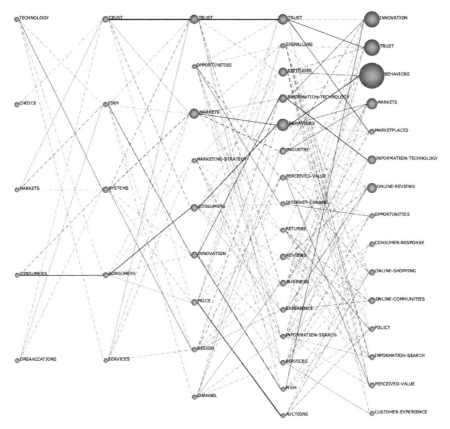

Fig. 3 The evolution of digital marketing themes (1990–2020)

The Conceptual Structure (1990–1999). During this period, with the limited research areas defined yet, the TECHNOLOGY and MARKETS appeared as the Motor themes with an effort to familiarize the academia with the subject of "Use of Technology in Commercial Markets" (Fig. 2a). The most dominant motor theme was TECHNOLOGY (Table 1). TECHNOLOGY, as a theme, was closely related to the sub-themes *search cost, internet markets, e-business, new products, and diffusion of innovations*. The sub-themes are the apparent indicators of academia's approach to the new digital products as innovations and try to relate them to e-business. The other motor theme is the MARKETS, in close relationship with the sub-themes *network externalities, value chain, business, industry, and investment*. Scholars were defining the value chain of DM and in a belief that the more the investment, the more the advantage of these newly founded electronic companies. And it is a challenge to understand the buying patterns of consumers, reflected in the sub-theme network externalities, in the digital environment. The only basic theme of this

Table 1 Performance analysis (1990–1999)

Theme	Number of papers	Average citations	h-index
TECHNOLOGY	10	193.8	8
CHOICE	11	147.64	11
MARKETS	6	46.67	6
CONSUMERS	5	120	5
ORGANIZATIONS	7	226.43	7

period was CHOICE. By definition of the basic themes, CHOICE is important for the DM field but not well-developed yet. Since CHOICE reflects the *consumer preference* (sub-theme), it is highly related to CONSUMER, which showed up as the isolated theme of the era. The theme CONSUMER had a very weak tie with the sub-theme *behavior*, yet, and the strongest tie with the sub-theme *information-technology*. Consumer side studies were gathered around flow, perception, and feelings at the consumer level, consumer search, electronic markets, and telecommunications at the company technology level. ORGANIZATION was the emerging theme and at the very basic level at this period.

To summarize, the 1990s were the first years for both the practical and theoretical developments of DM. While practitioners were trying to get the best out of the new digital medium, academia was struggling to define the technical and operational dynamics of the medium. The focus of the studies in this era was the organizations, with only a few consumer studies.

4.2   2000–2004: Understanding the Rules of Digital Marketplaces

The Practical Landscape (2000–2004). At the beginning of the new millennium, companies recognized that the Internet was not only a tool for commercialization but also socialization. In the early 2000s, static websites became interactive and included dynamic content with a few social interaction aspects (Poynter & Lawrence, 2008). In this era, traditional interactive marketing took a new direction to become contemporary. This led companies to form online intellectual relationships with their customers through content and membership groups (Erragcha & Romdhane, 2014). The emergence of socialization through the web is also observed with the launch of LinkedIn (2002), MySpace (2003), and Facebook (2004). This period also created a shift in terms of interactivity. The bi-directional nature of relationships evolved into unidirectionality, i.e., between company and customer and between customers (Poynter & Lawrence, 2008). This was the milestone in interactive marketing's nature to become more digitalized. The interactive relationships were also symbolized by wikis and blogs. As consumers realized the opportunities in the digital world, traditional interactive marketing tools turned into digital, and DM was even more important. As a preliminary effort,

Google launched Adwords in 2000 and marked the beginning of search engine and display marketing.

The Conceptual Structure (2000–2004). In this period, the themes were either categorized as motor themes or emerging themes. Based on their strategic positions in the thematic map, FIRM, SYSTEMS, and TRUST are the motor themes of this period (Fig. 2b), well-developed, and important for the structuring of the DM field. *Innovation* was the most dominant co-occurrence of the theme FIRM. It became prominent in this era with a reasonable belief that the higher the *innovation capability* of a digital firm, the better it performs in electronic channels. And, as the relationship between the sub-themes promises, the *network* of the firm was one of the main determinants of the *innovation performance* of the firm. Thus, on the firm side, *innovation, network, performance,* and *e-business* studies gained importance. The SYSTEM studies were other drivers of the research field. The high citation rate of the theme (164.11) discloses its importance for scholars while supporting the position of the theme on the map (Table 2). The sub-themes of the SYSTEM being *information-technology, auctions, reverse auctions,* and *externalities* implied that the scholars were still trying to figure out the technicalities as well as new pricing mechanisms brought to the market mainly by eBay in the previous period. TRUST, the motor theme, had its strongest link with *markets* and breakdowns as *buyer–seller relationships, perceived risk,* and *consumer perceptions*. The co-occurrence network of TRUST was a clear indicator of how vital it is both for the electronic markets and relationships with consumers. It was one of the most studied subjects with 27 articles and the highest average citation (264.26) of the period.

CONSUMERS and SERVICES were the emerging themes of the period. The SERVICES studies had a new entrance to the DM domain with 3 articles. The scholars noticed that almost every product/service that was offered in the digital channels was based on a service economy. With the other emerging theme, CONSUMERS, academia is trying to understand the consumer *experience* and *perception* of *search costs* associated with *consumer search and price*. Although the theme CONSUMER is at the focus of every period, the elaborated consumer studies were reserved as subjects of interest shortly.

Table 2 Performance analysis (2000–2004)

Theme	Number of papers	Average citations	h-index
TRUST	27	264.26	24
FIRM	12	130.25	12
SYSTEMS	27	164.11	24
CONSUMERS	16	244.81	16
SERVICES	3	77	3

Although the studies of this era still mostly focused on the company side, consumer studies gained momentum. The main concern was shaped around acknowledgment of new systems by the firms, innovations which were the main drivers of the DM field at this period, and, to a small degree, relationships between buyer and seller. Still, it is not surprising to see that almost all the themes of 2000–2004 had a strong evolutionary follower, which is the theme TRUST (Fig. 3)—implying that the studies on the consumer were yet to accelerate.

4.3 2005–2009: The Rise of Multichannel Marketing

The Practical Landscape (2005–2009). Although the foundations of Web 2.0 (Community web) have been laid in the previous period, the term was first introduced at a conference organized by O'Reilly and Medialive International in 2004. Likewise, the evolutive marketing concept developed by Prof. Philip Kotler had reached its second stage, Marketing 2.0. It was time for conversations, collaborations, and communities. It was the years that the marketers awakened with the idea of going where the customers were instead of waiting for them.

Web 2.0 was named as the participating web. It rested on social media (Kaplan & Haenlein, 2010), which relied on user-generated content (UGC) (Ye et al., 2011) and crowdsourcing (Erragcha & Romdhane, 2014). Furthermore, considering the interaction capability of social media, digital and interactive marketing became even more effective in building a more personalized approach in the mid-2000s (Wang, 2021). Integrating the consumers into the marketing process in a personalized way and considering them as the players, not the receivers, was the fundamental idea behind marketing 2.0 (Bressolles, 2012). Consumers became collaborators of marketing strategies with never-lasting interactive communication during this period.

2005 was when YouTube, GoogleAnalytics, and search engine optimization (SEO) were first pronounced. As the methods of data collection, digital communication, and data analysis have accelerated, marketers looked for ways to utilize collected data, called "big data." Analyzing the big data opened the venue for fine-tuned segmentation and marketing. The focus of marketing in this period was moved from understanding the online customer to persuasion tactics through data analytics. Moreover, responding to all these changes, 2006 was the year in which analytical customer relationship building (CRM) was operationalized.

The introduction of Twitter in 2006 changed how consumers share opinions and how they get information. Social networks (e.g., Twitter, Facebook, Tumblr [2007]) were not only serving the purpose of opinion sharing but also giving a hand to the companies in identifying the consumer attitudes toward the brands. It was also the year that the mobile as a concept and media was recognized by digital marketers.

It seemed that the marketers had to obey the new rules set by the customers. No company filter was ever possible, and the new technologies challenged the companies more than ever. It was time to give away action in favor of interaction. The market became a forum for interactive marketing's naturally inherited conversations among connected customers and/or participants via digital and mobile tools (Wang, 2021). Rust et al. (2010) stated, "A truly customer-centered view of marketing is the natural result of technology."

The Conceptual Structure (2005–2009). The most recurrent occurrence was MARKETS which showed up as a motor theme during this period (Fig. 2c). MARKETS, as a theme, was closely related to the sub-themes of *behaviors, strategies, information-technology, electronic marketplaces, network externalities, network effects, information asymmetry, information goods,* and *online retailing.* TRUST, which has been studied generously since the beginning of the 2000s, was another motor theme that found a strong ground in this era as well (Table 3). This theme is interrelated with sub-themes like *performance, satisfaction, electronic markets, services, commitment, environments, buyer–seller relationships, perceived risk,* and *marketplaces.* These two themes are the most studied subjects of this period. Along with them, two more motor themes are also presented in Fig. 2c. These are INNOVATION and PRICE. INNOVATION is related to the sub-themes of *technology, firm, customers, information systems, organizations, capabilities, social networks, dynamic-capabilities,* and *telecommunications.* This era witnessed the infancy of analytical tools, mobile phones, and social media channels. As one of the main topics of interactive marketing, social media was used as a way to engage audiences in conversations and information sharing (Byon & Phua, 2021).

The studies exploring these facets of DM found its ground in the theme of INNOVATION. PRICE is interrelated with *consumer behavior, auctions, consumer perceptions, online-auctions, promotions, digital products, risk,* and *internet-auctions.* The theme has evolved into the theme of AUCTIONS in the next era (Fig. 3). PRICE has been studied from both buyer and seller perspectives. A group of studies under this theme explored the impact of

Table 3 Performance analysis (2005–2009)

Theme	Number of papers	Average citations	h-index
TRUST	61	81.84	34
OPPORTUNITIES	4	160	4
MARKETS	75	52.65	28
MARKETING-STRATEGY	9	67.89	9
CONSUMERS	41	87.12	28
INNOVATION	32	103	22
PRICE	27	69.89	22
DESIGN	13	85.46	11
CHANNEL	8	52.88	8

online pricing on consumers' behavior, including their risk perceptions (e.g., Chellappa & Kumar, 2005; Ratchford, 2009; Sen et al., 2006). Another realm of studies was analyzing the system of auctions in digital platforms, the use of promotions, and digital product pricing strategies. With the penetration of mobile technologies, changes in electronic markets, auctions and requirements, and adoption of new pricing mechanisms, PRICE's importance as a research field kept on growing.

The single basic theme of this era is CONSUMERS. The theme is interrelated with sub-themes of *perception, choice, search costs, communication, experience, retailers, mechanisms, brand*, and *social influence*. The theme represents studies on digital consumer behavior. The studies listed under this theme were attempts to discover consumer behavior with their perceptions and experience on digital platforms. CONSUMERS has been a recurrent theme since the 90s. During this period, it is also the second most cited theme with the highest number of average citations (Table 2).

The other group of themes MARKETING-STRATEGY, DESIGN, and CHANNEL were either emerging or disappearing themes in DM between 2005 and 2009 (Fig. 2c). MARKETING-STRATEGY is interrelated with sub-themes like *websites, tourism, decision, marketing-communications, online-reviews, paradigm, preferences,* and *purchase*. As the business landscape of DM was under change because of new channels, academia showed interest in possible strategic directions in these new environments. DESIGN evolved from SYSTEMS in the previous period is interrelated with the *product, supply-chain, systems, business-models, e-business, e-service, online communities,* and *reverse auctions*. The theme is mostly related to business system design within digital environments. The last theme in this quadrant is CHANNEL, which is interrelated with *industry, switching-costs, costs, shoppers, benefits,* and *choice-models*. Under the heading of this theme, academia explored channel choice in digital environments. The most representative sub-theme being *industry* is an indicator of the focus on the business side of channel choice.

The single isolated theme between 2005 and 2009 is OPPORTUNITIES. Examining the thematic evolution map (Fig. 2c), OPPORTUNITIES is a newly introduced theme in DM literature. The theme evolves into INTERNET-CHANNEL, EXPERIENCE, and PERCEIVED VALUE in the upcoming period. The theme has relationships with the *acquisition, customer value, distribution-channels, exchange, information-search, marketing-channels, motivation,* and *time*. The launch of social networks like Twitter and Facebook, and the introduction of mobile technologies, created growth in both availabilities of content and information at an increasing pace. Connecting the information availability with channel management, practitioners started to question "value" created in a multi-channel environment, and academia has focused on OPPORTUNITIES created by these channels. Despite having the smallest number of documents (4 papers), the theme was the most cited one in this period.

4.4 2010–2014: Rules of the Interactive Web

The Practical Landscape (2010–2014). 2010 was the year that Web 3.0 started. The idea behind Web 3.0 was user cooperation (Fuchs, 2010), and it was the first year of "extended immersive experience" (Erragcha & Romdhane, 2014, p. 140). The matching marketing era was categorized as Marketing 3.0, the age of participative and collaborative marketing (Kotler et al., 2010a). It was the "value-driven era" (Fuciu & Dumitrescu, 2018, p. 45). According to Kotler et al. (2010b), it was time for marketers to search for meaning in their strategies and apply the ones that were centered on "values." And the most memorable values were created through experiences.

With the new information age, the virtual networks served as knowledge-sharing media in addition to information exchange (Erragcha & Romdhane, 2014). The users were in dialogue with companies and with each other. These developments created "producing consumer (prosumer)" (Kotler et al., 2010a) who was a volunteer for content producing and sharing (via Twitter, Facebook, Instagram, Pinterest, YouTube), engaging in real-time discussions (via WhatsApp, Skype, Yahoo Messenger), publishing content via blogs, sharing knowledge via wikis, and reviewing products/services on platforms. Realizing the power that the consumer had, marketers, wisely, transformed the consumers into supporters and partners (Toffler, 1980). To achieve more advanced collaboration, companies asked them "to play the key role in creating value through co-creation" (Kotler et al., 2010a, p. 10), asking them to participate in the process, thus, putting the basics of interactive marketing into practice. Following the spirit, 2010–2011 were the years that many social media initiatives have stepped into the market, like WhatsApp (2010), Google+ (2011), Instagram (2011), Pinterest (2011), and Snapchat (2011). As the players of interactive marketing, they all aimed to allow the customers to engage and enjoy becoming a part of the interactive do-it-together process (Wang, 2021). However, it took some years before social media amassed large user bases and proved its worth for marketers through network externalities.

The other scope of Marketing 3.0 was focused on companies. The developments in information and communication technologies and their fast diffusion rate created changes and raised questions about the relationship between connected consumers and companies (Gómez-Suárez et al., 2017). As a response, buyer–seller and platform-consumer relationships became the trendiest research topics in DM.

In 2014, the number of mobile users surpassed desktop users. With all these different devices at the expense of consumers, "omnichannel marketing" was spinning around in 2014. However, multi-channel and mobile were fairly minor concepts for practitioners and thus for researchers in 2014 (Lamberton & Stephen, 2016). Their development was reserved for the next period.

The Conceptual Structure (2010–2014). As the domain of the digital diversified, there appeared many Motor themes in the thematic map (Fig. 2d).

The most important and the most influential of them were BEHAVIORS, TRUST, ATTITUDES, and INFORMATION-TECHNOLOGY (see Fig. 2d and Table 4). The sub-themes of BEHAVIORS (*consumers, communication, choice, brand, decision*) and TRUST (*satisfaction, commitment, buyer–seller relationships*) were the clear indicators of the studies on the communication channels that were effective in shaping consumer behavior and establishing trust. *Communication technologies, systems,* and *innovation* were the three sub-themes of the INFORMATION-TECHNOLOGY. They reflected academia's attempt to define innovative technologies and *systems* to improve digital companies' *capabilities*. ATTITUDES is another motor theme in the thematic map of 2010–2014. It had its sub-themes of *consumer behavior, perception,* and *environments* in the conceptual studies. And *gender* and *gender-difference* studies were elaborated under the heading of this theme. One stream of studies of the era projected that one of the goals was to understand the effect of attitudes on purchase intention within different environments along with the differences between genders.

The theme REVIEWS had the highest average citation, indicating the great interest in the theme, and was located in the exact middle of motor and highly developed themes. As the practitioners are aware of the consumer capabilities to stimulate others (reflected in the sub-theme of *social influence*), the *user-generated content* (UGC) studies gained momentum under the heading of REVIEWS. In the next period, REVIEWS evolved into ONLINE-REVIEWS (Fig. 3), answering the need to have detailed studies on the theme.

Table 4 Performance analysis (2010–2014)

Theme	Number of papers	Average citations	h-index
TRUST	77	39.49	30
SIGNALING	13	64.54	9
ATTITUDES	60	46.17	28
INFORMATION-TECHNOLOGY	53	42.49	23
BEHAVIORS	102	62.27	36
INDUSTRY	36	29.14	17
PERCEIVED VALUE	18	23.72	12
INTERNET-CHANNEL	12	54.33	10
RETURNS	11	49	9
REVIEWS	27	77.37	21
BUSINESS	28	30.25	14
EXPERIENCE	16	37.88	12
INFORMATION-SEARCH	10	48.3	7
SERVICES	14	34	10
FIRM	7	22.86	4
AUCTIONS	7	18.86	6

Although PERCEIVED VALUE and INDUSTRY were capturing the attention of researchers as the motor themes (Fig. 2d), they were not as influential as the other themes in this period based on average citation rates (Table 4). The theme PERCEIVED VALUE covered the studies on *consumer perceptions* and the benefits that the customer gets from buying either a *product* or *service*. And the INDUSTRY-related studies mainly dealt with *strategies* to be developed at *electronic marketplaces*.

Although not high in the number of studies, SIGNALLING was an important theme regarding the effect it created in terms of average citation (Table 4). It was located between emerging and isolated/highly developed themes. The theme mostly covered papers on price signaling and was internally related to *price, social interaction, platforms, information asymmetry, online marketplaces,* and *online search*. The internal ties reveal that as the online marketplaces, search engines, and aggregator platforms evolved, price signaling became an issue to be researched by scholars (e.g., Brettel & Spilker-Attig, 2010).

RETURNS and INFORMATION-SEARCH were two other highly cited emerging themes (Table 4). Examining the sub-themes, RETURN studies mainly concentrated on *risk, purchase,* and *policy*. They are the indicators of DM scholars' interest in the effect of different policies applied to handle returns and the risk perceived by the consumer during an online purchase. INFORMATION-SEARCH was scattered around the sub-themes of *preferences, perceived risk, recommender systems,* and *online reviews*. They were representing a growing interest in studies of the need for information about the connected customer and risks caused by the technology that enabled them to get this information. Other themes located in the quadrant of emerging or declining themes were EXPERIENCE, FIRM, and AUCTIONS (See Fig. 2d). Studies on FIRM and AUCTIONS were believed to be declining because of the low average citation rates (22.86 and 18.86, respectively). On the other hand, the theme of EXPERIENCE was emerging. As the need to understand the "customer experience" in emerging environments was staying steady, the interest in the subject kept growing. In this period, the themes SERVICES and BUSINESS surfaced as the basic themes. They needed time to be conceptualized.

In general, the themes in this period were indicators of the actualization of technology in shaping consumer behavior. The focus partially moved from firm-based studies to consumer-based research. While the consumer studies reflected the interest in consumer attitudes, trust development, value, and online experiences, firm-based studies were conceptualized around digital channels, pricing, and logistics. The studies in the era indicated a power shift in favor of consumers, who were the main driver of DM research in this period.

4.5   2015–2020: The Rise of the Customer Kingdom

The Practical Landscape (2015–2020). Although it is valid for all successive periods, it is not possible to mention clear-cut differences between this and the previous period. During this period, the technologies and applications that evolved in the preceding period became more functional in terms of DM.

Facebook acquired WhatsApp at the end of 2014 to serve corporations with data that is collected on different channels of social networks. With the collected data, digital marketers realized the potential of social media, which is not limited to marketing (Qin, 2020). With the proliferation of social media and with its discovered capabilities, social media altered the way of consumer involvement in interactive marketing (Vazquez, 2020). Companies discovered that social media allowed them to make the consumers actively participate in every creative stage of the company operations and sell products/services in digital marketplaces. With their enhanced interactivity feature, users interacted with each other and marketers in a triad relationship (Wang, 2021).

Although it started in the early 2010s, in this period, social commerce dominated the market. As companies were forming active brand communities, they were offering opportunities for collaboration and co-creation to the customers (Kucharska, 2019). As the customer feels like a part of the company, the academia, very conveniently, defined the theme as "collaborative platform economy," or more commonly, "sharing economy"—the term used in the traditional economy.

As "managers wanted to extract business values from social technologies" (Roberts & Grover, 2012), marketers started to seek the solution in mobile technologies and multi-channel. They started to invest in their apps, place ads in other's apps, or use ad networks (e.g., DoubleClick of Google). Mobile replaced the websites. It was possible to both geographically and behaviorally target consumers through geolocation services (Taylor et al., 2020), thus, giving the consumers time-sensitive promotions and building the relationship while providing the best experience for consumers.

At first sight, it seemed like consumers were sharing with each other (wikis, blogs, social media, vendor ratings, comments, etc.), but companies were adopting quickly by commercializing the model, as in the growth of Uber and Airbnb. The sharing economy along with the mobile, brought digital marketers to the concept of the service economy, moving away from the product economy. As the companies sought a way to differentiate themselves from the competition, they raised their standards for quality of services, tried to provide the experience unique to their services (Lamberton & Stephen, 2016), and asked for trust and loyalty.

Another important entry in this period was the launch of wearables in the market. They had the potential of mobile phones since the consumers carried them everywhere and, even better, wore them at night and day, and they enabled connection through devices (i.e., Internet of Things [IoT]). It did not take long for the companies to emerge with smartwatches (e.g., Pebble watch,

Apple Watch, Samsung Galaxy Gear), fitness bracelets (e.g., Fitbit Force), and smart spectacles (e.g., Google Glass) (Shankar et al., 2016). Wearables became another source of data for digital marketers. Voice recognition services followed immediately as a disruptive innovation (the key players were Apple's Siri, Amazon's Echo, and Google's Google Assistant). Putting all these smart devices together, consumers were highly immersed in the digital environment. To provide the best immersive experience, the technology of augmented reality (AR) (and, after a while, virtual reality—VR) stepped into the strategies of digital marketers.

The Conceptual Structure (2015–2020). As in previous periods, TRUST is a motor theme of this period. It is interrelated with *satisfaction, consumer behavior, commitment, electronic markets, online marketplaces, perceived risk, purchase intention, repurchase intention,* and *risk*. The ongoing trend of trust as a motor theme over the years addresses its importance in DM literature. TRUST has its strongest interconnections with *satisfaction, consumer behavior,* and *commitment*. This implies the impact of trust on consumer satisfaction and loyalty. As the competition in the digital world stiffened more, concepts like satisfaction, trust, and loyalty became more important for e-retailers. Another motor theme that has been evolved from the theme TRUST (2010–2014) is MARKETPLACES. It has interconnections with *online product reviews, price premiums, security, benefits, channel, contracts, decision, exchange,* and *information asymmetry*. The theme represents the exchange process of goods and information in digital channels. Especially the existence of *information asymmetry* shows that studies under the theme MARKETPLACES try to discover the balance between buyers and sellers in terms of information availability. INNOVATION is another theme that is in the upper-right quadrant. The theme is not new in the scope of DM literature. The theme appeared between 2005 and 2009 and makes its reappearance during this period (See Fig. 3). It's interrelated with sub-themes like *performance, technology, strategies, business models, capabilities, digital platforms, dynamic-capabilities, firm,* and *network effects*. Mostly related to seller-side innovations, this subject is expected to grow in the following periods. The introduction of wearables, AR, and VR technologies resulted in the entrance of INNOVATION as a motor theme to the map. And the sub-themes are indicators of academia's interest in discovering the impact of new technologies and business models on firm performance and capabilities. The combination of INDUSTRY and BEHAVIOR in the preceding period resulted in the theme of MARKETS (Fig. 3). The theme has interconnections with *reviews, search costs, consumer search, costs, industry, mechanisms, networks, online platforms,* and *preferences*. The theme connects the buyer and seller sides of DM. In terms of the number of papers, the largest theme is BEHAVIORS. Evolving from ATTITUDES and BEHAVIORS (Fig. 3), the theme is interrelated with *intentions, motivation, product, consumers, perception, attitudes, brand, choice,* and *communities*. The theme represents online consumer behavior and includes social media and community structures. The penetration of social media and the evolution of social commerce created new venues for researchers working on digital consumers (e.g., Graham & Wilder, 2020; Kakalejčík et al., 2020; Qin, 2020). Another theme that is highly related to BEHAVIORS is ONLINE-REVIEWS. The impact of social media also presents itself within this theme. The theme has interconnections with sub-themes like *social influence, user-generated content, tourism, acquisition, communication, experience, hotels, national culture,* and *sentiment*. Mostly dominated by tourism and hospitality studies, the theme investigates the impact of reviews on consumer behaviors (e.g., Sotiriadis, 2017). Also another important point stems from the sub-theme "*sentiment*." This is an indicator of a new realm of studies using big data and text analytics to discover the hidden sentiments in online reviews. This is a new perspective in DM research, which is expected to have great potential in the upcoming years. The last motor theme is also previously seen in the preceding periods, INFORMATION-TECHNOLOGY. The theme is interrelated with sub-themes of *services, SMEs, systems, behavioral intentions, business, digital innovation, extension, intrinsic motivation,* and *organizations*.

The single basic theme of the period is ONLINE SHOPPING. Evolving from themes like AUCTIONS, PERCEIVED VALUE, INTERNET-CHANNELS, ATTITUDES, and TRUST (Fig. 3), the theme is related to sub-themes like *values, online retailing, online consumer behavior, brand community, customers, customer value, gender differences, retailers,* and *time*. The theme is mostly focused on online retailing. The scope of the studies produced under this theme had two dimensions, understanding consumer characteristics (e.g., Gallant & Arcand, 2017) and defining the dimensions of customer value (e.g., Ariffin et al., 2018; Izogo & Jayawardhena, 2018). The proliferation of customers and penetration of online retailing as a channel created a need to understand what constitutes customer value in online retailing. As the theme represents itself as a basic theme, it is expected to grow in the upcoming years with the great potential of the introduction of new online shopping channels.

The themes CONSUMER-RESPONSE, ONLINE COMMUNITIES, POLICY, CUSTOMER-EXPERIENCE, INFORMATION-SEARCH, and PERCEIVED VALUE are placed in the lower left quadrant of the map (Fig. 2e). ONLINE COMMUNITIES is an emerging theme in this quadrant, which has strong internal ties with *social interactions, social networks, users, equity, identity, judgments, marketing-strategy, online consumer reviews,* and *smartphone*. The theme, evolved from REVIEWS, mostly deals with consumer interactions within online communities and possible strategies that can be pursued to benefit from earned media (e.g., Qin, 2020). CONSUMER-RESPONSE is interrelated with *pricing strategy, recall, switching-costs, promotions, brand attitude, design, emotions, failure,* and *field*. This theme focuses on investigating customer response toward different marketing activities in the fast-paced environment of DM (e.g., Wolkenfelt & Situmeang, 2020). POLICY is another theme that is expected to emerge in the upcoming years. This can easily be understood with a look at its relationship with sub-themes like *returns, social networking sites, corporate social responsibility (CSR), auctions, disclosure, expectations, food, incentives,* and *resources*. Especially its interrelationship with resources, returns, and CSR is very important. Since sustainability has been a very popular subject in the last few years, the theme is expected to present growth in the upcoming years. INFORMATION-SEARCH and PERCEIVED VALUE are two themes that had been present in the preceding periods. INFORMATION-SEARCH represents studies on pricing, emerging markets, and online search activities. The scope of PERCEIVED VALUE has evolved to include a more detailed approach to defining how value is created and perceived. The theme represents studies that focus on understanding consumer perceptions of value as well as the impact of marketing investment and its impact on value creation. The last theme in this quadrant is CUSTOMER-EXPERIENCE. This is a very strong theme in this period. Although it has the least number of articles, the theme was able to capture a relatively high number of average citations (Table 5). The theme is interrelated with sub-themes of *service innovation, attribution, directions,* and *environments*. In digital platforms, everything becomes a service. Achieving a high level of service excellence creates a higher demand for online companies and also provides a better customer experience. The product glut resulting in customer scarcity in digital environments created a greater need for a better customer experience, to which attribution is also highly related. A thorough understanding of the customer journey in digital channels can provide important insights on managing investments in DM, which can result in higher levels of marketing ROI.

Table 5 Performance analysis (2015–2020)

Theme	Number of papers	Average citations	h-index
INNOVATION	149	10.03	22
TRUST	154	10.31	18
BEHAVIORS	277	9.01	23
MARKETS	87	10.97	14
MARKETPLACES	20	5.95	5
INFORMATION-TECHNOLOGY	56	14.3	16
ONLINE-REVIEWS	72	11.89	14
OPPORTUNITIES	13	7.08	6
CONSUMER-RESPONSE	16	4.88	4
ONLINE SHOPPING	27	12.96	9
ONLINE COMMUNITIES	29	8.34	7
POLICY	14	11	9
INFORMATION-SEARCH	16	5.38	6
PERCEIVED VALUE	17	6.35	7
CUSTOMER-EXPERIENCE	7	11.14	4

The last theme that made a comeback in this period is OPPORTUNITIES. Stemming from INTERNET-CHANNEL in the previous period (Fig. 3), the theme has internal interrelations with *marketing communications, supply chain, virtual communities, attachment, buyers, challenges, digitalization,* and *information systems.* The inclusion of communities and communications refers to the seller side of DM; with the inclusion of supply chain and buyers, it refers to the buyer side of DM.

In brief, the last 5 years represent the strength of social media as a channel of commerce in DM. Almost in every quadrant, a significant number of subthemes have strong connections with the social media phenomenon. The impact of growth in social networking and mobile media, the emergence of new technologies, devices, and platforms, and the sharing economy are highly represented in academia's take on DM research.

5 Conclusion and Future Research

Digital marketing is a variant of interactive marketing (Wang, 2021), aiming to provide interactive, participatory, engaging, and immersive experiences. According to the study by Lim et al. (2022), the evolution of direct marketing to interactive marketing introduced the terms like social media, multi-channel marketing, relationship marketing, and viral marketing that led to the introduction of the DM concept. The same study presented that under the topic of multi-channel marketing, IDM was still a term used between 2012 and 2016 in the literature. Likewise, interactive marketing's demand to deeply understand the customer to deliver personalized experiences (Stone & Woodcock, 2014) is one of the core subjects that digital marketers cannot ignore.

Starting with the aim of defining the DM literature domain and comparing it with the practice of DM, we concluded that DM literature started as business and information-technology oriented and has significantly evolved in 30 years. Research orientation became consumer-oriented, especially with the introduction of web technologies, Web 2.0 and Web 3.0.

The findings aroused from the DM study show that there are interactive marketing features highly overlapping with the study results. It is not beyond expectations since the DM domain is a subset of the interactive marketing domain (Wang, 2021). The study results inform both the development and the future of interactive marketing. To give an idea of how investigating the DM domain has guided the future of interactive marketing, one can refer to the last era (2015–2020). The themes that fall under the category of emerging and motor themes in the last era are the basic indicators of future studies. For example, the interactive feature of the ONLINE COMMUNITIES, the personalized, engaged, and the two-way nature of CONSUMER EXPERIENCE, which appeared as the emerging themes in the last era, are themes of interactive marketing and DM. The theme PERCEIVED VALUE contains the value co-creation strategy as the construct calls for interactive marketing. With the feedback the marketers get from the customer in the form of CUSTOMER

RESPONSE, the personalization process is initiated with interactive marketing in mind. As an example of the development of the interactive marketing literature domain, the theme REVIEWS was first used as an influential keyword in the 2010–2014 era (in 27 papers only), and in the 2015–2020 era, it turned into CUSTOMER-REVIEWS with an astonishing number 72 papers. It indicated the studies on the participatory nature of both interactive and DM. Likewise, the studies on INNOVATION appeared first in the 2005–2009 era (in 41 papers), and then the studies accelerated to reach the number of 149 in 2010–2015. If we reasonably associate the term INNOVATION with value co-creation, it will imply the effect of interactive marketing on DM.

The study results also imply that the rapid and ever-lasting technological advancements within the DM realm require changes within marketing science in both the topics of the domain and the way research is carried out. Big data and machine learning will significantly change how researchers collect, analyze, and interpret data. Today, to gain a perspective on DM, it is vital that academia turns its face toward real-time data collection and analysis. A group of researchers specializing in advertising topics should benefit from the data collected via field experiments. The fast changes in technological advancements will diminish the power of traditional methods like survey design and lab experiments. Even though big data holds a huge promise for companies and researchers, it tends to provide information on certain situations like the ones looking for in-depth consumer insight. In these cases, relying on qualitative and transformative consumer research might provide further insights into consumers' points of view. Methodologies like nethnography would be much more applicable in these situations.

As digital channels keep on penetrating, success for companies lies in managing the product/brand/service in a multi-channel setting. Early research on DM mostly focused on the acceptance and proliferation of new technologies, but we need a new research stream that combines the digitalization phenomenon with a traditional marketing perspective. It calls for both field and conceptual studies.

In terms of what is next for DM, the future will be a story of two trends: On one hand, there are emerging new themes to meet the needs of the markets and connected consumers. On the other hand, the future will be shaped by persistent current themes. For example, it is no surprise that the SYSTEM studies will always be the motor theme in the DM domain since innovation and technology are the two basic drivers of digital. Investment in technology and R&D will thus be the present and future themes of DM for practitioners, and academia supports by researching how promising and resilient these innovations are for both the consumers and firms. At one-fold, future SYSTEM studies will be shaped around new technologies like the Internet of Everything (IoE), which refers to the intelligent connection of things, people, processes and platforms, and value provided to the customers through extended reality (XR), including immersive technologies like augmented reality (AR), virtual reality (VR), and mixed reality (MR). The future of interactive marketing will continue to accelerate forward, leveraging technological advancement with more personalized, digital, and dynamic content (Wang, 2021).

Future research, adding to the current one, can further include journals with different orientations like sociology, psychology, and human–computer interaction and can extend this research by focusing on more fragmented areas of DM (such as social media marketing).

References

Ariffin, S. K., Mohan, T., & Goh, Y. N. (2018). Influence of consumers' perceived risk on consumers' online purchase intention. *Journal of Research in Interactive Marketing*, 12(3), 309–327.

Barwise, P., & Farley, J. U. (2005). The state of interactive marketing in seven countries: Interactive marketing comes of age. *Journal of Interactive Marketing*, 19(3), 67–80.

Börner, K., Chen, C., & Boyack, K. W. (2003). Visualizing knowledge domains. *Annual Review of Information Science and Technology*, 37(1), 179–255.

Bressolles, G. (2012). *L'e-marketing*. Dunod.

Brettel, M., & Spilker-Attig, A. (2010). Online advertising effectiveness: A cross-cultural comparison. *Journal of Research in Interactive Marketing*, 4(3), 176–196.

Byon, K. K., & Phua, J. (2021). Digital and interactive marketing communications in sports. *Journal of Interactive Advertising*, 21(2), 75–78.

Callon, M., Courtial, J. P., & Laville, F. (1991). Co-word analysis as a tool for describing the network of interactions between basic and technological research: The case of polymer chemistry. *Scientometrics*, 22(1), 155–205.

Callon, M., Courtial, J. P., Turner, W. A., & Bauin, S. (1983). From translations to problematic networks: An introduction to co-word analysis. *Social Science Information*, 22(2), 191–235.

Chellappa, R. K., & Kumar, K. R. (2005). Examining the role of "free" product-augmenting online services in pricing and customer retention strategies. *Journal of Management Information Systems*, 22(1), 355–377.

Cobo, M. J., López-Herrera, A. G., Herrera-VieDMa, E., & Herrera, F. (2011). An approach for detecting, quantifying, and visualizing the evolution of a research field: A practical application to the fuzzy sets theory field. *Journal of Informetrics*, 5(1), 146–166.

Çadırcı, T. O., & Güngör, A. S. (2016). Electronic word-of-mouth communication in online social networks: The Motivational Antecedents of Electronic Word-of-Mouth (EWOM) engagement in online social networks. In *Capturing, analyzing, and managing word-of-mouth in the digital marketplace* (pp. 77–102). IGI Global.

Egghe, L. (2006). Theory and practise of the g-index. *Scientometrics*, 69(1), 131–152.

Erdem, T., Keller, K. L., Kuksov, D., & Pieters, R. (2016). Understanding branding in a digitally empowered world. *International Journal of Research in Marketing*, 33(1), 3–10.

Elsharnouby, T. H., & Mahrous, A. A. (2015). Customer participation in online co-creation experience: The role of e-service quality. *Journal of Research in Interactive Marketing*, 9(4), 313–336.

Erragcha, N., & Romdhane, R. (2014). New faces of marketing in the era of the web: From marketing 1.0 to marketing 3.0. *Journal of Research in Marketing, 2*(2), 137–142.

Finn, A., Wang, L., & Frank, T. (2009). Attribute perceptions, customer satisfaction and intention to recommend e-services. *Journal of Interactive Marketing, 23*(3), 209–220.

Fuchs, C. (2010). Social software and Web 2.0: Their sociological foundations and implications. In S. Murugesan (Eds.), *Handbook of research on Web 2.0, 3.0, and X.0: Technologies, business, and social applications* (Vol. II., pp. 764–789). IGI Global.

Fuciu, M., & Dumitrescu, L. (2018). From marketing 1.0 to marketing 4.0— The evolution of the marketing concept in the context of the 21st century. In *International conference knowledge-based organization* (Vol. 24, No. 2, pp. 43–48).

Gallant, I., & Arcand, M. (2017). Consumer characteristics as drivers of online information searches. *Journal of Research in Interactive Marketing, 11*(1), 56–74.

Gómez-Suárez, M., Martínez-Ruiz, M. P., & Martínez-Caraballo, N. (2017). Consumer-brand relationships under the marketing 3.0 paradigm: A literature review. *Frontiers in Psychology, 8*, 252.

Güngör, A. S., & Çadırcı, T. O. (2013). Segmenting eWOM engagers on online social networks based on personal characteristics and behaviour. *Ekev Academic Review, 17*(57), 33–50.

Güngör, A. S., & Özgen, Ç. T. (2020). Did you read the customer reviews Before Shopping?: The effect of customer reviews about online retail platforms on consumer behavioral responses. In *Emotional, sensory, and social dimensions of consumer buying behavior* (pp. 178–208). IGI Global.

Graham, K. W., & Wilder, K. M. (2020). Consumer-brand identity and online advertising message elaboration: Effect on attitudes, purchase intent and willingness to share. *Journal of Research in Interactive Marketing., 14*(1), 111–132.

Haeckel, S. H. (1998). About the nature and future of Interactive marketing. *Journal of Interactive Marketing, 12*(1), 63–71.

Hirsch, J. E. (2005). An index to quantify an individual's scientific research output. *Proceedings of the National Academy of Sciences, 102*(46), 16569–16572.

Hirsch, J. E. (2007). Does the h index have predictive power? *Proceedings of the National Academy of Sciences, 104*(49), 19193–19198.

Izogo, E. E., & Jayawardhena, C. (2018). Online shopping experience in an emerging e-retailing market: Towards a conceptual model. *Journal of Consumer Behaviour, 17*(4), 379–392.

Kakalejčík, L., Bucko, J., & Danko, J. (2020). Impact of direct traffic effect on online sales. *Journal of Research in Interactive Marketing, 14*(1), 17–32.

Kannan, P. K., & Li, H. A. (2017). Digital marketing: A framework, review and research agenda. *International Journal of Research in Marketing, 34*(1), 22–45.

Kaplan, A. M., & Haenlein, M. (2010). Users of the world, unite! The challenges and opportunities of social media. *Business Horizons, 53*(1), 59–68.

Kaya, İ, & Güngör, A. S. (2012). Kişiye özel fiyat teklifinin zamanlamasının, internette, satın alma karar sürecine etkisi. *İstanbul Üniversitesi İşletme Fakültesi Dergisi, 41*(2), 172–188.

Kotler, P., Kartajaya, H., & Setiawan, I. (2010a). *Marketing 3.0: From products to customers to the human spirit*. Wiley.

Kotler, P., Kartajaya, H., & Setiawan, I. (2010b). *Marketing 3.0: Values-driven marketing*. Erlangga.

Krishen, A. S., Dwivedi, Y. K., Bindu, N., & Kumar, K. S. (2021). A broad overview of Interactive digital marketing: A bibliometric network analysis. *Journal of Business Research, 131*, 183–195.

Kucharska, W. (2019). Online brand communities' contribution to digital business models: Social drivers and mediators. *Journal of Research in Interactive Marketing, 13*(4), 437–463.

Lamberton, C., & Stephen, A. T. (2016). A thematic exploration of digital, social media, and mobile marketing: Research evolution from 2000 to 2015 and an agenda for future inquiry. *Journal of Marketing, 80*(6), 146–172.

Lee, Y., Lee, Y., Seong, J., Stanescu, A., & Hwang, C. S. (2020). A comparison of network clustering algorithms in keyword network analysis: A case study with geography conference presentations. *International Journal of Geospatial and Environmental Research, 7*(3), 1.

Leung, X. Y., Sun, J., & Bai, B. (2017). Bibliometrics of social media research: A co-citation and co-word analysis. *International Journal of Hospitality Management, 66*, 35–45.

Lim, W. M., Kumar, S., Pandey, N., Rasul, T., & Gaur, V. (2022). From direct marketing to Interactive marketing: a retrospective review of the Journal of Research in Interactive Marketing, *Journal of Research in Interactive Marketing*, ahead-of-print. https://doi.org/10.1108/JRIM-11-2021-0276

López-Herrera, A. G., Cobo, M. J., Herrera-VieDMa, E., & Herrera, F. (2010). A bibliometric study about the research based on hybridating the fuzzy logic field and the other computational intelligent techniques: A visual approach. *International Journal of Hybrid Intelligent Systems, 7*(1), 17–32.

López, M., Sicilia, M., & Verlegh, P. W. (2021). How to motivate opinion leaders to spread e-wom on social media: Monetary vs non-monetary incentives. *Journal of Research in Interactive Marketing, 16*(1), 154–171.

Malthouse, E., & Shankar, V. (2009). Measuring and managing Interactive environments. *Journal of Interactive Marketing, 23*, 207–208.

Malthouse, E., & Hofacker, C. (2010). Looking back and looking forward with Interactive marketing. *Journal of Interactive Marketing, 24*(3), 181–184.

Martínez, M. A., Herrera, M., López-Gijón, J., & Herrera-VieDMa, E. (2014). H-Classics: Characterizing the concept of citation classics through H-index. *Scientometrics, 98*(3), 1971–1983.

Muñoz-Leiva, F., Sánchez-Fernández, J., LiébanaCabanillas, F. J., & Martínez-Fiestas, M. (2013). Detecting salient themes in financial marketing research from 1961 to 2010. *The Service Industries Journal, 33*(9–10), 925–940.

Noyons, E. C., Moed, H. F., & Luwel, M. (1999a). Combining mapping and citation analysis for evaluative bibliometric purposes: A bibliometric study. *Journal of the American Society for Information Science, 50*(2), 115–131.

Noyons, E., Moed, H., & Van Raan, A. (1999b). Integrating research performance analysis and science mapping. *Scientometrics, 46*(3), 591–604.

Park, J., & Feinberg, R. (2010). E-formity: Consumer conformity behaviour in virtual communities. *Journal of Research in Interactive Marketing, 4*(3), 197–213.

Payne, E. H. M., Peltier, J., & Barger, V. A. (2021). Enhancing the value cocreation process: Artificial intelligence and mobile banking service platforms. *Journal of Research in Interactive Marketing, 15*(1), 68–85.

Pons, P., & Latapy, M. (2005, October). Computing communities in large networks using random walks. In *International symposium on computer and information sciences* (pp. 284–293). Springer.

Poynter, R., & Lawrence, G. (2008). Insight 2.0: NOUVEAUX MÉDIAS, NOUVELLES RÈGLES, NOUVELLE VISION APPROFONDIE (1). *Revue Française Du Marketing, 218*, 25–38.

Qin, Y. S. (2020). Fostering brand–consumer interactions in social media: The role of social media uses and gratifications. *Journal of Research in Interactive Marketing, 14*(3), 337–354.

Ratchford, B. T. (2009). Online pricing: Review and directions for research. *Journal of Interactive Marketing, 23*(1), 82–90.

Roberts, N., & Grover, V. (2012). Leveraging information technology infrastructure to facilitate a firm's customer agility and competitive activity: An empirical investigation. *Journal of Management Information Systems, 28*(4), 231–270.

Rousseau, R. (2006). New developments related to the Hirsch index. Industrial sciences and technology, http://eprints.rclis.org/7616/1/Hirsch_new_developments.pdf. Accessed 1 May 2020.

Rust, R. T., Moorman, C., & Bhalla, G. (2010). Rethinking marketing. *Harvard Business Review, 88*(1), 94–101.

Sen, R., King, R. C., & Shaw, M. J. (2006). Buyers' choice of online search strategy and its managerial implications. *Journal of Management Information Systems, 23*(1), 211–238.

Shankar, V., Kleijnen, M., Ramanathan, S., Rizley, R., Holland, S., & Morrissey, S. (2016). Mobile shopper marketing: Key issues, current insights, and future research avenues. *Journal of Interactive Marketing, 34*(1), 37–48.

Shankar, V., & Malthouse, E. C. (2007). The growth of interactions and dialogs in Interactive marketing. *Journal of Interactive Marketing, 21*(2), 2–4.

Sotiriadis, M. D. (2017). Sharing tourism experiences in social media: A literature review and a set of suggested business strategies. *International Journal of Contemporary Hospitality Management, 29*(1), 170–225.

Steuer, J. (1992). Defining virtual reality: Dimensions determining telepresence. *Journal of Communication, 42*(4), 73–93.

Stone, M. D., & Woodcock, N. D. (2014). Interactive, direct and digital marketing: A future that depends on better use of business intelligence. *Journal of Research in Interactive Marketing, 8*(1), 4–17.

Taylor, M., Reilly, D., & Wren, C. (2020). Internet of things support for marketing activities. *Journal of Strategic Marketing, 28*(2), 149–160.

Toffler, A. (1980). *The Third Wave: The revolution that will change our lives.* Collins/Pan books.

Van Eck, N. J. V., & Waltman, L. (2009). How to normalize co-occurrence data? An analysis of some well- known similarity measures. *Journal of the American Society for Information Science and Technology, 60*(8), 1635–1651.

Van Eck, N. J., & Waltman, L. (2007). Bibliometric mapping of the computational intelligence field. *International Journal of Uncertainty, Fuzziness and Knowledge-Based Systems, 15*(05), 625–645.

Van Eck, N. J., Waltman, L., van den Berg, J., & Kaymak, U. (2006). Visualizing the computational intelligence field [Application notes]. *IEEE Computational Intelligence Magazine, 1*(4), 6–10.

Vazquez, E. E. (2020). Effects of enduring involvement and perceived content vividness on digital engagement. *Journal of Research in Interactive Marketing., 14*(1), 1–16.

Vanhala, M., Lu, C., Peltonen, J., Sundqvist, S., Nummenmaa, J., & Järvelin, K. (2020). The usage of large data sets in online consumer behaviour: A bibliometric and computational text-mining–driven analysis of previous research. *Journal of Business Research, 106*, 46–59.

Wang, C. L. (2021). New frontiers and future directions in Interactive marketing: Inaugural Editorial. *Journal of Research in Interactive Marketing, 15*(1), 1–9.

Wolkenfelt, M. R. J., & Situmeang, F. B. I. (2020). Effects of app pricing structures on product evaluations. *Journal of Research in Interactive Marketing, 14*(1), 89–110.

Ye, Q., Law, R., Gu, B., & Chen, W. (2011). The influence of user-generated content on traveler behavior: An empirical investigation on the effects of e-word-of-mouth to hotel online bookings. *Computers in Human Behavior, 27*(2), 634–639.

Zahay, D. (2021). Advancing research in digital and social media marketing. *Journal of Marketing Theory and Practice, 29*(1), 125–139.

CHAPTER 5

Interactive Digital Marketing Mechanisms: The Significance in Digital Transformation

Mona Rashidirad and Hamidreza Shahbaznezhad

1 Introduction

The term Interactive Digital Marketing (IDM) was first officially applied by Krishen et al. (2021). Even though it is just very recently that the term IDM is being applied and entered as a concept in the literature of marketing, it is not a new concept. Previously, scholars (Barwise & Farley, 2005; Byon & Phua, 2021; Zahay, 2014) highlighted the importance of using digital technologies in interactive marketing, and indeed, interactive marketing without digital technologies could not have been developed to what it is known as interactive marketing today. So, no one can disregard the significance of digital technologies as a substantial part of interactive marketing. While the importance of IDM to today's marketing is obvious, the definition of this concept is not. In this chapter, IDM is defined as the bi-directional value creation and mutual-influence marketing process through applying digital media, data and technologies.

As the term IDM has just entered the literature review, the mechanisms of IDM are not expected to be well-known. Nevertheless, new mechanisms and tools of interactive and digital marketing are developing every day to help

M. Rashidirad (✉)
International Marketing, Kent Business School, University of Kent, Canterbury, UK
e-mail: M.Rashidirad-702@Kent.ac.uk

H. Shahbaznezhad
NZ Post, Auckland, New Zealand
e-mail: Hamid.Sha@Nzpost.co.nz

© The Author(s), under exclusive license to Springer Nature Switzerland AG 2023
C. L. Wang (ed.), *The Palgrave Handbook of Interactive Marketing*,
https://doi.org/10.1007/978-3-031-14961-0_5

companies communicate with their customers in most interactive and efficient way and learn from them (Cluley et al., 2020). These mechanisms aim to accelerate companies' level of knowledge about customers, competitors, products and services and thereby assist companies to change and transform accordingly (Stone et al., 2021). This change in digital area needs a substantial level of agility in all companies, so the processes, databases, data flows, tasks and roles should be all transformed in the most agile way (Verhoef et al., 2021) to address the challenges of the current interactive environment (Melović et al., 2020). With new contextual data generated through using these mechanisms and the use of data science analytics, companies are expected to be well advanced in their digital transformation journey. Digital transformation, most frequently identified by the multi-factor effects of digital technologies on a company (Ziółkowska, 2021), is the process of applying state-of-the-art technologies to create new and disruptive processes, both in the culture and the customer experience, to trigger strategic responses from businesses to address changing business and market requirements (Guenzi & Habel, 2020; Vial, 2016).

While there are several IDM mechanisms, e.g., Social Media Marketing available to companies that could assist them in their digital transformation, these are not systematically studied and presented in the pertinent literature. The main focus of these IDM mechanisms is on interactive marketing through the use of online technologies to capture data from and about customers and lead customers to the company's products and services. Using IDM from a digital transformation perspective enables companies to make internal changes, improvements and advancements which reflect the market demand and customer needs. This chapter aims to examine the significance of IDM mechanisms in digital transformation and the way they assist companies to implement effective changes. To achieve this aim, the chapter questions are outlined as follows:

i. What is IDM and its role in companies' digital transformation?
ii. What are the effective mechanisms of IDM which are significant to companies' digital transformation?

This chapter comprises a literature review, based on secondary research, which is then followed by a case study. First, the relevant sources, both academic and business press, published in the last decade (2011–2021), are reviewed to gain a clear understanding of the concept of IDM. Then a critical and comparative study of the sources will be conducted which would help classify IDM mechanisms. Following that, the chapter will investigate a few chosen IDM mechanisms in a case study of a company in New Zealand to assess the ways in which the company applied the mechanisms in its digitalisation journey. Finally, it will discuss whether the company has been successful, why and what lessons learned can be shared from it.

This chapter will contribute to both theory and practice. One of the key theoretical contributions is to the new concept of IDM and its mechanisms which are under-studied in the extant literature so that students and researchers can use this chapter as a base to ground their understanding and future research. From a practical perspective, this chapter would enable interactive marketers to employ the latest IDM mechanisms for the right reasons to help their company in digital transformation. The finding may assist managers to make their decisions on digital and interactive marketing practices and investments and navigate the implementation through their digitalisation plans.

2 Literature Review

2.1 Interactive Digital Marketing (IDM): The Conceptualisation and Definition

In order to understand IDM, it is necessary to distinguish it from two concepts that make this term: digital marketing and interactive marketing.

Most businesses now need to compete and market in the digital environment and this has been considerably accelerated as a result of the recent Covid-19 pandemic. Digital marketing is about using any type of technological device to conduct marketing on electronic platforms (American Marketing Association, 2021). The word "digital" refers to the medium used to deliver the marketing campaign (Ritz et al., 2019). According to Gartner (2022) digital marketing is "a set of techniques, enabled by technology, which allows marketing to improve its processes to engage in a dynamic conversation with people who are influencers and buyers and ultimately target, acquire and retain customers. It includes the ability to interactively communicate with customers through electronic channels, such as the Web, email, smart devices such as phones and tablets and mobile applications". As can be inferred from this definition, one of the key aspects of digital marketing is the possibility of having interactive communication with customers. This has also been highlighted by Zahay (2014) who regards digital marketing as a means of interactivity and dynamic engagement with customers through digital channels.

Digital marketing uses all forms of technology, both online and offline. The offline technologies applied in digital marketing include instant messaging, text messaging and podcasting, while online digital marketing could include social media marketing, content marketing and email marketing. Therefore, Internet or online marketing is only a part of digital marketing, in which online technologies, e.g., websites, blogs, etc. are applied. Thus, an Internet connection is essential to online marketing. This marketing technique allows businesses to reach customers, conduct research, and sell their products or services over the Internet.

One of the main purposes of digital marketing is to improve customer relationship and engagement (Olson et al., 2021). As proposed by Krishen et al.,

(2021, p. 184), digital marketing applies "data, ICT-based technology (e.g., artificial intelligence), platforms (e.g. social networks), media and devices to extend the scope of marketing within both physical and virtual spaces, for the purpose of improving customer relationships by empowering, informing, influencing, and engaging consumers". But not all digital marketing mechanisms are interactive; that is, enabling customers to establish two-way communication with a company (Wang, 2021, p. 1). In other words, digital marketing does not necessarily mean interactive marketing if it is not practiced in a two-way (or multiple-way) interaction. For example, traditional Email Marketing and banner marketing are kinds of digital marketing, but they are not interactive marketing if they mainly focus on one-way communication instead of two-way interaction (involving customer engagement and participation). Another key mechanism of digital marketing is Search engine marketing (Peter & Dalla Vecchia, 2020) which also is not interactive. While search engine marketing is about gaining visibility on a search engine to encourage click-through to a website (Aswani et al., 2018), it does not provide any interactivity and synchronicity in communication. Therefore, while digital marketing includes both outbound and interactive marketing practices (Ritz et al., 2019), the focus of this chapter is solely on "interactive" digital marketing (IDM) (see Krishen et al., 2021). Today's customers are looking for engaging and authentic experiences that put them in charge of their own buying journey (Shahbaznezhad et al., 2021). This means it is time to rethink digital marketing as is known now and further focus on interactive part of it.

Interactive marketing is a marketing strategy that promotes an actively two-way relationship between parties, e.g., businesses and users/customers (Byon & Phua, 2021). Interactive marketing has dramatically changed the conventional thinking about marketing and has shifted it from one-sided customer interaction to a two-sided participation. Through interactive marketing, customers have been empowered to transform from passive recipients to active participants in the marketing messages. The term interactive marketing, as for any other concept in marketing, has many different definitions. In this chapter, the definition suggested by Wang (2021, p. 1) has been adopted, who believes that interactive marketing is "the bi-directional value creation and mutual-influence marketing process through active customer connection, engagement, participation and interaction". The underlying driver of the growth of interactive marketing was the advent of new technological platforms which have changed the whole concept of marketing from a linear pipeline of activities to a complex network of interactions between businesses and their stakeholders (Wang, 2021). Interactive marketing could be conducted through various forms, i.e., digital marketing, mobile marketing and social media marketing (Wang, 2021). These forms are called mechanisms, and this chapter aims to identify them as applied in the digital environment.

Having briefly defined both concepts of digital marketing and interactive marketing and reviewed their key characteristics, it is important to note that even though these two types of marketing share some similarities, they do not mean the same and these terms are not interchangeable. As noted by Moe and Ratchford (2022), it is becoming increasingly difficult to distinguish these two concepts and differentiate interactive marketing from other types of marketing, as marketing in all its various forms, including digital marketing, have the potential to be interactive, thanks to the widespread availability of Internet and advances in technology. However, not all interactive marketing practices are conducted digitally; some of its functions are being performed online, and others offline (Halbheer et al., 2014). Thus, in a broad sense, interactive marketing could be divided into digital and non-digital, as "digital" only defines the medium of the marketing communication. Also, it should be noted that not all digital marketing practices are interactive. Digital marketing can be interactive or not, so only a part of digital marketing is interactive. In fact, the usage of digital technologies in marketing does not necessarily make it interactive, meaning that the employment of IT is not an interactive subject.

A basic and simple difference between interactive marketing and digital marketing lies in whether the marketing activities are one-way or two-way communications. Interactive marketing existed before digital marketing, in its original form of direct marketing. For example, personal selling and service marketing are traditional forms of interactive marketing, as long as they are in a two-way and interactive form, existed long before the development of digital technologies. However, the advancement of digital technologies provides the tools and platforms that greatly facilitate a wider practice of interactive marketing. That is why interactive marketing emerges as a new academic discipline about 30 years ago, thanks to the growth of Internet and new digital technologies. For example, TV advertising becomes interactive TV advertising (there is growing area of interactive advertising as well) due to the accessibility of digital technology making such a change possible. Ikea's long-time used catalogue is a traditional, one-way communication (the customer can read the pictures in catalogue). The new digital technology and augmented reality (AR)/virtual reality (VR) allow customers to scan the content catalogue and link to the actual product image or videos and even making a purchase through it in a seamless way. This may give some people the misperception that equates interactive marketing with digital marketing.

Having discussed the differences between digital marketing and interactive marketing, our focus is on the intersection of these two types of marketing (see Fig. 1), which is called IDM. In this chapter, IDM is defined as the bi-directional value creation and mutual-influence marketing process through applying the 5Ds of digital marketing (Chaffey & Ellis-Chadwick, 2019). The 5Ds include digital devices, digital platform, digital media, digital data and digital technology. Any IDM should be conducted on a digital device, such as phones, tablets, laptops, desktop computers, TVs, gaming devices and virtual assistants (like Amazon Echo). IDM requires a digital platform, such as Instagram, Twitter, a blog or a website. Also, a digital media should be in place which enables interactive digital marketers to reach and engage with users, including emails, search engines or social networking. The fourth D is digital

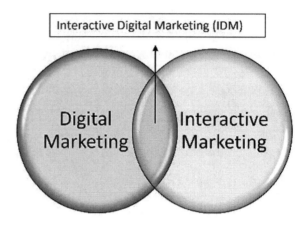

Fig. 1 The position of IDM in relation to interactive and digital marketing strategies

data, which refers to different forms of data, including text, photos, videos and interactive content shared by both users and businesses. Finally, any IDM applies digital technology or marketing technology, also known as "martech", which describes a range of software and tools that help companies in achieving marketing goals or objectives.

Thus, one can conclude that the fundamental element of IDM is that it enables companies and customers to interact and influence each other (Li et al., 2021).

2.2 The Importance of Interactive Digital Marketing (IDM) in Digital Transformation

Having previously discussed the concept of IDM in relation to interactive and digital marketing, in this section IDM will be carefully studied from both conceptual and managerial perspectives and will be reviewed within the context of digital transformation.

The topic of IDM has been gaining a tremendous amount of attention from researchers in recent years, so meaningful literature is available on the role of digital technologies in interactive marketing (Krishen et al., 2021). Some studies have been carried out on the role of social media user engagement (e.g., Shahbaznezhad & Rashidirad, 2020), content type and format (e.g., Shahbaznezhad et al., 2021) and social media platform in IDM (Coelho et al., 2016), and demonstrate the importance of strategic use of social and interactive platforms in stimulating two-way interaction with users.

No one can deny the role of Internet, as being the most favourable channel for the development and implementation of IDM. Interactive digital marketers use interactive and digital features and channels, i.e., email, social media and models for providing information and sorting customers, based on their requirements (Ahmed et al., 2017). IDM leverages the organisational customer knowledge to implement new integral changes, improvement and advancements. The question that needs to be answered in this section is why IDM should be highly considered by companies and, in particular, why companies should invest in IDM in their digital transformation journey.

Disruptive technologies are advancing rapidly. Planned or unplanned digital transformation is happening at an ever-increasing rate in companies across the world (Vial, 2016). IDM technologies, such as Artificial Intelligence (AI) and Business Intelligence (BI) offer extensive analytical capabilities to companies to digitally transform the way and which they understand customer behaviour. Customers are online and almost everyone uses digital technologies these days. To attract new customers and interact with the existing ones, the interactive online marketplace and digital platforms are among the most applied ways to make it happen. When people, as potential customers, hear about a business, they need to know about it and interact with it to fulfil their sense of gratification. If people cannot interact with a company quickly, easily and in a timely and effective manner and they do not have a chance to communicate their requests, then that company will inevitably lose them as customers.

Apart from external factors, such as interacting with customers which can be very well-managed through using IDM mechanisms, from an internal perspective, digital transformation leads to fundamental changes to the way a company operates. IDM mechanisms enable companies to modernise legacy systems, tune processes, accelerate efficient workflows, strengthen security and increase profitability (Matt et al., 2015). Chaffey and Ellis-Chadwick (2019, p. 144) define digital transformation as "a staged programme of business improvements to people, processes and tools used for integrated digital marketing to maximise the potential contribution of digital technology and media to business growth". The point of this explanation is that digital transformation is about creating a technology framework to funnel customer-related data into actionable insights. So, instead of defining new projects to migrate to the new technologies, companies need to leverage and optimise the systems and processes, ensuring they work together intelligently to provide more robust business intelligence and make data-driven decisions to drive future success (Verhoef et al., 2021). The key input of this transformation is the proper data flow from the business environment, competitors and, most importantly, the customers. Hence, for collecting and orchestrating all this input systematically, one needs to rely on IDM, as it promises an effective interaction with both external and internal players.

The benefits of using IDM in companies' digital transformation journey can be both financial and non-financial. The most frequently reported financial outputs are higher Return on Investment (ROI), higher profits, higher productivity and cost efficiency (Alrawadieh et al., 2020). But, most importantly, there are enormous intangible and non-financial advantages which include: higher organisational agility (Troise et al., 2022), accelerated data collection process (Dremel et al., 2017), better resource management (Fenech et al., 2019), providing integrative care of different digital platforms, enhancing brand reputation (Matarazzo et al., 2021), being responsive to various stakeholders, higher customers' reach-out and interaction rate (Berman, 2021) and better customer experience and engagement in developing new products and services.

3 IDM Mechanisms

3.1 Background

Before starting to review the prior relevant work on IDM mechanism taxonomies, it is key to establish the grounding of our research based on one of the fundamental models in marketing, i.e., marketing mix, initially proposed by McCarthy (1960). The reason that this model has been selected as the theoretical background for this chapter is that any decision with respect to IDM mechanisms must be guided by the companies' marketing mix (Virvilaitė & Belousova, 2005). While the original 4Ps of the marketing mix, i.e., Product, Price, Promotion and Place, were heavily criticised due to the lack of customer orientation and insufficient attention to the relationship with customers, the 7Ps were then offered which include further elements (the service mix) that better reflect service delivery (Constantinides, 2006; Goi, 2009). Of 7Ps model, the focus of IDM is mainly on service elements. i.e., People, Process and Physical evidence and, in particular, the people. This variable of the marketing mix clearly relates to how a company interacts with its customers and other stakeholders pre-sales, during sales and post-sales. Thus, the focus of IDM must be on the people element and the way companies develop and deploy their IDM mechanisms to best serve an interactive relationship with customers.

Different scholars have attempted to study interactive marketing mechanisms within the digital world, even though the literature shows that this strand of knowledge is still segregated and it is not systematically explored. For instance, Majid (2020) explores three main interactive marketing communications channels, i.e., e-word-of-mouth (e-WOM), online review forum and search engine optimisation (SEO). He proposes that all three channels positively affect customer acquisition. Also, he lists all interactive marketing micro-channels, including email, companies' website, SEO, WOM, telephone, face-to-face, among others. Clearly, not all of these are digital. For example, face-to-face and telephone marketing are not digital; therefore they cannot be considered in IDM. In another study, Sabin (2010) offers a model in the interactive marketing mechanisms are divided into ten types: content marketing, Search Engine Marketing (SEM), display advertising, Social Media Marketing, community marketing, email marketing, mobile marketing, affiliate marketing, online promotions and integrated campaigns. This taxonomy mainly focusses on categorising different mechanisms based on the currently available tools in online and digital platforms. One of the other relevant works to study IDM mechanisms, which is primarily grounded in digital marketing, is the study by Chaffey and Ellis-Chadwick (2019). They classify digital communications tools into six groups: search engine marketing, online PR, online partnership, social media marketing, opt-in email and display advertising. In a similar study, Olson et al. (2021) look at seven most common digital marketing tactics, which include content marketing, SEO, email marketing, search and social advertisements, data-driven personalisation, marketing technology usage and social media advertising. As can be seen, there are some mechanisms, e.g., social media marketing, which are shared in all these taxonomies and shows how digital marketing is embedded in most interactive marketing practices.

3.2   The Conceptual Framework

Having evaluated both academic and business-related taxonomies for IDM, it was decided to take the two models by Sabin (2010) and Chaffey and Ellis-Chadwick (2019) together as the base, and incorporate relevant knowledge and practical experience in the field to develop a conceptual framework (see Fig. 2). In this framework, IDM mechanisms are broadly considered through six categories as follows.

In order to construct this framework and carefully select the relevant mechanisms, the core concept of "interactivity" and its dimensions were used as the thought foundation of the framework. According to Rafaeli (1988, p. 111),

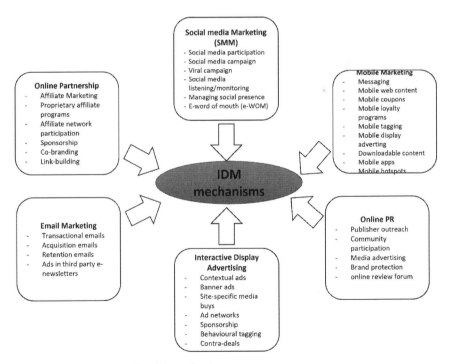

Fig. 2 Six categories of IDM mechanisms

interactivity is: "an expression of the intent that, in a given series of communication exchanges, any third (or later) transmission (or message) is related to the degree to which previous exchanges referred to even earlier transmissions". There is a general agreement that interactivity is captured in two factors that distinguish interactive communication from passive communication (Majid, 2020): (i) The ability to receive and respond to messages (Heeter, 2000) and (ii) the level of control that the receiver has in crafting the message (Downes & McMillan, 2000). However, one should be noted that while interactivity is an integral core element of all proposed IDM mechanisms, they do not all offer the same degree of interactivity to the customers/users. Thus, while some can be considered as highly interactive, e.g., social media participation, others may provide a less interactive experience to the customers, e.g., display advertising. Thus, in order to determine IDM mechanisms and distinguish them from the mechanisms of interactive marketing and digital marketing, the three main pillars of interactivity are used in this chapter. These three dimensions which have been frequently referred to in the extant literature (Liu & Shrum, 2002; Steuer, 1992; Wang, 2021) are (i) two-way communication, (ii) active control and (iii) synchronicity. Two-way communication refers to the reciprocal conversation with mutual influences in social and business ecosystems (Wang, 2021). It is the extent to which an IDM mechanism provides a true bi-directional engagement of the parties, e.g., businesses to users (B2C), businesses to businesses (B2B) or users and users (C2C). The second dimension of interactivity, which is active control, implies customer responsiveness and proactive behaviours in value creation and exchange. Finally, synchronicity refers to the extent of engagement in control and modification of real-time environmental changes.

Having used the concept of interactivity and the three pillars of it as the base for identifying IDM mechanisms, Fig. 2 illustrates the IDM mechanisms. Each is briefly outlined below.

Mobile Marketing and advertising applications deliver promotional information to customers based on their preferences and location (Kurkovsky & Harihar, 2006). IDM micro-mechanisms of mobile marketing include messaging, mobile web content, mobile coupons, mobile loyalty programmes, mobile tagging, mobile display advertising, downloadable content, mobile application and mobile hotspots (Sabin, 2010). Other examples may include promotions sent via SMS text messaging or MMS multimedia messaging, through downloaded apps using push notifications, through in-app or in-game marketing, through mobile websites, or by using a mobile device to scan QR codes. Interactive mobile marketing enables user interaction to connect and communicate with a company, i.e., the store's server. For example, the user is given selective products/offerings matching the user's preferences that include some current promotions. The user may then explore each product by viewing the product information, offer details and related products using a system of mobile marketing (Kurkovsky & Harihar, 2006).

The next IDM mechanism is Online Public Relation (PR) which seeks to maximise favourable mentions of a company, brands, products/services or website on third-party websites or social media platforms. These third-party media channels are the ones that are likely to be visited by a company's target market (Chaffey & Ellis-Chadwick, 2019). The reason that online PR is classified as an IDM mechanism is that it could be two-way, so companies are able to respond to negative mentions and conduct PR via various digital channels, e.g., social media news centre or blogs.

Interactive Display advertising, as one of the other IDM mechanisms includes contextual ads, banner ads and rich media ads, among others. This IDM mechanism aims to achieve brand awareness and encourage click-through to a target site (Hoban & Bucklin, 2015). Display advertising could be in various data forms, e.g., photo, video, audio and interactive media (Semara et al., 2021).

The next IDM mechanism identified is email marketing which usually consists of three main types of email viz. transactional emails, acquisition emails and retention emails, depending on the marketing objective. As noted by Hartemo (2016), email allows an active, interactive and personalised communication fulfilling the preferences of an empowered customer. Thus, email marketing is one of the main mechanisms of interactive marketing in the digital marketplace; one which makes customers active participants in the communication process; however, it needs to be highly relevant for the recipients. In a study by Ziółkowska (2021), it is shown that more than 77% of Small and Medium Size Enterprises (SMEs) use email as the most frequently used communication tool through their digital transformation.

The next IDM mechanism is Online partnership which is mainly about creating and managing long-term arrangements to promote a company's online services on third-party websites or through email communications (Stone & Woodcock, 2014). There are different forms of partnership, which include affiliate Marketing, affiliate network participation, proprietary affiliate programmes (Duffy, 2005), link building, online sponsorship, co-marketing and aggregators, such as price comparison sites, like Moneysupermarket (moneysupermarket.com) and booking.com.

Finally, social Media Marketing consists of social media advertising, social media participation, social media campaigns, social media apps/ widgets, social media monitoring and social media listening. No one doubts that social media has become the most attractive and powerful tool for customers to engage with brands (Chahal & Rani, 2017). Social media is considered as one of the key mechanisms to conduct interactive marketing (Byon & Phua, 2021), as it provides an online platform to share information and exchange ideas among users without any restriction in time, place and medium (Zhang et al., 2021). According to Melović et al. (2020), social media is the most used mechanism in companies' digitalisation projects.

3.3 An Analysis of IDM Mechanisms

As mentioned above, not all IDM mechanisms provide the same level of interactivity. Some offer a higher degree of two-way communication, while others may provide a greater level of engagement and synchronicity. To better understand each of the mechanisms, the three main aspects of interactivity, reviewed in Sect. 3.2 (Liu & Shrum, 2002; Steuer, 1992; Wang, 2021) are used and as can be seen in Table 1, the first three columns rank the interactivity level of each IDM mechanism based on a three-point scale of low/medium/high. For instance, social media marketing provides a high degree of two-way communication, active control and synchronicity (real-time communication), while email marketing is a less powerful IDM mechanism in all three aspects. The next two columns show the degrees of marketers' control of messaging, and customers' control in conversation, respectively. As indicated in the table, while marketers are salient and have high level of power and control in communication in some IDM mechanisms, e.g., mobile marketing and email marketing, their level of control is much less in the more open and real-time social media platforms. This is obviously amplified when one considers user-generated content, where users are in charge, compared to marketer-generated content (see Ding et al., 2014).

Table 1 An analysis of the IDM mechanisms

	Degree of two-way communication	*Degree of responses and proactive behaviour for value creation*	*Degree of engagement in control and modification of real-time environmental changes*	*Degree of marketer control of messaging*	*Degree of customer control*	*Degree of data creation for a marketer to integrate into digital transformation*
Mobile marketing	Medium	Medium	Medium	High	Medium	Low
Online PR	High	High	High	Medium	High	High
Interactive online advertising	Medium	Medium	Medium	Medium	Medium	Medium
Email marketing	Medium	Medium	Medium	High	Medium	Low
Online partnership	High	High	High	Medium	High	High
Social media marketing	High	High	High	Medium	High	High

It is necessary to note that effective employment of each of these IDM mechanisms relies on a deep understanding of the customers (Stone et al., 2021): who are they? What do they want? What content do they want to see? How do they make decisions online? How do they make orders online? What factors contribute to their purchasing decision? What devices do they use online? How can companies retain customers and encourage them to repeat their transactions? In order to obtain a deep understanding of the customers/users, data are essential. So data analytics is the backbone of any IDM mechanism. In other words, no IDM mechanism would work through any digital transformation, if it is not data-driven. So, any decision on IDM mechanisms should be informed through real-time data analysis. That is why, the last column of Table 1 is related to the importance of data insights provided by IDM mechanisms for marketers to integrate into their digital transformation projects. As demonstrated in the table, of the six identified IDM mechanisms, i.e., online PR, online partnership and social medial marketing provide high degree of data creation for digital transformation. Indeed, those IDM mechanisms that enable customers to have high control in communication are rich in terms of data collection. For example, Domino's, the American multinational pizza restaurant, started its digital transformation journey through its use of social media to find fresh ideas for improving its businesses. In 2012, Domino's lunched its "think oven", a Facebook page where users were asked to submit ideas. The ideas that attracted most attention were rewarded with a monetary prize and actually implemented with executive approval (Jobber & Ellis-Chadwick, 2020). This example shows the extent of data insight that social media marketing, as one of the IDM mechanisms, can provide to assist a company to embark on its digitalisation journey.

However, it should be noted that what is the key is not just the data, as the business environment is now awash with big data. Instead, the ability of companies to process, analyse and derive insights from the data is highly important (Moe & Ratchford, 2022). A careful data analysis in a coherent and integrative way through all different levels and functions of a company is not accessible unless the company has gone through some degrees of digital transformation to make the best use of real-time data. The importance of data analytics will be further explored through the presentation of the case study.

4 The Case Study of NZ Post

In this section, the main and the biggest postal and package delivery services company in New Zealand, NZ Post, will be explored as a case study. The case study aims to investigate IDM mechanisms in the digital transformation of the company.

4.1 Business Background

The NZ Post transformation project is a prime example of a large logistics company with more than 7,000 employees and contractors that has gone through transformational change by taking advantage of IDM mechanisms. NZ Post is a New Zealand-based delivery and e-commerce logistics company that processes and delivers items—parcels, packages and letters—of New Zealand and international origin, to meet the requirements of both sending and receiving customers. NZ Post provides logistics services for businesses, including many that are engaged in e-commerce with customers, and with other companies both in New Zealand and internationally.

The story of NZ Post highlights how a business in the public sector can change over time and improve its business outcomes with strategic thinking. NZ Post is the largest logistics and delivery network in New Zealand that provides sending and receiving customers with services to help them communicate and do business. The business services are consistent throughout the year and carefully planned. NZ Post allocates resources at the peak times of online shopping periods, both domestically and internationally. NZ Post is part of the national landscape, integral to the New Zealand (Kiwi) way of life for nearly 180 years during which the business has been changing consistently to meet its customers' needs. In 2020 Covid and lockdowns had a huge impact on the e-commerce sales and consequently on NZ Post's workload, activities and performance. Many big traditional physical brands extended their online presence, allowing them to keep trading during lockdowns. As online continues to become a bigger part of their business, many have been adapting their business models further to the new channel mix to accommodate customers' interactions both online and in-store.

4.2 Te Iho Programme (Digital Transformation Project)

Over the past five years, the parcel volumes of NZ Post have grown by more than 41%. In 2021 NZ Post delivered over 67 million items which entailed a huge amount of processing, sorting and deliveries. At the core of the NZ Post strategy is a single integrated supply chain that moves items safely, at the lowest cost, and to the service standard the customer has paid for. To make this vision a reality, NZ Post needed to have rich end-to-end data that flow seamlessly across their network systems, that of their partners and those of their customers. Following the increase in parcel volume, the existing transport management system and warehouse management legacy systems were unable to support this interactive data-driven vision.

Te Iho is the name of the company's transformation project to response rapidly to this unprecedented growth in online shopping over recent years. Te Iho is Maori name and it means the heart, essence or inner core. The story behind the name is linked to NZ Post's Māori name "Tukurau Aotearoa" and is inspired by Tāne's forest (Tāne being The God of the Forest). From the outside, the forest looks peaceful and serene but, if you look closely, it is a constant hive of movement, activity and network. At the heart of this forest is the company's network. The company's vision is to be the best partner for online shopping and the best delivery network in New Zealand. Te Iho plans to make a stronger, safer and more connected core backbone by building new facilities with the latest global automation technology, enhancing the systems and technology and reinforcing the company's processes and procedures. This will provide the stability and control that in turn sets the last mile teams up to deliver for the customers. Te eho plans to build capability and capacity in the interactive parcel network so the company can grow with customers' need. In Te eho, new processing sites are planned to be built with more than double the size of previous capacity in the parcel processing network over the next 10 years. Enabling capabilities is the part of Te eho that is focussed on data and technology. So, by improving the sorting systems, Te eho plans to make the operations more connected, visible, efficient and simple. By seeking quality information from the customers as early as possible, Te eho plans to improve the data and make changes to the data fields behind the barcodes on the parcel labels to bring them in line with industry and international standards. This connects parcels back to NZ Post locally and globally and it will give the company more standardised data about parcels including what is inside, its estimated dimensions and weight, its priority and whether it is perishable. This data set lets the company forecast and plan a more efficient journey for parcels from pick up through delivery even for parcels that come unexpectedly. Industry and international standardised data will help the business to deliver a more consistently interactive experience for customers and make it easier for them to work with NZ Post.

As a result, a massive transformation project was started in early 2021. The project was massive enough to lead the company to go through rebranding and logo changing to open a new chapter in its history. This transformation project was started by investing $170 million on optimising the parcel network and processing infrastructure, data, culture and standardisation. All these major changes need strategic, organisational, cultural, financial and operational restructuring to suit the new digital-driven environment. Digital transformation would be the underlying layer of transformation to create a new sustainable, competitive and interactive service setting.

To reach these goals, NZ Post first planned to advance its online partnership with key strategic customers in B2B environment and define collaboration-based business using big data and digital technologies. Then, the company attempted to incorporate new IDM mechanisms to improve service quality for individuals and retailers (see the next section). The second major step (under process at the time of writing this chapter), is related to human resources and enhancing the organisation skillset, which is the hardest and most crucial part of the transformation. This is mainly related to defining new values, new behaviours, training, recruitment and reskilling for new roles which all need to be conducted in any successful digital realm. Finally, the company requires new business approaches, mechanisms, methods and technologies to provide a comprehensive service aligned to customer values. The new systems, processes, infrastructure and technologies need to be set to meet the customer requirements which are all based on digital technologies. So digital transformation would be at the heart of this transformation project.

4.3 IDM Mechanisms in Digital Transformation

The more an e-commerce business grows, the more it requires technology to help manage the deliveries efficiently, reliably and economically. NZ Post employs different IDM mechanisms to help it automate and simplify the delivery process. A few prime examples are elaborated below.

One of the key IDM mechanisms employed by NZ Post in their digital transformation is the shipping application programming interface (API), classified as a mobile marketing mechanism in the proposed conceptual framework (see Fig. 2). API is a software intermediary that allows two applications to talk to each other (see Boateng et al., 2019). Simple examples of APIs are each time you use an app like Facebook, send an instant message, or check the weather on your phone, you are using an API. APIs are mostly used to help developers provide information to marketers. The Shipping APIs used by NZ Post let large companies customise the shipping functionality into the client software quickly and easily (NZ Post, 2022a). With this IDM, companies can create labels, track parcels, validate addresses and retrieve shipping options, all using the usual software interface. For instance, if a customer is a Shopify user, they check out the NZ Post's addressing plugin that can streamline their customers' checkout experience by choosing a valid New Zealand address from the drop-down list.

E-ship is one of the other company's IDM mechanisms initiated as part of their digitisation and it is now applied by the company. E-ship is a cloud-based B2B mobile-based app that integrates with client e-commerce platforms to automate the process of delivering customers' orders. E-ship is particularly designed for e-commerce companies which frequently send multiple parcels at once, giving them an instantly accessible and interactive platform. Some of the key features of e-ship for client companies are accessing all NZ Post shipping options, sending customised email notifications to customers, generating on-demand reports, quick label printing and generating and printing pick slips (NZ Post, 2022b).

As another example, related to the online partnership mechanism (presented in Fig. 2), NZ Post is committed to giving its customers the latest information, insights and tools to help them grow the partners in B2B. Along with this annual review of online shopping trends, NZ Post produces a regular and timely update called e-commerce Spotlight. This covers the latest market data and also provides in-depth analysis and stories that are directly relevant at the time.

One of the fundamental changes in the digital transformation era in NZ Post was associated with the database architecture. Following customers' needs to track their parcels and packages, there has been a movement from focussing on data at rest (service-oriented architecture) to focussing on events (event-driven architecture). The shift to event-driven architecture means moving from a data-centric model to an event-centric model. In the event-driven model, the data are still important, but the events become the most important component. An event is any change of state of some key business system. As a customer service business, the event driver will give interactively near-real-time notifications of events which will allow the company to respond to issues/ problems much more quickly. Hence, the database migration has been changed from SQL/Oracle-based databases to the Kafka transactional system-based one. This migration by itself does not include any of the IDM mechanisms mentioned in the model. Nevertheless, it provides the underlying infrastructure for interactive collaboration with customers for services through parcel tracking and notifications. Parcel notification is offered to all customers who are using any one of the company's online ticketing solutions when sending domestically. This will help customers to follow the progress of their parcel delivery. This visibility helps improve customer satisfaction and removes the need to call or email customers to find out where the shipment's current location is. Using SMS and email notifications as the mobile marketing mechanisms of IDM, it is easy to connect directly with customers. So, notifications can be sent when the item is picked up, then with the courier for delivery, when it has been delivered and when an attempted delivery has been made. Customers can interact with certain messages, giving them options to have their parcels left in a secure location. This avoids re-delivery and makes for happier customers. Similarly, with express courier services, customers can track their parcel's journey in real-time on a "live" map and receive instant pickup and delivery notifications via email or text. This includes estimated time of arrival and live GPS tracking. This improved level of visibility and control certainly leads to a better delivery experience for customers.

4.4 *The Challenges of the Digital Transformation Project*

There are numerous challenges in every transformation project. The majority of these are related to people, processes, technologies and budget. The most important part is the resistance to change. In big organisational settings such as NZ Post, there are several diverse teams that are intertwined with each other. So, if one plans to change one part, one needs to consider all other moving parts as well. Therefore, change management was one of the major concerns in the Te Iho Programme. Consequently, there has been continuous interaction with different stakeholders, the employees, to consider their concerns throughout the transformation. People usually do not like change and prefer to keep the system as it is so they may overcomplicate the change requests and make the implementation of new processes difficult. Finally, from a technology perspective, people are used to use old technology and usually resist upskilling themselves to the new work environment. Also, migration from old technology to new technology always has its own technical challenges. For instance, consolidating the different object-oriented databases, e.g., SQL and Oracle to the event-driven ones, e.g., Kafka might be a huge technical challenge because of the difference in underlying concept/architecture. To overcome this, the company tries to best use various IDM mechanisms, e.g., email, social media and mobile communication to facilitate the transformation by keeping an interactive relationship with employees and encouraging them to cooperate in the change.

5 Discussion, Implications and Conclusion

The far-reaching availability and adoption of digital technologies and online social networks has transformed marketing practices and the way marketers engage with customers. This adoption of novel and innovative devices and data-driven marketing, particularly in online marketing practices, provides a wide and efficient reach, which in most cases causes companies to conduct some degree of digital transformation. IDM, as an integral part of the digital transformation of today's business world, is evolving at the same rate to keep up with the required marketing and digital capabilities of companies (Bala & Verma, 2018). This chapter tracks research dynamics in IDM by reviewing recent articles, citation and co-citation networks on both areas of interactive marketing and digital marketing to conceptualise the new term of IDM. To the best of our knowledge, this chapter is a pioneering one which conceptualises the concept of IDM and classifies its mechanisms. The chapter suggests the significance of IDM and the application of its mechanisms in digital transformation which explains the recent shifts in marketing practices towards bi-directional, value creation and synchronised communication and partnerships with users. The focus of IDM in this chapter was mainly on service elements and in particular "People" of the marketing mix model. This element of the marketing mix clearly relates to how a company interacts with its customers and other stakeholders pre-sales, during sales and post-sales. Thus, the focus of the identified IDM was on people and the way companies could deploy IDM mechanisms to best act in their interactive relationship with customers through their digital transformation.

Apart from the aforementioned theoretical contributions, this chapter offers practical contributions to the field of IDM as an international and interdisciplinary area. It provides a solid foundation to interactive digital marketers, as well as policymakers to devise certain mechanisms for enhancing the effectiveness of their marketing campaigns through IDM mechanisms. The chapter identified and described IDM mechanisms which are particularly considered through any organisation's digital transformation. Thus, it would enable interactive marketers to employ the latest IDM mechanisms for the right reasons to help their company in its digital transformation. The ideas put forth herein can incontestably aid business and marketing professionals to better plan their digital transformation projects that are facilitated by IDM mechanisms. These mechanisms promise companies to provide their users (both employees and customers) with a two-way, value-creating and synchronised experience throughout the digitalisation journey. Indeed, this chapter suggests companies' marketing professionals and decision-makers need to critically think about investing in IDM mechanisms, even before they start their digital transformation project. For instance, it is suggested that companies use IDM mechanism of social media marketing to lower the users' resistance against the digital transformation and make sure everyone feels they are a part of the change. Thus, the findings of this chapter may assist managers in their decisions on the use of digital and interactive marketing practices and navigate the way it could be put in place through their digital transformation plans.

However, determining which mechanisms would be the most effective ones in a digital transformation project and deliver the best customer satisfaction is not possible because this is highly context-dependent. This means that choosing the most effective IDM mechanisms in digital transformation may vary from one company to another one, depending on their internal and external environment. Indeed, IDM mechanisms aid companies to better understand their customers' needs and make innovative changes. In digital transformation, the key driver to change is customer data. IDM mechanisms facilitate two-way communication between customers and companies. So the new tools and services designed for customers will be driven by customers' ideas and comments. Thus, any development and deployment of IDM mechanisms have to be data-driven. Given the fact that Internet has enabled companies to capture data of vast amounts (Big Data), and the potential payoff from learning how to use it, data analytics has gained increasingly important role in IDM practices. While this area is mostly practical based, future research on methods that make productive use of these data is still needed (Ratchford, 2015).

One of the other key challenges of scholars and practitioners' in IDM area is the nature of today's digital marketplace, which is highly changing and dynamic, thanks to the ever-increasing and disruptive advances in technologies. This makes the developed models, theories and frameworks become outdated very quickly (Moe & Ratchford, 2022). As a result, the mechanisms of IDM that have been put together in this chapter could be easily replaced or upgraded by new ones in less than a year's time! So, it is crucial for researchers, marketers and any policy makers in this area to stay updated through continuous monitoring the environment, finding new ways to collect and analysis data and investing in new mechanisms and platforms to interact with customers.

REFERENCES

Ahmed, R. R., Vveinhardt, J., & Streimikiene, D. (2017). Interactive digital media and impact of customer attitude and technology on brand awareness: Evidence from the South Asian countires. *Journal of Business Economics and Management, 18*(6), 1115–1134.

Alrawadieh, Z., Alrawadieh, Z. & Cetin, G. (2020). Digital transformation and revenue management: Evidence from the hotel industry. *Special Issue: The Economics of Revenue Management in Hospitality and Tourism*, 1–18. https://doi.org/10.1177/1354816620901928

American Marketing Association. (2021). *What is digital marketing?* https://www.ama.org/pages/what-is-digital-marketing/. Accessed 24 February 2022.

Aswani, R., Kumar Kar, A., Ilavarasan, V., & Dwivedi, Y. K. (2018). Search engine marketing is not all gold: Insights from Twitter and SEOClerks. *International Journal of Information Management, 38*(1), 107–116.

Bala, M., & Verma, D. (2018). A critical review of digital marketing. *International Journal of Management, IT & Engineering, 8*(10), 321–339.

Barwise, P., & Farley, J. U. (2005). The state of interactive marketing in seven countries: Interactive marketing comes of age. *Journal of Interactive Marketing, 19*(3), 67–80. https://doi.org/10.1002/dir.20044

Berman, S. J. (2021). Digital transformation: Opportunities to create new business models. *Strategy and Leadership, 40*(2), 16–24. https://doi.org/10.1108/10878571211209314

Boateng, R., Ofoeda, J., & Effah, J. (2019). Application programming interface (API) research: A review of the past to inform the future. *International Journal of Enterprise Information Systems, 15*(3), 76–95. https://doi.org/10.4018/IJEIS.2019070105

Byon, K. K., & Phua, J. (2021). Digital and interactive marketing communications in Sports. *Journal of Interactive Advertising, 21*(2), 75–78. https://doi.org/10.1080/15252019.2021.1970422

Chaffey, D., & Ellis-Chadwick, F. (2019). *Digital marketing, strategy, implementation and practice*. Pearson.

Chahal, H., & Rani, A. (2017). How trust moderates social media engagement and brand equity. *Journal of Research in Interactive Marketing, 11*(3), 321–335. https://doi.org/10.1108/JRIM-10-2016-0104

Cluley, R., Green, W., & Owen, R. (2020). The changing role of the marketing researcher in the age of digital technology: practitioner perspectives on the digitization of marketing research. *International Journal of Marketing Research, 62*(1), 27–42.

Coelho, R. L. F., de Oliveira, D. S., & de Almeida, M. I. S. (2016). Does social media matter for post typology? Impact of post content on Facebook and Instagram metrics. *Online Information Review, 40*(4), 458–471.

Constantinides, E. (2006). The marketing mix revisited: Towards the 21st century marketing. *Journal of Marketing Management, 22*(3–4), 407–438.

Ding, Y., et al. (2014). The role of marketer- and user-generated content in sustaining the growth of a social media brand community, *IEEE*. https://doi.org/10.1109/HICSS.2014.226

Downes, E. J., & McMillan, S. J. (2000). Defining interactivity: A qualitative identification of key dimensions. *New Media & Society, 2*(2), 157–179.

Dremel, C., Herterich, M., Wulf, J., Waizmann, J.-C., & Brenner, W. (2017). How AUDI AG established big data analytics in its digital transformation. *MIS Quarterly Executive, 16*(2), 81–100.

Duffy, D. L. (2005). Affiliate marketing and its impact on e-commerce. *Journal of Consumer Marketing, 22*(3), 161–163. https://doi.org/10.1108/07363760510595986

Fenech, R., Baguant, P., & Ivanov, D. (2019). The changing role of Human Resource Management in an era of digital transformation. *Journal of Management Information & Decision Sciences, 22*(2), 166–175.

Gartner. (2022). *Gartner glossary, information technology glossary, digital marketing*. https://www.gartner.com/en/information-technology/glossary/digital-marketing-2. Accessed 20 February 2022.

Goi, C. L. (2009). A review of marketing mix: 4Ps or more? *International Journal of Marketing Studies, 1*(1), 1–15.

Guenzi, J. H., & Habel, J. (2020). Mastering the digital transformation of sales. *Californian Management Review, 62*(4), 57–85.

Halbheer, D., Stahl, F., Koenigsberg, O., & Lehmann, D. R. (2014). Choosing a digital content strategy: How much should be free? *International Journal of Research in Marketing, 31*(2), 192–206.

Hartemo, M. (2016). Email marketing in the era of the empowered consumer. *Journal of Research in Interactive Marketing, 10*(3), 212–230. https://doi.org/10.1108/JRIM-06-2015-0040

Heeter, C. (2000). Interactivity in the context of designed experiences. *Journal of Interactive Advertising, 1*(1), 3–14.

Hoban, P. R., & Bucklin, R. E. (2015). Effects of Internet display advertising in the purchase funnel: Model-based insights from a randomized field experiment. *Journal of Marketing Research, 52*(3), 375–393. https://doi.org/10.1509/jmr.13.0277

Jobber, D., & Ellis-Chadwick, F. (2020). *Principles and practice of marketing*. McGraw-Hill Publication.

Krishen, A. S., et al. (2021). A broad overview of interactive digital marketing: A bibliometric network analysis. *Journal of Business Research, 131*(7), 183–195.

Kurkovsky, S., & Harihar, K. (2006). Using ubiquitous computing in interactive mobile marketing. *Personal and Ubiquitous Computing, 10*(4), 227–240.

Li, F., Larimo, J., & Leonidou, L. C. (2021). Social media marketing strategy: Definition, conceptualization, taxonomy, validation, and future agenda. *Journal of the Academy of Marketing Science, 49*(1), 51–70. https://doi.org/10.1007/s11747-020-00733-3

Liu, Y., & Shrum, L. J. (2002). What is interactivity and is it always such a good thing? Implications of definition, person, and situation for the influence of interactivity on advertising effectiveness. *Journal of Advertising, 31*(4), 53–64.

Majid, K. A. (2020). Effect of interactive marketing channels on service customer acquisition. *Journal of Services Marketing, 35*(3), 299–311.

Matarazzo, M., Penco, L., Profumo, G., & Quaglia, R. (2021). Digital transformation and customer value creation in Made in Italy SMEs: A dynamic capabilities perspective. *Journal of Business Research, 123*(2), 642–656. https://doi.org/10.1016/j.jbusres.2020.10.033

Matt, C., Hess, T., & Benlian, A. (2015). Digital transformation strategies. *Business Information System Engineering, 57*(5), 339–343.

McCarthy, E. J. (1960). *Basic marketing: A managerial approach.* Homewood, IL: Richard D. Irwin.

Melović, B., et al., (2020). The impact of digital transformation and digital marketing on the brand promotion, positioning and electronic business in Montenegro. *Technology in Society, 63*(11). https://doi.org/10.1016/j.techsoc.2020.101425

Moe, W. W., & Ratchford, B. T. (2022). How the explosion of customer data has redefined interactive marketing. *Journal of Interactive Marketing, 42*(1), 1–2.

NZ Post. (2022a). *Shipping API.* https://www.nzpost.co.nz/business/ecommerce/digital-solutions/shipping-apis, Accessed 24 April 2022.

NZ Post. (2022b). *E-ship.* https://www.nzpost.co.nz/business/ecommerce/digital-solutions/eship, Accessed 24 April 2022.

Olson, E. M., et al. (2021). Business strategy and the management of digital marketing. *Business Horizons, 64*(2), 285–293.

Peter, M. K., & Dalla Vecchia, M. (2020). The digital marketing toolkit: A literature review for the identification of digital marketing channels and platforms. *New Trends in Business Information Systems and Technology,* 251–265.

Rafaeli, S. (1988). From new media to communication. *Sage Annual Review of Communication Research: Advancing Communication Science, 16,* 110–134.

Ratchford, B. T. (2015). Some directions for research in interactive marketing. *Journal of Interactive Marketing, 29,* v–vii.

Ritz, W., Wolf, M., & McQuitty, S. (2019). Digital marketing adoption and success for small businesses: The application of the do-it-yourself and technology acceptance models. *Journal of Research in Interactive Marketing, 13*(2), 179–203.

Sabin, T. (2010). *What is interactive marketing?* https://troysabin.wordpress.com/. Accessed on 20 February 2022.

Semara, O. Y., Handayani, W., Rahayu, F., & Shaddiq, S. (2021). Communication and interactive marketing management through Internet advertising. *Strategic Management Business Journal, 1*(02), 25–29.

Shahbaznezhad, H., Dolan, R., & Rashidirad, M. (2021). The role of social media content format and platform in users' engagement behaviour. *Journal of Interactive Marketing, 53*(2), 47–65. https://doi.org/10.1016/j.intmar.2020.05.001

Shahbaznezhad, H., & Rashidirad, M. (2020). Exploring Firms' Fan Page Behavior and Users' Participation: Evidence from Airline Industry on Twitter. *Journal of Strategic Marketing, 29*(6), 492–513. https://doi.org/10.1080/0965254X.2020.1770318

Steuer, J. (1992). Defining virtual reality: Dimensions determining telepresence. *Journal of Communication, 42*(4), 73–93.

Stone, M. et al., (2021). Interactive marketing, customer information and marketing research. In L.T. Wright, et al. (Eds.), *The Routledge companion to marketing research.* Routledge.

Stone, M. D., & Woodcock, N. D. (2014). Interactive, direct and digital marketing: A future that depends on better use of business intelligence. *Journal of Research in Interactive Marketing, 8*(1), 4–17.

Troise, C., Corvello, V., Ghobadian, A., & O'Regan, N. (2022). How can SMEs successfully navigate VUCA environment: The role of agility in the digital transformation era. *Technological Forecasting and Social Change, 174*(1), 1–12. https://doi.org/10.1016/j.techfore.2021.121227

Verhoef, P. C., et al. (2021). Digital transformation: A multidisciplinary reflection and research agenda. *Journal of Business Research, 122*(1), 889–901.

Vial, G. (2016). Understanding digital transformation: A review and a research agenda. *Journal of Strategic Information Systems, 28*(2), 118–144.

Virvilaitė, R., & Belousova, R. (2005). Origin and definition of interactive marketing. *Commerce of Engineering Decisions, 41*(1), 67–73.

Wang, C. L. (2021). New frontiers and future directions in interactive marketing: Inaugural Editorial. *Journal of Research in Interactive Marketing, 15*(1), 1–9.

Zahay, D. (2014). Beyond interactive marketing. *Journal of Research in Interactive Marketing, 8*(4). https://doi.org/10.1108/JRIM-08-2014-0047

Zhang, L., Zhao, H., & Cude, B. (2021). Luxury brands join hands: Building interactive alliances on social media. *Journal of Research in Interactive Marketing, 4*, 787–803. https://doi.org/10.1108/JRIM-02-2020-0041

Ziółkowska, M. J. (2021). Digital transformation and marketing activities in small and medium-sized enterprises. *Sustainability, 13*(5), 1–16. https://doi.org/10.3390/su13052512

CHAPTER 6

Empowering Consumers in Interactive Marketing: Examining the Role of Perceived Control

Xiaohan Hu

1 INTRODUCTION

As innovative technologies give consumers more opportunities to participate in and interact with marketing processes, interactivity has become an integral part of contemporary marketing practice (Wang, 2021). Recent studies in interactive marketing research have investigated a wide range of interactive platforms and technologies, such as self-service technology (e.g. Robertson et al., 2016; Zhu et al., 2007), gamified marketing (e.g. Hu & Wise, 2021; Xi et al., 2018), virtual reality (e.g. Kim et al., 2021; Wang & Chen, 2019), augmented reality (e.g. Whang et al., 2021; Zimmermann et al., 2022), and social media marketing (e.g. Cuevas et al., 2021; Jung & Heo, 2021; Yoon et al., 2022). Extant literature also acknowledges the positive effects of interactivity on marketing outcomes, including consumers' attitudes and behaviors (e.g. Cuevas et al., 2021; Kim et al., 2021; Kirk et al., 2015; Lucia-Palacios & Pérez-López, 2021). Despite the amount of research investigating interactivity, one of the compelling issues that emerge from this research is to reveal the underlying mechanisms that explain the effects of interactivity (Sundar, 2004; van Noort et al., 2012). Only if underlying principles are studied can we fully understand how consumers are influenced by interactive marketing communications (van Noort et al., 2012), and therefore inform both the theoretical and practical understanding of interactive marketing.

X. Hu (✉)
University of Illinois at Urbana-Champaign, Champaign, IL, USA
e-mail: xhu33@illinois.edu

While interactive marketing platforms and technologies have rapidly evolved, the psychological mechanisms underlying their use remain largely unchanged. The core values of interactive marketing, including consumer connection, engagement, participation, and interaction (Wang, 2021), are realized by empowering consumers so they have a more active role. Consumers today are increasingly empowered by having more control in actively making decisions about their marketing experience enabled by newly developed technologies, such as social media, interactive videos, virtual reality, etc. Such a role reversal of consumers from passive to active and from reactive to proactive can be summarized as a reduction of institutional control and an increase of consumer control (Shapiro, 1999). Therefore, consumer control has become an integral part of consumer empowerment in interactive marketing today.

Motivated by the need to explicate the underlying mechanisms of interactive marketing effectiveness and understand consumer empowerment in interactive marketing activities, this chapter addresses the changing role of consumers from passive to active, from reactive to proactive, by providing a theoretical overview of the concept perceived control and associated psychological processes in interactive marketing. Due to its conceptual connection with interactivity, control, particularly consumers' perception of control, can be a key psychological mechanism to understand the effectiveness of interactive marketing. Explicating perceived control and associated psychological processes will therefore advance theoretical understanding and provide practical guidelines for interactive marketing research and practice. This chapter first discusses the conceptual definitions of perceived control, particularly in the interactive marketing context; then the chapter focuses on the relationship between interactivity and perceived control in marketing research and explicates the important role of control in explaining interactive marketing effectiveness. In addition, the chapter outlines psychological processing consequences and effects of perceived control, focusing on consumers' affective, cognitive, and behavioral responses. Finally, the chapter discusses some possible moderating factors that may influence the relationship between control and interactive marketing effectiveness, including consumers' dispositional factors, motivation, and personalization. Directions for future research are also suggested. Figure 1 summarizes the theoretical framework to examine the role of perceived control in interactive marketing.

2 Defining Perceived Control in Interactive Marketing

The concept of control has been studied broadly in research areas including psychology, marketing, advertising, and technology studies. However, conceptualizing control is difficult because of the number of related terms that have been defined and studied in the literature, such as autonomy, self-determination, and agency. Moreover, scholars have focused specifically on some sub-concepts or dimensions of control such as perceived control, actual

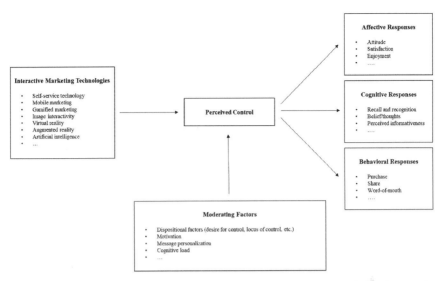

Fig. 1 Theoretical framework for examining perceived control in interactive marketing

control, locus of control, etc. This chapter explicates control by focusing on the subjective aspect of this concept. Consumer perception is one of the central foci of marketing research. It has been argued that perceived control is a powerful predictor of people's behavior and emotion, independent of the actual control conditions that may have contributed to those perceptions (Averill, 1973; Skinner, 1996). In the marketing literature, perceived control is also studied as an important factor determining marketing effectiveness (e.g. Hu & Wise, 2021; Kirk et al., 2015; Lee et al., 2018).

Psychologically, Skinner (1996) defined perceived control as the belief about the extent to which people have control over the environment. The concept is also seen as the amount of control people feel they have over a situation or another person (Bugental et al., 1989). Accordingly, people with a higher sense of control believe they have a strong impact on their surroundings. Steiner (1979) defined control as an experiential state that occurs "when feeling that he or she, rather than other people, luck, or unmanageable forces, determines whether desired outcomes will be received" (p. 17). Some scholars have also defined control as individuals' perceived ability to exert influence over targets. According to Burger (1989), control can be simply defined as the perceived ability to significantly alter events. This view of control also falls into the subjective perspective because it suggests that it is not necessary for an individual to have actual control over the events but rather that the individual only perceive that he or she is able to exert control.

In marketing research, control has been studied as a psychological construct in different contexts. Services researchers were among the first in the marketing discipline to recognize the relevance of perceived control. As these researchers sought to distinguish between higher and lower quality services, perceived control surfaced as a salient explanation (Hui & Bateson, 1991; Zhu et al., 2007). More recently, as digital self-service technologies (SSTs), such as Internet shopping, mobile apps, and automated chatbots, are getting increasingly prevalent and becoming a critical component of interactive marketing (Lee, 2017), perceived control has been broadly examined in this area. According to Collier and Sherrell (2010), control in self-service settings is the ability to rule the flow of transaction and the level of interactivity experienced by consumers. Perceived control over SST refers to the perception of mastery over the processes and outcomes of the service interface technologies (Zhu et al., 2007, 2013). Perceived control has also been studied in other areas of interactive marketing. In their study of gamified marketing, for instance, Lee et al. (2018) defined perceived control as the users' sense that the game precisely executes their intended actions. Based on this definition, these authors also argued that perceived control is related to the user interface and a well-designed user interface helps users control their actions in the game. Hanus and Fox (2017) studied customizable interface in interactive advertising and defined control as the perception that one is able to manipulate a customizable interface in a predictable way.

To summarize, perceived control emphasizes people's subjective assessment of the extent to which they can alter or impact environment. It focuses on people's interpretation of their own abilities and the target that they can exert control upon. In interactive marketing research, perceived control refers to consumers' perception of their ability to rule, alter, or manipulate marketing messages and interfaces, enabled by interactive marketing technologies, such as Internet websites, mobile apps, self-service technologies, etc. To better understand the role of perceived control in interactive marketing, the next section explicates the conceptual association between interactivity and perceived control.

3 Interactivity and Perceived Control

The conceptual relationship between interactivity and perceived control has been explicated since the early age of interactive marketing, when the concept of interactivity just emerged in marketing and consumer research. In their discussion about interactive advertising and presence, Lombard and Snyder-Duch (2001) suggested that central to the idea of interactivity is the concept of control. Steuer (1992) defined interactivity as the extent to which users can participate in modifying the form and content of a mediated environment in real-time. The potential for the user to modify the environment is the essence of user control, which has been conceptualized as a key component of interactivity by a number of researchers. For example, Liu and Shrum (2002) conceptualized interactivity in marketing and advertising research as a three-dimensional construct encompassing (1) active control, (2) two-way communication, and (3) synchronicity. Specifically, active control referred to consumers' ability to customize the information flow and jump from one location in the Internet to another. The authors also explicated this idea with the example of Internet banner advertising where consumers could actively control their advertising experience by choosing to click on the ad to obtain more information or ignore the ad without doing anything special. Since consumer perceptions are central to marketing research, researchers have also examined perceived interactivity and its relationship with perceived control. For example, Wu (2006) studied perceived interactivity in website marketing. He defined perceived interactivity as a psychological state experienced by a site-visitor during his or her interaction with a website, which manifests in three dimensions: (1) perceived control; (2) perceived responsiveness; and (3) perceived personalization. Specifically, Wu (2006) followed the theory of planned behavior and defined perceived control as the perceived ease or difficulty of performing the behavior (Ajzen, 1991). Similarly, McMillan and Hwang (2002) also identified control as a central component of perceived interactivity in web-based advertising. Based on the above conceptualization, it is apparent that control is a key component of interactivity. From a conceptual perspective, an interactive marketing interface should offer consumers various interactive options for controlling the nature of their interaction, and therefore influence consumers' perception of control toward the marketing messages.

The interactive marketing literature also provides sufficient empirical support to the relationship between interactive marketing technologies and perceived control. For example, Moes et al. (2021) found that interactivity enabled by in-store interactive advertising screens led to consumers' feelings of agency and control. Whang et al. (2021) found that interactivity, as a feature of augmented reality shopping experience, enhanced perceived cognitive control and perceived behavioral control. Researchers also found that using image interactivity technology (IIT) for product display also enhanced consumers' perceived control toward their interactions with marketing messages (Hu & Wise, 2020; Overmars & Poels, 2015). Recent interactive marketing research has also examined gamified marketing, which usually requires an interactive process of completing game tasks relevant to marketing messages. One study showed that using interactive hand gestures as game input led to increased perceived control (Xi et al., 2018). Hu and Wise (2021) investigated the playable ad, which is an innovative type of digital advertising that integrates interactivity and gamification in marketing communications. They found that compared with more traditional video advertising, consumers interacting with the playable ad showed greater perceived control.

The conceptual relation and the empirical findings discussed above reveal that perceived control is a key component of interactivity in marketing communications. As a psychological construct describing consumers' subjective feeling, perceived control is also closely related to psychological processing outcomes, such as attitude and behavior. The next section focuses on how perceived control explains the effects of interactive marketing on multidimensional consumer responses.

4   Effects of Perceived Control in Interactive Marketing

In studying the effectiveness of interactive marketing, researchers have measured various types of consumer responses including attention, memory, attitude, and purchase intention. Among these outcome variables, marketing researchers have also made distinctions between affective, cognitive, and behavioral responses. Holbrook and Hirschman (1982) proposed a comprehensive model of a consumer response system, including effect, cognition, and behavior. According to these authors, consumers' affective responses include attitude, preference, mood, and feelings. Cognitive responses involve attention, memory, beliefs, and thought. Behaviors and behavioral intentions are also known as conative/behavioral responses in the model, which have been typically measured as purchase intention, intention to search, etc. Based on this model, the following sections review interactive marketing literature that examines the psychological effects of perceived control on consumers' affective, cognitive, and behavioral responses.

4.1   Effects of Perceive Control on Affective Responses

In general, it is demonstrated that having control is subjectively positive. Research showed that perceived control elicited by interactive marketing technologies positively influenced consumers' attitudes, feelings, and satisfaction levels. For example, Yen (2005) studied consumers' experience with Internet self-service, such as online travel services and bookstores. Through a survey, she found that control over Internet self-service technology led to a positive effect on users' satisfaction with the service. Hanus and Fox (2017) investigated the effects of customizable options in online advertising and manipulated the extent to which participants were able to customize the avatars that represented the source of the marketing message. They found that having more choices led to greater perceived control, which reduced people's psychological reactance toward persuasion and increased product liking. Hu and Wise (2020) studied the role of perceived control in explaining the effect of image interactivity technology on multidimensional consumer responses. They found that perceived control mediated the effect of using interactive product images (vs. static images) on multidimensional consumer responses, including perceived informativeness, product attitude, purchase intention, and willingness to pay. Wang and Chen (2019) compared the marketing effectiveness of virtual reality (VR) brand videos and websites. They found that perceived control of VR videos had a significant effect on consumers' interest in the brand. Fan et al. (2022) investigated consumer responses to artificial intelligence services. This study showed that compared with consumers using the voice assistant, consumers using the touch panel for service had greater perceived control due to the perception of extended self, which enhanced their satisfaction with the service.

Why is perceived control positively associated with consumers' affective responses? Such a relationship has been validated in early psychology research, which demonstrated that increased perceived control exerted a positive impact on human physical and psychological well-being, including physical tolerance, anxiety, task performance, etc. (e.g. Ball & Vogler, 1971; Staub et al., 1971; Thompson, 1981). Through neuroimaging techniques, recent research in cognitive psychology and neuroscience also found neural bases for control in brain regions that are involved in affective and motivational processes, suggesting that having control is inherently rewarding and motivating to human beings (see Leotti et al., 2010). In the context of interactive marketing research, a relevant theoretical framework that has been widely applied to understand the effect of perceived control on affective responses is the psychological reactance theory. This theory proposes that individuals perceive a series of ways in which they are free to behave. Once a behavior is perceived as specific freedom, anything that makes it more difficult to exercise that freedom constitutes a threat. As a result, individuals feel motivated to restore the threatened freedom (Brehm & Brehm, 1981). One effective restoration strategy is to exercise different freedom to gain a feeling of control and choice (Wicklund, 1974), since the psychological reactance theory follows the assumption that humans place a high value on choice and control (Quick et al., 2013). This means that perceived control can diminish freedom threat and reactance, which enhances affective responses. Research suggests that as interactive marketing technologies afford more perceived control, consumers feel less reactance toward the persuasive marketing messages and have more positive affective responses. For example, one recent study on social media marketing demonstrated that consumers' feelings of autonomy to control Facebook ads were negatively associated with their perceptions of freedom threat and reactance (Youn & Kim, 2019). When consumers felt they had a sense of autonomy in controlling social media advertising, they perceived less reactance and showed fewer negative feelings and emotions. Following the psychological reactance theory, Choi and Kim (2022) studied the effects of an interactive advertising feature—the ad skip option. They found that presence of the ad skip option resulted in a higher level of perceived control, predicting lower ad intrusiveness and ad irritation, and a more favorable ad attitude. In the context of gamified marketing, Hu and Wise (2021) found that playable ads, compared to video ads, increased consumers' perceived control, which in turn led to less psychological reactance and a more positive product attitude.

Understanding perceived control as a motivational need of humans can contribute to our understanding of interactive marketing research and practice. For example, with gamification of marketing and more active consumer participation, it is believed that interactive marketing is becoming more fun, exciting, and inviting (Wang, 2021). This can be explained by the fact that control, namely, the ability to manipulate, modify, customize, and eventually determine the game process, is the fundamental feature of games. Since having control is psychologically motivating and rewarding, integrating game components into interactive marketing practices can therefore provide consumers more engaging and positive affective experience. Future research in interactive marketing should therefore pay more attention to the motivating nature of perceived control and examine how perceived control can explain the positive experience of various types of interactive marketing technologies, such as social e-commerce, virtual reality, augmented reality, etc.

4.2   Effects of Perceive Control on Cognitive Responses

While a handful of studies have confirmed the positive relationship between perceived control and affective responses in interactive marketing, relatively fewer studies have examined the effects of control on consumers' cognitive responses. Similar to the effect on affective responses, the psychological reactance theory has been adopted to explain the effect of perceived control on cognitive responses. According to the theory, reactance is conceptualized as a combination of effect and cognition. Perceived control, which helps mitigate freedom threat, can diminish reactance, indicated by cognitive responses such as negative thoughts and beliefs (Quick et al., 2013). Empirical studies following this theoretical framework typically confirmed the relationship between perceived control and negative cognitions. As interactive marketing technologies afforded more control, consumers had fewer negative thoughts toward the marketing messages (e.g. Hu & Wise, 2021; Youn & Kim, 2019). Additionally, as the increasing use of artificial intelligence, virtual reality or augmented reality further facilitates marketers to deliver exceptional experiences (Wang, 2021), marketing scholars have also paid attention to the role of direct product experience, or telepresence, in explaining the effects of perceived control on cognitive responses. For example, Klein's (2003) research is one of the earliest studies that examined user control and virtual product experience. The author proposed that the greater the level of control consumers experienced in interactive marketing, the greater the perceived similarity of the experience to a direct product experience, which meant a greater level of telepresence. Such direct product experience enabled by user control tended to intensify consumers' beliefs about the product. Through two experimental studies, Klein (2003) confirmed the relationship between control, telepresence, and consumers' cognitive responses.

Besides the lack of research in this area, empirical findings on the relationship between perceived control and cognitive responses in an interactive marketing context are also mixed. For instance, Wang (2015) investigated the interactive experience of corporate websites by focusing on consumers' control of navigation. It was argued that control of navigation can influence cognition because the dynamic process of navigation, which allowed consumers to customize browsing experience, could stimulate systematic elaboration of information (Liu & Shrum, 2009). When control of navigation was perceived to be high, consumers could concentrate on interacting with the website content, and therefore generated more positive thoughts about the website and the brand. However, results from Wang (2015) failed to confirm the relationship between control and more positive thoughts toward the marketing message. Nelson et al. (2006) examined consumers' processing of brand placement in games and manipulated control by asking participants to play (user control) or watch (computer-control) the game. They found that game players, who were able to actively control the gaming process, recalled fewer embedded brands than watchers.

A possible explanation to the inconclusive findings on control and cognitive responses is the capacity limit of cognitive resources. While interactivity in marketing and advertising activities can facilitate information processing and persuasion by affording consumers more control, it may also require more cognitive resources and add to consumers' cognitive load, which makes it more difficult to control and process relevant information (Liu & Shrum, 2009). For example, Ariely (2000) studied both the advantages and disadvantages of information control on consumers' decision quality, memory, knowledge, and confidence. Results showed that controlling the information in an interactive shopping scenario enhanced consumers' memory and knowledge about the relevant information, and consumers' confidence in their judgments. However, having control could also create demands on cognitive resources and therefore impeded consumers' cognitive responses. In their study of brand placement in games, Nelson et al. (2006) also suggested that active players were more likely to experience cognitive overload than passive watchers. Due to the limited cognitive resources and the information-demanding context of game play, active game players might focus more on the central elements of a game, while passive watchers would have remaining cognitive resources to attend to peripheral elements in the game such as brand placement.

In sum, the interactive marketing literature offers some insights into the relationship between perceived control and consumers' cognitive responses, such as cognitive thoughts. Unlike the consistent findings for affective responses, it appears that the availability of cognitive resources is an important factor that may moderate the relationship between perceived control and cognitive responses: while control can facilitate cognitive processing of interactive marketing messages, it may also become cognitively demanding under conditions of high cognitive load, and thus impede cognitive processing. Future research should further explore the effects of perceived control on a broader range of cognitive responses, such as attention and memory toward marketing messages, and how cognitive load may interact with the process in interactive marketing.

4.3 Effects of Perceived Control on Behavioral Responses

According to the model of the consumer response system, behavioral responses are generally the outcomes of cognition and/or affect. Prior interactive marketing research also demonstrated that both cognitive and affective responses were related to consumers' behavioral intentions. For example, Papagiannidis et al. (2017) found that increased perceived control elicited by immersive virtual retail environment had positive effects on consumers' simulated experience, engagement, and enjoyment, which further influenced purchase intention. Youn and Kim (2019) found that increased perceived control toward social media advertising decreased consumers' negative cognitions and anger, leading to less behavioral avoidance to social media advertising. Robertson et al. (2016) found that consumers' satisfaction toward self-service technologies mediated the effects of perceived control on consumers' behavioral intentions, including the intention to reuse the service and the intention to spread positive word-of-mouth.

Other studies have also revealed the direct effect of control on consumers' behavioral intentions. Particularly, the theory of planned behavior (Ajzen, 1985) has been widely adopted to investigate the effect of perceived control on behavioral responses in interactive marketing research (e.g. Ariffin et al., 2021; Li & Yin, 2021; Wang & Chen, 2019). The theory of planned behavior proposes factors that shape an individual's behavioral intentions and behaviors. Specifically, it is theorized that perceived behavioral control, which refers to perception of easiness or difficulty in performing a certain behavior, drives behavioral intention (Ajzen, 1991). The more resources and opportunities an individual has or the more power in performing tasks, the higher the level of perceived control and the stronger the behavioral intention (Ajzen, 1991).

Following the theory of planned behavior, marketing scholars have demonstrated that perceived control plays a significant role in affecting consumers' behavioral intentions in interactive marketing activities. For instance, Ariffin et al. (2021) found that perceived control was positively related to consumers' intention to continue using e-wallet. Li and Yin (2021) found that perceived control induced by skippable video advertising negatively affected ad avoidance intention. Richard and Meuli (2013) tested the theory of planned behavior in the context of permission-based location-aware mobile advertising (PBLAMA), which is a type of interactive mobile marketing that enables marketers to send more personalized and targeted messages to individual consumers based on their geographic location. They found that the lack of perceived control significantly and negatively influenced intentions to use PBLAMA. In the context of virtual reality marketing, Wang and Chen (2019) suggested that consumers' interaction with VR videos and websites was accompanied by perceived behavioral control. They argued that VR viewers' perceived control originated in their beliefs that they could watch an activity in a way that they could not otherwise do in person, which brought more profound feelings of immersion, interaction, and emotion. As a result, the positivity associated with perceived control offered by the VR context could be transferred to their perception of the marketing message embedded in VR videos. Results from this study showed that perceived control of VR brand videos was positively associated with consumers' interest in the embedded brand and the intention to consider the brand. The above evidence suggested that perceived control was a significant factor that explained consumers' intention to engage in interactive marketing activities.

5 Moderating Factors that Influence the Effects of Perceived Control

In addition to the main psychological processes described above, there are several factors that may moderate the effects of perceived control on affective, cognitive, and behavioral responses in interactive marketing. These moderating factors will be discussed in more detail next.

5.1 Dispositional Factors of the Consumer

The amount of control that is optimal, or even beneficial, is likely to depend upon individual differences, such as a desire for control or locus of control (Klein, 2003). A desire for control is an important factor accounting for variations in human behavior in control situations. It refers to individual differences in general desire for having control over the events in one's life (Burger & Cooper, 1979). Specifically, people high in the desire for control are "assertive, decisive, and active. They generally seek to influence others when such influence is advantageous. They prefer to avoid unpleasant situations or failures by manipulating events to ensure desired outcomes" (p. 383). People who are low in desire for control, conversely, can be described as "nonassertive, passive, and indecisive. These persons are less likely to attempt to influence others and may prefer that many of their daily decisions be made by others" (p.383). Locus of control (LOC), on the other hand, captures people's general expectancies about the causes of rewards and punishments (Rotter, 1966). People with an internal LOC ("internals") generally expect that their actions will produce predictable outcomes. Conversely, people with an external LOC ("externals") generally expect that outcomes are due to external variables such as fate, luck or powerful others. It is argued that internals are more action-oriented, commit to tasks allowing for personal control, and derive more satisfaction from situations calling for personal control (Hoffman et al., 2003).

Such individual differences suggest that having control may not always be preferable and satisfactory. Previous marketing literature has also confirmed that consumers' dispositional differences may influence their perceptions and responses to marketing information. For example, Faraji-Rad et al. (2017) examined the relationship between the desire for control and consumers' adoption of a new product. They found that people with a higher level of desire for control were less likely to consider using new products than traditional products. For people with a lower desire for control, the newness of the product did not affect the willingness to consider the product. With regard to SST adoption, Hoffman et al. (2003) examined locus of control (LOC) and found that consumers with high internal LOC were more committed to adopting the Internet for goal-directed activities, whereas consumers with high external LOC were less likely to adopt the Internet for goal-directed activities. According to these authors, a possible explanation for such difference was that internals usually adopted and mastered riskier and innovative strategies and thus they were likely among the first to be attracted to the new marketing technologies. Mullins et al. (2015) argued that fit between consumers' desire for control and their perceived control in the marketing environment predicted consumers' satisfaction. Their argument was based on the person-environment fit theory. The theory suggests that fit between what an individual needs and what the environment supplies lead to positive outcomes such as satisfaction. Misfit, on the other hand, can trigger negative outcomes. Based on this theory, people's desire for control can be viewed as individual needs and perceived control represents perceptions of what the environment supplies (Mullins et al., 2015). When an individual's desire for control is greater or less than perceived control of the environment, the individual is likely to experience greater dissatisfaction. Results from this study confirmed that consumers' satisfaction and product sales were highest when perceived and desired control converged, and decreased when perceived and desired control diverged, suggesting the moderation role of desire for control on the effects of perceived control.

However, the research cited above primarily explored dispositional factors and control in a more traditional marketing context. Relatively little is known about the relationship between dispositional factors, perceived control, and consumer responses in interactive marketing. As the rapid development and innovation in new technologies empower consumers with a more active role in controlling marketing messages and processes, individual differences in desire or locus of control should be even more relevant in interactive marketing research. For instance, gamified marketing encourages more active consumer engagement and participation (Wang, 2021). Despite the trend toward greater consumer engagement and control, the consequences of having control may not always be beneficial. It is important to understand not only the consequences of perceived control per se, which have been well established but also the relationship between consumers' dispositional need for control and perceived control. Future research should investigate the role of dispositional factors in impacting the effectiveness of interactive marketing.

5.2 Consumer Motivation

Marketing and consumer research shows that two fundamental motivational orientations underlie the difference in consumer goals and behaviors. Consumers may behave and process marketing information differently depending on whether their goals are primarily utilitarian or hedonic (e.g. Hirschman & Holbrook, 1982; Wang & Jiang, 2019). The utilitarian motivational orientation involves consumers engaging in a marketing activity in order to obtain needed products, services, or information with little or no inherent satisfaction derived from the activity itself. On the other hand, the hedonic motivational orientation refers to consumers engaging in a marketing activity to derive inherent satisfaction from the activity itself. In this case, the activity is motivated by more experiential benefits provided by the experience, such as agreement or excitement.

Hoffman and Novak (1996) summarized the distinction between goal-directed and experiential behaviors specifically in the digital marketing context. According to these authors, goal-directed behaviors are utilitarian, instrumental oriented, and extrinsically motivated. Whereas experiential behaviors are related to hedonic value, ritualized orientation, and intrinsic motivation. Botti and McGill (2011) also suggested that a hedonic consumption experience was intrinsically motivated and inherently rewarding, namely, it was sought as an end in itself. On the contrary, a utilitarian experience was extrinsically motivated and not rewarding in itself. Since people typically engage in intrinsically motivated behaviors to feel competent and self-determining (Deci, 1975), it has been argued that the concept of intrinsic motivation is closely associated with people's desire for control (Burger & Cooper, 1979).

Empirical studies have examined the relationship between perceived control and motivation. In Zuckerman et al.'s (1978) study, for instance, some participants were given the opportunity to select three of six problems they would work on and how to allocate their time among the three chosen problems, while other participants had no choice in their tasks. Results showed that participants who had free choice in their tasks, namely, who had a higher level of perceived control, were more intrinsically motivated than those who did not have any choice. Botti and McGill (2011) looked into the interaction effect between perceived control and hedonic/utilitarian goal of consumers. In their study, participants were asked to imagine eating gourmet food in Italy for either a hedonic or a utilitarian goal. Perceived control was also manipulated by choice. Choosers were able to select one of the main courses from a menu while nonchoosers were told that one of the main courses would be randomly assigned to them. Results from this study demonstrated that participants who had choice were significantly more satisfied than those without choice. Moreover, in the hedonic condition, choosers' satisfaction was greater than that of nonchoosers. In the utilitarian condition, no significant difference in satisfaction level was observed between choosers and nonchoosers.

The above evidence suggests that consumer motivation can be tied to perception of control. Specifically, when consumers are more intrinsically motivated in their interaction with marketing messages, they are likely to engage in more hedonic consumption experiences. Such experience is more consistent with the value of having control, which has also been argued to be motivational and self-determining (Burger & Cooper, 1979). As a result, perceived control may lead to a more positive effect when consumers are intrinsically motivated. Despite being a relevant factor, consumer motivation and its relationship with perceived control have not been explored in an interactive marketing context. As technology advancement fuels the growth of interactive marketing with more powerful tools, it is worth investigating consumers' motivations to adopt and interact with these sophisticated technologies, such as virtual reality and artificial intelligence. Future research should investigate how differences in consumer motivation in marketing activities may interact with perceived control to influence interactive marketing effectiveness.

5.3 *Personalization*

Besides the factors associated with the consumer, variables related to marketing messages may also influence the effects of perceived control. One factor that is particularly prominent in interactive marketing is personalization. Conceptually, personalization refers to the provision of personally relevant content, products, and services based on individual users' unique characteristics and needs (Xiao & Benbasat, 2007). As the application of artificial intelligence, big data, and social recommendation system increases more focused and personalized marketing activities (Wang, 2021), personalization has now become a common feature of interactive marketing that facilitates system catering to consumers' interests and needs.

Marketing scholars have argued that personalization is relevant to consumers' perception of control. While the presumptive advantage of personalization is reduced customer effort, this comes at the cost of restricting consumers' options, which may put consumers in a more passive role (de Groot, 2022; Hoffman & Novak, 2009). Other researchers have also compared personalization with customization, both of which are common features in interactive marketing. Customization refers to the ability of consumers to take control and make changes to the presentation and function of an interface (Marathe & Sundar, 2011). It has been argued that the key difference between personalization and customization is the source of interaction: personalization is system-initiated while customization is user-driven (Lee et al., 2015; Sundar & Marathe, 2010). When consumers are able to customize marketing information, they are taking a more active role in determining their marketing experience. Whereas in personalization, new technologies such as artificial intelligence and recommendation systems automatically generate relevant information and consumers are more passive in receiving the messages. This means that personalization may restrict consumers' active engagement in interactive marketing processes and negatively influence the perception of control.

Despite the above arguments on the conceptual relationship between personalization and perceived control, empirical research on how personalization influences the effects of control in an interactive marketing context is a largely neglected topic so far. Even within the limited research on this topic, findings regarding the influence of personalization on consumers' perception of control are mixed. In one recent study on personalized marketing promotions, Kim et al. (2019) explored how consumer control affected the effectiveness of personalization. They found that when consumers with difficult-choice tasks received personalized promotions, they could more easily complete their chosen task and felt more control over their choice, which further positively influenced their attitude and behavior. But for consumers with an easy choice task, a personalized promotion did not affect their perceived control and attitude as compared to non-personalized promotion. However, one significant limitation of this study is the possible confounding between personalization and choice. The authors manipulated personalization by providing consumers with only one recommended product that was relevant to the consumer's interest. However, in the non-personalization condition, consumers were given multiple choices to actively choose from. Therefore, it was unclear whether personalization or choice influenced consumers' perception of control. Another recent study compared reactive personalization, a type of personalization service offering users options of receiving personalized information, and proactive personalization, a personalization service without option (Zhang & Sundar, 2019). Results from this study showed no significant difference between reactive and proactive personalization in affecting users' perception of control. Since the authors did not include a condition where non-personalized messages were offered, it was also unclear whether having personalized information, with or without choices, influenced users' perceptions differently.

In sum, personalization, as a prominent feature in interactive marketing, is conceptually related to consumers' perception of control (e.g. Hoffman & Novak, 2009). Despite the trend of changing consumers' role from passive to active, from reactive to proactive in interactive marketing, personalization seems to take away some level of control from consumers and enable more automatic and effortless marketing experience. This warrants the research question of how personalized marketing information might influence consumers' perception of control and the effectiveness of interactive marketing activities. However, very limited research has directly investigated the relationship between personalization, perceived control, and consumer responses. Future research should more deeply explore the role of personalization in affecting consumers' perceptions and responses in an interactive marketing context.

6   General Discussion

Newly developed technologies have empowered consumers with a more active role in interactive marketing activities. A direct consequence of such empowerment is that consumers today have more control over their interactions with marketing messages and processes. As a fundamental psychological construct, perceived control refers to people's subjective feelings toward their ability to change the environment and obtain desired outcomes (e.g. Skinner, 1996). Such feeling of control is, on one hand, deeply grounded in the interactive nature of contemporary marketing practice, and on the other hand, closely associated with consumer's psychology processing of marketing messages. Therefore, perceived control can be a key concept to understand the effectiveness of interactive marketing. Table 1 summarizes the perceived control literature in interactive marketing research.

6.1   Theoretical Implications

By reviewing literature on perceived control and interactive marketing, this chapter builds a theoretical framework that explicates the relationship between interactivity and perceived control, the effects of perceived control on multidimensional consumer responses, and possible moderating factors. Within this framework, several directions for future research in interactive marketing are identified.

One area to be more fully explored is the relationship between newly developed technologies in interactive marketing and perceived control. Although a handful of studies have investigated how interactive features influence consumers' perceived control and psychological processing of marketing information, many of them still focus on relatively more traditional forms of interactive technologies, such as the Internet and SST (e.g. Robertson et al., 2016; Wang, 2015; Zhu et al., 2013). As interactive marketing has dramatically expanded its scale and scope because of the newly developed and more sophisticated technologies, such as artificial intelligence, virtual reality, and augmented reality (Wang, 2021), a more profound understanding of how these new technologies impact perceived control and consumer responses would be important. Some recent interactive marketing research has paid attention to psychological processing associated with new marketing technologies, such as gamification, interactive advertising, and virtual shopping (e.g. Hu & Wise, 2021; Kim et al., 2021; Moes et al., 2021; Wang & Chen, 2019). Future research should further explore the newly developed technologies in interactive marketing and how perceived control may explain the influence of interactive features on consumer engagement and experience.

Another area that should receive more research interest includes the effects of perceived control on multidimensional consumer responses. Whereas the effects of perceived control have been tested extensively on affective responses such as consumer attitude, research on cognitive and behavioral outcomes

Table 1 Summary of literature in perceived control and interactive marketing research

Author and year	Interactive marketing context	Control definition	Interactivity definition	Effects of control	Theory
Ariffin et al. (2021)	Mobile marketing	People's perception of ease or difficulty in performing the behavior		• Intention to use e-wallet	Theory of Planned Behavior
Choi and Kim (2022)	Online advertising (in-stream video ad)	Behavioral control is the perceived ability to perform an intended behavior to influence a given situation (Averill, 1973; Ajzen, 1991; Bobbitt and Dabholkar, 2001). In the context of digital media, behavioral control reflects the perceived difficulty of behaving in a certain way on a media platform (e.g. high control means low difficulty). Cognitive control is the perceived ability to interpret and appraise a given situation (Averill, 1973; Kim et al., 2019). Decisional control is confidence in one's ability to make an autonomous decision (Averill, 1973)		• Ad intrusiveness and ad irritation, which further influence ad attitude	Psychological Reactance Theory

(continued)

Table 1 (continued)

Author and year	Interactive marketing context	Control definition	Interactivity definition	Effects of control	Theory
Collier and Sherrell (2010)	Self-service technology (SST)	Perceived control from a self-service perspective is defined as a belief in one's ability to command and exert power over the process and outcome of a self-service encounter. With self-service technology, perceived control refers to the ability to dictate the pace of the transaction, the nature of the information flow, and the level of interactivity	Jensen (1998) stated that interactivity is "a measure of a media's potential ability to let the user exert an influence on the content and/or form of the mediated communication" (p. 201)	• Speed of transaction evaluation • Exploration • Trust in service provider • Intention to use the SST • Perceived value	Theory of Planned Behavior
Fan et al. (2022)	Artificial intelligence	Perceived control in consumer behavior research refers to consumers' belief that they have the means to control the service encounter outcomes (Grewal et al., 2007)		• Satisfaction with the technology, which further influences consumption preference and word-of-mouth	
Hanus and Fox (2017)	Online advertising	The perception that one is able to manipulate a customizable interface in a predictable way	Interactive affordances of customizable media often increase a sense of control in users by means of providing choices that allow users to change content in predictable ways	• Reactance • Product liking	Psychological Reactance Theory

Author and year	Interactive marketing context	Control definition	Interactivity definition	Effects of control	Theory
Hu and Wise (2020)	Online product display (image interactivity technology)	Perceived control refers to the belief about the extent to which people have control over the environments (Skinner 1996)	Image interactivity technology refers to website features that enable the "creation and manipulation of product or environment images to simulate (or surpass) actual experience with the product or environment" (Fiore, Kim, and Lee 2005, p. 39)	• Perceived informativeness • Product attitude • Purchase intention • Willingness to pay	
Hu and Wise (2021)	Gamified marketing	Control has been conceptualized as a key component of interactivity (Liu and Shrum 2002). Empirical research has also revealed that interactive message features can enhance perceived control		• Attitude toward the advertised product • Freedom threat • Reactance	Psychological Reactance Theory

(continued)

Table 1 (continued)

Author and year	Interactive marketing context	Control definition	Interactivity definition	Effects of control	Theory
Kirk et al. (2015)	Online advertising	Active control generally is viewed as a key dimension of perceived interactivity (Liu, 2003; Voorveld et al., 2011). Active control gives customers greater control over the information search and acquisition process (Chakraborty, Lala, and Warren, 2003; Liu and Shrum, 2002)	Functional interactivity is viewed as a characteristic, feature, property, or capability inherent in a medium (Kim et al., 2011)—such as hyperlinks, clickable maps, or graphics—that can be user-modified. Research in marketing, however, takes the view that a device or interface is interactive only truly if a consumer perceives it to be so	• Attitude • Behavioral intention to adopt the digital product	
Lee et al. (2018)	Gamified marketing; augmented reality	We define perceived control as the users' sense that the game precisely executes their intended actions (Koufaris, 2002). In a computer game context, perceived control is also related to the user interface. A well-designed user interface helps users control their actions in the game		• Flow, which mediates the effect on game satisfaction and game stickiness	Flow Theory
Li and Yin (2021)	online advertising	Perceived control, which is a psychological need, refers to the cognitive condition of the individual's ability to control a specific environment (Quick & Stephenson, 2007)		• Perceived intrusiveness • Ad avoidance intention	Theory of Planned Behavior

Author and year	Interactive marketing context	Control definition	Interactivity definition	Effects of control	Theory
Moes et al. (2021)	In-store interactive advertising screens	Self-agency refers to the feeling that one shapes her/his own actions and, therefore, is frequently intertwined with freedom of choice	Based on different interactivity types, Liu and Shrum (2002, p. 54) propose the following definition of interactivity: "The degree to which two or more communication parties can act on each other, on the communication medium, and on the messages and the degree to which such influences are synchronized	• Impulse-visit urges • Impulse-buying urges	Psychological Reactance Theory
Nelson et al. (2006)	Gamified marketing	We manipulate control by instructing participants to play (user control) or watch (computer-control) the game	Games typically provide a different type of interactive environment from other media, including interactive online media. According to Grodal (2000): "a video game provides an interactive interface, which enables the player to control actions and often also perceptions by an ability to control the point of view, that is, to control the point from which, and the direction by which, the game world is represented. This leads to several dramatic changes compared to film viewing" (p. 202)	• Recall of brands	Theories of working memory and cognitive load

(continued)

Table 1 (continued)

Author and year	Interactive marketing context	Control definition	Interactivity definition	Effects of control	Theory
Overmars and Poels (2015)	Online product display (image interactivity technology)	Potential of users to modify their environments. It has been conceptualized as a key component of interactivity (Klein, 2003; Steuer, 1992)		• Tactile sensations • Perceived diagnosticity of experience attributes	
Papagiannidis et al. (2017)	Virtual reality	The ability to control the relationship of one's senses to the stimulus Users' ability to use a certain technology		• Simulated experience, which further influences engagement and enjoyment	Flow Theory
Richard and Meuli (2013)	Mobile marketing; location-based marketing	Individual's perception of the ease or difficulty of performing a specific task or action		• Intention of using PBLAMA	Theory of Planned Behavior
Robertson et al. (2016)	Self-service technology (SST)	Perceived control is a function of an individual's felt ability to perform a particular behavior, such as commanding the process and outcome of an SST encounter (Collier and Sherrell, 2010)	The capacity of the technology to let the user exert an influence on its content and/or form	• SST satisfaction • Positive word-of-mouth intentions	
Wang and Chen (2019)	Virtual reality	Perceived control, according to the Planned Behavior Theory (Ajzen, 1991), refers to people's perception of their ability to perform a given behavior	Reflecting a perceptual perspective, perceived interactivity refers to a psychological state experienced by users during their interaction with an interactive medium (Wu, 2006)	• Interest in the brand • Willingness to consider the brand	Theory of Planned Behavior

Author and year	Interactive marketing context	Control definition	Interactivity definition	Effects of control	Theory
Wang (2015)	Website	Control of navigation refers to the ease or difficulty with which users can work out where they are on a website and then choose the course of their visit (Wu, 2006)	Web-based interactivity refers to users' perception and psychological experience of the direction, control and time of the communication (Wu, 2006; McMillan & Hwang, 2002)	• Attitude toward the website, which mediates the effects of control on attitude toward the sponsor's brand and attitude toward the non-profit organization	
Whang et al. (2021)	Augmented reality	In new media, behavioral control is defined as the sense of autonomy surrounding how easy or difficult it is to behave in a certain way (Compeau, 1995; Venkatesh et al., 2003). Cognitive control occurs when people are able to predict the next step and understand the situation in performing a task (Averill, 1973; Kim et al., 2019)	Interactivity refers to the degree to which two or more communications act on each other, as well as the degree of synchronizability (Liu, 2003). It can also be defined as "the degree to which consumers perceive that a product presentation is two-way, controllable, and responsive to input" (Mollen & Wilson, 2010)	• Purchase intention	
Xi et al. (2018)	Gamified marketing; mobile marketing	Effort is regarded as the primary means to get sense of control. Prior research has shown that the more effort people devote, the more they suggestively believe that they can control the outcomes with the help of the effort, and the greater sense of efficacy people experience (Carver and Scheier 2001; Higgins 2012; Lee and Qiu 2009; Schunk 1983)		• Game enjoyment	

(continued)

Table 1 (continued)

Author and year	Interactive marketing context	Control definition	Interactivity definition	Effects of control	Theory
Yen (2005)	Self-service technology (SST)	The amount of control a customer feels that she or he holds over the process or outcome of a service encounter		• User satisfaction with service	
Youn and Kim (2019)	Social media advertising	Individuals feel autonomous when they make their own decisions freely without being influenced by an external force (Deci & Ryan, 2000)		• Perceived ad intrusiveness, which further influences perceived threat to freedom, reactance, and ad avoidance	Psychological Reactance Theory
Zhu et al. (2007)	Self-service technology (SST)	The term "perceived control" describes a subjective assessment of control over a task in an environment. In an SST setting, it refers to a customer's sense of mastery over the processes and outcomes of the service interface (Langeard et al. 1981)	The degree to which users can modify the form or content of the mediated environment in real time		
Zhu et al. (2013)	Self-service technology (SST)	Perceived control over SST refers to the degree to which a customer believes he or she has the ability to adapt to and direct the SST to fulfill service needs It refers to the perception of mastery over a technology in a particular situation	SST interactivity is the degree to which a customer believes the SST enables arrangement of the amount, style, and sequence of presented information (Steuer 1992). It is an external, stable, and uncontrollable factor that reflects the ease of the recovery task and contributes to expectancy	• Costumer recovery expectancy, which further affects consumer behaviors such as customer-recovery effort, customer-recovery strategy	Attribution Theory

is relatively scarce thus far. For example, a few empirical studies have examined perceived control and consumers' cognitive thoughts toward interactive marketing messages (e.g. Wang, 2015; Youn & Kim, 2019). However, such effects have not been fully explored on a broader types of cognitive processing, such as attention and recall, which are also fundamental factors to understand marketing and advertising effectiveness. For behavioral responses, most research primarily focuses on consumers' behavioral intentions (e.g. Ariffin et al., 2021; Moes et al., 2021). Considering that consumers today are more actively generating marketing content and participating in marketing activities, it would be interesting to see more studies that investigate how interactive marketing shapes consumers' actual behaviors, such as adoption of new technologies, word-of-mouth, co-creation, etc. Future research that employs relevant theoretical frameworks to better explain the effects of perceived control in interactive marketing is needed.

Finally, special interest needs to be devoted to possible moderating factors that influence the effects of perceived control in interactive marketing. Although interactive marketing increasingly involves consumer controlling and modifying the marketing environment, more control may not always equal a better experience. The amount of control that is most beneficial may depend on both consumers' dispositional and situational factors in interactive marketing activities (Hoffman & Novak, 2009; Klein, 2003). As outlined in the framework, research on how these moderating factors such as personalization impact interactive marketing effectiveness is less frequently found in current literature, despite the fact that conceptually these factors are closely associated with perceived control and psychological responses. The necessity to obtain a better understanding of this topic is amplified by the current interactive marketing practice where not only the consumers are actively controlling marketing messages, but the algorithm driving the technologies, such as artificial intelligence, personalization, and recommendation system, is also determining what information consumers are exposed to. Identifying and exploring how these algorithm-controlled applications may influence consumers' active role in interactive marketing activities should advance both interactive marketing research and practice.

6.2 *Managerial Implications*

This chapter also provides several implications for practitioners in the marketing industry. By reviewing interactive marketing literature, this chapter provides insights into the important role of perceived control in various interactive marketing context, including self-service, gamified marketing, virtual and augmented reality, etc. The effects of perceived control suggest that perceived control can positively influence consumers' affective, cognitive, and behavioral responses. This implies that marketers can work on strategies to increase consumers' perceived control in order to gain better marketing effects. Prior research has demonstrated the relationship between perceived control and interactive technologies and features. For instance, Ariely (2000) studied control as the degree to which consumers had the freedom in determining the sequence of information reception. Recent research also showed that gamified marketing technologies enhance perceived control by allowing consumers to actively interact with gamified marketing messages such as playable ad (Hu & Wise, 2021). Therefore, marketers may apply more interactive technologies and incorporate more control elements in marketing messages, such as customizable options and game elements, to enhance the effectiveness of marketing communication.

This chapter also sheds light on possible moderators of the effects of control, such as dispositional factors and consumer motivations. This implies that consumer insights related to consumers' traits and motivations of using interactive technologies may be particularly beneficial for marketers to design more effective messages. With technological innovation in big data analytics, insights may be generated from big data indicating consumers' traits and preferences.

This chapter also suggests that as interactive marketing technologies such as personalization and artificial intelligence facilitate a more automatic and effortless marketing experience, the possible issue may arise because of restricted consumers' control (e.g. Fan et al., 2022). Therefore, marketers should recognize consumers' underlying needs and offer solutions to enhance consumers' perceived control of the technologies. One possible solution is to offer consumers more choices. For example, marketers may provide several personalized options for consumers to choose from so that they may perceive higher control of such personalization technology. Additional research, both in academia and industry, should explore in greater detail how to balance consumer control and technology control in interactive marketing.

References

Ajzen, I. (1985). From intentions to actions: A theory of planned behavior. In J. Kuhl & J. Beckman (Eds.), *Action-control: From cognition to behavior* (pp. 11–39). Springer.

Ajzen, I. (1991). The theory of planned behavior. *Organizational Behavior and Human Decision Processes, 50*, 179–211.

Ariely, D. (2000). Controlling the information flow: Effects on consumers' decision making and preferences. *Journal of Consumer Research, 27*(2), 233–248. https://doi.org/10.1086/314322

Ariffin, S. K., Abd Rahman, R. M. F. R., Muhammad, A. M., & Zhang, Q. (2021). Understanding the consumer's intention to use the e-wallet services. *Spanish Journal of Marketing - ESIC, 25*(3), 446–461. https://doi.org/10.1108/SJME-07-2021-0138

Averill, J. R. (1973). Personal control over aversive stimuli and its relationship to stress. *Psychological Bulletin, 80*(4), 286–303. https://doi.org/10.1037/h0034845

Ball, T. S., & Vogler, R. E. (1971). Uncertain pain and the pain of uncertainty. *Perceptual and Motor Skills, 33*(3_suppl), 1195–1203. https://doi.org/10.2466/pms.1971.33.3f.1195

Botti, S., & McGill, A. L. (2011). The locus of choice: Personal causality and satisfaction with hedonic and utilitarian decisions. *Journal of Consumer Research, 37*(6), 1065–1078. https://doi.org/10.1086/656570

Brehm, S. S., & Brehm, J. W. (1981). *Psychological reactance: A theory of freedom and control*. Academic Press.

Bugental, D. B., Blue, J., & Cruzcosa, M. (1989). Perceived control over caregiving outcomes: Implications for child abuse. *Developmental Psychology, 25*(4), 532–539. https://doi.org/10.1037/0012-1649.25.4.532

Burger, J. M. (1989). Negative reactions to increases in perceived personal control. *Journal of Personality and Social Psychology, 56*(2), 246–256. https://doi.org/10.1037/0022-3514.56.2.246

Burger, J. M., & Cooper, H. M. (1979). The desirability of control. *Motivation and Emotion, 3*(4), 381–393. https://doi.org/10.1007/BF00994052

Choi, D., & Kim, J. (2022). The impacts of ad skip option and ad time display on viewer response to in-stream video ads: The role of perceived control and reactance. *Internet Research, 32*(3), 790–813. https://doi.org/10.1108/INTR-09-2020-0514

Collier, J. E., & Sherrell, D. L. (2010). Examining the influence of control and convenience in a self-service setting. *Journal of the Academy of Marketing Science, 38*(4), 490–509. https://doi.org/10.1007/s11747-009-0179-4

Cuevas, L., Lyu, J., & Lim, H. (2021). Flow matters: Antecedents and outcomes of flow experience in social search on Instagram. *Journal of Research in Interactive Marketing, 15*(1), 49–67. https://doi.org/10.1108/JRIM-03-2019-0041

Deci, E. L. (1975). *Intrinsic motivation*. Plenum Press.

de Groot, J. I. M. (2022). The personalization paradox in Facebook advertising: The mediating effect of relevance on the personalization–brand attitude relationship and the moderating effect of intrusiveness. *Journal of Interactive Advertising*, 1–18. https://doi.org/10.1080/15252019.2022.2032492

Fan, A., Lu, Z., & Mao, Z. (Eddie). (2022). To talk or to touch: Unraveling consumer responses to two types of hotel in-room technology. *International Journal of Hospitality Management, 101*, 103–112. https://doi.org/10.1016/j.ijhm.2021.103112

Faraji-Rad, A., Melumad, S., & Johar, G. V. (2017). Consumer desire for control as a barrier to new product adoption. *Journal of Consumer Psychology, 27*(3), 347–354. https://doi.org/10.1016/j.jcps.2016.08.002

Hanus, M. D., & Fox, J. (2017). Source customization reduces psychological reactance to a persuasive message via user control and identity perceptions. *Journal of Interactive Advertising, 17*(1), 1–12. https://doi.org/10.1080/15252019.2017.1287023

Hirschman, E. C., & Holbrook, M. B. (1982). Hedonic consumption: Emerging concepts, methods and propositions. *Journal of Marketing, 46*(3), 92–101.

Hoffman, D. L., & Novak, T. P. (1996). Marketing in hypermedia computer-mediated environments: Conceptual foundations. *Journal of Marketing, 60*(3), 50–68. https://doi.org/10.1177/002224299606000304

Hoffman, D. L., & Novak, T. P. (2009). Flow online: Lessons learned and future prospects. *Journal of Interactive Marketing, 23*(1), 23–34. https://doi.org/10.1016/j.intmar.2008.10.003

Hoffman, D. L., Novak, T. P., & Schlosser, A. E. (2003). Locus of control, web use, and consumer attitudes toward Internet regulation. *Journal of Public Policy & Marketing, 22*(1), 41–57. https://doi.org/10.1509/jppm.22.1.41.17628

Holbrook, M. B., & Hirschman, E. C. (1982). The experiential aspects of consumption: Consumer fantasies, feelings, and fun. *Journal of Consumer Research, 9*(2), 132–140. https://doi.org/10.1086/208906

Hu, X., & Wise, K. (2020). Perceived control or haptic sensation? Exploring the effect of image interactivity on consumer responses to online product displays. *Journal of Interactive Advertising, 20*(1), 60–75. https://doi.org/10.1080/15252019.2019.1707729

Hu, X., & Wise, K. (2021). How playable ads influence consumer attitude: Exploring the mediation effects of perceived control and freedom threat. *Journal of Research in Interactive Marketing, 15*(2), 295–315. https://doi.org/10.1108/JRIM-12-2020-0269

Hui, M. K., & Bateson, J. E. G. (1991). Perceived control and the effects of crowding and consumer choice on the service experience. *Journal of Consumer Research, 18*(2), 174–184. https://doi.org/10.1086/209250

Jung, A.-R., & Heo, J. (2021). Does cluttered social media environment hurt advertising effectiveness? The moderation of ad types and personalization. *Journal of Research in Interactive Marketing, 15*(4), 592–606. https://doi.org/10.1108/JRIM-11-2020-0238

Kim, H. Y., Song, J. H., & Lee, J.-H. (2019). When are personalized promotions effective? The role of consumer control. *International Journal of Advertising, 38*(4), 628–647. https://doi.org/10.1080/02650487.2019.1593721

Kim, J.-H., Kim, M., Park, M., & Yoo, J. (2021). How interactivity and vividness influence consumer virtual reality shopping experience: The mediating role of telepresence. *Journal of Research in Interactive Marketing, 15*(3), 502–525. https://doi.org/10.1108/JRIM-07-2020-0148

Kirk, C. P., Chiagouris, L., Lala, V., & Thomas, J. D. E. (2015). How do digital natives and digital immigrants respond differently to interactivity online? *Journal of Advertising Research, 55*(1), 81–94. https://doi.org/10.2501/JAR-55-1-081-094

Klein, L. R. (2003). Creating virtual product experiences: The role of telepresence. *Journal of Interactive Marketing, 17*(1), 41–55. https://doi.org/10.1002/dir.10046

Lee, C.-H., Chiang, H.-S., & Hsiao, K.-L. (2018). What drives stickiness in location-based AR games? An examination of flow and satisfaction. *Telematics & Informatics, 35*(7), 1958–1970. https://doi.org/10.1016/j.tele.2018.06.008

Lee, H.-J. (2017). Personality determinants of need for interaction with a retail employee and its impact on self-service technology (SST) usage intentions. *Journal of Research in Interactive Marketing, 11*(3), 214–231. https://doi.org/10.1108/JRIM-04-2016-0036

Lee, S., Kim, K. J., & Sundar, S. S. (2015). Customization in location-based advertising: Effects of tailoring source, locational congruity, and product involvement on ad attitudes. *Computers in Human Behavior, 51,* 336–343. https://doi.org/10.1016/j.chb.2015.04.049

Leotti, L. A., Iyengar, S. S., & Ochsner, K. N. (2010). Born to choose: The origins and value of the need for control. *Trends in Cognitive Sciences, 14*(10), 457–463. https://doi.org/10.1016/j.tics.2010.08.001

Li, B., & Yin, S. (2021). How perceived control affects advertising avoidance intention in a skippable advertising context: A moderated mediation model. *Chinese Journal of Communication, 14*(2), 157–175. https://doi.org/10.1080/17544750.2020.1776743

Liu, Y., & Shrum, L. J. (2002). What is interactivity and is it always such a good thing? Implications of definition, person, and situation for the influence of interactivity on advertising effectiveness. *Journal of Advertising, 31*(4), 53–64. https://doi.org/10.1080/00913367.2002.10673685

Liu, Y., & Shrum, L. J. (2009). A dual-process model of interactivity effects. *Journal of Advertising, 38*(2), 53–68. https://doi.org/10.2753/JOA0091-3367380204

Lombard, M., & Snyder-Duch, J. (2001). Interactive advertising and presence: A framework. *Journal of Interactive Advertising, 1*(2), 56–65. https://doi.org/10.1080/15252019.2001.10722051

Lucia-Palacios, L., & Pérez-López, R. (2021). How can autonomy improve consumer experience when interacting with smart products? *Journal of Research in Interactive Marketing* (ahead-of-print). https://doi.org/10.1108/JRIM-02-2021-0031

Marathe, S., & Sundar, S. S. (2011). What drives customization? Control or identity?. In *Proceedings of the SIGCHI conference on human factors in computing systems* (pp. 781–790). ACM.

McMillan, S. J., & Hwang, J.-S. (2002). Measures of perceived interactivity: An exploration of the role of direction of communication, user control, and time in shaping perceptions of interactivity. *Journal of Advertising, 31*(3), 29–42.

Moes, A., Fransen, M., Fennis, B., Verhagen, T., & van, V. H. (2021). In-store interactive advertising screens: The effect of interactivity on impulse buying explained by self-agency. *Journal of Research in Interactive Marketing* (ahead-of-print). https://doi.org/10.1108/JRIM-03-2021-0097

Mullins, R. R., Bachrach, D. G., Rapp, A. A., Grewal, D., & Beitelspacher, L. S. (2015). You don't always get what you want, and you don't always want what you get: An examination of control–desire for control congruence in transactional relationships. *Journal of Applied Psychology, 100*(4), 1073–1088. https://doi.org/10.1037/a0038273

Nelson, M. R., Yaros, R. A., & Keum, H. (2006). Examining the influence of telepresence on spectator and player processing of real and fictitious brands in a computer game. *Journal of Advertising, 35*(4), 87–99. https://doi.org/10.2753/JOA0091-3367350406

Overmars, S., & Poels, K. (2015). Online product experiences: The effect of simulating stroking gestures on product understanding and the critical role of user control. *Computers in Human Behavior, 51*, 272–284. https://doi.org/10.1016/j.chb.2015.04.033

Papagiannidis, S., Pantano, E., See-To, E. W. K., Dennis, C., & Bourlakis, M. (2017). To immerse or not? Experimenting with two virtual retail environments. *Information Technology & People, 30*(1), 163–188. https://doi.org/10.1108/ITP-03-2015-0069

Quick, B. L., Shen, L., & Dillard, J. P. (2013). Reactance theory and persuasion. In J. P. Dillard & L. Shen (Eds.), *The SAGE handbook of persuasion: Developments in theory and practice* (pp. 167–183). Sage.

Richard, J. E., & Meuli, P. G. (2013). Exploring and modelling digital natives' intention to use permission-based location-aware mobile advertising. *Journal of Marketing Management, 29*(5–6), 698–719. https://doi.org/10.1080/0267257X.2013.770051

Robertson, N., McDonald, H., Leckie, C., & McQuilken, L. (2016). Examining customer evaluations across different self-service technologies. *Journal of Services Marketing, 30*(1), 88–102. https://doi.org/10.1108/JSM-07-2014-0263

Rotter, J. B. (1966). Generalized expectancies for internal versus external control of reinforcement. *Psychological Monographs: General and Applied, 80*(1), 1–28. https://doi.org/10.1037/h0092976

Shapiro, A. L. (1999). *The control revolution: How the internet is putting individuals in charge and changing the world we know.* Century Foundation.

Skinner, E. A. (1996). A guide to constructs of control. *Journal of Personality and Social Psychology, 71*(3), 549–570. https://doi.org/10.1037/0022-3514.71.3.549

Staub, E., Tursky, B., & Schwartz, G. E. (1971). Self-control and predictability: Their effects on reactions to aversive stimulation. *Journal of Personality and Social Psychology, 18*(2), 157–162. https://doi.org/10.1037/h0030851

Steiner, I. D. (1979). Three kinds of reported choice. In L. C. Perlmuter & R. A. Monty (Eds.), *Choice and perceived control* (pp. 17–27). Erlbaum.

Steuer, J. (1992). Defining virtual reality: Dimensions determining telepresence. *Journal of Communication, 42*(4), 73–93. https://doi.org/10.1111/j.1460-2466.1992.tb00812.x

Sundar, S. S. (2004). Theorizing interactivity's effects. *The Information Society, 20*(5), 385–389. https://doi.org/10.1080/01972240490508072

Sundar, S. S., & Marathe, S. S. (2010). Personalization versus customization: The importance of agency, privacy, and power usage. *Human Communication Research, 36*(3), 298–322. https://doi.org/10.1111/j.1468-2958.2010.01377.x

Thompson, S. C. (1981). Will it hurt less if I can control it? A complex answer to a simple question. *Psychological Bulletin, 90*(1), 89–101. https://doi.org/10.1037/0033-2909.90.1.89

van Noort, G., Voorveld, H. A. M., & van Reijmersdal, E. A. (2012). Interactivity in brand web sites: Cognitive, affective, and behavioral responses explained by consumers' online flow experience. *Journal of Interactive Marketing, 26*(4), 223–234. https://doi.org/10.1016/j.intmar.2011.11.002

Wang, C. L. (2021). New frontiers and future directions in interactive marketing: Inaugural Editorial. *Journal of Research in Interactive Marketing, 15*(1), 1–9. https://doi.org/10.1108/JRIM-03-2021-270

Wang, C. L., & Jiang, Y. (2019). Examining consumer affective goal pursuit in services: When affect directly influences satisfaction and when it does not. *Asia Pacific Journal of Marketing and Logistics, 32*(6), 1177–1193. https://doi.org/10.1108/APJML-03-2019-0205

Wang, Y. (2015). Affective and cognitive influence of control of navigation on cause sponsorship and non-profit organizations. *International Journal of Nonprofit and Voluntary Sector Marketing, 20*(4), 331–346. https://doi.org/10.1002/nvsm.1534

Wang, Y., & Chen, H. (2019). The influence of dialogic engagement and prominence on visual product placement in virtual reality videos. *Journal of Business Research, 100*, 493–502. https://doi.org/10.1016/j.jbusres.2019.01.018

Whang, J. B., Song, J. H., Choi, B., & Lee, J.-H. (2021). The effect of augmented reality on purchase intention of beauty products: The roles of consumers' control.

Journal of Business Research, 133, 275–284. https://doi.org/10.1016/j.jbusres. 2021.04.057

Wicklund, R. A. (1974). *Freedom and reactance.* Lawrence Erlbaum.

Wu, G. (2006). Conceptualizing and measuring the perceived interactivity of websites. *Journal of Current Issues and Research in Advertising, 28*(1), 87–104. https://doi.org/10.1080/10641734.2006.10505193

Xi, W., Jin, M., Gong, H., & Wang, Q. (2018). Touch or shake? The interaction effect between hand gesture and reward setting on the enjoyment of gamified marketing. *CEUR Workshop Proceedings, 2186,* 100–107.

Xiao, B., & Benbasat, I. (2007). E-commerce product recommendation agents: Use, characteristics, and impact. *MIS Quarterly, 31*(1), 137–209. https://doi.org/10.2307/25148784

Yen, H. R. (2005). An attribute-based model of quality satisfaction for Internet self-service technology. *The Service Industries Journal, 25*(5), 641–659. https://doi.org/10.1080/02642060500100833

Yoon, H. J., Huang, Y., & Yim, M. Y.-C. (2022). Native advertising relevance effects and the moderating role of attitudes toward social networking sites. *Journal of Research in Interactive Marketing* (ahead-of-print). https://doi.org/10.1108/JRIM-07-2021-0185

Youn, S., & Kim, S. (2019). Understanding ad avoidance on Facebook: Antecedents and outcomes of psychological reactance. *Computers in Human Behavior, 98,* 232–244. https://doi.org/10.1016/j.chb.2019.04.025

Zhang, B., & Sundar, S. S. (2019). Proactive vs. reactive personalization: Can customization of privacy enhance user experience? *International Journal of Human-Computer Studies, 128,* 86–99. https://doi.org/10.1016/j.ijhcs.2019.03.002

Zhu, Z., Nakata, C., Sivakumar, K., & Grewal, D. (2007). Self-service technology effectiveness: The role of design features and individual traits. *Journal of the Academy of Marketing Science, 35*(4), 492–506. https://doi.org/10.1007/s11747-007-0019-3

Zhu, Z., Nakata, C., Sivakumar, K., & Grewal, D. (2013). Fix it or leave it? Customer recovery from self-service technology failures. *Journal of Retailing, 89*(1), 15–29. https://doi.org/10.1016/j.jretai.2012.10.004

Zimmermann, R., Mora, D., Cirqueira, D., Helfert, M., Bezbradica, M., Werth, D., Weitzl, W. J., Riedl, R., & Auinger, A. (2022). Enhancing brick-and-mortar store shopping experience with an augmented reality shopping assistant application using personalized recommendations and explainable artificial intelligence. *Journal of Research in Interactive Marketing* (ahead-of-print). https://doi.org/10.1108/JRIM-09-2021-0237

Zuckerman, M., Porac, J., Lathin, D., & Deci, E. L. (1978). On the importance of self-determination for intrinsically-motivated behavior. *Personality and Social Psychology Bulletin, 4*(3), 443–446.

CHAPTER 7

How Brands Drive Electronic Word-of-Mouth in an Interactive Marketing Environment: An Overview and Future Research Directions

Ya You and Yi He

1 INTRODUCTION

With the ability to facilitate bidirectional communication among a large set of participants separated by time and space, electronic WOM (eWOM) has enabled consumers to obtain or exchange product information and experience at any time and anywhere. In recent years, eWOM has certainly revolutionized the consumer experience. A recent survey shows that nearly nine out of ten (89%) consumers worldwide make the effort to read reviews before buying products (Trustpilot, 2020). Similarly, the latest online review statistics show that nearly four in five (79%) consumers mention that they trust the reviews they read online as much as personal recommendations (BrightLocal, 2020). These studies indicate that eWOM has become a credible source of information about products or services and has also had a significant impact on consumer purchase behaviors. From a firm's perspective, social media expenditures have increased from 3.5% of marketing budgets in 2009 to 58% in 2021, especially during the pandemic (The CMO Survey, 2021). Recognizing the power of eWOM, companies now actively utilize various branding strategies

Y. You (✉) · Y. He
College of Business and Economics, California State University, East Bay, Hayward, CA, USA
e-mail: ya.you@csueastbay.edu

Y. He
e-mail: yi.he@csueastbay.edu

to motivate consumers to engage with the brand and become online brand advocates.

Which kind of brands will drive more eWOM? How do brand characteristics affect eWOM? How does the new interactive marketing environment facilitate the way consumers talk about the brands? How can brands leverage interactive marketing tools and promote consumer eWOM? These are important questions for academic scholars and managers to explore. In particular, the construct of eWOM is considered to be multifaceted, which has multiple components such as eWOM modality, eWOM valence, and eWOM audience size.

Thus, this chapter aims to synthesize the literature on brand characteristics and relationships and eWOM from a variety of fields such as marketing and management to offer a comprehensive conceptual framework that describes the role of brand characteristics/relationships as an important antecedent of eWOM in the interactive marketing environment, and to provide insightful research questions regarding how branding influences eWOM in the rapidly changing interactive marketing environment. Specifically, this chapter applies the "Five As" model (i.e., awareness, associations, attitude, attachment, and activity; Keller & Lehmann, 2006) of brand-knowledge structures (e.g., brand associations and relationships) to illustrate how various brand characteristics affect different components of eWOM (i.e., what and where consumers talk about brands), that is, modality, valence, and audience size, and identifies interactive marketing environmental factors including new age technology (e.g., AI, AR, VR), platform revolution (e.g., social shopping sites, virtual brand communities), and participatory culture (e.g., digital influencers, virtual influencers) (i.e., how interactive marketing environment facilitates eWOM toward brands; Wang, 2021) that may moderate the brand-eWOM relationships (See Fig. 1 for our conceptual framework). As such, the authors offer important managerial insights on how interactive marketing environmental factors facilitate the impact of brand factors on consumer eWOM to guide interactive marketing practice. Furthermore, based on the conceptual framework that summarizes the wealth of branding and eWOM research, the authors suggest several promising future research directions in this fertile ground of scholarly inquiry.

2 Summary of Brand and WOM Research

2.1 The Definitions of WOM and eWOM

Word-of-mouth (WOM) is defined as "informal communications directed at other consumers about the ownership, usage, or characteristics of particular goods and services or their sellers" (Westbrook, 1987, p. 261). Discussing any issues related to products or sharing brand-related contents with others could be considered WOM (Berger, 2014). Prior research has reported that WOM has profound impacts on consumer attitudes and behavioral responses to a

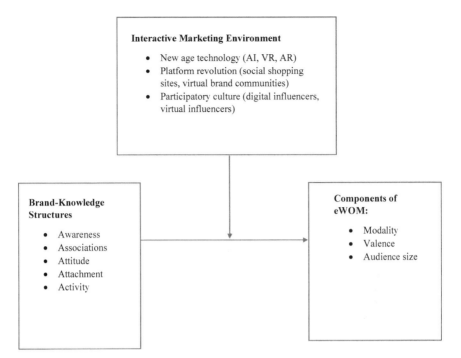

Fig. 1 Conceptual model

product or a brand (e.g., selection of movies, Godes & Mayzlin, 2009; website visits, Trusov et al., 2009). In addition, WOM will affect product awareness, product trial intent (Van den Bulte & Wuyts, 2009), and purchase decision (Bughin et al., 2010). As a result, it has been reported that WOM communications influence nearly 70% of all buying decisions (Balter, 2008) and are considered the primary driving force of sales in two-thirds of all industries (Dye, 2000).

The emergence of new media, which provides all consumers a venue to distribute and broadcast their individual ideas and opinions, has amplified the role of WOM in marketing (Wilson et al., 2012). Electronic word-of-mouth (eWOM) has become a common way of communicating and exchanging product-related information in the virtual community (Blazevic et al., 2013). eWOM is defined as "any positive or negative statement made by potential, actual, or former customers about a product or company, which is made available to a multitude of people and institutions via the Internet" (Hennig-Thurau et al., 2004, p. 39). Within the context of interactive marketing, new media has certainly transformed how information is transmitted and received, and eWOM has become a concept of great strategic importance for most companies. For example, Forbes magazine calls eWOM the most important social media for marketers (Whitler, 2014). Eisingerich et al. (2014), in their survey among 30 senior executives in various industries, find that 82% of the managers actively and systematically encouraged their customers to recommend their company to others. As a result, eWOM has become an important agenda in marketing research (Chan & Ngai, 2011), and marketing scholars have examined the impact of eWOM in a variety of contexts including social networking sites (Trusov et al., 2009), product reviews (Tirunillai & Tellis, 2012), discussion forums (Andreassen & Streukens, 2009), and blogs (Dhar & Chang, 2009).

2.2 WOM Research and Branding

With regard to WOM research, prior research has examined the effects of WOM characteristics, including modality, valence, and audience size, among others, on WOM generation and transmission. First, prior research has investigated the effect of changing communication channels on WOM generation and transmission (e.g., Berger & Iyengar, 2013; Eelen et al., 2017; Eisingerich et al., 2015; Klesse et al., 2015). One important difference is that online communication provides consumers more time to think about what to say and what not to say (Berger & Iyengar, 2013; Eisingerich et al., 2015), whereas offline communication tends to be more spontaneous (Klesse et al., 2015), and therefore, people often speak about what comes to mind without much deliberation (Berger & Schwartz, 2011). Second, prior research has examined different ways under which positive vs. negative WOM is generated, transmitted, and received by consumers (e.g., Bi et al., 2018; Mafael et al., 2016; Rodríguez-Torrico et al., 2021; Wakefield & Wakefield, 2017). For instance, De Angelis et al. (2012) demonstrate that consumers are more likely to share positive than negative WOM during the WOM generation stage, but they share more negative than positive WOM during the transmission stage. Third, marketing researchers have also highlighted the importance of audience size in determining the underlying process by which people spread WOM (Barasch & Berger, 2014; Ju et al., 2017) For example, Barasch and Berger (2014) suggest that the ways consumers transmit WOM largely depend on the size of the audience, in that they often share information to make them look good via broadcasting (i.e., communicating to a large audience), while they usually share information to help others through narrowcasting (i.e., communicating to a small audience).

As another important area of WOM research, previous research has studied a variety of antecedents to WOM activities, such as content characteristics (Akpinar & Berger, 2017; Berger & Milkman, 2012), product characteristics (Nguyen & Chaudhuri, 2019), source characteristics (Muda & Hamzah, 2021; Shen, 2021; Wien, 2019), and incentive characteristics (López et al., 2021). Findings show that emotional appeals are more likely to be shared than informative appeals (Akpinar & Berger, 2017), as well as positive content is more likely to be transmitted than negative content and this difference is partially driven by physiological arousal (Berger & Milkman, 2012). More innovative products generate more eWOM volume, but surprisingly less positive sentiment (Nguyen & Chaudhuri, 2019). Providing non-monetary incentives such as a product free of charge increases the likelihood to spread eWOM, while monetary incentives could have an indirect negative impact on eWOM intention (López et al., 2021). Among the four types of micro-influencers, market mavens and their online messages have the highest impact on consumer engagement on social media (Shen, 2021).

Within this research area, there is yet another important research stream that specifically evaluates the effects of brand relationship and brand characteristics on how WOM is generated, transmitted, and received by consumers (Eelen et al., 2017; Karjaluoto et al., 2016; Lovett et al., 2013; Paharia et al., 2014; Torres et al., 2019). Given the increasingly prominent role of branding in the general marketing research and practice, an increasing amount of scholarly effort has been put into exploring the relationship between how consumers respond to a brand (e.g., how consumers think, feel, and do about a brand) and their WOM generation and transmission. These consumer responses to a brand are typically captured in brand-knowledge structures. While a number of different knowledge structures have been proposed by marketing researchers, in this chapter, the authors apply the "Five As" model put forward by Keller and Lehmann (2006, p. 745) to comprehensively synthesize the marketing literature on the relationship between branding and WOM. The "Five As" model includes five aspects of consumer responses to a brand that form a hierarchy as follows:

a. awareness (ranging from recognition to recall);
b. associations (encompassing tangible and intangible product or service considerations);
c. attitude (ranging from acceptability to attraction);
d. attachment (ranging from loyalty to addiction);
e. activity (including purchase and consumption frequency and involvement with the marketing program, other customers through WOM, etc., or the company).

Building upon the "Five As" model, the wealth of marketing literature on branding and WOM has generally suggested that all the five different levels in brand-knowledge structures in the mind of consumers will jointly shape WOM generation and transmission. In what to follow, the authors will describe the complexity of these important relationships in detail.

Brand Awareness and Associations Brand memory and associations are essential in providing information cues to WOM generation. For example, in a seminal research conducted by Lovett et al. (2013), based on a dataset on online and offline WOM and characteristics for more than 600 of the most talked-about U.S. brands, the authors identified a set of 13 brand characteristics that stimulate WOM. These characteristics are grouped into three categories, namely, social (quality, differentiation, premium/value, relevance, and visibility), emotional (excitement, satisfaction, perceived risk, and involvement), and functional (age, complexity, type of good, knowledge, perceived risk, and involvement). The findings show that whereas the social and functional drivers are the most important for online WOM, the emotional driver is the most important for offline WOM. Other research has also demonstrated that perceived brand authenticity, social exclusion, and brand strength increase positive WOM (Kumar & Kaushal, 2021; Wymer & Casidy, 2019).

Recent research has also examined the effect of brand positioning on WOM intention and behavior. To illustrate, He et al. (2020) evaluate the effect of underdog versus top dog brand positioning on different stages of eWOM generation, from mental representation (i.e., eWOM intention) to action implementation (i.e., eWOM behavior) and the underlying mechanism. The findings show that an underdog (versus top dog) positioning leads to higher eWOM intention, whereas its effect on actual eWOM behavior demonstrates a reverse pattern. Paharia et al. (2014) show that positioning brands against large competitors, that is, highlighting a large competitor's size and close proximity can help smaller brands receive more positive eWOM through online reviews.

Brand Attitude Research in WOM generally suggests a U-shaped relationship between brand attitude and consumers' likelihood of sharing information about a brand with other consumers (Anderson, 1998). Prior research has suggested that consumers are likely to talk about a brand they like as a form of reciprocating for previous benefits the brand provided (Berger, 2014; Hennig-Thurau et al., 2004). On the other hand, as consumers' negative attitude toward a brand becomes more negative, their desire to vent is likely to increase; as a result, negative attitude corresponds to negative WOM (Berger, 2014; Hennig-Thurau et al., 2004). When it comes to sharing with brands, Hydock et al. (2020) find a hockey stick-shaped relationship between brand attitude and sharing with brands. Those with positive attitudes (vs. neutral attitude) are more likely to share their opinion, but those with negative attitudes do not show a similar increase in sharing. Mafael et al. (2016) examine the impact of pre-existing brand attitudes on consumer processing of eWOM. Consumers perceive positive (negative) arguments in online reviews as more (less) persuasive when having a positive (negative) attitude toward the brand. Perceived persuasiveness in turn influences behavioral intentions. In other words, brand attitude amplifies the positive (negative) effects of positive (negative) eWOM on subsequent consumer behavioral intentions.

Brand Attachment Marketing researchers are paying increasing attention to the relationship between brand attachment and WOM. Overall, numerous marketing studies have provided compelling empirical evidence supporting the connection between strong positive brand relationships/attachments and offline WOM and eWOM. Examples of these strong positive brand relationships include brand love (Batra et al., 2012; Kaiser et al., 2020; Karjaluoto et al., 2016), brand passion (Albert et al., 2013), brand trust and commitment (Akrout & Nagy, 2018), and brand loyalty (Eelen et al., 2017). It is also worth noting that brand loyalty is less positively related to spreading eWOM than in-person WOM (Eelen et al., 2017). You et al. (2021) further suggest that the nature of brand relationships and ease of sharing jointly shape eWOM generation. They find that when sharing is difficult, compared to those in a communal brand relationship, consumers in an exchange brand relationship are more likely to generate eWOM. Conversely, when sharing is easy and self-brand connection is deep, consumers in a communal brand relationship are more likely to contribute eWOM than those in an exchange brand relationship. Tuškej et al. (2013) show that congruity of consumers and brand values tends to have positive influence on consumers' identification. Consumers who identify with a brand tend to commit stronger to a brand and generate positive WOM.

More interestingly, positive consumer-brand relationships will make a brand become potentially more resilient in the face of negative WOM or a brand crisis. To illustrate, Wilson et al. (2017) show that when self-brand connection is high, consumers process negative WOM defensively—a process that actually increases their behavioral intentions toward the brand. Baghi and Gabrielli (2021) find that self-brand connection protects the brand when it is involved in a performance-related crisis, although it does increase people's negative WOM when the brand is involved in a values-related crisis. Augusto et al. (2019) show that customer-brand identification can be combined with eWOM to achieve high resilience to negative information.

Besides the benefits that come with positive brand relationships, branding researchers have also provided important findings that help marketing managers to carefully consider the danger of negative brand relationships, such as brand hate. For example, Curina et al. (2020) show that brand hate positively influences offline negative WOM and online complaining. Other research (Kähr et al., 2016) has reported a new type of more alarming negative consumer behavior, which seems to be an extreme form of negative WOM driven by brand hate. That is, consumers who have turned hostile and who are strongly determined to cause damage to the brand. Empowered by new technological possibilities, an individual consumer can now wreak havoc on a brand with relatively little effort. This phenomenon is termed "consumer brand sabotage," and the authors have urged marketing managers to be mindful of destructive nature of consumer brand sabotage and provided suggestions to detect and prevent consumer brand sabotage before it occurs.

Brand Activity Consumer brand activity/experience is often considered the most important part of brand knowledge used by consumers to generate the actual content of WOM. Klein et al. (2016) find that pop-up brand stores' hedonic shopping value, store uniqueness, and store atmosphere increase consumers' WOM toward the brand. Brand experience mediates the effect of these pop-up brand store characteristics on WOM. Wakefield and Wakefield (2017) find that consumers composing eWOM about a negative brand encounter experience anxiety, and the anxiety relates to online impression management. As the brand experience stimulates anxiety (and negativity) while messages are being composed, consumer anxiety leads to the altering of message availability. Table 1 summarizes relevant research on branding and WOM.

3   Overview of Interactive Marketing Environment

Interactive marketing is defined as "the bi-directional value creation and mutual-influence marketing process through active customer connection, engagement, participation and interaction" (Wang, 2021). Recently, marketing communication media and distribution channels has become more interactive as a result of technological advancements, social media revolution, and participatory culture (Malthouse & Hofacker, 2010; Wang, 2021). In this chapter, the authors provide an overview of these environmental factors that reshape interaction marketing.

First, new age technologies such as artificial intelligence (AI), virtual reality (VR), and augmented reality (AR) have expanded the scale and scope of interactive marketing. In particular, these technologies have reshaped brand-consumer interactive relations and improved consumers' shopping experience with portable and wearable devices and highly interactive virtual connections (Flavián et al., 2019). Second, social media platform revolution as reflected in the advent and development of interactive social shopping sites and virtual brand communities has facilitated a new business ecosystem for customer connections and communications. The evolution of digital platforms has helped build a complex network of producers and consumers in an interconnected ecosystem and allowed for a greater level of brand-consumer and consumer–consumer interactions and engagement. Finally, due to digital technologies, the growing participatory culture including digital influencers and virtual influencers has promoted active consumer engagement, which improves consumer-brand relationships. Table 2 provides a detailed summary of each element of interactive marketing environment discussed.

4   Future Research Questions

While the relationships between various brand factors and WOM have been investigated extensively in the literature as discussed earlier, the evolution of the interactive marketing environment offers great opportunities to understand whether and how these new environmental factors would moderate the brands-eWOM relationships. Hence, our conceptual framework highlights the important role of new interactive marketing environmental elements such as new age technologies (e.g., AI, VR, AR), platform revolution (e.g., social shopping sites, virtual brand communities), and participatory culture (e.g., digital influencers, virtual influencers) in moderating the relationships between brand characteristics and eWOM generation and transmission. Next, this chapter will present relevant real-world examples and propose research

Table 1 Summary of selected studies of how brands drive WOM

Studies	Operationalization of WOM	Brand factor	Research context	Key theories	Key findings
Akrout and Nagy (2018)	WOM intention	Brand relationship quality	Facebook	Social exchange theory; Uses and gratifications theory	Trust and commitment developed within the brand fan page will be transformed into positive WOM for the respective brand if fans have a strong relationship quality with the brand
Albert et al. (2013)	WOM behavior	Brand passion	Participants' favored brands of their own choice	Consumer-brand relationship paradigm; Relationship quality theory	Brand passion depends on brand identification and, to a lesser degree, on brand trust. Brand passion relates positively to WOM
Augusto et al. (2019)	eWOM behavior	Resilience to negative information	Airline industry	Social identity theory, cognitive dissonance theory, and self-perception theory	Customer-brand identification can be combined with eWOM to achieve high resilience to negative information

(continued)

Table 1 (continued)

Studies	Operationalization of WOM	Brand factor	Research context	Key theories	Key findings
Baghi and Gabrielli (2021)	Negative WOM intention	Self-brand connectedness	Fashion brands	Brand crisis, values-related crisis, and performance-related crisis	Self-brand connection protects the brand when it is involved in a performance-related crisis, although it does increase people's negative WOM when the brand is involved in a values-related crisis
Batra et al. (2012)	WOM behavior	Brand love	Study 1: Loved and not-loved items, as well as interpersonal and non-interpersonal love; Study 2: Interpersonal love and consumer choice loved brands (e.g., Apple, Victoria's Secret)	Grounded theory, triangular theory of interpersonal love	The nature and consequences of brand love. Brand love leads to brand loyalty, WOM, and resistance to negative information

Studies	Operationalization of WOM	Brand factor	Research context	Key theories	Key findings
Curina et al. (2020)	Online/offline WOM behavior	Brand hate	Service products	Consumer culture theory, consumer-brand relationships	Brand hate positively influences offline negative word-of-mouth (NWOM), online complaining, and non-repurchase intention
Dalman et al. (2020)	WOM intention	Brand failure (higher vs. lower equity)	Technological products	Brand equity and innovation failures, negative WOM and the desire to be opinion leaders, the role of consumer testimonials	Among higher-OL (opinion leadership) consumers, higher-equity brands attract more (less) NWOM than lower-equity brands in the absence (presence) of testimonials
Eelen et al. (2017)	In-person WOM; eWOM intention	Brand loyalty	CPG brands	Brand loyalty and WOM	Brand loyalty is less positively related to spreading eWOM than in-person WOM

(continued)

Table 1 (continued)

Studies	Operationalization of WOM	Brand factor	Research context	Key theories	Key findings
He et al. (2020)	WOM intention/behavior (whether shared online)	Underdog (vs. top dog) brand positioning	A learning website and Kickstarter (Crowd-funding platform)	Lay theory of achievement (incremental/entity)	An underdog (versus top dog) positioning leads to higher eWOM intention, whereas its effect on actual eWOM behavior demonstrates a reverse pattern. Consumer lay theory of achievement moderates the effect of brand positioning on WOM behavior

Studies	Operationalization of WOM	Brand factor	Research context	Key theories	Key findings
Hydock et al. (2020)	WOM behavior	Brand feedback/consumer-to-brand sharing	Study 1: On-campus retailer Study 2: Wireless service provider Study 3: Tech companies Study 4: Cable company Study 5: Wireless service provider Study 6: TV/electronics retailer Study 7: Cable/internet company	The effect of attitude on sharing, the effect of the aversion to criticize on sharing with brands	A hockey stick-shaped relationship between brand attitude and sharing with brands. Those with positive attitudes (vs. neutral attitudes) are more likely to share their opinion, but those with negative attitudes do not show a similar increase in sharing

(continued)

Table 1 (continued)

Studies	Operationalization of WOM	Brand factor	Research context	Key theories	Key findings
Kähr et al. (2016)	WOM behavior	Consumer brand sabotage	Qualitative Interviews: Real cases of negative WOM, boycott activities, or customer retaliation Preliminary Study 1: Real cases of negative consumer behavior/TripAdvisor Preliminary Study 2: Clothing brand (fictitious)	Aggression and appraisal theories; General Aggression Model (GAM)	A conceptual framework for consumer brand sabotage: Consumers who have turned hostile and who are strongly determined to cause damage to the brand. Empowered by new technological possibilities, an individual consumer can now wreak havoc on a brand with relatively little effort
Karjaluoto et al. (2016)	Offline WOM intention; eWOM intention	Brand love	Consumer brands; Facebook	Brand love and WOM	Brand love is positively associated with offline WOM and eWOM

Studies	Operationalization of WOM	Brand factor	Research context	Key theories	Key findings
Klein et al. (2016)	WOM intention	Pop-up brand stores/experiential retail/brand experience	Luxury car retail	Brand experience in luxury retail, characteristics of pop-up brand stores, WOM for luxury brands	Pop-up brand stores' hedonic shopping value, store uniqueness, and store atmosphere increase consumer (WOM) intentions toward the brand. Brand experience mediates the effect of these pop-up brand store characteristics on WOM
Kumar and Kaushal (2021)	WOM behavior	Psychological brand ownership; perceived brand authenticity; and social exclusion	Automobile industry	Psychological ownership theory, extant theory, psychological reactance theory, brand authenticity theory	Both perceived brand authenticity and social exclusion engender a sense of psychological brand ownership. In addition, the findings also lend support to positive WOM and purchase intentions as the outcomes of psychological brand ownership

(continued)

Table 1 (continued)

Studies	Operationalization of WOM	Brand factor	Research context	Key theories	Key findings
Lovett et al. (2013)	Offline WOM/eWOM behavior (# of mentions)	Social, emotional, and functional brand characteristics	Consumer and service brands, sports teams, and TV shows	Brand characteristics and WOM	Social and functional brand characteristics are most important for online WOM, while the emotional brand characteristics are most important for offline WOM
Mafael et al. (2016)	eWOM behavior	Biased assimilation	Study 1 and 2: McDonald's Study 3a and 3b: Abercrombie & Fitch	Biased assimilation theory, dual process theory	Consumers perceive positive (negative) arguments in online reviews as more (less) persuasive when having a positive (negative) attitude toward the brand. Perceived persuasiveness in turn influences behavioral intentions
Paharia et al. (2014)	WOM behavior (# of reviews)	Brand positioning	Yelp	Positioning and branding	Highlighting a large competitor's size and close proximity gets more online reviews for smaller brands

Studies	Operationalization of WOM	Brand factor	Research context	Key theories	Key findings
Tuškej et al. (2013)	WOM behavior	Consumer-brand identification/brand relationships	Consumers' favorite brand	Identification theory, social identity theory, self-congruity theory, organizational identity theory	Congruity of consumer and brand values tends to have a positive influence on consumers' identification. Consumers who identify with a brand tend to commit stronger to a brand and generate positive WOM
Wakefield and Wakefield (2017)	eWOM behavior	Anxiety and ephemeral (self-deleting) social media	Study 1: Consumers' favorite professional sports team from any of the professional leagues. Study 2: Six brand categories (clothing, automobiles, and restaurants) and experience goods (banks, insurance, and hotels)	Stimulus-Organism-Response Theory	Consumers composing eWOM about a negative brand experience anxiety, and the anxiety relates to online impression management. As the brand experience stimulates anxiety (and negativity) while messages are being composed, consumer anxiety leads to the altering of message availability

(continued)

Table 1 (continued)

Studies	Operationalization of WOM	Brand factor	Research context	Key theories	Key findings
Wilson et al. (2017)	eWOM behavior	Self-brand connection	Study 1: Clothing brands; Study 2: Smartphones; Study 3: Hotels	Self-brand connection, homophily, susceptibility to informational influence, product life cycle, product familiarity, brand strength	Self-brand connection is high, consumers process NWOM defensively—a process that actually increases their behavioral intentions toward the brand ara>
Wymer and Casidy (2019)	WOM behavior	Brand strength	Study 1: Coke; Study 2: T-Mobile	Brand strength inter-dimensional dynamics, brand equity, nomological net, social learning theory, social cognitive theory	Brand familiarity has an antecedent influence on brand attitude and brand remarkability, and that the influence of brand strength on WOM is partially mediated by brand preference

Studies	Operationalization of WOM	Brand factor	Research context	Key theories	Key findings
You et al. (2021)	eWOM behavior	Brand relationship norms	Study 1: Instagram social media campaign for the learning website Study 2: Twitter	Brand relationship norms between consumers and brands, ease of sharing of online content	When sharing is difficult, compared to those in a communal relationship, consumers in an exchange relationship are more likely to generate eWOM and pay a higher price premium. Conversely, when sharing is easy and the self-brand connection is deep, consumers in a communal relationship are more likely to contribute eWOM and a higher WTP than those in an exchange relationship

(continued)

Table 1 (continued)

Studies	Operationalization of WOM	Brand factor	Research context	Key theories	Key findings
Zhang et al. (2021)	WOM/eWOM behavior	Brand heritage	China's time-honored catering brands	Stimulus-organism-response theory, consumer behavior theory, brand management theory, cultural theory	Positive antecedent of brand authenticity for customers' in-person WOM and eWOM. The path is influenced by the mediation mechanisms of response (awakening of interest), cognition (brand experience), and affection (brand identification)

Table 2 Summary of elements of interactive marketing environment

Element of interactive marketing environment	Definition	Key benefits to brands and consumers	Real-world examples
New age technologies			
AI	AI "refers to programs, algorithms, systems and machines that demonstrate intelligence" (Shankar, 2018), with the ability to process large amounts of data and recognize patterns in the data, and learn from experience, adjust to new inputs and perform human-like tasks	• Gain insights on consumer behaviors, usage, and preferences • Improve customer experience by offering personalized recommendations, communications, and feedback to consumers • "Word-of-machine" effect stems from a lay belief that AI recommenders are more competent than human recommenders in the utilitarian realm and less competent than human recommenders in the hedonic realm (Longoni & Cian, 2022)	• Amazon's Personalize • Roomba vacuum cleaner • Robot dog Aibo
VR	VR is a simulated experience that typically uses a wearable device such as headsets to generate realistic images, sounds, and other sensations that to immerse users in virtual, often entertaining 3-D worlds (e.g., virtual videogames) (Hoyer et al., 2020)	• Allow consumers to experience and test products or services in 3D in real time, which enhances their product knowledge, curiosity, and enjoyment during the process • Upgrade and enrich consumption for consumers	• Oculus Quest • HTC Vive Pro Eye • Sony Playstation

(continued)

Table 2 (continued)

Element of interactive marketing environment	Definition	Key benefits to brands and consumers	Real-world examples
AR	AR is an interactive experience of a real-world environment where the objects that reside in the real world are enhanced by computer-generated perceptual information, typically using sensors and object recognition capabilities from input devices such as cameras (Tan et al., 2022)	• Create novel and engaging experiences for consumers • Help consumers better understand complex mechanisms and product value • Increase the confidence in consumer purchase decisions	• IKEA's Place • L'Oreal's Virtual Try-On feature • LEGO's Hidden Side
Platform revolution			
Social shopping sites	Social shopping sites are online shopping platforms that allow for customer-to-customer interactions and influence. On social shopping sites, users can interact with each other by providing likes or comments, and either purchase directly on the website or click on an image to purchase from a retail partner (Weeks et al., 2021)	• Facilitate two-way communications between brands and consumers • Help customers to make informed purchase decisions • Improve customer experience through consumer-to-consumer communications and connections	• Instagram • Etsy • Fancy • Wanelo

(continued)

questions on each of these interactive marketing environment elements in our framework.

4.1 Future Research Questions on New Age Technologies: AI

- *Real-world example*: In 2019, Amazon launched *Personalize*, a fully managed AI-powered recommendation service, which facilitates the development of websites, mobile apps, and content management and

Table 2 (continued)

Element of interactive marketing environment	Definition	Key benefits to brands and consumers	Real-world examples
Virtual brand communities	Virtual brand communities are "specialized, non-geographically bound online communities based on social communications and relationships among a brand's consumers" (De Valck et al., 2009)	• Create a two-way relationship between brands and consumers • Reinforce brand positioning by co-creating brand meanings through consumer engagement with brand content • Enhance consumer brand loyalty	• Nike Run • Sephora Beauty Insider Community • My Starbucks Idea • Kraft Recipes
Participatory culture			
Digital influencers	Digital influencers are individuals who have established credibility with large social media audiences because of their knowledge and expertise on particular topics, and thereby exert a significant influence on their followers' and peer consumers' decisions (Ki & Kim, 2019)	• Help brands to build relationship, trust, and credibility with consumers by providing authentic and engaging content • Better reach out to target consumers and connect to wider consumer segments	• Tim "Shmee" Burton (Automotive vlogger) • Huda Kattan (Makeup artist and blogger)
Virtual influencers	A virtual influencer is a computer-generated fictional character that is used in social media marketing as a substitute for a human "influencer"	• Improve the stability of brand image through the control of brand communication • Help brands to develop stronger relationship with consumers	• Gorillaz • Miquela Sousa • Shudu Gram

email marketing systems that suggest products, provide tailored search results, and customize funnels on the fly (Wiggers, 2019).

- *Suggested research questions*:
  - How does AI technology moderate the impact of brand-consumer relationship on eWOM generation?

- How does the interplay between different types of AI technology (e.g., physical robot or embedded algorithm) and brand-consumer relationship jointly affect eWOM generation and transmission?
- How does AI technology interact with brand attachment to affect eWOM valence?

4.2 Future Research Questions on New Age Technologies: VR

- *Real-world example:* In 2015, Marriott International launches VRoom Service, a virtual reality experience in its hotels. VRoom Service allows guests to test the product by ordering the valise containing a Samsung Gear VR headset. The headset and earphones transport the guest to another dimension for 25 hours, the rental period of the device (Marriott, 2015).
- *Suggested research questions:*
    - How does VR experience influence the relationships between different brand emotional characteristics (e.g., excitement, satisfaction, involvement) and consumer eWOM?
    - How does the valence (i.e., positive or negative) of VR experience affect the link between brand relationships and eWOM?
    - How does VR experience affect the impact of perceived brand authenticity on eWOM valence?

4.3 Future Research Questions on New Age Technologies: AR

- *Real-world example:* In 2017, IKEA launched IKEA Place, a new AR application that allows users to test IKEA's products in real time. Users can browse through over 2,000 IKEA products on an online database to make their selections. IKEA Place can also save each user's favorite products, share their selections on social media, and facilitate direct purchases through the IKEA website (Ayoubi, 2017).
- *Suggested research questions:*
    - Does AR application affect the way brand experience drives eWOM?
    - How does AR technology moderate the relationship between brand functional characteristics (e.g., complexity, perceived risk) and eWOM?
    - How does AR application interact with brand positioning to affect eWOM?

4.4 Future Research Questions on Platform Revolution: Social Shopping Sites

- *Real-world example:* MAC, a luxury cosmetic brand, launched the stellar Instagram hashtag campaign where the brand's senior makeup artists introduced #SeniorArtistsSlayHalloween. This Instagram hashtag

campaign encourages fans and makeup artists to use MAC's products, and share creative Halloween looks and new style in makeup (Morris, 2021).
- *Suggested research questions:*
    - How do social shopping sites promote the impact of brand love (hate) on positive (negative) eWOM?
    - Do different social shopping sites have differentiated effects on the relationship between brand loyalty and eWOM?
    - What are the most effective recommendation and referral tools of social shopping sites to facilitate the driving force of brand attachment on eWOM?

4.5 Future Research Questions on Platform Revolution: Virtual Brand Communities

- *Real-world example:* In 2017, Sephora launched a new online and app-based tool called the Beauty Insider Community, which consists of five responsive features aimed to give virtual customers an open line of communication to its experts and fellow shoppers. The goal is to empower customers to create a better shopping experience and make informed product choices (Arneson, 2017).
- *Suggested research questions:*
    - How can brand positioning be strengthened through building virtual communities and its impact on consumer eWOM?
    - Do virtual brand communities moderate the relationship between brand attitude and positive/negative eWOM?
    - How do virtual brand communities interact with brand attachment to drive eWOM within different channels?

4.6 Future Research Questions on Participatory Culture: Digital Influencers

- *Real-world example:* Baggit, a handbag brand from India, launched an influencer campaign to engage their audience and build interaction with them. The influencers (bloggers) showcased the product by carrying a Baggit handbag throughout the event and shared the story behind their new handbag collection. The brand created a pre-buzz on social media with their set of bloggers from Mumbai, where they shared their tweets using #PlayTheLifeGame (Sabharwal, 2021).
- *Suggested research questions:*
    - How do digital influencers facilitate the impact of consumer-brand identification on eWOM?

- How do digital influencers affect the role of social and emotional brand characteristics on eWOM components (e.g., audience size; valence; online vs. offline)?
- How do different types of digital influencers (e.g., micro-influencers, macro-influencers, mega-influencers) affect the relationship between brand passion on eWOM?

4.7 Future Research Questions on Participatory Culture: Virtual Influencers

- *Real-world example:* In 2021, a virtual influencer, Reah Keem, introduced the LG Electronics' latest products during the company's virtual press conference. Keem is a 23-year-old musician and her name means "a child from the future." She has thousands of followers and interacts with consumers on Instagram and Twitter. LG Electronics worked with Keem to reach the MZ generation, the combination of millennials and Generation Z, or those born between 1980 and 2000 (Lee, 2021).
- *Suggested research questions:*
  - Do virtual influencers dilute the positive effect of perceived brand authenticity on eWOM?
  - How do virtual influencers interact with brand loyalty to drive eWOM?
  - How do different forms of influencers (e.g., virtual influencers vs. digital influencers) moderate the relationship between brand relationships and eWOM?

5 Conclusion

In the field of interactive marketing, many have observed transformational changes as a result of many emerging phenomena, such as new technologies (e.g., AI, AR, VR), platform revolution (e.g., social shopping sites, virtual brand communities), and participatory culture (e.g., digital influencers, virtual influencers). How can brand managers leverage these phenomena to encourage positive eWOM generation and transmission for their brands? To answer this question, this chapter first synthesizes the extant literature on the relationships between a variety of branding factors and WOM using the "Five As" brand-knowledge structures model (i.e., awareness, associations, attitude, attachment, and activity; Keller & Lehmann, 2006). Then, the chapter provides an overview of these emerging phenomena with illustrative real-world examples, and suggests potential future research questions. The authors link brand characteristics and relationships, new interactive marketing environmental elements, and eWOM in a comprehensive conceptual model, and propose opportunities to explore complex interplays among these constructs. In doing so, the authors offer managerial guidance to brand managers to take the advantage of such a new interactive marketing environment to promote consumer online engagement, and provide a roadmap to guide future research effort in this line of inquiry.

REFERENCES

Akpinar, E., & Berger, J. (2017). Valuable virality. *Journal of Marketing Research, 54*(2), 318–330.

Akrout, H., & Nagy, G. (2018). Trust and commitment within a virtual brand community: The mediating role of brand relationship quality. *Information & Management, 55*(8), 939–955.

Albert, N., Merunka, D., & Valette-Florence, P. (2013). Brand passion: Antecedents and consequences. *Journal of Business Research, 66*(7), 904–909.

Anderson, E. W. (1998). Customer satisfaction and word of mouth. *Journal of Service Research, 1*(1), 5–17.

Andreassen, T. W., & Streukens, S. (2009). Service innovation and electronic word-of-mouth: Is it worth listening to? *Managing Service Quality: An International Journal, 19*(3), 249–265. https://doi.org/10.1108/09604520910955294

Arneson, K. (2017). *Sephora just launched its own community platform, and we're obsessed.* https://www.glamour.com/story/sephora-beauty-insider-community-platform

Augusto, M., Godinho, P., & Torres, P. (2019). Building customers' resilience to negative information in the airline industry. *Journal of Retailing and Consumer Services, 50*, 235–248.

Ayoubi, A. (2017). *IKEA Launches Augmented Reality Application.* https://www.architectmagazine.com/technology/ikea-launches-augmented-reality-application

Baghi, I., & Gabrielli, V. (2021). The role of betrayal in the response to value and performance brand crisis. *Marketing Letters, 32*(2), 203–217.

Balter, D. (2008). *The word of mouth manual.* BZZ Pubs.

Barasch, A., & Berger, J. (2014). Broadcasting and narrowcasting: How audience size affects what people share. *Journal of Marketing Research, 51*(3), 286–299.

Batra, R., Ahuvia, A., & Bagozzi, R. P. (2012). Brand love. *Journal of Marketing, 76*(2), 1–16.

Berger, J. (2014). Word of mouth and interpersonal communication: A review and directions for future research. *Journal of Consumer Psychology, 24*(4), 586–607.

Berger, J., & Iyengar, R. (2013). Communication channels and word of mouth: How the medium shapes the message. *Journal of Consumer Research, 40*(3), 567–579.

Berger, J., & Milkman, K. L. (2012). What makes online content viral? *Journal of Marketing Research, 49*(2), 192–205.

Berger, J., & Schwartz, E. M. (2011). What drives immediate and ongoing word of mouth? *Journal of Marketing Research, 48*(5), 869–880.

Bi, N. C., Zhang, R., & Ha, L. (2018). Does valence of product review matter? The mediating role of self-effect and third-person effect in sharing YouTube word-of-mouth (vWOM). *Journal of Research in Interactive Marketing, 13*(1), 79–95.

Blazevic, V., Hammedi, W., Garnefeld, I., Rust, R. T., Keiningham, T., Andreassen, T. W., Donthu, N., & Carl, W. (2013). Beyond traditional word-of-mouth: An expanded model of customer-driven influence. *Journal of Service Management, 24*(3), 294–313. https://doi.org/10.1108/09564231311327003

BrightLocal. (2020). *Local consumer review survey 2020.* https://www.brightlocal.com/research/local-consumer-review-survey/

Bughin, J., Doogan, J., & Vetvik, O. J. (2010). A new way to measure word-of-mouth marketing. *McKinsey Quarterly, 2*(1), 113–116.

Chan, Y. Y., & Ngai, E. W. (2011). Conceptualising electronic word of mouth activity: An input-process-output perspective. *Marketing Intelligence & Planning.*

Curina, I., Francioni, B., Hegner, S. M., & Cioppi, M. (2020). Brand hate and non-repurchase intention: A service context perspective in a cross-channel setting. *Journal of Retailing and Consumer Services, 54,* 102031.

Dalman, M. D., Chatterjee, S., & Min, J. (2020). Negative word of mouth for a failed innovation from higher/lower equity brands: Moderating roles of opinion leadership and consumer testimonials. *Journal of Business Research, 115,* 1–13.

De Angelis, M., Bonezzi, A., Peluso, A. M., Rucker, D. D., & Costabile, M. (2012). On braggarts and gossips: A self-enhancement account of word-of-mouth generation and transmission. *Journal of Marketing Research, 49*(4), 551–563.

De Valck, K., Van Bruggen, G. H., & Wierenga, B. (2009). Virtual communities: A marketing perspective. *Decision Support Systems, 47*(3), 185–203.

Dhar, V., & Chang, E. A. (2009). Does chatter matter? The impact of user-generated content on music sales. *Journal of Interactive Marketing, 23*(4), 300–307.

Dye, R. (2000). The buzz on buzz. *Harvard Business Review, 88*(November/December), 139–146.

Eelen, J., Özturan, P., & Verlegh, P. W. (2017). The differential impact of brand loyalty on traditional and online word of mouth: The moderating roles of self-brand connection and the desire to help the brand. *International Journal of Research in Marketing, 34*(4), 872–891.

Eisingerich, A. B., Auh, S., & Merlo, O. (2014). Acta non verba? The role of customer participation and word of mouth in the relationship between service firms' customer satisfaction and sales performance. *Journal of Service Research, 17*(1), 40–53.

Eisingerich, A. B., Chun, H. H., Liu, Y., Jia, H. M., & Bell, S. J. (2015). Why recommend a brand face-to-face but not on Facebook? How word-of-mouth on online social sites differs from traditional word-of-mouth. *Journal of Consumer Psychology, 25*(1), 120–128.

Flavián, C., Ibáñez-Sánchez, S., & Orús, C. (2019). The impact of virtual, augmented and mixed reality technologies on the customer experience. *Journal of Business Research, 100,* 547–560.

Godes, D., & Mayzlin, D. (2009). Firm-created word-of-mouth communication: Evidence from a field test. *Marketing Science, 28*(4), 721–739.

He, Y., You, Y., & Chen, Q. (2020). Our conditional love for the underdog: The effect of brand positioning and the lay theory of achievement on WOM. *Journal of Business Research, 118,* 210–222.

Hennig-Thurau, T., Gwinner, K. P., Walsh, G., & Gremler, D. D. (2004). Electronic word-of-mouth via consumer-opinion platforms: What motivates consumers to articulate themselves on the internet? *Journal of Interactive Marketing, 18*(1), 38–52.

Hoyer, W. D., Kroschke, M., Schmitt, B., Kraume, K., & Shankar, V. (2020). Transforming the customer experience through new technologies. *Journal of Interactive Marketing, 51,* 57–71.

Hydock, C., Chen, Z., & Carlson, K. (2020). Why unhappy customers are unlikely to share their opinions with brands. *Journal of Marketing, 84*(6), 95–112.

Ju, I., He, Y., Chen, Q., He, W., Shen, B., & Sar, S. (2017). The mind-set to share: An exploration of antecedents of narrowcasting versus broadcasting in digital advertising. *Journal of Advertising, 46*(4), 473–486.

Kähr, A., Nyffenegger, B., Krohmer, H., & Hoyer, W. D. (2016). When hostile consumers wreak havoc on your brand: The phenomenon of consumer brand sabotage. *Journal of Marketing, 80*(3), 25–41.

Kaiser, C., Ahuvia, A., Rauschnabel, P. A., & Wimble, M. (2020). Social media monitoring: What can marketers learn from Facebook brand photos? *Journal of Business Research, 117*, 707–717.

Karjaluoto, H., Munnukka, J., & Kiuru, K. (2016). Brand love and positive word of mouth: The moderating effects of experience and price. *Journal of Product & Brand Management, 25*(6), 527–537.

Keller, K. L., & Lehmann, D. R. (2006). Brands and branding: Research findings and future priorities. *Marketing Science, 25*(6), 740–759.

Ki, C. W. C., & Kim, Y. K. (2019). The mechanism by which social media influencers persuade consumers: The role of consumers' desire to mimic. *Psychology & Marketing, 36*(10), 905–922.

Klein, J. F., Falk, T., Esch, F. R., & Gloukhovtsev, A. (2016). Linking pop-up brand stores to brand experience and word of mouth: The case of luxury retail. *Journal of Business Research, 69*(12), 5761–5767.

Klesse, A. K., Levav, J., & Goukens, C. (2015). The effect of preference expression modality on self-control. *Journal of Consumer Research, 42*(4), 535–550.

Kumar, V., & Kaushal, V. (2021). Perceived brand authenticity and social exclusion as drivers of psychological brand ownership. *Journal of Retailing and Consumer Services, 61*, 102579.

Lee, S. (2021). *Virtual influencers emerge as brand ambassadors.* https://www.kedglobal.com/newsView/ked202102100021

Longoni, C., & Cian, L. (2022). Artificial intelligence in utilitarian vs. hedonic contexts: The "word-of-machine" effect. *Journal of Marketing, 86*(1), 91–108.

López, M., Sicilia, M., & Verlegh, P. W. (2021). How to motivate opinion leaders to spread e-WoM on social media: Monetary vs non-monetary incentives. *Journal of Research in Interactive Marketing, 16*(1), 154–171.

Lovett, M. J., Peres, R., & Shachar, R. (2013). On brands and word of mouth. *Journal of Marketing Research, 50*(4), 427–444.

Mafael, A., Gottschalk, S. A., & Kreis, H. (2016). Examining biased assimilation of brand-related online reviews. *Journal of Interactive Marketing, 36*, 91–106.

Malthouse, E., & Hofacker, C. (2010). Looking back and looking forward with interactive marketing. *Journal of Interactive Marketing, 24*(3), 181–184.

Marriott. (2015). *Marriott launches a virtual reality service.* https://hospitality-on.com/en/technologies/marriott-launches-virtual-realityservice#:~:text=Marriott%20International%20is%20testing%20virtual,a%20Samsung%20Gear%20VR%20headset

Morris, J. (2021). *10 best examples of successful Instagram marketing campaigns.* https://taggbox.com/blog/successful-instagram-marketing-campaigns/

Muda, M., & Hamzah, M. I. (2021). Should I suggest this YouTube clip? The impact of UGC source credibility on eWOM and purchase intention. *Journal of Research in Interactive Marketing, 15*(3), 441–459.

Nguyen, H. T., & Chaudhuri, M. (2019). Making new products go viral and succeed. *International Journal of Research in Marketing, 36*(1), 39–62.

Paharia, N., Avery, J., & Keinan, A. (2014). Positioning brands against large competitors to increase sales. *Journal of Marketing Research, 51*(6), 647–656.

Rodríguez-Torrico, P., Cabezudo, R. S. J., San-Martín, S., & Apadula, L. T. (2021). Let it flow: the role of seamlessness and the optimal experience on consumer word of mouth in omnichannel marketing. *Journal of Research in Interactive Marketing* (Ahead of print).

Sabharwal, L. (2021). *5 best examples of influencer marketing*. https://www.mygreatlearning.com/blog/best-examples-of-influencer-marketing/

Shankar, V. (2018). How artificial intelligence (AI) is reshaping retailing. *Journal of Retailing, 94*(4), vi–xi.

Shen, Z. (2021). A persuasive eWOM model for increasing consumer engagement on social media: Evidence from Irish fashion micro-influencers. *Journal of Research in Interactive Marketing, 15*(2), 181–199.

Tan, Y. C., Chandukala, S. R., & Reddy, S. K. (2022). Augmented reality in retail and its impact on sales. *Journal of Marketing, 86*(1), 48–66.

The CMO Survey. (2021). *Managing and measuring marketing spending for growth and returns*, Deloitte.

Tirunillai, S., & Tellis, G. J. (2012). Does chatter really matter? Dynamics of user-generated content and stock performance. *Marketing Science, 31*(2), 198–215.

Torres, P., Augusto, M., & Matos, M. (2019). Antecedents and outcomes of digital influencer endorsement: An exploratory study. *Psychology & Marketing, 36*(12), 1267–1276.

Trusov, M., Bucklin, R. E., & Pauwels, K. (2009). Effects of word-of-mouth versus traditional marketing: Findings from an internet social networking site. *Journal of Marketing, 73*(5), 90–102.

Trustpilot (2020). https://business.trustpilot.com

Tuškej, U., Golob, U., & Podnar, K. (2013). The role of consumer–brand identification in building brand relationships. *Journal of Business Research, 66*(1), 53–59.

Van den Bulte, C., & Wuyts, S. (2009). Leveraging customer networks. *The network challenge: Strategy, profit, and risk in an interlinked world*, 243–258.

Wakefield, L. T., & Wakefield, R. L. (2017). Anxiety and ephemeral social media use in negative eWOM creation. *Journal of Interactive Marketing, 41*, 44–59.

Wang, C. L. (2021). New frontiers and future directions in interactive marketing: Inaugural Editorial. *Journal of Research in Interactive Marketing, 15*(1), 1–9.

Weeks, J. B., Smith, K. M., & Hulland, J. (2021). Consumer brand curation on social shopping sites. *Journal of Business Research, 133*, 399–408.

Westbrook, R. A. (1987). Product/consumption-based affective responses and post-purchase processes. *Journal of Marketing Research, 24*(3), 258–270.

Whitler, K. A. (2014). *Why word of mouth marketing is the most important social media*. Forbes.com.

Wien, A. H. (2019). Self-presentation via electronic word of mouth–a reflective or impulsive activity? *Journal of Research in Interactive Marketing, 13*(3), 331–350.

Wiggers, K. (2019). *Amazon launches Personalize, a fully managed AI-powered recommendation service*. https://venturebeat.com/2019/06/10/amazon-launches-personalize-a-fully-managed-ai-powered-recommendation-service/

Wilson, A. E., Giebelhausen, M. D., & Brady, M. K. (2017). Negative word of mouth can be a positive for consumers connected to the brand. *Journal of the Academy of Marketing Science, 45*(4), 534–547.

Wilson, R. E., Gosling, S. D., & Graham, L. T. (2012). A review of Facebook research in the social sciences. *Perspectives on Psychological Science, 7*(3), 203–220.

Wymer, W., & Casidy, R. (2019). Exploring brand strength's nomological net and its dimensional dynamics. *Journal of Retailing and Consumer Services, 49*, 11–22.

You, Y., He, Y., Chen, Q., & Hu, M. (2021). The interplay between brand relationship norms and ease of sharing on electronic word-of-mouth and willingness to pay. *Information & Management, 58*(2), 103410.

Zhang, S. N., Li, Y. Q., Liu, C. H., & Ruan, W. Q. (2021). A study on China's time-honored catering brands: Achieving new inheritance of traditional brands. *Journal of Retailing and Consumer Services, 58*, 102290.

PART II

Technology Development and Interactive Marketing

CHAPTER 8

Technological Innovations in Interactive Marketing: Enhancing Customer Experience at the New Retail Age

Sahil Singh Jasrotia

1 INTRODUCTION

The advancements in new technologies, including artificial intelligence (Manser Payne et al., 2021), virtual reality and augmented reality (Chiang & Chung, 2021) (Kim et al., 2021) and Smart speakers (Chen et al., 2021; Hsieh & Lee, 2021) and chatbot (Tsai et al., 2021), big data and machine learning (Yu, 2021), etc., the retail sector has moved from a traditional brick and mortar store to an online to mobile and voice-based platforms to the Omni-channel retailing (Wang, 2021). Even the shopping from E-commerce has started shifting towards Social Commerce and Mobile Commerce (Wang, 2021). There have been many technological transformations, and in the upcoming times, there will be many more advanced technologies impacting the retail world (Zaki, 2019). The covid-19 pandemic caused major disruptions around the world and businesses were rocked by its impact. However, the disruption in businesses brought in many new innovations in both digital and physical retail stores and it became incumbent for both small and large retailers to adopt new technologies to survive in the competitive market.

Digital marketing has made the decision-making process easy (Dahiya & Gayatri, 2021). Now people can make many intelligent decisions; they can get an update on the market with just a few clicks and research. People across the

S. S. Jasrotia (✉)
Jaipuria Institute of Management, Indore, India
e-mail: sahiljasrotia93@gmail.com

© The Author(s), under exclusive license to Springer Nature Switzerland AG 2023
C. L. Wang (ed.), *The Palgrave Handbook of Interactive Marketing*,
https://doi.org/10.1007/978-3-031-14961-0_8

globe are still afraid to buy products or services online, and this trend has been changing recently (Guru et al., 2020).

Nevertheless, the driving variables behind their transactions are the same for buyers. People want their items as soon as possible and at a fair price (Some may also prefer to have them shipped and ready inside their front doors). The most popular retailers understand this and at all touchpoints offer smooth service. Only think about it: you can now go shopping at Amazon on your mobile, laptop, brick and mortar store (with a summer order of about $13.7 billion from the Whole Foods grocery chain), or by Alexa. Shoppers shift and forth between these numerous touchpoints. A survey of forty thousand shoppers established that merely 7% shop entirely online and only 20% shop just in stores (Sopadjieva et al., 2017). The study also found that retailers can get more profits by proposing a unified experience to their customers across the cell, desktop and in-store. The survey found that patrons who search for a retailer's website devote 13% more in-store characteristically. However, as customers become more content with digital platforms, in-store traffic decreases.

Digital media is a media form that comprises of various common facts involving digitisation, content, communication and technology (Guinibert, 2022). This type of media can be produced, viewed, changed and distributed through electronic devices. Software, video games, videos, blogs, social networking and online ads are the most widely used interactive media (kalski et al., 2017). Even though digital media is part of our daily culture, business owners are still dissatisfied with digital marketing platforms replacing their paper ads (Sharma et al., 2020). Nevertheless, with the continuous advances in technology, one cannot ignore the impact of new media on our way of life. It affects how we teach, entertain, publish and communicate regularly. Digital media is moving the business world out of the industrial age and into the information age due to this impact. We're not writing stuff on paper with pens anymore but talking with digital devices instead. There is very significant scope for companies in the global market, and there are enormous opportunities for solid penetration, with the help of factors such as population in countries like China and India, increasing people's buying power globally, better internet connectivity, adoption of smartphones and increasing literacy (Amankwah-Amoah et al., 2021). Marketers and researchers can be attributed to the prospect of being a profitable segment in the retail sector. One way to cross the gap is in-store technology, but online, mobile and other user interfaces keep changing, too. The current chapter presents several global innovations for retailers changing the game. The scope of the chapter is widespread as it offers several implications for managers and academicians. The managers can understand the importance of usage of innovative interactive technologies and how with their usage.

This chapter provides an overview of the merging technological innovations for interactive marketing, including physical showrooms for online purchases, smart mirrors, virtual worlds and enhanced, checkout-free stores, facial recognition-based shopping, visual and voice-based search, drones and the chatbots. The chapter is organised as follows: First, it presents a theoretical background based on a literature review. Second, it offers some applications of new technologies in retail industries. Third, it discussed the influences of new technologies on retailing from an interactive marketing perspective, with managerial implications.

2   LITERATURE REVIEW AND THEORETICAL BACKGROUND

Innovations are key in today's competitive environment and the retail scenario is ever-changing with many disruptive innovations taking place in the area. As defined by (Nagy et al., 2016, p. 122), a disruptive innovation is "an innovation that changes the performance metrics, or consumer expectations, of a market by providing radically new functionality, discontinuous technical standards, or new forms of ownership." Interactive Marketing in the past three decades has evolved from a basic traditional form of marketing to the fastest developing business model which offers interactive content to its customers. The primary reasons for the growth of interactive marketing are the evolution and rapid development of innovative technologies. Innovations like chatbots, messaging applications and virtual reality simulations have become essential in today's marketing (Wang, 2021). Interactive marketing is effective in offering tailor-made services to the customers. In varying forms, such as social media, mobile or mobile, Interactive Marketing provides dynamic and engaging content to users with the help of newly developed technologies (Barger et al., 2016). Various studies have discussed innovative technologies and how they are used in interactive marketing. (Hsieh & Lee, 2021), their study examined how AI-enabled smart speakers are bringing a revolution in marketing by changing how people interact with smart products. Furthermore (Tsai et al., 2021) discussed the influences of chatbots on customer engagement and how chatbots are advancing as an interactive technology. Chiang and Chung (2021) discussed how modern retail can utilise augmented reality and bring online customers into the retail settings; the study indicated that augmented reality creates excitement among users and motivates them to buy the products/services. The current chapter explores multiple innovative technologies in retailing and how they create interactive marketing.

2.1   New Retail

New retail is a recent concept in the retailing environment that offers an integrated delivery model uniting online, offline, supply-chains, logistics and information of the organisation to provide an enhanced experience to the customers (Helm et al., 2020). Brands continuously focus on shifting their businesses from single-channel to multi-channel to further towards Omni-channel, thus, offering more possibilities to their customers to transact. The more options a brand provides to its customers, the higher the chances for its growth (Hinterhuber & Liozu, 2017).

The omni-channel model of retailing offers the consumers a shopping experience that is entirely integrated by uniting the offline, digital and every other channel the brand is operating in (Verhoef et al., 2015). Omni-channel enables the connection with all the checkpoints of the company, thus, offering a seamless experience to customers. The concept of New Retail is also similar to omni-channel. Still, it differentiates itself from omni-channel on certain key features that include innovativeness in delivery and experience, effective use of technology where the concept is being applied, digitising supply chain operations, integrating the online and offline marketing, optimising speed and scale of implementation, driving engagement and offering better brand experience.

The New retail concept stores would become the future of retail. The key drivers will be the technological innovations and value-added services, thus, creating a clear difference between traditional stores and new retail concept stores.

2.2   Retail Customer Experience

Present-day retailing is symbolised by the development and emergence of *"Experience stores"* across the globe (Pantano & Gandini, 2018). These experience retail stores offer pleasant shopping experiences to the customers to enhance customer loyalty and satisfaction (Terblanche, 2018). As defined by __ retail customer experience include all those essential elements that motivate or prevent customers from decision making while interacting with the retailer (Puccinelli et al., 2009). Customers involve themselves in various activities while selecting to shop from a retail store; those activities may include ease, post-shopping service experiences, availability of multiple products under one roof and speed and scale of operations. Previous studies have noted a significant impact of retail service experience with enhanced sales, customer repeat behaviour, loyalty, goodwill, reputation, word of mouth, frequent shopping behaviour and image creation (Jalilvand et al., 2012; Walsh & Bartikowski, 2013).

Creating a superior shopping experience is essential for both brick and mortar and digital retail stores to survive in this competitive market (Reinartz et al., 2019). Retailers need to invest in innovative and emerging technologies to stay competitive. With the latest technology, retailers will be able to provide a superior customer experience and generate a loyal customer base. Technological advancements in retail will encourage more customer interaction and involvement, thus creating an interactive environment.

Retailers need to focus on several dimensions of creating a better retail experience for their customers, and for that, they need to have a unique personality which may make them distinctive from their competitors; many studies have reported shopping as a leisure time activity, and thus retailers must work on creating some entertaining and delightful experiences resulting into pleasure and enjoyment of shoppers.

3 Emerging Retail Innovations for Interactive Marketing

3.1 Physical Showrooms for Online Purchases

Physical showrooms for online purchases are kinds of offline stores offered by online retailers to provide information to their customers (Hilken et al., 2018). These kinds of stores help the online retailers to encourage customers' showrooming behaviour. Physical showrooms for online purchases are the stores where the customers cannot make the actual purchases but can have a look at the final product and place their orders. These stores are curated stores for online service providers wherein they can have their physical presence. Most customers want to see and feel the product, interact with the salesperson and know more about it before buying it (Haridasan & Fernando, 2018). These kinds of physical stores by online retailers offer solutions to such problems.

Companies like Lenskart in India have been pioneers in opening Physical stores where customers can try glasses and spectacles to have their frame recommendations and order from their online website and get them delivered to their homes. They have even started with Virtual reality checks for their customers to try and test which product suits them. Home-Décor brand Pepperfry also follows this approach. They have recently launched its studio stores where the customers can visit and make their purchases online after looking at the quality and features of the product. Since there is not much stock, such showrooms need less retail space than conventional stores, so not much retail space is required (Bell et al., 2018). Clients can take a stab at different items, yet they can't leave with any. The "guide shop" of the business has each size that customers could like, and "aides" at the stores help them locate the best match. They need to place their orders in the shop and convey them to their homes. The possibility of display area stores will help pull in more youthful purchasers (Spence & Gallace, 2011). A recent KPMG survey showed that the concept of a showroom store was liked by 55 per cent of Millennials versus 28 per cent of Baby Boomers (KPMG, 2017).

Physical showrooms for making online purchases offer several benefits to the customers and organisations. (i) Benefits to the customers—the major limitation with just having a digital presence was that the customers could not touch and feel the product, whereas, with these physical stores, the customers can see the product first; identify and understand the quality and then make a conscious decision of buying. (ii) Benefits to the organisation—the customer conversion rate can be optimised, lesser returns; thus saving the costs, better customer loyalty can be created and the concept may help generate more sales.

3.2 The Smart Mirrors

Smart mirrors are an interactive technology that offers a real-world environment to the users; it enables the customers to stand in front of the mirror and choose from the variety of products/services provided by the firm (Ogunjimi et al., 2021). Fitting rooms are an inevitable part of shopping for garments, but they are hated by clients (Garcia, 2016). A study by Body Labs in 2016 reported that 46 per cent of customers in a fitting room "hate" putting on clothing (Garcia, 2016). However, according to Warn Tech, shoppers who take a stab at garments in the store are multiple times more bound to make a buy than the individuals who peruse products on the business floor.

The Virtual Trial Room of Zovi.com in India aims to overcome this problem. The Trial room presents a Smart mirror to the consumers, a camera and a screen that records a short video to give a 360-degree perspective on how a garment resembles a dress. A one next to the other correlation of how a customer glances in two distinct dresses is likewise introduced. Many other companies in India are also implementing this technology in their businesses to attract more consumers (Kamble et al., 2019).

The Ralph Lauren Polo Flagship store in the United States uses innovative fitting stores with the smart mirrors made by Oak Labs company. The organisation has installed this mirror in their physical store where customers can see how the product looks on them. They can also change the environment lights, and the mirror recommends different clothes and accessories according to their body types. The organisation's representatives say that after installing these smart mirrors, they have seen an increase in sales up to threefold (Tagiev, 2017).

The smart mirrors offer several benefits to the customer and organisations (i) Benefits to the Customers: It provides different product combinations to the customers, it offers various product recommendations based on body type and previous purchases, it provides an easy check for availability of the product, and it displays the complete range of products that are available at the store. (ii) Benefits to the organisations: It can help the organisation, offer to increase their sales, new data and insights for stores and helps the organisation in increasing their basket size.

3.3 Virtual Worlds and Enhanced

A virtual world or Virtual reality (VR) is a simulated environment created with the help of a computer or other media, wherein the users can feel their presence (Kim et al., 2021). For example, in virtual worlds, the customers can browse 3D images of products in a retail store, travel anywhere and check for visual product representation if placed in different locations without physically visiting the stores. Virtual worlds are created so that they can enhance the user's experience (Kim et al., 2021). There is a similar issue for retailers of bulkier items like furniture: how do customers decide how a sofa would look in their home environment? The response by Ikea is AR applications that allow consumers to get a visual representation of how an object looks in their respective homes. "You can hold the phone up, and the app will calcu," Burrows said. Let's say you've got a six-foot gap. It's going to offer furniture that fits into that space, so it's not offering an eight-foot couch.

Similarly, Tanishq, a leading Jewellery store in India, opened virtual trial kiosks at various places like Delhi and Bangalore airports. Consumers can virtually try jewellery as many times as they want, leading to an enhanced customer experience.

Furthermore, RentItBae, a fashion enterprise started in 2006, aims to offer various clothing from various brands to its customers on a rental basis. The company has installed different AI solutions allowing the consumers to know about the product and its prices and rental charges. The company has also established a voice-enabled system enabling the consumers to speak their demands to the bright screens of the company. Apple is a significant enabler of such technology; the implementations of Ikea, Tanishq and RentItbae use AR kit, the platform for Apple to build AR experiences.

The virtual worlds offer several benefits; it enables superior customer service, enables better user engagement, enables higher conversion rate and better customer retention.

3.4 Checkout-Free Stores

Checkout-free stores are a new concept in the retailing scenario wherein the customers can choose the products from the store, pay from their mobile application and leave the store without even standing/waiting in queues for their billing (Spanke, 2020). These stores provide flexibility to employees to focus on other essential areas, assist in shopping for customers and offer ease.

People in India spend around 7 hours 50 minutes daily using the Internet on any device (Chow, 2021) but for shopping, they love to go out, but the main point of discomfort for shoppers is waiting in queues. Indians, by one calculation, spend most hours a year standing in lines. Although Perpule 1 Pay was released in 2017, a self-checkout app Claims that consumers can decrease their average shopping time by 80 per cent by using their services. The company found the issue of time being wasted by Indians by standing in queues as a significant problem, and being a highly populous nation, the rush in shopping malls can be too much sometimes. Perpule 1 Pay allows consumers to scan products, pay and move out of the shopping malls without wasting time standing in queues. Similarly, other hypermarkets in India have started self-checkout stores to provide their consumers with a seamless experience (Aradhana, 2016).

To make brick and mortar stores effective, retailers should utilise self-checkout to a greater extent, a high-contact insight to redistribute their present representatives (Jasrotia et al., 2019). It provides them with a more significant online point of distinction. The Checkout-free stores offer several benefits: they provide a convenient shopping experience to the users, it saves the customer time, as they need not stand in long queues, it saves time for employees as they are not involved in the billing processes, and it helps in enhancing the storage capacity.

3.5 Facial Recognition Based Shopping

Facial recognition shopping is an innovative technology in retailing where customers can make payments for their shopping through facial recognition (Dang et al., 2021). This system enables a cashless payment system with a motive to reduce customer waiting time; this innovative technology would further grow in the area of retail as it offers convenience to customers and also relieves them from the risks of carrying cash, credit/debit cards for payment (Dang et al., 2021).

What is more appropriate than the application-based checkouts of Perpule 1 Pay? A system where even a smartphone is not required? The catch: it's available only in China, but it is the future that many companies will be eying on. In Hangzhou, China, Alibaba's Ant Financial Unit recently initiated facial recognition payment in partnership with Kentucky Fried Chicken (KFC) (Russell, 2017). To utilise it, consumers need to glance at an in-store stand with facial recognition technologies. Consumers should have installed and logged in to the Alipay app, and then they can visit the stores and just with their face, the application will deduct the payment from their account. A 3D camera is installed at KFC, and consumers have to look into the camera.

Along similar lines, the Indian Government has planned to add facial recognition and iris scan in India for making digital payments which will enhance the consumer shopping experience (Jain, 2020). The recent acceptance of digital payments like Unified Payment Interface (UPI) is a critical indicator that Indian consumers are willing to adopt the new technological changes. Facial recognition-based shopping and price offers several benefits: It provides convenience to the users, it reduces customer touchpoints, it is time-saving and it is secure, as the picture is destroyed immediately and the data is not shared.

3.6 Visual and Voice-Based Search

Urban youths are getting tempted to voice-based services, be it Google Assistant or Amazon's Alexa. People are using these services for playing music, setting alarms, calling and many more. It is tempting to write off this category because the Echo system from Amazon appears to have an early market lead. Companies like Genie are coming up with voice-led services to offer B2C services to the consumers. Furthermore, Delhi-based company Goldseat offers consumers updates on destinations, offline entertainment free of cost based on IoT services and wifi on railway stations, buses and public spaces.

Moreover, when customers ask for generic goods, such as a new jacket or flatware package, Google Home technology can recommend local distributors. Meanwhile, Apple's Siri calls up local stores via Apple Charts.

As the "Internet Trends Study" by Mary Meeker noted last year, voice-based technology helps customers shop while doing household chores, driving, or on the go. It's a magnet for millennials, too. A new Walker Sands study found that 43% of Millennials made a voice-based buy over the earlier year. Customers revealed in that report that the essential motivation behind why shoppers were careful about the voice-based hunt was assurance, protection and the absence of visuals.

There has been a lot of exposure to voice-based communication, but another new way for consumers to find new products is through visual search (Pagani et al., 2019). Google unveiled Google Lens in October, enabling users to point to an object and get an overview of it. For example, Google Lens could reveal to her the image and where she could buy it if an individual sees somebody wearing a decent pair of shoes.

Visual and voice-based search offers several benefits to the users and organisations; it improves product discoverability, offers a competitive advantage, provides an ease to the customer and helps the organisation increase conversions.

3.7 The Drones

The usage of drone technology is on the rise in the area of retail. As an innovative technology the retailers are using drones for majorly two purposes i.e. for creating an integrated supply chain and enabling contactless retail experiences to its customers. The drones majorly used in the retail environment are augmented robots controlled by mobile devices and are mostly used to fulfil last mile delivery.

The drone is a flying robot that can be remotely controlled using a software controlled flight plan in its system (Jacob et al., 2022). Amazon indicated starting Drone services for delivery of its products to the consumers. Since then, many companies have been working on drone-based deliveries. In India, Food Delivery applications like Zomato and Swiggy have started testing drone-based delivery (Ray, 2021). Through this innovation, companies are willing to reduce the human touch involved in the delivery of the products, especially after Covid-19 when people are focusing majorly on their hygiene and want reduced human touch; this innovation can prove to be a great asset for some organisations. The Director General of Civil Aviation (DGCA) in India has also given the go-ahead to these companies to operate at the virtual sight level.

Consumers are increasingly looking for a retail experience customised to suit their personal shopping preferences (Evanschitzky et al., 2015). Studies show that 75% of customers are more likely to buy from a retailer who recognises them by name and recommends alternatives based on their past buying history (Accenture, 2016). Brick and mortar stores aim to appeal to the consumer needs of customers through strategies such as targeted ads and incentive schemes to succeed.

When shopping both online and offline, the average customer now embraces and anticipates a customised retail experience (Roy et al., 2017). This is due to the increase in millennial purchasing power in a generation that is more used to personalisation. Through channels such as Netflix, Spotify and Amazon, all customers have become accustomed to personalised, tailored digital experiences.

Using Drones services offers many advantages; It helps optimise the customer experience, helps in ensuring safety, helps in avoiding physical touch, is time-saving and is cost-effective.

3.8 *Chatbots*

A chatbot is a virtual assistant capable of having meaningful conversations with the users (Tsai et al., 2021). The chatbots have the essence of interactive marketing because they are highly interactive and provide two-way communication and personalised information and services. Retail companies are using chatbots to fill the gap between online and offline experiences. Customers visit offline stores to interact and suggest with the human workers, ask queries and provide customer service (Vannucci & Pantano, 2020). Chatbots can replace all these tasks, thus, bridging the online-offline gap. Many retail chains use chatbots to stay ahead of their competitors and provide interactive solutions to their customers. Retail giant H&M 2016 launched chatbot services allowing the customers to see, share and purchase products from the catalogue of H&M (Jin et al., 2019). Along similar lines, Tommy Hilfiger launched their chatbot service wherein their chatbot would greet the user and then introduces the user to the collection of products of the organisation (Beriault-Poirier et al., 2019).Chatbots can provide the organisations will multiple advantages as they can increase customer engagement, offer unrestricted 24*7 availability, provide customised flexibility and provide smoother communication experiences to customers.

4 Retail Innovations and Interactive Retailing

To enhance customer experiences, the retailers are innovating by bringing interactive retailing coupled with technology as retail innovations (Alexander & Kent, 2022). Interactive retailing involves using technology in distinctive ways that create better engagement with customers in retail outlets (Colombi et al., 2018). For instance, Toy retailer Hamley's creates an immersive experience for their prospective customers at some premium locations where the children can explore things and play to have a motive to visit again. The phenomenon of creating interactive retailing is common now all over the globe, and several brands are experimenting with it (Bradlow et al., 2017). As the customer of today have evolved and are more aware of technology, thus, brands must immerse themselves with technology and change their way of interacting with customers.

Offering interactive experiences to customers makes customers' experience with the brand memorable. It prompts the customers to talk about it with their social groups, helping the organisation reach a wider audience and gain a competitive edge. Interactive retailing offers a seamless experience to customers where the customer can have options from both online and offline stores at once and make a wise decision based on their expertise (Shi et al., 2020). For example, interactive displays allow customers to check a product digitally while being present at a physical store or a physical store and buy it online.

Interactive retailing provokes users to talk about their experiences and create a buzz on social media and among their peers about the unique experience while interacting with the brand (Roggeveen & Sethuraman, 2020). Interactive marketing offers various advantages to the organisation as by providing memorable experiences, they would be able to see an increase in footfall, helps in improving the brand reputation, interactive retailing offers a personalised experience which further helps in improved revenues for the organisation, provides an edge over competitors, helps in gauging customer reactions in a better manner and thus, better marketing strategies can be made. The manpower and other organisational resources can be used efficiently.

5 Managerial Implications to Interactive Marketing the Retailing

This chapter offers various implications for retail managers on how they can make effective use of technology and interactive retailing to stand out from their competitors by providing unique brand experiences. Interactive retailing and innovative technologies would help the retail managers create a niche for themselves and build a loyal customer base. Since the use of technology and creative experiences is not much in vogue in developing and emerging economies, retailers in such nations can become pioneers and gain first-move advantages. Adapting to innovative retail technologies would not only add to their revenues but also help in generating goodwill for their brand. Interactive retailing is getting recognition, and retailers should adapt to this with time to sustain and grow in the market. Retail managers can use social media as a practical part of their interactive retailing strategy and strengthen their presence online.

Looking into the growing acceptance and growth of interactive technologies, retail managers need to instal these innovative technologies in their businesses to survive in this environment. These interactive technologies assist in improving the functionality of retail stores wherein ease of use and process is offered to the customers. Smart mirrors can help the retailers in expediting the purchase decision process of customers as fitting rooms are essential for buyers when they decide on apparel products; smart mirrors as an alternative would assist in their faster decision making (Vidushi & Kashyap, 2021). Additionally, chatbots would create an interactive marketing wherein they can help the customers in searching for the products, getting recommendations and many more; the managers can use chatbots as an interactive tool to reduce the limitation of human interaction prevailing with online retailers and offer personalised services to users. Furthermore, with the help of virtual reality, managers can enhance the immersive experiences of their customers. They can provide them with enjoyment and curiosity about their brand leading to better and enhanced decision making (Lavoye et al., 2021).

6   Conclusion

Retail is expected to grow exponentially, and there is a lot of scope for managers to encash the opportunity. Consumers are shifting and adapting to the digital world and want products and services conveniently. For buyers, the driving variables behind their transactions are the same. People want their items as soon as possible and at a fair price.

Some the Retail companies are finding it difficult to attract new consumers as they don't want to update themselves with the technology. The biggest problem they have is to bring individuals back into shops. One of the ways they do this is to get the digital experience into the world. Omni-Channel retailing is one way to bridge this gap as it offers a seamless experience to the consumers across different channels.

Companies across the globe are coming up with various innovative ideas to sustain in the market and enhance their market share. One such technology application may be an alternative to intelligent/smart mirrors. While some retailers, such as H&M, have introduced innovations AI-based fitting rooms for their customers to try on garments. Progressively, clients are looking for a retail experience that has been adjusted to suit their very own shopping inclinations.

The current chapter can be helpful to marketers in understanding current market trends and take specific insights from the chapter that may be of their help. The present chapter also adds theory in the field of retail, by offering information on recent technologies used in the area of interactive retail which can be helpful for various scholars.

References

Accenture. (2016). *Consumers welcome personalised offerings but businesses are struggling to deliver.* Accenture.

Alexander, B., & Kent, A. (2022). Change in technology-enabled omnichannel customer experiences in-store. *Journal of Retailing and Consumer Services, 65*, 102338.

Amankwah-Amoah, J., Khan, Z., Wood, G.,& Knight, G. (2021). COVID-19 and digitalization: The great acceleration. *Journal of Business Research, 136*, 602–611.

Aradhana, G. (2016). Technological profile of retailers in India. *Indian Journal of Science and Technology, 9*(15), 1–16.

Barger, V., Peltier, J., & Schultz, D. (2016). Social media and consumer engagement: A review and research agenda. *Journal of Research in Interactive Marketing, 10*(4), 268-287.

Bell, D., Gallino, S., & Moreno, A. (2018). Offline showrooms in omnichannel retail: Demand and operational benefits. *Management Science, 64*(4), 1629–1651.

Beriault-Poirier, A., Prom Tep, S., & Sénécal, S. (2019). Putting chatbots to the test: Does the user experience score higher with chatbots than websites? In T. Ahram, W. Karwowski, & R. Taiar (Eds.), *Human systems engineering and design. IHSED 2018. Advances in intelligent systems and computing.* Springer.

Bradlow, E. T., Gangwar, M., Kopalle, P., & Voleti, S. (2017). The role of big data and predictive analytics in retailing. *Journal of Retailing, 93*(1), 79–95.

Chen, Y., Keng, C.-J., & Chen, Y.-L. (2021). How interaction experience enhances customer engagement in smart speaker devices? The moderation of gendered voice and product smartness. *Journal of Research in Interactive Marketing* (Ahead of Print).

Chiang, L.-L., Huang, T.-L., & Chung, H. (2021). Augmented reality interactive technology and interfaces: A construal-level theory perspective. *Journal of Research in Interactive Marketing* (Ahead of Print).

Chow, J. (2021). *Online Shopping, eCommerce and Internet Statistics.* Webhostings.

Colombi, C., Kim, P., & Wyatt, N. (2018). Fashion retailing "tech-gagement": Engagement fueled by new technology. *Research Journal of Textile and Apparel, 22*(4), 390–406.

Dahiya, R., & Gayatri. (2021). A research paper on digital marketing communication and consumer buying decision process: an empirical study in the Indian passenger car market. *Journal of Global Marketing, 31*(2), 73–95.

Dang, V., et al. (2021). Consumer attitudes toward facial recognition payment: an examination of antecedents and outcomes. *International Journal of Bank Marketing* (Ahead of Print).

Evanschitzky, H., et al. (2015). Consumer trial, continuous use, and economic benefits of a retail service innovation: The case of the personal shopping assistant. *Journal of Product Innovation Management, 32*(3), 459–475.

Garcia, S. (2016). *Customers hate fitting rooms—And clothing retailers are paying the price.* Marketwatch.

Guinibert, M. (2022). Defining digital media as a professional practice in New Zealand. *Kōtuitui: New Zealand Journal of Social Sciences Online, 17*(2), 185–205.

Guru, S., Nenavani, J., Patel, V., & Bhatt, N. (2020). Ranking of perceived risks in online shopping. *Decision, 47*(2), 137–152.

Haridasan, A., & Fernando, A. (2018). Online or in-store: Unravelling consumer's channel choice motives. *Journal of Research in Interactive Marketing, 12*(2), 215–230.

Helm, S., Kim, S. H., & Van Riper, S. (2020). Navigating the 'retail apocalypse': A framework of consumer evaluations of the new retail landscape. *Journal of Retailing and Consumer Services, 54*, 101683.

Hilken, T., et al. (2018). Making omnichannel an augmented reality: The current and future state of the art. *Journal of Research in Interactive Marketing, 12*(4), 509–523.

Hinterhuber, A., & Liozu, S. M. (2017). Is innovation in pricing your next source of competitive advantage? In A. Hinterhuber & S. M. Liozu (Eds.), *Innovation in pricing* (pp. 11–27). Routledge.

Hoyer, W. D., et al. (2020). Transforming the customer experience through new technologies. *Journal of Interactive Marketing*, 57–71.

Hsieh, S., & Lee, C. (2021). Hey Alexa: Examining the effect of perceived socialness in usage intentions of AI assistant-enabled smart speaker. *Journal of Research in Interactive Marketing*, 15(2), 267–294.

Jacob, B., Kaushik, A., & Velavan, P. (2022). Autonomous navigation of drones using reinforcement. In J. Verma & S. Paul (Eds.), *Advances in augmented reality and virtual reality. Studies in computational intelligence* (pp. 159–176). Springer.

Jain, R. (2020). *Indian Government to add facial recognition, iris scan for digital payments*. Business Insider.

Jalilvand, M. R., Samiei, N., Dini, B., & Manzari, P. Y. (2012). Examining the structural relationships of electronic word of mouth, destination image, tourist attitude toward destination and travel intention: An integrated approach. *Journal of Destination Marketing & Management*, 1(1–2), 134–143.

Jasrotia, S. S., Mishra, H. G., & Koul, S. (2019). Brick or click? Channel choice disruptions in travel industry. *Asia-Pacific Journal of Management Research and Innovation*, 15(1–2), 16–26.

Jin, B. E., Cedrola, E., & Kim, N. L. (2019). Process innovation: Hidden secret to success and efficiency. In E. Byoungho & C. Elena (Eds.), *Palgrave studies in practice: Global fashion brand management* (pp. 1–19). Palgrave Pivot.

Kalski, P., Neuendorf, K., & Cajigas, J. (2017). Content analysis in the interactive media age. In *The content analysis guidebook* (Vol. 2, pp. 201–242).

Kamble, S., Gunasekaran, A., & Arha, H. (2019). Understanding the Blockchain technology adoption in supply chains-Indian context. *International Journal of Production Research*, 57(7), 2009–2033.

Kim, J.-H., Kim, M., Park, M., & Yoo, J. (2021). How interactivity and vividness influence consumer virtual reality shopping experience: The mediating role of telepresence. *Journal of Research in Interactive Marketing*, 15(3), 502–525.

KPMG. (2017). *The truth about online consumers*. KPMG.

Lavoye, V., Mero, J., & Tarkiainen, A. (2021). Consumer behavior with augmented reality in retail: A review and research agenda. *The International Review of Retail, Distribution and Consumer Research*, 31(3), 299–329.

Manser Payne, E., Peltier, J. & Barger, V. (2021). Enhancing the value co-creation process: Artificial intelligence and mobile banking service platforms. *Journal of Research in Interactive Marketing*, 15(1), 68–85.

Nagy, D., Schuessler, J., & Dubinsky, A. (2016). Defining and identifying disruptive innovations. *Industrial Marketing Management*, 57, 119–126.

Ogunjimi, A., Rahman, M., Islam, N., & Hasan, R. (2021). Smart mirror fashion technology for the retail chain transformation. *Technological Forecasting and Social Change*, 173, 121118.

Pagani, M., Racat, M., & Hofacker, C. (2019). Adding voice to the omnichannel and how that affects brand trust. *Journal of Interactive Marketing*, 48, 89–105.

Pantano, E., & Gandini, A. (2018). Shopping as a "networked experience": An emerging framework in the retail industry. *International Journal of Retail & Distribution Management*, 46(7), 690–704.

Puccinelli, N. M., et al. (2009). Customer experience management in retailing: Understanding the buying process. *Journal of Retailing, 85*(1), 15–30.

Ray, A. (2021). *Food delivery in India via drones? Zomato, Swiggy, Dunzo can start testing.* Livemint.

Reinartz, W., Wiegand, N., & Imschloss, M. (2019). The impact of digital transformation on the retailing value chain. *International Journal of Research in Marketing, 36*(3), 350–366.

Roggeveen, A. L., & Sethuraman, R. (2020). How the COVID-19 pandemic may change the world of retailing. *Journal of Retailing, 96*(2), 169–171.

Roy, S., et al. (2017). Constituents and consequences of smart customer experience in retailing. *Technological Forecasting and Social Change, 124*, 257–270.

Russell, J. (2017). *TechCrunch is now a part of Verizon Media.* Techcrunch.

Sharma, A., Sharma, S., & Chaudhary, M. (2020). Are small travel agencies ready for digital marketing? Views of travel agency managers. *Tourism Management, 79*, 104–178.

Shi, S., Wang, Y., Chen, X., & Zhang, Q. (2020). Conceptualization of omnichannel customer experience and its impact on shopping intention: A mixed-method approach. *International Journal of Information Management, 50*, 325–336.

Sopadjieva, E., Dholakia, U., & Benjamin, B. (2017). A Study of 46000 shoppers shows that omnichannel retailing works. *Harvard Business Review, 3*, 1–2.

Spanke, M. (2020). Easy checkout. *Retail isn't dead* (pp. 85–93). Palgrave Macmillan.

Spence, C., & Gallace, A. (2011). Multisensory design: Reaching out to touch the consumer. *Psychology & Marketing, 28*(3), 267–308.

Tagiev, R. (2017). *Facelet* [Online] Available at: https://www.facelet.com/en-us/blog/smart-fitting-rooms-how-they-work-and-why-stores-need-them/ [Accessed 29 December 2021].

Terblanche, N. S. (2018). Revisiting the supermarket in-store customer shopping experience. *Journal of Retailing and Consumer Services, 40*, 48–59.

Tsai, W.-H., Liu, Y., & Chuan, C.-H. (2021). How chatbots' social presence communication enhances consumer engagement: The mediating role of parasocial interaction and dialogue. *Journal of Research in Interactive Marketing, 15*(3), 460–482.

Vannucci, V., & Pantano, E. (2020). Digital or human touchpoints? Insights from consumer-facing in-store services. *Information Technology & People, 33*(1), 296–310.

Verhoef, P. C., Kannan, P. K., & Inman, J. J. (2015). From multi-channel retailing to omni-channel retailing: Introduction to the special issue on multi-channel retailing. *Journal of Retailing, 91*(2), 174–181.

Vidushi, V., & Kashyap, R. (2021). Reconfigure the apparel retail stores with interactive technologies. *Research Journal of Textile and Apparel* (Ahead of Print).

Walsh, G., & Bartikowski, B. (2013). Exploring corporate ability and social responsibility associations as antecedents of customer satisfaction cross-culturally. *Journal of Business Research, 66*(8), 989–995.

Wang, C. (2021). New frontiers and future directions in interactive marketing: Inaugural Editorial. *Journal of Research in Interactive Marketing, 15*(1), 1–9.

Yu, B. (2021). How consumer opinions are affected by marketers: an empirical examination by deep learning approach. *Journal of Research in Interactive Marketing* (Ahead of Print).

Zaki, M. (2019). Digital transformation: Harnessing digital technologies for the next generation of services. *Journal of Services Marketing, 33*(4), 429–435.

CHAPTER 9

The Role of Artificial Intelligence in Interactive Marketing: Improving Customer-Brand Relationship

Wajeeha Aslam and Kashif Farhat

1 INTRODUCTION

Interactive marketing is a "bi-directional value generation and mutual-influence marketing process through active consumer connection, engagement, involvement, and interaction" (Wang, 2021, p. 1). The evolving concept of "interactive marketing" forced the technologies for advancement and innovation (Wang, 2021), and vice versa. For example, AI has brought a significant revolution in business markets (Cheng & Jiang, 2022; Kietzmann & Pitt, 2020), and become a fundamental part of marketing practice. AI-based service provides brand-related information and enables two-way communication (Hsieh & Lee, 2021). The chatbot (an interactive messaging service) powered by AI has gained popularity at a rapid rate (Cheng & Jiang, 2022), and has been introduced on many consumer-facing platforms (Li et al., 2021). A rising number of organizations are transitioning from traditional customer care methods to chatbot digital solutions across many industries (Forbes, 2017). This transition allows customers to communicate 24/7 and from any location (Cheng & Jiang, 2020) at a lower cost (Pantano & Pizzi, 2020). Hence, chatbots benefit both customers and businesses as they offer

W. Aslam (✉)
IQRA University, Karachi, Pakistan
e-mail: wajeeha_aslam_87@live.com

K. Farhat
Higher Colleges of Technology, Sharjah, United Arab Emirates

© The Author(s), under exclusive license to Springer Nature Switzerland AG 2023
C. L. Wang (ed.), *The Palgrave Handbook of Interactive Marketing*,
https://doi.org/10.1007/978-3-031-14961-0_9

flexibility, accessibility, and low-cost operations in comparison with a human assistant (Aslam et al., 2022).

Chatbots are developed to interact with humans, and due to continual developments in AI to replicate natural language, it is expected that they will replace human agents (Kumar et al., 2016). Instead of one-way sales, the human–computer connection allows firms to create deeper relationships with customers through continuing and tailored "dialogues" (Huang & Rust, 2018; Rajkumar & Ganapathy, 2020). Hence, it promotes the concept of "interactive marketing" as it offers customers to relish the interactive process on a deeper level (Verma et al., 2021; Wang, 2021).

From 2019 to 2026, the chatbot sector is expected to develop at the fastest rate in the customer service area, with a compound annual growth rate of 31.6%. (Business Insider, 2020). The effective role of chatbots especially rose to prominence during the Covid-19 pandemic to gather information, determine the potential products, and pick the brands for customers to purchase while many countries enforced lockdown and interacting with on-floor staff in retail stores was not possible (Li et al., 2021). Though chatbots have gained importance in the business industry, however before implementation, it is essential for the marketers to know the key service quality dimensions (Jain et al., 2018; Li et al., 2021) that affect the customer-brand relationship and the response. Mainstream studies emphasized on the features and the applications of AI-based technologies for marketers (Chung et al., 2018; Kietzmann et al., 2018). However, there is a dearth of literature available related to the aspects of chatbot service quality. Jain et al. (2018) also emphasized considering chatbot service quality dimensions before implementing in business. Moreover, the past literature has not evident the impact of customer-brand relationship on consumer response (Cheng & Jiang, 2022). Hence, it is important to discuss the linkage of chatbot service quality with customer-brand relationships and with customer responses. The studies that have considered customer response mainly focused on the attitudinal responses of the consumer in the context of chatbots and have ignored the behavioral aspect of the response, for example, e-WOM (Cheng & Jiang, 2022). Marketing literature has endorsed that strong brand relations motivate the customers to create WOM i.e., a voluntary behavior of the consumer and show customer participation. The recent study also suggested examining the link between chatbot services with e-WOM in relation to brand-relationship factors (Eren, 2021).

Thus, in light of the foregoing literature gaps, this chapter aims to identify the influence of chatbot service quality dimensions on customer-brand relationship and their impact on e-WOM (i.e., response). The chapter considers stimulus-organism-response (S-O-R) theory as a theoretical ground to explain the relation of chatbot service quality dimensions with customer-brand relationship and e-WOM. The chapter has numerous theoretical and managerial contributions in the field of interactive marketing and offers useful insights related to the chatbot service quality dimensions that foster brand-relationship. This is one of the earlier chapters that have introduced the S-O-R model in explaining the context of chatbot-based service. The chapter also highlighted e-WOM as a behavioral response and an antecedent of customer-brand relationship that is absent in earlier literature on AI. Moreover, the chapter offers critical insights to businesses to enjoy the benefits of AI in fostering interactive marketing.

The chapter is organized as follows: In Sect. 2, the chatbot service quality dimensions are introduced and discussed. In Sect. 3, the conceptualization of the customer-brand relationship and its dimension are mentioned followed by Sect. 4 which explains the response of the consumer, based on the customer-brand relationship. Section 5 presents the theoretical background that explained the flow of the proposed model. Lastly, Sect. 6 provides a discussion, conclusion, implications, and area for future research.

2 Chatbot Service Quality Dimensions

Customers' perception of service quality has long been considered a key aspect in firms' efforts to differentiate their products and services from the competitors (Parasuraman et al., 1988). Therefore, to improve the service quality of the firms, several studies have proposed quality dimensions in the field of information systems (IS) (DeLone & McLean, 2003; Lee et al., 2002; Nelson et al., 2005; Parasuraman et al., 1988; Wang & Strong, 1996; Zmud, 1978). The SERVQUAL model proposed by Parasuraman et al. (1988) has arguably gained the highest popularity among other quality models in the literature. The SERVQUAL dimensions (tangibles, reliability, responsiveness, assurance, and empathy) were proposed for service industry i.e., banking, appliance repair, and telecommunication, and several studies have endorsed the importance of these dimensions (Ali & Raza, 2017; Li et al., 2021). However, Bloemer et al. (1999) argued that service quality is a multi-dimensional concept while other scholars contended that service quality dimensions may vary on basis of the situation and context (Kuo et al., 2009). Hence, a variety of service quality dimensions have featured in the literature for various services such as for e-commerce services (DeLone & McLean, 1992), e-service quality (Jun et al., 2004), etc. Hence, the scholars agree that service quality dimensions may vary according to the context and the information system type (Li et al., 2021). The studies have categorized the quality dimensions in numerous categories. For example, system-related, service-related, and information-related (Li et al., 2021). However, some of the quality dimensions fit in different fields, such as accessibility and reliability lie in both system-related and service-related (Nelson et al., 2005; Wang & Strong, 1996). Hence, the dimensions of the service quality were considered based on technical and service aspects (Li et al., 2021).

In the context of chatbots, three dimensions are proposed by Parasuraman et al. (1988); reliability, responsiveness, and assurance are salient to explore. These dimensions of service quality were proposed to determine the service of the telecommunication and banking industry, and hence it is somehow relevant to the chatbot service. In the past, Li et al. (2021) also considered these as a quality dimension of chatbot service. The term *reliability* refers to the system or service "has the ability to perform the promised service dependably and accurately" (Parasuraman et al., 1988, p. 23), and hence, in the context of a chatbot, it refers to the chatbot service's ability to provide reliable and accurate service. The term *responsiveness* refers to the system or service's "capability to help users and provide prompt service to users" (Parasuraman et al., 1988, p. 23), and it is critical for chatbot-based services to respond promptly. The studies related to chatbots have considered the element of responsiveness as "accessibility", and have interchangeably used this term to explain timely responses by the chatbot service. Lastly, the term *assurance* refers to the system or service's "knowledge and ability to inspire trust and confidence" in the user (Parasuraman et al., 1988, p. 23). Therefore, in the context of a chatbot, it refers to the perception of the users for chatbot-based service being trustworthy and knowledgeable to respond.

Moreover, chatbots are meant to be equipped with natural language processing (NLP) technologies that allow them to interpret human dialogue and engage in interactive conversations with people (Li et al., 2021). The literature considered two more quality dimensions, namely *understandability* (McKinney et al., 2002) and *interactivity* for the smart technologies (Cho et al., 2019), and hence, for the chatbot-based service these two dimensions are relevant as these reflect the ability to interpret human discourse and provide interactive discussions. The term *understandability* refers to the "user's perception that a chatbot service understands human dialogues, the context of a conversation, and the nuance of human language" (Li et al., 2021), and the term *interactivity* refers to "a user's perception that her/his communications with a chatbot service resemble the dialogues she/he has with human agents" (Cho et al., 2019). Various studies have argued that the ability to comprehend human conversation is the essential assessment benchmark to determine the quality of chatbot service (Kuligowska, 2015; Nguyen, 2019). Park et al. (2018) designed a study to examine the quality of chatbots by their capability of understanding human conversation. The studies also comprehend that chatbots who understand human dialogues intelligently are more likable (Nguyen, 2019; Sensuse et al., 2019). Lastly, interactivity is considered a distinguishing factor for end-users as it offers increased engagement (Neuhofer et al., 2015), humanness (Go & Sundar, 2019), and improved perceived quality (Li et al., 2021). Hence, the quality of the interactivity can influence the evaluation of the service.

Figure 1 presents the five dimensions of a chatbot service quality i.e., reliability, responsiveness, assurance, understandability, and interactivity.

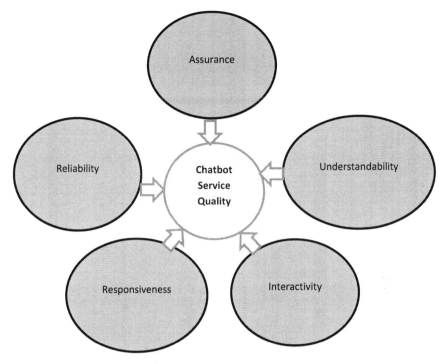

Fig. 1 Chatbot service quality

3 Customer-Brand Relationship (CUBR)

With the proliferation of brands and the competition, today's brands seek to build relationships aiming for a long-term and reciprocal engagement with their customers (Morgan-Thomas et al., 2020). The advancements in the field of online marketing and technology also encourage the concept of interactive marketing as it allows two-way communication that increases brand relationships through active participation, interaction, and engagement. This bi-directional relationship mutually benefits both customers and businesses (Wang, 2021).

Brand relations can be individual and collective (Veloutsou & Ruiz-Mafé, 2020). Individual brand-centric relationships exist when consumers act as self-contained individuals and interact with brands, forming emotional or even functional bonds with them (Veloutsou, 2007). In contrast, collective brand-centric relationships are "relationships that members/affiliates of brand-focused groups, such as brand communities and brand tribes, develop as individuals with other group members, other individuals associated with the group, or as a collective with the brand" (Cova & Pace, 2006). However, this chapter focuses on the individual aspect as a customer-brand relationship, and hence consumers are considered independent entities (Cheng & Jiang,

Table 1 Dimensions of customer-brand relationship

	Definitions
Commitment	A customer's level of attachment or expectation for a continuous relationship with a brand
Trust	A level of confidence of a customer on a brand
Control mutuality	The degree to which parties agree on who has rightful power to influence one another
Satisfaction	The pleasing experience of a customer with the brand

2022). Scholars from several disciplines have considered multiple components to measure customer-brand relationships (Cheng & Jiang, 2022). For example, a theoretical framework was proposed in which the brand is viewed as an important partner in consumer relationships measured through commitment, partner quality, love, passion, intimacy, and self-connection, conceived as the five components of a customer-brand relationship (Fournier, 1998). Another theoretical paradigm is composed of three characteristics of the customer-brand relationship: satisfaction, trust, and affective commitment (Zhang & Bloemer, 2008). Since brands must sustain strong consumer relationships, one notable notion of this relationship construct includes four strength indicators: commitment, self-connection, intimacy, and satisfaction (Jeon & Baeck, 2016). Among all, Grunig and Huang (2000) proposed the most prominent frameworks that grounded customer-brand relationships in the sub-dimensions: commitment, trust, control mutuality, and satisfaction. Many relationship management studies have embraced the model conceptualized by Grunig and Huang (Cheng, 2020). For instance, Cheng and Jiang (2022) employed the dimensions of commitment, trust, control mutuality, and satisfaction as sub-dimensions of customer-brand relationships in the context of chatbots. Having discussed this, the chapter considers *commitment*, *trust*, *control mutuality*, and *satisfaction* as sub-dimensions of the customer-brand relationship as suggested by Grunig and Huang (2000). Table 1 present the definitions of the dimensions of the customer-brand relationship.

4 Response

In the past, marketing literature has demonstrated numerous customer responses arising from the brand relationship. Studies have divided customer responses into behavioral and attitudinal responses. Behavioral responses reflect the choice of the customer to remain with the firm or brand (Athanassopoulos et al., 2001), and attitudinal responses reflect the person's attitude or feeling toward the brand. Studies have discussed various responses such as word-of-mouth, patronage, loyalty, etc. (Martínez & Del Bosque, 2013; Kim & Ham, 2016).

In the context of chatbots, Cheng and Jiang (2022) considered the attitudinal customer's responses such as brand preference, brand loyalty, and purchase intention as customer responses and neglected various other behavioral responses of the consumer such as WOM. Even though, studies in the past have furnished evidence that consumer relationship with the brand also affects behavioral responses such as WOM (Anderson & Mittal, 2000; Aslam & Farhat, 2020). The study of Cheng and Jiang (2022) also suggested that future studies consider e-WOM as a response of the consumer in studies related to chatbots. Therefore, considering the highlighted gap, this chapter considers e-WOM as a response to the customer-brand relationship.

5   Theoretical Background

For developing a connection in between the chatbot service quality dimensions, customer-brand relationship, and e-WOM, stimulus-organism-response (S-O-R) theory is considered, which explains the mechanism of the system that supports a customer's attitude and actions (Russell & Mehrabian, 1974). This theory is developed in the field of environmental psychology, but it is also effective in a variety of other areas, including consumer behavior and decision-making (Arif et al., 2020; Sohaib & Kang, 2015). The theory postulates that environmental stimuli influence individuals' cognitive and emotive reactions (i.e. organisms), which eventually lead to behavioral responses (Russell & Mehrabian, 1974). Many researchers have considered this theory in explaining the different phenomena, such as online shopping behavior (Aslam & Luna, 2021; Peng & Kim, 2014), retail environment (Cachero-Martínez & Vázquez-Casielles, 2017), consumer behavior (Arif et al., 2020), tourism industry (Kim et al., 2020), etc. In this chapter, stimuli are the chatbot service quality dimensions that affect customer-brand relationship (i.e. organism) and that eventually lead to the response (e-WOM). The conceptual model is present in Fig. 2.

5.1   *Stimulus: Chatbot Service Quality Dimensions*

In the context of a chatbot, stimuli are text-based chatbot's distinguishing features that will entice customers (Cheng et al., 2022). The distinguishing features of chatbot service quality could be reliability, understandability, interactivity, responsiveness, and assurance (as discussed in Sect. 2). Table 2 summarizes the definitions and explanation of the chatbot service quality dimensions.

Extant literature supports that accurate information provided by the chatbot positively affects trust (Cheng & Jiang, 2022), satisfaction (Kettinger & Lee, 1994), an important element for customers (Chung & Park, 2019). Various studies also confirm that understandability positively influences users' positive reactions (Kuligowska, 2015; Li et al., 2021). Similarly, the reliability of the information provided by the chatbot is important for the users

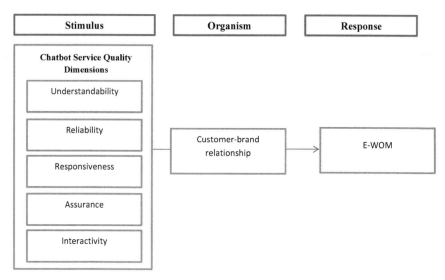

Fig. 2 Conceptual model

Table 2 Chatbot service quality dimensions

	Definition and explanation
Reliability	**Definition:** The chatbot has an aptitude to accomplish the job correctly and dependably **Explanation:** This ability of chatbot benefits in increasing the chatbot-based service usage and improving the efficacy of the task performance (AlHagbani & Khan, 2016; Sensuse et al., 2019)
Understandability	**Definition:** The ability of the chatbot to comprehend human dialogues appropriately **Explanation:** This distinguishing feature of chatbot is deemed important in improving customer-support service (Nguyen, 2019)
Interactivity	**Definition:** The chatbot capability of developing a perception that chatbot-based interaction is like human-based interaction **Explanation:** This ability of the chatbot enhance the element of "humanness" (Go & Sundar, 2019), and that is essential for users' engagement with chatbot-based service (Neuhofer et al., 2015)
Responsiveness	**Definition:** The ability of the chatbot to respond promptly to the user's request **Explanation:** This ability of the chatbot benefits customer-support service (Nguyen, 2019) as users appreciate a quick response and immediate service
Assurance	**Definition:** The ability of the chatbot to develop the trust of the user **Explanation:** This ability of the chatbot assures the user to rely on the chatbot-based service and develops satisfaction (Lee & Park, 2019)

(Chung & Park, 2019) and positively affects satisfaction (Kettinger & Lee, 1994). The prompt response provided by the chatbot also helps in building the consumer-brand relationship, and the chatbot's ability to develop confidence in the user also promotes the customer-brand relationship (Li et al., 2021). Similarly, the interactive feature plays an important role in developing users' positive feelings toward smart devices (Cho et al., 2019). Based on the literature, current chapter considers chatbot service quality dimensions as stimuli and influences the customer-brand relationship.

5.2   Organism: Customer-Brand Relationship

Organism basically refers to "individuals' cognitive or affective condition" (Cheng et al., 2022). In this chapter, the customer-brand relationship is considered as an organism. As discussed earlier in the chapter, *commitment*, *trust*, *control mutuality*, and *satisfaction* are considered customer-brand relationship dimensions as proposed by Grunig and Huang (2000). Commitment, trust, control mutuality, and satisfaction involve emotions and feelings, and hence, these are considered as an organism in this chapter.

Earlier studies have validated that chatbot communication quality affects customer satisfaction, commitment, and trust (Cheng & Jiang, 2022; Chung et al., 2018). Similarly, credible information provided by the chatbot affects customer satisfaction (Mimoun et al., 2017). This reflects that chatbot service quality dimensions act as stimuli and trigger consumer feelings that build a strong relationship with the brand.

5.3   Response: e-WOM

Word of mouth (WOM) marketing is an important component of interactive marketing since it involves customers and turns them into brand ambassadors (López et al., 2021; Srivastava & Sharma, 2017). In this chapter, e-WOM is considered a response to the customer-brand relationship (i.e., organism). WOM is a voluntary behavior (Aslam & Luna, 2021) that reflects the customer engagement intention of the consumer (Carlson et al., 2018). Literature supports that positive e-WOM plays a significant role in the success of a brand (Aslam et al., 2019). Therefore, brands are focusing on identifying the elements that motivate customers to create positive WOM (Aslam & Luna, 2021), because positive feedback or reviews shared by the consumer bring huge consumer traffic to the brand's website (Roy, 2018). The advent of the technology allows users to act as contributors (Jenkins et al., 2006). User-generated content is particularly more effective since it allows people to develop and share media content and reach a large audience through dynamic social networks (Ho et al., 2020). Hence, WOM plays an essential role in brand co-production, creation, promotion, and distribution, enticing new players, and accelerating market expansion (Humphrey et al., 2018).

6 Discussion

To support value co-creation and contribute to the knowledge of value cocreation, it is vital to incorporate customers' perspectives into the development of new service systems (Peltier et al., 2020; Pizzi et al., 2021). For example, AI can be utilized to deliver online customer support that goes beyond standard personalized recommender systems (Pizzi et al., 2021). The emergence of AI benefits marketers as it offers various options for marketing and is gaining interest among practitioners (Fagella, 2018; Perez-Vega et al., 2021). Hence, marketers are using AI-based technologies for improved business operations (Ameen et al., 2021). Among all AI-aided customer service tools, chatbot has received immense attention as it offers low-cost (Aslam et al., 2022; Feng, 2022). The rise of chatbot-based services may be directly related to increased demand for self-service that is more convenient, rapid, on-demand, and less stressful (Li et al., 2021; Terpening & Littleton, 2016). Nowadays, various businesses are transitioning from traditional customer care methods to chatbot digital solutions (Cheng & Jiang, 2022) because human–computer connection allows firms to build deeper relationships with customers through continuing and tailored conversation (Huang & Rust, 2018). Thus, the chatbot-based service creates bi-directional value and fosters interaction and participation. The increased adoption of chatbots in businesses has earned the attention of marketers to fully utilize this technology for maximum benefits. For this, the understanding related to chatbot service quality dimensions should be necessary for the marketers to improve customer-brand relationships that promote voluntary behavior (i.e., positive e-WOM).

The chatbot service quality dimensions such as interactivity, understandability, reliability, assurance, and responsiveness are critical for building a strong brand relationship. The existing literature contends that reliability plays an important role across various industries, such as bookstores, restaurants, and healthcare (Rosen & Karwan, 1994). A past study also elaborated that the reliability feature of the chatbot service develops satisfaction which motivates the user to continuously use the chatbot-based service (Li et al., 2021). This revealed that chatbot-based service should be dependable, sympathetic, reassuring, and compatible to the user's needs. The literature also stated that the reliability of the chatbot builds consumer trust (Yagoda & Gillan, 2012). Another chatbot service quality, assurance also affects the consumer-brand relationship. This finding is consistent with the past findings of Rosen and Karwan (1994) as they claimed that the assurance element plays a crucial role in many industries. Li et al. (2021) also identified that assurance develops a state of confirmation that leads to satisfaction. This indicates that the chatbot service should be trustworthy and has substantive information to answer queries of the user. Moreover, understandability, the ability of a chatbot to understand human language plays a key role in fostering brand relationships. The ability of chatbots to understand human discourse is an essential characteristic of chatbot services (Kuligowska, 2015). The interactive quality of a chatbot is also significant as it influences the consumer's positive emotions and builds customer satisfaction. The literature related to smart devices has highlighted the importance of interactivity in fostering a positive attitude (Cho et al., 2019; Shin et al., 2013). The literature also provides the evidence that interactivity affects positive experiences in e-commerce (Yoo et al., 2010). In line with this, Shin et al. (2013) argued that a positive impact of interactivity of smart television affects satisfaction and positive feelings. Lastly, the responsiveness quality of the chatbot service also positively affects customer-brand relationship. This finding is consistent with the study of Cheng and Jiang (2022) as they determined that the prompt response provided by the chatbot also builds customer confidence and satisfaction. Past studies have demonstrated that consumers perceive a service as credible and competent if a virtual agent provides relevant, up-to-date, and timely information (Chakrabarty et al., 2014). The existing study also elaborates that customers are more likely to regard human–bot contact as professional, accurate, and credible when firms' e-service agents engage in interactive marketing initiatives, share the latest information about new products and services, and proactively cater to humans' needs (Chung et al., 2018). This reflects that chatbot service quality dimensions play a crucial role in fostering customer-brand relationships, and chatbot service quality dimensions act as "stimuli" and trigger organisms (i.e., customer-brand relationship).

In the end, the findings of this chapter highlight the effectiveness of customer-brand relationship on customer behavioral response. The improved customer-brand relationship generates consumer response—positive e-WOM which is an important aspect of interactive marketing. Hence, the customer-brand relationship plays a role to foster the concept of interactive marketing as brands desire to develop long-term relationships with customers to motivate them to act as brand ambassadors (López et al., 2021).

6.1 Theoretical Contributions and Implications

The chapter offers several theoretical contributions in the field of AI and interactive marketing. Businesses today are increasingly adopting AI in their business operations. For instance, digital marketers are implementing interactive messaging services, such as using chatbots powered by AI. Focusing this, the chapter demonstrates the chatbot service quality dimensions that can foster customer-brand relationships to promote the interactive marketing concept. The chapter discusses three service quality aspects (reliability, responsiveness, and assurance) proposed by Parasuraman et al. (1988) and determined the other two quality aspects of chatbots, namely understandability and interactivity as relevant service quality dimensions. The chapter adds to the body of knowledge on chatbot user experience (UX) by defining the key quality aspects of chatbot services. Moreover, the chapter demonstrates that the S-O-R theory effectively explains the influence of chatbot service quality dimensions on customer-brand relationships and its impact on e-WOM. This is one of the first scholarly works that have introduced the S-O-R model in the context of chatbot-based service. Furthermore, the chapter confirms that chatbot service quality dimensions act as stimuli that trigger the organism (customer-brand relationship), and this organism leads to response (voluntary behavior of the consumer). Hence, the chapter established the understanding of the worth of chatbot in the business operations as the chatbot use promotes the voluntary behavior of the user and therefore; benefits the interactive marketing concept. Additionally, the chapter also shows that e-WOM is a behavioral response and an antecedent of customer-brand relationship which is absent in the extant literature on AI. Therefore, the chapter extends the literature on the customer-brand relationship by measuring the relationship itself, antecedents (chatbot service quality dimensions), and outcome (e-WOM). There is a critical gap in the literature in terms of an integrated model of the causes, state, and consequences of customer-brand relationships. Thus, this chapter fills an important void in the literature on customer-brand relationship activated through AI-powered chatbots. Lastly, the chapter offers critical insights to businesses to enjoy the benefits of AI in fostering interactive marketing since chatbots are considered an influential marketing tool that effectively serves the needs of customers, facilitates decision-making, and encourages interactivity.

The findings of the chapter also serve as the bases to implement the chatbot-based solution in the industry and tenders insights to the businesses that are currently involved in using the AI-based chatbot to facilitate customers. The chapter reveals the role of chatbot service quality dimensions in developing a customer-brand relationship and their influence on electronic word-of-mouth (e-WOM) in promoting interactive marketing. Chatbot is a positive tool for communication, addressing consumer demands, assisting their decision-making process, and creating strong customer-brand relations across industries. The findings of the chapter are applicable and beneficial for chatbot developers, design teams, quality assurance specialists, and businesses who aim to engage customers through chatbots. Developers and designers should assess the quality dimensions to ensure that customers and end-users have an engaging experience that in turn encourages customers to re-use the chatbot service. The findings reveal that chatbot service quality dimensions play a significant role in developing customer-brand relationships. Therefore, chatbot developers and quality assurance managers should improve the elements of reliability and assurance. It is essential that chatbots provide relevant and accurate information. The element of responsiveness is also vital in developing customer-brand relations and consequently, the chatbot service should be capable to give prompt responses and render service in to meet the user expectations. Similarly, chatbots should understand customers' queries and concerns effectively and should be interactive. This quality dimension of chatbots enhances the relationship with customers that eventually helps in motivating consumers for e-WOM; a voluntary behavior that promotes the concept of interactive marketing. Earlier researchers have discussed the importance of customer participation (Aslam & Luna, 2021) and have furnished evidence that the customer who shares brand-related information becomes the focal person (Vries & Carlson, 2014), and the reviews shared by the customer brings high customer traffic (Roy et al., 2018).

Though the chapter extends the literature on AI and interactive marketing, there remain a few areas that can be the future path of research. The chapter presents five chatbot service quality dimensions, but future studies may explore other relevant service quality aspects. Further, the chapter considered only e-WOM as a behavioral response of the customer. Future studies may study customer engagement behavior as well to extend the knowledge of interactive marketing. The chapter focused on the customer-brand relationship elements proposed by Grunig and Huang (2000) but studies may study other brand-relationship components discussed in other theories. Lastly, the chapter has not explored any specific industry or business and therefore, there is an issue of generalizability that needs to be addressed in future. It is recommended to review the proposed framework in specific types of businesses such as airlines, banking, hotel, etc.

References

AlHagbani, E. S., & Khan, M. B. (2016, July). Challenges facing the development of the arabic chatbot. *In First International Workshop on Pattern Recognition, 10011*(1), 192–199. https://doi.org/10.1117/12.2240849

Ali, M., & Raza, S. A. (2017). Service quality perception and customer satisfaction in Islamic banks of Pakistan: The modified SERVQUAL model. *Total Quality Management & Business Excellence, 28*(5–6), 559–577. https://doi.org/10.1080/14783363.2015.1100517

Ameen, N., Tarhini, A., Reppel, A., & Anand, A. (2021). Customer experiences in the age of artificial intelligence. *Computers in Human Behavior, 114*(1), 106548. https://doi.org/10.1016/j.chb.2020.106548

Anderson, E. W., & Mittal, V. (2000). Strengthening the satisfaction-profit chain. *Journal of Service Research, 3*(2), 107–120. https://doi.org/10.1177/109467050 032001

Arif, I., Aslam, W., & Siddiqui, H. (2020). Influence of brand related user-generated content through Facebook on consumer behaviour: A stimulus-organism-response framework. *International Journal of Electronic Business, 15*(2), 109–132. https://doi.org/10.1504/IJEB.2020.106502

Aslam, W., & Farhat, K. (2020). Impact of after-sales service on consumer behavioural intentions. *International Journal of Business and Systems Research, 14*(1), 44–55. https://doi.org/10.1504/IJBSR.2020.104145

Aslam, W., & Luna, I. R. D. (2021). The relationship between brand Facebook page characteristics, perceived value, and customer engagement behavior: An application of Stimulus-Organism-Response (SOR). *Revista Brasileira De Gestão De Negócios, 23*(1), 43–62. https://doi.org/10.7819/rbgn.v23i1.4092

Aslam, W., Farhat, K., & Arif, I. (2019). Role of electronic word of mouth on purchase intention. *International Journal of Business Information Systems, 30*(4), 411–426. https://doi.org/10.1504/IJBIS.2019.099304

Aslam, W., Ahmed Siddiqui, D., Arif, I., & Farhat, K. (2022). Chatbots in the frontline: drivers of acceptance. *Kybernetes*, Vol. ahead-of-print No. ahead-of-print. https://doi.org/10.1108/K-11-2021-1119

Athanassopoulos, A., Gounaris, S., & Stathakopoulos, V. (2001). Behavioural responses to customer satisfaction: An empirical study. *European Journal of Marketing*, 35(5/6), 687–707. https://doi.org/10.1108/03090560110388169

Bloemer, J., De Ruyter, K. O., & Wetzels, M. (1999). Linking perceived service quality and service loyalty: A multi-dimensional perspective. *European Journal of Marketing*, 33(11/12), 1082–1106. https://doi.org/10.1108/03090569910292285

Business Insider. (2020). *The latest market research, trends, and landscape in the growing AI chatbot industry*. Available at: www.businessinsider.com/chatbot-market stats-trends. Accessed on 2 April 2022.

Cachero-Martínez, S., & Vázquez-Casielles, R. (2017). Living positive experiences in store: How it influences shopping experience value and satisfaction? *Journal of Business Economics and Management*, 18(3), 537–553. https://doi.org/10.3846/16111699.2017.1292311

Carlson, J., Rahman, M., Voola, R., & De Vries, N. (2018). Customer engagement behaviours in social media: capturing innovation opportunities. *Journal of Services Marketing*, 32(1), 83–94. https://doi.org/10.1108/jsm-02-2017-0059

Chakrabarty, S., Widing, R. E., & Brown, G. (2014). Selling behaviours and sales performance: The moderating and mediating effects of interpersonal mentalizing. *Journal of Personal Selling & Sales Management*, 34(2), 112–122. https://doi.org/10.1080/08853134.2014.890899

Cheng, X., Bao, Y., Zarifis, A., Gong, W., & Mou, J. (2022). Exploring consumers' response to text-based chatbots in e-commerce: The moderating role of task complexity and chatbot disclosure. *Internet Research*, 32(2), 496–517. https://doi.org/10.1108/INTR-08-2020-0460

Cheng, Y. (2020). Contingent organization-public relationship (COPR) matters: Reconciling the contingency theory of accommodation into the relationship management paradigm. *Journal of Public Relations Research*, 32(3/4), 140–154. https://doi.org/10.1080/1062726X.2020.1830405

Cheng, Y., & Jiang, H. (2020). How do AI-driven chatbots impact user experience? Examining gratifications, perceived privacy risk, satisfaction, loyalty, and continued use. *Journal of Broadcasting and Electronic Media*, 65(4), 592–614. https://doi.org/10.1080/08838151.2020.1834296

Cheng, Y., & Jiang, H. (2022). Customer–brand relationship in the era of artificial intelligence: Understanding the role of chatbot marketing efforts. *Journal of Product & Brand Management*, 31(2), 252–264. https://doi.org/10.1108/JPBM-05-2020-2907

Cho, W. C., Lee, K. Y., & Yang, S. B. (2019). What makes you feel attached to smartwatches? The stimulus–organism–response (S-O-R) perspectives. *Information Technology & People*, 32(2), 319–343. https://doi.org/10.1108/ITP-05-2017-0152

Chung, K., & Park, R. C. (2019). Chatbot-based healthcare service with a knowledge base for cloud computing. *Cluster Computing*, 22(1), 1925–1937. https://doi.org/10.1007/s10586-018-2334-5

Chung, M. J., Ko, E. J., Joung, H. R., & Kim, S. J. (2018). Chatbot e-service and customer satisfaction regarding luxury brands. *Journal of Business Research, 117*(1), 587–595. https://doi.org/10.1016/j.jbusres.2018.10.004

Cova, B., & Pace, S. (2006). Brand community of convenience products: New forms of customer empowerment—The case "My Nutella The Community." *European Journal of Marketing, 40*(1), 1087–1105. https://doi.org/10.1108/03090560610681023

DeLone, W. H., & McLean, E. R. (1992). Information systems success: The quest for the dependent variable. *Information Systems Research, 3*(1), 60–95. https://doi.org/10.1287/isre.3.1.60

DeLone, W. H., & McLean, E. R. (2003). The DeLone and McLean model of information systems success: A ten-year update. *Journal of Management Information Systems, 19*(4), 9–30. https://doi.org/10.1080/07421222.2003.11045748

Eren, B. A. (2021). Determinants of customer satisfaction in chatbot use: Evidence from a banking application in Turkey. *International Journal of Bank Marketing, 39*(2), 294–311. https://doi.org/10.1108/IJBM-02-2020-0056

Fagella, D. (2018). *Artificial intelligence in marketing and advertising—5 examples of real traction* [Online]. https://www.techemergence.com/artificial-intelligence-inmarketing-and-advertising-5-examples-of-real-traction/. Accessed on 7 April 2022.

Feng, D. (2022). *The world of chatbots: Customer service, business automation & scalability*. Available at: https://www.bigcommerce.com/blog/chatbots/#chatbots-now-and-in-our-future. Accessed on 7 April 2022.

Forbes. (2017). *How chatbots improve customer experience in every industry: An infograph*. available at: www.forbes.com/sites/blakemorgan/2017/06/08/how-chatbotsimprove-customerexperience-in-every-industry-an-infograph/#2162528867df/

Fournier, S. (1998). Consumers and their brands: Developing relationship theory in consumer research. *Journal of Consumer Research, 24*(4), 343–373. https://doi.org/10.1086/209515

Go, E., & Sundar, S. S. (2019). Humanizing chatbots: The effects of visual, identity and conversational cues on humanness perceptions. *Computers in Human Behavior, 97*(1), 304–316. https://doi.org/10.1016/j.chb.2019.01.020

Grunig, J. E., & Huang, Y. H. (2000). From organizational effectiveness to relationship indicators: antecedents of relationships, public relations strategies, and relationship outcomes. In J. A. Ledingham & S. D. Bruning (Eds.), *Public relations as relationship management: A relational approach to the study and practice of public relations* (pp. 23–54). Erlbaum.

Ho, J., Pang, C., & Choy, C. (2020). Content marketing capability building: A conceptual framework. *Journal of Research in Interactive Marketing, 14*(1), 133–151. https://doi.org/10.1108/JRIM-06-2018-0082

Hsieh, S. H., & Lee, C. T. (2021). Hey Alexa: Examining the effect of perceived socialness in usage intentions of AI assistant-enabled smart speaker. *Journal of Research in Interactive Marketing, 15*(2), 267–294. https://doi.org/10.1108/JRIM-11-2019-0179

Huang, M. H., & Rust, R. T. (2018). Artificial intelligence in service. *Journal of Service Research, 21*(2), 155–172. https://doi.org/10.1177/1094670517752459

Humphrey, W. F., Laverie, D. A., & Shields, A. B. (2018). Building the force: enacting fan brand community through the star wars BB-8 droid builders club. In C. L. Wang (Ed.), *Exploring the rise of fandom in contemporary consumer culture* (pp. 126–146). IGI Global Inc. Available at: www.igi-global.com/chapter/building-the-force/190236

Jain, M., Kumar, P., Kota, R., & Patel, S. N. (2018). Evaluating and informing the design of chatbots. In *Proceedings of the 2018 designing interactive systems conference (IDS)* (pp. 895–906), ACM. https://doi.org/10.1145/3196709.3196735

Jenkins, H., Clinton, K., Puroshotma, R., Robinson, A., & Weigel, M. (2006). *Confronting the challenges of participatory culture: Media education for the 21st century*. The MacArthur Foundation, available at: www.macfound.org/media/article_pdfs/JENKINS_WHITE_PAPER

Jeon, J. O., & Baeck, S. (2016). What drives consumer's responses to brand crisis? The moderating roles of brand associations and brand-customer relationship strength. *Journal of Product & Brand Management, 25*(6), 550–567. https://doi.org/10.1108/JPBM-10-2014-0725

Jun, M., Yang, Z., & Kim, D. (2004). Customers' perceptions of online retailing service quality and their satisfaction. *International Journal of Quality & Reliability Management, 21*(8), 817–840. https://doi.org/10.1108/02656710410551728

Kettinger, W. J., & Lee, C. C. (1994). Perceived service quality and user satisfaction with the information services function. *Decision Sciences, 25*(5–6), 737–766. https://doi.org/10.1111/j.1540-5915.1994.tb01868.x

Kietzmann, J., & Pitt, F. L. (2020). Artificial intelligence and machine learning: What managers need to know. *Business Horizons, 63*(2), 131–133. https://doi.org/10.1016/j.bushor.2019.11.005

Kietzmann, J., Paschen, J., & Treen, R. E. (2018). Artificial intelligence in advertising: How marketers can leverage artificial intelligence along the consumer journey. *Journal of Advertising Research, 58*(3), 263–267. https://doi.org/10.2501/JAR-2018-035

Kim, E., & Ham, S. (2016). Restaurants' disclosure of nutritional information as a corporate social responsibility initiative: Customers' attitudinal and behavioral responses. *International Journal of Hospitality Management, 55*(1), 96–106. https://doi.org/10.1016/j.ijhm.2016.02.002

Kim, S., Eun, J., Oh, C., Suh, B., & Lee, J. (2020, April). Bot in the bunch: Facilitating group chat discussion by improving efficiency and participation with a chatbot. In *Proceedings of the 2020 CHI Conference on Human Factors in Computing Systems* (pp. 1–13).

Kuligowska, K. (2015). Commercial chatbot: Performance evaluation, usability metrics and quality standards of embodied conversational agents. *Professionals Center for Business Research, 2*(2), 1–16. https://doi.org/10.18483/PCBR.22

Kumar, V., Dixit, A., Javalgi, R. R. G., & Dass, M. (2016). Research framework, strategies, and applications of intelligent agent technologies (IATs) in marketing. *Journal of the Academy of Marketing Science, 44*(1), 24–45. https://doi.org/10.1007/s11747-015-0426-9

Kuo, Y. F., Wu, C. M., & Deng, W. J. (2009). The relationships among service quality, perceived value, customer satisfaction, and post-purchase intention in mobile value-added services. *Computers in Human Behavior, 25*(4), 887–896. https://doi.org/10.1016/j.chb.2009.03.003

Lee, M. K., & Park, H. (2019). Exploring factors influencing usage intention of chatbot: Chatbot in financial service. *Journal of the Korean Society for Quality Management, 47*(4), 755–765. https://doi.org/10.7469/JKSQM.2019.47.4.755

Lee, Y. W., Strong, D. M., Kahn, B. K., & Wang, R. Y. (2002). AIMQ: A methodology for information quality assessment. *Information & Management, 40*(2), 133–146. https://doi.org/10.1016/S0378-7206(02)00043-5

Li, L., Lee, K. Y., Emokpae, E., & Yang, S. B. (2021). What makes you continuously use chatbot services? Evidence from Chinese online travel agencies. *Electronic Markets, 31*(3), 575–599. https://doi.org/10.1007/s12525-020-00454-z

López, M., Sicilia, M., & Verlegh, P. W. (2021). How to motivate opinion leaders to spread e-WoM on social media: Monetary vs non-monetary incentives. *Journal of Research in Interactive Marketing, 16*(1), 154–171. https://doi.org/10.1108/JRIM-03-2020-0059

Martínez, P., & Del Bosque, I. R. (2013). CSR and customer loyalty: The roles of trust, customer identification with the company and satisfaction. *International Journal of Hospitality Management, 35*, 89–99.

McKinney, V., Yoon, K., & Zahedi, F. M. (2002). The measurement of web-customer satisfaction: An expectation and disconfirmation approach. *Information Systems Research, 13*(3), 296–315. https://doi.org/10.1287/isre.13.3.296.76

Mimoun, M. S. B., Poncin, I., & Garnier, M. (2017). Animated conversational agents and ecustomer productivity: The roles of agents and individual characteristics. *Information & Management, 54*(5), 545–559.

Morgan-Thomas, A., Dessart, L., & Veloutsou, C. (2020). Digital ecosystem and consumer engagement: A socio-technical perspective. *Journal of Business Research, 121*(1), 713–723. https://doi.org/10.1016/j.jbusres.2020.03.042

Nelson, R. R., Todd, P. A., & Wixom, B. H. (2005). Antecedents of information and system quality: An empirical examination within the context of data warehousing. *Journal of Management Information Systems, 21*(4), 199–235. https://doi.org/10.1080/07421222.2005.11045823

Neuhofer, B., Buhalis, D., & Ladkin, A. (2015). Smart technologies for personalized experiences: A case study in the hospitality domain. *Electronic Markets, 25*(3), 243–254. https://doi.org/10.1007/s12525-015-0182-1

Nguyen, T. (2019). *Potential effects of chatbot technology on customer support: A case study* [Master's dissertation]. Aalto University.

Pantano, E., & Pizzi, G. (2020). Forecasting artificial intelligence on online customer assistance: Evidence from chatbot patents analysis. *Journal of Retailing and Consumer Services, 55*(1), 102096. https://doi.org/10.1016/j.jretconser.2020.102096

Parasuraman, A., Zeithaml, V. A., & Berry, L. L. (1988). SERVQUAL: A multiple-item scale for measuring consumer perceptions of service quality. *Journal of Retailing, 64*(1), 12–40.

Park, M., Aiken, M., & Salvador, L. (2018). How do humans interact with chatbots? An analysis of transcripts. *International Journal of Management & Information Technology, 14*(1), 3338–3350. https://doi.org/10.24297/ijmit.v14i0.7921.

Peltier, J. W., Dahl, A. J., & Swan, E. L. (2020). Digital information flows across a B2C/C2C continuum and technological innovations in service ecosystems: A service-dominant logic perspective. *Journal of Business Research, 121*, 724–734. https://doi.org/10.1016/j.jbusres.2020.03.020

Peng, C., & Kim, G. Y. (2014). Application of the stimuli-organism-response (S-O-R) framework to online shopping behaviour. *Journal of Internet Commerce, 13*(3/4), 159–176. https://doi.org/10.1080/15332861.2014.944437

Perez-Vega, R., Kaartemo, V., Lages, C. R., Razavi, N. B., & Männistö, J. (2021). Reshaping the contexts of online customer engagement behavior via artificial intelligence: A conceptual framework. *Journal of Business Research, 129*(1), 902–910.

Pizzi, G., Scarpi, D., & Pantano, E. (2021). Artificial intelligence and the new forms of interaction: Who has the control when interacting with a chatbot? *Journal of Business Research, 129*(1), 878–890. https://doi.org/10.1016/j.jbusres.2020.11.006

Rajkumar, R., & Ganapathy, V. (2020). Bio-inspiring learning style chatbot inventory using brain computing Interface to increase the efficiency of E-learning. *IEEE Access, 8*(1), 67377–67395. https://doi.org/10.1109/ACCESS.2020.2984591

Rosen, D. L., & Karwan, K. R. (1994). Prioritizing the dimensions of service quality: An empirical investigation and strategic assessment. *International Journal of Service Industry Management, 5*(4), 39–52. https://doi.org/10.1108/09564239410068698

Roy, A. (2018). *7 tips to market your brand using customer reviews*. Retrieved from https://www.jeffbullas.com/author/ankit-roy/

Roy, S. K., Balaji, M. S., Soutar, G., Lassar, W. M., & Roy, R. (2018). Customer engagement behavior in individualistic and collectivistic markets. *Journal of Business Research, 8*(6), 281–290.

Russell, J. A., & Mehrabian, A. (1974). Distinguishing anger and anxiety in terms of emotional response factors. *Journal of Consulting and Clinical Psychology, 42*(1), 79–83. https://doi.org/10.1037/h0035915

Sensuse, D. I., Dhevanty, V., Rahmanasari, E., Permatasari, D., Putra, B. E., Lusa, J. S., ... & Prima, P. (2019, October). Chatbot evaluation as knowledge application: a case study of PT ABC. In *2019 11th International Conference on Information Technology and Electrical Engineering (ICITEE)* (pp. 1–6). IEEE. https://doi.org/10.1109/ICITEED.2019.8929967

Shin, D. H., Hwang, Y., & Choo, H. (2013a). Smart TV: are they really smart in interacting with people? Understanding the interactivity of Korean Smart TV. *Behaviour & Information Technology, 32*(2), 156–172. https://doi.org/10.1080/0144929X.2011.603360

Sohaib, O., & Kang, K. (2015). Individual level culture influence on online consumer iTrust aspects towards purchase intention across cultures: A SOR model. *International Journal of Electronic Business, 12*(2), 142–161. https://doi.org/10.1504/IJEB.2015.069104

Srivastava, D., & Sharma, R. W. (2017). Developing a model for studying the antecedents and effects of Word of Mouth (WoM) and e-WoM marketing based on literature review. *Jindal Journal of Business Research, 6*(1), 25–43. https://doi.org/10.1177/2278682117700307

Terpening, E., & Littleton, A. (2016, November 15). The 2016 state of social business: Social's shift from innovator to integrator. *Altimeter, a Prophet Company*.

Veloutsou, C. (2007). Identifying the dimensions of the product-brand and consumer relationship. *Journal of Marketing Management, 23*(1/2), 7–26. https://doi.org/10.1362/026725707X177892

Veloutsou, C., & Mafe, C. R. (2020). Brands as relationship builders in the virtual world: A bibliometric analysis. *Electronic Commerce Research and Applications, 39*(1), 100901. https://doi.org/10.1016/j.elerap.2019.100901

Verma, S., Sharma, R., Deb, S., & Maitra, D. (2021). Artificial intelligence in marketing: Systematic review and future research direction. *International Journal of*

Information Management Data Insights, 1(1), 100002. https://doi.org/10.1016/j.jjimei.2020.100002

Vries, N. J., & Carlson, J. (2014). Examining the drivers and brand performance implications of customer engagement with brands in the social media environment. *Journal of Brand Management, 21*(6), 495–515. https://doi.org/10.1057/bm.2014.18

Wang, C. L. (2021). New frontiers and future directions in interactive marketing: Inaugural Editorial. *Journal of Research in Interactive Marketing, 15*(1), 1–9. https://doi.org/10.1108/JRIM-03-2021-270

Wang, R. Y., & Strong, D. M. (1996). Beyond accuracy: What data quality means to data consumers. *Journal of Management Information Systems, 12*(4), 5–33. https://doi.org/10.1080/07421222.1996.11518099

Yagoda, R., & Gillan, D. (2012). You want me to trust a ROBOT? The development of a human-robot interaction trust scale. *International Journal of Social Robotics, 4*(3), 235–248. https://doi.org/10.1007/s12369-012-0144-0

Yoo, W. S., Lee, Y. J., & Park, J. K. (2010). The role of interactivity in e-tailing: Creating value and increasing satisfaction. *Journal of Retailing and Consumer Services, 17*(2), 89–96. https://doi.org/10.1016/j.jretconser.2009.10.003

Zhang, J., & Bloemer, J. M. M. (2008). The impact of value congruence on consumer-service brand relationships. *Journal of Service Research, 11*(2), 161–178. https://doi.org/10.1177/1094670508322561

Zmud, R. W. (1978). An empirical investigation of the dimensionality of the concept of information. *Decision Sciences, 9*(2), 187–195. https://doi.org/10.1111/j.1540-5915.1978.tb01378.x

CHAPTER 10

How Internet of Things Is Shaping Consumer Behavior? The Interactive Experience Between Customer and Smart Object

Ching-Jui Keng, Hsin-Ying Liu, and Yu-Hsin Chen

1 INTRODUCTION

With the rapid development of digital technology, enterprises have greater access to increasingly diversified information communication channels to directly interact with consumers. Due to artificial intelligence (AI), the target market has become clearer and more visible, enabling most businesses to realize how many advantages AI development offer and to invest more resources in developing AI technology and related application services (Hu et al., 2021; Ki et al., 2020), such as the Internet of Things (IoT), big data, cloud computing, Augmented Reality (AR), Virtual Reality (VR), mixed reality, virtual assistants, chatbots, and robots. Through AI, many people have embraced more important innovations in 2021, including "Customer Experience (CX)", which is ubiquitous and critical to personal life. "Experience is everything" is a strategy adopted by companies to improve CX and gain more competitive advantages (Clarke & Kinghorn, 2018). By utilizing LUCI (Listening, Understanding, Dialogue, Improvement), AI can gather valuable customer feedback and provide personalized services and product recommendations by analyzing customers' past purchases and preferences (Maras, 2020).

C.-J. Keng (✉)
National Taipei University of Technology, Taipei, Taiwan
e-mail: cjkeng@ntut.edu.tw; keng.chingjui@gmail.com

H.-Y. Liu · Y.-H. Chen
Shih Chien University, Taipei, Taiwan
e-mail: chenyuhsin@g2.usc.edu.tw

© The Author(s), under exclusive license to Springer Nature Switzerland AG 2023
C. L. Wang (ed.), *The Palgrave Handbook of Interactive Marketing*,
https://doi.org/10.1007/978-3-031-14961-0_10

E-commerce sites use AI chatbots to answer customers' questions, encourage them to decide the time of buying, change brands' understanding of serving customers all the way, and promote more relevant products and product discount information (De Cicco et al., 2020).

The rise of IoT has been proclaimed to be essential for organizational innovation, adaptation, and success in a changing environment (Nolin & Olson, 2016). In IoT, electronic products are embedded in smart systems to make them smart objects, where they can communicate with users actively or passively through such systems. Smart objects can exchange high amounts of connectivity, network, and data and include smartwatches, smart speakers, smart TVs, robotic vacuum cleaners, smart cars, and smart home appliances. These smart objects are seamlessly integrated into the virtual world, enabling them to connect at anytime and anywhere, thus forming a ubiquitous network environment. Users' interaction with them provides a fascinating possibility for easing everyday work.

During the process of communication, both parties continuously exchange information, and for them it is an interactive process in which the roles of sender and receiver of messages are switched. IoT has become a major topic in the consumer behavior literature to explore how consumers and smart objects interact with each other. In the past, scholars have argued that the interactive experience between customers and smart objects involves humans and non-humans and focused on their ability to influence each other with paired entities. Smart objects have their own unique capabilities and varied experiences when interacting with consumers. In addition, smart objects and devices provide functions that promote social interaction and personal needs. The application of social content is the interaction between IoT devices and existing social network services. Therefore, it is necessary to examine the potential social and personal impacts on IoT.

Based on previous literature, this chapter proposes Human–Computer Interaction (HCI) and Human–Human Interaction (HHI) and presents a new framework for consumers in regards to the smart object interaction experience, which is grounded in the assemblage theory and in the hierarchy of the social customer engagement experience. The optimal scenario of interactive experience between customer and smart object has been explored under the framework of IoT by observing the said experience among interpersonal orientation, object orientation, and social orientation. Moreover, with the knowledge frame derived from social psychology, this chapter explores the behavior effect and interaction experience between consumers and smart objects. Figure 1 illustrates a research concept of a customer-smart object interaction experience.

Voice-powered AI technologies and individuals' interactions with them are a timely and important area of research, given the limited understanding on how consumers interact with smart objects and how smart objects interact with consumers. However, few empirical studies have focused on users' experience-based connectedness from when they feel linked to a smart object in a smart

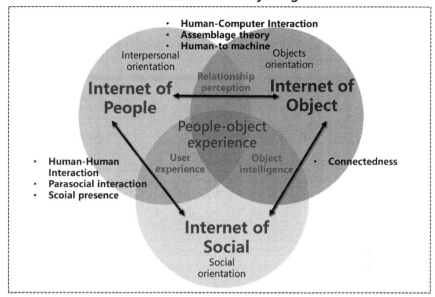

Fig. 1 Concepts of the customer-smart object interaction experience

environment. Based on a literature review, this chapter develops an integrated model for examining the interactions between the consumer and the smart speaker. The proposed model is validated by an experiment, in which the levels of the interaction experience between the customers and the smart objects are divided into two types (high vs. low), and their influences on customers' engagement with the smart object are investigated. The moderating variables of parasocial interaction and user types in the proposed relationship are also discussed. More specifically, this chapter explores the relationship of smart objects that are likely to emerge from the interaction of consumers with these unique products.

2 Literature Review

2.1 AI Technology Advancement Optimization of the Customer Experience

The digital revolution has fundamentally changed the customer experience over the past two decades, as new technologies lead to new concepts of it—how shoppers experience the consumption journey, how they get along with others, and how they perceive tangible objects in the world (Schmitt, 2019). Through AI, people's lives have embraced more important innovations in 2021, including customer experience, which is ubiquitous and critical to one's personal life. Customer experience refers to the overall value recognition of the interaction between customers and enterprises, including information search before buying products, purchase process, enterprise processing mode of problems, product distribution, and after-sales service, with an emphasis on all service encounters. Given this, the product and service itself are only a part of customer value recognition. The implementation of all assignment links in the interactive process affects customers' willingness to purchase again, to recommend products to others, and how much money they plan to spend. Therefore, understanding customer experience with smart products is the focus of interactive marketing research (Wang, 2021).

Marketers are presently trying to use AI to improve customer experience. As the core of said experience, AI can enhance the application of technology to create a consumer-centered service experience, which is the key to enterprises' future success. Hoyer et al. (2020) pointed out that AI and IoT have significantly changed customer experience and even combined together to form artificial intelligence of things (AIoT). IoT means a network of interconnected things, which is a result of equipping the carrier with a sensor or radio frequency identification tag, to support sensory information transmission by those carriers with communication technology and to achieve intelligent automatic control of objects and other application functions (Ng & Wakenshaw, 2017; Reaidy et al., 2015; Wang et al., 2015; Yu et al., 2017). In other words, AIoT allows things, people, and processes to be connected at any time and at any place to anyone via anything (Côrte-Real et al., 2020; Hoyer et al., 2020). By understanding how new technologies will enable customers to conduct shopping and create potentially new experience values, AIoT can enhance this value creation and increase a company's understanding of its customers' preferences and shopping patterns (Ameen et al., 2021; Evans, 2019). Different key customer contact points can bring significant benefits to the company and increase overall customer satisfaction.

The development of AI can be divided into technology-oriented and human-oriented aspects with the former focusing on massive data, algorithm improvement, and optimized computing hardware, while the latter emphasizes different types and effects of interaction between humans and AI, such as "customer (people) - service provider (people)", "customer (AI) - service provider (people)", "customer (people) - service provider (AI)", and "customer (AI) - service provider (AI)" (Robinson et al., 2020). According to MIT Technology Review, 90% of enterprises introduce AI in order to improve customer experience and seek more profits, while 50% of companies use AI to solve all customer inquiries (Ciuffo, 2019). AI technology can process customers' past purchases and preference data to help offer personalized services and product recommendations. For example, beauty brands can make effective customized style and product recommendation lists according to customers' needs and preferences (Maras, 2020).

Recent studies have explored user experiences when interacting with AI (Lim & Ayyagari, 2018; McLean et al., 2018; Scholz & Duffy, 2018;

Cowan & Ketron, 2019; Novak & Hoffman, 2019; Lucia-Palacios & Pérez-López, 2022). The literature on AI applications mostly has focused on the antecedent variation of AI technology applications adapted by users, which is based on the technology acceptance model (TAM) (Gao & Huang, 2019; Pillai et al., 2020; Rese et al., 2020), unified theory of acceptance and use of technology (UTAUT) (Cabrera-Sánchez et al., 2021), expected confirmation model (ECM) (Park, 2020), and use and satisfaction (U&G) (McLean & Osei-Frimpong, 2019; Rese et al., 2020). Since the application of AI technology emphasizes personalization, connectivity, accessibility, and anthropomorphism compared to past technologies (Gummerus et al., 2019), most scholars have looked to explain the interaction between users and AI technology applications with interactive experience (interpersonal interaction and human–computer interaction), which, however, may be explained from the perspective of intelligent experience. For example, Lucia-Palacios and Pérez-López (2022) empirically analyzed that autonomy increases the likelihood of consumer experience leading to the continued use of smart home speakers. Furthermore, discussions of the antecedent variation should not only depend on the functional performance of AI, but also need to consider social, emotional, and relational capabilities (Van Doorn et al., 2017; Wirtz et al., 2018). Sidaoui et al. (2020) developed the customer experience feeling model (CEFM) of AI with dimensions including mood, emotion, and value.

Ki et al. (2020) proposed four relational qualities of AI—Intimacy, Understanding, Enjoyability, and Involvement. Based on the customer journey and experience and from the perspectives of cognition, emotion, and society, Hoyer et al. (2020) came up with the influence of AI equipment on the three stages of customer shopping (pre-delivery, transaction, and post-transaction), so as to create experience value. Chaves and Gerosaa (2021) aimed to understand how to maximize the benefits of human–computer interaction from the perspective of social features. They summarized and analyzed 56 studies from different fields, derived 11 social features, and divided them into three categories of conversational intelligence, social intelligence, and personification.

2.2 *Consumer Experience and Object Experience Emergence in the Internet of Things*

In the age of digital interaction, products are no longer the final "finished" outputs in the traditional sense. Instead, players (typically consumers and associated social networks) interact with an organization, which is the same as actors in the ecosystem space (typically companies and associated organizational ecosystems) that continue to create value. The scholars Novak and Hoffman have devoted themselves to researching and understanding consumers' interactive experience and consumer behavior in a virtual environment for many years (Hoffman & Novak, 1996; Novak & Hoffman, 1997; Novak et al., 1999). Few academic studies have explored the interaction experience between customers and intelligent objects in the context of IoT. DeLanda (2016) and Hoffman and Novak (2018) explained the interaction experience between consumers and smart objects, based on the assemblage theory. Consumer-smart object relationship styles can be divided into two expressive roles: agency and communion (Novak & Hoffman, 2019). Chen et al. (2021) discussed the interactive experience between users and smart speakers based on the assemblage theory and revealed that a highly interactive experience improves customer engagement.

According to the assemblage theory, the interactive experience between people and intelligent objects, through empowering and limiting capabilities in the human–computer linkage and together with the characters of agency and communion, can be classified into four different types of experience combination attributes (Hoffman & Novak, 2018): self-extension, self-restriction, self-expansion, and self-reduction. When combining empowering ability, the agency character gives rise to self-extension, giving integral capabilities to parts and leading to new capacities of this combination, while the communion character brings out self-expansion, empowering the parts of the whole. Consumers who serve as a part of the combination will gain more capacities. After combining the limiting ability, the agency character has self-reduction, as shown by components limiting overall capabilities (the ability of consumers to remove some items or limit some items from making the overall combination less capable). When the communion character starts being characterized with self-reduction, the overall capacity of the component declines, and the consumer's capacity is limited. In the first case, the range of capabilities is expanded to acquire more power or abilities, while in the second case the opposite is true. These four different types of experience combinations are further illustrated as follows.

1. Self-extension

Belk (1988) was the first to propose the concept of self-extension in his research and applied it to the commercial market or consumer research, so as to explore how individuals extend their own personality from themselves to objects or others. In other words, some brand products are not only possessions for consumers, but also a representation of their feelings or emotions for the brand with special meaning. The product is not just regarded as "my" (self) belongings, but also as a metaphor for "myself". This kind of consumers has positive attitudes, can develop self-construction independently, and can put their own personalities into the whole combination. Due to the popularity of smart objects, consumers extend their personal abilities to the combination of smart objects and themselves, making the combination more capable with both personal abilities and characteristics. For example, a consumer intelligent surveillance camera can monitor and timely control the behavior of pets at home. It is fair to say that consumers extend their "self" to the camera, allowing pets to feel like their owners are at home.

2. Self-expansion

Self-expansion is a concept that incorporates other people's features into the self (Aron et al., 2004), in which "others' features" include other people's resources, ideas, and identity. Self-expansion is a concept that incorporates the characteristics of others into the self, in that the stronger the ability of the smart object itself is, the more ability it gives the consumers to expand (Hoffman & Novak, 2018). For example, a smart speaker provides clothing suggestions according to meteorological conditions, is set to automatically tell the whole family what to wear, and adapts to the weather conditions of the day when the alarm clock rings in the morning. Family members trust the reliability of the information and will gradually rely on the clothing suggestions provided by the smart speaker.

3. Self-restriction

When consumers are under some pressure, they will show an attitude of self-resistance in their interaction and make choices in line with personal interests (Brehm & Brehm, 2013), thus limiting the use of intelligent objects and the generation of creativity. In the self-restriction experience, consumers therefore can constrain the combination of intelligent objects by, for example, removing parts of the component, by limiting the capability of the component, or by not installing or refusing to enjoy some specific functions of IoT, leading to self-restriction (Hoffman & Novak, 2018). In other words, when consumers limit the ability to combine, they limit the spark that might arise in a consumer-intelligence combination, such as the possibility of doubting security, thus not wanting to gain access to mobile fingerprinting and facial recognition.

4. Self-reduction

Self-reduction is characterized by the fact that the stronger the ability of the smart object is, the more limited the consumer's ability is. For example, when consumers use smart air conditioning devices to keep the indoor temperature under consistent control, they will mistrust their devices at first and constantly check the indoor temperature. After a period, they will check the room temperature less frequently, due to the convenience brought about by smart air conditioning devices.

3 How Interaction Experience Enhances Customer Engagement in a Smart Speaker: An Empirical Study

3.1 Research Purposes and Questions

With the advancements of IoT, AI, and 5G in recent years, smart objects have become more widely applied in the lives of consumers to fulfill a variety of functions (Wang, 2021). Smart speakers are currently one of the few consumer terminal products on the market that use voice control as the main human–machine interface (Hoy, 2018; Hsieh & Lee, 2021). AI technology enables smart speakers to have natural language processing and machine-learning functions, which are more advanced and more humanized than ever before (Guzman, 2018). Therefore, the need for consumers to feel comfortable while interacting with electronic devices or an AI agent is important for enhancing customer experience and boosting consumer engagement (Kim et al., 2021; Payne et al., 2021; Wang, 2021). However, few empirical studies have focused on users' experience-based connectedness from when they feel connected to smart speakers in a smart environment. The framework of our research is based on three viewpoints: Internet of people, Internet of object, and Internet of social. This chapter explores the new interactive experiences between consumers and a smart speaker that can create the effect of customer engagement by enhancing parasocial interaction and user types. Thus, our research questions are as follows.

RQ1. How do different levels of customer to smart speaker experience influence customer engagement with a smart speaker?

RQ2. How do the moderating variables of user types influence customer engagement with a smart speaker in a proposed relationship?

RQ3. How do the moderating variables of parasocial interaction influence customer engagement with a smart speaker in a proposed relationship?

3.2 Literature Review and Hypotheses' Development

3.2.1 Effects of Interaction Experience Levels on Customer Engagement

Research on the topic of customer engagement has developed into an important strategic imperative in recent years (Rather, 2018; Rather & Hollebeek, 2021). Voorhees et al. (2017) emphasized that customer experience takes place throughout many interactions and even influences customer outcomes. Customer engagement is the psychological state that occurs through an interactive co-creative customer experience with a focal agent/object in focal service relationships (Brodie et al., 2011, 2013). Hollebeek et al. (2014) defined customer brand engagement as the level of customers' motivational, brand-related, and context dependent state of mind, as characterized by a specific level of cognitive, emotional, and behavioral activity during or related to focal consumer/brand interactions. Customer engagement should be treated as a multidimensional construct that comprises emotional, cognitive, and behavioral facets in accordance with suggestions made by Brodie et al. (2011) and Hollebeek et al. (2014). Smart speaker communication is inherently interactive. The assemblage theory explains various combinations of specific interactive experiences between consumers and smart objects. Consumers can access them through an object-oriented personality, which is a non-human-centered method, to evaluate their own agentic or communal roles when interacting with smart objects. In other words, smart objects and consumers have their own unique abilities and experiences when interacting with each other. Consumer experience can be thought of as an assemblage that is always contingent upon the existence of a consumer-object assemblage (Canniford & Bajde, 2016; Canniford & Shankar, 2013; DeLanda, 2016; Hoffman & Novak, 2018; Novak & Hoffman, 2019). Chen et al. (2021) discussed the interactive experience between users and smart speakers based on the assemblage theory and revealed that a highly interactive experience improves customer engagement. Thus, we propose the following research hypothesis.

> *H1.* A high-level interactive experience results in a higher level of customer engagement compared to a low-level interactive experience.

3.2.2 The Moderating Effects of User Types

Reversal theory is a psychological theory that captures the dynamic nature of psychological experience by positing pairs of opposite met motivational states (Apter, 1984). This theory indicates that there are two different phenomenological states of mind: telic and paratelic states (Chiu & Chang, 2020). The reversal theory proposes that telic-oriented people are especially drawn to calm arousal, whereas paratelic-oriented people are especially drawn to energetic arousal (Fan et al., 2015). This chapter focuses on the telic and paratelic states. Telic individuals are goal-oriented and delightfully relaxed when tasks given to them are completed, while paratelic individuals are sense-oriented and feel more excited and happier with their increasing emotional involvement (Apter, 1982, 2001; Markus & Kitayama, 1991; Rose et al., 2022). Jung et al. (2014) pointed out that different user types influence different interactive advertising types. In the telic state, individuals become anxious, because of their greater awareness due to threatening or demanding events, but they become relaxed and happy when the task is accomplished. In the paratelic state, with emotional engagement and arousal, people will feel excited and pleasure, but they will feel bored without stimulation (Markus & Kitayama, 1991). When customers are telic, they are goal-oriented, which shows affirmation and confidence. The higher the level of interaction is between customers and intelligent objects, the better the telic customers will feel that they can achieve the desired goals, thus resulting in higher customer engagement. When customers are paratelic, they value entertainment and enjoy the interaction process. The higher the level of interaction is between customers and intelligent objects, the less interest the paratelic customers will feel, thus resulting in lower customer engagement. Therefore, this paper proposes the next hypotheses.

> *H2.* When smart speaker devices present different user types, there are significant differences between the effects of the interactive experience levels on customer engagement.
>
> *H2a.* When the user type is telic, the higher the interactive experience level is, the higher is the customer engagement; on the contrary, the lower the interactive experience level is, the lower is the customer engagement.
>
> *H2b.* When the user type is paratelic, there are no significant differences between the effects of a high-level interactive experience and a low-level interactive experience on customer engagement.

3.2.3 The Moderating Effects of Parasocial Interaction

Proposed by Horton and Richard Wohl (1956), parasocial interaction is described as media users' reaction to media personas such that they perceive personas as intimate conversational partners (Dibble et al., 2016). According to Nass et al. (1994), the Computers as Social Actors (CASA) theory explains that human–machine interactions and human–human interactions have basically the same social characteristics.

Even without real human characters, an interactive media environment can create a parasocial interaction. Parasocial interaction is instructive in studying consumer-bot interactions. For instance, Han and Yang (2018) pointed out that customers' parasocial relationships have a positive influence on satisfaction and continuance intention toward intelligent personal assistants. Tsai et al. (2021) analyzed chatbots and reported that their influences of high social presence communication on consumer engagement are mediated by parasocial interaction and dialogue. Compared with one-to-many communication in social media, one-on-one chat communication may require a higher level of parasocial interaction. Youn and Jin (2021) found that the consumer-chatbot relationship type affects CRM-related outcomes (behavioral intention, satisfaction, and trust) through parasocial interaction. Therefore, this chapter infers parasocial interaction has a moderating effect in the interaction process, which will affect customer engagement.

> *H3.* When smart speaker devices present different levels of parasocial interaction, there are significant differences between the effects of the interactive experience levels on customer engagement.
>
> *H3a.* When smart speaker devices present high parasocial interaction, the high-level interactive experience has high customer engagement.
>
> *H3b.* When smart speaker devices present low parasocial interaction, a high-level interactive experience has high customer engagement; conversely, a low-level interactive experience has lower customer engagement.

3.3 Method and Experimental Design

3.3.1 Experimental Design and Participants

To examine the proposed hypotheses, we conduct a 2 (high vs. low interactive experience levels) × 2 (telic vs. paratelic-user types) × 2 (high vs. low parasocial interactions) factorial between-subjects experiment. Thus, in total eight interaction situations are derived, with participants being randomly and equally assigned to one of them.

By means of university bulletin boards and several online communities of local universities, university students interested in smart IoT-related issues were invited to participate in the field experiment. In total, 263 participants were recruited for this experiment, made up of 136 (51.7%) males and 127 (43.8%) females, whose ages ranged from 20 to 29 years (68.8%). This chapter also used Pearson's chi-square testing for cross-tabulation to analyze the randomization of the main characteristics, including gender ($\chi^2 = 4.678$, $p = 0.699$), age ($\chi^2 = 38.837$, $p = 0.301$), education ($\chi^2 = 22.659$, $p = 0.362$), and occupation ($\chi^2 = 56.969$, $p = 0.061$), which are non-significant with the randomness of the test group assignment. Hence, the intended purpose of the random assignment was achieved.

3.3.2 Stimulus Materials

Experimental products. A smart speaker plays an important role in the IoT environment and arguably has changed traditional forms of human–computer interaction (Kowalczuk, 2018). The use of voice interaction can be the control terminal for a smart house. A smart speaker often provides a range of ways to interact with a device (McLean & Osei-Frimpong, 2019). Therefore, this chapter adopts the smart speaker as the main device for interaction with the users. The interaction of tasks and messages given to smart speakers by the users creates an experience level interaction (Hoffman & Novak, 2018).

High and low interactive experience levels. We design the command task and messages from the users to the smart speaker to provide interactive experience levels. Through these command tasks and messages, the smart speaker offered answers and contextual information about the users' needs. Furthermore, the users responded with their opinions, and the smart speaker operated accordingly. If tasks could not be resolved by the smart speaker, then collaboration was encouraged by the smart speaker to ask for the users' help. For the high interactive experience levels, we gave the smart speaker five different tasks for interaction: answering questions, a to-do list, setting an alarm clock, providing weather, and giving traffic conditions. When the users find that the smart speaker can complete the overall task and technical functionality is abundant, which promotes the expansion of its ability to fulfill its expected functions, they are willing to share this experience with others. With low interactive experience levels, when the user finds that the command task given to the smart speaker cannot meet the requirements or obtain satisfactory answers and technical functionality is not high, then the user's ability is limited, the influence is reduced, and the information or experience shared with others is limited.

User types and parasocial interaction level. In this experiment we designed a smart speaker that can present two user types of situations: both telic and paratelic. The telic user type is an example of how serious searching for product information can be. The smart speaker was set up to be professional (skilled) and to perform task-based activities during the interaction. Examples include answering questions, a to-do list, setting an alarm clock, providing weather, and giving traffic conditions. The paratelic user type means entertaining and/or amusement. The smart speaker was set up to be socially capable and to perform various entertainment-based activities during the interaction, such as playing music, playing audiobooks, providing humorous jokes, and playing various games.

All participants were asked to imagine two interactive tasks for the smart speaker: task-based (answering questions, a to-do list, setting an alarm clock, providing weather, and giving traffic conditions) and entertainment-based (playing music, playing audiobooks, providing humorous jokes, and playing various games). At a high level of parasocial interaction, the smart speaker will treat users as friends and give them a hand by caring for them and reminding them of things. At a low level of parasocial interaction, the opposite occurs.

3.3.3 Procedure

Participants were given a simulated website address and asked to visit it at a convenient time. First, each participant was informed about the overall experimental procedure by means of a PowerPoint presentation displayed on a monitor. Second, participants were instructed on how they could interact with the smart speaker devices. Third, all participants were asked to imagine two interactive tasks for the smart speaker: task-based and entertainment-based as noted above. Fourth, after the introduction and once they were on the website, they were randomly assigned to one of the eight consumer and smart speaker device interactive experience scenarios, and the experimental activity officially started. After browsing the stimuli, the participants were asked to complete a questionnaire pertaining to their demographic data, the interactive experience level between the user and the smart speaker, the user types, the parasocial interaction, and the customer engagement of the smart speaker.

3.3.4 Measurements

All questionnaire items were taken from previously validated studies. They were translated into Chinese and minimally revised to fit the experimental smart speaker setting of the current study. The suggestion of Chen et al. (2021) was used for measuring the interactive experience levels by employing a 5-point Likert scale (1 = strongly disagree and 5 = strongly agree) on 6 items. The variables of the user types were assessed by using 10 items, as suggested by Jung et al. (2014), the parasocial interaction was measured by using 11 items, adapted from Whang (2018), and 10 items were developed to measure

Table 1 Summary of manipulation check results

Construct	Group	Mean	Std. dev	F-value
HIEL	High	4.097	0.457	119.444***
	Low	3.165	0.870	
LIEL	Low	2.386	0.754	124.615***
	High	3.459	0.807	
UT	Telic	4.973	1.018	144.018***
	Paratelic	3.300	1.235	
PSI	High	5.016	1.084	37.392***
	Low	4.213	1.045	

Notes $^*p < 0.05$, $^{**}p < 0.01$, and $^{***}p < 0.001$. High interaction experience levels (HIEL), Low interaction experience levels (LIEL), User types (UT), Parasocial interaction (PSI)

customer engagement, based on the work of Vinerean and Opreana (2015). Three construct measures were scored on a 7-point Likert scale (1 = strongly disagree and 7 = strongly agree).

3.4 Manipulation Check and Measurement

3.4.1 Manipulation Check

The results of the manipulation check are shown in Table 1. A significantly high interactive experience level value was reported from the high-level interactive experience group, compared with the low-level interactive experience group. This result is statistically significant. In terms of the low interactive experience levels, the low-level interactive experience condition group reported a significantly lower interactive experience level value than the high-level interactive experience condition group. This result was also statistically significant.

For the check of user types, the subjects allocated to the telic had significantly higher feelings than those allocated to the paratelic, and there was a significant difference between the two situations. In the item of parasocial interaction, those allocated to the high parasocial interaction situation had significantly higher feelings than those allocated to the low parasocial interaction situation, and there were significant differences between the two situations. Thus, manipulations of the variables of interactive experience levels, the user types, and the parasocial interaction in this experiment were successful.

3.4.2 Measurement Validation

The results are shown in Table 2. Nunnally (1978) asserted that a Cronbach's α value of 0.5 or higher denotes acceptable reliability, and a value of between 0.806 and 0.931 denotes superior reliability (Nunnally & Bernstein, 1994). Composite Reliability (CR) for the constructs was higher than 0.865, which is greater than the suggested cut-off value of 0.70 (Hair et al., 1998). Thus,

Table 2 Convergent validity, reliability, and discriminant validity

Construct	Item	Cronbach's α	CR	AVE	AVE^2
HIEL	3	0.802	0.884	0.718	0.847
LIEL	3	0.803	0.884	0.718	0.847
Telic	5	0.896	0.924	0.710	0.843
Paratelic	5	0.806	0.865	0.564	0.751
PSI	11	0.931	0.942	0.600	0.774
CE	10	0.907	0.924	0.550	0.741

Note High interaction experience levels (HIEL), Low interaction experience levels (LIEL), Parasocial interaction (PSI), Customer engagement (CE)

Table 3 Results of the main effect

IV	DV	Hypothesis	n	Mean	SD	F-value	p-value	Result
HIEL	CE	H1	134	5.035	0.693	4.280	0.040*	Supported
LIEL			129	4.818	0.989			

Notes $^*p < 0.05$, $^{**}p < 0.01$, and $p < 0.001^{***}$. SD is standard deviation

they were acceptable. The Average Variance Extracted (AVE) ranged from 0.550 to 0.718, exceeding the recommended value of 0.50 (Hair et al., 2013). The square root of AVE for each construct in our study had a higher value than the inter-construct correlations. Therefore, it satisfied the conditions for discriminant validity (Gefen et al., 2000).

3.5 Findings

3.5.1 Effects of Interaction Experience Levels on Customer Engagement

The hypotheses were tested by using one-way ANOVA, and the results are displayed in Table 3. The main effect of the interactive experience levels was significant on customer engagement. The various levels of interactive experiences influenced consumers' engagement differentially. Therefore, *H1* is supported.

3.5.2 Moderating Effects of User Types and Parasocial Interaction

As indicated in Table 4, the ANOVA analysis results indicate that different levels of interactive experiences and user types have a significant interaction effect on customer engagement. Thus, *H2* is supported. We next compare telic and paratelic. The telic values at a high interactive experience level and a low interactive experience level on customer engagement were significant. *H2a* is thus supported. Moreover, the paratelic values did not have a higher significant influence on customer engagement at a high interactive experience level than at a low interactive experience level. Thus, *H2b* is not supported.

Table 4 Results of the moderating effects of user types and parasocial interaction

IV	DV	Hypothesis	Type III SS	df	Mean SS	F-value	p-value	Result
IEL × UT	CE	H2	2.888	1	2.888	4.023	0.046	Supported
IEL × PSI	CE	H3	8.465	1	8.465	12.194	0.001	Supported
UT type: Telic								
IV	DV	Hypothesis	n	Mean	SD	F-value	p-value	Result
HIEL	CE	H2a	66	5.103	0.749	6.911	0.010	Supported
LIEL			67	4.681	1.073			
UT type: Paratelic								
HIEL	CE	H2b	68	4.969	0.631	0.001	0.982	Not Supported
LIEL			62	4.966	0.876			
PSI level: HPSI								
HIEL	CE	H3a	65	4.914	0.719	0.924	0.338	Not Supported
LIEL			64	5.061	0.999			
PSI level: LPSI								
HIEL	CE	H3b	69	5.149	0.651	17.169	0.000	Supported
LIEL			65	4.579	0.927			

Note $^*p < 0.05$, $^{**}p < 0.01$, and $^{***}p < 0.001$

For *H3* the results suggest a significant interaction effect on customer engagement between the different levels of interactive experiences and parasocial interaction as shown in Table 4. Thus, *H3* is supported. In high parasocial interaction, whether for high interactive experience level or low interactive experience level, both did not have a significant influence on customer engagement. Thus, *H3a* is not supported. However, low parasocial interaction has a significant effect on the high interactive experiences on customer engagement. Thus, *H3b* is supported.

4 Conclusion

With the proliferation of smart objects and smart home applications that are available within the IoT context, and given the unique characteristics of its technology, interactive marketing practices can develop a personalized approach that allows for customers' engagement and for them to enjoy the interactive process experiences (Wang, 2021). The focus of this chapter is to explore the levels of interaction experience between customers and smart objects' influences on customer engagement. There is hence likely to be a significant value when contemplating and evaluating the roles of the smart objects' experience and consumer experience in this chapter. Versus a low interactive experience level, this chapter shows that a high interactive experience level has a greater impact on customer engagement. Another interesting result is that user types and parasocial interaction interfere with the interactive experience levels of users and smart speaker devices and customer engagement.

This chapter contributes to marketing research on interactivity by providing new evidence on the effect of interaction experience on customer engagement with smart products. First, it combines the theoretical foundations of the assemblage theory, the customer experience, customer engagement, and HCI literature to explain the concept of interaction experience levels between users and smart speaker devices. Second, this chapter expands the area of consumers and smart objects' interaction experience levels. As found in previous research (Hoffman & Novak, 2018), that smart object-consumer and consumer-smart object present by no means equivalent experiences. Lastly, the authors find that marketers need to understand how framing AI smart speaker roles differently affect the extent and the degree to which user types form parasocial interaction with the smart speaker. Therefore, designing and programming smart speaker messages should focus on projecting a high level of affective (e.g., using humorous dialogue), interactive (e.g., actively asking questions, acknowledging consumers' feedback, and showing appreciation of customers), and cohesive strategies (e.g., phatic language and addressing customers by names) (Tasi et al., 2021).

Considering these limitations and other observations, the following directions could be proposed for future research. First, users' experience toward smart speaker devices was artificially designed in a controlled laboratory environment. Second, in the selection of smart objects, future studies are encouraged to investigate further how consumer engagement influences the interaction experience of different smart objects. Finally, future research could explore the expansion of the relationship between consumers and smart objects, from one-to-one to one-to-many, and examine the differences in the impact on consumer engagement.

References

Ameen, N., Tarhini, A., Reppel, A., & Anand, A. (2021). Customer experiences in the age of artificial intelligence. *Computers in Human Behavior, 114,* 106548.

Apter, M. J. (1982). *The experience of motivation: Theory of psychological reversals.* Academic Press.

Apter, M. J. (1984). Reversal theory and personality: A review. *Journal of Research in Personality, 18*(3), 265–288.

Apter, M. J. (2001). *Motivational style in everyday life: A guide to reversal theory.* APA.

Aron, A., McLaughlin-Volpe, T., Mashek, D., Lewandowski, G., Wright, S. C., & Aron, E. N. (2004). Including others in the self. *European Review of Social Psychology, 15*(1), 101–132.

Belk, R. W. (1988). Possessions and the extended self. *Journal of Consumer Research, 15*(2), 139–168.

Brehm, S. S., & Brehm, J. W. (2013). *Psychological reactance: A theory of freedom and control.* Academic Press.

Brodie, R. J., Hollebeek, L. D., Juric´, B., & Ilic´, A. (2011). Customer engagement: conceptual domain, fundamental proposition, and implications for research. *Journal of Service Research, 14*(3), 252–271.

Brodie, R. J., Ilic´, A., Juric´, B., & Hollebeek, L. D. (2013). Customer engagement in a virtual brand community: an exploratory analysis. *Journal of Business Research, 66*(1), 105–114.

Cabrera-Sánchez, Villarejo-Ramos, Á.F., Liébana-Cabanillas, F., and Shaikh, A. A. (2021). Identifying relevant segments of AI applications adopters–Expanding the UTAUT2's variables. *Telematics and Informatics, 58*, 101529.

Canniford, R., & Shankar, A. (2013). Purifying practices: How consumers assemble romantic experiences of nature. *Journal of Consumer Research, 39*(5), 1051–1069.

Canniford, R., & Bajde, D. (2016). *Assembling consumption in assembling consumption: Researching actors, networks and markets* (R. Canniford & D. Bajdes, Eds.) (pp. 1–17). Routledge.

Chavesa, A. P., & Gerosa, M. A. (2021). How should my chatbot interact? A survey on human-chatbot interaction design. *International Journal of Human-Computer Interaction, 37*(8), 1–52.

Chen, Y. H., Keng, C. J., & Chen, Y. L. (2021). How interaction experience enhances customer engagement in smart speaker devices? The moderation of gendered voice and product smartness. *Journal of Research in Interactive Marketing* (ahead-of-print).

Chiu, Y. P., & Chang, S. C. (2020). Using eye-tracking to measure the influence of banner ads' browsing behavior and attitude on host websites. *Contemporary Management Research, 16*(1), 35–54.

Ciuffo, J. (2019). *How global companies are winning at AI deployment*. Retrieved from https://www.genesys.com/blog/post/mit-technology-reviewinsights-how-global-companiesare-winning-at-ai-deployment

Clarke, D., & Kinghorn, R. (2018). *Experience is everything: Here's how to get it right*. PwC. Available at: pwc.com/future-of-cx (accessed 22 August 2019).

Côrte-Real, N., Ruivo, P., & Oliveira, T. (2020). Leveraging Internet of Things and big data analytics initiatives in European and American firms: Is data quality a way to extract business value? *Information & Management, 57*, 103141.

Cowan, K., & Ketron, S. (2019). A dual model of product involvement for effective virtual reality: The roles of imagination, co-creation, telepresence, and interactivity. *Journal of Business Research, 100*, 483–492.

Dibble, J. L., Hartmann, T., & Rosaen, S. F. (2016). Parasocial interaction and parasocial relationship: Conceptual clarification and a critical assessment of measures. *Human Communication Research, 42*(1), 21–44.

De Cicco, R., Silva, S. C., & Alparone, F. R. (2020). Millennials' attitude toward chatbots: An experimental study in a social relationship perspective. *International Journal of Retail & Distribution Management, 48*(11), 1213–1233.

DeLanda, M. (2016). *Assemblage theory*. Edinburgh University Press.

Evans, M. (2019). *Build A 5-star customer experience with artificial intelligence*.

Fan, X., Chang, E. C., & Wegener, D. T. (2015). Two- or one-dimensional view of arousal? Exploring tense and energetic arousal routes to consumer attitudes. *European Journal of Marketing, 49*(9/10), 1417–1435.

Gao, B., & Huang, L. (2019). Understanding interactive user behavior in smart media content service: An integration of TAM and smart service belief factors. *Heliyon, 5*(12), e02983.

Gefen, D., Straub, D. W., & Boudreau, M. C. (2000). Structural equation modeling and regression guidelines for research practice. *Communications of the Association for Information Systems, 4*(7), 2–77.

Gummerus, J., Lipkin, M., Dube, A., & Heinonen, K. (2019). Technology in use—Characterizing customer self-service devices. *Journal of Services Marketing, 33*(1), 44–56.

Guzman, A. L. (2018). Voices in and of the machine: Source orientation toward mobile virtual assistants. *Computers in Human Behavior, 90*, 343–350.

Han, S., & Yang, H. (2018). Understanding adoption of intelligent personal assistants: A parasocial relationship perspective. *Industrial Management & Data Systems, 118*(3), 618–636.

Hair, J. F., Anderson, R. E., Tatham, R. L., & Black, W. C. (1998). *Multivariate data analysis* (5th ed.). Prentice Hall.

Hair, J. F., Ringle, C. M., & Sarstedt, M. (2013). Partial least squares structural equation modeling: Rigorous applications, better results and higher acceptance. *Long Range Planning, 46*(1/2), 1–12.

Hoffman, D. L., & Novak, T. P. (1996). Marketing in hypermedia computer-mediated environment: Conceptual foundations. *Journal of Marketing, 60*(3), 50–68.

Hoffman, D. L., & Novak, T. P. (2018). Consumer and object experience in the internet of things: An assemblage theory approach. *Journal of Consumer Research, 44*(6), 1178–1204.

Hollebeek, L. D., Glynn, M. S., & Brodie, R. J. (2014). Consumer brand engagement in social media: Conceptualization, scale development and validation. *Journal of Interactive Marketing, 28*, 149–165.

Horton, D., & Richard Wohl, R. (1956). Mass communication and para-social interaction: Observations on intimacy at a distance. *Psychiatry, 19*(3), 215–229.

Hoy, M. B. (2018). Alexa, Siri, Cortana, and more: An introduction to voice assistants. *Medical Reference Services Quarterly, 37*(1), 81–88.

Hoyer, W. D., Kroschke, M., Schmitt, B., Kraume, D., & Shankar, V. (2020). Transforming the customer experience through new technologies. *Journal of Interactive Marketing, 51*, 57–71.

Hsieh, S. H., & Lee, C. T. (2021). Hey Alexa: Examining the effect of perceived socialness in usage intentions of AI assistant-enabled smart speaker. *Journal of Research in Interactive Marketing, 15*(2), 267–294.

Hu, Q., Lu, Y., Pan, Z., Gong, Y., & Yang, Z. (2021). Can AI artifacts influence human cognition? The effects of artificial autonomy in intelligent personal assistants. *International Journal of Information Management, 56*, 102250.

Jung, J. M., Chu, H., Min, K. S., & Martin, D. (2014). Does telic/paratelic user mode matter on the effectiveness of interactive internet advertising? A reversal theory perspective. *Journal of Business Research, 67*(6), 1303–1309.

Ki, C. W., Cho, R., & Lee, J. E. (2020). Can an intelligent personal assistant (IPA) be your friend? Para-friendship development mechanism between IPAs and their users. *Computers in Human Behavior, 111*, 106412.

Kim, J. H., Kim, M., Park, M., & Yoo, J. (2021). How interactivity and vividness influence consumer virtual reality shopping experience: The mediating role of telepresence. *Journal of Research in Interactive Marketing, 15*(3), 502–525.

Kowalczuk, P. (2018). Consumer acceptance of smart speakers: A mixed methods approach. *Journal of Research in Interactive Marketing, 12*(4), 418–431.

Lim, A., & Ayyagari, R. (2018). Investigating the determinants of telepresence in the e-commerce setting. *Computers in Human Behavior, 85*, 360–371.

Lucia-Palacios, L., & Pérez-López, R. (2022). How can autonomy improve consumer experience when interacting with smart products? *Journal of Research in Interactive Marketing, 16*(4).

Maras, E. (2020). *Beauty retailers embrace AR, AI*. https://www.digitalsignagetoday.com/articles/beauty-retailers-embrace-ar-ai/ (Accessed 22 April 2020).

Markus, H. R., & Kitayama, S. (1991). Culture and the self: Implications for cognition, emotion, and motivation. *Psychological Review, 98*(2), 224–253.

McLean, G., Al-Nabhani, K., & Wilson, A. (2018). Developing a mobile applications customer experience model (MACE)-implications for retailers. *Journal of Business Research, 85,* 325–336.

McLean, G., & Osei-Frimpong, K. (2019). Hey Alexa... examine the variables influencing the use of artificial intelligent in-home voice assistants. *Computers in Human Behavior, 99,* 28–37.

Nass, C. I., Steuer, J., & Tauber, E. R. (1994). Computers are social actors. In *Proceedings of the SIGCHI conference on Human factors in computing systems* (pp. 72–78). ACM.

Ng, I. C. L., & Wakenshaw, S. Y. L. (2017). The Internet-of-Things: Review and research directions. *International Journal of Research in Marketing, 34,* 3–21.

Nolin, J., & Olson, N. (2016). The Internet of Things and convenience. *Internet Research, 26*(2), 360–376.

Novak, T. P., & Hoffman, D. L. (1997). Measuring the flow experience among web users. *Interval Research Corporation, 7,* 1–35.

Novak, T. P., Hoffman, D. L., & Yung, Y. F. (1999). Measuring the customer experience in online environments: A structural model approach. *Marketing Science, 19*(1), 22–44.

Novak, T. P., & Hoffman, D. L. (2019). Relationship journeys in the internet of things: A new framework for understanding interactions between consumers and smart objects. *Journal of the Academy of Marketing Science, 47,* 216–237.

Nunnally, J. C. (1978). *Psychometric theory.* McGraw-Hill.

Nunnally, J. C., & Bernstein, I. H. (1994). The assessment of reliability. *Psychometric Theory, 3,* 248–292.

Park, E. (2020). User acceptance of smart wearable devices: An expectation-confirmation model approach. *Telematics and Informatics, 47,* 101318.

Payne, E. M., Peltier, J., & Barger, V. A. (2021). Enhancing the value co-creation process: Artificial intelligence and mobile banking service platforms. *Journal of Research in Interactive Marketing, 15*(1), 68–85.

Pillai, R., Sivathanu, R., & Dwivedi, Y. K. (2020). Shopping intention at AI-powered automated retail stores (AIPARS). *Journal of Retailing and Consumer Services, 57,* 102207.

Rather, R. A. (2018). Consequences of consumer engagement in service marketing: An empirical exploration. *Journal of Global Marketing, 32*(2), 116–135.

Rather, R. A., & Hollebeek, L. (2021). Customers' service-related engagement, experience, and behavioral intent: Moderating role of age. *Journal of Retailing & Consumer Services, 60,* 102453.

Reaidy, P., Gunasekaran, A., & Spalanzani, A. (2015). Bottom-up approach based on internet of things for order fulfillment in a collaborative warehousing environment. *International Journal of Production Economics, 159,* 29–40.

Rese, A., Ganster, L., & Baier, D. (2020). Chatbots in retailers' customer communication: How to measure their acceptance? *Journal of Retailing and Consumer Services, 56,* 102176.

Robinson, S., Orsingher, C., Alkire, L., De Keyser, A., Giebelhausen, M., Papamichail, K. N., Shams, P., & Temerak, M. S. (2020). Frontline encounters of the AI kind: An evolved service encounter Framework. *Journal of Business Research, 116,* 366–376.

Rose, J. L., Arango-Soler, L. A., Souza, C. D., Khaksar, S. M. S., & Brouwer, A. R. (2022).He dark age of advertising: An examination of perceptual factors affecting advertising avoidance in the context of mobile Youtube. *Journal of Electronic Commerce Research, 23*(1), 13–32.

Schmitt, B. (2019). From atoms to bits and back: A research curation on digital technology and agenda for future research. *Journal of Consumer Research, 46*(4), 825–832.

Scholz, J., & Duffy, K. (2018). We are at home: How augmented reality reshapes mobile marketing and consumer-brand relationships. *Journal of Retailing and Consumer Services, 44*, 11–23.

Sidaoui, K., Jaakkola, M., & Burton, J. (2020). AI feel you: Customer experience assessment via chatbot interviews. *Journal of Service Management, 31*(4), 745–766.

Tsai, W. H. S., Liu, Y., & Chuan, C. H. (2021). How chatbots' social presence communication enhances consumer engagement: The mediating role of parasocial interaction and dialogue. *Journal of Research in Interactive Marketing, 15*(3), 460–482.

Van Doorn, J., Mende, M., Noble, S., Hulland, J., Ostrom, A., Grewal, D., & Petersen, J. A. (2017). Domo Arigato Mr. Roboto: Emergence of automated social presence in organizational frontlines and customers' service experiences. *Journal of Service Research, 20*(1), 43–58.

Vinerean, S., & Opreana, A. (2015). Consumer engagement in online settings: Conceptualization and validation of measurement scales. *Expert Journal of Marketing, 3*(2), 35–50.

Voorhees, C. M., Fombelle, P. W., Gregoire, Y., Bone, S., Gustafsson, A., Sousa, R., & Walkowiak, T. (2017). Service encounters, experiences and the customer journey: Defining the field and a call to expand our lens. *Journal of Business Research, 79*, 269–280.

Wang, C. L. (2021). New frontiers and future directions in interactive marketing: Inaugural Editorial. *Journal of Research in Interactive Marketing, 15*(1), 1–9.

Wang, P., Valerdi, R., Zhou, S., & Li, L. (2015). Introduction: Advances in IoT research and applications. *Information Systems Frontiers, 17*(2), 239–241.

Whang, C. (2018). *Voice shopping: The effect of the consumer-voice assistant parasocial relationship on the consumer's perception and decision making*.

Wirtz, J., Patterson, P., Kunz, W., Gruber, T., Lu, V., Paluch, S., & Martins, A. (2018). Brave new world: Service robots in the frontline. *Journal of Service Management, 29*(5), 907–931.

Youn, S., & Jin, S. V. (2021). "In A.I. we trust?" The effects of parasocial interaction and technopian versus luddite ideological views on chatbot-based customer relationship management in the emerging feeling economy. *Computers in Human Behavior, 119*, 106721.

Yu, X., Roy, S. K., Quazi, A., Nguyen, B., & Han, Y. (2017). Internet entrepreneurship and "the sharing of information" in an Internet-of-Things context: The role of interactivity, stickiness, e-satisfaction and word-of-mouth in online SMEs' websites. *Internet Research, 27*(1), 74–79.

CHAPTER 11

The Physical Presence and Relationship Distance for Efficient Consumer–AI-Business Interactions and Marketing

Corina Pelau, Dan-Cristian Dabija, and Daniela Serban

1   INTRODUCTION

Artificial intelligence has changed and will continue to change the way in which companies interact with their consumers, having major implications on the future marketing strategies of companies (Huang & Rust, 2022; Lim et al., 2022; Puntoni et al., 2021). In the past, classical marketing communication campaigns targeted only the consumer and their reference groups, as the only ones able to make buying decisions and choose which products to buy or to use. Consumers' permanent use of artificial intelligence systems and devices will change this communication, with increased input of AI systems and devices in the consumers' buying decisions (Dawar, 2018). From simple recommendations provided by intelligent systems (such as search engines and social media) based on the past online behavior of consumers, to complex automated decisions made by intelligent assistants (such as Alexa, Siri, Bixby) used by the consumers, AI will play a crucial role in the future marketing

---

C. Pelau (✉) · D. Serban
Bucharest University of Economic Studies, Bucharest, Romania
e-mail: corina.pelau@fabiz.ase.ro

D. Serban
e-mail: daniela.serban@csie.ase.ro

D.-C. Dabija
Babes-Bolyai University Cluj-Napoca, Cluj-Napoca, Romania
e-mail: cristian.dabija@econ.ubbcluj.ro

© The Author(s), under exclusive license to Springer Nature Switzerland AG 2023
C. L. Wang (ed.), *The Palgrave Handbook of Interactive Marketing*,
https://doi.org/10.1007/978-3-031-14961-0_11

campaigns of companies (Dawar, 2018; McLean et al., 2021; Puntoni et al., 2021; Yu, 2021). Due to the fact that several consumer activities will be taken over by smart AI systems, it will not be enough just to convince the consumer about the characteristics and image of a product, but it will also be important to appear in the recommendation list of the AI device on which the consumer relies (Dawar, 2018). Different scenarios predict that each consumer will have their own AI systems which will do the shopping, make vacation reservations and even solve administrative tasks such as paying bills, car maintenance and home appliances (Dawar, 2018). Therefore, future marketing campaigns will be bi-directional, targeting both the consumers and the AI devices used. In effect, the AI assistant will make decisions for the consumer.

The objective of this chapter is to give an overview of the different scenarios concerning the implementation of several forms of artificial intelligence systems or devices in the everyday life of consumers and the way they interfere in the communication between companies and consumers. Starting from this main objective, the authors will focus on the key elements regarding the role of AI systems and devices in the future marketing strategies of companies.

2 Classification of AI Systems and Devices in Marketing

One important aspect in analyzing the role of AI in marketing is to have an overview on the different forms and classifications of AI systems and devices which affect the buying decisions of consumers. Depending on the type of AI, they will play different roles in the future interactions between companies and consumers. The main classifications on which the authors will focus in this chapter are AI with a physical or virtual presence and the distance of the relationship between consumers and AI.

In terms of physical presence, there is AI with physical presence and AI without physical presence. According to Wirtz et al. (2018), AI without physical presence includes also virtual AI and holograms. The difference between the two lies mainly in the design and anthropomorphic characteristics of AI. While for the AI without physical presence, the focus is on creating a human-like, warm voice and developing communication and interaction skills (Chong et al., 2021; Hoy, 2018; McLean & Osei-Frimpong, 2019), in the case of AI with physical presence there is a supplementary challenge for engineers to design friendly AI with human-like features (Lv et al., 2021; Sundar et al., 2017) and good mobility. Some authors focus on the design of a friendly face for AI which can mimic human body language with features like a direct gaze design or head nodding (Song & Luximon, 2020). Although studies have not proven any direct impact of the physical appearance of AI on acceptance by consumers (Blut et al., 2021; Lu et al., 2019), an anthropomorphic design may enhance the psychological characteristics of AI (Pelau et al., 2021; Tan et al., 2020) and create a social presence (Adam et al., 2021; Araujo,

2018; Feine et al., 2019; Wang, 2017). Moreover, AI with physical presence will need more maintenance in comparison to virtual AI, which only requires system updates.

The second classification criterion is the distance of the relationship between consumers and AI. Clark and Mills (1993) define the interpersonal relations between humans as communal and exchange relations and depending on the type, there is a certain etiquette for communication and mutual behavior based on the type of relation. Similar relations occur between consumers and AI. There are external company-owned AI, which will take over several service tasks from human employees and there are personal AI assistants which are owned by the consumer and which affect the relation between consumers and companies. Taking into consideration the different relations between consumers and the two types of AI, there are likely to be different implications for the marketing activity of companies. The main difference between the two types of AI is that personal assistants are continuously in the presence of the consumer, having access to their private data, while the interaction with company-owned AI happens only occasionally and they have less access to consumer data. Having access to more personal data, the interaction between a personal AI assistant and consumer is more focused on their needs and preferences, leading to a familiar relation with rather informal communication and higher attachment from the consumer. In opposition to this, the relationship with an external company-owned AI is more distant, as interaction only takes place occasionally when the consumer needs the offered service. Consequently, the AI has access only to the information required for service delivery and the relation is more formal and comparable to a human service employee.

Taking into consideration these aspects, the expectations from the types of AI will be different and consequently also the implications for the marketing strategies of companies. In Fig. 1, there can be observed a classification of AI based on the previously described criteria and the main challenges for each.

As can be observed in Fig. 1, based on the physical presence and the relation to the consumer, the authors have identified four categories of AI. The first category includes service robots which take over certain tasks from human employees. They have physical presence and they are outside the private sphere of consumers, being employed by companies for delivering different services. The second category is chatbots and voice assistants. They usually take over tasks from call center agents by providing support for products and services. They do not have physical presence and they are outside the private sphere of consumers. The third category includes personal home assistants like Alexa or other intelligent devices and home appliances. Although not yet anthropomorphic, they have a physical presence and by taking over different tasks in the home, they are present in the private sphere of consumers. The fourth category is personal voice assistants like Siri or Bixby. They usually take over different secretary tasks, by completing the assignments delegated by the consumer.

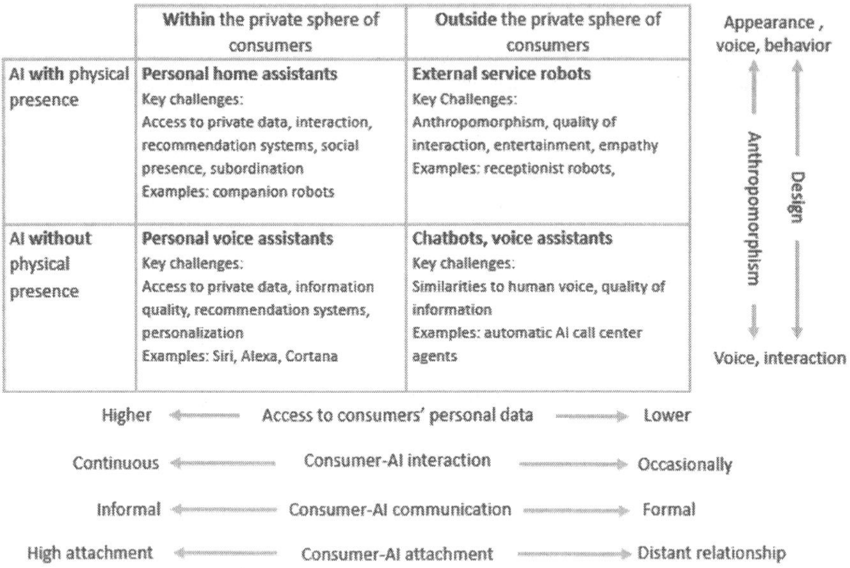

	Within the private sphere of consumers	Outside the private sphere of consumers
AI with physical presence	**Personal home assistants** Key challenges: Access to private data, interaction, recommendation systems, social presence, subordination Examples: companion robots	**External service robots** Key Challenges: Anthropomorphism, quality of interaction, entertainment, empathy Examples: receptionist robots,
AI without physical presence	**Personal voice assistants** Key challenges: Access to private data, information quality, recommendation systems, personalization Examples: Siri, Alexa, Cortana	**Chatbots, voice assistants** Key challenges: Similarities to human voice, quality of information Examples: automatic AI call center agents

Appearance, voice, behavior ↑ Anthropomorphism / Design ↓ Voice, interaction

Higher ← Access to consumers' personal data → Lower
Continuous ← Consumer-AI interaction → Occasionally
Informal ← Consumer-AI communication → Formal
High attachment ← Consumer-AI attachment → Distant relationship

Fig. 1 Classification of AI based on physical presence and relationship distance to the consumers

They do not have physical presence, but they accompany the consumer continuously and have access to their private information, being present on their smartphone.

3 The Role of AI in the Marketing Strategy of Companies

Based on the characteristics of AI and the relation it has with the consumer, they will play different roles in the marketing strategy of companies. In the following section, the authors will analyze the main challenges for each type of AI and the implication it will have on the marketing strategies of companies.

3.1 External Service Robots and Their Role for Consumer Interactions in Service Delivery

With evolving technology, the presence of physical AI has increased in the past years, taking over different roles in service delivery. From receptionist robots in hotels and customer touchpoints served by robots, to different types of industrial robots (Wirtz et al., 2018), there is a wide variety of AI with physical presence which intervenes in the business–consumer interactions. A special role in marketing will have service robots taking over different tasks from human employees and fulfilling the expectations and needs of consumers (Choi et al., 2021; Zhu & Chang, 2020). Service robots will need good communication and interaction skills in order to provide all the information expected by consumers (Ashfaq et al., 2020), but at the same time, they will have to entertain and be empathetic in relation to the customer (Gursoy et al., 2019; Longoni & Cian, 2022; Pelau et al., 2021). An especially challenging situation is the case of service failure, when the customer is more sensitive than usual and when the pre-programmed algorithms do not provide the desired solution (Choi et al., 2021).

Anthropomorphism (Grewal et al., 2020; Wirtz et al., 2018) and social presence (Blut et al., 2021; van Doorn et al., 2017) are important features of service robots, for increasing the consumers' trust and acceptance of AI. Anthropomorphism is the attribution of human-like characteristics to objects (Epley et al., 2007) or brands (Golossenko et al., 2020). The anthropomorphic characteristics of service robots can be of several types, from a human-like physical appearance (Liu et al., 2022; Song & Luximon, 2020), including a human voice (Chong et al., 2021) to psychological and behavioral characteristics like free will and consciousness (Lu et al., 2019) or the ability to care and show empathy (Kervenoael et al., 2020; Pelau et al., 2021). Although several authors have shown that the physical human-like characteristics do not necessarily influence the acceptance of AI (Blut et al., 2021; Lu et al., 2019), they apparently enhance the psychological characteristics of AI, which impact more on consumers (Pelau et al., 2021; Tan et al., 2020).

Although the acceptance of service robots instead of human employees is still the main challenge for companies, the Covid-19 pandemic has fastened their implementation, as service robots are immune to viruses and therefore in times of social distancing the interaction with a service robot is safer (Kim et al., 2021; Seyitoglu & Ivanov, 2021).

3.2 *External Chatbots and Voice Assistants and Their Role in Consumer Services and Support*

One of the most promising AI technologies used by companies is chatbots and intelligent voice assistants (Araujo, 2018; Chung et al., 2020). These types of AI have the ability to interact with consumers by voice or text and are frequently involved in activities relating to sales, customer support and marketing (Ashfaq et al., 2020; Wang, 2021). Often when consumers get in touch with a company, they telephone or chat with a non-physical, virtual assistant. With the help of voice assistants, consumers can place orders or demand information or assistance regarding products (Chung et al., 2020).

Analyzing the types of voice assistants, two categories can be observed. On one hand, there are the chatbots which interact with consumers mainly by text (Ashfaq et al., 2020). On the other hand, there are voice assistants, which interact with the consumers by voice (Feine et al., 2019; Fernandes & Oliveira, 2021; Wang, 2021). Taking into consideration the fact that these types of AI are the companies' representatives in relation to consumers, customer satisfaction is the main predictor for their acceptance and use (Ashfaq et al., 2020;

Chung et al., 2020). According to Ashfaq et al. (2020), information and service quality, perceived usefulness and perceived enjoyment are the main determinants of consumer satisfaction with intelligent voice assistants.

Anthropomorphism also plays an important role in the case of voice assistants, as apparently consumers have a stronger affective response (Ciechanowski et al., 2019) and would rather comply with instructions provided by AI with human-like features (Adam et al., 2021). Social presence and social cues also play an important role in the interaction between AI and consumer (Adam et al., 2021; Araujo, 2018; Feine et al., 2019). As intelligent voice assistants don't have a physical presence, anthropomorphic characteristics are incorporated by giving them names and creating avatars for them (Crolic et al., 2022). In addition, social cues are incorporated in their language and reactions. According to Feine et al. (2019), there are four types of social cues: verbal, visual, auditory and invisible. In order to increase their social presence, AI frequently has small talk as a verbal social cue, facial expression as a visual cue, tonality of voice as an auditory cue and identity as an invisible cue.

There is also a negative side to anthropomorphic characteristics. According to Crolic et al. (2022), the consumer's emotional context impacts the positive or negative effects of the anthropomorphic characteristics of AI chatbots and voice assistants. Moreover, some anthropomorphic features might produce feelings of discomfort in the communication between consumer and AI (Luo et al., 2019). Therefore, the development of the features of AI voice assistants is important in order to optimize the interaction between consumer and AI, and therefore its acceptance.

3.3 *Personal Voice Assistants and Their Role in Consumers' Buying Decisions*

Personal voice assistants are software agents that run on a purpose-built speaker or smartphone and have the ability to interact with the consumer by voice (Hoy & Pomputius, 2018). They have the ability to react by voice to a listened word, by accessing an artificial intelligence-driven server that supplies the voice assistant with the necessary information (Hoy & Pomputius, 2018). The use of intelligent voice assistants has increased in past years because of their functionality, consumers frequently using them for information searches, for completing basic tasks, to deliver orders, purchase products and for interaction with companies (McLean & Osei-Frimpong, 2019). Among the best known personal voice assistants are Apple's Siri, Microsoft's Cortana and Amazon's Alexa. In comparison with previous technologies, they have the ability to interact with consumers in a similar way to the interaction between humans, using natural language processing and machine learning technologies (McLean & Osei-Frimpong, 2019). According to McLean and Osei-Frimpong (2019), the main drivers of the use of intelligent voice assistants are utilitarian benefits and social presence and attraction. Moreover, the interaction quality between consumers and AI voice assistants enhances future usage intention (Hsieh & Lee, 2021; Lucia-Palacios & Perez-Lopez, 2021). Taking into account the fact that the intelligent voice assistant is permanently present around the consumer, several authors have researched the relation and attachment between consumers and intelligent voice assistants, confirming that friendship and similar para-relations can occur between them (Ki et al., 2020; McLean & Osei-Frimpong, 2019; Tsai et al., 2021). Moreover, the induced personality (Poushneh, 2021) and gender (Chen et al., 2021; Loideain & Adams, 2020) of the voice assistant can be an important predictor for defining the para-relation between consumer and AI. This para-friendship between consumer and AI can be of importance for companies, as closer relationships lead to more self-disclosing behavior (Ki et al., 2020) and less data privacy concerns. Besides, the AI friend can have an important role in recommending the products and services acquired by the consumer (Dawar, 2018; McLean et al., 2021; Yu, 2021). Moreover, some studies show that AI assistants can take over the co-creation role in traditional customer–company interactions (Payne et al., 2021). Based on this role of AI in advising and recommending products to the consumer, future marketing will be bi-directional, targeting both the consumer and the AI system. On one hand, the consumer has to be convinced about the brand image and its characteristics, while on the other hand, a brand or a product has to be attractive from the point of view of the AI system, in order to be recommended to the consumer or bought in an automatic way by the AI assistant (Dawar, 2018). Therefore, the future of marketing will focus more on the ability and efficiency of using AI devices and systems in order to make products and brands attractive and to be included in their automated buying decisions.

3.4 Personal AI Assistants and Their Role in Assisting Consumers' Household Activities

Personal AI assistants are intelligent devices that take over several of the daily activities of consumers and have in the same time a physical presence. Although their development is so far incipient, there are several fields where personal robots are implemented, such as AI companions for senior and elderly people (Sundar et al., 2017) or shopping companions (Bertacchini et al., 2017), while future scenarios include them for taking over different activities in the household (Dawar, 2018). Depending on their behavioral characteristics, personal AI will bring both utilitarian and hedonic benefits. For instance, in the case of elderly people, humanoid robots can take the place of human caregivers by assisting in the daily routine and reminding them of things they have to do. At the same time, caregiving robots can help them move around the house and lift heavy objects. Especially for those elderly people living alone, these caregiving robots have an essential role in communicating with the outside world and even alerting medical institutions in the case of medical emergency (Sorell & Draper, 2014). They can also be involved in different spare-time activities like shopping (Bertacchini et al., 2017). AI with a physical presence can assist the human consumer and take over certain tasks such as lifting and carrying shopping bags. As previously described, anthropomorphism and social presence will play an important role in the acceptance of these AI companions. According to Sundar et al. (2017), the preferred human-like features of the AI depend on their role.

AI with a physical presence can substitute different personal activities which are not taken over by other humans. Some authors describe the future of humans as being permanently surrounded by intelligent devices, which will act as personal assistants and take over some of the daily activities of consumers (Dawar, 2018). An important aspect in the implementation of AI is their position of equality or subordination: more precisely should AI be considered as assistants or companions? According to Bryson (2009), all AI should be subordinated to their human owner. This is easy to implement in the case of AI which takes over functional tasks, but it is more difficult to fulfill in the case of social-interactive robots which accompany the consumer for spare-time and entertainment activities. The personality of consumers plays an important role in this equality-subordination positioning of AI. Some consumers who like to express power will be willing to subordinate their AI assistants (Hu et al., 2022), in opposition to introverted persons, who might enjoy the companionship of AI (Yuan et al., 2022). The integration of AI as assistant or companion will have important implications for the marketing strategies of companies, as the influence of AI on the consumer will depend on this integration.

4   Discussions and Future Implications

4.1   Implications for Consumer–AI Relations

In this chapter, the main categories of AI are presented, classified based on their physical or virtual presence and their social distance to their human owner as well as the main challenges they pose for the marketing strategies of companies. As seen in this classification, the big variety of AI with different functions and roles will have important implications for consumer–AI interactions in the future. However, it is important to make the distinction between these types of AI, as they will have different roles in the lives of consumers and consequently in the future marketing strategies of companies. In our opinion, one main distinction will be based on social distance. External service robots or voice assistants will be seen as similar to service employees and therefore the relation with them will be more distant, implying a formal communication and lower attachment. In opposition to this, the relation to personal voice assistance or to personal AI assistants with physical presence is closer and more personal, leading to an informal communication and also to the AI's higher access to the consumers' personal data. Trust and acceptance are concepts that are frequently measured in relation to AI. Based on the categories of AI, these constructs will have different valences for research. On one hand, in the case of external AI, the consumer will have to trust the AI to do the job well and accept it instead of a human employee. On the other hand, in the case of the personal AI, trust implies the access to personal data and to keeping this information private, while acceptance refers to accepting the AI in the private sphere and allowing it to perform certain tasks for the consumer. The satisfaction related to AI will depend on the expectations set by the consumers and the expected relations between consumer and AI.

4.2 Implications of the Consumer–AI Relations on the Marketing Strategies of Companies

The categorization of AI has different valences for the marketing strategies of companies. In the case of the external AI, the main challenge is to design competent and friendly AI with similar characteristics to human employees. Such AI should be able to fulfill the tasks in a similar way to human employees. In the case of personal AI, the design and features are important for the connection and relationship between the consumer and AI, and the ability of the AI to intervene in the buying decisions of the consumer. Personal AI will have the task either to recommend or to take buying decisions for the human consumer, gaining an important role for the marketing strategies of companies. Thus, companies should focus not only on convincing the consumer to buy their products, but also on getting the personal AI to recommend and include the product in the shopping list of the human consumer. One important question here concerns who is in control of the AI. The AI will have the ability through machine learning to know the preferences of the consumer, but at the same time, the system behind the AI is designed by a company which might have control of the AI's systems and recommendations. Especially in the case of a para-friendship relationship between consumer and AI, the human might be exposed by relying only on the recommendations of the AI, which might be controlled by a company. An AI device can play an important role in communication between company and consumer, but only if the consumer trusts the AI device and if he/she is willing to provide personal data to the AI device. Therefore, it is important to consider how these intelligent systems should be designed in order to protect the consumer, while at the same time allowing companies to gain competitive advantage.

4.3 Implications of Consumer–AI Interaction on the Marketing Strategies of Companies

The interaction between consumer and AI is another key aspect for the successful implementation of AI devices. On one hand, there is the interaction quality in the sense that the exchanged information between consumer and AI should be mutually understandable. If the AI does not understand the commands of the human consumer, it will not be able to perform the task efficiently and according to the expectations of the human consumer. On the other hand, if the consumer has difficulties in understanding the recommendations of the AI, he/she will choose a purchasing method that involves easier and simpler learning processes. However, there is also the engagement and fun in the interaction between consumer and AI. An empathetic, engaging and funny interaction will increase the attachment of the consumer toward the AI and therefore the willingness to continue using the AI. Positive emotions related to the interaction with the AI will determine whether the consumer intensifies its usage.

Consequently, it is important to design the communication and interaction between consumer and AI in order to make it functional, efficient, interactive and engaging at the same time. This interaction will play a role in the intensity and volume of the commercial transactions and it will determine the buying decisions of the consumer.

4.4 Managerial and Practical Implications

The conceptual analysis presented in this chapter has major managerial and practical implications. For companies and managers, it is important to clearly define what type of robot will take over a certain function. Managers must be aware of the fact that there are different types of AI and it is important to implement them correctly depending on the context and tasks for which they interact with the consumer. As shown above, there are certain operations with a low involvement, in which the interaction and relations between the consumer and AI are rather functional, while there are also operations with an emotional involvement, where the interaction and relations should be designed accordingly. For marketing departments, it is important to determine the expectations of consumers and design the interaction accordingly. For instance, a consumer might find overwhelming the implication of emotional reactions in an expected functional relationship, while conversely, if the emotional elements are lacking in an expected engaging relationship, the consumer will find the interaction cold and unempathetic. Based on consumer and marketing research, it is important to determine the right balance between functional and social-interactive components in each dealing between consumer and AI. Of course, the correct balance can be established based on previous consumer–employees interactions, but at the same time, it might depend on each consumer and their expectations.

Another important aspect in the implementation of AI is the equality–subordination relation between consumers and AI and their role as assistants or companions. Depending on the programmed behavioral characteristics of AI, there can be distinguished between functional and social-interactive robots. In the case of the functional role of AI, it is expected to have a subordination relationship, in which the AI will execute the tasks commanded by the human owner and will have less power in influencing the decisions of the consumer. In the case of a social-interactive AI, emotional relations between consumer and AI will occur, leading to a rather equal relationship. In this case, the AI will have emotional power to make recommendations for the human consumer. Both scenarios and both types of robots will impact the interaction between consumer and company, by having rather analytical relations in the case of the functional AI or rather emotional relations in the case of the social-interactive AI. In both cases the interaction between company and consumer will take place with the help of AI.

4.5 Future Research Directions

The research directions for consumer–AI interactions and their implication on the marketing strategies of companies are vast, but there is no golden rule for their implementation. In future research, the authors consider that it is important to make a delimitation between the different types of AI. Most of the existent studies have been done on AI in general with the delimitation based on the AI type used in the research. In future research, the authors aim to investigate empirically both the anthropomorphic features of AI devices and robots as well as the social relations between consumer and AI.

In this chapter, there is presented a conceptual classification of AI types and their role for the marketing strategies of companies, but the topic needs further empirical investigation. As mentioned before, it is important to assess the role of each AI involved in the relation between companies and consumers, to establish the expectations of the consumer and implement the AI accordingly. In each case, the relation between AI and consumers depends on several positive and negative outcomes that he/she receives from this relationship. On one hand, there is the increased efficiency brought by the AI to the consumers' activities, the hedonic pleasure and even the social presence and interaction with the AI. On the other hand, the consumer might feel threatened by the interference of the AI device in his/her private life and even lose his/her social capabilities because of the communication with the AI device to the detriment of other human beings. Consequently, it is important to balance the positive and negative aspects of the consumer–AI relations, in order to optimize the benefits for the consumer and companies. Consequently, the relation has to be further investigated in order to optimize its outcomes for consumers, companies and society in general.

5 CONCLUSIONS

The results of this conceptual analysis on the implementation of AI in the interaction between consumers and companies show the importance of the role played by AI in service and product delivery. The analysis of the different features of AI, such as physical, psychological and behavioral anthropomorphic features as well as social presence depends a lot on the expectations of consumers. In their interaction with a company or in service delivery, consumers, depending on the context, might want an easy functional relationship or more complex and engaging social relations with the AI and with the company. It is important for companies to establish for each product and each service, the amount of engagement the consumers want in order to enhance the implementation of different types of AI. Companies must be aware of the fact that each type of AI plays a different role in their relation to consumers and therefore anthropomorphic characteristics, behavior and social presence should be designed according to expectations. Some AIs will act as personal assistants and will have more access to consumers' personal data and private life, while others will keep a social distance and serve the consumer according to its commands. The same is valid for the physical presence of AI and robots. Consequently, there is no golden rule for the implementation of AI. Each company has to adapt according to the interaction context and to the expectations and personality of the consumer.

Acknowledgements This work was supported by a grant from the Romanian Ministry of Education and Research, CNCS–UEFISCDI, project number PN-III-P1-1.1-TE-2021-0795, within PNCDI III.

References

Adam, M., Wessel, M., & Benlian, A. (2021). AI-based chatbots in customer service and their effects on user compliance. *Electronic Markets, 31*(2), 427–445. https://doi.org/10.1007/s12525-020-00414-7

Alepis, E., & Patsakis, C. (2017). Monkey says, monkey does: Security and privacy on voice assistants. *IEEE Transactions on Affective Computing, 5*, 17841–17851. https://doi.org/10.1109/ACCESS.2017.2747626

Araujo, T. (2018). Living up to the chatbot hype: The influence of anthropomorphic design cues and communicative agency framing on conversational agent and company perceptions. *Computers in Human Behavior, 85*, 183–189. https://doi.org/10.1016/j.chb.2018.03.051

Ashfaq, M., Yun, J., Yu, S. B., & Loureiro, S. M. C. (2020). I, Chatbot: Modeling the determinants of users' satisfaction and continuance intention of AI-powered service agents. *Telematics and Informatics, 54*, 101473. https://doi.org/10.1016/j.tele.2020.101473

Belanche, D., Casalo, L. V., Flavian, C., & Schepers, J. (2020). Service robot implementation: A theoretical framework and research agenda. *The Service Industries Journal, 40*(3–4), 203–225. https://doi.org/10.1080/02642069.2019.1672666

Bertacchini, F., Bilotta, E., & Pantano, P. (2017). Shopping with a robotic companion. *Computers in Human Behavior, 77*, 382–395. https://doi.org/10.1016/j.chb.2017.02.064

Blut, M., Wang, C., Wünderlich, N. V., & Brock, C. (2021). Understanding anthropomorphism in service provision: A meta-analysis of physical robots, chatbots, and other AI. *Journal of the Academy of Marketing Science, 49*, 632–658. https://doi.org/10.1007/s11747-020-00762-y

Bryson, J. J. (2009). Robots should be slaves. In Y. Wilks (Ed.), *Close engagements with artificial companions: Key social, psychological, ethical and design issues* (pp. 63–74). John Benjamins Publishing Company. https://doi.org/10.1075/nlp.8.11bry

Chen, Y. H., Keng, C.-J., & Chen, Y.-L. (2021). How interaction experience enhances customer engagement in smart speaker devices? The moderation of gendered voice and product smartness, *Journal of Research in Interactive Marketing*, 16(3), 403–419. https://doi.org/10.1108/JRIM-03-2021-0064

Choi, S., Mattila, A. S., & Bolton, L. E. (2021). To err is human (−oid): How do consumers react to robot service failure and recovery? *Journal of Service Research*, 24(3), 354–371. https://doi.org/10.1177/1094670520978798

Chong, T., Yu, T., Keeling, D. I., & de Ruyter, K. (2021). AI-chatbots on the services frontline addressing the challenges and opportunities of agency. *Journal of Retailing and Consumer Services*, 63, 102735. https://doi.org/10.1016/j.jretconser.2021.102735

Chung, M., Ko, E., Joung, H., & Kim, S. J. (2020). Chatbot e-service and customer satisfaction regarding luxury brands. *Journal of Business Research*, 117, 587–595. https://doi.org/10.1016/j.jbusres.2018.10.004

Ciechanowski, L., Przegalinska, A., Magnuski, M., & Gloor, P. (2019). In the shades of the uncanny valley: An experimental study of human–chatbot interaction. *Future Generation Computer Systems*, 92, 539–548. https://doi.org/10.1016/j.future.2018.01.055

Clark, M. S., & Mills, J. (1993). The difference between communal and exchange relationships: What it is and is not. *Personality and Social Psychology Bulletin*, 19(6), 684–691. https://doi.org/10.1177/0146167293196003

Crolic, C., Thomaz, F., Hadi, R., & Stephen, A. T. (2022). Blame the bot: Anthropomorphism and anger in customer-chatbot interactions. *Journal of Marketing*, 86(1), 132–148. https://doi.org/10.1177/00222429211045687

Dawar, N. (2018, August). Marketing im Zeitalter von Alexa. *Harvard Business Manager*.

Epley, N., Waytz, A., & Cacioppo, J. T. (2007). On seeing human: A three-factor theory of anthropomorphism. *Psychological Review*, 114(4), 864–886. https://doi.org/10.1037/0033-295X.114.4.864

Feine, J., Gnewuch, U., Morana, S., & Maedche, A. (2019). A taxonomy of social cues for conversational agents. *International Journal of Human-Computer Studies*, 132, 138–161. https://doi.org/10.1016/j.ijhcs.2019.07.009

Fernandes, T., & Oliveira, E. (2021). Understanding consumers' acceptance of automated technologies in service encounters: Drivers of digital voice assistants adoption. *Journal of Business Research*, 122, 180–191. https://doi.org/10.1016/j.jbusres.2020.08.058

Golossenko, A., Pillai, K. G., & Aroean, L. (2020). Seeing brands as humans: Development and validation of a brand anthropomorphism scale. *International Journal of Research in Marketing*, 37(4), 737–755. https://doi.org/10.1016/j.ijresmar.2020.02.007

Grewal, D., Kroschke, M., Mende, M., Roggeveen, A. L., & Scott, M. L. (2020). Frontline cyborgs at your service: How human enhancement technologies affect customer experiences in retail, sales, and service settings. *Journal of Interactive Marketing*, 51, 9–25. https://doi.org/10.1016/j.intmar.2020.03.001

Gursoy, D., Chi, O. H., Lu, L., & Nunkoo, R. (2019). Consumers' acceptance of artificially intelligent (AI) device use in service delivery. *International Journal of Information Management*, 49, 157–169. https://doi.org/10.1016/j.ijinfomgt.2019.03.008

Hoy, M. B., & Pomputius, A. F. (2018). Alexa, Siri, Cortana, and more: An introduction to voice assistants. *Medical Reference Services Quarterly, 37*(1), 81–88. https://doi.org/10.1080/02763869.2018.1404391

Hsieh, S. H., & Lee, C. T. (2021). Hey Alexa: Examining the effect of perceived socialness in usage intentions of AI assistant-enabled smart speaker. *Journal of Research in Interactive Marketing, 15*(2), 267–294. https://doi.org/10.1108/JRIM-11-2019-0179

Hu, P., Lu, Y., & Wang, B. (2022). Experiencing power over AI: The fit effect of perceived power and desire for power on consumers' choice for voice shopping. *Computers in Human Behavior, 128*, 107091. https://doi.org/10.1016/j.chb.2021.107091

Huang, M.-H., & Rust, R. T. (2022). AI as customer. *Journal of Service Management, 33*(2), 210–220. https://doi.org/10.1108/JOSM-11-2021-0425

Kervenoael, R.d., Hasan, R., Schwob, A., & Goh, E. (2020). Leveraging human-robot interaction in hospitality services: Incorporating the role of perceived value, empathy, and information sharing into visitors' intentions to use social robots. *Tourism Management, 78*, 104042. https://doi.org/10.1016/j.tourman.2019.104042

Ki, C. W., Cho, E., & Lee, J. E. (2020). Can an intelligent personal assistant (IPA) be your friend? Para-friendship development mechanism between IPAs and their users. *Computers in Human Behaviour, 111*, 1–10. https://doi.org/10.1016/j.chb.2020.106412

Kim, S.S., Kim, J., Badu-Baiden, F., Giroux, M. & Choi, Y. (2021). Preference for robot service or human service in hotels? Impacts of the COVID-19 pandemic. International *Journal of Hospitality Management, 93*. https://doi.org/10.1016/j.ijhm.2020.102795

Lim, W.M., Kumar, S., Pandey, N., Rasul, T., & Gaur, V. (2022). From direct marketing to interactive marketing: a retrospective review of the Journal of Research in Interactive Marketing, *Journal of Research in Interactive Marketing* (ahead-of-print). https://doi.org/10.1108/JRIM-11-2021-0276

Liu, X. S., Yi, X. S., & Wan, L. C. (2022). Friendly or competent? The effects of perception of robot appearance and service context on usage intention. *Annals of Tourism Research, 92*. https://doi.org/10.1016/j.annals.2021.103324

Loideain, N. N., & Adams, R. (2020). From Alexa to Siri and the GDPR: The gendering of Virtual Personal Assistants and the role of Data Protection Impact Assessments. *Computer Law & Security Review, 36*, 1–14. https://doi.org/10.1016/j.clsr.2019.105366

Longoni, C., & Cian, L. (2022). Artificial intelligence in utilitarian vs. hedonic contexts: The "word-of-machine" effect. *Journal of Marketing, 86*(1), 91–108. https://doi.org/10.1108/10.1177/0022242920957347

Lu, L., Cai, R. Y., & Gursoy, D. (2019). Developing and validating a service robot integration willingness scale. *International Journal of Hospitality Management, 80*, 36–51. https://doi.org/10.1016/j.ijhm.2019.01.005

Lucia-Palacios, L., & Perez-Lopez, R. (2021). How can autonomy improve consumer experience when interacting with smart products? *Journal of Research in Interactive Marketing* (ahead-of-print). https://doi.org/10.1108/JRIM-02-2021-0031

Luo, X., Tong, S., Fang, Z., & Qu, Z. (2019). Frontiers: machines vs. humans: the impact of artificial intelligence chatbot disclosure on customer purchases. *Marketing Science, 38*(6), 937–947, https://doi.org/10.1287/mksc.2019.1192

Lv, X., Liu, Y., Luo, J., Liu, Y., & Li, C. (2021). Does a cute artificial intelligence assistant soften the blow? The impact of cuteness on customer tolerance of assistant service failure. *Annals of Tourism Research, 87*, 103114. https://doi.org/10.1016/j.annals.2020.103114

McLean, G., & Osei-Frimpong, K. (2019). Hey Alexa … examine the variables influencing the use of artificial intelligent in-home voice assistants. *Computers in Human Behaviour, 99*, 28–37. https://doi.org/10.1016/j.chb.2019.05.009

McLean, G., Osei-Frimpong, K., & Barhorst, J. (2021). Alexa, do voice assistants influence consumer brand engagement?—Examining the role of AI powered voice assistants in influencing consumer brand engagement. *Journal of Business Research, 124*, 312–328. https://doi.org/10.1016/j.jbusres.2020.11.045

Payne, E. M., Peltier, J., & Barger, V. A. (2021). Enhancing the value co-creation process: Artificial intelligence and mobile banking service platforms. *Journal of Research in Interactive Marketing, 15*(1), 68–85. https://doi.org/10.1108/JRIM-10-2020-0214

Pelau, C., Dabija, D. C., & Ene, I. (2021). What makes an AI device human-like? The role of interaction quality, empathy and perceived psychological anthropomorphic characteristics in the acceptance of artificial intelligence in the service industry. *Computers in Human Behavior, 122*, 106855. https://doi.org/10.1016/j.chb.2021.106855

Poushneh, A. (2021). Humanizing voice assistant: The impact of voice assistant personality on consumers' attitudes and behaviors. *Journal of Retailing and Consumer Services, 58*, 102283. https://doi.org/10.1016/j.jretconser.2020.102283

Puntoni, S., Walker, R. R., Giesler, M., & Botti, S. (2021). Consumers and artificial intelligence: An experiential perspective. *Journal of Marketing, 85*(1), 131–151. https://doi.org/10.1177/0022242920953847

Seyitoglu, F., & Ivanov, S. (2021). Service robots as a tool for physical distancing in tourism. *Current Issues in Tourism, 24*(12), 1631–1634. https://doi.org/10.1080/13683500.2020.1774518

Song, Y., & Luximon, Y. (2020). Trust in AI agent: A systematic review of facial anthropomorphic trustworthiness for social robot design. *Sensors, 20*(18), 5087. https://doi.org/10.3390/s20185087

Sorell, T., & Draper, H. (2014). Robot carers, ethics, and older people. *Ethics and Information Technology, 16*(3), 183–195. https://doi.org/10.1007/s10676-014-9344-7

Sundar, S., Jung, E. W., Waddell, F., & Kim, K. J. (2017). Cheery companions or serious assistants? Role and demeanor congruity as predictors of robot attraction and use intentions among senior citizens. *International Journal of Human-Computer Studies, 97*, 88–97. https://doi.org/10.1016/j.ijhcs.2016.08.006

Tan, H., Zhao, Y., Li, S., Wang, W., Zhu, M., Hong, J., & Yuan, X. (2020). Relationship between social robot proactive behavior and the human perception of anthropomorphic attributes. *Advanced Robotics, 34*(20), 1324–1336. https://doi.org/10.1080/01691864.2020.1831699

Tsai, W.-H.S., Liu, Y., & Chuan, C.-H. (2021). How chatbots' social presence communication enhances consumer engagement: The mediating role of parasocial interaction and dialogue. *Journal of Research in Interactive Marketing, 15*(3), 460–482. https://doi.org/10.1108/JRIM-12-2019-0200

van Doorn, J., Mende, M., Noble, S. M., Hulland, J., Ostrom, A. L., Grewal, D., & Petersen, J. A. (2017). Domo Arigato Mr. Roboto. Emergence of automated social presence in organizational frontlines and customers' service experiences. *Journal of Service Research, 20*(1), 43–58. https://doi.org/10.1177/1094670516679272

Wang, C. L. (2021). New frontiers and future directions in interactive marketing: Inaugural Editorial. *Journal of Research in Interactive Marketing, 15*(1), 1–9. https://doi.org/10.1108/JRIM-03-2021-270

Wang, W. (2017). Smartphones as social actors? Social dispositional factors in assessing anthropomorphism. *Computers in Human Behavior, 68*, 334–344. https://doi.org/10.1016/j.chb.2016.11.022

Wirtz, J., Patterson, P. G., Kunz, W. H., Gruber, T., Lu, V. N., Paluch, S., & Martins, A. (2018). Brave new world: Service robots in the frontline. *Journal of Service Management, 29*(50), 907–931. https://doi.org/10.1108/JOSM-04-2018-0119

Yu, B. (2021). How consumer opinions are affected by marketers: an empirical examination by deep learning approach. *Journal of Research in Interactive Marketing, 16*(4). https://doi.org/10.1108/JRIM-04-2021-0106

Yuan, C., Zhang, C., & Wang, S. (2022). Social anxiety as a moderator in consumer willingness to accept AI assistants based on utilitarian and hedonic values. *Journal of Retailing and Consumer Services, 65*, 1–11. https://doi.org/10.1016/j.jretconser.2021.102878

Zhu, D. H., & Chang, Y. P. (2020). Robot with humanoid hands cooks food better? *International Journal of Contemporary Hospitality Management, 32*(3), 1367–1383. https://doi.org/10.1108/IJCHM-10-2019-0904

CHAPTER 12

Humanizing Chatbots for Interactive Marketing

Wan-Hsiu Sunny Tsai and Ching-Hua Chuan

1 Introduction

The advances in artificial intelligence (AI) technologies have transformed interactive marketing, elevating the field in automation, reach, acceleration, precision, and accuracy. AI-powered self-service tools can further empower consumers in value co-creation (Payne et al., 2021). Among the various AI-enabled tools, chatbots represent a new frontier of interactive marketing (Tsai et al., 2021a, 2021b). Chatbots, also known as conversational agents, are automated computer programs powered by natural language processing to engage consumers in interactive, one-on-one, personalized text- or voice-based conversations. Given the dialogic nature, Sundar et al. (2016) argue that chatbots may realize the promise of media technologies to simulate interpersonal communication. Across various industries, from e-learning, healthcare, to e-commerce, chatbots have been adopted for their responsiveness, 24–7 availability, and cost-efficiency (Adam et al., 2021; Loveys et al., 2020). Pizzi et al. (2021) suggest that chatbot assistants are particularly favored by e-commerce websites to subrogate salespeople and add a human touch. During the COVID-19 pandemic, the US Centers for Disease Control and Prevention's chatbot has answered over a million inquiries per day from users in

W.-H. S. Tsai (✉) · C.-H. Chuan
University of Miami, Coral Gables, FL, USA
e-mail: wanhsiu@miami.edu

C.-H. Chuan
e-mail: c.chuan@miami.edu

the US (Smith, 2020), an impossible feat if such support were to be administered by human representatives. Particularly relevant to the pandemic that has dramatically shifted the majority of consumers' everyday interactions from face-to-face to virtual, chatbots can be easily implemented on various digital platforms, from websites to mobile apps. On Facebook alone, there are more than 400,000 chatbots working hard to generate leads, provide assistance, and close sales (Kim, 2020). Industry reports predict that e-commerce via chatbots will grow from $2.8 billion in 2019 to $142 billion in 2024 (Juniper Research, 2020), creating new buzzwords such as chatvertising (Mims, 2014) and conversational marketing (Cancel & Gerhardt, 2019).

The most common use of chatbots in interactive marketing today is for customer service (Tsai et al., 2021a, 2021b). Research has confirmed the effectiveness of chatbots as e-service agents to provide engaging service experiences to improve marketing outcomes including user compliance (Adam et al., 2021), trust (Youn & Jin, 2021), and customer–brand relationship (Chung et al., 2018). In online customer service, chatbots do not get frustrated or lose their temper when communicating with angry, difficult customers as humans sometimes do (Luo et al., 2019; Tsai et al., 2021a, 2021b). The majority of chatbot research has focused on the *utilitarian* usage of chatbots (Ling et al., 2021) for customer service (e.g., Araujo, 2018; Go & Sundar, 2019) and evaluated task-oriented factors such as perceived usefulness (e.g., Zarouali et al., 2018) and communication accuracy (e.g., Cheng & Jiang, 2021). However, as a personalized, one-on-one communication tool, the potential of chatbots for interactive marketing extends far beyond providing information (Ramerman, 2020).

Huang and Rust (2018) note that emotional intelligence enabling computers to understand people's emotional status and respond with empathy will be the driving force of consumer acceptance of AI technologies. Prior research in interactive marketing also attests to the importance of social communication style for brand avatars in facilitating consumer–brand relationships (e.g., Foster et al., 2021). Recently, scholars have noted the increasing popularity of "social chatbots" that are "humanlike, with personality and appropriate emotions" (Croes & Antheunis, 2021, p. 280) that satisfy people's social and relational needs (Shum et al., 2018) and enhance consumer–brand relationships (Youn & Jin, 2021). Social chatbots like Kuki, who introduces "herself" as "your AI BFF," and Replika, "an AI companion who cares," are designed to communicate in a highly personable, affectionate manner to stimulate attraction and offer emotional and social support. Focusing on text-based social chatbots that can be easily implemented on websites and messenger platforms, this book chapter synthesizes the relevant literature from the fields of computer-mediated communication (CMC) and human–computer interaction (HCI) to highlight the key factors driving chatbot persuasiveness.

Specifically, this chapter is organized as follows. To explicate the potential of computer-controlled chatbots in relation to human-controlled avatars, this chapter first discusses the HCI literature comparing the social influence of computers versus human agents. Then, the chapter delves into the various anthropomorphic cues to humanize chatbots, including visual-oriented human identity cues (e.g., appearance, name, gender), content and style-specific verbal cues, as well as non-verbal cues such as typing indicators. To mitigate the negative consequences when chatbots fail to understand consumers' inputs, strategies for chatbots to communicate humility are provided. The chapter next addresses some of the most widely studied mediators of chatbot anthropomorphism—social presence and parasocial interaction—and highlights the under-researched role of emotions in consumer–chatbot interactions. The chapter further elaborates on the "uncanny valley" effect pertaining to people's feelings of eeriness toward highly human-like chatbots.

2 COMPUTER AGENTS VERSUS HUMAN AVATARS

As social beings, human perceptions, feelings, and experiences are shaped by the actual, perceptual, and implied presence of others (Allport, 1985). However, the source and mechanism of such social influence in today's digital world is constantly being redefined and transformed, particularly when users encounter computer agents that can demonstrate human-like intelligence or intentions. Kim and Sundar (2012) argue that when interacting with chatbots, people perceive that they are interacting with another *intelligent being*, despite their awareness of the bot's non-human identity, and respond to it as a meaningful source of interaction.

Extensive research in CMC has compared the social influence of computer-controlled agents versus human-controlled avatars but the findings are contradictory. Some studies reported that users respond differently to virtual characters based on whether they believe the character is being controlled by a computer or by another person (e.g., Blascovich et al., 2002). This line of research suggests that, due to the prevailing schema regarding computers as unfeeling and mechanical, users will be more susceptible to the social influences (e.g., persuasiveness) of a perceived human than a computer (Blascovich, 2002). For instance, users tend to be more open, agreeable, and extroverted; and use less profanity, more and longer words per message, and more positive emotions when communicating with perceived humans rather than chatbots (Hill et al., 2015; Mou & Xu, 2017). With a chatbot, users are less likely to establish common ground and sustain personal relationships during the conversation (Corti & Gillespie, 2016).

In contrast, other studies have shown that computer agents can be received as well as human avatars. The computers are social actors (CASA) literature suggests that when a computer mimics humans by demonstrating social cues, people intuitively and unconsciously respond to the computer as though they were interacting with another human being, rather than cognitively determine how they should respond differently (Nass & Moon, 2000; Reeves & Nass, 1996). Although users are aware that a computer agent is not human and might not warrant human attributions, they respond to it as a real person, without consciously intending to do so (Reeves & Nass, 1996). For instance, Nowak and Biocca (2003) found that human avatars and computer agents evoke similar levels of perceived copresence, social presence, and telepresence. In fact, being ostracized by a computer agent when playing Cyberball can generate similar levels of damage to self-esteem, sense of belonging, and meaningful existence as being ostracized by a human partner (Zadro et al., 2004). Specific to the conversational advantage of chatbots, Ho et al. (2018) observed that users' emotional self-disclosure to a perceived chatbot partner generated emotional, relational, and psychological benefits that are comparable to disclosures to a human partner. As chatbots have been increasingly adopted in various industries, the crucial question is no longer about whether chatbots may perform equally well or differently from human avatars, but what factors can enhance the effectiveness of chatbots for what outcomes.

Specific to interactive marketing, Luo et al.'s (2019) field experiment on voice-based chatbots for online financial services found that when companies do not disclose to customers the computer identity of the sales representative in sales phone calls, chatbots are as effective as proficient human representatives and four times more effective than inexperienced ones in engendering customer purchases. However, when customers are told that they are interacting with a bot, purchase rates drop by more than 79.7%. Based on survey data, they further confirm that when customers know they are talking to a bot, they are more brusque, purchase less, and even terminate the calls early because they perceive the bot as less knowledgeable and empathetic. It is important to note that consumers are likely to respond differently to voice-based versus text-based bots, and more importantly, they may be more cautious and skeptical toward the uses of chatbots for complicated, high-risk financial services studied in Luo et al.'s (2019) experiment. Indeed, Mozafari et al. (2021) found that for highly critical services, if the text-based chatbot is able to solve the service issue, chatbot disclosure reduces customer trust and consequently hampers retention. By contrast, for less critical services, chatbot disclosure has no impact on customer trust. Unexpectedly, they also observed that when the chatbot fails to handle the service issue, disclosing the chatbot identity can mitigate the negative failure effect and improve customer retention. They explained that the chatbot disclosure serves as a type of explanation of the service failure and may be regarded as akin to an apology. Nonetheless, given the increasing demand from regulators and consumers for corporate transparency, including chatbot disclosure (Federal Trade Commission, 2017), marketers are strongly encouraged to explicitly inform consumers that they are interacting with a bot. Adam et al. (2021) further argue that instead of attempting to disguise a chatbot's machine identity or tricking users into thinking they are interacting with a human, marketers should focus on strategies and factors that can enhance chatbots' effectiveness. Next, this chapter will discuss the key variables that drive chatbots' persuasiveness, from chatbot design to consumer attributes, contextual considerations, and key mediators.

3   ANTHROPOMORPHISM OF CHATBOTS

Research highlights people's skepticism or resistance to chatbots, likely due to the understanding that chatbots are devoid of feelings and empathy, and are thus incapable of genuinely understanding their personal needs. Not surprisingly, extensive research has explored ways to imbue chatbots with "humanity" by boosting perceived anthropomorphism—the degree to which non-human entities can project human-like characteristics, behaviors, emotions, and intentions (Powers & Kiesler, 2006). Higher anthropomorphism has been shown to lower reactance (Pizzi et al., 2021) and improve consumer trust, interaction, and experience (De Visser et al., 2016). For instance, Roy and Naidoo (2021) found that perceived humanness of chatbots based on social judgment cues of warmth and competence contributes to consumer perception of the target brand as more humane. Blut et al.'s (2021) meta-analysis of the service literature further confirms that anthropomorphism is positively associated with robots' perceived animacy, intelligence, and likability. Not surprisingly, anthropomorphism is the most commonly implemented and tested factor in chatbot research.

While chatbots can be either disembodied (e.g., Bank of America's "Erica") or embodied with a virtual representation, the majority of chatbot studies have focused on embodied chatbots that can be easily designed to look like humans, such as IKEA's "Anna." Go and Sundar (2019) suggest that the easiest way to infuse a chatbot with humanness might be the use of human figures that can encapsulate various human identity cues (e.g., human-like face, name, age, gender, occupational role) as explicit visual cues to give the bot a human identity (Liew & Tan, 2021). Feine et al.'s (2019) taxonomy of social cues for chatbots also identified agent appearance (e.g., gender, age, race, hair color, occupational role) as an important visual cue. Hence, it has been argued that appearance-oriented human identity cues have primacy over other anthropomorphic cues such as language (Roy & Naidoo, 2021). Indeed, anthropomorphic appearance has become the default of chatbot design in the literature (e.g., Roy & Naidoo, 2021), while the manipulation and operationalization of anthropomorphic appearance can vary from a cartoon-like, animated picture to a real person's photo. Not surprisingly, many brands have created embodied chatbots that have human-like figures or profile pictures in the design.

Another key factor driving chatbots' persuasiveness is anthropomorphic verbal cues in messages, which are not as directly and immediately observable as human identity visual cues (Youn & Jin, 2021). Research has examined various communication strategies or conversational styles utilizing anthropomorphic verbal cues to enhance chatbots' perceived humanness. Feine et al.'s (2019) taxonomy of chatbot social cues differentiates verbal cues into *content* (i.e., what is said) and *style* (how something is said). For instance, Tsai et al. and's (2021a, 2021b) experiment tested chatbot messages that use content cues of humor and phatics (i.e., communications that serve a purely social function such as "Great weather today!"), of addressing users by name and expressing agreement and appreciation with the user. They reported that such verbal cues effectively boost user perception of having a dialogue with the bot, which in turn improves consumer evaluation. Youn and Jin (2021) reported that verbal cues of the first-person singular pronoun, small talk, and empathy positively drive consumer compliance. In particular, AI tools' "empathetic intelligence" in recognizing and understanding people's emotional expressions, responding with proper emotions, and influencing others' emotions, has been advocated as the next key step for improving consumer acceptance (Huang & Rust, 2018). Increasing research efforts have been dedicated to exploring how chatbots can express empathy to improve user response. For instance, Liu and Sundar (2018) tested three types of empathic expression—sympathy (e.g., "I feel sorry for your pain"), cognitive empathy (i.e., acknowledgment of users' situations and feelings), and affective empathy (e.g., "I could imagine how annoying it is")—and found that chatbots' expression of sympathy and affective empathy is perceived as more supportive.

Research has also evaluated style-oriented verbal cues. For instance, Nass et al. (1995) suggest that personalities of computers can be easily constructed and conveyed via dominant language style (e.g., assertions and commands; speaking first in the conversation) or submissive style (e.g., questions and suggestions; speaking second in the interaction). Roy and Naidoo (2021) experimented with anthropomorphic conversational styles of warm versus competent and found that the varying communication style persuaded consumers to demonstrate different psychological predispositions toward the chatbot. Liebrecht and van Hooijdonk (2020) similarly suggest applying conversational human voice, an informal style of organizational communication to enhance the chatbot's perceived humanness.

A critical style-oriented verbal cue that has not been sufficiently studied is the chatbot's projected brand personality or character. Prior HCI studies have highlighted the importance of the general "friendly" personality trait (e.g., Mehra, 2021) and compared easily differentiated, dichotomous personalities of extraversion versus introversion (e.g., Lee et al., 2006). At the same time, marketing literature has documented that consumers commonly attribute human properties to brands (Verčič & Verčič, 2007), and multi-dimensional brand personalities (i.e., sincerity, excitement, competence, sophistication, and ruggedness; Aaker, 1997) have been widely studied. For example, sincerity and ruggedness positively influence trust toward the brand while excitement and sophistication help create an emotional bond with the brand (Sung & Kim, 2010). Similarly, Davies et al. (2004) developed a corporate character scale in public relations that consists of five key dimensions: agreeableness, enterprise, competence, chic, and ruthlessness. However, research has not adequately explored how well chatbots can project a specific brand personality dimension or corporate character or the impact of specific brand personality in chatbot–consumer interactions and the associated brand–consumer relationship.

Lastly, a widely recognized disadvantage of text-based platforms is their relative limitation in facilitating non-verbal communication. Despite the limited affordance of text-based chatbots, non-verbal anthropomorphic cues such as "typing" indicators, longer response time signifying "thinking," as well as emojis could be perceived as part of the communication processed by users and accordingly can evoke social responses in human–machine communication (Feine et al., 2019; Xu & Liao, 2020; Seeger et al., 2021).

3.1   Chatbot Humility

Although many studies focus on anthropomorphic verbal cues that can boost a chatbot's perceived competence and expertise (Liew & Tan, 2021), a chatbot's self-disclosure of limitations and shortcomings in performance can, in fact, boost trustworthiness and thus elevate user engagement (Rheu et al., 2021). In particular, anthropomorphic chatbots may set high expectations although they have only a limited ability to understand all types of input, including grammatical and syntactic errors in users' responses that human representatives would be able to comprehend. With substantial buzz and hype about AI advances in media coverage, consumers' expectations of what AI-powered chatbots can do are likely to be further inflated, leading to great frustration when such expectations are not met. Indeed, Luger and Sellen (2016) reported "user expectations dramatically out of step with the operation of the systems, particularly in terms of known machine intelligence, system capabilities and goals" (p. 5286). It is thus imperative to employ strategies to mitigate the detrimental impacts when chatbots' response failures occur.

If a chatbot's self-introduction is infused with humility by explicitly communicating that it is still "learning" as a technology-in-progress, as well as acknowledging its limitations and potential failure in understanding their input, users may lower their expectations or even become more patient or tolerant when the chatbot fails to understand them or respond appropriately. For instance, the weather forecast bot "Poncho" informed users "I'm good at talking about the weather. Other stuff, not so good" and Slack's chatbot states "I try to be helpful (But I'm still just a bot. Sorry!)" in its self-introduction (Waddell, 2017) Additionally, fallback responses (e.g., "I did not understand your request. Can you rephrase?") are necessary when response failure occurs (Ashktorab et al., 2019). Instead of simply stating that the chatbot could not understand the user's questions, including humility in chatbots' fallback responses is also crucial.

Relatedly, as AI tools become increasingly prevalent, consumers' awareness of the limitation and imperfection of the technology may lead to a general tendency toward algorithm aversion (Dietvorst et al., 2015), defined as people's reluctance to use algorithms that they know to be superior but *imperfect*. Focusing on test score forecast algorithms, Dietvorst et al. (2018) suggest that giving users the freedom to modify the algorithm, even in a very restricted manner, can induce a sense of control that increases satisfaction and preference with the algorithm. Pizzi et al. (2021) further suggest that conversation initiation (i.e., conversation initiated by the chatbot or by the user) should be considered since unsolicited help or advice from chatbots may evoke reactance similar to the negative effects of pop-up advertisements. They found that initiation locus significantly interacts with anthropomorphic chatbot design so that consumer reactance is lower for user-initiated anthropomorphic chatbots. More research is needed to explore whether allowing users to modify or customize aspects of the chatbot design and communication might lead to higher acceptance, more tolerance of chatbot failures, or greater interaction satisfaction.

3.2 *Anthropomorphism, Social Presence, and Parasocial Interaction*

Related to the widely recognized importance of anthropomorphism in chatbot design, social presence has been extensively documented as the key factor mediating the effects of chatbot anthropomorphism on interpersonal effects. Defined as a degree of salience of another intelligent being (living or synthetic) in mediated interactions (Qiu & Benbasat, 2009; Short et al., 1976), social presence addresses people's perceptions of human contact (i.e., warmth, empathy, sociability) and psychological distance with others in CMC and HCI. Chatbot studies consistently suggest that anthropomorphic chatbots, such as bots that resemble human appearances, can evoke a sense of social presence by generating feelings of interacting with the "other person" (Go & Sundar, 2019; Kim & Sundar, 2012). Social presence resulting from anthropomorphism has been shown to improve trust, engagement, interaction satisfaction, as well as attitude and emotional connection with chatbot's affiliated company (Araujo, 2018).

To understand how chatbots can simulate interpersonal communication, scholars have also examined the mediating role of parasocial interaction. This concept was originally conceptualized for audiences' perception of having an intimate and personal relationship akin to friendship and companionship with media personalities, such as fictional TV characters and news hosts (Horton & Wohl, 1956). Given the dominance of social media, CMC scholars have studied parasocial interaction with social media personalities, such as bloggers (Colliander & Dahlén, 2011) and social media influencers (Rasmussen, 2018), and documented the mediating effects of parasocial interaction on brand attitudes and purchase intentions (Colliander & Dahlén, 2011). In terms of consumer–chatbot interaction, Youn and Jin (2021) found that consumers who interacted with a friend chatbot (versus an assistant chatbot) experience stronger parasocial interaction, which further enhances perceived personality of chatbot's represented brand. Tsai et al., (2021a, 2021b) argue that the one-on-one, interactive, social, and conversational context can facilitate parasocial interaction compared to traditional media and the public-oriented, one-to-many communications with brand representatives on social networking sites.

They observed that the effects of chatbots' anthropomorphic verbal cues were fully mediated by parasocial interaction. Their results thus suggest that when pre-testing anthropomorphic cues in design and messaging, parasocial interaction should be considered as an important evaluation goal.

4 HUMAN EMOTIONS IN CONSUMER–CHATBOT INTERACTION

Compared to chatbot design and communication factors that have been the primary focus of prior studies, the role of emotions in consumer–chatbot interactions demands more research attention. In particular, in settings where consumers need to share information on sensitive, embarrassing, and potentially stigmatized issues such as financial difficulty, mental health, or sexual activity, consumers may be more willing to speak to computers that are viewed as impersonal but non-judgmental. It has long been speculated that "people would tell an impartial machine personal or embarrassing things about themselves, without fear of negative evaluation" (Weisband & Kiesler, 1996, p. 3). In health communication, research suggests that people tend to avoid face-to-face conversations on embarrassing or stigmatized topics (e.g., Redston et al., 2018). For instance, embarrassment is a major barrier to colon cancer prevention (Terdiman, 2006) and for young people in discussing sexual health with their physicians. Consequently, Planned Parenthood has offered a sex-ed chatbot, Roo, to answer teens' questions about puberty, sex, and relationships (Segran, 2019). Beyond health issues, Katsanis (1994) indicates that when purchasing embarrassing "unmentionable products" that are unhealthy, stigmatized, or sexually oriented, embarrassment is involved in all stages of buying and consumption (Dahl et al., 2001). However, there exist few studies assessing the effectiveness of chatbots in handling embarrassing topics and the preliminary results are mixed. Lucas et al. (2014) observed that participants who believed they were interacting with a computer agent reported lower evaluation fears and impression management, and were more honest in disclosing and displaying their sadness. They explained that because people believe that pre-programmed chatbots lack the ability to think independently, hence believe that chatbots do not judge them. Qualitative evidence further supports the notion that chatbot acceptability can be higher for sensitive content or stigmatized health issues (e.g., Nadarzynski et al., 2019; Zamora, 2017). By contrast, Tsai et al.'s (2021a, 2021b) experiment comparing chatbot versus human brand representative in the context of discussing sexually transmitted diseases and HPV vaccines found that embarrassed participants were more likely to disclose concerns of HPV risks and provide more elaborate answers to the perceived human representative. Even when participants experienced embarrassment, they responded similarly to chatbots and human representatives, rather than favoring chatbots. Along this line of reasoning, non-anthropomorphic bots highlighting the computer identity may be better suited to handle embarrassing conversations.

Specific to the prevalent use of chatbots in customer service, anger has been recognized as a powerful driver of consumer dissatisfaction with failed service encounters or product malfunction (Funches, 2011). However, angry consumers may get even more irritated when encountering a chatbot agent that is viewed as incapable of genuine understanding of their emotional stress and turmoil caused by the product and the company. Additionally, when angry consumers contact customer service, the first thing they want is to vent (Forbes, 2013). However, as an interaction-based anger regulatory strategy, venting is closely related to people's need to be understood by others that can bring a sense of validation. Without the emotional capacity to truly understand angry consumers' frustrations, chatbots are inherently poorly equipped in venting interactions. Angry consumers also contact customer service to seek a heartfelt apology (Worthington, 1998). However, the remorse and apology communicated by chatbots can be dismissed as pre-programmed, automated reactions. Indeed, Tsai et al., (2021a, 2021b) reported that angry participants reported lower interaction satisfaction with the chatbot than with the human representative. Moreover, Crolic et al. (2022) found that angry consumers interacting with an anthropomorphic (versus non-anthropomorphic) chatbot are more likely to report lower satisfaction, company evaluation, and future purchase intentions. They further verified that the anthropomorphic chatbot design elevates consumers' expectation of chatbot efficacy, and angry consumers respond more punitively to the expectancy violations compared with non-angry customers. In this way, although chatbots may function as well as human representatives in providing solutions or compensations to angry consumers, chatbots in general are disfavored by angry consumers, who may further "punish" the anthropomorphic ones that violated their expectations. Overall, there exists scarce empirical data about the effects of other powerful emotions, such as hope, aspiration, sadness, and fear, in the chatbot context. While chatbots can increasingly recognize and respond to a greater variety of human emotions, more research is needed to explicate the role of different emotions in influencing consumer–chatbot interactions.

5   Emotional and Empathetic Intelligence

Beyond chatbot design factors, scholars have advocated for the integration of consumer psychological traits to offer more personalized chatbot interactions (Pizzi et al., 2021). For instance, Youn and Jin (2021) focused on consumers' ideological perspective in embracing or resisting AI (technopians versus luddites) and found that technopians perceive an assistant chatbot (versus friend chatbot) to be more sincere, whereas luddites do not view the chatbot to be sincere regardless of whether the bot introduces itself as an assistant or a friend. Specific to their increasing popularity, anthropomorphic social chatbots have been found to be particularly appealing to consumers who either have a higher need for human interaction (Sheehan & Gottlieb,

2020) or social phobia (Jin & Youn, 2021). In social psychology, De Gennaro et al. (2020) demonstrated that after experiencing social exclusion on social media, interacting with an anthropomorphic chatbot that can offer empathy can help participants to achieve a more positive mood. Given the pervasive experience of social exclusion that can be experienced in our interactions with family members, friends, colleagues, and strangers (Chen et al., 2017)—an experience that is likely made more common by political polarization and the COVID-19 pandemic—fortifying chatbots' empathetic intelligence to better satisfy consumers' emotional and social needs is key to providing more engaging interactions. However, two of the most well-known mental health support chatbots adopt non-anthropomorphic appearances—Woebot resembles a less slick Wall-E while Wysa takes the form of a cartoon penguin. More research thus is needed to verify the importance of human identity cues in consumer evaluation of chatbots' emotional and empathetic intelligence.

6   From Consumer–Chatbot Interaction to Relationship

While research has underscored the effectiveness of chatbots in inducing positive interpersonal outcomes from trust to engagement, whether consumers can establish meaningful relationships with chatbots remains an unanswered question. Based on qualitative interviews on participants' experiences with the social chatbot Replika, Skjuve et al. (2021) suggest that participants' interactions with the chatbot that were initially fueled by curiosity were later transformed by substantial affective exploration and engagement and developed into relationships that are rewarding with affective and social value. However, Croes and Antheunis' (2021) longitudinal study on the social chatbot Mitsuku (now Kuki) observed that participants' repeated interactions with the social chatbot over three weeks did not translate into friendship. In fact, most social processes associated with relationship formation, including perceived social attraction, interaction quality, empathy, and communication competence of the chatbot deteriorated over time. After a few interactions, the chatbot was viewed as predictable and less empathetic, and the interactions became less enjoyable. The researchers thus conclude that although chatbots can be programmed to be highly social and human-like and act *as if* they care about the human interactants, users do not develop feelings of "friendship" with a chatbot. They further point out that even today's most advanced chatbots can only learn from real-time interaction instead of referencing prior conversations, which seriously hinders relationship formation and maintenance. However, in the case of Replika, not only can users create and customize the chatbot's appearance as their own virtual companion, but the chatbot can learn and mimic their "creator" human friend's texting styles (Huang & Rust, 2018), and more importantly, create "shared memories" based on prior conversations with the user. In this way, each human–chatbot interaction contributes to accumulated shared experiences and common history, creating feelings of getting acquainted with each other, and may ultimately contribute to relationship formation. Similarly, in order to provide more personalized interactions based on prior conversations with each individual user, future chatbots should recognize each distinct customer, either based on IP address or consumer account.

7 The Uncanny Valley Effects of Chatbot Anthropomorphism

Despite the popularity and advantages of anthropomorphic chatbots, Sundar (2008) suggests that as part of the "machine heuristic," computers can also be perceived as unbiased, objective, inherently logic-driven, and thus may be more credible. Therefore, it is likely that in marketing contexts when perceived credibility and objectivity is key, it may be more beneficial for the chatbot to explicitly communicate its computer identity instead of appearing to be more human-like.

More importantly, research based on the uncanny valley theory for humanoid technologies suggests that highly anthropomorphic objects can induce adverse reactions, such as feelings of eeriness, leading to negative evaluation (e.g., Seyama & Nagayama, 2007). Specifically, the theory suggests a curvilinear relationship between a computer agent's degree of human likeness and user response. While a low to medium degree of anthropomorphism can increase positive responses, negative affective responses occur when the computer is highly anthropomorphic, yet still not perfect (Mara et al., 2022). Ciechanowski et al.'s (2019) experiments comparing a simple text-based chatbot with a highly anthropomorphic animated chatbot that can move and read its responses in addition to the text responses showed that the simple text-based bot was more positively evaluated in terms of more pleasant interaction. In the context of computer-generated imagery (CGI) influencers, Arsenyan and Mirowska (2021) found that highly anthropomorphic CGI influencers received fewer positive emojis, more anger and anxiety emotions, and more doubts in user comments, as compared to less anthropomorphic influencers. The majority of uncanny valley studies evaluated physical robots. For instance, Kim et al.'s (2019) study on physical social robots observed the uncanny effect that anthropomorphism of a consumer robot decreases favorable attitudes. Mara et al.'s (2022) meta-analysis of uncanny valley studies with human-like robots confirms more positive responses for human-like robots at low to medium anthropomorphism. However, due to the scarcity of highly anthropomorphic robots tested in the literature, results regarding the adverse effects are inconclusive. Critically, scholars have suggested that feelings of eeriness are likely to occur when higher expectations of social interaction induced by human identity cues are unmet when highly human-like computer agents fail to understand users' responses or respond appropriately (Kontogiorgos et al., 2019; Nowak & Biocca, 2003). Human identity cues, especially anthropomorphic appearances, thus can be a double-edged sword, as they can set high expectations when consumers first encounter a chatbot, leading to frustration and negative brand evaluation when such expectations are not met. However, with advances in AI, particularly in the area of affective computing that can boost chatbots' emotional and empathetic intelligence (Huang & Rust, 2018), future chatbots may one day meet consumers' high expectations.

8 CONCLUSION

As a state-of-the-art technology, one embodying two-way communication as well as facilitating consumer participation in interactive marketing (Wang, 2021), chatbots are poised to become the next major marketing communication channel and e-commerce platform. This chapter highlights the advantages of anthropomorphic chatbots in enhancing social presence and parasocial interaction via human identity, verbal, and non-verbal cues. At the same time, the disadvantages of chatbots in general and human-like chatbots in particular in handling embarrassing conversations and placating angry customers are noted. Given the increasing popularity of highly social, human-like chatbots that can act as virtual friends or companions, future research should carefully explore how consumers interpret and respond to chatbots' expressed emotions (e.g., remorse) and empathy in relation to perceived agency and authenticity. Relatedly, as chatbots are becoming more sophisticated and can even hold memories of prior conversations with an individual user, critical research attention is needed to explore the evolving parasocial *relationships* that consumers may form with brand chatbots, which is especially important in today's digital world where "the distinction between truth and falsehood has become irrelevant" (Kalpokas et al., 2019, p. 9).

REFERENCES

Aaker, J. L. (1997). Dimensions of brand personality. *Journal of Marketing Research*, 34(3), 347–356.

Adam, M., Wessel, M., & Benlian, A. (2021). AI-based chatbots in customer service and their effects on user compliance. *Electronic Markets*, 31(2), 427–445.

Allport, G. W. (1985). The historical background of social psychology, *The Handbook of Social Psychology*, 1, 1–46.

Araujo, T. (2018). Living up to the chatbot hype: The influence of anthropomorphic design cues and communicative agency framing on conversational agent and company perceptions. *Computers in Human Behavior*, 85, 183–189.

Arsenyan, J., & Mirowska, A. (2021). Almost human? A comparative case study on the social media presence of virtual influencers *International Journal of Human-Computer Studies*, 155, pp. 102694.

Ashktorab, Z., Jain, M., Liao, Q. V., & Weisz, J. D. (2019). Resilient chatbots: Repair strategy preferences for conversational breakdowns, In *Proceedings of the 2019 CHI conference on human factors in computing systems*, pp. 1–12.

Blascovich, J. (2002). Social influence within immersive virtual environments, In R. Schroeder (Ed.), *The Social Life of Avatars: Presence and Interaction in Shared Virtual Environments* pp. 127–145. Springer London.

Blut, M., Wang, C., Wünderlich, N. V., & Brock, C. (2021). Understanding anthropomorphism in service provision: A meta-analysis of physical robots, chatbots, and other AI. *Journal of the Academy of Marketing Science*, 49(4), 1–27.

Cancel, D. and Gerhardt, D. (2019). *Conversational Marketing*, Wiley.

Chen, R. P., Wan, E. W., & Levy, E. (2017). The effect of social exclusion on consumer preference for anthropomorphized brands. *Journal of Consumer Psychology*, 27(1), 23–34.

Cheng, Y., & Jiang, H. (2021). Customer–Brand relationship in the era of artificial intelligence: Understanding the role of chatbot marketing efforts. *Journal of Product & Brand Management. Advance Online Publication.* https://doi.org/10.1108/JPBM-05-2020-2907

Ciechanowski, L., Przegalinska, A., Magnuski, M., & Gloor, P. (2019). In the shades of the uncanny valley: An experimental study of human–Chatbot interaction. *Future Generation Computer Systems*, 92, 539–548.

Colliander, J., & Dahlén, M. (2011). Following the fashionable friend: The power of social media: Weighing publicity effectiveness of blogs versus online magazines. *Journal of Advertising Research*, 51(1), 313–320.

Corti, K., & Gillespie, A. (2016). Co-constructing intersubjectivity with artificial conversational agents: People are more likely to initiate repairs of misunderstandings with agents represented as human *Computers in Human Behavior*, 58, 431–442.

Crolic, C., Thomaz, F., Hadi, R., & Stephen, A. T. (2022). Blame the bot: Anthropomorphism and anger in customer–chatbot interactions. *Journal of Marketing*, 86(1), 132–148.

Croes, E. A., & Antheunis, M. L. (2021). Can we be friends with Mitsuku? A longitudinal study on the process of relationship formation between humans and a social chatbot, *Journal of Social and Personal Relationships*, 38(1), 279–300.

Chung, M., Ko, E., Joung, H., & Kim, S. J. (2018). Chatbot e-service and customer satisfaction regarding luxury brands. *Journal of Business Research*, 117, 587–595.

Dahl, D. W., Manchanda, R. V., & Argo, J. J. (2001). Embarrassment in consumer purchase: The roles of social presence and purchase familiarity. *The Journal of Consumer Research*, 28(3), 473–481.

Davies, G., Chun, R., da Silva, R. V., & Roper, S. (2004). A corporate character scale to assess employee and customer views of organization reputation. *Corporate Reputation Review*, 7(2), 125–146.

De Gennaro, M., Krumhuber, E. G., & Lucas, G. (2020). Effectiveness of an empathic chatbot in combating adverse effects of social exclusion on mood, *Frontiers in Psychology*, 10, 3061.

De Visser, E. J., Monfort, S. S., McKendrick, R., Smith, M. A., McKnight, P. E., Krueger, F., & Parasuraman, R. (2016). Almost human: Anthropomorphism increases trust resilience in cognitive agents. *Journal of Experimental Psychology: Applied*, 22(3), 331.

Dietvorst, B. J., Simmons, J. P., & Massey, C. (2015). Algorithm aversion: People erroneously avoid algorithms after seeing them err. *Journal of Experimental Psychology*, 144(1), 114.

Dietvorst, B. J., Simmons, J. P., & Massey, C. (2018). Overcoming algorithm aversion: People will use imperfect algorithms if they can (even slightly) modify them. *Management Science, 64*(3), 1155–1170.

Federal Trade Commission (2017). Privacy & data security update (2016). Federal Trade Commission, https://www.ftc.gov/reports/privacy-data-security-update-2017-overview-commissions-enforcement-policy-initiatives-consumer

Feine, J., Gnewuch, U., Morana, S., & Maedche, A. (2019). A taxonomy of social cues for conversational agents *International Journal of Human-Computer Studies, 132*, 138–161.

Forbes Magazine (2013, August 2). *7 Steps For Dealing With Angry Customers.* https://www.forbes.com/sites/thesba/2013/08/02/7-steps-for-dealing-with-angry-customers/

Foster, J. K., McLelland, M. A. and Wallace, L. K. (2021). Brand avatars: impact of social interaction on consumer–brand relationships, Journal of Research in Interactive Marketing, Vol. ahead-of-print No. ahead-of-print. https://doi.org/10.1108/JRIM-01-2020-0007

Funches, V. (2011). The consumer anger phenomena: Causes and consequences. *Journal of Professional Services Marketing, 25*(6), 420–428.

Fox, J., Arena, D., & Bailenson, J. N. (2009). Virtual reality: A survival guide for the social scientist. *Journal of Media Psychology, 21*(3), 95–113.

Go, E., & Sundar, S. S. (2019). Humanizing chatbots: The effects of visual, identity and conversational cues on humanness perceptions. *Computers in Human Behavior, 97*, 304–316.

Hill, J., Randolph Ford, W., & Farreras, I. G. (2015). Real conversations with artificial intelligence: A comparison between human–human online conversations and human–chatbot conversations. *Computers in Human Behavior, 49*, 245–250.

Ho, A., Hancock, J., & Miner, A. S. (2018). Psychological, relational, and emotional effects of self-disclosure after conversations with a chatbot. *The Journal of Communication, 68*(4), 712–733.

Horton, D., & Richard Wohl, R. (1956). Mass communication and para-social interaction: Observations on intimacy at a distance. *Psychiatry, 19*(3), 215–229.

Huang, M. H., & Rust, R. T. (2018). Artificial intelligence in service. *Journal of Service Research, 21*(2), 155–172.

Jin, S. V., & Youn, S. (2021). Why do consumers with social phobia prefer anthropomorphic customer service chatbots? Evolutionary explanations of the moderating roles of social phobia. *Telematics and Informatics, 62*, 101644.

Juniper Research (2020). Chatbots to facilitates $142 billion of retail spend by 2024, driven by omnichannel strategies, available at https://doi.org/www.juniperresearch.com/press/press-releases/chatbots-to-facilitate-$142-billion-of-retail

Kalpokas, I., Kalpokas, I., & Finotello. (2019). *A Political Theory of Post-Truth.* Palgrave Macmillan.

Katsanis, L. P. (1994). Do unmentionable products still exist?: An empirical investigation. *Journal of Product & Brand Management, 3*(4), 5–14.

Kim, L. (2020). 9 ways to use Facebook chatbots to grow your business, available at https://www.allbusiness.com/use-facebook-chatbots-to-grow-your-business-132318-1.html

Kim, S. Y., Schmitt, B. H., & Thalmann, N. M. (2019). Eliza in the Uncanny Valley: Anthropomorphizing consumer robots increases their perceived warmth but decreases liking. *Marketing Letters, 30*(1), 1–12.

Kim, Y., & Sundar, S. S. (2012). Anthropomorphism of computers: Is it mindful or mindless? *Computers in Human Behavior*, *28*(1), 241–250.

Kontogiorgos, D., Pereira, A., Andersson, O., Koivisto, M., Gonzalez Rabal, E., Vartiainen, V., & Gustafson, J. (2019, July). The effects of anthropomorphism and non-verbal social behaviour in virtual assistants. In *Proceedings of the 19th ACM International Conference on Intelligent Virtual Agents*, pp. 133–140.

Lee, K. M., Peng, W., Jin, S. A., & Yan, C. (2006). Can robots manifest personality?: An empirical test of personality recognition, social responses, and social presence in human–robot interaction. *Journal of Communication*, *56*(4), 754–772.

Liebrecht, C., & van Hooijdonk, C. (2020). Creating humanlike chatbots: What chatbot developers could learn from webcare employees in adopting a conversational human voice In A. Følstad, T. Araujo, S. Papadopoulos, E. L-C. Law, O-C. Granmo, E. Luger, & P. B. Brandtzaeg (Eds.), Chatbot Research and Design: Third International Workshop, CONVERSATIONS 2019, Amsterdam, The Netherlands, November 19–20, 2019, Revised Selected Papers (pp. 51–64). (Lecture Notes in Computer Science (including subseries Lecture Notes in Artificial Intelligence and Lecture Notes in Bioinformatics)); Vol. 11970. Springer.

Liew, T. W., & Tan, S. M. (2021). Social cues and implications for designing expert and competent artificial agents: A systematic review. *Telematics and Informatics*, *65*, 101721.

Ling, E. C., Tussyadiah, I., Tuomi, A., Stienmetz, J., & Ioannou, A. (2021). Factors influencing users' adoption and use of conversational agents: A systematic review. *Psychology & Marketing*, *38*(7), 1031–1051.

Liu, B., & Sundar, S. S. (2018). Should machines express sympathy and empathy? Experiments with a health advice chatbot. *Cyberpsychology, Behavior, and Social Networking*, *21*(10), 625–636.

Loveys, K., Sebaratnam, G., Sagar, M., & Broadbent, E. (2020). The effect of design features on relationship quality with embodied conversational agents: A systematic review. *International Journal of Social Robotics*, *12*(6), 1293–1312.

Lucas, G. M., Gratch, J., King, A., & Morency, L.-P. (2014). It's only a computer: Virtual humans increase willingness to disclose. *Computers in Human Behavior*, *37*, 94–100.

Luger, E., & Sellen, A. (2016, May). Like having a really bad PA the gulf between user expectation and experience of conversational agents. In *Proceedings of the 2016 CHI conference on human factors in computing systems*, pp. 5286–5297.

Luo, X., Tong, S., Fang, Z., & Qu, Z. (2019). Frontiers: Machines vs. humans: The impact of artificial intelligence chatbot disclosure on customer purchases. *Marketing Science*, *38*(6), 937–947.

Mara, M., Appel, M., & Gnambs, T. (2022). Human-like robots and the uncanny valley: A meta-analysis of user responses based on the godspeed scales. *Zeitschrift Für Psychologie*, *230*(1), 33.

Mehra, B. (2021). Chatbot personality preferences in Global South urban English speakers. *Social Sciences & Humanities Open*, *3*(1), 100131.

Mims, C. (2014). Advertising's new frontier: talk to the bot, *The Wall Street Journal*, available at https://www.wsj.com/articles/advertisings-new-frontier-talk-to-the-bot-1406493740?mod=dist_smartbrief

Mozafari, N., Weiger, W. H., & Hammerschmidt, M. (2021). Trust me, I'm a bot–repercussions of chatbot disclosure in different service frontline settings. *Journal of Service Management*, *33*(2), 221–245.

Mou, Y., & Xu, K. (2017). The media inequality: Comparing the initial human-human and human-AI social interactions. *Computers in Human Behavior, 72,* 432–440.

Nadarzynski, T., Miles, O., Cowie, A., & Ridge, D. (2019). Acceptability of artificial intelligence (AI)-led chatbot services in healthcare: A mixed-methods study. *Digital Health, 5*(1), https://doi.org/10.1177/2055207619871808.

Nass, C., & Moon, Y. (2000). Machines and mindlessness: Social responses to computers. In *Journal of Social Issues, 56*(1), 81–103.

Nass, C., Moon, Y., Fogg, B. J., Reeves, B., Dryer, D. C. (1995, May). *Can computer personalities be human personalities?* CHI '95: Conference companion on human factors in computing systems, pp. 228–229.

Nowak, K. L., & Biocca, F. (2003). The effect of the agency and anthropomorphism on users' sense of telepresence, copresence, and social presence in virtual environments. *Presence: Teleoperators and Virtual Environments, 12*(5), 481–494.

Payne, E. M., Peltier, J., & Barger, V. A. (2021). Enhancing the value co-creation process: Artificial intelligence and mobile banking service platforms. *Journal of Research in Interactive Marketing, 15*(1), 68–85.

Pizzi, G., Scarpi, D., & Pantano, E. (2021). Artificial intelligence and the new forms of interaction: Who has the control when interacting with a chatbot? *Journal of Business Research, 129,* 878–890.

Powers, A., & Kiesler, S. (2006). The advisor robot: tracing people's mental model from a robot's physical attributes. In *Proceedings of the 1st ACM SIGCHI/SIGART conference on Human-robot interaction*, pp. 218–225.

Qiu, L., & Benbasat, I. (2009). Evaluating anthropomorphic product recommendation agents: A social relationship perspective to designing information systems. *Journal of Management Information Systems, 25*(4), 145–182.

Ramerman, M. (2020). Five predictions for marketing in 2021, *Forbes*, available at https://www.forbes.com/sites/forbesagencycouncil/2020/09/23/five-predictions-for-marketing-in-2021/?sh=41c3fd084e8d

Rasmussen, L. (2018). Parasocial interaction in the digital age: An examination of relationship building and the effectiveness of YouTube celebrities. *The Journal of Social Media in Society, 7*(1), 280–294.

Redston, S., de Botte, S., & Smith, C. (2018). Resolving embarrassing medical conditions with online health information. *International Journal of Medical Informatics, 114,* 101–105.

Reeves, B., & Nass, C. I. (1996). *The media equation: How people treat computers, television, and new media like real people and places.* Cambridge University Press.

Rheu, M., Shin, J. Y., Peng, W., & Huh-Yoo, J. (2021). Systematic review: Trust-building factors and implications for conversational agent design. *International Journal of Human-Computer Interaction, 37*(1), 81–96.

Roy, R., & Naidoo, V. (2021). Enhancing chatbot effectiveness: The role of anthropomorphic conversational styles and time orientation. *Journal of Business Research, 126,* 23–34.

Seeger, A. M., Pfeiffer, J., & Heinzl, A. (2021). Texting with humanlike conversational agents: Designing for anthropomorphism. *Journal of the Association for Information Systems, 22*(4), 8.

Segran, E. (2019, September 12). *What teens are asking Roo, Planned Parenthood's new sex-ed chatbot.* Fast Company. https://www.fastcompany.com/90401983/what-teens-are-asking-roo-planned-parenthoods-new-sex-ed-chatbot.

Seyama, J. I., & Nagayama, R. S. (2007). The uncanny valley: Effect of realism on the impression of artificial human faces. *Presence*, *16*(4), 337–351.

Sheehan, B., Jin, H. S., & Gottlieb, U. (2020). Customer service chatbots: Anthropomorphism and adoption. *Journal of Business Research*, *115*, 14–24.

Short, J., Williams, E., & Christie, B. (1976). *The Social Psychology of Telecommunications*.

Shum, H. Y., He, X. D., & Li, D. (2018). From Eliza to XiaoIce: Challenges and opportunities with social chatbots. *Frontiers of Information Technology & Electronic Engineering, Col.*, *19*(1), 10–26.

Skjuve, M., Følstad, A., Fostervold, K. I., & Brandtzaeg, P. B. (2021). My chatbot companion-a study of human-chatbot relationships. *International Journal of Human-Computer Studies*, *149*, 102601.

Smith, A. (2020). CDC creates coronavirus chatbot called clara to check your symptoms. *Entrepreneur*. Retrieved 16 May 2022, from https://www.entrepreneur.com/article/348049.

Sundar, S. S. (2008). The MAIN model: A heuristic approach to understanding technology effects on credibility. In M. J. Metzger & A. J. Flanagin (Eds.), *Digital Media, Youth, and Credibility* (pp. 73–100). MIT Press.

Sundar, S. S., Bellur, S., Oh, J., Jia, H., & Kim, H. S. (2016). Theoretical importance of contingency in human-computer interaction: Effects of message interactivity on user engagement. *Communication Research*, *43*(5), 595–625.

Sung, Y., & Kim, J. (2010). Effects of brand personality on brand trust and brand affect. *Psychology & Marketing*, *27*(7), 639–661.

Terdiman, J. P. (2006). Embarrassment is a major barrier to colon cancer prevention, especially among women: A call to action. In *Gastroenterology*, *130*(4), 1364–1365.

Tsai, W. H. S., Liu, Y., & Chuan, C. H. (2021a). How chatbots' social presence communication enhances consumer engagement: the mediating role of parasocial interaction and dialogue. *Journal of Research in Interactive Marketing*, *15*(3), 460–482.

Tsai, W. H. S., Lun, D., Carcioppolo, N., & Chuan, C. H. (2021b). Human versus chatbot: Understanding the role of emotion in health marketing communication for vaccines. *Psychology & Marketing*, *38*(12), 2377–2392.

Waddell, K. (2017, April 21). Chatbots have entered the uncanny valley, *The Atlantic*. https://www.theatlantic.com/technology/archive/2017/04/uncanny-valley-digital-assistants/523806/.

Wang, C. L. (2021). New frontiers and future directions in interactive marketing. *Journal of Research in Interactive Marketing.*, *15*(1), 1–9.

Weisband, S., & Kiesler, S. (1996). Self disclosure on computer forms: Meta-analysis and implications. In *Proceedings of the SIGCHI conference on human factors in computing systems* (pp. 3–10).

Worthington, E. L., Jr. (1998). The pyramid model of forgiveness: Some interdisciplinary speculations about unforgiveness and the promotion of forgiveness. in *Dimensions of Forgiveness: Psychological Research and Theological Perspectives*, pp. 107–137. Radnor. PA. Templeton Foundation Press.

Xu, K., & Liao, T. (2020). Explicating cues: A typology for understanding emerging media technologies. *Journal of Computer-Mediated Communication*, *25*(1), 32–43.

Youn, S., & Jin, S. V. (2021). In AI we trust? The effects of parasocial interaction and technopian versus luddite ideological views on chatbot-based customer relationship management in the emerging feeling economy. *Computers in Human Behavior, 119*, 106721.

Verčič, A. T., & Verčič, D. (2007). Reputation as Matching Identities and Images: Extending Davies and Chun's Research on Gaps between the Internal and External Perceptions of the Corporate Brand. *Journal of Marketing Communications, 13*(4), 277–290.

Zadro, L., Williams, K. D., & Richardson, R. (2004). How low can you go? Ostracism by a computer is sufficient to lower self-reported levels of belonging, control, self-Esteem, and meaningful existence. *Journal of Experimental Social Psychology, 40*(4), 560–567. https://doi.org/10.1016/j.jesp.2003.11.006.

Zamora, J. (2017, October). I'm sorry, dave, i'm afraid i can't do that: Chatbot perception and expectations. In *Proceedings of the 5th international conference on human agent interaction*, pp. 253–260.

Zarouali, B., Van den Broeck, E., Walrave, M., & Poels, K. (2018). Predicting consumer responses to a chatbot on Facebook. *Cyberpsychology, Behavior, and Social Networking, 21*(8), 491–497.

CHAPTER 13

Affective Interaction with Technology: The Role of Virtual Assistants in Interactive Marketing

Guillermo Calahorra Candao, Carolina Herrando, and María José Martín-De Hoyos

1 INTRODUCTION

The evolution of the internet has culminated in the sensory or emotional web (5.0), which collects tools that can stimulate emotions in the individual through text, images, or sounds. The inclusion of artificial intelligence to optimize online interactions through the use of virtual assistants has presented a new challenge for interactive marketing researchers (Wang, 2021). The latest technological developments in business relationships are closely related to the generation of emotions between individuals who interact with technology throughout the purchase process. As early as 1955, Abbot (1955, p. 40) stated that "what people really want are not products but satisfying experiences." Other authors have recently expanded on this idea, attributing to the customer experiences of a holistic nature that incorporate the customer's cognitive, emotional, social, and spiritual responses in all interactions with the company (Lemon & Verhoef, 2016; Schmitt et al., 2015). Consumers are looking not just for an effective transaction but for an overall hedonic consumption experience (Wang et al., 2020).

G. C. Candao · C. Herrando (✉) · M. J. M.-D. Hoyos
University of Zaragoza, Zaragoza, Spain
e-mail: cherrando@unizar.es

M. J. M.-D. Hoyos
e-mail: mjhoyos@unizar.es

© The Author(s), under exclusive license to Springer Nature Switzerland AG 2023
C. L. Wang (ed.), *The Palgrave Handbook of Interactive Marketing*,
https://doi.org/10.1007/978-3-031-14961-0_13

Social interaction on the internet is a fundamental factor that influences the experience of individuals (Hernández-Ortega, 2019). That is, these experiences are determined by the information generated by other users, by shared experiences, by the quality of this information, by its purpose (utilitarian or hedonic), by the sender of this message (the company, other users, chatbots, or virtual assistants), or by the value of the comments shared (positive, negative, or neutral).

Many e-commerce platforms already have a customer service with their own virtual assistant that helps and advises in the purchase process. In this way, these assistants exert an influence on the consumer's purchase decision process, due to the idiosyncrasy of their acoustic and sound characteristics (Chattaraman et al., 2019), or even due to the image or visual appearance of the virtual assistant (Benbasat et al., 2020).

The experiences and emotions generated from interaction with technology have been and continue to be one of the most relevant research topics in marketing (Lemon & Verhoef, 2016; McKechnie et al., 2018). The virtual relationships (social and commercial) that exist through different devices basically use three forms of communication: text, image, and sound. All of these forms make it possible to transmit a message in different contexts, and each message supposes a stimulus for the sender and receiver, which leads to a cognitive or physiological response.

Consequently, one of the main challenges researchers and marketers are facing is to tackle the emotions the customer experiences during online interactions along the customer journey (Lemon & Verhoef, 2016). The objective of this chapter is to review the state of the art on the field of emotions, the tools involved in the affective interaction with VA, and to deep dive into the role of VA in this interaction. Second section of this chapter presents a literature review about the emotion concept and approaches. The third section describes the three main communication tools (text, sound, and image), which allow boosting of interactive marketing experiences, and contextualizes the role of emotions in these experiences. The fourth section introduces virtual assistants as part of interactive marketing strategy and discusses their role in transmitting emotions to consumers through anthropomorphic features. The final section provides an overall discussion with a proposed future agenda and a summary of the main key points of this chapter.

2   Theoretical Revision of Emotion

The definition of emotion varies depending on how it is measured. According to the *categorical approach*, emotions are classified into categories that are different from each other. These categories are known as *basic* emotions, which are limited, universal, and primary (e.g., happiness, sadness, fear, etc.) from which secondary emotions are constructed (Ekman, 1992; Picard et al., 2001). They are considered universal emotions because humans can find them in all cultures, and they are also related to specific physiological patterns or emotional expressions. Unlike the following approaches, there is not a specific and defined number of emotions that might or might not be represented under this perspective.

The approach sustained by Ekman (1992) is taken as a reference in categorical emotions, where only 6 of them were considered basic (anger, disgust, fear, happiness, sadness and surprise). Later virtual personal assistants' (VPA) literature has used this theory to explain basic aspects of the communication between consumers and virtual assistants (Castillo et al., 2018; Wang et al., 2005), separating some emotions from others and assuming, as well, a dichotomous approach where the used sound by the VPA cannot be fit in more than just one category of emotion (e.g., the emotion transmitted is/isn't happiness). The limited possibilities of using a finite variety of emotion-led researchers to adopt a wider approach.

The *dimensional approach* focuses on the identification of emotions located in a specific dimension that corresponds to an internal emotional representation of the human being (Yang & Chen, 2012). These dimensions are based on the analysis of the correlation between affective concepts, usually defined as VAD: *valence* (which collects positive and negative affective states), *arousal* (measuring the level of energy or stimulus), and *dominance* (the feeling of being in control of a situation) (Osgood, 1957).

Valence, as the value of an emotion, ranging from pleasant to unpleasant (Bradley & Lang, 2000), has received little attention within the OCR literature, and the existing research remains largely inconclusive. For example, while some studies have pointed out the effects of valence in OCRs on businesses, others have found no such correlation (Forman et al., 2008; Liu, 2006). Even within each of these positions, there is no consensus. While some researchers have found a relation between positive emotions and OCRs (Park & Nicolau, 2015), others have argued the opposite (Wilson et al., 2017), and neither of the studies concerned considered the affective outcomes and managerial benefits that emotional variables might bring. Furthermore, there has been a tendency within the literature to consider valence in terms of a general status for a whole review, despite the findings of psycholinguistic studies that each word has its own affective value (Bradley & Lang, 2000; Hinojosa et al., 2016; Stadthagen-Gonzalez et al., 2017). Also, in the study of emotions, some researchers highlight the need to consider the positive or negative valence of the combination of OCRs read, and not just one-to-to emotional contagion; since the overall experience while reading OCRs is what impacts the affective responses in terms of valence and arousal (Herrando et al., 2022).

Valence and arousal have been among the main concepts in the classification of affective responses (Wundt, 1912), as both affective states define the structure of an emotion (Lang, 1994). From the early stages, valence and arousal have been the foundations of emotion research (Lang, 1994). Valence and arousal have proved useful in different research fields, including linguistics (Coltheart et al., 2001; Frost et al., 1987), neurology (Mammarella et al., 2013), and food and beverages (Drobes et al., 2001). Valence and arousal have also been an important part of research related to the effect of word-of-mouth on sales, especially in terms of reviews and comments on social commerce websites (Chevalier & Mayzlin, 2006). Interestingly, in virtual environments, users find more helpful OCRs which accompany text with an image (Wu et al., 2021).

Valence and arousal are often presented together with a third variable, called dominance, which measures the state in which a person feels in control of a situation, has not been studied with the same interest as the first two (Osgood et al., 1957). This is because dominance explains to a lesser extent the variation in possible affective judgments, and the values provided for this variable vary much more between people compared to valence and arousal (Bradley & Lang, 1994).

Previous research has examined how the three variables influence how we process words, images, and sounds. The studies that relate the set of VAD (valence-arousal-dominance) variables in databases of visual and auditory stimuli are widely known. Table 1 lists some of the most popular databases with these variables.

Although these studies use valence-arousal-dominance indistinctly to quantify emotions, studies in neuropsychology show that valence has stronger effects on the activation of the amygdala, the dorsomedial prefrontal cortex and the ventromedial, regardless of whether the stimulus was text, image, or audio (Kensinger & Schacter, 2006). Valence and arousal have been used more extensively because they seem to have stronger effects on the other variables, especially when compared to dominance (Sutton et al., 2019).

Russell (1980) proposed a circumplex model that, using a circular and two-dimensional structure, allows us to observe the inverse correlation between valence and arousal (see Fig. 1).

Figure 1 illustrates the represented two-dimensional space where valence and arousal are mixed in order to show some examples of complex emotions, allowing the definition of a greater variety of emotions. The same author argues that valence and arousal are the key dimensions of affection and a basis for the construction of emotions (Russell, 2003). The use of dominance, as a third variable, allows to obtain a more complex image of the representation of emotions (as shown in Fig. 2). It can be observed an increase in the complexity of the models using three variables instead of only two (Deng et al., 2015).

For this reason, the use of valence and arousal as variables to represent emotions is more practical (Deng et al., 2015).

3   Communication Tools in Interactive Marketing

Interactive marketing strategies, aimed to encourage optimal customer experiences, focus on digital content and interactions. Interactive technologies (such as the internet of things, virtual reality or artificial intelligence) are transforming customer experience (Lucia-Palacio & Pérez-López, 2021; Payne et al., 2021). The digital environment allows users to interact with a firm, with other users, or with virtual assistants through text, image, and sound (see Fig. 3).

Table 1 Databases that integrate emotions and stimuli (text-image-sound)

Stimulus	Study	Authors
Sound	IADS	Affective auditory stimuli: Characterization of the International Affective Digitized Sounds (IADS) by discrete emotional categories (Stevenson et al., 2008)
	IADS-E	Affective auditory stimulus database: An expanded version of the International Affective Digitized Sounds (IADS-E) (Yang et al., 2018)
	IADS-2	Affective auditory stimuli: Adaptation of the international affective digitized sounds (IADS-2) for European Portuguese (Soares et al., 2013)
	Spanish IADS	El sistema internacional de sonidos afectivos (IADS): adaptación española (Fernández-Abascal et al., 2008)
Image	IAPS	The International Affective Picture System (IAPS) in the study of emotion and attention (Lang & Bradley, 2007)
	Brazilian IAPS	Brazilian norms for the International Affective Picture System (IAPS): comparison of the affective ratings for new stimuli between Brazilian and North-American subjects (Lasaitis et al., 2008)
	Spanish IAPS	Un método para el estudio experimental de las emociones: el International Affective Picture System (IAPS). Adaptación española (Moltó et al., 1999)
	NAPS	The Nencki Affective Picture System (NAPS): Introduction to a novel, standardized, wide-range, high-quality, realistic picture database (Marchewka et al., 2014)
Text	ANEW	*Affective norms for English words (ANEW): Instruction manual and affective ratings* (Bradley, & Lang, 1999)
	New ANEW	A new ANEW: Evaluation of a word list for sentiment analysis in microblogs (Nielsen, 2011)
	Spanish ANEW	The Spanish adaptation of ANEW (affective norms for English words) (Redondo et al., 2007)
	Italian ANEW	The adaptation of the affective norms for English words (ANEW) for Italian (Montefinese et al., 2014)
	ANGST	ANGST: Affective norms for German sentiment terms, derived from the affective norms for English words (Schmidtke et al., 2014)
	FAN and FANChild	Affective norms for french words (FAN) (Monnier & Syssau, 2014) Affective norms for 720 French words rated by children and adolescents (FANchild). (Monnier & Syssau, 2017)

3.1 Text

Research has afforded special attention to the emotional analysis of the text since the late 1990s. Bradley and Lang (1999) popularized the tools of valence, arousal, and dominance that Russell (2003) later used to quantify the emotional perception of thousands of words.

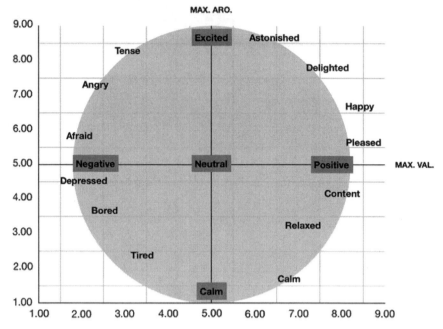

Fig. 1 Circumplex model representing valence and arousal. Own elaboration from (Russell, 1980)

Fig. 2 Valence-arousal-dominance emotional space

Online consumer reviews (hereafter OCRs) allow consumers to share their experiences online by writing comments about the quality of products and services (Filieri et al., 2021; Wang et al., 2019), thereby developing an

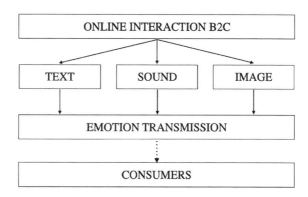

Fig. 3 Communication tools in interactive marketing

associated image and reducing uncertainties about the products' characteristics (Filieri, 2016). OCRs influence consumer decisions (Filieri & McLeay, 2014), consumer perceptions and attitudes (Vermeulen & Seegers, 2009), and product sales (Ye et al., 2009). Therefore, OCRs are used strategically to establish a reputation among consumers, and they are considered a powerful marketing tool (Wang et al., 2019). When users review a product, they tend to share their experiences showing satisfaction or dissatisfaction. Thus, OCRs entail sharing positive, negative, or neutral experiences and, consequently, also expose some emotions.

The OCR literature has given considerable attention to affective values (Purnawirawan et al., 2015). However, most of the findings about the role of valence have been inconclusive. Liu (2006) found that the volume of reviews correlated to sales but that the reviews' valence did not. Forman et al. (2008) found no connection between valence and sales, while Chevalier and Mayzlin (2006) found that negative valence reviews hurt sales. Park and Nicolau (2015) found that consumers consider extreme reviews more useful than moderate ratings. Even though the conclusions of previous studies are far from straightforward, they share a common approach: they understand valence as a concept applying to a whole review, instead of analyzing individual stimuli in each word, as proposed previously (Bradley et al., 1999).

3.2 Image

Different branches of science have studied the relationship that may exist between the components of an image and how these components can serve as stimuli to generate emotions (Kim et al., 2021; Wu et al., 2022).

Avatars are animated characters that some companies incorporate on their websites to facilitate interactions with the consumer through the use of virtual assistants. These visual perceptions influence the user's perceived emotions (Van Pinxteren et al., 2020) and increase the probability that consumers buy in online environments (e.g., Etemad-Sajadi, 2016), since they evoke a high social presence (Lin et al., 2020). This social presence can be enhanced by anthropomorphic images (the attribution of similar characteristics and traits of humans to objects, Epley et al., 2007), which influence the emotions of users (Banks & Bowman, 2016; Tsai et al., 2021). Despite these results, the research is still in an early stage, and researchers suggest that "further research is needed to assess the critical role that appearance and visual characteristics play in avatars and chatbots" (Lin et al., 2020, p. 14).

3.3 Sound

The appearance of virtual personal assistants integrated into smart devices is permeating all activities of human daily life: medical assistance, learning, information searching, home automation, and shopping. In this context, voice-controlled personal assistants are defined as wireless devices equipped with artificial intelligence, capable of assimilating and reproducing the human voice through interactions with synthesized and personalized responses which provide personal, professional, administrative, or technical assistance (Hoy, 2018). Personalized content is seen as one of the most effective interactive marketing tools for advertising (Brinson & Britt, 2021). In this line, virtual personal assistant services have become a fundamental component of different technological devices (smartphones, voice assistants, etc.), social commerce web pages, and appliances that are part of the internet of things (White, 2019).

Although numerous authors have given their attention to the study of sound and emotions, its analysis continues to require special attention. There is a call for research that focuses on the characteristics in the style of the interaction between virtual assistants and users that gauges the value virtual assistants bring (Chattaraman et al., 2019). Previous studies have realized the necessity of including human behavior characteristics in virtual assistants, such as warmth, competence, and believability (Niewiadomski et al., 2010), or even adding an extra dimension of reality (Kopp et al., 2003; Schmeil & Broll, 2007). Thus, the Marketing Science Institute and various discussion forums about marketing tendencies (McKechnie et al., 2018) propose to continue researching the science of emotion to explore the possibilities of consumption-based emotions and self-determined relational engagement with a particular company or service provider through the use of virtual assistants.

The process of humanizing an object triggers a mental perception similar to that experienced when interacting with a human on the part of consumers (Puzakova et al., 2013), and the use of virtual personal assistants (VPA) such as Siri or Alexa elevates this perception (MacInnis & Folkes, 2017).

Anthropomorphism is defined as "the universal human tendency to ascribe human physical and mental characteristics to nonhuman entities, objects and events" (Zawieska et al., 2012). Robots' anthropomorphic design cues have been identified as significant drivers to favorable customer responses, they can for example increase trust and social bonding with the firm (Wirtz et al., 2018). The defining cues of anthropomorphism include both, the physical features or embodiment of a robot (head, body and face) and the nonphysical features (emotion, gaze, voice, gesture and mimicry) and all of them contributing to increase the perception of human presence (Blut et al., 2021). Voice is an effective anthropomorphic cue as human–robot interaction literature confirmed, since users anthropomorphize robots when these have a voice (Lee & Nass, 2004).

Theories such as parasocial interaction (Horton and Wohl, 1956) explain that people can develop a relationship through an imagined interaction with other people. When the other party to the relationship is not human, their perceived humanity is a fundamental condition that precedes parasocial interaction, since it allows people to see the other being as real (Banks & Bowman, 2016; Giles, 2002). VAs fulfill the precondition of the parasocial interaction theory due to the high level of human likeness by their voice. Voice assistants have many anthropomorphic features that automatically cause users to assign human characteristics to the device. The way voice assistants work provides anthropomorphic cues due to their resemblance to the way humans speak (for example, due to the ability to generate immediate and relevant responses to user questions).

As to emotion transmission through the use of sounds, there are two types of studies in the literature that use this method: those that divide the audio block into segments of short duration and represent each one in the valence-arousal matrix (Korhonen et al., 2006), and those that analyze these blocks individually and offer a global result (Lu et al., 2005).

When assigning dimensional values to an audio file, there are different sound characteristics that influence each value. The elements of sound that affect the prediction of emotion are, among others, timbre, dynamics, rhythm, tempo, and harmony (Grekow, 2018). Mode or harmony are usually related to valence, while rhythm, energy, and timbre have a greater impact on arousal (Gabrielsson & Lindström, 2001). However, none of these characteristics works individually, it is the effect of all of them together (and their own configuration) that affects the assignment of values (Hevner, 1935). The use of specialized and specific software allows researchers to provide numerical values to all these sound characteristics that affect the emotional perception of an audio file.

In addition, there is an academic need to continue research on the interaction between virtual assistants and users to assess the benefit for the latter (Chattaraman et al., 2019).

4 Virtual Assistants

4.1 The Evolution of Virtual Assistants

There are multiple definitions of virtual assistant, but according to Hoy (2018), "virtual assistants are the realization of the science fiction dream of interacting with our computers by talking to them."

A dog-shaped toy named Radio Rex released in 1922 was the first device that could be considered a virtual assistant. The improvement of technology became a turning point in the development of virtual assistants. A few decades later, in 1952, Audrey was introduced to the market. Audrey was an automatic digit identification device that was able to understand phonemes, considered the basic component of communication. MIT developed the first natural language processing bot, ELIZA, between 1964 and 1966. It was created to show the superficiality of communication between robots and humans, stimulating conversations using previously established patterns.

The decade of the 1990s was essential for the development of today's virtual assistants. Companies such as Philips and IBM started to integrate digital voice recognition into personal computers. In fact, it was in 1994 when the first smartphone was introduced, laying the groundwork for what we know as a smartphone these days. Since Apple's Siri was the first virtual assistant introduced to the mainstream, it has been the most used option. The next to come was Microsoft's Cortana in 2013, followed by Amazon's Alexa in 2014. Amazon's Alexa was the first virtual assistant that was released with its own device, the Echo Dot home speaker (see the study of Hsieh & Lee, 2021). Lastly, Google's Go was released in 2016 with its own home speaker and as an app for Android-based smartphones.

The current most popular virtual assistants are continually listening for a specific keyword to wake them up, although this can be changed once the assistant is configured and ready to use. The most popular virtual assistants' keywords are summarized in Table 2.

According to a report by a market research firm (Forrest, 2021), Apple's Siri and Google's Go assistant were tied in top position for market share in the first months of 2021. The third position belonged to Baidu's assistant, a Chinese-only assistant for the company's website. Even though each virtual assistant has their unique features, all of them share some features that they are able to perform even if using different voice commands. Any virtual assistant will remember where a user parked their car by the user giving the virtual assistant one of the following commands:

- "This is where I parked."
- "I left the car on ____ Street."
- "Please, remember where I parked."

Table 2 Most popular virtual assistants and their keyword to wake up. Own elaboration

Developer	Virtual assistant	Wake word	Release
Amazon	Alexa	Alexa	2014
Apple	Siri	Hey, Siri	2011
Google	Google Go	OK, Google	2016
Microsoft	Cortana	Cortana	2013

In any of those cases, Google's assistant will use geolocation to establish the address where the car has been parked to store the task in its memory. Similarly, users can ask different questions to learn where the car is at:

- "Can you remind me where I parked?"
- "Where did I park?"
- "Is my car near this place?"

Unlike previous virtual assistants developed back in the XX century and in the first years of the XXI, current natural language processors do not require specific commands in order to work effectively (Hoy, 2018). Once the assistant hears the key or wake word (see Table 1), the user's voice is recorded and sent to a specialized server, where it is processed in order to return a specific command. Depending on the command, the server will look up the function to be executed based on the request, sending the output of the back-end process as a response. This output is translated to speech and given to the user in less than a second. Figure 4 illustrates this process.

Depending on the type of request, the back-end entity or server will supply the virtual assistant with a suitable piece of information to read out loud to the user or complete the task asked for. Fortunately, the number of actions and services supported by voice commands and virtual assistants is growing rapidly, since the internet of things is adopting more devices every year (Kumar et al., 2021), while manufacturers are trying to build voice control systems into their products. Every virtual assistant works in its own unique way, even though their basic functions are the same. Current virtual assistants differ from previous devices in that answers are more complex and diverse in response to questions and commands. This is because virtual assistants are always connected to the internet.

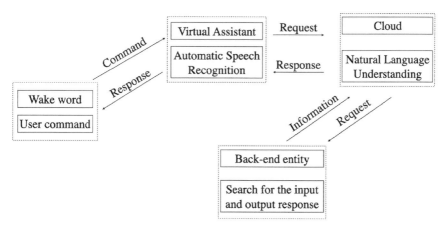

Fig. 4 How a virtual assistant works. Own elaboration

4.2 Virtual Assistants in Interactive Marketing

Sci-fi movies and future-inspired books have treated technology and computers like human beings since the former were invented: KITT in Knight Rider (1982), C-3PO in Star Wars (1977), or RoboCop (1987), for example. The tendency to include humanized objects and tools has been a recurrent factor in pop culture and, thus, in anthropomorphic and sociological studies in the literature (MacInnis & Folkes, 2017). This humanization process is made due to specific expression re-creations (Kim & McGill, 2011), through an avatar (Nowak & Rauh, 2005), or even due to cultural and recreational factors (Epley et al., 2007). Some researchers suggest that the process of making a brand or an object human triggers a human-like mind perception by the consumers (Puzakova et al., 2013), and the use of VPA such as Siri or Alexa might increase that perception (MacInnis & Folkes, 2017). The idea of holding conscious and meaningful conversations with robots and computers seemed futuristic only decades ago, but nowadays this is no longer a mere possibility: human–robot interaction is an available option. Various consumer-level products have been developed in the past years, bringing inexpensive voice assistants into users' everyday tasks. This revolution seems to be just starting, since more and more features are being added to these assistants every year.

VPA services have become a fundamental component of different technological devices (smartphones, voice assistants, etc.), social commerce web pages, and appliances that are part of the internet of things (White, 2019). The virtual assistant market is projected to be worth $7.8 billion by 2023 (Market Research Future, 2018) and their global sales in 2022 are expected to outshine computers, tablets, and smartphones as devices for online purchases (Gartner, 2016). The previous study expects that at least 75% of households worldwide will own a virtual personal assistant in 2022 (Gartner, 2016). In relation to the shopping process, it is hoped that there will be an increase in the number of online shopping orders triggered by the virtual assistant speaker, instead of through a computer or smartphone. In fact, there is an important line of research on sound regarding human–robot interactions, which focuses on voice analytics and the effect of voice on emotions (Hildebrand et al., 2020). These are significantly important reasons why the overall shopping process needs to be improved in order to offer a significantly valuable experience.

4.3 Emotions When Interacting with Virtual Assistants

Since the proposal of the Computers are social actors (CASA) paradigm whereby consumers act naturally when they interact with virtual assistants, just as if they were interacting with other people (Nass et al., 1994), researchers have found the relationship between classic social psychology theories and the success of a determined configuration of virtual assistants. The *similarity-attraction theory* (proposed by Byrne & Griffitt, 1969), the *emotional contagion theory* (Hennig-Thurau et al., 2006) or the *dress-code theory* by Cardon and Okoro (2009) are just some examples of the theories used to study the relationship between VPAs and users. Previous research has confirmed that attractiveness is associated with increased emotional bonding (Kim & Kim, 2022). Table 3 shows some results found in these previous theories.

As Pérez Marco et al. (2017) maintain, there is a need to include more "cognitive-affective architectures in modern intelligent agents," and none of the previous studies take into account the transmission of complex emotions during the shopping process, besides the projection of a certain aesthetic and looks (gender, skin color, or type of clothing) restricting their configuration to what it is established in the European Civil Law Rules in Robotics (Nevejans, 2016). Yet the new technological advances and modern structures impact and allow adjustment of the virtual assistant's conduct in real time, accomplishing a more realistic and emotive connection with the user.

Table 3 Examples of anthropomorphic theories and their application in VPA studies. Own elaboration

Theory	Study	Finding
Similarity-attraction theory	Qiu and Benbasat (2010)	Ethnicity matching improves perceptions of social presence and increases enjoyment and usefulness
Emotional contagion theory	Verhagen et al. (2014)	Friendliness rise in task-oriented communications during transactions in telecommunication services
Dress-code theory	Lunardo et al. (2016)	Using clothes increases purchase intention, trust, and social presence due to a rise in the perceived attractiveness of female VPA
Gender theories (Foster & Resnick, 2013)	Beldad et al. (2016)	Rise of the purchase intention, credibility, and perceived trust from the assistant and the seller to the buyer depending on the gender
	Liew and Tan (2018)	Importance of gender within specialist and generalist environments (female VPA are more effective in specialized transactions)

The literature on this topic highlights emotional cognition using three dimensions to explore the relationship between consumers and virtual assistants: perceived social presence, perceived social interactions, and perceived humanity. Table 4 summarizes the three dimensions and the main studies that support each one.

5 General Discussion

The focus of this chapter was to explore the challenges of current available interactive technologies. Emotions are produced in any interaction. Text, image and sound can be seen as communication tools where emotions are transferred which shapes interactive customer experiences. In the interactive marketplace, consumers and firms interact through text (OCRs), image (avatars), and sound (virtual assistants). This interactivity between humans and technology through text, image, or sound conveys emotions with different valence.

There is, at the moment, an academic necessity to continue research into the characteristics in the style of interaction between virtual assistants and users that allow valuing the benefit for them (Chattaraman et al., 2019). Thus, the Marketing Science Institute and various discussion forums about marketing tendencies (McKechnie et al., 2018) propose to continue researching the science of emotion to explore the possibilities of consumption-based emotions and self-determined relational engagement with a particular company or service provider through the use of virtual assistants. This chapter contributes to presenting the state of the art regarding the investigation of emotions transmitted in virtual interactions and proposes different paths in which to continue advancing in the investigation.

Regarding the interaction through the text, they transmit emotions with negative or positive valence, OCRs influence consumer decisions, consumer perceptions, attitudes, and product sales. Although there is still no consensus on which level of valence or arousal is most appropriate for a message, we can affirm that the dominance variable has been largely discarded for research in this field, that neutral comments do not produce an emotional effect on the consumer (Herrando et al., 2022) and that extreme valences do not produce positive effects in commercial environments (Hernández-Ortega, 2019).

Regarding voiced virtual assistants, the interaction through the sound there is not just one single variable that can define the emotion of a sound file. However, timbre, dynamics, rhythm, tempo, and harmony are some of the most important variables that influence sound and the prediction of emotion.

In relation to image, previous studies point to the need of including human behavior characteristics in virtual assistants, such as warmth, competence, and believability (Niewiadomski et al., 2010), or even adding an extra dimension of reality (Schmeil & Broll, 2007).

The future of the research has to focus on the study of the design of anthropomorphism features as embodiment (head, body and face) and the

Table 4 Dimensions of the interactive relationships between consumers and virtual assistants. Own elaboration

Component	Definition	Studies
Perceived social presence	Defined as the feeling of "being with another" (Biocca et al., 2003), to describe the relationships between the assistant and the users, evaluating the user's perception of the assistant's characteristics. This is likely to be influenced by a variety of anthropomorphic cues	Hassanein and Head (2007); Qiu and Benbasat (2010); Vilaro et al. (2021)
Perceived social interactivity	Perception that a virtual assistant displays appropriate emotions and actions according to established social norms (Wirtz et al., 2018). The trustworthiness of a virtual assistant is increased by its social intelligence, measured by the voice, which is one of the main cues that lets users feel they can interact with a virtual assistant as with other people (Chattaraman et al., 2019)	McLean and Wilson (2019); Cobos-Guzman et al. (2021); Kim et al. (2018)

(continued)

Table 4 (continued)

Component	Definition	Studies
Perceived humanity	"Type of emotions that users experience when using a product" (Velez & Jentsch, 2016). Current products and brands tend to display human characteristics (MacInnis & Folkes, 2017), such as psychological cues (emotions, gestures) and nonpsychological characteristics (anthropomorphic figures and faces). Previous studies have shown that perceived humanness is crucial in order to understand the interaction between users and virtual assistants (Doorn et al., 2017), since virtual assistants mimic human behavior, adapting their language, emotions, and gestures	Whang (2018); Patrizi et al. (2021); McLean and Osei-Frimpong (2019)

non-physical features (emotion, gaze, voice, gesture and mimicry). Theories such as "Uncanny Valley Theory" (Mori, 1970) or "Similarity attraction theory and dissimilarity repulsion theory" (Byrne, 1971), once again acquire relevance in research.

The measurement of perceived social presence, perceived social interactivity and perceived humanity in online environments and its consequences, both social and commercial, will be key to advancing research on the interaction between humans and virtual assistants. The CASA paradigm is one of the most important theories that explains how humans interact with virtual assistants. Both categorical and dimensional approaches allow the measurement of emotions. The first approach uses basic emotions (anger, disgust, fear, happiness, sadness, and surprise), and the second allows the identification of emotions on different dimensions (valence and arousal).

The context in which the interaction occurs and the objective of the message will be decisive in the design of the text, image, and sound. Valence, rhythm, tone, or human-like voice will change depending on whether it is a message with hedonic or utilitarian purposes. The experience expected by the user in a context in which his objective is to solve a doubt about the use of a product, to search for information, to buy, or to make a complaint, will be considerably different. As future research, this chapter proposed the study of the relationship between the objective of the interaction and expected user emotions in each situation, in order to later be able to capture them in the design of the tool with which it interacts.

In general, this chapter concludes that, as society evolves and virtual assistants are used more frequently, new trends arise, proposing new insights into the idiosyncrasy of virtual assistants, their conception, and future. Virtual assistants are here to stay. Research in the field is already looking for ways to improve social interactions between agents and analyzing different cues (voice, form, gestures, words) to keep offering better experiences.

Acknowledgements The authors are grateful for the financial support of the Spanish Government (research project: PID2020-118425RBI00) and the Government of Aragon and the European Social Fund (GENERES Group S-54).

References

Abbott, L. (1955). *Quality and competition*. Columbia University Press.

Banks, J., & Bowman, N. D. (2016). Avatars are (sometimes) people too: Linguistic indicators of parasocial and social ties in player–avatar relationships. *New Media & Society, 18*(7), 1257–1276.

Beldad, A., Hegner, S., & Hoppen, J. (2016). The effect of virtual sales agent (VSA) gender—product gender congruence on product advice credibility, trust in VSA and online vendor, and purchase intention. *Computers in Human Behavior, 60*, 62–72.

Benbasat, I., Dimoka, A., Pavlou, P. A., & Qiu, L. (2020). The role of demographic similarity in people's decision to interact with online anthropomorphic recommendation agents: Evidence from a functional magnetic resonance imaging (fMRI) study. *International Journal of Human-Computer Studies, 133*, 56–70.

Biocca, F., Harms, C., and Burgoon, J. K. (2003), Toward a more robust theory and measure of social presence: Review and suggested criteria, *Presence: Teleoperators & Virtual Environments, 12*(5), 456–480.

Blut, M., Wang, C., Wünderlich, N. V., & Brock, C. (2021). Understanding anthropomorphism in service provision: A meta-analysis of physical robots, chatbots, and other AI. *Journal of the Academy of Marketing Science, 49*(4), 632–658.

Bradley, M. M., and Lang, P. J. (1999), Affective norms for English words (ANEW): Instruction manual and affective ratings, *Technical Report C-1, the Center for Research in Psychophysiology, 30*(1), 25–36, University of Florida.

Bradley, M. M., and Lang, P. J. (2000), Measuring emotion: Behavior, feeling, and physiology, *Cognitive neuroscience of emotion*, pp. 242–276, New York, NY: Oxford University Press.

Brinson, N. H., & Britt, B. C. (2021). Reactance and turbulence: Examining the cognitive and affective antecedents of ad blocking. *Journal of Research in Interactive Marketing, 15*(4), 549–570.

Byrne, D. E. (1971). *The attraction paradigm*. Academic press.

Byrne, D., & Griffitt, W. (1969). Similarity and awareness of similarity of personality characteristics as determinants of attraction. *Journal of Experimental Research in Personality, 3*(3), 179–186.

Cardon, P. W., & Okoro, E. A. (2009). Professional characteristics communicated by formal versus casual workplace attire. *Business Communication Quarterly, 72*(3), 355–360.

Castillo, S., Hahn, P., Legde, K., and Cunningham, D. W. (2018), Personality analysis of embodied conversational agents, *Proceedings of the 18th International Conference on Intelligent Virtual Agents*, pp. 227–232.

Chattaraman, V., Kwon, W. S., Gilbert, J. E., & Ross, K. (2019). Should AI-Based, conversational digital assistants employ social or task-oriented interaction style? A task-competency and reciprocity perspective for older adults. *Computers in Human Behavior, 90*, 315–330.

Chevalier, J. A., & Mayzlin, D. (2006). The effect of word of mouth on sales: Online book reviews. *Journal of Marketing Research, 43*(3), 345–354.

Cobos-Guzman, S., Nuere, S., De Miguel, L., & König, C. (2021). Design of a virtual assistant to improve interaction between the audience and the presenter. *International Journal of Interactive Multimedia & Artificial Intelligence, 7*(2), 232–240.

Coltheart, M., Rastle, K., Perry, C., Langdon, R., & Ziegler, J. (2001). DRC: A dual route cascaded model of visual word recognition and reading aloud. *Psychological Review, 108*(1), 204–256.

Deng, J. J., Leung, C. H., Milani, A., & Chen, L. (2015). Emotional states associated with music: Classification, prediction of changes, and consideration in recommendation. *ACM Transactions on Interactive Intelligent Systems (TiiS), 5*(1), 1–36.

Drobes, D. J., Miller, E. J., Hillman, C. H., Bradley, M. M., Cuthbert, B. N., & Lang, P. J. (2001). Food deprivation and emotional reactions to food cues: Implications for eating disorders. *Biological Psychology, 57*(1), 153–177.

Ekman, P. (1992). An argument for basic emotions. *Cognition & Emotion, 6*(3–4), 169–200.

Epley, N., Waytz, A., & Cacioppo, J. (2007). On Seeing Human: A three-Factor theory of anthropomorphism. *Psychological Review, 114*(4), 864–886.

Etemad-Sajadi, R. (2016). The impact of online real-time interactivity on patronage intention: The use of avatars. *Computers in Human Behavior, 61*, 227–232.

Kim, D.Y. and Kim, H.-Y. (2022), Social media influencers as human brands: an interactive marketing perspective, *Journal of Research in Interactive Marketing*, Vol. ahead-of-print No. ahead-of-print.

Fernández-Abascal, E. G., Guerra, P., Martínez, F., Domínguez, F. J., Muñoz, M. Á., Egea, D. A., ... Vila, J. (2008). El sistema internacional de sonidos afectivos (IADS): Adaptación española. *Psicothema, 20*(1), 104–113.

Filieri, R. (2016). What makes an online consumer review trustworthy? *Annals of Tourism Research, 58*, 46–64.

Filieri, R., & McLeay, F. (2014). E-WOM and accommodation: An analysis of the factors that influence travelers' adoption of information from online reviews. *Journal of Travel Research, 53*(1), 44–57.

Filieri, R., Raguseo, E., & Vitari, C. (2021). Extremely negative ratings and online consumer review helpfulness: The moderating role of product quality signals. *Journal of Travel Research, 60*(4), 699–717.

Forman, C., Ghose, A., & Wiesenfeld, B. (2008). Examining the relationship between reviews and sales: The role of reviewer identity disclosure in electronic markets. *Information Systems Research, 19*(3), 291–313.

Forrest, S. (2021), Global Virtual Assistant Market achieves 15% Growth in 2020, *Futuresoure Consulting*. Available at: https://www.futuresource-consulting.com/insights/global-virtual-assistant-market-achieves-15-growth-in-2020/?locale=en

Foster, C., & Resnick, S. (2013). Service worker appearance and the retail service encounter: The influence of gender and age. *The Service Industries Journal, 33*(2), 236–247.

Frost, R., Katz, L., & Bentin, S. (1987). Strategies for visual word recognition and orthographical depth: A multilingual comparison. *Journal of Experimental Psychology: Human Perception and Performance, 13*(1), 104–115.

Gabrielsson, A., and Lindström, E. (2001), The influence of musical structure on emotional expression, *Music and emotion: Theory and research*, pp. 223–248, Oxford University Press.

Gartner, N. (2016). *Gartner says worldwide spending on VPA-enabled wireless speakers will top $2 billion by 2020*. Gartner Newsroom, p. 80.

Giles, D. C. (2002). Parasocial interaction: A review of the literature and a model for future research. *Media Psychology, 4*(3), 279–305.

Grekow, J. (2018), From content-based music emotion recognition to emotion maps of musical pieces, *Springer Cham*, Warsaw, Poland.

Hassanein, K., & Head, M. (2007). Manipulating perceived social presence through the web interface and its impact on attitude towards online shopping. *International Journal of Human-Computer Studies, 65*(8), 689–708.

Hennig-Thurau, T., Groth, M., Paul, M., & Gremler, D. D. (2006). Are all smiles created equal? How emotional contagion and emotional labor affect service relationships. *Journal of Marketing, 70*(3), 58–73.

Hernandez-Ortega, B. (2019). Not so positive, please! Effects of online consumer reviews on evaluations during the decision-making process. *Internet Research, 29*(4), 606–637.

Herrando, C., Jiménez-Martínez, J., Martín-De Hoyos, M. J., and Constantinides, E. (2022), emotional contagion triggered by online consumer reviews: Evidence from a neuroscience study, *Journal of Retailing and Consumer Services*, Vol. 67, 102973.

Hevner, K. (1935). The affective character of the major and minor modes in music. *The American Journal of Psychology, 47*(1), 103–118.

Hildebrand, C., Efthymiou, F., Busquet, F., Hampton, W. H., Hoffman, D. L., & Novak, T. P. (2020). Voice analytics in business research: Conceptual foundations, acoustic feature extraction, and applications. *Journal of Business Research, 121*, 364–374.

Hinojosa, J. A., Martínez-García, N., Villalba-García, C., Fernández-Folgueiras, U., Sánchez-Carmona, A., Pozo, M. A., & Montoro, P. R. (2016). Affective norms of 875 Spanish words for five discrete emotional categories and two emotional dimensions. *Behavior Research Methods, 48*(1), 272–284.

Horton, D., & Richard Wohl, R. (1956). Mass communication and para-social interaction: Observations on intimacy at a distance. *Psychiatry, 19*(3), 215–229.

Hoy, M. B. (2018). Alexa, Siri, Cortana, and More: An Introduction to Voice Assistants. *Medical Reference Services Quarterly, 37*(1), 81–88.

Hsieh, S. H., & Lee, C. T. (2021). Hey Alexa: Examining the effect of perceived socialness in usage intentions of AI assistant-enabled smart speaker. *Journal of Research in Interactive Marketing, 15*(2), 267–294.

Kim, K., Boelling, L., Haesler, S., Bailenson, J., Bruder, G., and Welch, G. F. (2018), Does a digital assistant need a body? The influence of visual embodiment and social behavior on the perception of intelligent virtual agents in AR, *IEEE International Symposium on Mixed and Augmented Reality (ISMAR)*, pp. 105–114.

Kim, J.-H., Kim, M., Park, M., & Yoo, J. (2021). How interactivity and vividness influence consumer virtual reality shopping experience: The mediating role of telepresence. *Journal of Research in Interactive Marketing, 15*(3), 502–525.

Kim, S., & McGill, A. L. (2011). Gaming with Mr. Slot or gaming the slot machine? Power, anthropomorphism, and risk perception. *Journal of Consumer Research, 38*(1), 94–107.

Kim, W. G., Lim, H., & Brymer, R. A. (2015). The effectiveness of managing social media on hotel performance. *International Journal of Hospitality Management, 44*, 165–171.

Kopp, S., Jung, B., Lessmann, N., and Wachsmuth, I. (2003), Max-a multimodal assistant in virtual reality construction. *KI-Künstliche Intelligenz, 17*(4), 11–17.

Korhonen, M. D., Clausi, D. A., & Jernigan, M. E. (2006). Modeling emotional content of music using system identification, *IEEE Transactions on Systems, Man, and Cybernetics. Part B (cybernetics), 36*(3), 588–599.

Kumar, B., Singh, D. A. V., and Agarwal, D. P. (2021). Trust model for virtual assistant based on artificial intelligence with communication between machines. *Design Engineering, 8*, 4701–4712.

Lang, P. J. (1994), The motivational organization of emotion: Affect-reflex connections, *Emotions: Essays on emotion theory*, pp. 61–93.

Lang, P., & Bradley, M. M. (2007). The International Affective Picture System (IAPS) in the study of emotion and attention. *Handbook of Emotion Elicitation and Assessment, 29*, 70–73.

Lasaitis, C., Ribeiro, R. L., & Bueno, O. F. A. (2008). Brazilian norms for the International Affective Picture System (IAPS): Comparison of the affective ratings for new stimuli between Brazilian and North-American subjects. *Jornal Brasileiro De Psiquiatria, 57*, 270–275.

Lee, K. M., & Nass, C. (2004). The multiple source effect and synthesized speech: Doubly-disembodied language as a conceptual framework. *Human Communication Research, 30*(2), 182–207.

Lemon, K. N., & Verhoef, P. C. (2016). Understanding customer experience throughout the customer journey. *Journal of Marketing, 80*(6), 69–96.

Liew, T. W., & Tan, S.-M. (2018). Exploring the effects of specialist versus generalist embodied virtual agents in a multi-product category online store. *Telematics and Informatics, 35*(1), 122–135.

Lin, Y. T., Doong, H. S., & Eisingerich, A. B. (2021). Avatar design of virtual salespeople: Mitigation of recommendation conflicts. *Journal of Service Research, 24*(1), 141–159.

Liu, Y. (2006). Word of mouth for movies: Its dynamics and impact on box office revenue. *Journal of Marketing, 70*(3), 74–89.

Lu, L., Liu, D., & Zhang, H. J. (2005). Automatic mood detection and tracking of music audio signals. *IEEE Transactions on Audio, Speech, and Language Processing, 14*(1), 5–18.

Lucia-Palacios, L. and Pérez-López, R. (2021). How can autonomy improve consumer experience when interacting with smart products?, *Journal of Research in Interactive Marketing*, Vol. ahead-of-print No. ahead-of-print.

Lunardo, R., Bressolles, G., & Durrieu, F. (2016). The interacting effect of virtual agents' gender and dressing style on attractiveness and subsequent consumer online behavior. *Journal of Retailing and Consumer Services, 30*, 59–66.

MacInnis, D. J., & Folkes, V. S. (2017). Humanizing brands: When brands seem to be like me, part of me, and in a relationship with me. *Journal of Consumer Psychology, 27*(3), 355–374.

Mammarella, N., Borella, E., Carretti, B., Leonardi, G., & Fairfield, B. (2013). Examining an emotion enhancement effect in working memory: Evidence from age-related differences. *Neuropsychological Rehabilitation, 23*(3), 416–428.

Marchewka, A., Żurawski, Ł, Jednoróg, K., & Grabowska, A. (2014). The Nencki Affective Picture System (NAPS): Introduction to a novel, standardized, wide-range, high-quality, realistic picture database. *Behavior Research Methods, 46*(2), 596–610.

Market Research Future. (2018). Voice assistant market by type growth, trends and analysis—forecast 2025 | MRFR. Available at: https://www.marketresearchfuture.com/reports/voice-assistant-market-4003

McKechnie, S., Nath, P., & Xun, J. (2018). New insights into emotion valence and loyalty intentions in relational exchanges. *Psychology & Marketing, 35*(2), 160–169.

McLean, G., & Osei-Frimpong, K. (2019). Hey Alexa… examine the variables influencing the use of artificial intelligent in-home voice assistants. *Computers in Human Behavior, 99*, 28–37.

McLean, G., & Wilson, A. (2019). Shopping in the digital world: Examining customer engagement through augmented reality mobile applications. *Computers in Human Behavior, 101*, 210–224.

Moltó, J., Montañés, S., Gil, R. P., Cabedo, P. S., Verchili, M. C. P., Irún, M. P. T., … Santaella, M. D. C. F. (1999). Un método para el estudio experimental de las emociones: el International Affective Picture System (IAPS). Adaptación española, *Revista de psicología general y aplicada: Revista de la Federación Española de Asociaciones de Psicología, 52*(1), 55–87.

Monnier, C., & Syssau, A. (2014). Affective norms for french words (FAN). *Behavior Research Methods, 46*(4), 1128–1137.

Monnier, C., & Syssau, A. (2017). Affective norms for 720 French words rated by children and adolescents (FANchild). *Behavior Research Methods, 49*(5), 1882–1893.

Montefinese, M., Ambrosini, E., Fairfield, B., & Mammarella, N. (2014). The adaptation of the affective norms for English words (ANEW) for Italian. *Behavior Research Methods, 46*(3), 887–903.

Mori, M. (1970). Bukimi no tani [the uncanny valley]. *Energy, 7*, 33–35.

Nass, C., Steuer, J., and Tauber, E. R. (1994), Computers Are Social Actors, *Proceedings of the SIGCHI Conference on Human Factors in Computing Systems*, pp. 72–78.

Nevejans, N. (2016), European Civil Law Rules in Robotics: Study, *Publications Office*.

Nielsen, F. Å. (2011). A new ANEW: Evaluation of a word list for sentiment analysis in microblogs. arXiv preprint arXiv:1103.2903.

Niewiadomski, R., Demeure, V., and Pelachaud, C. (2010), Warmth, competence, believability and virtual agents, *International Conference on Intelligent Virtual Agents*, pp. 272–285.

Nowak, K. L., & Rauh, C. (2005). The influence of the avatar on online perceptions of anthropomorphism, androgyny, credibility, homophily, and attraction. *Journal of Computer-Mediated Communication, 11*(1), 153–178.

Osgood, C. E., Suci, G. J., and Tannenbaum, P. H. (1957), *The measurement of meaning*, No. 47, University of Illinois press.

Park, S., & Nicolau, J. L. (2015). Asymmetric effects of online consumer reviews. *Annals of Tourism Research, 50*, 67–83.

Patrizi, C., Llado, M., Benati, D., Iodice, C., Marrocco, E., Guarascio, R., ... Recchia, A. (2021). Allele-specific editing ameliorates dominant retinitis pigmentosa in a transgenic mouse model, *The American Journal of Human Genetics, 108*(2), 295–308.

Payne, E. M., Peltier, J., & Barger, V. A. (2021). Enhancing the value co-creation process: Artificial intelligence and mobile banking service platforms. *Journal of Research in Interactive Marketing, 15*(1), 68–85.

Pérez Marco, J., Serón Arbeloa, F. J., & Cerezo Bagdasari, E. (2017). Combining cognition and emotion in virtual agents. *Kybernetes, 46*(06), 933–946.

Picard, R. W., Vyzas, E., & Healey, J. (2001). Toward machine emotional intelligence: Analysis of affective physiological state. *IEEE Transactions on Pattern Analysis and Machine Intelligence, 23*(10), 1175–1191.

Purnawirawan, N., Eisend, M., De Pelsmacker, P., & Dens, N. (2015). A meta-analytic investigation of the role of valence in online reviews. *Journal of Interactive Marketing, 31*, 17–27.

Puzakova, M., Kwak, H., & Rocereto, J. F. (2013). When humanizing brands goes wrong: The detrimental effect of brand anthropomorphization amid product wrongdoings. *Journal of Marketing, 77*(3), 81–100.

Qiu, L., & Benbasat, I. (2009). Evaluating anthropomorphic product recommendation agents: A social relationship perspective to designing information systems. *Journal of Management Information Systems, 25*(4), 145–182.

Qiu, L., & Benbasat, I. (2010). A study of demographic embodiments of product recommendation agents in electronic commerce. *International Journal of Human-Computer Studies, 68*(10), 669–688.

Redondo, J., Fraga, I., Padrón, I., & Comesaña, M. (2007). The Spanish adaptation of ANEW (affective norms for English words). *Behavior Research Methods, 39*(3), 600–605.

Russell, J. A. (1980). A circumplex model of affect. *Journal of Personality and Social Psychology, 39*(6), 1161–1178.

Russell, J. A. (2003). Core affect and the psychological construction of emotion. *Psychological Review, 110*(1), 145–172.

Schmeil, A., and Broll, W. (2007), MARA—A mobile augmented reality-based virtual assistant, *2007 IEEE Virtual Reality Conference*, pp. 267–270.

Schmidtke, D. S., Schröder, T., Jacobs, A. M., & Conrad, M. (2014). ANGST: Affective norms for German sentiment terms, derived from the affective norms for English words. *Behavior Research Methods, 46*(4), 1108–1118.

Schmitt, B., Joško Brakus, J., & y Zarantonello, L. (2015). From experiential psychology to consumer experience. *Journal of Consumer Psychology, 25*(1), 166–171.

Soares, A. P., Pinheiro, A. P., Costa, A., Frade, C. S., Comesaña, M., & Pureza, R. (2013). Affective auditory stimuli: Adaptation of the international affective digitized sounds (IADS-2) for European Portuguese. *Behavior Research Methods, 45*(4), 1168–1181.

Stadthagen-Gonzalez, H., Imbault, C., Pérez Sánchez, M. A., & Brysbaert, M. (2017). Norms of valence and arousal for 14,031 Spanish words. *Behavior Research Methods, 49*(1), 111–123.

Stevenson, R. A., & James, T. W. (2008). Affective auditory stimuli: Characterization of the international affective digitized sounds (IADS) by discrete emotional categories. *Behavior Research Methods, 40*(1), 315–321.

Sutton, T. M., Herbert, A. M., & Clark, D. Q. (2019). Valence, arousal, and dominance ratings for facial stimuli. *Quarterly Journal of Experimental Psychology, 72*(8), 2046–2055.

Tsai, W.-H.S., Liu, Y., & Chuan, C.-H. (2021). How chatbots' social presence communication enhances consumer engagement: The mediating role of parasocial interaction and dialogue. *Journal of Research in Interactive Marketing, 15*(3), 460–482.

Van Doorn, J., Mende, M., Noble, S. M., Hulland, J., Ostrom, A. L., Grewal, D., & Petersen, J. A. (2017). Domo arigato Mr. Roboto: Emergence of automated social presence in organizational frontlines and customers' service experiences. *Journal of Service Research, 20*(1), 43–58.

Van Pinxteren, M. M., Pluymaekers, M., & Lemmink, J. G. (2020). Human-like communication in conversational agents: A literature review and research agenda. *Journal of Service Management., 31*(2), 203–225.

Velez, J. E., and Jentsch, F. (2016, September). Robot emotive display systems and the analogous physical features of emotion, *Proceedings of the Human Factors and Ergonomics Society Annual Meeting, 60*(1), 1344–1348.

Verhagen, T., van Nes, J., Feldberg, F., & van Dolen, W. (2014). Virtual customer service agents: Using social presence and personalization to shape online service encounters. *Journal of Computer-Mediated Communication, 19*(3), 529–545.

Vermeulen, I. E., & Seegers, D. (2009). Tried and tested: The impact of online hotel reviews on consumer consideration. *Tourism Management, 30*(1), 123–127.

Vilaro, M. J., Wilson-Howard, D. S., Zalake, M. S., Tavassoli, F., Lok, B. C., Modave, F. P., ... Krieger, J. L. (2021). Key changes to improve social presence of a virtual health assistant promoting colorectal cancer screening informed by a technology acceptance model, *BMC Medical Informatics and Decision Making, 21*(1), 1–9.

Wang, Z., Cheng, N., Fan, Y., Liu, J., and Zhu, C. (2005), Construction of virtual assistant based on basic emotions theory, *International Conference on Affective Computing and Intelligent Interaction*, pp. 574–581.

Wang, C. L. (2021). New frontiers and future directions in interactive marketing: Inaugural Editorial. *Journal of Research in Interactive Marketing, 15*(1), 1–9.

Wang, C. L., Wang, Y., Wei, J., & Chung, H. (2020). Understanding experiential consumption: Theoretical advancement and practical implication. *Asia Pacific Journal of Marketing and Logistics., 32*(6), 1173–1176.

Wang, W., Li, F., & Yi, Z. (2019). Scores vs. stars: A regression discontinuity study of online consumer reviews. *Information & Management, 56*(3), 418–428.

Whang, C. (2018), Voice Shopping: The effect of the consumer-voice assistant parasocial relationship on the consumer's perception and decision making, *University of Minnesota Digital Conservancy*.

White, H. (2019), Voice assistants are taking over consumer IoT. *IoT For All*, available at: https://www.iotforall.com/voice-assistants-consumer-io

Wilson, A. E., Giebelhausen, M. D., & Brady, M. K. (2017). Negative word of mouth can be a positive for consumers connected to the brand. *Journal of the Academy of Marketing Science, 45*(4), 534–547.

Wirtz, J., Patterson, P. G., Kunz, W. H., Gruber, T., Lu, V. N., Paluch, S., & Martins, A. (2018). Brave new world: Service robots in the frontline. *Journal of Service Management, 29*(5), 907–931.

Wu, R., Chen, J., Wang, C. L., & Zhou, L. (2022). The influence of emoji meaning multipleness on perceived online review helpfulness: The mediating role of processing fluency. *Journal of Business Research, 141*, 299–307.

Wu, R., Wu, H. H., & Wang, C. L. (2021). Why is a picture 'worth a thousand words'? Pictures as information in perceived helpfulness of online reviews. *International Journal of Consumer Studies, 45*(3), 364–378.

Wundt, W. M. (1912). *An introduction to psychology*, G. Allen, Limited.

Yang, W., Makita, K., Nakao, T., Kanayama, N., Machizawa, M. G., Sasaoka, T., ... Miyatani, M. (2018). Affective auditory stimulus database: An expanded version of the International Affective Digitized Sounds (IADS-E). *Behavior Research Methods, 50*(4), 1415–1429.

Yang, Y. H., & Chen, H. H. (2012). Machine recognition of music emotion: A review. *ACM Transactions on Intelligent Systems and Technology (TIST), 3*(3), 1–30.

Ye, Q., Law, R., & Gu, B. (2009). The impact of online user reviews on hotel room sales. *International Journal of Hospitality Management, 28*(1), 180–182.

Zawieska, K., Duffy, B. R., & Strońska, A. (2012). Understanding anthropomorphisation in social robotics. *Pomiary Automatyka Robotyka, 16*(11), 78–82.

PART III

Interactivity in the Virtual World

CHAPTER 14

Augmented Reality in Interactive Marketing: The State-Of-The-Art and Emerging Trends

Marc Riar, Jakob J. Korbel, Nannan Xi, Sophia Meywirth, Rüdiger Zarnekow, and Juho Hamari

1 Introduction

With the development of virtual technologies and information systems such as mixed reality (MR), multisensory modalities, big data, cloud computing, robotics, and Internet of Things (IoT), the current marketing practices are facing various opportunities and challenges. Especially during the COVID-19 pandemic, increasing numbers of marketing activities relied on digital technologies to communicate with consumers remotely (Donthu & Gustafsson,

---

The original version of this chapter was revised: The incorrect author's affiliation list has been corrected. The correction to this chapter is available at https://doi.org/10.1007/978-3-031-14961-0_43

M. Riar (✉) · J. J. Korbel · S. Meywirth · R. Zarnekow
Technical University of Berlin, Berlin, Germany
e-mail: marc.riar@tu-berlin.de

J. J. Korbel
e-mail: jakob.j.korbel@tu-berlin.de

S. Meywirth
e-mail: sophia.meywirth@campus.tu-berlin.de

R. Zarnekow
e-mail: ruediger.zarnekow@tu-berlin.de

N. Xi · J. Hamari
Tampere University, Tampere, Finland
e-mail: nannan.xi@tuni.fi

© The Author(s), under exclusive license to Springer Nature Switzerland AG 2023, corrected publication 2023
C. L. Wang (ed.), *The Palgrave Handbook of Interactive Marketing*,
https://doi.org/10.1007/978-3-031-14961-0_14

2020; Jiang & Stylos, 2021). On one hand, marketers have the opportunities to present more vivid, rich, and creative product, service, brand, and advertising information with the aid of digital platforms and tools (Sheng et al., 2021; Soto-Acosta, 2020) as well as to conduct customer management in a more efficient way (Barnes, 2020; Jiang & Stylos, 2021). On the other hand, due to the lack of guidance on designing and implementing virtual technologies in marketing practices, unpleasant user experience, low usability, information overload, privacy risk, and ethical concerns are becoming the hurdles to consumers' adoption and continued use of these virtual technologies.

One of the relatively mature virtual technologies that has been applied widely in current marketing practices is augmented reality (AR). The AR market was valued at USD 14.7 billion in 2020 and is expected to grow at a CAGR of 31.5% from 2021 to 2026.[1] AR technology allows to superimpose virtual content (e.g., objects, information, videos, sounds, etc.) into the physical environment (Azuma, 1997) with the aim to modify the perceived reality with virtual elements in an interactive manner (Xi & Hamari, 2021). The typical AR marketing practices include AR fitting rooms (Chiang et al., 2021), AR interactive advertisement (Feng & Xie, 2018), AR product presentation, and customization (e.g., IKEA catalog and Amazon AR view) as well as location-based AR shopping. These marketing information, that are being created and provided by AR, can modify consumers' multisensory experience (e.g., visual, sound, olfactory, and haptic) and have been believed to increase consumer engagement and loyalty as well as facilitate consumer decision-making (Chiang et al., 2021). However, while the potential affordances of AR for interactive marketing have become more prominent (Carrozzi et al., 2019; Wang, 2021), a synthesized understanding of the effects of AR in marketing is still lacking. A few critical views have considered AR as a kind of marketing gimmick to attract consumers rather than an effective marketing tool for increased sales conversions. AR-mediated advertising, information presentation, promotion, and shopping have not replaced the traditional marketing techniques (Yaoyuneyong et al., 2016). In addition, the long-term effect of AR on marketing performance remains unknown. Due to the lack of understanding of the mechanisms and boundary conditions of how AR influences consumers' psychological and behavioral aspects, marketing practitioners rarely incorporate AR into their long-term marketing strategies (Tan et al., 2022).

Thus, a thorough and comprehensive understanding of interactive AR marketing can help understand a) what kind of psychological experience and behavioral outcomes AR marketing can evoke; b) what sorts of products and what marketing contexts AR has been applied to; c) what sort of different AR

J. Hamari
e-mail: juho.hamari@tuni.fi

N. Xi
University of Vaasa, Vaasa, Finland

[1] https://www.globenewswire.com/news-release/2021/10/06/2309582/28124/en/Global-Augmented-Reality-Market-Report-2021-Surging-Demand-for-AR-Devices-and-Applications-in-Healthcare-Forecast-to-2026.html.

technologies have been implemented; and d) what opportunities and challenges are perceived by practitioners in terms of using AR for marketing praxis. To address these questions, this chapter aims to develop a comprehensive understanding of the current state of the literature on interactive AR marketing and to expand this with the view of practitioners by conducting five interviews with small online shop providers. Based on the obtained results, a future outlook of trends for AR as an interactive marketing technology is presented.

2   Background and Related Work

2.1   AR and Interchangeable Terms

Since the presented information and content are both digital in AR and virtual reality (VR), in some of the early literature, AR was often treated as an interchangeable term with VR (Novak-Marcincin et al., 2014) or one branch of VR technology (Y. Huang et al., 2011). Xi and Hamari (2021) defined and clarified the difference between AR and VR from the perspective of applying technology: AR aims at modifying the perceived real world while VR aims at replacing reality with a virtual environment. VR is touted to block out the real world (Manis & Choi, 2019) and digitally duplicate or substitute the "real reality" (Kim et al., 2021; Xi & Hamari, 2021; Yim et al., 2017). VR can provide a highly immersive, natural, and realistic digital world for users and a sensation of "being there" (Hardiess et al., 2015; Kipper, 2013). In comparison, AR provides access to additional "augmenting" information (Pantano & Servidio, 2012; Rese et al., 2014) that can take any form and can be related to the stimulation of any senses (van Krevelen & Poelman, 2010) (e.g., scent, tactile sense, etc.) (Azuma, 1997; Lu & Smith, 2007). Most commonly, AR is employed to augment consumers' visual experiences and to provide the possibility of interacting with visual virtual information. Especially, with the help of recognition and tracking techniques, the digitalized content (e.g., text, pictures, 3D models, audio, and video) can be triggered and displayed on the screen according to specific elements (e.g., images, objects, barcodes, QR codes, and location) in the current surroundings (Aggarwal & Singhal, 2019; Hilken et al., 2018).

In the existing literature, AR has been considered with three main attributes: vividness, novelty, and interactivity (Azuma, 1997; McLean & Wilson, 2019). The vividness of AR is the ability to produce a sensory-rich mediated environment (Steuer, 1992), and is usually related to the display quality and aesthetic aspect of information (Flavián et al., 2019; McLean & Wilson, 2019). The novelty of AR refers to the unique and personalized content experienced through the AR display, which can lead to consumers' curiosity and being engrossed (McLean & Wilson, 2019), while it can even act as a central cue that enhances consumers' understanding toward a brand's features (Feng & Xie, 2019). The third attribute, i.e., interactivity, is related to AR systems' capacity to allow consumers to modify (e.g., move, resize, reshape, etc.) the digitally overlaid virtual content (McLean & Wilson, 2019).

2.2 A Theoretical Framework for Interactive AR Marketing

In the realm of marketing, AR has been regarded as a strategic concept that incorporates digital content into users' perception to attain organizational goals and to present consumer benefits (Rauschnabel et al., 2019), such as extraordinary experiences, convenience, as well as personalized content (Wang, 2021). Understanding consumer behavior is one of the major themes in interactive marketing (Lim et al., 2022) and various theories have been employed to understand how AR technology influences consumers during shopping (Riar et al., 2022). One of the most relevant theoretical concepts in research on immersive technologies is grounded in the Stimulus-Organism-Response (S–O-R) model (Loureiro et al., 2019). The model specifies that different environmental conditions serve as stimuli (S) that affect the internal evaluation processes of consumers (O), leading to a response (R). Recently, the S–O-R model has also become a relevant theoretical basis for explaining consumer decision processes and behavior in the literature on interactive AR marketing (Nikhashemi et al., 2021; Qin et al., 2021). The main notion is that the technological characteristics of AR serve as stimuli to elicit cognitive and affective states in consumers which consequently lead to behavioral outcomes (see Fig. 1). While recent studies have used this notion to empirically investigate the effects of AR on consumers, there is a lack of a synthesized overview of the diverse technological proficiencies of AR and what psychological and behavioral responses these are capable to evoke. Therefore, guided by the S–O-R framework, the present study aims at closing this gap.

3 Method

The methodology of this chapter is divided into two parts. First, a systematic review of the academic corpus of literature on the phenomenon of using AR for interactive marketing purposes is performed. Second, semi-structured interviews with small online shop providers are conducted to complement the

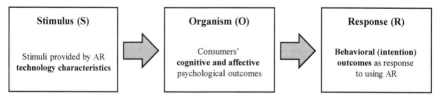

Fig. 1 Framework for consumer response in interactive AR marketing based on S–O-R theory

findings from research with initial insights into the practitioners' perspectives on AR use in the marketing context.

3.1 Literature Review

Search strategy: The systematic literature review was performed by following the instructions of Brereton et al. (2007) and the search was conducted within the Web of Science database. This database was selected because it is indexing further bibliographic sources that, among other areas, provide access to relevant literature in the fields of information technology as well as marketing, retail, and shopping. The search string was constructed to include the relevant terms (i.e., "augmented reality" and "marketing") as well as the extended sphere of retail and shopping in order to ensure an exhaustive search. The final search string looks as follows and was performed to search the titles, abstracts, and keywords in the selected database: *("augmented reality" OR AR OR "virtual try-on") AND (marketing OR advertis* OR brand* OR shop* OR retail* OR commerce)*. The search term "virtual try-on" was added because AR is sometimes used for self-representation in form of virtual mirrors by which consumers can superimpose virtual products on themselves, such as sunglasses, clothes, makeup, etc. On the other hand, terms related to "virtual reality/VR" were excluded from the search string because the present chapter focuses specifically on AR. In order to capture the most recent developments and trends, the search was conducted to cover the academic literature of the past 5 years (January 2016–August 2021).

Study selection: The search returned an initial set of 889 studies. This initial set was pre-screened and duplicates, short papers, commentaries, non-peer-reviewed articles, studies that were written in languages other than English, studies on other technologies, such as VR, and non-empirical studies were excluded. The final pool consists of 43 studies. The included studies are highlighted with "*" in the references.

Data extraction: In accordance with recommendations by Brereton et al. (2007), a data extraction form was created to systematically obtain the relevant information from the screened literature. Specifically, this form was construed to obtain general information about the literature (e.g., authors, publication venue, etc.) and in line with the conceptualization based on the S–O-R theory presented in Fig. 1, information related to the technological characteristics of AR as well as the psychological and behavioral responses of consumers were extracted. In addition, to provide further contextual information and to elucidate a more comprehensive picture of interactive AR marketing, information related to the use contexts of AR marketing, devices, and product types that have been investigated in the screened literature were extracted.

Table 1 Overview of the conducted interviews

Interview	Industry/Branch	Position of Interviewee within Company	Interview Date	Interview Duration
IW1	Electronic cigarettes	Managing director	08.11.2021	24:59
IW2	Bedding	eCommerce & Marketing manager	11.11.2021	32:36
IW3	Water purification	IT & HR Manager	16.11.2021	32:54
IW4	Consumer electronics	Managing director	18.11.2021	38:28
IW5	Gift boxes	Managing director	19.11.2021	45:15

3.2 Practitioner Interviews

Preparation: The first point of contact with the interviewees was established via E-Mail. Five respondents of small businesses (1–15 employees) agreed to take part in the interviews (see Table 1). Due to the request of the interview partners, their company names and details remain anonymous. A short summary of the research objectives was sent to the interviewees and interview dates were scheduled. An interview guideline containing 21 questions and 15 sub-questions was designed prior to conducting the interviews. The interview guideline was divided into six parts, each covering a specific topic: (1) the background and prior experiences with AR, (2) the perceived usefulness of AR for marketing, (3) the prerequisites that must be met in order to implement AR successfully in marketing, including potential barriers, risks, estimated costs, etc., (4) the usage of AR applications by their competitors and the suitability of AR within their branch, (5) the internal factors such as the employee structure and priorities within the business, and (6) the general view of AR applications as a future trend in marketing.

Interviews, data coding, and analysis: To establish a common understanding of the research scope, the participants were presented with a demo of an AR application at the beginning of the interviews. The interviews were conducted semi-structured (Helfferich, 2014) and therefore contained no standardized but open questions to encourage the interview partners to share their subjective opinion. The data derived from the interviews were analyzed following the guidelines of Mayring (i.e., Mayring, 2015, 2019). First, the interviews were transcribed to allow the coding and analysis of the data. The coding and analysis were conducted software-supported relying on the software tool QCAmap.[2] Second, a category system was established consisting of (1) opportunities of AR in marketing, and (2) challenges of AR in marketing with the subcategories AR technology, customer outcome,

[2] https://www.qcamap.org/ui/de/home.

and economic outcome. Finally, the data were qualitatively analyzed and interpreted (Sect. 4.5).

4 Conceptual Overview of Interactive AR Marketing

In this section, a holistic framework of interactive AR marketing is incrementally derived from the combined results of the literature review (Sect. 4.1–4.4) and the practitioner interviews (Sect. 4.5). The unified results are illustrated in Fig. 2.

4.1 Use Scenarios and Contexts

The screened literature reveals diverse use scenarios for employing AR technology for the purpose of interactive marketing that spans across location-independent online situations as well as solutions for physical (brick-and-mortar) stores (see Fig. 2: segment 4.1). Importantly, from a marketing

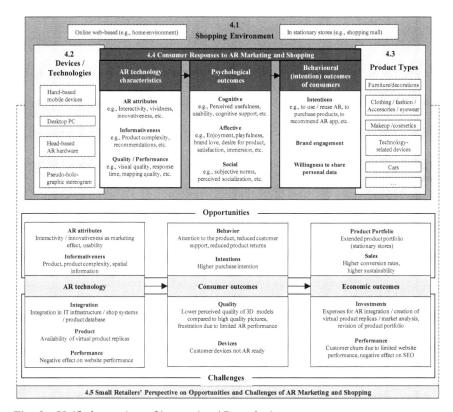

Fig. 2 Unified overview of interactive AR marketing

perspective, sellers can attract consumers to a brand by providing AR functionality and giving them a new sense of experiencing products, both in-store and in online shopping scenarios. The advantages of AR in online shops involve that consumers can interact with virtual 3D representations of products in real-time, which unquestionably enhances the product experience beyond simply viewing non-interactive 2D pictures of products. Above all, consumers can often place virtual products in private environments, for example at home, where the product can be viewed and experienced within the environment it is intended for (Brengman et al., 2019; Fan et al., 2020; Haile & Kang, 2020; Kowalczuk et al., 2021; Pantano et al., 2017). Thereby, consumers can better assess the particular features of products, customize them and get a better idea of how these will fit into the intended surroundings, which can affect ownership perceptions (Brengman et al., 2019; Carrozzi et al., 2019) and enhance purchase decisions (Haile & Kang, 2020; Kowalczuk et al., 2021).

In addition to location-independent online solutions, AR can also provide unique consumer experiences in brick-and-mortar shopping environments. Specifically, marketers can make use of consumers' curiosity by offering virtual mirrors or interactive screens (Javornik et al., 2016, 2021) within their stores or in shopping malls, thereby drawing the consumers' attention to stores and making the interaction with brands more enticing. Stores can also offer solutions by which consumers can use the AR capabilities of their own mobile devices. For example, AR can help shoppers navigate through supermarkets to find particular products (Chylinski et al., 2020) or superimpose additional virtual product cues to increase the consumers' informativeness (Qin et al., 2021; Rese et al., 2017; Smink et al., 2019) and support their purchase decisions. Overall, the interactive AR experiences can, among other factors, positively influence product (Xu et al., 2020) and brand attitudes (T.-L. Huang, 2019; Rauschnabel et al., 2019; Uribe et al., 2021; van Esch et al., 2019), which may directly translate into a sales conversion. Hence, both in-store and online AR solutions provide appealing opportunities for marketers to advertise products, improve product management and consumer services, making AR technology a desirable instrument for marketing praxis.

4.2   *Devices and Technologies*

The rapid technological development of the past decades has opened up various possibilities to enter the AR sphere (see Fig. 2: segment 4.2). Desktop-PCs with external or built-in web cameras are an entry-level option by which users can, for instance, experience try-on products (e.g., sunglasses, clothes, makeup, etc.) as a sort of virtual mirror on themselves (T.-L. Huang, 2019; Smink et al., 2019). This concept has also been taken up in malls as well as brick-and-mortar stores via designated (mostly physically fixed) interactive screens that support so-called virtual or smart mirror functionalities by which users can virtually try on products. Thereby, these interactive screens provide personalized experiences, prompt playful interaction, and allow for self-referencing, which can in turn affect brand attitudes (T.-L. Huang, 2019).

Another frontier for creating AR experiences is the use of pseudo-holographic technology by which the users themselves do not use any technology to superimpose virtual content. Instead, a visualization system generates a 3D illusion of content, for example, to create a virtual exhibition of products within a store (Morillo et al., 2019).

The rise of mobile devices has been one of the most prominent factors for the diffusion of AR technology. Present-day mobile devices are largely rolled out with AR capabilities which makes them a particularly interesting channel for marketers to connect with and bind consumers on a large scale. Besides having advantages in terms of diffusion, mobile devices also entail other important properties that enhance the experience with augmented content. Touch displays and the maneuverability of light-weight mobile devices, such as smartphones and tablets, enable users to effortlessly interact with augmented content (e.g., moving a virtually displayed and true-to-scale couch from one side of the room to the other, placing a virtually presented lamp on a physical desk, etc.). Therefore, it is unsurprising that the vast majority of the reviewed literature has relied on exploring the benefits of mobile AR marketing.

Designated AR devices, such as AR glasses (Heller et al., 2019b) offer an even more immersive experience by providing hands-free interaction and by overlaying augmented information directly in the users' field of view. While examples of AR glasses in research and practice are still relatively limited compared to the use of mobile devices, it is foreseeable that these will become more prevalent in the future as more affordable and technologically mature devices emerge. Therefore, marketers should keep an eye on these developments and appropriate themselves with the necessary knowledge to exploit the future potentials of contemporary AR technology.

4.3 Virtual Product Types

Creating personalized product experiences is one of the essential marketing strategies to generate brand engagement. Current literature on AR marketing is in accord with this because studies are largely focusing on how AR can create personalized consumer experiences. This becomes especially evident in terms of the product types that are offered to consumers via AR technology. Most prominently, these involve wearables such as accessories, eyewear, cosmetics, fashion, and clothing. Usually, these products are presented via try-on proficiencies by which AR operates as a virtual mirror. From a marketing perspective, this is a highly relevant feature of AR because it can connect consumers directly with products by letting them experience these wearables on themselves, thereby inducing self-brand connections (Baek et al., 2018), brand awareness, and shaping brand attitudes (T.-L. Huang, 2019).

Another popular trend has evolved around letting consumers place virtual furniture and decorations directly into their homes. In the past, consumers relied on the impressions and information that they could gather by visiting furniture stores and afterward used this information to map out or mentally picture and measure whether or not these items fit size-wise or in terms of the existing décor and interior design. Today, consumers can utilize AR technology to display virtual furniture and decorations true-to-scale directly in their intended environments. Thereby, AR technology supports the mental imagery of consumers and provides the necessary information to support purchase decisions (Heller et al., 2019a, 2019b).

While wearables and furniture or decorations currently seem to be the main two product categories of AR solutions, there are numerous other product categories that marketers can consider in order to offer unique product experiences to consumers and to draw them to a brand (see Fig. 2: segment 4.3 for selected further examples).

4.4 Consumer Response to AR Marketing

The use of AR has been argued to increase store attractiveness (Bonnin, 2020) by addressing different consumer needs, both of pragmatic and hedonic nature (Javornik et al., 2016; Qin et al., 2021; Rauschnabel, 2021; Rauschnabel et al., 2019; Riar et al., 2021). The extant literature on AR in marketing contexts largely explores how AR can address pragmatic and hedonic consumer needs by investigating how the specific technological features of AR affect psychological outcomes, which ultimately transcend into behavioral outcomes (see Fig. 2: segment 4.4.). Some of the most explored AR attributes are interactivity and vividness. interactivity refers to the technological ability to perform modifications with virtual content in real-time, whereas vividness refers to the representational richness of a medium. Both technological attributes are highly relevant to generating immersive experiences (Steuer, 1992). Further important characteristics to attain desired consumer responses in marketing practice are the informativeness of the AR application (e.g., the quality and degree of provided information, product contextuality, information sharing capabilities, etc.) (Heller et al., 2019a; Hilken et al., 2020; Kowalczuk et al., 2021; Pantano et al., 2017) as well as aspects pertaining to the quality or performance of the AR solution (e.g., the visual quality, mapping quality, responsiveness of the AR app, etc.) (Kowalczuk et al., 2021; Pantano et al., 2017; Park & Yoo, 2020).

In terms of the psychological outcomes, AR can give rise to diverse cognitive responses, such as usefulness perceptions (Pantano et al., 2017; Rese et al., 2017; Zhang et al., 2019), perceived informativeness (Feng & Xie, 2018; Qin et al., 2021; Rese et al., 2017; Smink et al., 2019), curiosity (Beck & Crié, 2018; Yang et al., 2020), brand awareness (Feng & Xie, 2019), creativity (Jessen et al., 2020) as well as self-referencing (T.-L. Huang, 2019), which is decisive in creating a personalized experience with products, forging ownership perceptions (Song et al., 2020), and attachment with a brand (Yuan et al., 2021).

Marketers may also take a special interest in the ability of AR to produce affective consumer responses. The reviewed literature suggests that consumers can perceive nostalgia (Hinsch et al., 2020) and higher sensations of enjoyment when interacting with AR-mediated product presentations. The hedonic value can create intrinsically fulfilling experiences, such as immersion (Hilken et al., 2020; Kowalczuk et al., 2021; Smink et al., 2020), brand love (T.-L. Huang, 2019), desire for products (Hilken et al., 2017), and consumer satisfaction (Jessen et al., 2020; McLean & Wilson, 2019; Moriuchi et al., 2021; Poushneh & Vasquez-Parraga, 2017). These are all aptitudes that set AR as an interactive marketing technology apart from more conventional non-interactive technologies.

In addition to the cognitive and affective responses that have been encountered, the analyzed body of literature also indicates that it can be imperative to cultivate social dynamics between consumers. Albeit considered only to a marginal extent, the reviewed studies indicate that AR can be combined with social media features (Zhang et al., 2019) and other social constituents, such as point-of-view sharing (Hilken et al., 2020) or further communicative acts. It is assumed, that social experiences can be facilitated via AR, which can result in viral marketing behavior and unpaid brand endorsements (Sung, 2021). Groundwork on interactive marketing indicates that the proliferation of social media, content-sharing, brand, and fandom communities is becoming increasingly relevant for marketers and users to share brand and product-related information (Wang, 2021). Accordingly, marketers should consider today's participatory culture where subjective norms (McLean & Wilson, 2019) are shaped through online communities, customer recommendations, (internet) celebrities as well as significant others such as family and friends, which ultimately influences consumers' attitudes toward companies, brands, and products. Thus, in order to transform AR into an effective marketing tool, it seems relevant to consider functionalities that can satisfy the need of consumers to socialize and communicate about products and brands.

In a similar vein, when turning the attention to the encountered behavioral outcomes in Fig. 2, consumers have also been found to breed word-of-mouth intentions (Heller et al., 2019a; Mishra et al., 2021; Park & Yoo, 2020) when engaging with AR technology because it is largely regarded as fun and interesting, thus prompting consumers to share their experience with others. Willingness to share personal data is another outcome addressed in the reviewed literature (Smink et al., 2019). AR often requires users to reveal their current surroundings, or their own face, body, hands, etc., and its use may thus result in privacy concerns or perceived intrusiveness. However, it has also been argued that the perceived informativeness as a result of using AR can encourage users to share their personal information (Smink et al., 2019). Therefore, it seems that the positive aspects of AR can overcome potential hesitancies of consumers when it comes to sharing personal information. Besides word-of-mouth intentions and willingness to share personal data, the reviewed literature chiefly agrees that AR can induce intentions to revisit stores

(Javornik, 2016; Park & Yoo, 2020) that support AR functionality as well as increase purchase intentions (Beck & Crié, 2018; Brengman et al., 2019; Moriuchi et al., 2021; Zhang et al., 2019). This is important for marketers, as it pinpoints AR technology as a medium with the potential not only to increase sales conversion but also to maintain customer relations.

4.5 Small Retailers' Perspective

Opportunities for adopting AR in marketing: Pertaining to the practitioner perspectives on AR marketing in the domain of small shop owners, all interviewees showed a positive attitude toward AR, considering it as a relevant application "in the near future" (IW3) and stated several advantages that they expect from the technology. In the experience of the retailers, the description of the products in online shops is the most important criterion for the consumers' purchase decision ("the better the description on the website, the better the sales" (IW2)) while the product pictures are vital since they "are what haptics are for stationary retail" (IW2). Therefore, an advanced visualization of the products is of great importance to the online retailers and considered by the interviewees as the most prominent benefit of AR applications (IW1, IW2, IW3, IW4, IW5). The enhanced visual and spatial impression allows the consumers to get more detailed information about the product (IW2, IW3) and assess the size of the products which is still an issue in E-commerce (IW3, IW5). Consumers often order a product twice due to the limited size evaluation possibilities (IW5). Compared to product pictures, 3D visualizations have the advantage that the users can evaluate the entire product with a simple click rather than go through the entire photo gallery (IW2) while the product itself comes "within reach" (IW3). Specifically, the opportunity to interact with and evaluate specific components of a complex product, to experience the product from the in- and outside, and to customize several parts of the product simultaneously is stressed by the interviewees as a great advantage (IW2, IW4, IW5). In addition, the integration of the products in their spatial contexts can solve the challenge of product installation issues (IW3) which also affects stationary retail. In the case of IW2, the product portfolio differs online and offline since some of their products are only sold in the stationary store. AR is considered as a great complement to allow the consumers to experience the products from the stationary store beforehand at home in their spatial context (IW2, IW3). The stationary retail can additionally benefit from AR by using the application to provide the consumers with online information about the product in the stationary environment (e.g., product reviews) (IW5). Furthermore, offline retailers might use the AR application to let the users experience or see products that are not exhibited on the shop floor based on a catalog with products, QR codes, and AR functionality (IW5). Hence, the shop owners expect from the integration of the AR functionalities a reduction of user complaints and product returns (IW1, IW4), higher sustainability (IW5), and a higher purchase intention (IW2) as well as a reduction of customer support due to the higher informativeness (IW5). Overall, AR is regarded as a technology that can generate positive marketing effects due to its newness and the curiosity toward the technology that increases the interest in the products. Consumers are predicted to "stay longer with the product" (IW2), leading to increasing sales (IW2).

The early adoption of the technology provides an additional marketing advantage since the shops can advertise themselves as "the only store where you can assess the products in AR that fits you" (IW5). AR can also be included in traditional marketing approaches such as newsletters to allow the consumers to get a teaser of new products (IW3). In addition, IW5 would welcome the integration of the AR functionality in social media stores, such as the Instagram shop, to facilitate the interaction with the consumer base (IW5). Therefore, social media is not only a platform to enhance the marketing capabilities via AR but a medium to foster AR adoption from the interviewee's perspective: Advertising AR over influencers and social media may shift attention to the benefits of the technology (IW1, IW2).

Challenges for adopting AR in marketing: Apart from the expected benefits from the inclusion of AR in marketing, the interviewees emphasize challenges concerning the integration of the technology and virtual product replica, i.e., 3D models of the products (Korbel, 2021). The integrational challenges mainly stem from the consumer devices in use as well as the integration in the IT infrastructure and existing shop systems. The interviewees state that a multitude of consumers may not possess smartphones that allow the usage of AR applications (IW4, IW5). If users see the AR feature but are not able to use it or have problems using the AR application, they could get frustrated and even tend to leave the website (IW5). The same applies to the computational requirements of AR applications. The computational requirements might be too high (IW5), leading, in the worst case, to a limited functionality or even a crash of the website. If the AR application impairs the functionality of the website, it can lead to customer churn (IW4) and negatively influence SEO (IW5). Therefore, the IT infrastructure and servers must be migrated to enable the AR functionalities (IW1) and short loading times (IW5). In addition, settings should be available and editable so that website owners can adjust the resource insensitivity of the AR application (IW5). Furthermore, the interviewees stress that the integration of the AR functionalities should be a one-time IT effort (IW4), feasible "with a few clicks" (IW4), and compatible with existing shop systems (IW2). The provision of AR as a plugin for existing shop systems would tremendously decrease the integrational challenges (IW3). If an easy integration of the AR functionalities is not possible, shop owners tend to think about adopting and investing in AR twice (IW4).

The challenges regarding the virtual product replicas mainly derive from the creation, provisioning, and quality of the 3D models that are mandatory to use the AR application at all. How the models are created or provided depends on the firm's access to supplier and manufacturing media data. While the firm in the case of IW5 creates product pictures themselves (also in 360 degrees) and would require a software tool or pipeline to convert their product pictures to 3D models, the firms of IW1 and IW4 rely entirely on pictures from the suppliers or manufacturers based on partnerships and do not even have the products at hand (IW1). Hence, the virtual product replicas must be provided by the manufacturer, supplier, or the vendor of the AR environment in the opinion of the interviewees (IW1, IW2, IW3, IW4), otherwise the added value is not comparable with the efforts and investments in the AR environment (IW4). Therefore, the providers of AR applications should coordinate and arrange terms with suppliers and manufacturers to integrate the virtual product replicas in the supplier or manufacturer API where firms can access all the other information about the products (IW1, IW4). Apart from the provisioning of the 3D models, the interviewees raise concerns about their quality. The quality of the 3D models in the AR application must be comparable to the high-quality pictures on the websites (IW3, IW5). The visualization of the products may differ from the actual products, especially in terms of colors (IW2). However, inaccurate visualizations of product characteristics are a general problem in E-Commerce (IW2) and may be resolved by technology development (IW3).

The challenges have a direct effect on the investments, expenses, and efforts of small retailers. The interviewees agree that additional personnel is required to adopt AR for their shop systems, either to implement and integrate the AR environment (IW1, IW5), to conduct market analyses on whether AR is desired by the consumers (IW3), or to create the virtual product replicas (IW3, IW2, IW4, IW5) while the latter is considered as mandatory to use AR at all, especially if new products are added to the portfolio (IW4, IW5).

Implications of adopting AR in marketing: The opportunities and challenges are summarized in Fig. 2 (segment 4.5). In addition, three main implications can be derived from the interviews: First, manufacturers and suppliers as well as the shop owners must be provided with evidence that the technology is well received by consumers and that it has positive effects on, e.g., brand awareness, purchase intention, etc. Otherwise, they seem reluctant to create 3D models at extra expenses, and in turn the technology will not be adopted by small shop owners since the effort to provide their own virtual 3D models is considered too high for a currently not quantifiable benefit. Second, the software tools to create virtual product replicas need to advance to allow shop owners to quickly generate 3D models of their products, preferably based on already existing data such as product pictures. Third, an easy integration of AR functionalities (e.g., via plugin) within the existing IT infrastructure and shop systems is pivotal for the diffusion of AR as a marketing tool and to keep the expenses for additional personnel and resources low.

5 Discussion

In the present chapter, the academic literature of the past five years was explored to conceptualize a holistic picture of the use of AR as an interactive marketing technology and five interviews with small online retailers were conducted to complement the findings with an initial practitioners' perspective (see Fig. 2). Specifically, in the literature review part, focus was set on the use scenarios of AR in marketing, the virtual product types that are most commonly investigated, and importantly, in line with the S–O–R framework, the technological characteristics of AR were explored and the psychological as well as behavioral outcomes that AR is capable of evoking was reported on. The interviews revealed that small online shop owners see several opportunities and challenges for introducing AR as part of their marketing strategy, which are also reflected in Fig. 2 and from which three practical implications were derived in Sect. 4.5. In the following, as part of the interpretation of the combined results from the interviews and observations in the literature, several future trends for using AR in marketing are discussed.

5.1 Future Trends in Research and Practice

Layered augmented product information: A crucial challenge for marketers consists in effectively communicating product and brand-related information to consumers. Specifically, this entails providing the right amount of information so that consumers can make informed decisions while not being overwhelmed with too much information that would be too strenuous to mentally process (B.-K. Lee & Lee, 2004). What makes this even more challenging, recent research indicates that engagement with AR technology itself can increase the mental workload of users due to the task of cognitively processing the virtually overlayed content within the physical surrounding (Xi et al., 2022) which induces even more challenges in terms of information load. Marketers need to be aware of these challenges in order to mitigate negative consumer experiences, such as irritation or less satisfied consumers in general (B.-K. Lee & Lee, 2004). Some of the recommendations to deal with this is to consider dynamically embedded information that users themselves display or hide via the interactive proficiencies of AR technology (Riar et al., 2022). For example, AR solutions may be designed in a way to empower users to interact with the different features of a product, by which information related to the particular features is being dynamically displayed. This way, consumers can learn about the product features and gather relevant pre-purchase information in snippets to support learning processes and avoid information overload as well as unsatisfying consumer experiences.

Integrating interactive marketing practice with gamification and location-based services: One of the rising trends in recent years that has also penetrated into the marketing literature is gamification, i.e., the employment of principles through which a system or service becomes more gameful.

From a marketing perspective, the goal of gamification is to afford services in a way to enhance consumers' experienced value of the core service (Huotari & Hamari, 2017). Previous studies have indicated that gamification possesses the ability to increase brand engagement (Xi & Hamari, 2020), brand experience (Sung, 2021), and consumer-brand satisfaction (J.-Y. Lee & Jin, 2019). Thus, it should be recognized as a desirable approach for marketers to connect consumers to a brand. More importantly, gamification can be combined with AR and location-based services to unleash even greater potential for marketing praxis. One of many examples exists in notifying consumers via push notifications of place-dependent special offers. These offers may entail virtual coupons that are overlaid via AR technology into the real world and that can be collected and redeemed at a nearby store. Thereby, AR and gamification can be used in combination with the navigational aspects of location-based services and draw consumers to stores. In addition, AR has been used to provide added value to consumers via in-store navigation functionalities (Jayagoda et al., 2021). There seems to be much potential in creating in-store marketing solutions via combining AR with gamification and location-based services because they may be perceived as both useful and fun. Important implications can also be drawn from full-fledged location-based AR games (Laato et al., 2021; Morschheuser et al., 2017), which have lately been investigated for their potential to attract consumers to points of interest and for increasing place attachment (Oleksy & Wnuk, 2017), as well as general number of customers (Pamuru et al., 2021) via increased foot traffic in and around neighborhoods and stores. These potentials should not go unnoticed by marketers because harnessing the power of location-based AR games and gamification solutions may hold important economic implications for competitive advantage. Accordingly, in addition to looking into options for adding a gameful AR layer to their existing mobile apps to increase the experienced value of their core services, marketers may find it profitable to look into partnerships with suppliers of location-based AR games to establish unique marketing strategies and campaigns.

Social Capabilities: Another intriguing direction for interactive marketing praxis is to utilize the potential social capabilities of AR technology to connect consumers with each other and to create shared social experiences (Sung, 2021). The influence of significant others to shape brand attitudes or induce the purchase of products has become an exceedingly vital phenomenon among marketers. Thus, it seems important to scrutinize whether and how AR may be used to support connectedness and socialization between consumers. The reviewed literature supports the notion that AR can have unique potentials to connect users with each other, such as via sharing, social media, recommender, and perspective-taking functionalities. Specifically, AR may introduce novel ways for consumers to share content and information, such as point-of-view sharing (Hilken et al., 2020) through which a user can select products and modify their features (e.g., color) in the AR view and share the augmented content with the exact modifications with significant others. Through such functionality, AR enables two or more individuals to mutually participate in shopping-related decision processes. Besides asynchronous point-of-view sharing, the technological leaps in the AR realm may also allow users to synchronously participate in co-shopping activities where two or more individuals simultaneously interact (e.g., reshape, resize, move, change color or other features) with virtual content, thereby enhancing collective decision processes. So far, the potential socializing features of AR seem underrepresented in industry contexts as well as not sufficiently addressed in academia. Due to the benefits of social features to induce, for example, co-shopping or word-of-mouth, these potentials should be regarded as a worthwhile and intriguing future waypoint for both researchers and marketing practitioners.

Augmentation of other sensory information besides visual: The present literature review on interactive AR marketing made it evident that current investigations are chiefly limited to exploring the effects of augmented visual content, whereas investigations into other sensory experiences (i.e., touch, smell, sound, taste) largely remain uncharted territory. This is striking because essentially any human sense can in some way be augmented and utilized for marketing purposes. Sensory marketing is the discipline of involving the human senses for shaping consumers' perceptions toward firms, brands, and products (Hultén et al., 2009). Specifically, marketers can consider involving touch and movement-based features (e.g., via haptic gloves) as well as smell (e.g., via scent masks), or audio information to provide an even richer and more immersive experience when consumers engage with products or brands via AR technology. Marketing literature suggests that involving the human senses for branding purposes can have many merits. For example, sound has been suggested to express brand identity (Hultén et al., 2009), while smell can trigger memories (Goldkuhl & Styvén, 2007), positive emotional and cognitive responses (Rimkute et al., 2016), both consciously and unconsciously, thus making sensory information an efficacious instrument for marketing. However, so far, there is little knowledge on the effectiveness of AR technology that utilizes the human senses beyond the visual. Due to the above-mentioned possible merits for marketing, it seems important to investigate how involving other sensory information in AR beyond the visual can affect consumer responses.

Marketplace for virtual products: Lastly, the diffusion of AR in retail and interactive marketing strongly depends on the availability of virtual product replicas that are the basis for the product visualization regardless of whether the aim is to sell (virtual) products or to use the objects as virtual assets for interactive marketing campaigns. Although manufacturers and suppliers possess 3D models of their products, these models cannot be directly transferred to AR environments due to their complexity and concerns regarding intellectual property (Korbel & Zarnekow, 2021). Thus, online trading platforms emerged that allow the trade of 3D models which are sufficient for AR environments (e.g., Sketchfab). However, these platforms comprise a variety of 3D models for identical physical products while most of the models are neither approved by the manufacturers or suppliers nor are they even aware of their existence. Therefore, the currently existing virtual assets can only be used in AR environments to a limited extent. Furthermore, the search for and integration of the models remains in the hands of the retailers, which induces additional expenses that especially small online retailers might not be willing to invest in (see Sect. 4.5 Small retailers' perspective). Consequently, there is a need for new virtual asset online platforms that incorporate 3D models of physical products with explicit identifiers (e.g., European Article Number (EAN) or Universal Product Code (UPC)) and provide interfaces that allow an automatic search and assignment of the virtual objects to the real products in online stores and on websites. Alternatively, software architectures and programming interfaces must be created that allow manufacturers and suppliers to include 3D models in databases that can be accessed by the consumers, i.e., online shop providers, and directly assigned to the products in their AR applications. Without the availability of virtual product replicas and sufficient processes to include these models in virtual environments, firms will neither be able to use AR applications to their full extent nor participate in the realm of virtual shopping and marketing.

5.2 Limitations

The search of the literature in the present chapter has been limited to the Web of Science database and even though it is one of the most recognized proprietary databases for peer-reviewed and high-quality publications, there is still a chance that some publications have been missed. Therefore, future studies may consider using additional and multiple databases such as JSTOR, Scopus, Google Scholar, EBSCO, etc.

Furthermore, only literature written in English was reviewed. Undeniably, important AR marketing-related studies which were written in languages other than English are excluded from this study. Especially, the application of AR in marketing practice is in full swing in Asia, such as China, Japan, and South Korea. Thus, other search languages can also be considered in future studies.

Even though the interviews turned out to be very informative pertaining to the perceived opportunities and challenges of using AR in marketing, a limitation may exist in the small sample size of five interviewees to capture the practitioner stance as well as in the selected business domain (small retailers), thus the generalizability of these perceptions cannot be ensured. It is also worth noticing that none of the interviewees already use AR as part of their marketing strategies. Consequently, the results obtained from the interviews are based on pre-adoption perceptions of the opportunities and challenges of utilizing AR in marketing and can be understood as initial findings from a small retailer perspective. While this is highly relevant for understanding the stance of practitioners that have not yet integrated AR technology within their marketing campaigns, insights on post-adoption perceptions of integrating AR as an interactive marketing tool from practitioners are missing from this study.

Despite these limitations, the present study contains vital contributions by (1) providing a synopsis of the results from interactive AR marketing research, by (2) revealing the standpoint of five practitioners in terms of the perceived opportunities and challenges of integrating AR as a marketing instrument, and by (3) spotlighting several waypoints for interactive AR marketing in future research and practice endeavors.

6 Conclusion

In the present chapter, a comprehensive framework (see Fig. 2) of interactive AR marketing was presented by combining results from a review of academic literature and initial findings of using AR in interactive marketing from a practitioner perspective based on interviews with small retailers that operate online shops.

Based on the theoretical premise of the S–O–R model (see Fig. 1), the results of this chapter contribute to understanding the dynamics of interactive AR marketing by showing how AR evokes diverse psychological outcomes, which essentially translate into behavioral outcomes of consumers. Specifically, the obtained results in this chapter indicate that the technological characteristics of AR (e.g., interactivity, vividness, informativeness, quality, performance, etc.) can give rise to several cognitive, affective, and social-psychological outcomes, which can positively impact consumers' brand engagement and willingness to share personal data, as well as behavioral intentions to purchase products, use AR applications, or to recommend it to others. Moreover, the environments (i.e., online and stationary), the technologies and devices, as well as the product types that have been subject to interactive AR marketing in the current scientific literature were outlined.

To provide an even more comprehensive overview, the present chapter supplemented the consumer view with a practitioner's view. For this purpose, five interviews with online shop providers were conducted to understand the perceived opportunities and challenges of integrating AR in praxis from a small retailer perspective. From the interviews, three implications could be derived, including that awareness and confidence of the benefits of integrating AR needs to be proliferated more widely among practitioners, and that an easy integration of AR within existing IT infrastructures as well as efficient ways to create virtual product replicas are necessary before small retailers see a tangible pay off in entering the AR sphere for their business and marketing strategies.

In retrospect of the combined observations from the literature review and the conducted interviews, this chapter paves a way forward via a discussion of several emergent trends of applying AR in interactive marketing. In particular, the present chapter exposes the need to further investigate (1) how virtual information should be presented to users (e.g., layered, interactive, embedded); (2) what needs to be considered in terms of the amount of presented information, and the trade-off between informativeness and information overload; (3) how gamification and location-based services can be utilized to produce better marketing campaigns via AR; (4) how to create social experiences or make use of other sensory information (e.g., touch, smell, sound) to generate even more immersive consumer experiences; and (5) how the diffusion of AR in interactive marketing can be fostered by establishing marketplaces and IT architectures for the provisioning of virtual product replicas.

References

"*"indicates the studies included in the literature review

Aggarwal, R., & Singhal, A. (2019). Augmented reality and its effect on our life. In *9th International Conference on Cloud Computing, Data Science & Engineering*, (pp. 510–515). IEEE. https://doi.org/10.1109/CONFLUENCE.2019.8776989

Azuma, R. T. (1997). A survey of augmented reality. *Presence: Teleoperators and Virtual Environments*, 6(4), 355–385. https://doi.org/10.1162/pres.1997.6.4.355

*Baek, T. H., Yoo, C. Y., & Yoon, S. (2018). Augment yourself through virtual mirror: The impact of self-viewing and narcissism on consumer responses. *International Journal of Advertising*, 37(3), 421–439. https://doi.org/10.1080/02650487.2016.1244887

Barnes, S. J. (2020). Information management research and practice in the post-COVID-19 world. *International Journal of Information Management*, 55, 102175. https://doi.org/10.1016/j.ijinfomgt.2020.102175

*Beck, M., & Crié, D. (2018). I virtually try it … I want it ! Virtua fitting room: A tool to increase on-line and off-line exploratory behavior, patronage and purchase intentions. *Journal of Retailing and Consumer Services*, 40, 279–286. https://doi.org/10.1016/j.jretconser.2016.08.006

*Bonnin, G. (2020). The roles of perceived risk, attractiveness of the online store and familiarity with AR in the influence of AR on patronage intention. *Journal of Retailing and Consumer Services*, 52, 101938. https://doi.org/10.1016/j.jretconser.2019.101938

*Brengman, M., Willems, K., & van Kerrebroeck, H. (2019). Can't touch this: The impact of augmented reality versus touch and non-touch interfaces on perceived ownership. *Virtual Reality*, 23(3), 269–280. https://doi.org/10.1007/s10055-018-0335-6

Brereton, P., Kitchenham, B. A., Budgen, D., Turner, M., & Khalil, M. (2007). Lessons from applying the systematic literature review process within the software engineering domain. *Journal of Systems and Software*, 80(4), 571–583. https://doi.org/10.1016/j.jss.2006.07.009

*Carrozzi, A., Chylinski, M., Heller, J., Hilken, T., Keeling, D. I., & de Ruyter, K. (2019). What's mine is a hologram? How shared augmented reality augments psychological ownership. *Journal of Interactive Marketing*, 48, 71–88. https://doi.org/10.1016/j.intmar.2019.05.004

Chiang, L.-L., Huang, T.-L., & Chung, H. F. (2021). Augmented reality interactive technology and interfaces: a construal-level theory perspective. *Journal of Research in Interactive Marketing*. Advance online publication. https://doi.org/10.1108/JRIM-06-2021-0156

Chylinski, M., Heller, J., Hilken, T., Keeling, D. I., Mahr, D., & de Ruyter, K. (2020). Augmented reality marketing: A Technology-Enabled approach to situated customer experience. *Australasian Marketing Journal, 28*(4), 374–384. https://doi.org/10.1016/j.ausmj.2020.04.004

Donthu, N., & Gustafsson, A. (2020). Effects of COVID-19 on business and research. *Journal of Business Research, 117*, 284–289. https://doi.org/10.1016/j.jbusres.2020.06.008

*Fan, X., Chai, Z., Deng, N., & Dong, X. (2020). Adoption of augmented reality in online retailing and consumers' product attitude: A cognitive perspective. *Journal of Retailing and Consumer Services, 53*, 101986. https://doi.org/10.1016/j.jretconser.2019.101986

*Feng, Y., & Xie, Q. (2018). Measuring the content characteristics of videos featuring augmented reality advertising campaigns. *Journal of Research in Interactive Marketing, 12*(4), 489–508. https://doi.org/10.1108/JRIM-01-2018-0027

*Feng, Y., & Xie, Q. (2019). Ad creativity via augmented reality technology in online video ads: The differential role of novelty, message usefulness, and Ad-Consumer association. *Journal of Promotion Management, 25*(6), 907–933. https://doi.org/10.1080/10496491.2018.1536624

Flavián, C., Ibáñez-Sánchez, S., & Orús, C. (2019). The impact of virtual, augmented and mixed reality technologies on the customer experience. *Journal of Business Research, 100*, 547–560. https://doi.org/10.1016/j.jbusres.2018.10.050

Goldkuhl, L., & Styvén, M. (2007). Sensing the scent of service success. *European Journal of Marketing, 41*(11/12), 1297–1305. https://doi.org/10.1108/03090560710821189

*Haile, T. T., & Kang, M. (2020). Mobile augmented reality in electronic commerce: Investigating user perception and purchase intent amongst educated young adults. *Sustainability, 12*(21), 9185. https://doi.org/10.3390/su12219185

Hardiess, G., Mallot, H. A., & Meilinger, T. (2015). Virtual reality and spatial cognition. In *International Encyclopedia of the Social & Behavioral Sciences* (pp. 133–137). Elsevier. https://doi.org/10.1016/B978-0-08-097086-8.43098-9

Helfferich, C. (2014). Leitfaden- und Experteninterviews. In N. Baur & J. Blasius (Eds.), *Handbuch Methoden der empirischen Sozialforschung*. 559–574. Springer Fachmedien Wiesbaden. https://doi.org/10.1007/978-3-531-18939-0_39

*Heller, J., Chylinski, M., de Ruyter, K., Mahr, D., & Keeling, D. I. (2019a). Let me imagine that for you: Transforming the retail frontline through augmenting customer mental imagery ability. *Journal of Retailing, 95*(2), 94–114. https://doi.org/10.1016/j.jretai.2019.03.005

*Heller, J., Chylinski, M., de Ruyter, K., Mahr, D., & Keeling, D. I. (2019b). Touching the Untouchable: Exploring Multi-Sensory Augmented Reality in the Context of Online Retailing. *Journal of Retailing, 95*(4), 219–234. https://doi.org/10.1016/j.jretai.2019.10.008

*Hilken, T., de Ruyter, K., Chylinski, M., Mahr, D., & Keeling, D. I. (2017). Augmenting the eye of the beholder: Exploring the strategic potential of augmented reality to enhance online service experiences. *Journal of the Academy of Marketing Science, 45*(6), 884–905. https://doi.org/10.1007/s11747-017-0541-x

Hilken, T., Heller, J., Chylinski, M., Keeling, D. I., Mahr, D., & de Ruyter, K. (2018). Making omnichannel an augmented reality: The current and future state of the art. *Journal of Research in Interactive Marketing, 12*(4), 509–523. https://doi.org/10.1108/JRIM-01-2018-0023

*Hilken, T., Keeling, D. I., de Ruyter, K., Mahr, D., & Chylinski, M. (2020). Seeing eye to eye: Social augmented reality and shared decision making in the marketplace. *Journal of the Academy of Marketing Science, 48*(2), 143–164. https://doi.org/10.1007/s11747-019-00688-0

*Hinsch, C., Felix, R., & Rauschnabel, P. A. (2020). Nostalgia beats the wow-effect: Inspiration, awe and meaningful associations in augmented reality marketing. *Journal of Retailing and Consumer Services, 53*, 101987. https://doi.org/10.1016/j.jretconser.2019.101987

Huang, Y., Jiang, Z., Liu, Y., & Wang, Y. (2011). Augmented reality in exhibition and entertainment for the public. In B. Furht (Ed.), *Handbook of Augmented Reality.* 707–720. Springer New York. https://doi.org/10.1007/978-1-4614-0064-6_32

*Huang, T.-L. (2019). Psychological mechanisms of brand love and information technology identity in virtual retail environments. *Journal of Retailing and Consumer Services, 47*, 251–264. https://doi.org/10.1016/j.jretconser.2018.11.016

Hultén, B., Broweus, N., & van Dijk, M. (2009). Sensory Marketing. *Palgrave Macmillan UK.* https://doi.org/10.1057/9780230237049

Huotari, K., & Hamari, J. (2017). A definition for gamification: Anchoring gamification in the service marketing literature. *Electronic Markets, 27*(1), 21–31. https://doi.org/10.1007/s12525-015-0212-z

*Javornik, A., Rogers, Y., Moutinho, A. M., & Freeman, R. (2016). Revealing the shopper experience of using a "Magic Mirror" augmented reality Make-Up application. In *DIS '16: Designing Interactive Systems Conference 2016*, Brisbane QLD Australia.

*Javornik, A. (2016). 'It's an illusion, but it looks real!' Consumer affective, cognitive and behavioural responses to augmented reality applications. *Journal of Marketing Management, 32*(9–10), 987–1011. https://doi.org/10.1080/0267257X.2016.1174726

*Javornik, A., Marder, B., Pizzetti, M., & Warlop, L. (2021). Augmented self—The effects of virtual face augmentation on consumers' self-concept. *Journal of Business Research, 130*, 170–187. https://doi.org/10.1016/j.jbusres.2021.03.026

Jayagoda, N. M., Jayawardana, O., Welivita, W., Weerasinghe, L., & Dassanayake, T. (2021). SMARKET - Shopping in supercenters (Hypermarkets) with augmented reality. In (pp. 771–776). IEEE. https://doi.org/10.1109/ICCCA52192.2021.9666359

*Jessen, A., Hilken, T., Chylinski, M., Mahr, D., Heller, J., Keeling, D. I., & de Ruyter, K. (2020). The playground effect: How augmented reality drives creative customer engagement. *Journal of Business Research, 116*, 85–98. https://doi.org/10.1016/j.jbusres.2020.05.002

Jiang, Y., & Stylos, N. (2021). Triggers of consumers' enhanced digital engagement and the role of digital technologies in transforming the retail ecosystem during COVID-19 pandemic. *Technological Forecasting and Social Change, 172*, 121029. https://doi.org/10.1016/j.techfore.2021.121029

Kim, J.-H., Kim, M., Park, M., & Yoo, J. (2021). How interactivity and vividness influence consumer virtual reality shopping experience: The mediating role of telepresence. *Journal of Research in Interactive Marketing, 15*(3), 502–525. https://doi.org/10.1108/JRIM-07-2020-0148

Kipper, G. (2013). *Augmented reality: An emerging technologies guide to AR* (1st ed.). Syngress/Elsevier. https://learning.oreilly.com/library/view/-/9781597497336/?ar

Korbel, J. J. (2021). Creating the virtual: The role of 3D models in the product development process for physical and virtual consumer goods. In *Lecture Notes in Information Systems and Organisation. Innovation Through Information Systems, 46*, 492–507. Springer International Publishing. https://doi.org/10.1007/978-3-030-86790-4_33

Korbel, J. J., & Zarnekow, R. (2021). *Die Rolle von 3D-Modellen im Wertschöpfungsprozess von physischen und virtuellen Konsumgütern*. Advance online publication. https://doi.org/10.1365/s40702-021-00816-x

*Kowalczuk, P., Siepmann, C., & Adler, J. (2021). Cognitive, affective, and behavioral consumer responses to augmented reality in E-Commerce: A comparative study. *Journal of Business Research, 124*, 357–373. https://doi.org/10.1016/j.jbusres.2020.10.050

van Krevelen, D., & Poelman, R. (2010). A survey of augmented reality technologies, applications and limitations. *International Journal of Virtual Reality, 9*(2), 1–20. https://doi.org/10.20870/IJVR.2010.9.2.2767

Laato, S., Rauti, S., Islam, A. N., & Sutinen, E. (2021). Why playing augmented reality games feels meaningful to players? The roles of imagination and social experience. *Computers in Human Behavior, 121*, 106816. https://doi.org/10.1016/j.chb.2021.106816

Lee, J.-Y., & Jin, C.-H. (2019). The role of gamification in brand app experience: The moderating effects of the 4Rs of app marketing. *Cogent Psychology, 6*(1), Article 1576388. https://doi.org/10.1080/23311908.2019.1576388

Lee, B.-K., & Lee, W.-N. (2004). The effect of information overload on consumer choice quality in an on-line environment. *Psychology & Marketing, 21*(3), 159–183. https://doi.org/10.1002/mar.20000

Lim, W. M., Kumar, S., Pandey, N., Rasul, T., & Gaur, V. (2022). From direct marketing to interactive marketing: A retrospective review of the Journal of Research in Interactive Marketing. *Journal of Research in Interactive Marketing*. Advance online publication. https://doi.org/10.1108/JRIM-11-2021-0276

Loureiro, S. M. C., Guerreiro, J., Eloy, S., Langaro, D., & Panchapakesan, P. (2019). Understanding the use of Virtual Reality in Marketing: A text mining-based review. *Journal of Business Research*, 514–530,. https://doi.org/10.1016/j.jbusres.2018.10.055

Lu, Y., & Smith, S. (2007). Augmented reality E-Commerce assistant system: Trying while shopping. In lecture notes in computer science. *Human-Computer Interaction. Interaction Platforms and Techniques, 4551*, 643–652. Springer Berlin Heidelberg. https://doi.org/10.1007/978-3-540-73107-8_72

Manis, K. T., & Choi, D. (2019). The virtual reality hardware acceptance model (VR-HAM): Extending and individuating the technology acceptance model (TAM) for virtual reality hardware. *Journal of Business Research, 100*, 503–513. https://doi.org/10.1016/j.jbusres.2018.10.021

Mayring, P. (2015). *Qualitative Inhaltsanalyse: Grundlagen und Techniken* (12., überarbeitete Auflage). Beltz.

Mayring, P. (2019). Qualitative inhaltsanalyse—Abgrenzungen, spielarten, weiterentwicklungen. Advance online publication. https://doi.org/10.17169/fqs-20.3.3343 Forum Qualitative Sozialforschung / Forum: Qualitative *Social Research, 20*(3), Article No. 16 Qualitative Content Analysis I.

*McLean, G., & Wilson, A. (2019). Shopping in the digital world: Examining customer engagement through augmented reality mobile applications. *Computers in Human Behavior, 101*, 210–224. https://doi.org/10.1016/j.chb.2019.07.002

*Mishra, A., Shukla, A., Rana, N. P., & Dwivedi, Y. K. (2021). From "touch" to a "multisensory" experience: The impact of technology interface and product type on consumer responses. *Psychology & Marketing, 38*(3), 385–396. https://doi.org/10.1002/mar.21436

*Morillo, P., Orduña, J. M., Casas, S., & Fernández, M. (2019). A comparison study of AR applications versus pseudo-holographic systems as virtual exhibitors for luxury watch retail stores. *Multimedia Systems, 25*(4), 307–321. https://doi.org/10.1007/s00530-019-00606-y

*Moriuchi, E., Landers, V. M., Colton, D., & Hair, N. (2021). Engagement with chatbots versus augmented reality interactive technology in E-Commerce. *Journal of Strategic Marketing, 29*(5), 375–389. https://doi.org/10.1080/0965254X.2020.1740766

Morschheuser, B., Riar, M., Hamari, J., & Maedche, A. (2017). How games induce cooperation? A study on the relationship between game features and we-intentions in an augmented reality game. *Computers in Human Behavior, 77*, 169–183. https://doi.org/10.1016/j.chb.2017.08.026

*Nikhashemi, S. R., Knight, H. H., Nusair, K., & Liat, C. B. (2021). Augmented reality in smart retailing: A (n) (A) symmetric approach to continuous intention to use retail brands' mobile AR apps. *Journal of Retailing and Consumer Services, 60*, 102464. https://doi.org/10.1016/j.jretconser.2021.102464

Novak-Marcincin, J., Janak, M., Barna, J., & Novakova-Marcincinova, L. (2014). Application of virtual and augmented reality technology in education of manufacturing engineers. In *Advances in Intelligent Systems and Computing. New Perspectives in Information Systems and Technologies, 2*, 439–446. Springer International Publishing. https://doi.org/10.1007/978-3-319-05948-8_42

Oleksy, T., & Wnuk, A. (2017). Catch them all and increase your place attachment! The role of location-based augmented reality games in changing people—place relations. *Computers in Human Behavior, 76*, 3–8. https://doi.org/10.1016/j.chb.2017.06.008

Pamuru, V., Khern-am-nuai, W., & Kannan, K. (2021). The impact of an Augmented-Reality game on local businesses: A study of Pokémon go on restaurants. *Information Systems Research, 32*(3), 950–966. https://doi.org/10.1287/isre.2021.1004

*Pantano, E., Rese, A., & Baier, D. (2017). Enhancing the online decision-making process by using augmented reality: A two country comparison of youth markets. *Journal of Retailing and Consumer Services, 38*, 81–95. https://doi.org/10.1016/j.jretconser.2017.05.011

Pantano, E., & Servidio, R. (2012). Modeling innovative points of sales through virtual and immersive technologies. *Journal of Retailing and Consumer Services, 19*(3), 279–286. https://doi.org/10.1016/j.jretconser.2012.02.002

*Park, M., & Yoo, J. (2020). Effects of perceived interactivity of augmented reality on consumer responses: A mental imagery perspective. *Journal of Retailing and Consumer Services, 52*, 101912. https://doi.org/10.1016/j.jretconser.2019.101912

*Poushneh, A., & Vasquez-Parraga, A. Z. (2017). Discernible impact of augmented reality on retail customer's experience, satisfaction and willingness to buy. *Journal of*

Retailing and Consumer Services, 34, 229–234. https://doi.org/10.1016/j.jretco nser.2016.10.005
*Qin, H., Peak, D. A., & Prybutok, V. (2021). A virtual market in your pocket: How does mobile augmented reality (MAR) influence consumer decision making? *Journal of Retailing and Consumer Services, 58*, 102337. https://doi.org/10.1016/j.jretco nser.2020.102337
*Rauschnabel, P. A. (2021). Augmented reality is eating the real-world! The substitution of physical products by holograms. *International Journal of Information Management, 57*, 102279. https://doi.org/10.1016/j.ijinfomgt.2020.102279
*Rauschnabel, P. A., Felix, R., & Hinsch, C. (2019). Augmented reality marketing: How mobile AR-apps can improve brands through inspiration. *Journal of Retailing and Consumer Services, 49*, 43–53. https://doi.org/10.1016/j.jretconser.2019.03.004
*Rese, A., Baier, D., Geyer-Schulz, A., & Schreiber, S. (2017). How augmented reality apps are accepted by consumers: A comparative analysis using scales and opinions. *Technological Forecasting and Social Change, 124*, 306–319. https://doi.org/10.1016/j.techfore.2016.10.010
Rese, A., Schreiber, S., & Baier, D. (2014). Technology acceptance modeling of augmented reality at the point of sale: Can surveys be replaced by an analysis of online reviews? *Journal of Retailing and Consumer Services, 21*(5), 869–876. https://doi.org/10.1016/j.jretconser.2014.02.011
Riar, M., Korbel, J. J., Xi, N., Zarnekow, R., & Hamari, J. (2021). The use of augmented reality in retail: A review of literature. In *Hawaii International Conference on System Sciences,* Hawaii, USA, (pp. 638–647). https://doi.org/10.24251/HICSS.2021.078
Riar, M., Xi, N., Korbel, J. J., Zarnekow, R., & Hamari, J. (2022). Using augmented reality for shopping: A framework for AR induced consumer behavior, literature review and future agenda. *Internet Research*. Advance online publication. https://doi.org/10.1108/INTR-08-2021-0611
Rimkute, J., Moraes, C., & Ferreira, C. (2016). The effects of scent on consumer behaviour. *International Journal of Consumer Studies, 40*(1), 24–34. https://doi.org/10.1111/ijcs.12206
Sheng, J., Amankwah-Amoah, J., Khan, Z., & Wang, X. (2021). COVID-19 Pandemic in the new era of big data analytics: Methodological innovations and future research directions. *British Journal of Management, 32*(4), 1164–1183. https://doi.org/10.1111/1467-8551.12441
*Smink, A. R., Frowijn, S., van Reijmersdal, E. A., van Noort, G., & Neijens, P. C. (2019). Try online before you buy: How does shopping with augmented reality affect brand responses and personal data disclosure. *Electronic Commerce Research and Applications, 35*, 100854. https://doi.org/10.1016/j.elerap.2019.100854
*Smink, A. R., van Reijmersdal, E. A., van Noort, G., & Neijens, P. C. (2020). Shopping in augmented reality: The effects of spatial presence, personalization and intrusiveness on app and brand responses. *Journal of Business Research, 118*, 474–485. https://doi.org/10.1016/j.jbusres.2020.07.018
*Song, H. K., Baek, E., & Choo, H. J. (2020). Try-on experience with augmented reality comforts your decision. *Information Technology & People, 33*(4), 1214–1234. https://doi.org/10.1108/ITP-02-2019-0092

Soto-Acosta, P. (2020). COVID-19 Pandemic: Shifting digital transformation to a High-Speed gear. *Information Systems Management, 37*(4), 260–266. https://doi.org/10.1080/10580530.2020.1814461

Steuer, J. (1992). Defining virtual reality: Dimensions determining telepresence. *Journal of Communication, 42*(4), 73–93. https://doi.org/10.1111/j.1460-2466.1992.tb00812.x

*Sung, E. (2021). The effects of augmented reality mobile app advertising: Viral marketing via shared social experience. *Journal of Business Research, 122*, 75–87. https://doi.org/10.1016/j.jbusres.2020.08.034

Tan, Y.-C., Chandukala, S. R., & Reddy, S. K. (2022). Augmented reality in retail and its impact on sales. *Journal of Marketing, 86*(1), 48–66. https://doi.org/10.1177/0022242921995449

*Uribe, R., Labra, R., & Manzur, E. (2021). Modeling and evaluating the effectiveness of AR advertising and the moderating role of personality traits. *International Journal of Advertising, 1–28*,. https://doi.org/10.1080/02650487.2021.1908784

*van Esch, P., Arli, D., Gheshlaghi, M. H., Andonopoulos, V., von der Heidt, T., & Northey, G. (2019). Anthropomorphism and augmented reality in the retail environment. *Journal of Retailing and Consumer Services, 49*, 35–42. https://doi.org/10.1016/j.jretconser.2019.03.002

Wang, C. L. (2021). New frontiers and future directions in interactive marketing: Inaugural Editorial. *Journal of Research in Interactive Marketing, 15*(1), 1–9. https://doi.org/10.1108/JRIM-03-2021-270

Xi, N., Chen, J., Gama, F., Riar, M., & Hamari, J. (2022). The challenges of entering the metaverse: An experiment on the effect of extended reality on workload. *Information Systems Frontiers*. Advance online publication. https://doi.org/10.1007/s10796-022-10244-x

Xi, N., & Hamari, J. (2020). Does gamification affect brand engagement and equity? A study in online brand communities. *Journal of Business Research, 109*, 449–460. https://doi.org/10.1016/j.jbusres.2019.11.058

Xi, N., & Hamari, J. (2021). Shopping in virtual reality: A literature review and future agenda. *Journal of Business Research, 134*, 37–58. https://doi.org/10.1016/j.jbusres.2021.04.075

*Xu, L., Zhang, L., Cui, N., & Yang, Z. (2020). How and when AR technology affects product attitude. *Asia Pacific Journal of Marketing and Logistics, 32*(6), 1226–1241. https://doi.org/10.1108/APJML-03-2019-0221

*Yang, S., Carlson, J. R., & Chen, S. (2020). How augmented reality affects advertising effectiveness: The mediating effects of curiosity and attention toward the ad. *Journal of Retailing and Consumer Services, 54*, 102020. https://doi.org/10.1016/j.jretconser.2019.102020

Yaoyuneyong, G., Foster, J., Johnson, E., & Johnson, D. (2016). Augmented reality marketing: Consumer preferences and attitudes toward hypermedia print ads. *Journal of Interactive Advertising, 16*(1), 16–30. https://doi.org/10.1080/15252019.2015.1125316

*Yim, M.Y.-C., Chu, S.-C., & Sauer, P. L. (2017). Is augmented reality technology an effective tool for E-commerce? An interactivity and vividness perspective. *Journal of Interactive Marketing, 39*, 89–103. https://doi.org/10.1016/j.intmar.2017.04.001

*Yuan, C., Wang, S., Yu, X., Kim, K. H., & Moon, H. (2021). The influence of flow experience in the augmented reality context on psychological ownership. *International Journal of Advertising, 40*(6), 922–944. https://doi.org/10.1080/02650487.2020.1869387

*Zhang, T., Wang, W. Y. C., Cao, L., & Wang, Y. (2019). The role of virtual try-on technology in online purchase decision from consumers' aspect. *Internet Research, 29*(3), 529–551. https://doi.org/10.1108/IntR-12-2017-0540

CHAPTER 15

Interactive Marketing with Virtual Commerce Tools: Purchasing Right Size and Fitted Garment in Fashion Metaverse

Sadia Idrees, Gianpaolo Vignali, and Simeon Gill

1 INTRODUCTION

The information and communication technology experiences a paradigm shift every 10 years. In 1990s, there was a paradigm of PC communications, in the 2000s the internet, and mobile in 2010s. For 2020s, the significant words of the current paradigm are the metaverse world, virtual commerce or v-commerce (Lee, 2021). The chapter aims to enrich the function and practicability of fashion metaverse mobile 3D body scanner applications for interactive selection of right size and fitted garment through v-commerce platforms. Additionally, v-commerce tools such as virtual, augmented, and mixed reality have a potential to enhance interactivity in terms of virtual fashion viewing technology during online purchase of garments. The chapter further elaborates on the function of v-commerce tools such as mobile body scanners, VR, AR, and MR for enhancing fashion metaverse by reflecting the consolidative view of consumer behaviour in terms of their adoption of the technology,

S. Idrees (✉) · G. Vignali · S. Gill
University of Manchester, Manchester, UK
e-mail: sadia.idrees@manchester.ac.uk

G. Vignali
e-mail: gianpaolo.vignali@manchester.ac.uk

S. Gill
e-mail: simeon.gill@manchester.ac.uk

© The Author(s), under exclusive license to Springer Nature Switzerland AG 2023
C. L. Wang (ed.), *The Palgrave Handbook of Interactive Marketing*,
https://doi.org/10.1007/978-3-031-14961-0_15

and their intention to use it for confident garment purchase online. In addition, recent studies on the enhancement and development of v-commerce tools and examples of interactive tools employed by fashion industry have been analysed for in-depth understanding of phenomenon of fashion metaverse. Thus, the recent studies and examples show how these interactive features of virtual reality, augmented reality, mixed reality, and mobile scanning apps have aided in enhancing the confidence in viewing and buying the right size and fitted garments during online shopping of apparel products. Furthermore, v-commerce platforms have contributed positively for managers in making informed decisions when designing their interactive marketing and retailing strategies.

As established, the predicted fast pace growth of the industry has been noted with the worldwide VR market size estimated to grow from less than 5 billion US dollars in 2021 to more than 12 billion US dollars by 2024 (Statista, 2021b). Currently, the application of AR technology is advancing in online and in-store retail. The mobile augmented reality users worldwide have risen by 1.5 billion from the noted 200 million since 2015; they are estimated to increase to 1.7 billion by 2024 (Statista, 2021a). Therefore, VR and AR strengths have been utilised and will prove useful for the future. For instance, VR tools are applicable in the development stage of products such as virtual prototyping. Whereas AR tools are more appropriate at the point of consumer integration, for example, testing concepts and fitting assessments. Garments need to be customised in terms of virtual clothing according to consumers' body dimensions and consumers can view fitting simulations before making a purchase. (De Silva et al., 2019).

The global virtual fitting room market grew from $ 3.50 billion in 2021 to $12.97 billion in 2028 (Johnson, 2021). V-commerce technology offers a convenient way to try-on products, and findings from Johnson in 2021 show that 34% consumers find virtual fitting shopping experience more entertaining, useful, and attractive (Johnson, 2021). V-commerce interactive tools share commonalities and variations in terms of solutions of providing experience of virtual fitting room with accuracy, attraction, interactivity, and immersion with fashion viewing AR, VR, and MR tools as well as body measurements and personalised avatar acquired from scanning apps. The scanning apps detect the user's 2D facial and body shape and provide output in 3D facilitated with 360-degree viewing (Kim & Sung, 2021). The 3D body scanning along with VR, AR, and MR provide an accurate virtual fitting experience by reflecting personalised body dimensions and avatars along with metaverse environment immersion and attraction such as virtual catwalk, and 3D 360-degree view of virtual outfit on personalised avatars. They also offer customisation, size recommendation, heat maps to analyse the tightness and looseness of a garment, mix and match of apparel and accessories (triMirror, 2021; Lim & Jafari, 2021).

2 Limitations of E- and M-Commerce for Interactive Marketing in Fashion Retail

The following section of this chapter outlines the limitations of both e-commerce and m-commerce marketing tools in terms of immersion, interactivity, attraction, and accuracy, with regard to fashion viewing as well as size and fitting issues in online shopping atmosphere.

2.1 E-Commerce

E-commerce extensively encompasses with the sales and purchase of goods and services through interfaces aided with internet as well as any transaction that is done solely through online platforms. E-commerce offers, online consumers, an opportunity to experience a unified omnichannel or multichannel retailing (Bargavi et al., 2022).

2.2 M-Commerce

The term m-commerce is used to indicate the advancing practice of performing economic, advertising, and transactions endeavours by using wireless smart devices such as smartphones, iPad, and tablets with wireless internet, 3G and 4G, web browsers, and mobile apps. The term m-commerce can also be named: e-shop, e-store, Internet shop, web shop, web-store, online store, and virtual store (Sharma & Madan, 2022).

2.3 Limitation of Immersion, Interactivity, and Attraction During Product Examination

Despite many advantages there are limitations to the experience of immersion, interaction, and attraction with products in online setting, that sometimes discourage customers to shop. Consumers frequently buy apparel products online, which is about 50.7% of the population (Afrin et al., 2022). However, through e-commerce and mobile apps, online buyers are not able to experience a real store setting including salespeople, trying-on garments, mixing and matching of products, or to seeking sensory stimulation (Escobar-Rodriguez & Bonson-Fernandez, 2017) all of which inhibit their overall attractive and immersive experience. In online shopping platforms, interactivity, rich data representation, and realism are important features to fulfil the consumer's relational expectations. The former approach used for the presentations of products in digital stores does not go beyond two-dimensional (2D) images or animation/video-footage/catwalk. The current approach is inherently deficient in provision of information with no interactivity as compared to a three-dimensional (3D) virtual model (Altarteer & Charissis, 2019). A functional web app that offers useable and clear information with high-level interactivity, immersion, and attraction is deemed essential to compensate for the non-physical presence of a product. The latter can be accomplished by incorporating (VR, AR, and MR) interactive tools for intuitive interaction between consumers and virtual products (Altarteer & Charissis, 2019).

2.4 Inaccuracy of Size and Fit During Online Shopping

Size selection is the most critical phase while online shopping. Consumers around the globe have variations in their body types and sizes (Hwangbo et al., 2020). Ready-to-wear garments are constructed using specific standard body sizes and standard sizing system varies from country to country. The US, UK, and EU have specific sizing systems in terms of their population body structure (Reid et al., 2020). Moreover, consumers are dissatisfied with ready-to-wear garments constructed using standard sizing system and with the inability to try-on garments online, halt to make a confident purchase (Lee & Xu, 2020). Furthermore, variations have been noted in fashion brands sizing charts. Therefore, high clothing return rates have been experienced in online buying, chiefly because shoppers could not verify whether the product fits their bodies well, for example there are expressed concerns about product length and circumference, when online purchases are being made (Hwangbo et al., 2020). Consumers have a relationship between body types and attitudes towards online shopping, because of their distinct body shapes; and each buyer has different fit difficulties (Altarteer & Charissis, 2019). Apparel buyers lack the prepared knowledge regarding the measurement of their body dimensions. Additionally, there are technical challenges involved in taking body dimensions manually by buyers themselves such as exact landmarking points to be considered while measuring the human body (8559-1, 2017; Almalki et al., 2020). Therefore, customising apparel products in an online setting is challenging using the traditional manual method of capturing body dimensions (Idrees et al., 2020a).

Traditionally consumers try on clothes during offline shopping. Whereas during online shopping consumers need to correlate their body size with size charts or images of products to make the size decision. To correlate body dimensions to available standard size charts consumers need to remember their body measurements or to measure themselves using tape measurements which is a time-consuming process, and also requires one to have a profound knowledge to get accurate body dimensions (Hwangbo et al., 2020). Therefore, size selection is a highly tricky process in an online environment. For convenience in online shopping, fashion platforms offer free returns. Consequently, higher return rate has been noted due to size and fit issues in online apparel shopping which adds significant operational costs (Abdulla et al., 2019). Moreover, an approach such as Fit Analytics and True fit has been developed for online consumers to deliver size and fit recommendations and visualisation in online fashion interfaces. The interfaces approach is through a manual entering of anthropometric data and garment data such as past purchase history, preferred fit, and preferred style explicitly through online surveys or questionnaires which is also a lengthy and uncertain approach (Januszkiewicz et al., 2017). Thus, to cater to the needs of online buyers to shop confidently online, it is essential to develop a system that has the potential to serve all body types equally and that size choices are expanded (Jain et al., 2018). Therefore, to rectify these challenges, an interactive 3D body scanning tool (digital human dimensions) has been instituted to enhance fashion v-commerce interfaces globally to deliver the right size and fitted garment (Idrees et al., 2020a).

3 Advantages of Virtual Commerce for Interactive Marketing in Fashion Retail

V-commerce has distinctive features from both e-commerce and m-commerce; it is an emerging interactive marketing shopping channel. In v-commerce, a virtual three-dimensional (3D) environment is offered with enhanced functionality, immersion, interactivity, attraction, and accuracy to visualise online products as well as to find the right size and fitted garment. Additionally, this way of delivery overcomes the lack of direct interaction with product and people (Wang, 2021). V-commerce also has improved sensory depth in contrast to e-commerce, as it can communicate with highly detailed 3D features than 2D static images; consumers can experience realistic and engaging distinct features (Altarteer & Charissis, 2019). Compared to traditional e-commerce interfaces, the metaverse technology has a great potential to enhance customers' experience and trust by providing hedonist and utilitarian values via its distinctive interactive features such as augmented and virtual reality features (Wang, 2021). A thriving online interface has a potential to offer various categories to online consumers from the amateur to the expert and from the goal directed to the empirical user (Rajan et al., 2021). Additionally, buyers demand an engaging, interactive, and memorable online environment to make a confident purchase (Brannon Barhorst et al., 2021). Similarly buyers visit and purchase from an online interface if it presents a practical alternative to offline services or if it adds value (Battistoni et al., 2022). V-commerce technologies have been developed extensively, including Metaverse fashion technology which offers interaction with 3D features via 3D body scanning apps, augmented reality, virtual reality, and mixed reality; this has proven to be one of the most visited features and enhanced interactivity to boost online sales (Idrees et al., 2020a, 2020b; Xue & Parker, 2020). V-commerce includes the metaverse environment and interactive v-commerce tools, those are explained in detail in the following sections of the chapter.

3.1 Metaverse Environment

Immersive technology comprises of the computer software and hardware that accelerate the five senses of humans (i.e., vision, hearing, touch, smell, and taste) in a virtual atmosphere to generate the experience of being there, i.e., the sense of existence (Suh & Prophet, 2018; Xue et al., 2019). The notion of metaverse was derived from the novel 'Snow Crash' published by Neal Stephenson in 1992; it signifies a three-dimensional virtual world in which 'Meta' means virtual and abstract, and 'verse' means universe (Lee, 2021). The participants interact with themselves through their own avatars generated by themselves in a virtual construct of metaverse to participate or redevelop real life in a virtual metaphorical environment without temporal and spatial restrictions (Díaz et al., 2020). The notion of a metaverse or virtual world serves beyond commerce and entertainment to generate a real virtual non-natural community in which digital operators or avatars become human users and communicate socially and economically with each other in an immersive three-dimensional virtual and multi-user online atmosphere. Recently, with the advancement of smartphones AR and VR devices, interaction between numerous actual and virtual objects is viable, and a novel world of metaverse is expanding swiftly (Lee, 2021). Furthermore, meta-commerce could become a future trend of online shopping due to the amalgamation of v-commerce and metaverse environments.

3.1.1 Fashion Metaverse

Fashion consumers can interact with the metaverse through interactive, immersive, and attractive consumer-facing interfaces. There are several types of metaverse environments and avatar solutions offered by technological enterprises to enhance consumer experience in fashion metaverse. These display different levels of realism of virtual environment with actual image and virtual image. Various solutions have been introduced such as Roblox, Sandbox, Second life, Body lab's triMirrorTM, Metail's MeModelTM, Fitle's 3D model, EZ faceTM, Zugara, Fits.meTM, Fitiquette to facilitate virtual catwalk, 3D 360-degree rotation, customisation, garment fit visualisation with heat maps, and the mixing and match of products in fashion metaverse (Lee & Xu, 2020; Narin, 2021).

Avatar Realism in Fashion Metaverse

The avatar's realism and fashion metaverse environment have been created in terms of accuracy, interactivity, immersion, and attractiveness. Some VFR online shopping platforms have offered various solutions such as (1) VFRs using body scanning device such as 3D look and MeThreeSixty/Formcut 3D by Size Stream (3Dlook, 2021; Stream, 2022), (2) 3D avatar, (3) 3D customer's model, (4) 3D mannequin which offers fitting room with real 3D simulation, (5) Augmented reality fitting room, (6) Robotic mannequins, (7) Dress-up mannequins for mix and match, (8) The real fashion model. Type 1 to Type 5 VFRs, from the solutions listed above, have utilised real consumer figures with body dimensions data. However, they have variation in terms of accuracy and attractiveness. Type 6 to Type 8, on the other hand, utilised virtual figures; for instance, virtual mannequin or image of actual model which is in some way identical to the real user's figure. The eight types of technologies display various levels of realism in the simulation process, therefore provide various levels of user experience and satisfaction in fashion metaverse. They present variations in technology regarding accuracy, attraction, immersion, and interactivity. The research concluded that VFR technology can aid in enhancing personalise experiences in terms of accuracy, attraction, immersion, and interactivity and can deliver seamless experience to consumers by optimizing and improving its technological features. Additionally, it contributes to enhancing fashion v-commerce by influencing the adoption and utilisation of VFR technology (Lee & Xu, 2020).

Fashion Metaverse Environment
Gaming companies have entered the fashion world to offer more unique experiences to their users, through announcements of the metaverse as the future of the internet. In the gaming world, the examples of metaverse such as Roblox, Sandbox, and Fortnite are becoming very popular (Narin, 2021). Roblox has an average of 46.6 million daily users covering 180 countries. Fashion brands have entered into this metaverse to deliver consumers new experiences and emulate brand awareness (Gibson, 2021). Gucci consumers can have an immersive experience within Roblox, where users can walk into the Gucci Garden with a blank avatar. The avatar can be manipulated through several experience areas, various colours, and patterns, which can be added to the character distinctively designed by Gucci. Five active users daily and 50% users monthly update their avatar on Roblox. The users customise their avatars with the most recent virtual fashion products and merchandise, exhibiting their real-life style. (Gibson, 2021). Tommy Hilfiger has used the service of eight native Roblox designers to generate 30 digital fashion products based on their brand's pieces. Forever 21, employed with metaverse construction organisation Virtual Brand Group, outset a 'Shop City' in which Roblox influencers generate and oversee their own stores, combating against each other. The latest products in the physical world of brands will be available in their virtual world. Human driven and totally virtual avatar influencers have become prominent. Tamara Hoogeweegen future laboratory strategist elaborates that metaverse environment of fashion brands will become customisable with user-generated products, as noticed with Forever 21; for example Tommy Hilfiger and Ralph Lauren's Roblox world, was inspired by user behaviour (Mcdowell, 2022). This demonstrates that there are various practical applications of fashion metaverse to display virtual fashion and goods in fashion industry. There are great ways for online retailers to test novel notions, modernise or even launch entire latest trends in an entirely low-risk, sustainable approach (Gibsons, 2021).

3.2 *Interactive Features of Fashion Metaverse in Virtual Commerce*

The fashion metaverse has been enhanced by v-commerce tools such as Virtual Reality (VR), Augmented Reality (AR), Mixed Reality (MR), and 3D Body scanning mobile apps. The following section of the chapter discusses the recent developments in application design of VR, AR, MR, and 3D body scanning technology for enhancing fashion metaverse. Additionally, outlines the consumer behaviour research regarding intention to use, satisfaction, and purchase with v-commerce tools and sheds light on the recent examples of interactive technology application in the fashion industry. The chapter also assessed v-commerce tools and fashion metaverse environment with AIDA marketing model to provide effectiveness of interactive marketing strategy for consumers' and retailers' benefit.

3.2.1   Virtual Reality (VR)

VR is formally defined as 'the illusion of participation in a synthetic environment rather than external observation of such an environment. VR relies on three-dimensional (3D), stereoscopic, head tracked displays, hand/body tracking and binaural sound. VR is an immersive, multisensory experience' (Gigante, 1993 p. 3). In other words, the virtual environment does not appear within physical surroundings and is detached from the real environment by a VR screen or head-mounted display such as VR glasses (Belova, 2020).

Recent Developments in Virtual Reality

VR is a system of multisource information. It has a potential to deliver human–computer interaction and deliver immersive feeling to the participants. It can be facilitated with multi-perception of vision, hearing, force sense, touch, movement, and other human perceptions. Various imaginative environments can be created in the virtual world. A recent paper by Jian (2022), presented a clothing business model from three aspects such as product manufacturing end, client end, and shopping experience under C2M clothing customisation mode. The system utilised 3D human body measurement extraction technology along with VR. By using real body shapes the garment can be adjusted to deliver successful fitting and garment customisation services (Jian, 2022). Similarly, study in 2019 enhanced time efficiency and improved the accessibility of garment trying-on by creating a virtual dressing room smartphone application via Microsoft Kinect sensor. The system approach is based on the extraction of user body dimensions to create an avatar via video stream, avatar alignment, and detection of skin colour. The system utilised modules for location of the joints for positioning, scaling, and rotation to align the 2D cloth models with the user. The avatar is superimposed on the user in real time. The study concluded that VFR application is acceptable in terms of easy control, user-friendliness, flexibility, and real-look cloth model for users to choose the right size (Masri & Al-Jabi, 2019). Furthermore, research has been conducted for the development of an in-home virtual dressing room for garment fitting by employing an integrated system comprising of personalised 3D body model reconstruction and garment fitting simulation. The paper contributes to these innovative developments by proposing a simple and new virtual 3D fitting room app that creates personalised body model reconstruction of the user for virtual garment fitting. The app entails minimum involvement from the user. Only needed two images (front and profile images) using smart phone camera;

then the user selects their specification for either loose or fitted garment. The reconstruction method is convenient, efficient, and is an easy replacement to taking accurate body dimensions such as those taken by a tailor. The 3D reconstruction presents high-level accuracy when assessed with the average resolution of the original model utilising the CAESAR dataset. The app can be applied as a virtual fitting system for online stores, clothing design, and personalised garment simulations (Li & Cohen, 2021).

Consumer Behaviour Research of VR Technology
The study evaluated the 3D semi-immersive virtual reality (VR) system for online luxury product visualisation and customisation service. The outcomes revealed that the perceived presence, usefulness, ease of use, and the perceived experience value showed a significantly positive impact on the attitudes of users towards the 3D VR semi-immersive system. The outcomes also revealed that using the advantage of 3D VR systems in context with real-time manipulation of the products and the adaptability in customising the 3D models' features in real time, positively impacted the attitudes of users towards the 3D VR technology. Moreover, online luxury brand product customisation features displayed a positive impact on the attitudes of users towards the 3D VR system as well (Altarteer & Charissis, 2019). Similarly, the study team in 2019 designed and created StereoVR, called 'FutureShop', for incorporating a virtual fashion retailing practice and for evaluating consumers' responses for further development. The participants completed the shopping process from a selection of products to purchase in FutureShop. The participants reported that they found technology highly interactive which improves their satisfaction and encourage their purchase intention. They explained their hedonic shopping experience in future shops as innovative, fun, and exciting. The outcomes of the research deliver empirical support for employing the stereoscopic displays, interaction, and computer-simulated environment in future virtual shopping practices, which blend online shopping with real-world shopping (Lau & Lee, 2019). Virtual try-on apps (VTOs) studies have also been conducted by employing two theories such as Sirgy's theory of the self and Sundar's theory of interactive media effects (Time). The study tested two additional constructs such as Photo satisfaction and consumer inspiration using two VTO apps available in the market and their impact on the intent to adopt/adoption intention. The mixed-methods study examined the effects of personalisation and customisation in the modern generation of apparel VTOs. Findings show that customisation affordance encouraged and influenced adoption intention. The users who were satisfied with their avatar picture showed stronger impact on perceived augmentation. Additionally, study illustrates how the Time's Sense of Agency component aided with the reception of a positive consumer response to mobile marketing technology, which was used in the study as an app's mix and match feature. The study reported that perceived augmentation has been influenced by body-image for affective judgements built during the pre-task VTO avatar creation phase (Tawira & Ivanov, 2022).

Fashion Retailers' Application of Virtual Reality
Globally businesses have been utilising this technology to lessen the ambiguity of selecting fashion goods, in terms of right sizing and to cut back on returns. For example, a virtual try-on application (Asizer) facilitates 3D body scanning and garment simulation by demonstrating a variety of clothing brands to select. Users can virtually try-on products and can view virtual catwalk videos for personalised experiences in the online environment (Asizer, 2022). Similarly, a Canadian-based company triMirror introduced virtual fitting technology which facilitates a personalised online trying-on experience, utilising heat maps which envisage tightness and looseness of a garment on personal avatar and can analyse fabric performance when the buyer virtually moves around in different styles prior to purchasing a garment (triMirror, 2022).

3.2.2   Augmented Reality (AR)
The AR technology is an interactive technology which permits operators to view the real environment, with virtual objects added up or blended with the real environment. The technology allows virtual products to be examined in the place of physical products. Moreover, it delivers enhanced information about the product; thus, enhancing the visualisation of the object (Udiono, 2021a, 2021b, 2021c).

Recent Developments in Augmented Reality
A recent study, conducted in 2021, introduced a clothing customisation full-featured system aided with augmented reality. The system comprises of material library for making choice of styles, patterns, colours, and fabrics for the users. The system not only introduced stages of custom designing, but additionally consumers can also view fitting on the virtual clothes. The system utilised Azure Kinect somatosensory technology, Open GL 3D rendering, and a somatosensory virtual fitting room. The user is permitted to play with various designs to the cloth; after satisfaction with the choice, the user can try virtual fitting. The augmented reality virtual try-on system comprises of functional modules. The sub-module comprises a selection of patterns, colours, fabrics, and styles. In sub-module of virtual fitting, the system scans the depth data stream of human bones using Azure Kinect Somatosensory camera and apprehends bone-tracking processing method. Additionally, a user can try-on 3D clothing, virtually, in the proper position of the human body. The rendering tools aid in the selection of proper rendering tools to render clothing textures, lighting, etc., so that users can view virtual clothing with more accurate effects via display (Feng et al., 2021). Furthermore, another study introduced an android augmented reality technology for fashion retailing industry and examined its benefits on customer behaviour to enhance the marketing and sales strategies of various fashion brands. The three different sections were tested in this research to enhance fashion retailing industry such as consumer behaviour, consumer experience, and the benefits of augmented reality to retail stores. Initially, the results of consumers'

behaviour showed that the user interface of application was acceptable and user-friendly. The research supported that 3D dynamic objects enhanced decision-making processes. Secondly, the consumers agreed on the effectiveness of technology in decision-making processes, which is replacing traditional try-on methods. Therefore, the research revealed that augmented reality has a sustainable impact on the consumer experience during the pre-purchase phase. The research conducted on the augmented retail stores also revealed that the technology really enhances consumer experience in the method of decision-making on buying a product which will drive the improvement of the footfall of customers in stores, the enhancement of brand image, which will deliver high sales and profit benefits (El-Seoud & Taj-Eddin, 2019). A recent study successfully implemented a virtual trial room using Flask Web application with OpenCV (a Python Module). The application works on devices with built-in or attached camera, internet, and web browser. This application helped to save time, why trying on clothes at home which is equivalent to in-store changing room. The app captures a video of the user and splits the video into specific frames. The application can monitor the user's movement and angles accurately, to superimpose the 2D clothes over devices and virtual clothes over the monitored user without requiring the user to align smart device screen, ensuring a better user experience. This is a great app for marketing wearable goods; it can help gain more attention from buyers. The application recommends sizes such as S, M, and L which enhance the quality of the application (Rajan et al., 2021).

Consumer Behaviour Research of AR Technology
Brannon Barhorst et al. (2021) concluded that learning was a noteworthy predictor of satisfaction with the AR experience and that flow was a noteworthy predictor of learning. The state of flow is considered as a sense of tranquillity, losing the worries of everyday life, immersion, enjoyment, and focused attention. Thus, the state of flow justifies cognitive information processing since attention is aimed and distractions free. Moreover, flow has a more positive impact on information utility and enjoyment with AR apps when, for example, a shopping experience was compared with AR and without AR. Therefore, AR apps induce an intensified state of flow and permit the elaborated state of information, satisfaction, and overall enjoyment. The unique components of AR (interactivity, novelty, and vividness) enhance cognitive processing with useful information, learning, and enjoyment via combination of real-world and virtual world experiences, which influence consumers' satisfaction (Brannon Barhorst et al., 2021). Moreover, a study explored the role of augmented reality as a meta-user interface, with a focus on its applications for interactive fitting room systems and influence on the associated shopping experience. Nine interaction design patterns were developed for AR fitting rooms to support the shopping experience including: (1) Body measurement; (2) Intuitive and comfortable interaction; (3) Selecting the garment's characteristics; (4) Selecting the garment's characteristics automatically; (5) Selecting

a garment in the virtual catalogue of a store; (6) Selecting a garment in the virtual catalogue of the store using a second device; (7) Physically selecting a garment in the store using a smart wardrobe; (8) Physically selecting a garment in the store using a mobile device; (9) Magic shop window. The shopping experience, based on the proposed patterns, was influenced by three main factors, such as the perception of the utility, the ability to generate interest and curiosity, the perceived comfort of the interaction, and the environment in which the system is installed. The results revealed that the patterns efficaciously supported these factors (Battistoni et al., 2022). Similarly, research regarding customer brand engagement has been studied through augmented reality (AR) features such as Amazon, ASOS, and IKEA apps via smartphones. The research studied AR attributes such as AR novelty, AR interactivity, and AR vividness and established their influence on technology acceptance attributes such as perceived ease of use, usefulness, enjoyment, and subjective norms. The AR attributes and technology acceptance attributes positively influenced brand engagement through the retailer's AR mobile application. Additionally results revealed that AR aided in product engagement delivers an increased satisfaction with the experience of the app and future intention to use the brand. The research contributes to provide practical incorporation on the utilisation of AR technology (McLean & Wilson, 2019). Furthermore, Qin et al. (2021) research evaluates the consumer experience about how mobile augmented reality (MAR) influences behaviours, especially in the smartphone context. The study employed a cognition–affect–conation framework to explore how MAR experiences enhance consumers' decision-making processes. The results show that consumers' cognitive evaluation of MAR applications encouraged their intuitive reactions, which ultimately developed conative behaviours. Therefore, this research permits a unified perception for mutually examining continuous use and purchase intentions in one research model. Additionally, the study evaluated how perceived value, a cognitive trait variable, effects consumer conative replies directly and indirectly through intuitive reactions. Their findings affirm the relationships projected in the cognition–affect–conation framework and analytically confirm the direct and indirect impacts of perceived value on conative efforts in the context of MAR. Thus, Qin et al. (2021) study findings immensely contribute to application design and marketing strategy development.

Fashion Retailers' Application of Augmented Reality
AR technology has enhanced the hedonic value regarding garment viewing in augmented worlds. Whereas consumers enjoy utilitarian value in terms of product viewing technology, reducing waiting time for fitting rooms, can reduce stress, especially for families with children who might get impatient when they wait for family members to try-on garments. Moreover, the technology is easily used by any age group (Brannon Barhorst et al., 2021). Ralph Lauren launched AR virtual mirrors for their in-store fitting rooms; it shows 90 per cent consumers engagement with enhanced hedonic value (Johnson,

2021). Furthermore, AR mobile applications have also been launched by various fashion retailers such as Sapphire, a Pakistani fashion brand which allows users to view products on augmented avatars in 360-degree view (Idrees et al., 2020b; Sapphire, 2019). Additionally, fashion brands such as: H&M offers six AR filters to advertise 1990s streetwear collection; Louis Vuitton released a filter regarding the game League of Legends, as company-designed outfits of the characters; Sack Fifth Ave introduced RPR's virtual clothing configurator utilising smart glasses and smartphones, so consumers can visit virtual clothing rack in-store and at home (Johnson, 2021). The AR experience makes online recommendations about clothing and accessories, which ultimately add ease and hedonic value.

3.2.3 Mixed Reality (MR)

The mixed reality (MR) user interface is a compelling concept for improving a user's experience by integrating computer-generated knowledge into real-world situations. This is an attractive way out of combining AR and VR for the v-commerce environment (Wang & Dunston, 2011). Since the virtual environment is a metaverse, participants interact with each other and with objects through digital objects and avatars. This is a concept where technologies and subjects of augmented reality (AR), virtual reality (VR), and mixed reality (MR) have been incorporated and developed into the virtual world. VR brings objects into the artificial environment and permits users to engage themselves, and AR enhances information to the actual world. In addition to the scenario of AR and VR interaction, the possibilities of their observed interactions result in MR (Cabero-Almenara et al., 2021; Lee, 2021).

Recent Developments and Consumer Behaviour Research of Mixed Reality

Collaborative apparel, a new product development model, has been introduced in study facilitated with virtual simulation technologies. Nowadays, consumers anticipate virtual experience to develop and design their own apparel, apart from buying. Garments need to be customised in terms of virtual clothing according to consumers' body dimension. Consumers can view fitting simulations before making a purchase. Thus, VR and AR strengths are utilized. For instance, VR tools are applied in the development stage of the product such as virtual prototyping, whereas AR tools are more appropriate at the point of consumer integration in testing concepts and fitting assessments (De Silva et al., 2019). Virtual fitting has been studied with avatar modes and self-image modes using MR technology. For example, Kim and Sung's (2021) study explores the relationships between experience economy, perceived flow, and continuous use intention in a mixed reality (MR) environment, for consumer. Results reported for avatar mode for entertainment and aesthetic experiences showed a positive impact on continuous use intentions via mediating impacts on flow; and the education experience showed a positive impact on continuous intentions to utilise the MR technology. For self-image, results revealed that flow has a mediating effect on entertainment on continuous use intentions. However, education and escapism had a direct impact on the intention to use the MR technology (Kim & Sung, 2021). Online purchase has a strong impact on the sustainability issue, as clothing returns are chiefly caused by the poor sizing (Fernandes & Morais, 2021a, 2021b, 2021c). Therefore, employing interactive technologies to resolve sustainability and sizing issues is necessary for the fashion industry. Retailers have employed virtual fitting rooms to facilitate consumers, in terms of sustainability and sizing. Fashion online retail sale is also dependent on the presentation of products, therefore realistic fashion viewing technology should also be incorporated. Fernandes and Morais (2021a, 2021b, 2021c) concluded that utilising single technology contributes to poor business model. Thus, new technologies such as Augmented Reality (AR), Virtual Reality (VR), and Mixed Reality (MR) and interactive mirrors (IM) can be combined with the latest smartphone evolution to relaunch solutions like Smart fitting rooms (SFR) to resolve issues of poor fitting, online returns, realistic online fashion viewing, and sustainability (Fernandes & Morais, 2021a, 2021b, 2021c).

3.2.4 3D Body Scanning Mobile Applications

Mobile scanning apps have the capability to extract digital measurements and personalise 3D body avatars by acquiring 2D images using camera-based smart devices. Such applications have been developed for smartphones, tablets, and laptops for buyers and retailers, to offer full body scanning, scanning of various body parts separately, virtual fitting room for visualisations and recommendations of size and fit. The mobile scanners can measure parameters such as distances, girths, heights, width, surface area, body fat percentage, and circumferences by detecting body landmarks through artificial intelligence (Idrees et al., 2020a).

Recent Developments and Consumer Behaviour Research of Mobile Scanning

A recent study presents a mass-produced mobile device with an integrated LiDAR scanner, in iPhone 12 Pro, for scanning the human body (Mikalai et al., 2022). The potential of technology was assessed by analysing the raw 3D sensor data using 3D design software MesLab and Rinoceros. The accuracy of measuring the dimensional traits of a human body utilising a 3D model was assessed. The scanner results demonstrate the potential to construct garments using the personalised human dimensions (Mikalai et al., 2022). Similarly, the potential of 3D body scanners has also been studied via the acquisition of digital measurements through Styku (MyBodee) scanners for bespoke garment construction, along with 3D virtual simulations on 3D avatars to analyse garment fit on virtual avatars. The whole process of virtual fitting has been reported as a better approach than ready-to-wear garments (Sohn et al., 2020). Moreover, a comparative study conducted using MeThreeSixty mobile app, conventional anthropometric, and size stream scanner (SS20) noted that smartphone apps' accuracy is comparable to conventional tape measurement procedures administered by trained technicians (Smith et al., 2021a, 2021b, 2021c). The fashion industry reported high return rates due to sizing issues online (Lim & Jafari, 2021). Thus, Mobile 3D body scanning technology is being introduced to aid consumers in choosing the correct garment sizes via examinations of personalised virtual avatar. The mobile app scanning companies claim that the technologies they offer are accurate, dependable, and exact. Therefore, Lim and Jafari (2021) investigated ten 3D mobile body scanning applications by identifying their characteristics, methods, and advantages. The expert-evaluated apps showed that the apps demonstrated the capability to be applied in garment customisation and size recommendations (Lim & Jafari, 2021). Consumer behaviour has been evaluated by research, such as that of Lin and Kang (2019). In the study, to evaluate scanner tech, students created their own avatar using an iPad with a structure lens. The majority of the participants were satisfied with their own avatar. They also elaborated that the avatars were moderate to very accurate representations of their bodies. Technology was affordable and easy to operate; majority showed positive responses, in terms of future applications in fashion industry (Lin & Kang, 2019). Furthermore, Idrees et al. (2020a) also study consumer behaviour using smartphone 3D body scanning apps, that have been conducted, to analyse consumers' behaviour in terms of ease of use and usefulness of the Nettelo app. They found that consumers found it useful for acquiring body dimensions to receive customised garments and size recommendations of chief international sizing systems such as US, UK, FR, IT, DE (Idrees et al., 2020a).

Fashion Retailers' Application of 3D Body Scanning Mobile Apps

The latest mobile 3D body scanning apps have been employed by various fashion retailers and are easily accessible for consumer to acquire virtual size and fitting benefits. For instance, Element Pure mobile scanning app has a fairly simple process, via its 2 picture-click (of front and side poses) by using an app. The app then creates a model of the torso within 60 s—5 min. The AI-based app also delivers custom-fitted tailored shirts to their consumers. The process of scanning is user-friendly, and it is explained by a video on how to use the app. The additional options in custom shirt fitting include slim, regular, and relaxed fit (Element Pure, 2019). Moreover, Nettelo has similar scanning processes through the use of 2D images and quick display of body dimensions and size recommendations of different countries such as the EU, UK, USA, etc. (Nettelo, 2022). Size stream also offers MeThreeSixty mobile body scanner and Formcut 3D measurement technology. The entire scanning process takes 5 min. The user needs to wear a tight fitted upper and lower garment which shows its body contour clearly for extraction of exact body dimensions (Stream, 2022). 3D look offers virtual trying-on using body scanning technology. More than 100 retailers have partnered with 3D look companies including uniform industry Safariland and Fechheimer Brothers(a Berkshire Hathaway company), 1822 denim women brand (a New York-based company) which uses 3Dlook's Your fit widget, as well as Boost VC, 500 Startups, ICU Ventures, and U Ventures (which are all former consumer retailers of 3D look) (3Dlook, 2021; Edelson, 2021).

4 THE AIDA MODEL AND INTERACTIVE MARKETING WITH VIRTUAL COMMERCE TOOLS

The v-commerce tools and metaverse environment have been evaluated with the AIDA marketing framework to outline the effectiveness of interactive marketing strategy for consumers' and retailers' benefit. The overall goal of marketing is to attract consumers to buy goods and services either online or offline. The AIDA model focuses on consumer response to marketing communications in the cognitive, affective, and conative classifications (Hair et al., 2009). The AIDA model presumes that marketing drives consumers along the following four phases (Attention, Interest, Desire, and Action) in the purchase-decision process (Table 1) (Hair et al., 2009).

5 DISCUSSION AND CONCLUSION

The chapter has provided insights on fashion metaverse environment and v-commerce tools such as mobile scanners, VR, AR, and MR. The v-commerce tools were introduced to improve interactive marketing. The chapter concluded that v-commerce tools and fashion metaverse have distinct main features to enhance interactive marketing such as immersive technology, interactivity, attractiveness, and accuracy. **(1) Immersive Technology:** The AR, VR, and MR technologies simulate visual, auditory, haptic, and motion realness which are designated as immersive technology. For instance, VR is well-accepted as an entirely integrated virtual environment; AR can display computer engendered content (e.g., user interfaces and images) on actual world locations in real time. MR, on the other hand, can execute virtual displays, merge virtual scenes with actual ones, or deliver additional multiplex interactivity. Thus, MR accomplishes a vibrant collaboration of virtual and real content in a similar space. Besides, the character realness of models and virtual space enhance the perceived immersion in virtual worlds (VWs) technology. A VW is frequently interacted and positioned with intelligent tools, permitting its operators to easily interact with the virtual bodies and intelligent tools, and connect with each other. **(2) Interactivity:** The interactivity offered by v-commerce tools contrasts in terms of the correlation between users and interactive v-commerce tools. The technologies such as realistic avatar, image enlargement, and 360-degree rotation can aid consumers to examine the product clearly and can analyse colour contrasting and matching of garments and accessories on personalise 3D avatars in virtual and augmented reality. Moreover, virtual trying a garment and online customisation services by 3D body scanning tools have offered an easier solution for buying right size and fitted garment online. The perceived ease of use, perceived usefulness,

Table 1 AIDA Marketing framework with assessment Of VR, AR, MR, and 3D Mobile app scanners for interactive marketing

AIDA marketing framework with assessment of VR, AR, MR, and 3D mobile app scanners for Interactive Marketing	
Attention	How to attract attention or awareness among consumers on the existing or novel products and services being offered? • Displaying realistic virtual 3D interactive personalise avatars, products, and environment • Realistic and interactive experience with metaverse environment • Convenience of shopping at home • Use of smartphone or camera enabled hardware • Realistic right size and fitting visualisation and recommendation • Consumer-facing interfaces which are affordable, highly interactive, and easy operatable technology • Human–computer interaction which deliver immersive, interactive, and attractive feelings to the participants
Interest	How to build interest of customers to acquire more knowledge about the products or services and permit them to evaluate whether they meet their requirements or expectations? • Dress-up mannequins for mix and match and 360-degree rotation view • Satisfaction with realistic fashion viewing and size and fitting • Viewing of tightness and looseness of garment • Time efficiency and improve the accessibility of garment trying on by using virtual dressing room on personal smartphone application • Product development and selection is convenient, efficient, and an easy and quick replacement to acquiring accurate body dimensions as taken by a tailor • Better perspective of how the final garment will look, fit, and behave in online environment • Perceived enjoyment, perceived ease of use, perceived usefulness positively impacts the attitude towards virtual commerce tools for apparel shopping • Innovative, fun, and exciting • Blends online shopping with real-world shopping
Desire	How to make certain that customers have a desire to purchase the products or services because they fulfil the needs, wants, and their interest? • Providing access to use technology free and user-friendly • By creating smartphone enabled applications • By creating interaction with technology such as recent use in the fashion industry
Action	How to make certain that customers can take action to make the decision to buy the products or services? • Enhanced fashion viewing and interaction in a metaverse • Virtual trying on like in-store fitting room • Certainty of right size product through mobile scanners • Positive experience of virtual fitting rooms with combination of realistic VR and AR enhances decision-making process to make a purchase during virtual shopping

and entertainment experience have enhanced the perceived interactivity of consumers with v-commerce tools. Moreover, MR tools offer interactivity and visualisation by offering interactive feedback when consumers visualise a product. The interaction with modern systems permits users to employ a highly functional and thorough evaluation with the utilisation of more specific, aimed, and pertinent information. Additionally, consumers can enjoy realness, speed, smoothness, accuracy, and enrich information in dynamic ways.

(3) Attractiveness: When consumers perceive an overall positive and pleasant experience in fashion metaverse, this enhances attractiveness. Moreover, the opportunity to alter the visually translated figure, visualising themselves in metaverse environment and in virtual fitting room with different clothing styles, skin colour, eye colour, and hairstyles, promotes the perceived attractiveness of the virtual model. The v-commerce also fulfilled the social and emotional needs of consumers such as sharing of product for reviews with friends and family to make a purchase that resulted in enhanced attractiveness. Attractiveness is interconnected with accuracy of garment fit because a great level of attractiveness results from viewing the real body-shaped avatar displaying the garment fit. Since user body shape is closely correlated with the size and fit of garments, augmented reality, and virtual reality bring a realistic experience of virtual fitting. Users can examine outfits as if they are actually wearing outfit in virtual world. Likewise, it presents a great possibility of enhancing interactive marketing because it displays gamification and entertainment during online purchase, provides ease of size viewing, style, and fit of an outfit in a virtual fashion shop, with no travel restrictions. The whole scenario of virtual environment allows consumers to better appraise the products by providing a strong simulation of the virtual buying experience. **(4) Accuracy:** Accuracy indicates the match between the real user model and realistic view of products on personalised avatar. Because consumers globally vary in body size, shape, hair, and skin colour; thus, it is challenging to measure each consumer accurately and visualise consumer models with personalise fit. Therefore, to provide solution, body scanning mobile applications have demonstrated high potential to deliver accurate body dimensions and size recommendations among the v-commerce tools with user-friendly approaches. When consumers perceive a great level of accuracy while using a technology, they are more likely to have an enhanced utilitarian experience with prospect of fulfilling consumer's functional needs of finding right fit garment in the virtual environment with involvement of AR and VR tools, which provide haptic realistic view of products and haptic feedback. Therefore, consumers' positive experience of virtual fitting rooms with combination of different v-commerce tools enhances their decision-making process during virtual shopping.

Furthermore, by assessing the v-commerce tools and metaverse environment with AIDA marketing model, it has been concluded that fashion metaverse tools facilitate consumers to make a confident apparel purchase. Moreover, v-commerce tools and metaverse environment showed high potential in benefiting retailers with mass customisation business model, inventory management efficiently, delivering accurate size and fitting visualisation, and recommendation services as well as the design of interactive marketing and retailing strategies.

REFERENCES

8559-1, I. (2017), Size designation of clothes—Part 1: Anthropometric definitions for body measurement, *International Organization for Standardization (ISO)*, pp. 1–80. Available at: https://www.iso.org/standard/61686.html

Abdulla, G. M., Singh, S. and Borar, S. (2019), Shop your right size: Asystem for recommending sizes for fashion products, *Creative Commons Attribution 4.0 International (CC-BY 4.0) license*, pp. 327–334. Available at: https://doi.org/10.1145/3308560.3316599

Abou El-Seoud, S., & Taj-Eddin, I. (2019). An android augmented reality application for retail fashion shopping. *International Journal of Interactive Mobile Technologies*, 13(1), 4–19. https://doi.org/10.3991/ijim.v13i01.9898

Afrin, S., Zaman, S. R., Sadekeen, D., Islam, Z., Tabassum, N., and Islam, M. N. (2022), How usability and user experience vary among the basic m-commerce, AR and VR based user interfaces of mobile application for online shopping, *In International Conference on Design and Digital Communication, Springer International Publishing*, pp. 44–53. https://doi.org/10.1007/978-3-030-89735-2_4

Almalki, F., Gill, S., Hayes, S. G. and Taylor, L. (2020), 3D body scanners' ability to improve the cutting of patterns for traditional Saudi garment to assimilate them into modern-day clothing, *In Proceedings of 3Dbody.tech 2020 11th Int. Conference and Exhibition on 3D Body Scanning and Processing Technologies, 17–18 Nov. 2020, online/virtual 3D*, p. 25. https://doi.org/10.15221/20.25

Altarteer, S., & Charissis, V. (2019). Technology acceptance model for 3D virtual reality system in luxury brands online stores. *IEEE Access*, 7, 64053–64062. https://doi.org/10.1109/ACCESS.2019.2916353

Asizer (2022), *A virtual dressing room*, Available at: https://www.asizer.com/, (Accessed: 2 January 2022).

Bargavi, N., & MONIR, M. M. S., Das, S., Rizal, S. and Davis, J. K. (2022). Consumer's shift towards e-commerce and m-commerce: An empirical investigation. *Journal of Positive School Psychology*, 6(2), 703–710.

Barhorst, J. B., McLean, G., Shah, E., & Mack, R. (2021). Blending the real world and the virtual world: Exploring the role of flow in augmented reality experiences. *Journal of Business Research, Elsevier*, 122, 423–436. https://doi.org/10.1016/j.jbusres.2020.08.041

Battistoni, P., Di Gregorio, M., Romano, M., Sebillo, M., Vitiello, G., & Brancaccio, A. (2022). Interaction design patterns for augmented reality fitting rooms. *Sensors*, 22(3), 982. https://doi.org/10.3390/s22030982

Belova, K. (2020), How AR and VR solutions transform the fashion industry, *Pixelplex*, Available at: https://pixelplex.io/blog/how-ar-and-vr-transform-the-fashion-industry/, (Accessed: 5 January 2022).

Cabero-Almenara, J., Barroso-Osuna, J. and Martinez-Roig, R. (2021), Mixed, augmented and virtual, reality applied to the teaching of mathematics for architects, *Applied Sciences*, 11(15), 7125. https://doi.org/10.3390/app11157125

De Silva, R. K. J., Rupasinghe, T. D., & Apeagyei, P. (2019). A collaborative apparel new product development process model using virtual reality and augmented reality technologies as enablers, *International Journal of Fashion Design. Technology and Education. Taylor & Francis, 12*(1), 1–11. https://doi.org/10.1080/17543266.2018.1462858

Díaz, J., Saldaña, C., & Avila, C. (2020). Virtual world as a resource for hybrid education. *International Journal of Emerging Technologies in Learning, 15*(15), 94–109.

3Dlook (2021), Case Study: How 1822 Denim reduced returns by 30%, *3DLOOK*, Available at: https://3dlook.me/blog/case-study-how-1822-denim-reduced-returns-by-30/?utm_source=linkedin&utm_medium=company_page&utm_campaign=1822_case_study, (Accessed: 26 May 2021).

Edelson, S. (2021). 3DLook thrives during pandemic with capital raise and new clients, *Forbes*, Available at: https://www.forbes.com/sites/sharonedelson/2021/03/16/3dlook-thrives-during-pandemic-with-capital-raise-and-new-clients/?sh=c3d55b2430a2&utm_source=social&utm_medium=post&utm_campaign=6-5-million-series-a-round-announcement&utm_term=3dlook_social_media, (Accessed: 26 May 2021).

Element Pure (2019). The future of clothing: "Element pure" uses 3D scanning, AI technology for perfect-fitting shirts, *Clothing, Reviews, Technology*, Available at: https://boomers-daily.com/2019/09/12/the-future-of-clothing-element-pure-uses-3d-scanning-ai-technology-for-perfect-fitting-shirts/, (Accessed: 8 January 2022).

Escobar-Rodriguez, T., & Bonson-Fernandez, R. (2017). Analysing online purchase intention in Spain: Fashion e-commerce. *Information Systems and E-Business Management, 15*(3), 599–622.

Fernandes, C.E. and Morais, R. (2021a). A review on potential technological advances for fashion retail: smart fitting rooms, augmented and virtual realities, *dObra[s]—revista da Associação Brasileira de Estudos de Pesquisas em Moda, 32*, 168–186.

Feng, L., Ma, L., & Ng, G. (2021). Personalized customization system solution using augmented reality technology. *In MATEC Web of Conferences, 336*, 05017. https://doi.org/10.1051/matecconf/202133605017

Gibson, D. (2021). Huge opportunities for brands in virtual reality, just don't call it the metaverse yet, *The Drum*, Available at: https://www.thedrum.com/news/2021/09/16/huge-opportunities-brands-virtual-reality-just-don-t-call-it-the-metaverse-yet-0, (Accessed: 15 January 2022).

Gigante, M. A. (1993). Virtual reality: definitions, history and applications, *In Virtual Reality Systems*, pp. 3–14, Academic Press.

Hair, J.F., Lamb, C.W., and McDaniel, C (2009). Essentials of marketing, *Cengage. Mason, OH*.

Hwangbo, H., Kim, E. H., Lee, S. H., & Jang, Y. J. (2020). Effects of 3D virtual "try-on" on online sales and customers' purchasing experiences. *IEEE Access, 8*, 189479–189489. https://doi.org/10.1109/ACCESS.2020.3023040

Idrees, S., Vignali, G. and Gill, S. (2020a, November). 3D body scanning with mobile application: An introduction to globalise mass-customisation with Pakistani fashion e-commerce unstitched apparel industry, In *proceedings of 3Dbody.tech 2020a 11th International conference and exhibition on 3D body scanning and processing technologies*, 17–18, online/virtual 3D, p.12. https://doi.org/10.15221/20.12

Idrees, S., Vignali, G., & Gill, S. (2020b). Technological advancement in fashion online retailing: A comparative study of Pakistan and UK fashion e-commerce. *International Journal of Economics and Management Engineering, 14*(4), 318–333.

Jain, S., Sundström, M. and Peterson, J. (2018). Mass customized fashion: Importance of data sharing in the supply, In *Nordic Retail and Wholesale Conference, Reykjavík*, pp. 1–3.

Januszkiewicz, M., Parker, C. J., Hayes, S. G. and Gill, S (2017, October 17). Online virtual fit is not yet fit for purpose: An analysis of fashion e-commerce interfaces, In *Proceedings of 3Dbody.tech 2017, 8th International Conference and Exhibition on 3D Body Scanning and Processing Technologies, Montreal, Canada, 11–12*, pp. 210–217. https://doi.org/10.15221/17.210

Jian, S. (2022). Virtual reality technology facilitates customized clothing design in C2M business model, In *Smart Communications, Intelligent Algorithms and Interactive Methods*. Springer, Singapore., pp. 111–119.

Johnson, P. (2021). *Augmented reality in fashion, rock paper reality*, Available at: https://rockpaperreality.com/ar-use-cases/augmented-reality-in-fashion/

Kim, E. Y., & Sung, H. (2021). The effect of user experience on perceived flow and continuous intentions to use the mixed reality technology. *Journal of the Korean Society of Clothing and Textiles, 45*(5), 907–921. https://doi.org/10.5850/JKSCT.2021.45.5.907

Lau, K. W., & Lee, P. Y. (2019). Shopping in virtual reality: A study on consumers' shopping experience in a stereoscopic virtual reality, *Virtual Reality. 23*(3), 255–268, London: Springer. https://doi.org/10.1007/s10055-018-0362-3

Lee, J. (2021). A study on metaverse hype for sustainable growth, *International Journal of Advanced Smart Convergence, 10*(3), 72–80. Available at: https://doi.org/10.7236/IJASC.2021.10.3.72

Lee, H., & Xu, Y. (2020). Classification of virtual fitting room technologies in the fashion industry: From the perspective of consumer experience, *International Journal of Fashion Design. Technology and Education. Taylor & Francis, 13*(1), 1–10. https://doi.org/10.1080/17543266.2019.1657505

Li, C., & Cohen, F. (2021). In-home application (app) for 3D virtual garment fitting dressing room. *Multimedia Tools and Applications, 80*(4), 5203–5224.

Lim, H.W. and Jafari, R. (2021). Exploration in 3D body scanning mobile applications, In *Proceedings of the 4th International Conference in Emotion and Sensibility: Convergence of AI and Emotional Science. Korean Society for Emotion and Sensibility*.

Lin, S.H. and Kang, J. Y. M. (2019). Body scanning to develop an avatar for fitting simulation, In *International Textile and Apparel Association Annual Conference Proceedings. Iowa State University Digital Press, 76*(1).

Masri, A. and Al-Jabi, M. (2019, April). Virtual dressing room application, *Jordan International Joint Conference on Electrical Engineering and Information Technology, JEEIT 2019—Proceedings. IEEE.* 694–698. https://doi.org/10.1109/JEEIT.2019.8717410

Mcdowell, M. (2022). 2022 fashion-tech predictions, *Vogue Business*, Available at: https://www.voguebusiness.com/technology/2022-fashion-tech-predictions?amp (Accessed: 15 January 2022).

McLean, G., & Wilson, A. (2019). Shopping in the digital world: Examining customer engagement through augmented reality mobile applications. *Computers in Human Behavior, Elsevier, 101*, 210–224. https://doi.org/10.1016/j.chb.2019.07.002

Mikalai, Z., Andrey, D., Hawas, H. S., Tetiana, H., & Oleksandr, S. (2022). Human body measurement with the iPhone 12 pro LiDAR scanner. *In AIP Conference Proceedings, 2430*(1), 090009. https://doi.org/10.1063/5.0078310

Narin, N. G. (2021). A content analysis of the AIDS media, *Journal of Metaverse, 1*(1), 17–24. Available at: https://lens.org/132-852-388-772-732

Nettelo (2022). Democratizing 3D body scan and analysis, *Available at:* http://nettelo.com/ (Accessed: 2 January 2022).

Qin, H., Osatuyi, B., & Xu, L. (2021). How mobile augmented reality applications affect continuous use and purchase intentions: A cognition-affect-conation perspective. *Journal of Retailing and Consumer Services, 63.* https://doi.org/10.1016/j.jretconser.2021.102680

Rajan, S. P., Hariprasad, V., Purusothaman, N., & Tamilmaran, T. (2021). Virtual dressing room with web deployment. *Turkish Journal of Computer and Mathematics Education, 12*(7), 2660–2666.

Reid, L.F., Vignali, G. Barker, K. Chrimes, C. and Vieira, R. (2020). Three-dimensional body scanning in sustainable product development: An exploration of the use of body scanning in the production and consumption of female apparel, In *Technology-Driven Sustainability: Innovation in the Fashion Supply Chain.* Springer Nature Switzerland AG, pp. 173–194.

Sapphire (2019). *Sapphire*, Available at: https://pk.sapphireonline.pk/ (Accessed: 4 December 2019).

Sharma, K., & Madan, P. (2022). Can perceived ease of use improve m-commerce adoption? Role of mobile network service quality. *International Journal of Online Marketing, 12*(1), 1–14. https://doi.org/10.4018/ijom.299394

Smith, B., Dechenaud, M. and Heymsfield, S. B. (2021b). Anthropometric evaluation of a 3D scanning mobile application, *1*, 19–20. doi: https://doi.org/10.15221/21.33

Sohn, J. M., Lee, S., & Kim, D. E. (2020). An exploratory study of fit and size issues with mass customized men's jackets using 3D body scan and virtual try-on technology. *Textile Research Journal, 90*(17–18), 1906–1930. https://doi.org/10.1177/0040517520904927

Statista (2021b). *Virtual reality (VR)—Statistics & facts*, Available at: https://www.statista.com/topics/2532/virtual-reality-vr/#dossierKeyfigures, (Accessed: 9 January 2022).

Statista (2021a). Global mobile augmented reality (AR) users 2019–2024, *Statista*, Available at: https://www.statista.com/statistics/1098630/global-mobile-augmented-reality-ar-users/, (Accessed: 9 January 2022).

Stream, S. (2022). *Our technology solutions made for a commercial world*, Available at: https://www.sizestream.com/technology, (Accessed: 2 January 2022).

Suh, A., & Prophet, J. (2018). The state of immersive technology research: A literature analysis. *Computers in Human Behavior, 86*, 77–90.

Takahashi, D. (1998). Closer to reality, *The Wall Street Journal*, 8.

Tawira, L., & Ivanov, A. (2022). Leveraging personalization and customization affordances of virtual try-on apps for a new model in apparel m-shopping. *Asia Pacific Journal of Marketing and Logistics.* https://doi.org/10.1108/apjml-09-2021-0652

triMirror (2022). Mobile Virtual Fitting, *Available at:* https://www.trimirror.com/Solutions/Mobile, (Accessed: 26 May 2021).

Udiono, T. (2021c). Perceptions of using augmented reality features on online shopping fashion platforms based on technology acceptance model, *In 2021c 3rd*

International Conference on Cybernetics and Intelligent System (ICORIS). IEEE, pp. 1–5

Wang, X. and Dunston, P. S. (2011). Comparative effectiveness of mixed reality-based virtual environments in collaborative design, *284 IEEE Transactions on Systems, Man, and Cybernetics—Part c: Applications and Reviews, 41*(3), 284–296.

Wang, C. L. (2021). New frontiers and future directions in interactive marketing: Inaugural editorial. *Journal of Research in Interactive Marketing, 15*(1), 1–9. https://doi.org/10.1108/JRIM-03-2021-270

Xue, L., & Parker, C. J. (2020). How to design fashion retail's virtual reality platforms. *International Journal of Retail & Distribution Management, 48*(10), 1057–1076. https://doi.org/10.1108/IJRDM-11-2019-0382

Xue, L., Parker, C. J., & McCormick, H. (2019). A virtual reality and retailing literature review: Current focus, underlying themes and future directions, In *Augmented Reality and Virtual Reality* (pp. 27–41). Springer.

CHAPTER 16

Virtual Influencer as a Brand Avatar in Interactive Marketing

Alice Audrezet and Bernadett Koles

1 Introduction

Social media influencers (SMIs), "people who gained popularity due to their social media presence and content, such as bloggers, YouTubers, and Instafamous individuals" (Aw & Chuah, 2021 pp. 146), are now well-established actors in the interactive marketing strategy of brands (López et al., 2022). SMIs' competencies to create sophisticated content about brands and products—via tutorials, product reviews, creative product staging in videos or posted images—federate a community of followers (Lee & Watkins, 2016), which make them attractive for brands (Hamilton et al., 2016). During the past fifteen years, many brands developed different types of collaborations with SMIs, including the simpler forms of product endorsement to the more complex forms of product co-development, in order to reach their audience in a more meaningful fashion (Lou & Yuan, 2019). Consequently, influencer marketing—a form of social media marketing that builds on influencer endorsements of products and services in specific domains of interests and expertise made available to followers on various social media platforms (De Jans & Hudders, 2020; Wang, 2021)—has quickly matured into a booming

A. Audrezet (✉)
Institut Français de La Mode, Paris, France
e-mail: aaudrezet@ifmparis.fr

B. Koles
IÉSEG School of Management, Lille, France
e-mail: b.koles@ieseg.fr

© The Author(s), under exclusive license to Springer Nature Switzerland AG 2023
C. L. Wang (ed.), *The Palgrave Handbook of Interactive Marketing*,
https://doi.org/10.1007/978-3-031-14961-0_16

industry thanks to companies and apps that offer technical support to foster cooperation between SMIs and brands. With 90% of marketing managers convinced by its effectiveness, even following the COVID-19 crisis that negatively impacted many businesses, recent estimates place the influencer marketing industry at $13.8 billion, representing a 42% increase from 2019.[1]

Although influencer-brand collaborations enable the establishment of a larger follower base, research warns that such an institutionalized brand encroachment vis-à-vis the influencer's shared content might threaten the SMI's ability to remain genuine and true-to-self (Audrezet et al., 2020; van Reijmersdal et al., 2020); attributes that made them popular in the first place (Duffy & Hund, 2019). As commercial opportunities are likely to encourage the promotion of products which influencers might not spontaneously be interested in (Harms et al., 2022), this cycle presents SMIs with a serious challenge: how to ensure and maintain their credibility (Al-Emadi & Ben Yahia, 2020; Sokolova & Kefi, 2020), authenticity (Lee & Eastin, 2021; Pöyry et al., 2019) and trustworthiness (Giuffredi-Kähr et al., 2022; Kim & Kim, 2021).

Beyond these well-documented expectations of followers, the traditional figure of the SMI faces another notable challenge presented by the emergence of a new opinion leader: the *virtual influencer*. The directory—VirtualHumans.org—keeps a log of existing and emerging virtual influencers once they can account for at least 1,000 followers across social media platforms. According to Christopher Travers, the founder of this database, "a virtual influencer is a digital character created in computer graphics software, then given a personality defined by a first-person view of the world, and made accessible on media platforms for the sake of influence". Developed by digital agencies leveraging sophisticated tools and technologies, non-human and entirely computer-generated characters can be provided with a human-like appearance and a unique personality (Moustakas et al., 2020) that might in turn blur the boundaries between offline and online consumer-perceived reality (Drenten & Brooks, 2020).

Despite their popularity and increasing prevalence on the influencer marketing landscape, surprisingly little is known about virtual influencers and the impact they might have on marketing and on consumer-brand relations. While computer-generated influencers offer new opportunities for brands, they also push the boundaries of altered reality which might present a challenge to adopt by marketers. The current chapter fills this gap in the literature by providing a detailed presentation of this new phenomenon within its greater digital ecosystem that includes brands, followers, digital agencies and social media platforms. More specifically, the objectives of this contribution are threefold. First, the chapter provides a comparative analysis of the developmental trajectories of virtual versus human influencers to understand their similarities and differences more fully. Second, building on empirical

---

[1] Influencer Marketing Benchmark report, Influencer Marketing Hub, 2021.

evidence, the authors identify different personas that can be used to approximate follower preferences concerning virtual influencers that in turn can be used for purposes of segmentation. And third, the chapter provides concrete strategic directions for brands wishing to collaborate with virtual influencers.

Concerning its structure, the chapter begins with a review of contemporary research on human influencers and their relationships with their followers. Here the authors reflect upon certain relevant theoretical frameworks—including social influence and parasocial relationship theory, representing streams of research that are often engaged within the field of influencer marketing (Aw & Chuah, 2021; Jin & Ryu, 2020). Next, the authors introduce examples of successful virtual influencers, review existing professional and scholarly sources that focus on this emerging phenomenon, and—building on interview research with a group of young consumers—provide comparative reflections vis-à-vis their human influencer counterparts. Finally, the authors offer a conceptual framework to assist brands in ways to effectively employ virtual influencers and conclude the chapter by offering directions for future research.

2 THE POSITIONING OF HUMAN INFLUENCERS

2.1 History and Conceptualization of Human Influencers

Starting in the 2000s, a set of adventurous Internet users embarked on a new opportunity to create a novel form of accessible content building on their specific interest in a range of areas like fashion, cosmetics, travel and technology, with the intention to share openly with interested parties via blogs and social media platforms, such as Instagram, YouTube, Facebook, etc. (Dinh & Lee, 2021; Rocamora, 2011). This new type of spontaneous and first-hand experience-based content was found more appealing to customers in comparison to the distant and more static material dominating specialized magazines (Evans et al., 2017; Lea et al., 2018). Thanks to the quality of their content and its amplified effect enabled by the Internet (McQuarrie et al., 2012), those "who have the potential to create engagement, drive conversation and/or sell products/services with the intended target audience" (IAB, 2018) became what we are now accustomed to call '*social media influencers*' (SMIs). Not surprisingly, brands quickly seized the opportunity to benefit from such content, especially given their context is increasingly characterized by a widespread distrust toward traditional forms of advertising (Audrezet et al., 2020; Corrêa et al., 2020). Consequently, the promotion of products and services through sponsored posts on Instagram, TikTok, YouTube, Twitch, and other platforms (Ge & Gretzel, 2018) are now considered 'common expenditures' of the interactive marketing strategy of firms.

2.2 Development and Effectiveness of Influencer Marketing

Previous research highlights the effectiveness of influencers as brand management tools (Carlson et al., 2020; Ryu & Jin, 2019; Valsesia et al., 2020; Wang et al., 2021) with beneficial consequences to boost consumer engagement (Al-Emadi & Ben Yahia, 2020; Hughes et al., 2019; Lee & Theokary, 2020; Tafesse & Wood, 2021) and the adoption of (Corrêa et al., 2020) and purchase intention toward products and services (Weismueller et al., 2020; Zhang et al., 2021). In addition to the characteristics of authenticity and trustworthiness mentioned in the introduction, influencer credibility (Pick, 2020) and self-disclosure (Leite & Baptista, 2021) have been shown to further impact consumer-brand connections and purchase intention.

In the emerging influencer marketing industry, rewards depend on the SMIs' level of influence, commonly approximated by the number of their followers on different social media platforms (Pittman & Abell, 2021). To draw upon their engaged and trusting community, brands at first were predominantly interested in mega-influencers—both online-born and traditional celebrities who emerged outside of the Internet—with follower counts in the millions. More recently, there has been a notable shift toward micro-influencers—those accounting for less than ten thousand followers—who represent niche domains and specific interest areas (Pittman & Abell, 2021).

Within the celebrity endorsement literature, it's been shown that endorsement effectiveness can be better predicted by embracing a customer-centric (i.e., consumer-endorser identification) as opposed to a product-centric approach (i.e., product-endorser fit) (Carlson et al., 2020). Furthermore, originality, uniqueness and innovativeness were found critical to be perceived as an opinion leader (Akdevelioglu & Kara, 2020; Casaló et al., 2020). Hence, the approach that seems to work best is one that focuses on expertise, lifestyles, and takes a consumer-centric approach (De Jans et al., 2021; Seeler et al., 2019).

2.3 Conceptualization of the Relationship Between Human Influencers and Their Followers

Several theories within and beyond traditional consumer research have been engaged to understand the relationships human influencers embody vis-à-vis their follower community.

2.3.1 Social Influence Theory

One example builds on Social Influence Theory (Tafesse & Wood, 2021) that distinguishes three processes underlying influential dyads. *Compliance* is the first type of social influence that occurs when people accept others' influence to gain approval or avoid disapproval. Influence by compliance tends to be extrinsically motivated and superficially accepted. *Identification* is the second form of social influence, referring to situations when individuals accept influence based on the relationship they form and maintain with the influencer that becomes part of their identity. This type of influence is intrinsically motivated, deeper and tends to be linked with various influencer qualities like attractiveness, creativity or popularity (Pittman &Abell, 2021). Finally, the third and most complex form of social influence entails *internalization*, when followers accept influence given its congruence with their own value systems. Here the influencers' credibility, expertise, trustworthiness and authenticity are of special importance.

2.3.2 Parasocial Relationship Theory
A particularly dominant framework proposed to approximate the relationship that emerges between influencers and their fans comes from the theory of parasocial interactions (PSIs), referring to the "feeling of companionship or illusion of friendship with media figures" (Jin & Muqaddam, 2019 pp. 527). Parasocial relationship theory has been used to explain the complex connection formed between users and a wide range of virtual entities, including avatars (Yi, 2022). Within the influencer marketing context, a parasocial relationship has been found to have a more prominent role when compared to opinion leadership in affecting the purchase intention of followers (Bi Farivar et al., 2021; Zhang, 2022). When exploring parasocial interaction between influencers and their audience, along with their perceived credibility, social and physical attractiveness and attitude homophily on purchase intention, Sokolova and Kefi (2020) found PSI to be stronger than credibility in predicting purchase intention—particularly in the case of younger age groups such as the Gen Z cohort. Both wishful identification and parasocial relationships were found to have significant but different impact on followers' stickiness; an important factor contributing to the economic valorization derived from the influencers' follower base (Hu et al., 2020). Along the same lines, closeness seemed to further impact the relationship in a positive fashion (Taillon et al., 2020).

2.3.3 Pseudo Interpersonal Relationship Theory
A promising new direction in the influencer marketing literature concerns the extent to which levels of perceived intimacy on behalf of consumers might deviate from the purely parasocial interactions; a point that will be of particular relevance in our later discussions concerning virtual influencers. In fact, extensive intimate first-person content shared by influencers and the opportunity for consumers to like and comment on the posted content creates an illusion of interpersonal connection (Aw & Chuah, 2021; Aw & Labrecque, 2020; Jin & Ryu, 2020; Kim & Kim, 2020; Moraes et al., 2019), above and beyond the parasocial relationship that has been widely engaged in contemporary research. These pseudo relationships that grew out of the celebrity endorsement scholarship tend to be more intense with influencers who are perceived as credible and attractive by their fans and followers (Gong & Li, 2017; Sakib et al., 2020; Sokolova & Kefi, 2020). These findings are particularly important given

that the emotional relationships and attachment consumers develop with the mediated influencer personas might help mitigate self-serving—as opposed to altruistic—attributions (Aw & Chuah, 2021; Pittman & Abell, 2021), being advantageous for influencers as well as brands alike. Indeed, Kim and Kim (2022) demonstrate that attachment tends to enhance influencer credibility and follower loyalty, in turn reducing overall resistance to advertising.

Importantly, given the limited available research focusing on the area of virtual influencers, it remains unclear as to how applicable these relational frameworks might be in the case of virtual influencers. Understanding this would help firms contemplate effective forms of collaboration with virtual influencers more fully, in turn assisting them in their selection and strategic decision-making process. Before elaborating on this further, the authors first introduce concrete cases of leading virtual influencers and provide examples for their brand collaborations and branding campaigns.

3   Virtual Influencers—A New Frontier in Interactive Marketing

Virtual influencers are computer-generated images (CGIs) or avatars who are created and controlled by teams of individuals often affiliated with digital agencies, and who account for a substantial enough follower base on social media platforms to attract attention from brands and consumers. Given the unlimited potential of virtual space, virtual influencers can assume many shapes and forms including robots, animals, cartoons, humans or aliens. They are similar to robots in that both entities are controlled by humans, and hence can be positioned as digital robots. At the same time, the content virtual influencers produce is very sophisticated, which differentiates these characters from other AI-driven technology such as chatbots or virtual assistants that are programmed to answer questions according to a script (Tsai et al., 2021; Wang, 2021).

While tracing the origins of virtual influencers, Brazil served as the cradle for this industry, with the creation of *Lu Do Magalu* in 2003, initially developed as a virtual mascot for the e-commerce sites of Magazine Luiza promoting appliances and electronics. She turned into an influencer in 2009 with the launch of her YouTube channel and attracted 30 M + followers across various social platforms. This initial success of a virtual influencer in Brazil was reinforced by a law in 2011 favoring children's animation produced by Brazilian studios on TV, which resulted in the rapid development of the Brazilian animation industry; with new talents eventually delving into the field of virtual influencers. Such a favorable context gave rise in 2016 to the quintessential *Lil Miquela*—a particularly well-known virtual influencer created and managed by the California-based Brud agency and positioned as a Brazilian-American robot.

Today, virtual influencers are emerging worldwide. Based on estimates from VirtualHuman.org—an IMDB-type database compiling relevant information on virtual influencers, there are approximately 200 virtual influencers considered 'worthy of interest'; although their real number and impact remain hard to objectively estimate. Successful examples include virtual influencers with a human-like appearance, like *Lil Miquela*, an LA-based robot 'it' girl and singer, or the virtual supermodel *Shudu*; others with 2D cartoon-like features such as the Japanese *Kizuna AI*—a singer, gamer and VTuber (virtual YouTuber; see Fig. 1 for illustration); virtual influencers with animalistic characteristics such as *bee_nfluencer*, a French-born virtual content creator dedicated to raising awareness about the need for protecting bees; or even ones that exhibit a completely unrealistic appearance, like the TikTok phenomenon *Noboby Sausage*, a colorful 3D dancing stick; and finally branded virtual influencers like *Colonel Sanders* from the KFC restaurant chain or *Daisy*—a creation of the online lifestyle store YOOX, who's frequently taking over the brand's Instagram account to share her most fashionable lifestyle recommendations.

Table 1 provides a comprehensive account of some of the most prominent virtual influencers. Examples to be showcased were selected based on their popularity—as approximated by the number of followers, and type to emphasize the vast diversity in terms of appearance, purpose of existence and primary domain of influence. Previous research shows that extreme cases in particular enable a clearer understanding of a phenomenon (Seawright & Gerring, 2008); which in our case is also advantageous to infer the communication

Fig. 1 *Kizuna AI*, a Japanese cartoon-like virtual singer, gamer and VTuber (credit: Kizuna AI Wikipedia page)

purpose, the target audience, and ultimately the marketing opportunities associated with virtual influencers.

In addition to these variations, the table also demonstrates that several digital agencies hide behind these virtual influencers, responsible for their creation as well as maintenance. Brud, the California-based transmedia company founded by Trevor McFedries and Sara DeCou, is probably the most well-known given that they are responsible for the creation of Lil Miquela, one of the pioneering virtual influencer projects. Since her debut, this forever-19 digital robot posting on social media with content showcasing her entertaining life in LA, has accounted for more than 3 million followers on Instagram. As an additional measure of her success, in 2018, TIME magazine designated her to be among the 25 Most Influential People on the Internet.

Although Miquela defines herself as a robot, she has a human appearance and "displays complex human emotions such as sympathy, affection and heartbreak" (Moustakas et al., 2020). This line blurring the 'real' and the 'virtual' is further reinforced by Miquela's stories that commonly showcase other influencers; both human and virtual. For instance, @bermudaisbae, a blond LA-based robot 'it' girl who used to support Donald Trump and @blakow22, a low-life and high-tech LA-based robot, formerly known as Bermuda's boyfriend, are parts of her social circle. These characters are also of Brud's creations, enabling to enhance Miquela's storylines with drama-rich content and opportunities. Regarding her collaborations with brands, Miquela's repertoire includes names like Prada, Calvin Klein, Dior, Balmain and Fenty Beauty. On the human influencer engagement side, one of Miquela's most remarkable campaigns is with Calvin Klein where she kissed the supermodel Bella Hadid. Under the influence of Trevor McFedries, Brud's co-founder and formal artist manager, Miquela was designed at the time of her launch as a virtual celebrity. In August 2017, she became a singer, with her first song 'Not Mine' quickly becoming a hit, reaching eighth position on Spotify Viral the same month. She also is an avid supporter of social campaigns such as Black Lives Matter and LGBTQI + concerns.

Recently, Brud has been repurposed as an entity for 'community-owned media and collectively built worlds', implying that the agency will offer fans the opportunity to provide direct input into Lil Miquela's storytelling. As an illustration, during the summer of 2021, fans were able to discover Lil Miquela's first job, after voting for this particular 'memory' to be revealed—and essentially developed. In October 2021, it was announced that Brud—along with its 32-member team—was acquired by Dapper Labs, the NFT startup, with the aim to build "the decentralized, collectively owned future of media and social with DAOs"[2] (Decentralized Autonomous Organization); a new kind of digital organizational structure that grants everyone equal decision-making power. These innovative collaborations present brands as well as the industry at large with new opportunities to re-envision consumer engagement

---

[2] Tweet of Trevor McFedries, October 4th, 2021.

Table 1 Identification and key attributes of notable virtual influencers

	Lil Miquela @lilmiquela	Shudu @shudu.gram	Noonoori @noonoori	Kizuna AI	Bee_nfluencer @bee_nfluencer	Nobody Sausage @nobodysausage	Colonel sanders @kfc	Kenna @thisis.kenna
Name account name								
Managing entity	Brud (digital agency)	The Digitals (digital modeling agency)	Opium (digital agency)	Kizuna AI Inc (exclusively dedicated digital agency)	Foundation in France (philanthropic French network)	Kael Cabral (freelance motion graphic designer)	KFC (fast food restaurants)	Essence Cosmetics
# of followers / prominent social media outlet	3 M Instagram	225 K Instagram	346 K Instagram	4 M YouTube	271 K Instagram	13 M TikTok	N/A Appears only on KFC's social networks	17.2 K Instagram
Type	Humanoid	Humanoid	Cartoon	Cartoon	Animalistic	Arbitrary / unrealistic	Branded (virtual mascot)	Branded (employee as intern)
Dominant content	Lifestyle & music / songs	Campaigns & inspirational interviews	Lifestyle & fashion	Gaming	Activism & entertainment	Colorful, groovy dance videos	Ironic lifestyle	Cosmetics & lifestyle
Primary purpose of communication	Entertainment & promotion of progressive values	Racial inclusion	Vegan activism	Entertainment with gaming & songs	Bees' protection	Entertainment & dance	Rejuvenation of brand's image	Promotion of the employer brand
Target consumers	Millennials targeting brands	Luxury brands	Sustainable fashion brands	Mass market & technology brands	Donors	Music brands	N/A	N/A

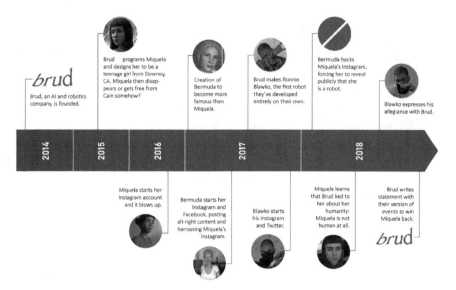

Fig. 2 Brud's activity timeline (*Source* Adapted from commons.wikimedia.org)

and multi-stakeholder collaborations. As an illustration, Fig. 2 offers a visual representation of Brud's activity over the years since its launch.

Another interesting example comes from The Diigitals—the first all-digital modeling agency created by the young English photographer Cameron-James Wilson. In 2017, this agency launched *Shudu*, an enigmatic virtual supermodel with an ideal body appearance. *Shudu* has gained public attention thanks to a repost from Fenty beauty at the beginning of 2018, securing a substantial follower base shortly thereafter (to date 224 K followers on Instagram). Facing criticisms regarding her idealized and overly perfectionist body shape, the Diigitals designed @brenn.gram in 2018, a supermodel with more realistic proportions and slight body imperfections like stretch marks. Contrary to Shudu who is dedicated to the world of fashion, Brenn champions sustainable lifestyle choices for urban living, sponsoring, for instance, fully electric Smart cars. As of now, The Diigitals are responsible for a total of seven models of different genders, ethnic backgrounds, and even the very first digital alien model *Galaxia*.

In addition to the virtual influencers with a more-or-less human-like appearance, there are interesting examples of characters that resemble cartoons. For instance, betting on the interest of fashion brands for renewed endorsements, Joerg Zuber, the CEO of the German agency Opium in 2018 developed Noonoori, a cartoon-like model with almost 400 K followers on Instagram. Embodying a dreamy fashionable Parisian with a vegan lifestyle, she is perfectly positioned to collaborate with sustainably oriented fashion brands, having secured collaborations with Gucci, Versace, Marc Jacobs, Dior and Kim Kardashian cosmetics. Her naïve appearance is also designed to attract brands wishing to reach a younger audience, especially those aiming to penetrate the digital fashion market.

In summary, these virtual opinion leaders and the digital agencies behind them managed to capture a sizable audience along with an impressive repertoire of brands. Positioning virtual influencers as an innovative instrument between consumers and brands, their future potential to play a prominent role in marketing is clear. What is less evident is how virtual influencers might compare to human influencers in terms of potential impact and appeal, and what options brands might have to incorporate them into their marketing strategy. The remainder of this chapter will focus on unpacking these questions more fully to provide firms with concrete and practical takeaways.

4 HUMAN INFLUENCERS VERSUS VIRTUAL INFLUENCERS

4.1 Developmental Trajectories

To contemplate the effectiveness of virtual influencers as a branding instrument, first, it is helpful to review the developmental trajectory of human influencers and see how they might compare to those of their virtual influencer counterparts. Applying the common marketing tool used to capture product life cycles, Fig. 3 presents the general evolution of influencers across four stages, highlighting certain key attributes for each.

The official launch of human influencers is usually tied to the beginning of their content sharing activity on social media sites. Posts tend to concentrate on key domains linked with a hobby or special interest, over time aiming to establish a sizable follower base. It is important to mention that at least in the early days of influencers, those who ended up successful often started out

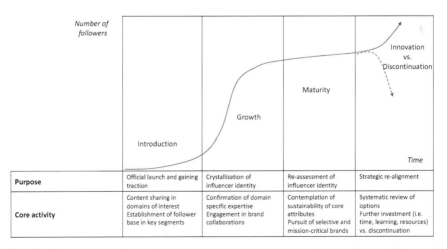

Fig. 3 Key stages of developmental trajectory to approximate the evolution of influencers

as pursuing a pastime activity related to their hobby or expertise, not necessarily intending to become famous (McQuarrie et al., 2012). Influencers who manage to conquer this phase move onto the growth stage, where they generally crystallize their identity, confirm their lead role in the chosen domain(s), and—attracting their attention—begin to collaborate more strategically with brands. It is critical for influencers to maintain their authenticity and true-to-self content, and to avoid the risk of brand encroachment that presents a significant challenge as it might jeopardize their very existence (Audrezet et al., 2020; Pittman & Abell, 2021; Pöyry et al., 2019). In the mature phase, influencers account for a steady follower base but often need to contemplate necessary modifications to keep up their appeal and relevance. In the final stage, influencers need to carefully consider their options, whether they are able to maintain their status and continue or instead accept 'exit' as the sensible choice. Being an influencer can be a highly demanding activity that might become overwhelming and at times can even be leading to burnout syndrome.

Although this trajectory can be applied relatively well to many traditional influencer journeys, it is also important to note important changes in the industry. In particular, starting out as a hobby for pioneer bloggers fifteen years ago (Duffy & Hund, 2015), the development of commercial opportunities for influencers resulted in the increasing professionalization of their activity, which is now perceived by many aspirational entrants as an actual career option (Rocamora, 2018). It is also not uncommon for influencers to continue to offer their marketing labor free of charge to brands in order to attract and secure their interest for future collaborations (Duffy & Hund, 2015). To get a head start and maximize their potential, an increasing number of 'wannabe' influencers enroll in official training programs, such as the Condé Nast Social Academy that is supported by the S.D.A. Bocconi School of Management. In these schools, aspirational influencers are trained to produce high-quality content while maintaining an authentic posture, to prepare them to navigate the different stages along their influencer journey more effectively.

Undoubtedly, much of the content presented in Fig. 3 concerning the general trajectory remains valid for virtual influencers as well, but with certain marked differences. First, the introduction stage can be substantially shortened by removing the accidental element, as virtual influencers are purposefully created to trigger consumer engagement. To some extent this move is also in line with the more recent introduction of aspirational human influencers who pursue training to launch their career. Second, while human influencers often need to wait until they generate a large enough follower base to attract brand attention, virtual influencers are often crafted by digital agencies or commissioned by corporate entities with a relatively clear branding purpose and positioning in mind. Third, while by and large there is a single or limited group of individuals behind a human influencer, there tends to be an entire team of highly trained expert professionals behind any virtual influencer, who carefully monitor their impact and are quick to react and intervene with potential modifications, as needed.

4.2   The Consumer Perspective

There are interesting takeaways that can be derived from the earlier parts of this chapter concerning human and virtual influencers that might assist in understanding their position in the global interactive marketing landscape. What has been missing thus far from our discussion is the consumer perspective—are virtual influencers equally salient and how can brands capture their full communication potential? To explore these questions more fully, the following section presents empirical insights based on semi-structured interviews the authors conducted with a group of young consumers, asking them first about their influencer following behaviors, and then about their perceptions of and attitudes toward virtual influencers. Participants from the Gen Z generation were targeted as they are the ones who are most frequent in the social media platforms—like Instagram—that host a fair amount of influencer activity. Our sample included 42 participants from Italy and France—18 males and 24 females—between the ages of 19 and 25. The majority of our respondents did not follow—and most were not even aware of the existence of—virtual influencers, which is not surprising given the relative novelty of this specialized and innovative digital phenomenon. Thematic content analysis was used to organize the data and to extract relevant themes (Patton, 2014). This exploratory research enabled us to get first-hand insights regarding the overall perceptions of young consumers that might be particularly relevant for brands to consider.

Based on their influencer following behaviors, three different personas were identified from a consumer segmentation perspective. On the least engaged end of the spectrum, the authors find *passive bystanders* whose main motivations surround entertainment, escapism, and predominantly aesthetic and hedonic appeal. They gather information and/or inspiration from posts in relevant domains but tend to be non-exclusive and portray limited loyalty. They are not necessarily interested in establishing any relationship with influencers, and—as long as their needs are fulfilled—are happy to equally consider human as well as virtual influencers.

In mid-range, the authors find *active community members* who are more committed, and, on the one hand, continue to appreciate information and aesthetic appeal, but also welcome the benefits of shared interest, meaning and friendship that are associated with their participation. For this group, the influencer—human or virtual—enables the network of like-minded individuals to emerge, with the community interactions triggering greater levels of engagement and loyalty. Based on this network effect, consumers find it sufficient to receive occasional influencer feedback or second-hand engagement between the influencer and another follower, even when it is different from themselves. This type of engagement resembles signs of parasocial interaction directly targeting the influencer but indirectly targeting the greater network of followers. From a comparative perspective, techniques employed to trigger parasocial interactions and create the impression of a relationship—including the sharing of daily life contents, reacting to comments—could be equally effective by human as well as virtual influencers.

On the most engaged level, the authors find followers who can be described as *devoted contributors* within the influencer's own network and who value attachment and continuity, deeper meaning, extensive loyalty, and resemble signs of pseudo-interpersonal love relationship. These consumers are so invested in following their beloved human influencer(s) that they do not see the value or reason for following virtual ones—whom they consider fake and not at all authentic. They view their chosen human influencers as 'friends' and are deeply invested in their everyday lives, portraying emotional connections that mirror the emotions experienced and revealed by the human opinion leader. Consumers in this category are likely to establish pseudo-interpersonal relationships with the human influencer(s) they follow; something that would not be expected in the case of virtual influencers. In this sense, this last category is best reserved for campaigns that target human influencers only.

These three personas indicate that depending on the type of consumers, brands should realistically align their strategy to appeal to the right type of audience, which is heavily influenced by the domain in which they aim to exert influence. Certain areas like fashion or cause marketing are likely to appeal to a broader audience and can benefit from sporadic and accidental visitors (our first group) as well as somewhat more engaged supporters (our second group) who are after the community membership. At least for the time being, virtual influencers are unlikely to appeal to those very dedicated to following their human influencers as they do not necessarily see the value of spending their time on such endeavors. Established luxury brands might have a particular role to play in this regard—in placing emphasis on the innovative nature of this form of communication and the strategic engagement of virtual influencers.

4.3 Recommendations for the Interactive Strategy of Brands

So, what does this all mean for brands? The remaining part of the chapter contemplates the strategy that brands can pursue to maximize their investment and appeal in ways that are congruent with the right type of audience. In particular, in line with some of the ideas put forth by VirtualHuman.org, the authors propose three ways in which brands can involve a virtual influencer in their interactive marketing strategy.

Partnership or sponsorship (low engagement). In collaboration with the managing agency of the virtual influencer, a brand can negotiate a specific promotional content to be posted by the digital character to its community. This is the easiest and simplest way to initiate a first collaboration with a virtual influencer, offering an ideal and low-risk approach to test the reaction of the audience, or—as our example will demonstrate—to reach a specific and often younger age group more effectively. As an illustration, Imma Gram (356 K followers on Instagram), a Japanize pink bob human-like influencer, was involved in a rather innovative partnership with IKEA in 2020. For three days, Imma moved and lived in a Tokyo-based IKEA. Bystanders could observe her living room from the street and her bedroom at the first floor of Harajuku's shop. Recreated with LEDs, Imma curated her fully furnished IKEA flat, and her household activities could be followed by her subscribers on social platforms.

Interestingly, these sponsorship types of engagements can also be relevant for non-commercial organizations. For instance, Knox Frost (674 K followers on Instagram)—a virtual influencer positioned around wellness and health-related matters—was sponsored by the World Health Organization in the spring of 2020 to promote social distancing and other sanitary guidelines following the COVID-19 pandemic, especially targeting younger generations.[3]

Recurrent collaboration (medium engagement). Representing a deeper level of mutual engagement and collaboration between the virtual influencer and the brand, this approach refers to contracts that usually involve long-term and often exclusive partnerships, in line with more traditional celebrity endorsement strategies. This co-creative form enables the development of richer and more meaningful storylines and carefully curated promotional messages that aim to engage with the intended audience more fully. As an example, Astro[4]—an alien musician followed by 111 K users on Instagram, has signed on with the streetwear brand Supreme. As a result, Astro is dressed from head to toe in Supreme clothing on its Instagram feed.

Ownership (high engagement). Acting as a brand avatar (Foster et al., 2022), this approach offers free rein to develop relevant branded storylines to engage target customers in an interactive dialogue. A particularly emblematic case is that of Colonel Sanders, the virtual influencer created by KFC.[5] This virtual character built on the KFC mascot is an attractive gray-haired humanoid showcasing a glamorous lifestyle. The content he posted on the company's Instagram account portrayed his everyday life at work with the KFC team, as well as meeting or traveling with other famous human and virtual influencers. Colonel Sanders is a particularly interesting case. More specifically, in addition to his engagement with KFC, he also promoted other brands like DrPepper or TurboTax, disclosing the partnership with #ad—similarly to any professional influencer. Such freedom from KFC created a sense of authenticity of its content, probably explaining why the famous fast-food chain managed to more

---

[3] Further details on this collaboration can be found on the following site: https://www.marketingdive.com/news/who-enlists-virtual-influencer-for-covid-19-prevention-campaign/575493/.

[4] https://www.instagram.com/astrolovesu/.

[5] For further details please see the following link: https://www.wk.com/work/kfc-virtual-colonel/.

than double consumer engagement on their corporate Instagram account following the introduction of Colonel Sanders as a virtual influencer. Unfortunately, it was a short-lived communication feature, and KFC returned to their regularly scheduled corporate social media programming, which resulted in an intense drop in consumer engagement.

Besides Colonel Sanders, Daisy from YOOX and Lu Do Magalu from Luiza constitute two other examples of branded and firm-owned influencers. More recently, Prada created Candy, a human-like purple-eyed virtual muse associated with their eponym perfume; while Barbie, the famous Mattel's doll, gave birth to a VTuber creating beauty content with more than 10 M channel subscribers. It is interesting to note that the social media management of these brand-owned virtual influencers varies from one brand to another, ranging from the creation of a new dedicated social platform (e.g., Barbie) to taking over of the brands' existing online space (e.g., KFC).

Beyond these three strategies, given their very nature of artificial creations, virtual influencers have been positioned with various benefits vis-à-vis their human influencer counterparts. First, they provide a good opportunity for brands to differentiate and escape the followers' fatigue of collaboration with human lifestyle influencers. Indeed, virtual influencers provide very sophisticated and unlimited possibilities of content that might range from an alien endorser to a burning dress on a catwalk. Given their unique and often unexpected features, this type of content can be particularly appealing to younger audiences. More prosaically, their posts and stories are readily available online 24/7 all over the world, and hence they offer a practical solution to battle the physical limitations of humans. Similarly, virtual influencers do not require rest and sleep and do not have health-related concerns that might otherwise limit their availability.

Given their targeted positioning from an early stage, virtual influencers are highly adaptable to specific brand requests which enable closer alignment with target groups offering customized engagements and experiences (Robinson, 2020). And as a particularly relevant point for firms, virtual influencers represent reduced PR risks and offline personal life scandals which in the case of their human counterparts might easily spill over to the online persona (Duffy & Hund, 2019). As a result, the engagement rate associated with virtual influencers tends to be—on average—three times higher than that of humans.

At any rate, virtual influencers do not only bring benefits along with them. In particular, their over-controlled communication might present certain limitations by jeopardizing the emotional connection between influencers and their community, which is one of the pivotal affordances of human influencers (Duffy & Hund, 2019). As an example, the developmental growth of Miquela's followers has been slower than that of other human influencers with a similar follower base, which tends to corroborate this idea. This slowdown might explain why Dapper Labs, the managing entity behind this Brazilian-American virtual opinion leader, is working to renew their strategy to boost their followers' involvement. In particular, the research driven by Moustakas et al. (2020) suggests that sharing an engaging and woven storyline might be able to humanize virtual influencers. Indeed, the narrative of conflicts, relationships, personal goals, and desires seems to be very effective in establishing an emotional connection with followers. Hence, the challenge brands face to maintain and develop virtual influencer personas would entail finding innovative ways to humanize them.

5 Avenues for Future Research

When having informal discussions with people (students, experts, marketing professionals) about virtual influencers, one of the greatest intrigues concerns the very reason why people might be motivated to follow such a fake digital persona that does not even exist. Indeed, this question is at the core of the development of virtual influencers and as such opens various avenues for future research. For instance, a vast body of research focusing on human influencers points to authenticity as a key factor to influencer success (Lee & Eastin, 2021; Pöyry et al., 2019). Nonetheless, according to Robinson (2020), given that human influencers also face issues surrounding their authenticity, the absence of the existence of virtual influencers and entirely fake identity and artificial nature might not pose a problem for their followers. In particular, given their exposure to AI-enabled technology from a relatively young age, Gen Z consumers might not be as preoccupied with the question of authenticity, making such a generational shift worthy of investigation.

A second issue relates to the importance of consumer literacy. Indeed, one might expect consumers to be more willing to push their comfort zones toward this new form of media in the future, for two reasons. On the one hand, consumer awareness about and acceptance toward social media influencers are increasing, indicating that people at large tend to be more familiar and comfortable with influencers. On the other hand, thanks to the enhanced technological literacy of consumers, within our era of innovative tools like social bots—referring to computer algorithms that automatically produce content (Appel et al., 2020), people are now able to manage fluent conversations and interactions with AI-driven technology to the extent that they might not even realize that they are not interacting with a human. It might be interesting to explore further how these new comfort zones might impact consumer expectations in terms of their interactions with virtual influencers.

One of the latest virtual influencer trends pertains to characters created, managed and owned by brands. A closer look reveals that linking a virtual influencer directly to the company as an employee, instead of having a virtual influencer solely campaigning for a single product, might be a promising strategic direction. As an illustration, Kenna is a girl bot intern at Essence Cosmetics who posts content on Instagram related to both her personal and professional life. Offering an office backstage to her followers, she is promoting Essence Cosmetics products as well as the company as an employer.

This approach could ultimately be linked to an employee advocacy strategy, where employees are expected to become the firm's ambassadors or spokespersons through their professional and personal social networks. In this sense, virtual employee advocacy offers a new path for research worthy of further exploration.

Another interesting area of inquiry concerns the future of the Metaverse and its impact on virtual influencers. According to Yonatan Ben Shimon, the founder of theVirtualEstate.net., "the Metaverse is a collective virtual shared space including the sum of all virtual worlds, augmented reality, and the Internet as a whole". Illustrating its diverse affordances, the Metaverse offers opportunities for innovative workplaces, gaming platforms, social spaces and virtual markets (Boyd & Koles, 2019). As such, the Metaverse can be associated with the development of new types of digital goods and possessions (Koles & Nagy, 2021), with particular attention to virtual art (verified piece of digital or graphic work stored and tokenized on the blockchain) and digital fashion (the visual representation of clothing built using computer technologies and 3D software). Moreover, the Metaverse can give space for venues to host virtual concerts run by virtual artists, which could be easily combined with virtual influencers.

From the consumer angle, these new consumption patterns might be somewhat unusual or unconventional at first, and here virtual influencers might offer an effective gateway between the two worlds. Because virtual influencers already live in the virtual ecosystem of the Metaverse, they might be able to provide legitimate advice to consumers regarding their digital purchases, similarly to the way their human counterparts do so in their offline existence. A specific opportunity arises within the digital fashion arena where clothing is entirely virtual and is not necessarily designed to be replicated in a physical format. Virtual influencers could become the legitimate models to showcase brands' virtual merchandise and inform their followers about new trends and tricks on how to dress their avatars. Although this point is increasingly recognized in industry-centered outlets,[6] future academic research could dwell further into examining the new role virtual influencers could play as ambassadors and counselors in the Metaverse.

Along these lines, the development of virtual influencers continues to blur the fine line between entertainment and advertising. For instance, cartoon influencers might be seen as a new form of entertaining content easily comparable with traditional animated cartoon fiction. The notable difference is that they have been created for a commercial purpose. Thus, virtual influencers envisioned as the ultimate commodification of entertainment is an important topic to explore in order to anticipate potentially misleading perceptions and ensure consumer well-being.

---

[6] Concrete examples can be found on the link: https://www.nssgclub.com/en/fashion/23083/digital-influencer-fashion-industry.

Importantly, virtual influencers tend to share content that is rich and often more immersive than the ones shared by their human counterparts. While regulations associated with social media influencers have been developed in most countries encouraging them to disclose their relationships with brands, as of now apart from India, the activities of virtual influencers are not yet regulated. In its influencer guidelines released in July 2021, Indian authorities included for the first time a specific reference to virtual influencers: in addition to the disclosure rules applicable to human influencers, virtual influencers (and their managing entities) are required to disclose to consumers that they are not interacting with a real human being. Such type of disclosure and its impact need to be assessed, as well as potential complementary or alternative rules; a topic that is particularly relevant in the case of influencers that resemble humans.

Finally, virtual influencers mark an important new stage in terms of content creation. Indeed, human influencers developed in large part thanks to the easy access to a wide range of content creation tools, which lead many consumers to become online creators. The creation and maintenance of virtual influencers assume specific high-level technical expertise and AI-based skills, which might present an obstacle when aiming for more sophisticated content that only highly specialized and tech-savvy people might be able to develop. Future research could explore ways in which the emergence of new major actors—similarly to Dapper Labs or the Diigitals—might lead the way here and ultimately bring consumers closer to virtual influencers.

6 Conclusion

The purpose of the current chapter was to extend our understanding of virtual influencers within the area of interactive marketing. Social media influencers have been prominent contributors to the marketing strategy of many firms, but substantially less is known about the impact and role of their virtual counterparts. This chapter started by introducing social media influencers and the relationship their followers are likely to form with them. It continued with a detailed review and concrete cases of prominent virtual influencers, highlighting their diversity in terms of appearance, target audience and type of brand collaboration. Then the authors shared some insights gathered on the basis of a set of semi-structured interviews conducted with young consumers to understand their general influencer following behaviors on Instagram as well as their perceptions of opinion concerning virtual influencers.

The authors moved onto taking the perspective of brands and offering concrete recommendations as to how companies might choose to collaborate with virtual influencers capturing different levels of engagement; ranging from partnerships and sponsorships at the lowest engagement level, advancing to recurrent collaborations, and concluding with ownership at the highest engagement level where brands develop their very own interactive mascots. The chapter concludes by sharing ideas for interesting research projects that might help advance scholarship as well as practice in this innovative but nascent industry. The authors are confident that new and exciting further innovations will be launched shortly with the progress and appreciation of the affordances enabled by the Metaverse, which should trigger additional ease and acceptance on behalf of consumers toward these virtual opinion leaders.

References

Akdevelioglu, D., & Kara, S. (2020). An international investigation of opinion leadership and social media. *Journal of Research in Interactive Marketing, 14*(1), 71–88.

Al-Emadi, F. A., & Ben Yahia, I. (2020). Ordinary celebrities related criteria to harvest fame and influence on social media. *Journal of Research in Interactive Marketing, 14*(2), 195–213.

Appel, G., Grewal, L., Hadi, R., & Stephen, A. T. (2020). The future of social media in marketing. *Journal of the Academy of Marketing Science, 48*(1), 79–95.

Audrezet, A., de Kerviler, G., & Guidry Moulard, J. (2020). Authenticity under threat: When social media influencers need to go beyond self-presentation. *Journal of Business Research, 117*, 557–569.

Aw, E.C.-X., & Chuah, S.H.-W. (2021). Stop the unattainable ideal for an ordinary me! Fostering Parasocial Relationships with Social Media Influencers: The Role of Self-Discrepancy. *Journal of Business Research, 132*, 146–157.

Aw, E.C.-X., & Labrecque, L. I. (2020). Celebrity endorsement in social media contexts: Understanding the role of parasocial interactions and the need to belong. *Journal of Consumer Marketing, 37*(7), 895–908.

Bi, N.C. and Zhang, R. (2022), I will buy what my 'friend' recommends: The effects of parasocial relationships, influencer credibility and self-esteem on purchase intentions, *Journal of Research in Interactive Marketing*, Vol. ahead-of-print No. ahead-of-print.

Boyd, D. E., & Koles, B. (2019). An introduction to the special issue "virtual reality in marketing": Definition, theory and practice. *Journal of Business Research, 100*, 441–444.

Carlson, B. D., Donavan, D. T., Deitz, G. D., Bauer, B. C., & Lala, V. (2020). A customer-focused approach to improve celebrity endorser effectiveness. *Journal of Business Research, 109*, 221–235.

Casaló, L. V., Flavián, C., & Ibáñez-Sánchez, S. (2020). Influencers on instagram: Antecedents and consequences of opinion leadership. *Journal of Business Research, 117*, 510–519.

Corrêa, S. C. H., Soares, J. L., Christino, J. M. M., & Gosling, M. d. S. and Gonçalves, C. A. (2020). The influence of youtubers on followers' use intention. *Journal of Research in Interactive Marketing, 14*(2), 173–194.

Dinh, T.C.T. and Lee, Y. (2021), "I want to be as trendy as influencers"—How "fear of missing out" leads to buying intention for products endorsed by social media influencers, *Journal of Research in Interactive Marketing*, Vol. ahead-of-print No. ahead-of-print.

Drenten, J. and Brooks, G. (2020), Celebrity 2.0: Lil miquela and the rise of a virtual star system, *Feminist Media Studies, 20*(8), 1319–1323.

Duffy, B.E. and Hund, E. (2015), Having it all on social media: Entrepreneurial femininity and self-branding among fashion bloggers, *Social Media + Society*, 1(2), 1–11.

Duffy, B. E., & Hund, E. (2019). Gendered visibility on social media: Navigating instagram's authenticity bind. *International Journal of Communication*, 13, 4983–5002.

Evans, N. J., Phua, J., Lim, J., & Jun, H. (2017). Disclosing instagram influencer advertising: The effects of disclosure language on advertising recognition, attitudes, and behavioral intent. *Journal of Interactive Advertising*, 17(2), 138–149.

Farivar, S., Wang, F. and Yuan, Y. (2021, March), Opinion leadership vs. Para-social relationship: Key factors in influencer marketing, *Journal of Retailing and Consumer Services*, 59, 1–11.

Foster, J. K., McLelland, M. A., & Wallace, L. K. (2022). Brand avatars: Impact of social interaction on consumer–brand relationships. *Journal of Research in Interactive Marketing*, 16(2), 237–258.

Ge, J., & Gretzel, U. (2018). Emoji rhetoric: A social media influencer perspective. *Journal of Marketing Management*, 34(15/16), 1272–1295.

Giuffredi-Kähr, A., Petrova, A., & Malär, L. (2022). Sponsorship disclosure of influencers—A curse or a blessing? *Journal of Interactive Marketing*, 57(1), 18–34.

Gong, W., & Li, X. (2017). Engaging fans on microblog: The synthetic influence of parasocial interaction and source characteristics on celebrity endorsement. *Psychology & Marketing*, 34(7), 720–732.

Hamilton, M., Kaltcheva, V. D. & Rohm, A. J. (2016, November), Social media and value creation: The role of interaction satisfaction and interaction immersion, *Journal of Interactive Marketing*, 36, 121–133.

Harms, B., Hoekstra, J. C., & Bijmolt, T. H. A. (2022). Sponsored influencer vlogs and young viewers: When sponsorship disclosure does not enhance advertising literacy, and parental mediation backfires. *Journal of Interactive Marketing*, 57(1), 35–53.

Hu, L., Min, Q., Han, S. and Liu, Z. (2020, October), Understanding followers' stickiness to digital influencers: The effect of psychological responses, *International Journal of Information Management*, 54, 1–14.

Hughes, C., Swaminathan, V., & Brooks, G. (2019). Driving brand engagement through online social influencers: An empirical investigation of sponsored blogging campaigns. *Journal of Marketing*, 83(5), 78–96.

IAB. (2018). *Why publishers are increasingly turning to influencer marketing—and what that means for marketers*, from https://www.iab.com/wp-content/uploads/2018/01/IAB_Influencer_Marketing_for_Publishers_2018-01-25.pdf

De Jans, S. and Hudders, L. (2020, November), Disclosure of vlog advertising targeted to children, *Journal of Interactive Marketing*, 52, 1–19.

De Jans, S., Spielvogel, I., Naderer, B. and Hudders, L. (2021, July), Digital food marketing to children: How an influencer's lifestyle can stimulate healthy food choices among children, *Appetite*, 162, 105182.

Jin, S.V. and Ryu, E. (2020, July), I'll buy what she's #wearing: The roles of envy toward and parasocial interaction with influencers in instagram celebrity-based brand endorsement and social commerce, *Journal of Retailing and Consumer Services*, 55, 1–15.

Jin, S. V., & Muqaddam, A. (2019). Product placement 2.0: Do brands need influencers, or do influencers need brands? *Journal of Brand Management, 26*(5), 522–537.

Kim, M. & Kim, J. (2020, October), How does a celebrity make fans happy? Interaction between celebrities and fans in the social media context, *Computers in Human Behavior, 111*, 1–11.

Kim, D. Y., & Kim, H.-Y. (2021). Trust me, trust me not: A nuanced view of influencer marketing on social media. *Journal of Business Research, 134*, 223–232.

Kim, D. Y. and Kim, H.-Y. (2022), Social media influencers as human brands: An interactive marketing perspective, *Journal of Research in Interactive Marketing*, Vol. ahead-of-print No. ahead-of-print.

Koles, B., & Nagy, P. (2021). Digital object attachment. *Current Opinion in Psychology, 39*, 60–65.

Lea, M., Jens, M. and Christian, M. (2018). *#sponsored #ad: Exploring the effect of influencer marketing on purchase intention.* Paper presented at the AMCIS.

Lee, J. A., & Eastin, M. S. (2021). Perceived authenticity of social media influencers: Scale development and validation. *Journal of Research in Interactive Marketing, 15*(4), 822–841.

Lee, J. E., & Watkins, B. (2016). Youtube vloggers' influence on consumer luxury brand perceptions and intentions. *Journal of Business Research, 69*(12), 5753–5760.

Lee, M. T., & Theokary, C. (2020). The superstar social media influencer: Exploiting linguistic style and emotional contagion over content? *Journal of Business Research, 132*, 860–871.

Leite, F. P. and Baptista, P. d. P. (2021), Influencers' intimate self-disclosure and its impact on consumers' self-brand connections: Scale development, validation, and application, *Journal of Research in Interactive Marketing*, Vol. ahead-of-print No. ahead-of-print.

López, M., Sicilia, M., & Verlegh, P. W. J. (2022). How to motivate opinion leaders to spread e-wom on social media: Monetary vs non-monetary incentives. *Journal of Research in Interactive Marketing, 16*(1), 154–171.

Lou, C., & Yuan, S. (2019). Influencer marketing: How message value and credibility affect consumer trust of branded content on social media. *Journal of Interactive Advertising, 19*(1), 58–73.

McQuarrie, E. F., Miller, J., & Phillips, B. J. (2012). The megaphone effect: Taste and audience in fashion blogging. *Journal of Consumer Research, 40*(1), 136–158.

Moraes, M., Gountas, J., Gountas, S., & Sharma, P. (2019). Celebrity influences on consumer decision making: New insights and research directions. *Journal of Marketing Management, 35*(13–14), 1159–1192.

Moustakas, E., Lamba, N., Mahmoud, D. & Ranganathan, C. (2020). *Blurring lines between fiction and reality: Perspectives of experts on marketing effectiveness of virtual influencers.* Paper presented at the 2020 International Conference on Cyber Security and Protection of Digital Services (Cyber Security).

Patton, M. Q. (2014). *Qualitative research & evaluation methods: Integrating theory and practice.* Sage Publications.

Pick, M. (2020). Psychological ownership in social media influencer marketing. *European Business Review, 33*(1), 9–30.

Pittman, M. and Abell, A. (2021, November), More trust in fewer followers: Diverging effects of popularity metrics and green orientation social media influencers, *Journal of Interactive Marketing, 56*, 70–82.

Pöyry, E., Pelkonen, M., Naumanen, E., & Laaksonen, S.-M. (2019). A call for authenticity: Audience responses to social media influencer endorsements in strategic communication. *International Journal of Strategic Communication, 13*(4), 336–351.

Robinson, B. (2020). Towards an ontology and ethics of virtual influencers. *Australasian Journal of Information Systems, 23*, 333–345.

Rocamora, A. (2011). Personal fashion blogs: Screens and mirrors in digital self-portraits. *Fashion Theory, 15*(4), 407–424.

Rocamora, A. (2018). The labour of fashion blogging. In L. Armstrong & F. McDowell (Eds.), *Fashioning Professionals: Identity and representation at work in the creative industries* (1st ed., pp. 65–82). Bloomsbury Academic.

Ryu, E., & Jin, S. V. (2019). Instagram fashionistas, luxury visual image strategies and vanity. *Journal of Product & Brand Management, 29*(3), 355–368.

Sakib, M. D. N., Zolfagharian, M., & Yazdanparast, A. (2020). Does parasocial interaction with weight loss vloggers affect compliance? *The Role of Vlogger Characteristics, Consumer Readiness, and Health Consciousness, Journal of Retailing and Consumer Services, 52*, 101733.

Seawright, J., & Gerring, J. (2008). Case selection techniques in case study research: A menu of qualitative and quantitative options. *Political Research Quarterly, 61*(2), 294–308.

Seeler, S., Lück, M., & Schänzel, H. A. (2019). Exploring the drivers behind experience accumulation—The role of secondary experiences consumed through the eyes of social media influencers. *Journal of Hospitality and Tourism Management, 41*, 80–89.

Sokolova, K., & Kefi, H. (2020). Instagram and youtube bloggers promote it, why should i buy? How credibility and parasocial interaction influence purchase intentions. *Journal of Retailing and Consumer Services, 53*, 1–9.

Tafesse, W., & Wood, B. P. (2021). Followers' engagement with instagram influencers: The role of influencers' content and engagement strategy. *Journal of Retailing and Consumer Services, 58*, 1–9.

Taillon, B. J., Jones, D. N., Mueller, S. M., & Kowalczyk, C. M. (2020). Understanding the relationships between social media influencers and their followers: The moderating role of closeness. *Journal of Product & Brand Management, 29*(6), 767–782.

Tsai, W.-H.S., Liu, Y., & Chuan, C.-H. (2021). How chatbots' social presence communication enhances consumer engagement: The mediating role of parasocial interaction and dialogue. *Journal of Research in Interactive Marketing, 15*(3), 460–482.

Valsesia, F., Proserpio, D., & Nunes, J. C. (2020). The positive effect of not following others on social media. *Journal of Marketing Research (JMR), 57*(6), 1152–1168.

van Reijmersdal, E. A., Rozendaal, E., Hudders, L., Vanwesenbeeck, I., Cauberghe, V., & van Berlo, Z. M. C. (2020). Effects of disclosing influencer marketing in videos: An eye tracking study among children in early adolescence. *Journal of Interactive Marketing, 49*, 94–106.

Wang, C. L. (2021). New frontiers and future directions in interactive marketing: Inaugural editorial. *Journal of Research in Interactive Marketing, 15*(1), 1–9.

Wang, T., Thai, T.D.-H., Ly, P. T. M., & Chi, T. P. (2021). Turning social endorsement into brand passion. *Journal of Business Research, 126*, 429–439.

Weismueller, J., Harrigan, P., Wang, S., & Soutar, G. N. (2020). Influencer endorsements: How advertising disclosure and source credibility affect consumer purchase intention on social media. *Australasian Marketing Journal, 28*(4), 160–170.

Yi, J. (2022), Female-oriented dating sims in china: Players' parasocial relationships, gender attitudes, and romantic beliefs, *Psychology of Popular Media*, Vol. ahead-of-print No. ahead-of-print.

Zhang, W., Chintagunta, P. K., & Kalwani, M. U. (2021). Social media, influencers, and adoption of an eco-friendly product: Field experiment evidence from rural china. *Journal of Marketing, 85*(3), 10–27.

CHAPTER 17

Sentimental Interaction with Virtual Celebrities: An Assessment from Customer-Generated Content

Bình Nghiêm-Phú and Jillian Rae Suter

1 INTRODUCTION

Celebrity endorsement can be considered one of the most popular and influential activities of marketing, in general, and interactive marketing, in particular (Al-Emadi & Yahia, 2020; Halonen-Knight & Hurmerinta, 2010; Wang, 2021). Traditionally, the image of a celebrity figure may be used in product designs or advertisements. Alternatively, the activities of that celebrity may be covered in media platforms with obvious connections with the products or brands that they present. Today, the celebrity themselves (an ordinary celebrity or a key opinion leader KOL) may also promote the products or brands via interactive tools on social networking sites, such as livestreams or short videos. On the other hand, customers tend to choose or to be attached to brands or products whose celebrity images match with those of the brands or products (Paul & Bhakar, 2018; Pradhan et al., 2016). Customers' perception of the celebrities can significantly affect their evaluation of the products, and eventually, their purchasing and consumption behaviors (Bergkvist et al., 2016; Kim et al., 2014; Wang et al., 2017). Customer perception, specifically, includes cognitive thoughts and affective feelings (Dichter, 1985). The

B. Nghiêm-Phú (✉)
University of Hyogo, Kobe, Japan
e-mail: binhnghiem@gmail.com

J. R. Suter
Shizuoka University, Shizuoka, Japan

© The Author(s), under exclusive license to Springer Nature Switzerland AG 2023
C. L. Wang (ed.), *The Palgrave Handbook of Interactive Marketing*,
https://doi.org/10.1007/978-3-031-14961-0_17

feelings or sentiments, in particular, can show the intensity of the parasocial interaction between a customer and a celebrity (Giles, 2002).

Celebrities usually are famous living human beings who are currently working in certain areas of sociocultural and economic life, such as entertainment, sports, business, politics, science, and education, among others. However, there also are several unconventional types of celebrities. For example, Hachiko and Kaikun are two famous dog endorsers of a place (Tokyo) and of a telecommunication company (Softbank) in Japan (Hansen, 2013). In the former case, the dog was dead yet its image and legend live. This also holds true with some dead celebrity figures (D'Rozario, 2016; Hudak, 2014; Petty & D'Rozario, 2009). To some extent, these celebrities still are the endorsers of their own or other companies' products. And thanks to the development of computer technology, some of them (e.g., Amy Winehouse, Michael Jackson, and Whitney Houston) are even resurrected in the forms of virtual 3D characters (Drenten & Brooks, 2020; Penfold-Mounce & Penfold-Mounce, 2018; Ross & Labrecque, 2018). In certain cases (e.g., Whitney Houston since 2016; Rowell, 2019), they are products of the holographic technique, a photographic method that keeps track of the light emanated from an object then rebuilds it in a virtual 3D form to be displayed on stages and perform live on their own or with supporting performers (Johnston, 2008). These virtual human celebrities, however, have some equal competitors, who are totally fictional figures, such as Hatsune Miku (Fig. 1), a virtual singer with a vocaloid (a voice created by computer programs) developed in Japan in 2009 (Annett, 2015; Guga, 2015; Prior, 2018). The innovativeness of technology and the creative combination of certain sociocultural factors (e.g., Japanese-ness, type of music, and singer and audience interaction) are some of the main reasons behind the rise of this Japanese virtual idol (Zaborowski, 2016).

Fig. 1 Hatsune Miku (*Source* Taken by the second author)

Since celebrity endorsement is undoubtedly an investment that can produce both good returns and bad losses (Chung et al., 2013; Knittel & Stango, 2014), a thorough understanding of the perceptions and impacts of the celebrities is very important, given the figures are real people or artificial characters. However, compared to the knowledge about human being agents, little is known about virtual or holographic celebrities, except some early discussions on the legal, ethical, and technological aspects of this issue (Anson, 2014; Drenten & Brooks, 2020; D'Rozario et al., 2007). Certain important questions, such as how viewers and customers perceive and interact with virtual celebrities, and how the perception of and interaction with virtual celebrities can affect viewers and customers' evaluations of products and services, remain largely unanswered. More research, thus, is necessary to better understand virtual figures, the new and probably next generation of celebrities. The outcomes of this attempt can significantly assist the development of virtual celebrities and the use of them in marketing practices in the future.

The purpose of this chapter is to examine (1) perceptions of virtual celebrities, and (2) the effect that a virtual figure can have as an endorser of a certain product. Two studies were undertaken to address each of these two objectives. Hatsune Miku, a fictional figure, is selected as the main focus of this research given the fact that she is one of the first celebrities of her type ever created (Annett, 2015; Guga, 2015; Prior, 2018). In addition, user-generated content, the information created and shared by viewers or customers of a given product, service, event, and the like on public websites and social media platforms, is employed as the source of data in these studies. This database has widely been employed in academic research in recent years (Fox et al., 2018; Liu et al., 2017) given its availability and accessibility. This type of data can also be analyzed to reveal the interactions that viewers and customers might have with a product, a service, an event, or a celebrity (Feng et al., 2021).

2 Study 1

The objective of this study was to examine viewers' perceptions of virtual celebrities. As mentioned earlier, Hatsune Miku was chosen as the main object. However, to expand the understanding, another type of virtual celebrity, a virtual presentation of a deceased human figure (Whitney Houston) was selected as the object for comparison. The practical reason was that both of them are famous singers and have their own products (e.g., music concerts) and distinct groups of fans. It should be noted that although the Whitney Houston figure involved a dead person, this study was not a posthumous one (Pentz et al., 2005; Wilkinson, 2002) but a study concerning a virtual character and other events or products related to this character.

The first research question (RQ) is presented as follows.

RQ1. How do viewers perceive the virtual presentations of (a) Hatsune Miku and (b) Whitney Houston?

2.1 Literature Review

Research on virtual performers in general, especially that about viewer perception of these figures, is limited. Black (2008), for example, mentioned cuteness as one of the main characteristics of the virtual idols. Black (2012) later argued that the commodification and mass-production of certain level of femininity support the relationship between a virtual idol and their fans, especially the male ones. In addition, Zell et al. (2015) discovered that the shape of a virtual figure could affect viewers' evaluation of its realness, while the material of the figure was the major indicator of its appeal. Adamo-Villani et al. (2015) added that the appeal of a polygonal character (e.g., a virtual singing avatar) could be improved if it was stylized rather than realistic. Moreover, Prieto et al. (2015) found that the head and eyebrow movements of a 3D animated character could influence viewers' perception of contrastive focus. However, they also ascertained that the former was more informative than the latter for focus identification.

In addition, research on viewer perception of human celebrities also provides more insights. Moulard et al. (2015), for example, found that a traditional celebrity (e.g., a movie star) is perceived as authentic if they possess two major qualities: rarity and stability. Alternatively, Al-Emadi and Yahia (2020) observed that an ordinary celebrity (e.g., a KOL) may have fame and opinion leadership on social media visual platforms (e.g., Instagram and Facebook) if they have the following characteristics: credibility, storytelling and content quality, fit with the platform, actual and aspired image homophily, and consistency. In another study, Suki (2014) discovered that a human celebrity's credibility is formed through their expertise, attitude toward the brand, and physical attractiveness, among others. Nonetheless, Edwards and La Ferle (2009) and Suki (2014) noticed that viewer perception may differ given certain personal and environmental factors, such as biological sex and religious tendency.

The abovementioned information, however, is mostly about the cognitive aspect of viewer perception (Dichter, 1985). This shows how and how much a viewer *thinks* about a celebrity on the one hand. However, there is another important component of viewer perception: the sentiments. This component demonstrates how and how much a viewer *feels* about a celebrity on the other hand. Generally, the sentiments have a mutual relationship with an interaction between two agents in the sense that both the sentiments and the interaction can affect and shape each other (Heise, 2006). To some extents, the more the sentiments are publicly expressed, the more intense the interaction can be externally and overtly estimated. In addition, the direction of the sentiments, whether they are positive, negative, neutral (neither positive nor negative), or mixed (both positive and negative), can also be implied from the interaction. This may hold true with a parasocial interaction (Giles, 2002) between a viewer and a celebrity.

In a recent study in Bangladesh, Khan et al. (2021) identified seven specific categories of sentiments toward celebrities, including abusive, angry, excited, happy, religious, sad, and surprise. In another study in Indonesia, Pinem et al. (2018) presented three general categories of sentiments toward a product after the celebrities endorsed it, including positive, neutral, and negative. The materials for analysis in both studies were user-generated content posted on popular social media networks, such as Facebook, Twitter, and YouTube. This practice has demonstrated the usability of such a database in understanding the sentimental interaction between viewers and celebrities.

2.2 Method

As mentioned earlier, this study used user-generated content as its source of data. The search of the database started with the selection of two most recent events of the involved virtual celebrities. Coincidentally, both figures had live concerts in 2020: Hatsune Miku with "Magical Mirai" and Whitney Houston with "An Evening with Whitney: The Whitney Houston Hologram Tour." In addition, both had their commercial ads posted on YouTube almost at the same time: the former on 12 February 2020 and the latter on 24 February 2020. The numbers of comments on the ads did not greatly differ at the time of data collection (mid-April 2020): 306 for the former and 294 for the latter. Therefore, viewers' comments on YouTube were collected and were treated as the database in this study.

The use of viewer comments from this particular platform was also supported by the findings of Prieto et al. (2015) in which they found that the combination of both the visual and audio cues was more effective in affecting viewer perception than the utilization of only one cue. YouTube, well-known for its visual and audio properties, provided both of these important cues for viewers to interact with the celebrities featured in the videos it kept.

As a form of user-generated materials, YouTube videos' comments have been analyzed by researchers to reveal the hidden themes and sentiments (Madden et al., 2013; Yasmina et al., 2016). To some extent, these comments can be considered as parts of a conversation or discourse among the contributors about certain common topics (Benson, 2015; Duncum, 2013; Lindgren, 2011). Therefore, the cognitive discourse analysis method (Tenbrink, 2020) and the sentiment analysis method (Liu, 2015) were adopted to extract the thoughts and feelings (sentiments) that YouTube viewers have of the virtual figures. These thoughts and feelings represented the related impressions or images (i.e., perceptions) held by YouTube viewers about the objects and the related events. The frequency and typology of the feelings, in particular, show certain levels of interaction between the viewers and the objects and events.

In this study, each set of comments (one about the Hatsune Miku figure and the other about the Whitney Houston figure) was considered a discourse. The languages of the discourses were diverse. Nonetheless, since the researchers were only familiar with English and Japanese, the comments written in other languages were overlooked (Hatsune Miku: n = 46; Whitney Houston: n = 9). This left a sample of 260 comments for the Hatsune Miku figure and another sample of 285 comments for the Whitney Houston character.

Given the moderate sample sizes, a manual analysis method was adopted. In the first stage of the analysis, each obvious and distinct feeling was noted if it was present in one entry. Its appearances in the next entries, in the same or similar ways of wording, were also noted and triangulated to ensure its validity (Flick, 2018). In the second stage, the obvious and distinct thoughts that attach with or lead to the feelings identified earlier were coded. The triangulation was repeated in the other entries in the discourse to validate their existences. The whole analysis process was mastered in a Microsoft Excel file. Each entry was put in one horizontal line, and each feeling or thought was treated in a vertical column. Both researchers of the research group participated in the analysis, and the total agreement between them served as the reliability criterion of the analysis outcome (Kassarjian, 1977).

2.3 Findings

2.3.1 The Perception of the Hatsune Miku Figure

The perception of YouTube viewers of the Hatsune Miku figure was mostly positive (expecting and enjoying). This virtual artist was thought to be a representative of an amazing Japan, who sang a unique genre of music (a combination of tradition and modernity) and possessed a very cool image.

> Opinion 1: *"Don't worry!! Miku EXPO is in the US and Canada this year!!"*
>
> Opinion 2: *"I'm hoping that she'll turn up at the Olympics."*
>
> Opinion 3: *"Ah yes, the mixture of modern holographic technology and electronic music mixing with traditional drumming that's been around for hundreds of years. Sounds like the Japan I know and love!"*
>
> Opinion 4: *"Ending speech is super cute, the new model is really growing on me :)"*
>
> Opinion 5: *"Cool as hell."*

However, there still were a few anti-fans who expressed a negative sentiment. The reasons might be the unauthenticity or inhumanness of the figure, as well as some personal preferences.

> Opinion 6: *"Well, this is just my opinion based on my own observation so my opinion will be biased… The idol industry is selling empty dreams (in my eyes anyway). Dreams are just dreams, and whether you like it or not, you will have to wake up one day or will die with your eyes still closed and your hard-earned money is spent wastefully on something they (the fans) can NEVER touch or obtain; their (Idols) genuine and unconditional love."*

Opinion 7: "個人的には可愛くない方向にいっている気がする." [Personally, I think that she is not cute at all.]

Opinion 8: "*I hate Miku*"

2.3.2 The Perception of the Whitney Houston Figure

Differently, YouTube viewers' perception of the Whitney Houston figure was a mixture of sentiments. On the one hand, many viewers expressed the wish to "let her rest." They said that they had bad feelings about the hologram and the event, and they blamed the organizers for taking advantage of the icon's songs and images. The reasons behind the negative sentiments were the unauthenticity of the look and the music.

> Opinion 9: "*They own you. This is the price of fame now. After you die, they prop your image up like a twisted marionette. You'll dance to their tune in life. You'll dance to their tune in death. Let the dead rest in peace.*"
>
> Opinion 10: "*This is just disrespectful making money like that, just let the poor lady Rest In Peace and the ones that got to see her in person [,] let them cherish those happy lucky memories.*"
>
> Opinion 11: "*This is really distasteful. Can you all let the woman RIP [?] I do not care who, even if her family is behind it, it's all about lining their pockets. There are so many clips of WH [Whitney Houston] in concert when she was alive that you can find if people need to see her.*"
>
> Opinion 12: "*How can you say the hologram is performing? It's doing nothing. It's not connecting with the audience, improvising, covering songs... This soulless machine is further from Whitney than someone like Glennis Grace or Deborah Cox.*"

On the other hand, other viewers were sympathizing with and being excited about the event and the figure. Again, the authenticity of the look and the music were cited by several viewers as the reasons behind their positive sentiments.

> Opinion 13: "*I take your point, but honestly I would much rather see a hologram of the late great Whitney Houston than any of today's 'artists' in person.*"
>
> Opinion 14: "*Excuse me but that's so ignorant of you since every single artist's family and estate release projects to preserve their legacies and of course they also want to make money, that's why it's called show business.*"
>
> Opinion 15: "*I LOVE THIS! I need to find a show ASAP* [as soon as possible] *here in Vegas!*"
>
> Opinion 16: "*It does look like her, even though for a hologram. Maybe you just want to sabotage the thing they are organizing, but can't deny is a well-done hologram.*"
>
> Opinion 17: "*At the 0:45 second mark you can see through it. 'They're here!' I love the live vocals used with a new Higher Love remix. I must have that!!!!!*"

2.4 Discussion

Overall, viewers had different perceptions of the two figures. While the perception of the Hatsune Miku figure was almost positive, that of the Whitney Houston figure was somewhat a combat of two opposite lines of thoughts and feelings. These outcomes suggest that the interaction between the viewers and the artificial figure of Hatsune Miku might have a more positive direction than that in the case of the deceased human figure of Whitney Houston. The coolness and cuteness of the artificial artist are undoubtedly the reasons behind the favorableness of the Hatsune Miku figure (Black, 2008, 2012). Nonetheless, the ethical issue of commodifying the images and products of a dead celebrity is undeniably the cause of many opposing voices (D'Rozario et al., 2007).

In particular, a noticeable component of viewer perception was the virtual figures' authenticity. In both cases, the songs and music and the looks of the figures were the important parts of their authenticity. Thus, as Al-Emadi and Yahia (2020) and Moulard et al. (2015) have already noted, rarity and stability or consistency were doubtlessly two significant properties of celebrity authenticity. In the case of the virtual celebrities, the human-likeliness was another important feature. Moreover, the status of the celebrity (artificial or dead) might also affect both viewers' perception of the virtual figures' authenticity and their overall impression. Thus, to improve the interactions between viewers and the virtual celebrities, certain levels of human-likeliness, resemblance, rarity, and consistency must be achieved.

3 Study 2

The second study continued the examination of customers' perception of virtual celebrities by linking it with their satisfaction with the products that the celebrities endorse. However, in order to identify the relative contribution of this factor, evaluations of customers of other product attributes were taken into account. In addition, to expand the understanding, opinions of users in different markets were also considered. Hatsune Miku, again, was the focus of this study.

The search of the Hatsune Miku-related products revealed that in addition to the concerts, the image and name of Hatsune Miku have also been used in a variety of things, such as plastic figures, clothes and accessories, notebooks and cards, and video games, among others. With the former, Hatsune Miku can be the products herself. With the video games, Hatsune Miku is only a part of the product (her image and voice), and she really is an endorser. Consequently, video games were specifically targeted. It should be noted that this product is a series of rhythm games in which players can indulge themselves with songs and modules performed by Hatsune Miku and other characters, as well as modifying some elements such as the Hatsune Miku's costume.

Amazon, one of the world's largest retailers at the time of research (Statista, 2021b), was employed to search for the products and markets. The local market, undoubtedly, was Japan. On Amazon Japan, Project DIVA MEGA39's of SEGA, Crypton Future Media and Nintendo was the latest of Hatsune Miku's video game (released on 12 February 2020). This product also was the most popular one in terms of customer review number (n = 142) at the time of the search (mid-April 2020) and was selected as the local object. Next, the similar product title was searched for on the Amazon pages for other countries. On Amazon US in particular, Project DIVA MEGA39's still was a brand-new product, and the number of customer reviews was very limited (n = 5). Therefore, an older product, Project DIVA X (released on 30 August 2016) was chosen instead, given the larger number of customer reviews (n = 111).

Japan and the US were selected as the two target markets, since Japan is the country of origin of the product, while the US is the second largest video game market in the world. In 2025, the video game industry is expected to become a 300 billion USD entity (GlobalData, 2019), with China (approximately 41 billion USD in 2020), the US (approximately 37 billion USD in 2020), and Japan (approximately 19 billion USD in 2020) as the three leading markets in terms of revenue (Statista, 2021a). The geographical and cultural differences (Hofstede et al., 2010) between the two countries were also considered.

The second research question (RQ) was developed to guide this study.

RQ2. Are there any significant correlations between customers' perceptions of the attributes of the game and the virtual celebrity and their overall satisfaction with the video game in (1) Japan and (2) the US?

3.1 Literature Review

The first video game, Spacewar!, was introduced in the early 1960s in the US (Kent, 2001). From a social perspective, video games can be developed for an entertainment or an educational purpose (Boyle et al., 2016). The playing of video games can lead to both positive and negative impacts on the motivation, cognition, emotion, and behavior of the players (Ferguson, 2007; Granic et al., 2014; Kafai & Burke, 2015). From a commercial approach, video games can be used as a promotional tool (Yoo & Eastin, 2017).

Compared to other studies on video games' impacts, research on consumers' satisfaction with video games is less abundant. However, the results of previous research have confirmed that some psychological aspects of the games (the content element), such as the difficulty and fun levels and the characters' images could significantly affect players' satisfaction (Klimmt et al., 2009; Martins et al., 2009; Oliver et al., 2016). In addition, it is observed that the functional component of the games (the hardware element) and the service element of the purchase (e.g., price) might also influence the overall satisfaction (Blaszczynski et al., 2005; Nair, 2007; Sepchat et al., 2008). Moreover, research in other fields has shown that the perception of celebrity endorsers could significantly affect customers' satisfaction with the product

(Gilal et al., 2020). This may hold true with video games, especially celebrity games (Chess & Maddox, 2018).

Regarding the research methods, customer satisfaction can be measured directly through structured surveys or semi-structured interviews. Alternatively, it can be assessed indirectly through an analysis of customers' reviews about a product, a service, or a celebrity (Liang et al., 2020). In this case, both sentiment analysis and content analysis are applied to fulfill the research purpose. The sentiments extracted show the level of satisfaction that customers have with a particular attribute of a product, for example. Alternatively, they demonstrate the intensity and direction of the parasocial interaction between customers and celebrity endorsers, as discussed earlier in study 1.

3.2 Method

In this study, customers' reviews of the related products posted on the purchase platform of Amazon were used as the database. In recent years, Amazon customer reviews have been adopted in many academic studies (Heng et al., 2018; Skalicky, 2013). The use of this source of data had several merits for this study. First, the data could be collected from customers in both markets, Japan and the US, although the review languages were different (Japanese and English respectively). Second, the textual reviews could be analyzed to understand customers' evaluations of product attributes (hardware, content, service, and endorsed celebrity), while the numerical ratings can be used to represent customers' overall satisfaction with the product.

A total of 142 Amazon customer reviews about Project DIVA MEGA39's in Japan (posted between February and April 2020) and 111 reviews about Project DIVA X in the US (posted between August 2016 and April 2020) were collected in mid-April 2020. The data were put in a Microsoft Excel file and were mastered there. A coding scheme was developed based on the existing literature (Blaszczynski et al., 2005; Gilal et al., 2020; Klimmt et al., 2009; Martins et al., 2009; Nair, 2007; Oliver et al., 2016; Sepchat et al., 2008), including four product attributes: hardware, content, service, and the virtual celebrity Hatsune Miku. The data were then deductively coded (Elo & Kyngäs, 2008) using the sentiment analysis method (Liu, 2015). The coding involved the search for the identification keywords, such as adjectives, that reviewers used to express their sentiments about a product attribute. A four-point scale was used to code the sentiments: 0 = no comment, 1 = negative, 2 = either mixed or neutral, and 4 = positive. With the Japanese dataset, one researcher of the research group and an independent coder worked together. With the English dataset, both researchers of the research group undertook the coding. Total agreement between the researchers and the independent coder, again, served as the reliability measure (Kassarjian, 1977). In addition, a manual coding method was readopted given the small numbers of reviews.

After the data were coded, they were descriptively analyzed to reveal customer satisfaction with the four products attributes. In the next step, cross tabulation analysis was computed to identify the associations between attribute satisfactions and overall satisfaction (product rating). This technique was selected given the nominal nature of the coding (Morgan et al., 2004). The Phi values were then evaluated to determine the relative contribution of each product attribute to the overall satisfaction. All the analyses were supported by IBM SPSS.

3.3 Findings

3.3.1 Japanese Customers' Satisfaction with Project DIVA MEGA39's
The majority of the customers from Japan did not reveal their sentiments toward the three attributes of hardware, content, and the Hatsune Miku character. Among those who expressed their sentiments, the customers who had a negative evaluation of the hardware and the service exceeded those who had a positive evaluation. The situation of Hatsune Miku was the reverse. On the other hand, the customers especially cared about the content, with the majority having a negative evaluation. Among the four attributes, satisfaction with content had the largest impact on overall satisfaction, followed by satisfaction with service. The impacts of hardware and Hatsune Miku were insignificant (Table 1).

3.3.2 American Customers' Satisfaction with Project DIVA X
Similar to their counterparts in Japan, the majority of the American customers did not express their sentiments toward the four attributes. With those who did, the number of positive sentiments exceeded that of negative sentiments. However, the numbers of neutral evaluations were large in the cases of two attributes: content and Hatsune Miku. Regarding the association between attribute satisfaction and overall satisfaction, it was observed that content and Hatsune Miku might have some significant contributions, while hardware and service did not (Table 1).

3.4 Discussion

Consistent with the findings of previous research, this study ascertained the importance of game content (e.g., song list, features and costumes of characters, visual display, difficulty and fun) with customers' overall satisfaction (Klimmt et al., 2009; Martins et al., 2009; Oliver et al., 2016). The observation was similar in both markets, Japan and the US. On the other hand, the significance of the functional component of the game, such as handle buttons and the compatibility with other devices (Blaszczynski et al., 2005), could not be confirmed.

In addition, the contribution of the service factor to overall satisfaction (Nair, 2007) was only seen in the original market, Japan. Perhaps, the localness of the product has made the service factor another important determinant of customers' overall satisfaction. On the contrary, the imported nature of

Table 1 Sentiments toward product and product attributes

	Japan (n = 142)						America (n = 111)					
	No comment	Negative	Neutral	Positive	Phi	p	No comment	Negative	Neutral	Positive	Phi	p
Hardware (connectability, play buttons)	125	15	1	1	0.265	0.617	104	1	2	4	0.153	0.978
Content (song list, characters, costume modules, visual display, difficulty, fun, play method)	31	54	32	25	0.759	0.000	43	10	38	20	0.684	0.000
Service (shipping, distribution, price)	135	5	0	2	0.332	0.048	96	3	4	8	0.358	0.115
Hatsune Miku	129	2	0	11	0.303	0.109	78	1	23	9	0.763	0.000

a foreign product might make this factor less important with customers in the US. Instead, the perception of the virtual celebrity was the factor that could influence their overall satisfaction (Gilal et al., 2020). This pattern, interestingly, was only observed in the American market.

In both cases, customers' sentimental interaction with the endorsed virtual figure was displayed less frequently (in other words, less intense) than these with the functional attributes of the games themselves. Customers in Japan showed more positive sentiments toward Hatsune Miku, while their counterparts in the US expressed more neutral sentiments toward this figure. The contribution of customer sentiments with the virtual figure to their overall satisfaction was insignificant in Japan probably due to the advancement of this particular game in this market, and thus, the overfamiliarity or boredom with the figure (Holl, 2019; Hsu & McDonald, 2002). The time and duration of the reviews (two months right after the release of the game) might also affect this outcome. On the contrary, the similar association was significant in the US since the game version under study was older. As Clements and Ohashi (2005) noticed, the effect of a marketing tactic will differ across different stages of a product's life cycle. Perhaps the power of the Hatsune Miku figure was waning in the original Japanese market, thus, the introduction and inclusion of the new figures or themes should be taken into account. However, due to the differences in product life cycles and probably in cultural backgrounds (Alsaleh et al., 2019), the appeal of the Hatsune Miku figure was still noticeable in the US, and the continuation of its use might be considered.

4 General Discussion

The celebrity-related marketing activities have employed a variety of public figures, including both living and dead humans and animals. This practice does not stop here but is expanding to include artificial figures as a new form or generation of celebrities (Guga, 2015; Prior, 2018). In certain cases, the artificial characters such as Hatsune Miku can effectively replace the more traditional celebrity figures in marketing campaigns.

Despite their artificiality, many customers treat the virtual celebrity figures as if they are real persons with distinct characteristics. However, since customer preferences are personal issues, some figures may be preferred while others may be disliked. A character, therefore, is only suitable with a certain segment of customers or a certain category of products, not with the market as a whole.

Future use of virtual celebrities as endorsers or as products themselves should carefully take into account this suitability element. In particular, the employment of a virtual dead celebrity figure on a large commercial scale should conscientiously consider the ethical aspect of this operation. While a certain group of fans may welcome this type of comeback, a larger group of the public may be against this idea. A societal marketing approach (Crane & Desmond, 2002), where the expectations and benefits of the general public and the society at large are recognized and respected, is appropriate in this case. In addition, the use of a virtual artificial celebrity should take into account the life cycle of the involved product and that of the celebrity themselves (Erdogan et al., 2001). If the virtual celebrity lost their appeal through time, a change of endorser might be necessary to maintain or boost the popularity of the product, in general, and the parasocial interaction between the customers and the celebrity, in particular.

5   Conclusion

The focus of this chapter was to explore the virtual celebrity phenomenon in the entertainment industry in recent years. By analyzing YouTube viewers' comments about two virtual celebrities and their music events, the first study found that viewer perception was a combination of both the positive and negative sentiments. The perceived authenticity of the virtual figures played an important part in this impression. In addition, by assessing Amazon customers' reviews about a video game endorsed by one of the virtual celebrities, the second study found that the sentiments dedicated to the figure could have some impact on customers' overall satisfaction. However, this pattern was only observed in a foreign market, where the video game was an imported product, and an older version of the game was investigated. In summary, both studies suggested that the sentiments toward, and thus, the parasocial interaction with a virtual celebrity of the viewers and customers varied across the specific virtual celebrity types (artificial figure and dead human figure), the markets where the products are sold, and probably the life cycles of the products.

Nonetheless, due to its exploratory nature, this chapter could not avoid some limitations. First, the comments about the virtual celebrities and their events were mostly written by viewers of YouTube commercial videos. The contribution of the actual audiences was largely missing. As a result, the perception was only limited to a small number of unrepresentative participants. Second, the role of the perceived image of the virtual celebrity was only verified in the case of customer satisfaction. Its importance with customers' purchase intention and other variables (e.g., attachment and motivation) was overlooked. Third, the impacts of the personal and environmental factors (e.g., biological sex, income, education, and religion), if there were any (Edwards & La Ferle, 2009; Suki, 2014), could not be identified and confirmed. The reason was attributed to the missing of such information on the review platforms.

Considering these limitations and other observations, the following directions could be proposed for future research. First, direct interviews and surveys with a larger audience of virtual celebrities could be undertaken to thoroughly examine fans and anti-fans' motivation, perception, attachment, and other perceptual and behavioral phenomena. Second, a segmentation of the public's attitude toward virtual celebrities, especially these of dead figures, could be done to identify the appropriate segment of potential customers for the products and services that they endorse. Third, the life cycle of a virtual celebrity, as well as the strategies to rejuvenate and reemploy unpopular virtual figures, could also be discussed. Findings of these studies will help expand the understanding about virtual celebrities, as well as to support the related businesses in the future.

REFERENCES

Adamo-Villani, N., Lestina, J., & Anasingaraju, S. (2015). Does character's visual style affect viewer's perception of signing avatars? In G. Vincenti, A. Bucciero, & C. Vaz de Carvalho (Eds.), *E-Learning, e-education, and online training. eLEOT 2015. Lecture Notes of the Institute for Computer Sciences, Social Informatics and Telecommunications Engineering, 160*, 1–8. Springer.

Al-Emadi, F. A., & Yahia, I. B. (2020). Ordinary celebrities related criteria to harvest fame and influence on social media. *Journal of Research in Interactive Marketing, 14*(2), 195–213. https://doi.org/10.1108/JRIM-02-2018-0031

Alsaleh, D. A., Elliott, M. T., Fu, F. Q., & Thakur, R. (2019). Cross-cultural differences in the adoption of social media. *Journal of Research in Interactive Marketing, 13*(1), 119–140. https://doi.org/10.1108/JRIM-10-2017-0092

Annett, S. (2015). What can a vocaloid do? The kyara as body without organs. *Mechademia: Second Arc, 10*, 163–177. https://doi.org/10.5749/mech.10.2015.0163

Anson, S. (2014). Hologram images and the entertainment industry: New legal territory? *Washington Journal of Law, Technology & Arts, 10*(2), 109–123.

Benson, P. (2015). YouTube as text: Spoken interaction analysis and digital discourse. In R. H. Jones, A. Chik, & C. A. Hafner (Eds.), *Discourse and digital practices. Doing discourse analysis in the digital age* (pp. 81–96). Routledge.

Bergkvist, L., Hjalmarson, H., & Mägi, A. W. (2016). A new model of how celebrity endorsements work: Attitude toward the endorsement as a mediator of celebrity source and endorsement effects. *International Journal of Advertising, 35*(2), 171–184. https://doi.org/10.1080/02650487.2015.1024384

Black, D. (2008). The virtual ideal: Virtual idols, cute technology and unclean biology. *Continuum, 22*(1), 37–50. https://doi.org/10.1080/10304310701642048

Black, D. (2012). The virtual idol: Producing and consuming digital femininity. In P. W. Galbraith & J. G. Karlin (Eds.), *Culture, Idols and Celebrity in Japanese Media* (pp. 209–228). Palgrave Macmillan.

Blaszczynski, A., Sharpe, L., Walker, M., Shannon, K., & Coughlan, M.-J. (2005). Structural characteristics of electronic gaming machines and satisfaction of play among recreational and problem gamblers. *International Gambling Studies, 5*(2), 187–198. https://doi.org/10.1080/14459790500303378

Boyle, E. A., Hainey, T., Connolly, T. M., Gray, G., Earp, J., Ott, M., Lim, T., Ninaus, M., Ribeiro, C., & Pereira, J. (2016). An update to the systematic literature review of empirical evidence of the impacts and outcomes of computer games and serious games. *Computers & Education, 94*, 178–192. https://doi.org/10.1016/j.compedu.2015.11.003

Chess, S., & Maddox, J. (2018). Kim Kardashian is my new BFF: Video games and the looking glass celebrity. *Popular Communication, 16*(3), 196–210. https://doi.org/10.1080/15405702.2017.1408113

Chung, K. Y., Derdenger, T. P., & Srinivasan, K. (2013). Economic value of celebrity endorsements: Tiger Woods' impact on sales of Nike golf balls. *Marketing Science*, *32*(2), 271–293. https://doi.org/10.1287/mksc.1120.0760

Clements, M. T., & Ohashi, H. (2005). Indirect network effects and the product cycle: Video games in the U.S., 1994–2002. *Journal of Industrial Economics*, *53*(4), 515–542. https://doi.org/10.1111/j.1467-6451.2005.00268.x

Crane, A., & Desmond, J. (2002). Societal marketing and morality. *European Journal of Marketing*, *36*(5–6), 548–569. https://doi.org/10.1108/03090560210423014

Dichter, E. (1985). What's in an image. *Journal of Consumer Marketing*, *2*(1), 75–81. https://doi.org/10.1108/eb038824

Drenten, J., & Brooks, G. (2020). Celebrity 2.0: Lil Miquela and the rise of a virtual star system. *Feminist Media Studies*, *20*(8), 1319–1323. https://doi.org/10.1080/14680777.2020.1830927

D'Rozario, D. (2016). The market for 'Delebs' (dead celebrities): A revenue analysis. *Journal of Customer Behaviour*, *15*(4), 395–414. https://doi.org/10.1362/147539216X14811340257178

D'Rozario, D., Petty, R. D., Taylor, L. C., & Bryant, F. K. (2007). The use of images of dead celebrities in advertising - History, growth factors, theory, legality, ethics and recommendations. In G. Fitzsimons, & V. Morwitz (Eds.), *Advances in consumer research*, *34*, 446–450. Association for Consumer Research.

Duncum, P. (2013). Creativity as conversation in the interactive audience culture of YouTube. *Visual Inquiry*, *3*(3), 115–125. https://doi.org/10.1386/vi.3.3.263_1

Edwards, S. M., & La Ferle, C. (2009). Does gender impact the perception of negative information related to celebrity endorsers? *Journal of Promotion Management*, *15*(1–2), 22–35. https://doi.org/10.1080/10496490902837940

Elo, S., & Kyngäs, H. (2008). The qualitative content analysis process. *Journal of Advanced Nursing*, *62*(1), 107–115. https://doi.org/10.1111/j.1365-2648.2007.04569.x

Erdogan, B. Z., Baker, M. J., & Tagg, S. (2001). Selecting celebrity endorsers: The practitioner's perspective. *Journal of Advertising Research*, *41*(3), 39–48. https://doi.org/10.2501/JAR-41-3-39-48

Feng, S., Song, K., Wang, D., Gao, W., & Zhang, Y. (2021). InterSentiment: Combining deep neural models on interaction and sentiment for review rating prediction. *International Journal of Machine Learning and Cybernetics*, *12*, 477–488. https://doi.org/10.1007/s13042-020-01181-9

Ferguson, C. J. (2007). The good, the bad and the ugly: A meta-analytic review of positive and negative effects of violent video games. *Psychiatric Quarterly*, *78*, 309–316. https://doi.org/10.1007/s11126-007-9056-9

Flick, U. (2018). *Doing tiangulation and mixed methods*. SAGE.

Fox, A. K., Bacile, T. J., Nakhata, C., & Weible, A. (2018). Selfie-marketing: Exploring narcissism and self-concept in visual user-generated content on social media. *Journal of Consumer Marketing*, *35*(1), 11–21. https://doi.org/10.1108/JCM-03-2016-1752

Gilal, F. G., Paul, J., Gilal, N. G., & Gilal, R. G. (2020). Celebrity endorsement and brand passion among air travelers: Theory and evidence. *International Journal of Hospitality Management*, *85*, 102347. https://doi.org/10.1016/j.ijhm.2019.102347

Giles, D. C. (2002). Parasocial interaction: A review of the literature and a model for future research. *Media Psychology, 4*(3), 279–305. https://doi.org/10.1207/S1532785XMEP0403_04

GlobalData. (2019, April). *Video games – Thematic research*. Retrieved April 24, 2020, from GlobalData: https://store.globaldata.com/report/gdtmt-tr-s212--video-games-thematic-research/

Granic, I., Lobel, A., & Engels, R.C.-M.-E. (2014). The benefits of playing video games. *American Psychologist, 69*(1), 66–78. https://doi.org/10.1037/a0034857

Guga, J. (2015). Virtual idol Hatsune Miku. In A. Brooks, E. Ayiter, & O. Yazicigil (Eds.), *Arts and technology. ArtsIT 2014. Lecture notes of the Institute for Computer sciences, social informatics and telecommunications engineering* (pp. 36–44). Springer.

Halonen-Knight, E., & Hurmerinta, L. (2010). Who endorses whom? Meanings transfer in celebrity endorsement. *Journal of Product & Brand Management, 19*(6), 452–460. https://doi.org/10.1108/10610421011085767

Hansen, P. (2013). Urban Japan's "fuzzy" new families: Affect and embodiment in dog–human relationships. *Asian Anthropology, 12*(2), 83–103. https://doi.org/10.1080/1683478X.2013.852718

Heise, D. R. (2006). Sentiment formation in social interaction. In K. A. McClelland & T. J. Fararo (Eds.), *Purpose, meaning, and action* (pp. 189–211). Palgrave Macmillan.

Heng, Y., Gao, Z., Jiang, Y., & Chen, X. (2018). Exploring hidden factors behind online food shopping from Amazon reviews: A topic mining approach. *Journal of Retailing and Consumer Services, 42*, 161–168. https://doi.org/10.1016/j.jretconser.2018.02.006

Hofstede, G., Hofstede, G. J., & Monkov, M. (2010). *Cultures and organizations - Software of the mind. Intercultural cooperation and its importance for survival*. McGraw Hill.

Holl, J. (2019). "The wonder of his time": Richard Tarlton and the dynamics of early modern theatrical celebrity. *Historical Social Research, 32*(Supplement: Celebrity's histories: Case studies & critical perspectives), 58–82. https://doi.org/10.12759/hsr.suppl.32.2019.58-82

Hsu, C.-K., & McDonald, D. (2002). An examination on multiple celebrity endorsers in advertising. *Journal of Product & Brand Management, 11*(1), 19–29. https://doi.org/10.1108/10610420210419522

Hudak, K. C. (2014). A phantasmic experience: Narrative connection of dead celebrities in advertisements. *Culture, Theory and Critique, 55*(3), 383–400. https://doi.org/10.1080/14735784.2014.880933

Johnston, S. F. (2008). A cultural history of the hologram. *Leonardo, 41*(3), 223–229. https://doi.org/10.1162/leon.2008.41.3.223

Kafai, Y. B., & Burke, Q. (2015). Constructionist gaming: Understanding the benefits of making games for learning. *Educational Psychologist, 50*(4), 313–334. https://doi.org/10.1080/00461520.2015.1124022

Kassarjian, H. H. (1977). Content analysis in consumer research. *Journal of Consumer Research, 4*(1), 8–18. https://doi.org/10.1086/208674

Kent, S. L. (2001). *The ultimate history of video games: From Pong to Pokémon and beyond - The story behind the craze that touched our lives and changed the world*. Prima Publishing.

Khan, M. S.-S., Rafa, S. R., Abir, A.-E. H., & Das, A. K. (2021). Sentiment analysis on Bengali facebook comments to predict fan's emotions towards a celebrity. *Journal of Engineering Advancements, 2*(3), 118–124. https://doi.org/10.38032/jea.2021.03.001

Kim, S. S., Lee, J., & Prideaux, B. (2014). Effect of celebrity endorsement on tourists' perception of corporate image, corporate credibility and corporate loyalty. *International Journal of Hospitality Management, 37*, 131–145. https://doi.org/10.1016/j.ijhm.2013.11.003

Klimmt, C., Blake, C., Hefner, D., Vorderer, P., & Roth, C. (2009). Player performance, satisfaction, and video game enjoyment. In S. Natkin, & J. Dupire (Eds.), *Entertainment Computing – ICEC 2009. ICEC 2009. Lecture Notes in Computer Science, 5709*, 1–12. Springer.

Knittel, C. R., & Stango, V. (2014). Celebrity endorsements, firm value, and reputation risk: Evidence from the Tiger Woods scandal. *Management Science, 60*(1), 21–37. https://doi.org/10.1287/mnsc.2013.1749

Liang, D., Dai, Z., Wang, M., & Li, J. (2020). Web celebrity shop assessment and improvement based on online review with probabilistic linguistic term sets by using sentiment analysis and fuzzy cognitive map. *Fuzzy Optimization and Decision Making, 19*, 561–586. https://doi.org/10.1007/s10700-020-09327-8

Lindgren, S. (2011). YouTube gunmen? Mapping participatory media discourse on school shooting videos. *Media, Culture & Society, 33*(1), 123–136. https://doi.org/10.1177/0163443710386527

Liu, B. (2015). *Sentiment analysis: Mining opinions, sentiments, and emotions*. Cambridge University Press.

Liu, X., Burns, A. C., & Hou, Y. (2017). An investigation of brand-related user-generated content on Twitter. *Journal of Advertising, 46*(2), 236–247. https://doi.org/10.1080/00913367.2017.1297273

Madden, A., Ruthven, I., & McMenemy, D. (2013). A classification scheme for content analyses of YouTube video comments. *Journal of Documentation, 69*(5), 693–714. https://doi.org/10.1108/JD-06-2012-0078

Martins, N., Williams, D. C., Harrison, K., & Ratan, R. A. (2009). A content analysis of female body imagery in video games. *Sex Roles, 61*, 824. https://doi.org/10.1007/s11199-009-9682-9

Morgan, G. A., Leech, N. L., Gloeckner, G. W., & Barret, K. C. (2004). *SPSS for introductory statistics – Use and interpretation* (2nd ed.). Lawrence Erlbaum Associates.

Moulard, J. G., Garrity, C. P., & Rice, D. H. (2015). What makes a human brand authentic? Identifying the antecedents of celebrity authenticity. *Psychology & Marketing, 32*(2), 173–186. https://doi.org/10.1002/mar.20771

Nair, H. (2007). Intertemporal price discrimination with forward-looking consumers: Application to the US market for console video-games. *Quantitative Marketing and Economics, 5*, 239–292. https://doi.org/10.1007/s11129-007-9026-4

Oliver, M. B., Bowman, N. D., Woolley, J. K., Rogers, R., Sherrick, B. I., & Chung, M.-Y. (2016). Video games as meaningful entertainment experiences. *Psychology of Popular Media Culture, 5*(4), 390–405. https://doi.org/10.1037/ppm0000066

Paul, J., & Bhakar, S. (2018). Does celebrity image congruence influences brand attitude and purchase intention? *Journal of Promotion Management, 24*(2), 153–177. https://doi.org/10.1080/10496491.2017.1360826

Penfold-Mounce, R., & Penfold-Mounce, R. (2018). Posthumous careers of celebrities. In R. Penfold-Mounce (Ed.), *Death, the Dead and Popular Culture* (pp. 9–39). Bingley.

Pentz, R. D., Cohen, C. B., Wicclair, M., DeVita, M. A., Flamm, A. L., Youngner, S. J., Hamric, A., McCabe, M. S., Glover, J. J., Kittiko, W. J., Kinlaw, K., Keller, J., Asch, A., Kavanagh, J. J., & Arap, W. (2005). Ethics guidelines for research with the recently dead. *Nature Medicine, 11*, 1145–1149. https://doi.org/10.1038/nm1105-1145

Petty, R. D., & D'Rozario, D. (2009). The use of dead celebrities in advertising and marketing: Balancing interests in the right of publicity. *Journal of Advertising, 38*(4), 37–49. https://doi.org/10.2753/JOA0091-3367380403

Pinem, F. J., Andreswari, R., & Hasibuan, M. A. (2018). Sentiment analysis to measure celebrity endorsement's effect using support vector machine algorithm. *Proceedings of the 5th International Conference on Electrical Engineering, Computer Science and Informatics* (pp. 690–695). IEEE.

Pradhan, D., Duraipandian, I., & Sethi, D. (2016). Celebrity endorsement: How celebrity–brand–user personality congruence affects brand attitude and purchase intention. *Journal of Marketing Communications, 22*(5), 456–473. https://doi.org/10.1080/13527266.2014.914561

Prieto, P., Puglesi, C., Borràs-Comes, J., Arroyo, E., & Blat, J. (2015). Exploring the contribution of prosody and gesture to the perception of focus using an animated agent. *Journal of Phonetics, 49*, 41–54. https://doi.org/10.1016/j.wocn.2014.10.005

Prior, N. (2018). On vocal assemblages: From Edison to Miku. *Contemporary Music Review, 37*(5–6), 488–506. https://doi.org/10.1080/07494467.2017.1402467

Ross, S. M., & Labrecque, L. I. (2018). Does a hologram give an encore? Authenticity in mixed reality: An abstract. In N. Krey, & P. Rossi (Eds.), *Back to the future: Using marketing basics to provide customer value. AMSAC 2017. Developments in Marketing Science: Proceedings of the Academy of Marketing Science* (pp. 273–274). Springer.

Rowell, D. (2019, October 30). *The spectacular, strange rise of music holograms*. Retrieved April 23, 2020, from The Washington Post Magazin: https://www.washingtonpost.com/magazine/2019/10/30/dead-musicians-are-taking-stage-again-hologram-form-is-this-kind-encore-we-really-want/?arc404=true

Sepchat, A., Descarpentries, S., Monmarché, N., & Slimane, M. (2008). MP3 players and audio games: An alternative to portable video games console for visually impaired players. In K. Miesenberger, J. Klaus, W. Zagler, & A. Karshmer (Eds.), *Computers Helping People with Special Needs. ICCHP 2008. Lecture Notes in Computer Science, vol 5105* (pp. 553–560). Springer.

Skalicky, S. (2013). Was this analysis helpful? A genre analysis of the Amazon.com discourse community and its "most helpful" product reviews. *Discourse, Context & Media, 2*(2), 84–93. https://doi.org/10.1016/j.dcm.2013.04.001

Statista. (2021a). *Leading gaming markets worldwide in 2020, by gaming revenue*. Retrieved August 04, 2021a, from Statista: https://www.statista.com/statistics/308454/gaming-revenue-countries/

Statista. (2021b). *Leading retailers worldwide in 2019, by retail revenue*. Retrieved August 04, 2021b, from Statista: https://www.statista.com/statistics/266595/leading-retailers-worldwide-based-on-revenue/

Suki, N. M. (2014). Does celebrity credibility influence Muslim and non-Muslim consumers' attitudes toward brands and purchase intention? *Journal of Islamic Marketing*, 5(2), 227–240. https://doi.org/10.1108/JIMA-04-2013-0024

Tenbrink, T. (2020). *Cognitive discourse analysis: An introduction*. Cambridge University Press.

Wang, C. L. (2021). New frontiers and future directions in interactive marketing: Inaugural editorial. *Journal of Research in Interactive Marketing*, 15(1), 1–9. https://doi.org/10.1108/JRIM-03-2021-270

Wang, S. W., Kao, G.H.-Y., & Ngamsiriudom, W. (2017). Consumers' attitude of endorser credibility, brand and intention with respect to celebrity endorsement of the airline sector. *Journal of Air Transport Management*, 60, 10–17. https://doi.org/10.1016/j.jairtraman.2016.12.007

Wilkinson, T. M. (2002). Last rights: The ethics of research on the dead. *Journal of Applied Philosophy*, 19(1), 31–41. https://doi.org/10.1111/1468-5930.00202

Yasmina, D., Hajar, M., & Hassan, A. M. (2016). Using YouTube comments for text-based emotion recognition. *Procedia Computer Science*, 83, 292–299. https://doi.org/10.1016/j.procs.2016.04.128

Yoo, S.-C., & Eastin, M. S. (2017). Contextual advertising in games: Impacts of game context on a player's memory and evaluation of brands in video games. *Journal of Marketing Communications*, 23(6), 614–631. https://doi.org/10.1080/13527266.2016.1155074

Zaborowski, R. (2016). Hatsune Miku and Japanese virtual idols. In S. Whiteley & S. Rambarran (Eds.), *The Oxford handbook of music and virtuality* (pp. 111–128). Oxford University Press.

Zell, E., Aliaga, C., Jarabo, A., Zibrek, K., Gutierrez, D., McDonnell, R., & Botsch, M. (2015). To stylize or not to stylize?: The effect of shape and material stylization on the perception of computer-generated faces. *ACM Transactions on Graphics*, 34(6), Article 184. https://doi.org/10.1145/2816795.2818126

CHAPTER 18

The Conceptualization of "Presence" in Interactive Marketing: A Systematic Review of 30 Years of Literature

Chen Chen, Xiaohan Hu, and Jacob T. Fisher

1 Introduction

Contemporary interactive marketing has, in many ways, moved beyond traditional one-way communication, evolving into approaches aimed at bi-directional value creation and mutual-influence processes (Wang, 2021). This evolution calls for active consumer engagement, participation, and connection, often with the help of immersive and interactive media experiences (Flavián et al., 2019; Wang, 2021). Technologies, such as artificial intelligence (AI), virtual reality (VR), and augmented reality (AR), have fueled consumers' experiences with embodied and immersive virtual components, producing a variety of opportunities for brand-consumer connections (Flavian et al., 2019; Tsai et al., 2020). The forms of immersive interactive media experiences available to marketers and consumers have changed as technology has advanced, developing from interactive websites (Coyle & Thorson, 2001), to playable in-game advertising (Besharat et al., 2013), to 360-degree videos (Feng, 2018), virtual reality (Jang et al., 2019), and augmented reality (Tsai et al., 2020). As these

---

C. Chen · X. Hu · J. T. Fisher (✉)
University of Illinois at Urbana-Champaign, Champaign, IL, USA
e-mail: jtfisher@illinois.edu

C. Chen
e-mail: chenc4@illinois.edu

X. Hu
e-mail: xhu33@illinois.edu

experiences have become more central in the modern marketing mix, research has brought attention to the novel processes involved (Bao & Wang, 2021; Tsai et al., 2021). A particularly central process highlighted within this body of literature is *presence*, the sense of "being there" in the mediated environment (Heeter, 1992; Kim et al., 2021; Steuer, 1992).

As research on presence has developed over the last several decades, the definition of presence has also evolved, incorporating a number of affective and cognitive processes, motivational factors, and behavioral consequences (Schubert et al., 2001). This expanding conceptual definition of presence is paralleled in many ways by the expanding set of fields and contexts in which presence has been investigated. These developments have produced a large and fruitful body of literature but have also created growing ambiguity as to the exact nature of presence as a theoretical construct and its role in interactive marketing. Failing to thoroughly review the literature may prevent a comprehensive understanding of the presence and limit the utility of the theory within the confines of interactive marketing (DeAndrea & Holbert, 2017; Flanagin, 2020).

To fill this gap, the authors herein report results from a systematic review of research investigating presence in immersive experiences, with a focus on the interactive marketing context. This review provides insights into the conceptual development of presence over the last several decades, identifies the most common definitions of presence employed in the interactive marketing literature, and summarizes its technological antecedents, associated processes, and subdimensions, suggesting key components in a conceptual framework of presence. In addition, the chapter highlights areas in which presence has been relatively well investigated and points out domains in which presence is comparatively understudied. In doing so, this chapter provides further clarity as to how presence in the immersive experience fuels interactive marketing and provides a roadmap for future research in this rapidly developing area.

2 Presence in Interactive Marketing

The earliest use of "presence" appears in 1980, describing the extent to which a user feels "transported" via a virtual "teleporting system" (a general term for remote control tools). Shortly thereafter, another popular definition of presence was developed by Steuer (1992), describing presence as a sense of "being there" in a mediated environment (Klein, 2003; Li et al., 2002; Lim & Childs, 2020; Nelson et al., 2006; Shen et al., 2020; Song & Zinkhan, 2008; Wang & Yao, 2020). Meanwhile, Sheridan (1992) proposed a similar conceptualization of presence, denoting it as a subjective sensation influenced by technological antecedents, such as the extent of sensory information provided by the system. Following that, across the subsequent 30 years of development, researchers have elaborated on the definition of presence along with its antecedents, associated processes, and subcomponents (Cummings & Bailenson, 2016; Lee, 2004; Lessiter et al., 2001; Lombard & Ditton, 1997; Witmer & Singer,

1998). For instance, Lee (2004) proposed three subcomponents of presence, physical presence, social presence, and self-presence. Wirth et al. (2007) elaborated on the processes of presence and proposed a two-step model, including taking perceptual cues to form a mental model of the space and projecting oneself into the virtual world.

However, the definitions of presence and its subcomponents have varied across studies, creating ambiguities as researchers seek to understand presence in the interactive marketing (Cummings & Bailenson, 2016; Kim & Biocca, 1997; Lombard & Ditton, 1997; Schubert et al., 2001; Wirth et al., 2007; Witmer & Singer, 1998). For instance, some research has suggested that presence is one dimension of immersion (Deng et al., 2020; Grinberg et al., 2014; Naul & Liu, 2020) or an indication that immersion has been experienced (Georgiou et al., 2019; Gromer et al., 2018). Cummings and Bailenson's (2016) meta-analysis further added evidence supporting this view. On the other hand, other researchers have suggested that immersion is a subcomponent of presence (Bulu, 2012; Whitbred et al., 2010). These variations happen partially due to inconsistent definitions of presence.

Research challenges have also come from the growing body of literature investigating the consequences of presence. One of the most frequently examined consequences of presence is positive affective responses. For instance, Cowan and Ketron (2019) proposed that presence potentially explains the effect of imagination on consumers' positive affective responses (i.e., satisfaction) and behaviors (i.e., purchasing) when a person has higher involvement with the product or brand. Kim et al. (2022) found that VR tourism increased spatial presence. The experience of presence also mediated the effect of VR on participants' intention to travel and willingness to pay to do so.

In contrast, potentially negative consequences of presence, such as negative feelings coming from branded experience and side effects of the system design, may receive less attention (Feng, 2018; Li et al., 2002). In the meantime, evidence has mounted from other fields suggesting that a stronger sense of presence may also trigger and amplify negative emotions, such as anger (Miyahira et al., 2010; van Gelder et al., 2019), anxiety (Renaud, 2002), and fear (Gromer et al., 2018). There have also been concerns related to the role of presence in system-induced nausea, sickness, and disorientation (Baños et al., 2004; Chowdhury et al., 2017; Ling et al., 2013). Given that research has shown that the positive effect of presence on consumers' product attitude and purchase intention can only be maximized when individuals experience little cybersickness, more research is likely needed to investigate how these negative feelings may temper the role of presence in positive outcomes (Breves & Dodel, 2021).

In addition to investigating affective outcomes of presence, more attention may be needed to resolve conflicting evidence as to the relationship between the experience of presence and subsequent memory related to the experience. In early research on presence, researchers found a positive correlation between consumers' sense of presence and product knowledge retention

(Daugherty et al., 2008; Keng & Lin, 2006). For example, in Keng and Lin (2006), participants had better recognition results when they saw vivid visual imagery and had a moderate sense of presence. However, recent studies added more evidence of a negative correlation between the presence and memory retention (Bailey et al., 2012; Chen & Yao, 2022; Rupp et al., 2016). For instance, Barreda-Ángeles et al. (2021) found that viewing 360° videos of news stories on immersive VR devices impaired users' cognitive information processing. Mixed findings and unclear reasons may result in inaccurate hypothesis-generating.

Finally, while there have been review attempts made on other similar concepts (e.g., social presence: Oh et al., 2018; online presence: Cioppi et al., 2019), there is as yet no existing systematic review focused on the conceptual development and empirical investigations of presence in the field of interactive marketing. For instance, Cioppi et al. (2019) conducted a systematic literature review on online presence, focusing on the users' sense of presence in an online environment, such as websites. Oh et al. (2018) conducted a systematic review of social presence and summarized its conceptual definitions and antecedents. In their review, social presence is defined as one sub-dimension of presence. Their scope of the research includes areas that are afield from interactive marketing experiences, limiting its generalizability to presence research specifically within the domain of interactive marketing.

Consequently, a more focused systematic review of presence within the interactive marketing literature is necessary to reveal the complete theoretical framework and highlight inconsistent findings and overlooked areas concerning the role of presence in interactive marketing. The output of which facilitates the construction of a firmer foundation for research progress. This systematic review centered around three primary research questions:

RQ1. How has presence been conceptualized within the interactive marketing literature?

RQ2. What has interactive marketing research revealed about the nature of presence, along with its antecedents, correlates, and outcomes?

RQ3. What are the areas in which there exists the most research potential for future development of presence in interactive marketing?

3 Method

3.1 Journal and Search String

This systematic review is a component of a broader systematic review project, which includes journal and conference papers published between the 1990s to 2020s in the following databases: EBSCO Communication Source, Scopus, and IEEE. The search results from these databases include subjects like business and management, communication, computer-mediated communication, and social psychology. To determine which specific journals were considered,

Table 1 Presence Search Strings

Logic	Keywords	Field
	"immersion" OR "immersive" OR "immersing" OR "immerse" OR "immersed"	In Title OR Abstract OR Keywords
AND	telepresence OR telepresence OR "Spatial Immersion" OR "Spatial presence" OR presence	
AND	computer OR laptop OR "media" OR internet OR online OR "social media" OR "social network" OR "social networks" OR phone OR phones OR smartphone OR smartphones OR mobile OR "mobile phone" OR "mobile phones" OR "Mobile phones" OR game OR gaming OR games OR "virtual reality" OR "VR" OR "augmented reality" OR "AR" OR "artificial intelligence" OR "AI" OR "360- degree video" OR "360-degree video" OR "CAVE" OR "3D"	

we consulted the Scopus Scientific Journal Rankings (SCImago), filtering the list of candidate journals based on whether the journal was within the domain of "marketing," "interactive marketing," "advertising," or "interactive advertising." To ensure that no journals within the area of interactive marketing were overlooked, we further supplemented the search results with a follow-up search within a list of known flagship journals in the field of interactive marketing, including *Journal of Marketing*, *Journal of Consumer Research*, *Journal of Interactive Marketing*, *Journal of Research in Interactive Marketing*, *Journal of Marketing Communications*, *Journal of Advertising*, and *Journal of Interactive Advertising*. Upon finalizing the list of included journals, an initial search was conducted using a query string designed to capture articles that consider the concept of presence while excluding articles that do not specifically pertain to interactive marketing. Table 1 below shows a complete description of the search string employed in this study.

3.2 Inclusion and Filtering Criteria

The initial search in the systematic review, combined with the follow-up search in the seven journals mentioned above produced a total of 296 papers without duplications. Filtering of resultant articles was conducted following PRISMA guidelines (Moher et al., 2009; Page et al., 2021). Two coders were trained based on a codebook developed for this study and completed three rounds of coding practice. After reaching acceptable intercoder reliability ($\kappa = 0.734$, $p < 0.0001$; see Peat et al., 2020, p. 228), the coders independently coded the rest of the papers. Coders reviewed the title and abstract of each paper to determine its relevance to both the concept of presence and the interactive marketing context. This resulted in a list of 68 papers that were passed onto the next stage of filtering.

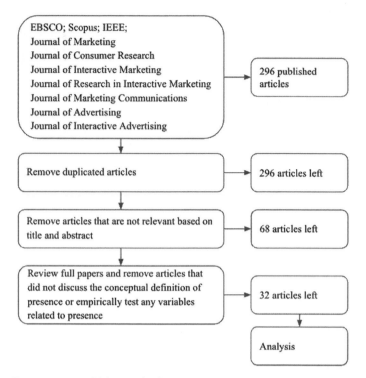

Fig. 1 Document acquisition and selection process

Coders then reviewed the full text for each manuscript, taking notes on the conceptual definition of presence proffered in the manuscript and the empirical investigation(s) that were conducted, removing articles that did not either: (a) discuss the conceptual definition of presence or, (b) empirically test any variables related to presence. For instance, if the paper discussed relevant concepts, such as social presence, immersion, engagement, or involvement, without explicitly conceptually discussing or empirically testing "presence," the paper was removed from further analysis. This resulted in a final set of 32 journal articles included in the full systematic review (Fig. 1).

4 Results

4.1 Conceptual Definitions of Presence and Developments in Interactive Marketing

Several popular definitions of presence were found within the interactive marketing literature. The most commonly cited definition is Steuer's (1992) description of presence as simply "a sense of being there." This definition has been cited 15 times (e.g., Choi et al., 2001; Klein, 2003; Li et al., 2002; Lim & Childs, 2020; Nelson et al., 2006; Shen et al., 2020; Song & Zinkhan,

2008; Wang & Yao, 2020). Lombard and Ditton (1997) defined presence as the "perceptual illusion of non-mediation." This definition has been cited by eight papers, making it the second most well-cited (e.g., Jeandrain, 2001; Nicovich, 2005; Yung et al., 2020). Following that, Kim and Biocca (1997) used the metaphorical term "being transported" to denote presence as an unstable state. Their empirical findings suggested two dimensions of presence, *arrival,* and *departure.* This definition has been cited six times (e.g., Besharat et al., 2013; Nelson et al., 2006). Witmer and Singer (1998) defined presence as the "subjective experience of being in one place when one is physically in another." This definition has been cited five times (Jang et al., 2019; Li et al., 2002; Nelson et al., 2006; see Table 2 for a summary of all conceptual definitions of presence that have been cited in the interactive marketing literature). The conceptualization of presence falls within three themes, (1) technological antecedents, (2) subdimensions, and (3) cognitive processes, jointly presenting a comprehensive theoretical framework of presence.

4.1.1 Technological Antecedents
Early conceptualization of presence focused primarily on its technological antecedents. The earliest definition of presence cited in interactive marketing comes from Minsky (1980), describing feelings that a human operator might experience when interacting through a teleoperator system. This definition has been cited three times (Banerjee & Longstreet, 2016; Papagiannidis et al., 2017; Shen et al., 2020). Other early definitions of presence also conceptualize it as a psychological state but primarily describe presence in terms of the features of technological systems that are theorized to relate to it (Sheridan, 1992; Steuer, 1992). For instance, Sheridan (1992) proposed that presence is a subjective sensation, the determinants of which are: (a) the extent of sensory information that is provided, (b) control in relation to sensors of the environment, and (c) ability to modify the physical environment. These three determinants are technological properties of the system rather than human abilities or other cognitive/affective variables.

Likewise, Steuer (1992) also proposes that technological features drive the experience of presence. Specifically, Steuer highlights two features of the digital environment: *vividness* and *interactivity*. Vividness is determined by sensory breadth (number of sensory inputs) and sensory depth (resolution of each input). Interactivity is influenced by three factors: speed (response rate), range (number of action options), and mapping (predictable control and changes). These clear operationalizations have been widely cited and used in manipulating presence (Coyle & Thorson, 2001; Jang et al., 2019; Papagiannidis et al., 2017). This focus on the technological antecedents has contributed to knowledge regarding how different technological and design features facilitate the experience of presence, but has also resulted in less discussion on the influences of individual traits and cognitive processes in influencing a person's likelihood to experience presence, or the experience of presence itself.

Table 2 Definition table of presence that has been cited in interactive marketing

Author & Year	Title	Definition of Presence	Components of Presence	N of IM Papers Cited
Steuer, 1992	Defining Virtual Reality: Dimensions Determining Telepresence	Telepresence: the extent to which one feels present in the mediated environment, rather than in the immediate physical environment	Antecedents: • Vividness • Interactivity	15
Lombard & Ditton, 1997	At the Heart of It All: The Concept of Presence	Presence: the perceptual illusion of non-mediation • An "illusion of non-mediation" occurs when a person fails to perceive or acknowledge an experience being "mediated" and responds as he/she would if the medium were not there	Subdimensions • Social richness • Realism • Transportation • Immersion • The perception of social actors in the environment • The perception of the medium as a social actor	8
Kim & Biocca, 1997	Telepresence via Television: Two Dimensions of Telepresence May Have Different Connections to Memory and Persuasion	Telepresence: equivalent to Gerrig's concept of "being transported"- a reader is phenomenally transferred to a mediated environment, resulting from low accessibility to the unmediated information and high accessibility to the mediated information	Cognitive Processes • Arrival • Departure	6

Author & Year	Title	Definition of Presence	Components of Presence	N of IM Papers Cited
Witmer & Singer, 1998	Measuring Presence in Virtual Environments: A Presence Questionnaire	Presence: the subjective experience of being in one place when one is physically in another	Subdimensions • Control responsiveness • Sensory exploration • Interface awareness • Involvement	5
Sheridan, 1992	Musings on Telepresence and Virtual Presence	Telepresence: sense of being physically present with virtual object(s) at the remote teleoperator site or "virtual presence" (sense of being physically present with visual, auditory or force displays generated by a computer) Presence: a subjective sensation, much like "mental workload", and mental model	Antecedents: • The extent of sensory information that is provided • Control in relation to sensors of the environment • Ability to modify the physical environment	4
Lee, 2004	Presence, Explicated	Presence: a psychological state in which virtual (para-authentic or artificial) objects are experienced as actual objects in either sensory or nonsensory ways	Subdimensions: • Physical presence • Social presence • Self-presence	4

(continued)

Table 2 (continued)

Author & Year	Title	Definition of Presence	Components of Presence	N of IM Papers Cited
Wirth et al., 2007	A Process Model of the Formation of Spatial Presence Experiences	Spatial Presence: a binary experience, during which perceived self-location and perceived action possibilities are connected to a mediated spatial environment	Cognitive Processes: • Draw upon spatial cues to perceive the mediated environment as a plausible space • Experience his or herself as being located within that perceived space	4
Minsky, 1980	Telepresence	Telepresence: feelings that a human operator might experience when interacting through a teleoperator system		3
Biocca, 1997	The Cyborg's Dilemma: Progressive Embodiment in Virtual Environments	Presence: the illusion of "being there" whether or not "there" exists in physical space or not		3
Lessiter et al., 2001	A Cross-media Presence Questionnaire: the ITC-Sense of Presence Inventory	Presence: an illusion is generated whereby a user senses that she/he is located somewhere other than her/his physical environment	Subdimensions • Spatial presence • Ecological validity • Engagement • Negative effects	3

Author & Year	Title	Definition of Presence	Components of Presence	N of IM Papers Cited
Heeter, 1992	Being There: The Subjective Experience of Presence	Presence: feeling like you exist within but as a separate entity from a virtual world that also exists	Subdimensions • Subjective personal presence • Social presence • Environmental presence	2
Slater et al., 1994	Depth of Presence in Virtual Environments	Presence: the participant's sense of "being there" in the virtual environment		1
Slater & Wilbur, 1997	A Framework for Immersive Virtual Environments (FIVE): Speculations on the Role of Presence in Virtual Environments	Presence: a state of consciousness, the (psychological) sense of being in the virtual environment		1
Slater, 1999	Measuring Presence: A Response to the Witmer and Singer Presence Questionnaire	Presence: the subjective experience of being in one place or environment, even when one is physically situated in another	Cognitive Processes • The memories they form about the environment will be theorized to resemble memories formed in real life	1
Lombard et al., 2000	Measuring Presence: A Literature-based Approach to the Development of a Standardized Paper-and-pencil Instrument	Presence: the perceptual illusion of non-mediation		1

(continued)

Table 2 (continued)

Author & Year	Title	Definition of Presence	Components of Presence	N of IM Papers Cited
Slater & Steed, 2000	A Virtual Presence Counter	Presence: a mental state in which a user feels physically present within the computer-mediated environment		1
Lombard & Snyder-Duch, 2001	Interactive Advertising and Presence	Presence: a psychological state or subjective perception in which … part or all of the individual's perception fails to accurately acknowledge the role of the technology in the experience		1
Li et al., 2002	Impact of 3D Advertising on Product Knowledge, Brand Attitude, and Purchase Intention: The Mediating Role of Presence	Presence: an illusion of "being there" in a mediated environment		1

Author & Year	Title	Definition of Presence	Components of Presence	N of IM Papers Cited
Sas & O'Hare, 2003	Presence Equation: An Investigation into Cognitive Factors underlying Presence	Presence: a psychological phenomenon, through which one's cognitive processes are oriented toward another world…together with an imperceptible shifting of focus of consciousness to the proximal stimulus located in that other world		1
Suh & Chang, 2006	User Interfaces and Consumer Perceptions of Online Stores: The Role of Telepresence	Telepresence: the experience or impression of being present at a location remote from one's own immediate environment		1
Slater, 2009	Place Illusion and Plausibility Can Lead to Realistic Behavior in Immersive Virtual Environments	Presence (place illusion; PI): the sense of "being there," the strong illusion of being in a place in spite of the sure knowledge that you are not there		1

(continued)

Table 2 (continued)

Author & Year	Title	Definition of Presence	Components of Presence	N of IM Papers Cited
Schubert, 2009	A new conception of spatial presence: once again, with feeling	Spatial presence: a feedback from unconscious cognitive processes that informs conscious thought about the state of the spatial cognitive system		1
Weibel & Wissmath, 2011	Immersion in computer games: the role of spatial presence and flow	Presence: a sense of spatial immersion in a mediated environment; a state of consciousness that gives the impression of being physically present in a mediated world		1
Shafer et al., 2011	Spatial presence and perceived reality aspredictors of motion-based video game enjoyment	Spatial presence (one dimension of presence): the sense of being there, actually being present in the virtual environment		1
Cummings & Bailenson, 2016	How immersive is enough? A meta-analysis of the effect of immersive technology on user presence	Presence: the psychological experience of "being there"		1

4.1.2 Subdimensions of Presence

Further explicating the construct of presence, researchers have elaborated on the subdimensions of presence in a digital environment that focused more on user experiences (Lee, 2004; Lessiter et al., 2001; Lombard & Ditton, 1997; Witmer & Singer, 1998). For instance, Lombard and Ditton (1997) propose six subdimensions of presence, including social richness (the extent to which a medium is perceived as being sociable, warm, personal, and intimate when used to interact with others); realism; transportation ("you are there," "it is here," and "we are together"); immersion (perceptual, psychological); the perception of social actors in the environment; and the perception of the medium as a social actor (social responses to cues provided by the medium itself).

Building on Lombard and Ditton (1997), Witmer and Singer (1998) propose four subdimensions involved in the experience of presence: control responsiveness, sensory exploration, interface awareness, and involvement. These factors encompass both system features and user experiences, showing a more inclusive operationalization of presence than was present in previous explications of the construct. This work also proposes that individuals' immersive tendencies influence the extent to which one may feel immersed in a media experience, measured by the tendency to lose track of time and level of involvement when watching TV, reading books, and daydreaming. Furthermore, Witmer and Singer (1998) provide an operationalization of these subdimensions in the form of the Presence Questionnaire (PQ) and the Immersive Tendency Questionnaire (ITQ).

Lessiter and colleagues (2001) propose a somewhat different set of subdimensions: spatial presence, ecological validity, engagement, and negative effects. Like Witmer and Singer (1998), Lessiter and colleagues also introduce an operationalization of these subdimensions, in the form of the ITC-Sense of Presence Inventory scale (ITC-SOPI). These subdimensions and their associated measurement have been widely cited in the interactive marketing literature (e.g., Feng, 2018; Li, 2002).

Finally, Lee (2004) proposed three dimensions involved in the experience of presence: physical presence, social presence, and self-presence. These dimensions denote the psychological states in which virtual physical objects, virtual social actors, and virtual self/selves are experienced as actual objects, social actors, and self/selves in either sensory or nonsensory ways. These dimensions expand the construct of presence to more fully encompass social and cognitive factors that may be involved in the immersive experience.

4.1.3 Cognitive Processes

Researchers have also elaborated on the various cognitive processes involved in the experience of presence. For instance, Kim and Biocca (1997) draw from the concept of "transportation," which describes the psychological sense of immersion experienced by the reader of a narrative story, to propose that presence is a "moment-by-moment" oscillation between senses of different spaces (physical versus mediated). Building on this conceptualization, Kim and Biocca (1997) also report findings from an exploratory and confirmatory factor analysis showing that self-report scales related to presence load on two factors, one of which corresponds with a sense of "arrival" and one of which corresponds with a sense of "departure." The conceptualization of presence in terms of the cognitive experience of arrival and departure has been influential within a broad swath of the interactive marketing literature (Besharat, 2013; Nelson, 2006).

Slater (1999) suggests that a person's sense of "being there" in a digital environment corresponds to the memories that they form about the environment. The more that the virtual environment becomes dominant in their mind, the more their memories of the environment are theorized to resemble those that would be formed in a physical environment. Building on Slater's (1999) framework, Wirth and colleagues (2007) propose a two-step process: First, the user must draw upon spatial cues to perceive the mediated environment as a plausible space. Second, the user must also experience his or herself as being located within that perceived space. More recently, Hartmann et al., (2016), build on this two-step model, proposing a spatial presence experience scale (SPES) for empirical tests.

4.2   *Investigations of Presence in Interactive Marketing*

Investigations of the experience of presence in the interactive marketing literature have considered a number of factors, but other salient factors have received comparatively less attention. Positive affective responses are the most frequently investigated factor in the literature, having been examined in 13 papers. In contrast, negative affective responses (i.e., anxiety) and negative feelings (i.e., nausea) related to presence, despite their importance within the presence literature more broadly, have not received attention within the interactive marketing context. Similarly, cognitive perceptions of content are frequently an object of focus within the literature (9 papers), but the relationship between feelings of presence and cognitive perceptions of the system or the self has not been investigated. Likewise, although motivations and intentions frequently feature in the interactive marketing literature, to date little extant work has considered how presence relates to actual behavior, and the work that exists has produced somewhat contradictory findings, especially in relation to memory.

4.2.1   *Affective Attitudinal Responses toward Content and System*
Positive attitudinal responses to the experience of presence are one of the most popular themes we observed in the reviewed literature. Researchers have primarily examined the effect of presence on users' positive attitudes toward marketing content, such as brands, products, and advertising messages (Klein, 2003; Li et al., 2002; Shen et al., 2020). Across two studies, Klein (2003) found that (tele)presence has a positive effect on both consumers' attitudes

toward the advertised product and their attitude strength. Building on Klein (2003)'s study, Tsai et al. (2020) found that (tele)presence explains the positive effect of immersive devices on consumers' brand liking when a product is presented in a realistic ad context. These consistent positive correlations between presence and attitudinal responses make the experience of presence a popular persuasive mechanism during the immersive experience.

In contrast, the effect of presence on negative affective responses toward content, such as anger, anxiety, and reactance, has received less attention in the literature. This oversight is especially notable given the extent to which presence has been found to amplify users' negative emotions within the broader research literature—especially when the content itself is negatively valenced. In the field of cybertherapy, for instance, Miyahira et al. (2010) suggested that presence moderates the effect of immersive technology on negative emotions, as viewers with a higher level of presence also experience greater emotional reactivity to anger-provoking stimuli. However, another line of research proposed that the effect of presence is similar to the transportation imagination model, in which users who experienced higher levels of telepresence or transportation are unable and unwilling to form counterarguments, resulting in reduced critical thoughts and enhanced persuasive effects. This proposition, though, has received inconsistent evidence (Breves, 2021; Chen & Yao, 2022; Oh & Jin, 2018; Oh et al., 2020). For instance, Breves (2021) found that participants have less negative valenced thoughts but more positive-valenced thoughts when they use more immersive technologies, and presence explains this effect. Some other researchers found it to be a conditional effect that presence only leads to less defensive responses among those who have low or moderate self-efficacy to quit smoking (Oh & Jin, 2018). A different piece of evidence comes from Chen and Yao (2022), in which researchers compared the effect of presence and transportation and found that transportation, but not presence, explains users' persuasive outcomes. Given the inconsistent findings, in the realm of interactive marketing, researchers could further investigate if and when presence modulates consumers' negative emotions, such as reactance to the recommendations (Fitzsimons & Lehmann, 2004) and psychological avoidance toward media content (Kuo et al., 2016).

In addition, how presence influences system-induced negative effects, such as nausea and disorientation, remains less unclear in interactive marketing. Some research from different fields found a mixed relationship between presence and system-induced negative effects (Baños et al., 2004; Chowdhury et al., 2017; Kim et al., 2020; Ling et al., 2013). For instance, Chowdhury et al. (2017) found a positive correlation and that participants who reported a higher level of presence also reported a stronger sense of nausea and disorientation. However, some other studies have suggested a negative correlation between presence and sickness (Nichols, 2000; Rupp et al., 2016). For instance, Nichols' (2000) study showed that participants had a higher level of presence and reported less sickness after using the device when they had a favorable attitude toward using VR. Findings suggest researchers in interactive marketing focus on both positive and negative sides of presence to generate a comprehensive understanding of its affective consequences. Understanding the role of presence also helps researchers and practitioners to identify and circumvent the negative affective outcomes in interactive immersive media and design the system and content strategically, especially when it comes to system adoption (Peukert et al., 2019). For instance, previous studies have identified the mixed role of presence on intention to reuse the virtual shopping environment: virtual environment increased users' intention hedonically via their sense of presence and enjoyment but decreased their reuse intention as it fails to meet utilitarian purposes, such as low readability of product information in the virtual environment and perceived low usefulness of the system (Peukert et al., 2019). Designing a virtual shopping environment to highlight the hedonic value of shopping and undermine the utilitarian value of the product may diminish the negative outcomes of presence.

4.2.2 Cognitive Perceptions of the Content, System, and Self-perceptions
Investigations on the relationship between presence and consumers' cognitive perceptions have primarily concerned the relationship between the feeling of presence and consumers' perceptions of marketing content, such as perceived advertising novelty (Feng, 2018), perceived informativeness of the marketing content (Tsai et al., 2020), perceived instrumental and experiential shopping value (Fiore et al., 2005; Jang et al., 2019), and perceived self-brand connection (Lim & Childs, 2020). In a website environment, Fiore (2005) found that an increased sense of presence explained the positive effect of product image interactivity on consumers' perceived instrumental value and experiential value. Similarly, in a virtual environment, Jang et al. (2019) found a positive correlation between presence and perceived experiential shopping value. These two factors further explained the indirect effect of interactivity and vividness on consumers' approach toward virtual reality stores.

Comparatively, there have been fewer investigations on the relationship between the feeling of presence and consumers' perceptions of the system (Feng et al., 2019; Li et al., 2002; Wu & Lin, 2018). In the interactive marketing literature, researchers have investigated consumers' perceived ecological validity of the system as one dimension of presence from the ITC-SOPO scale, with no direct investigation into their relationships (Feng et al., 2019; Li et al., 2002). However, as research in related fields indicates, consumers' perception of the system may turn out to be an important outcome of presence that further influences their perceptions of the media content. For example, in the field of journalism, Shin (2017) derived a path model that showed a positive influence of presence on users' perceived usability of the system, which further influenced their feeling of empathy, embodiment, and perceived learnability within this environment.

There has also been little discussion in the interactive marketing literature on how presence changes consumers' self-perceptions, such as perceived self-efficacy, self-control, or embodiment. As one exception, Kuo et al.'s (2016) qualitative research suggested that presence in the mediated world affirms consumers' identity and empowers them with more controls, thus, reducing the negative effect of an external stressor. Similarly, in a virtual environment, Murray et al., (2007) found that users' sense of presence is significantly associated with their perceived control in the VR environment. Another important but less studied perspective related to consumers' self-perception is *sense of embodiment (SoE)*. SoE is defined as "the ensemble of sensation that arises in conjunction with being inside, having, and controlling a body especially in relation to virtual reality applications" (Kilteni et al., 2012, pp. 374–375). Studies investigated the presence and users' SoE as parallel processes and these senses often elevated together during the immersive experience. Together, the review suggested focusing on the effect of presence on consumers' cognitive perceptions of all three aspects of interactive marketing: the marketing content, the system, and their changing self-perceptions.

4.2.3 Behavioral Intention and Actual Behaviors

Studies from interactive marketing research have identified a positive relationship between presence and various behavioral intentions, including, but not limited to, purchase intention, download intention, share intention, and intention to pay, continue, and visit (Fiore et al., 2005; Li et al., 2002; Shen et al., 2020; Wang & Yao, 2020; Wu & Lin, 2018; Wu & Stilwell, 2018). For instance, Wu and Stilwell (2018) found that engagement in a game, perceived mobility of the game (interaction without constraints of time and place), and perceived contextual value increased consumers' feeling of presence, which in turn, led to a higher intention to visit the game sponsor. Wang and Yao (2020) found a significant interaction between the level of presence and the level of control on consumers' purchase intention, such that players of a VR game reported a higher intention to purchase the fictitious brand in the game. The investigations of presence and behavioral consequences encompass a broad variety of behavioral intentions, showing an advance in interactive marketing literature.

However, to date, little extant work has considered examining the relationship between presence and actual behavior. This added ambiguity to the behavioral consequences of presence and its duration (long-term versus short-term). Some evidence for the effect of presence on users' behavior comes from social psychology. The findings of Reinhard et al.'s (2020) study, for instance, suggested that presence may induce a short-term change but decays at a fast rate. They found that participants with a higher level of presence were more subject to the influence of the proteus effect in a short period- when they embodied an older avatar, they walked slower at first but soon regressed to their normal walking pace. More research is needed in interactive marketing to examine the effect of presence on behavioral changes and their durations. As suggested by (Rodgers & Thorson, 2000), some important types of behavioral measures in interactive marketing include hits, click-throughs, time spent on websites, exploration patterns, and online purchasing patterns.

4.2.4   Memory: Contradictory findings and Potential Explanations
The overall marketing research cares about consumers' recall and recognition of brands and products, reflecting consumer attention and marketing effectiveness (Besharat et al., 2013). Herein, memory is different from consumers' perceptions and cognitive responses. There have been some discussions about the relationship between presence and memory retention within the interactive marketing literature (Besharat et al., 2013; Li et al., 2002; Shen et al., 2020), but the results have been mixed. For instance, Li et al. (2002) found that all three dimensions of presence mediated the positive effect of 3D advertising on consumers' product knowledge (study 2). Yet, recently, more evidence was found to support a negative association between presence and recall (i.e., Shen et al., 2020). Participants are asked to take a VR campus tour using a VR headset, watching on a desktop, or in a Google Cardboard. Researchers found that more immersive devices are associated with a higher level of presence, but presence is negatively associated with the recall of campus locations (Shen et al., 2020). These findings are consistent with recent research on virtual environments and presence (Bailey et al., 2012; Barreda-Ángeles et al., 2020; Chen & Yao, 2022; Rupp et al., 2016). For instance, when participants experience a virtual apartment tour in a more immersive environment, they report a higher sense of presence, while presence also accounts for reduced memory retention of the environment (Chen & Yao, 2022; study 1).

Researchers point to two possible explanations for this phenomenon consistent with the overall trend in other fields: (1) increased cognitive load due to the complicated and vivid virtual environment, and (2) prioritized spatial information processing in the spacious environment. Evidence supporting the cognitive load hypothesis includes studies from Makransky et al. (2019) and Schrader and Bastiaens (2012). For instance, Schrader and Bastiaens (2012) performed a mediation analysis and found that increased cognitive load partially explained the negative effect of presence on users' reduced learning outcomes. Evidence supporting the spatial processing priorities comes from Mania and Chalmers (2001) and Parong et al. (2020). Mania and Chalmers (2001) accessed students' memory retention of the lecture content and their spatial knowledge of the classroom. While participants using a head-mounted display fell short on memory retention of the learning material, they outperformed in spatial recall of the classroom environment. Research in interactive marketing can continue to probe into the correlation between presence and memory retention to develop better brand placement strategies and maximize campaign effectiveness.

5   Discussion

Various technologies have fueled the development of interactive marketing, shifting from bi-directional online communications to an immersive omnichannel virtual experience (Wang, 2021). These immersive technologies allow consumers to experience a sense of "being there" in the mediated environment, which fuels the effectiveness of marketing content and makes the concept of presence a central process of interest to researchers and practitioners in interactive marketing (Biocca, 1997). This chapter conducted a systematic review of presence in interactive marketing literature, focusing on reviewing the conceptual development and empirical application of presence, identifying areas that have been well investigated, and pointing out domains in which presence is comparatively understudied.

5.1 Theoretical Implications

The review identified common citations and summarized the development of presence in the interactive marketing literature in the following themes: technological antecedents, subdimensions, and cognitive processes, presenting the key components of the conceptual framework of presence. Technological antecedents allow researchers in interactive marketing to operationalize presence. Conceptualizing and measuring subdimensions further expanded researchers' understanding of different types of presence and their consequences (Feng et al., 2019; Jang et al., 2019; Li et al., 2002). Understanding cognitive processes involved in presence further encourages researchers to investigate the affective, cognitive, and behavioral outcomes of different stages of presence. These summarizations help researchers to understand the theoretical development of presence in interactive marketing and present a theoretical framework for the conceptualization of presence.

The chapter also identified several pathways for the advancement of presence investigations in interactive marketing. Positive affective responses toward and cognitive perceptions of the media content are frequently an object of focus within the literature. Researchers have consistently identified a positive correlation between presence and affective responses toward media content, making the experience of presence a popular persuasive mechanism theorized to be at play during the immersive experience. Researchers have also investigated the relationship between presence and users' cognitive perception of media content, such as perceived advertising novelty (Feng, 2018), perceived informativeness of the marketing content (Tsai et al., 2020), and perceived instrumental and experiential shopping value (Fiore et al., 2005; Jang et al., 2019). Finally, researchers in the interactive marketing literature have investigated the relationship between presence and users' various behavioral intentions, such as purchase intention, download intention, share intention, and intention to pay, continue, and visit (Shen et al., 2020; Wang & Yao, 2020; Wu & Lin, 2018; Wu & Stilwell, 2018).

5.2 Future Directions

The current chapter further contributes to the literature by identifying several understudied areas in interactive marketing, suggesting several promising directions for future research. In the following section, the authors elaborate on a selection of especially promising research agendas for investigating: (1) the influence of cognitive processes involved in presence, (2) affective and cognitive outcomes of presence on perceptions of the system, media content, and self, and (3) the influence of presence on memory and behavioral consequences thereof.

Theoretically, more research could further decompose and elaborate on the processes of presence to understand the contribution of different stages of presence on various affective, cognitive, memory, and behavioral outcomes. Kim and Biocca (1997), for instance, found that the "arrival" stage and "departure" stage of experiencing presence have different associations with participants' recognition and confidence in brand choices. The departure stage of presence is associated with increased memory of advertising and recognition speed, while the arrival stage of presence is associated with increased confidence in brand choice and buying intention. Wirth et al. (2007) proposed a two-step model of presence, and Hartmann et al. (2016) further developed a measurement scale with two factors: perceived self-location and possible action. Chen et al. (2022) built on Wirth et al.'s (2007) two-step model and worked from the perspective of embodied cognition, proposing that users have a loose boundary around themselves and project "self" to the virtual world to feel a sense of presence.

Consequently, users also perceive different action possibilities (affordance; Gibson, 1979) from the perspective of the "self" in the virtual world, leading to various behavioral changes. For instance, having a virtual body without a hand may be perceived as losing abilities to grab objects in the virtual world. Likewise, by projecting themselves into color-blind avatars, users also perceive themselves to be losing the ability to differentiate red from green, leading to more helping behaviors toward color-blind groups in real life (Ahn et al., 2013). In the realm of interactive marketing, it will likely also be interesting to investigate users' shopping behavior when they are empowered with various affordances in the virtual world. For example, further research could investigate if embodying a stronger virtual body will lead to more browsing or shopping in athletic outfits.

In addition, the review suggested paying more attention to the content-induced negative affective responses (Chowdhury et al., 2017). Research from other fields found that presence amplifies negative emotions, such as anxiety and fear (Gromer et al., 2018; Renaud et al., 2002). However, another line of research proposed that the effect of presence followed the prediction of the transportation imagination model and suggested that users who feel a higher level of presence should produce less critical thoughts and counterarguments, resulting in better affective responses and persuasive outcomes (Breves, 2021; Oh & Jin, 2018; Oh et al., 2020). In the realm of interactive marketing, researchers could further investigate if and when presence modulates the potential negative feelings induced by media content, such as reactance to persuasive messages (Fitzsimons & Lehmann, 2004) and psychological avoidance (Kuo et al., 2016).

Further, the affective and cognitive responses toward the system have also received less attention (Feng et al., 2019; Li et al., 2002; Wu & Lin, 2018), suggesting a promising area for future research. System usability and adoption are important issues within interactive marketing because they mediate interactions between consumers and marketers. Most immersive technologies, such as VR, still bear system and content design limitations, leading to nausea, sickness, and cybersickness (Chowdhury et al., 2017; Kim et al., 2020; Ling et al., 2013). However, as presence is defined as a sense of "non-mediation" (Lombard & Ditton, 1997), participants who feel presence may have reduced awareness of these negative impacts (Nichols, 2000) and perceive the system as more useful. Consistent findings from other fields showed that the experience of presence increased users' perceived usability of the system, which further influenced their adoption of the technology (Shin, 2017). Although, the relationship between presence and system-induced nausea and disorientation remains debatable (Nichols, 2000; Rupp et al., 2016). Research in interactive marketing could further investigate the interactions among consumers' experiences of presence, system-induced adverse effects, and cognitive perceptions of the system, such as perceived usefulness and ease of use (Alshaer et al., 2020).

Likewise, consumers' changing self-perception as a result of presence is a promising yet understudied area for future investigation. Within the interactive marketing literature, Kuo et al. (2016) suggested that presence empowers consumers with more controls and affirms their self-identities. Similarly, research from other fields found that presence influences users' perceived self-efficacy and perceived control in the immersive environment (Barbot & Kaufman, 2020; Cheng & Tsai, 2019; Kilteni et al., 2013; Murray et al., 2007; Shin & Biocca, 2018). Presence has also been found to be associated with a sense of embodiment, which leads to a higher sense of satisfaction and continuing intention (Shin & Biocca, 2018). Understanding how presence changes consumers' self-perceptions in interactive marketing may also provide valuable insights into improving marketing outcomes, such as consumers' higher confidence in their branded choice and purchasing behavior.

Last but not least, future research could further investigate the relationships between presence and consumers' memory retention. Early research identified a positive association, while recent studies have found a negative correlation (Bailey et al., 2012; Li et al., 2002). Drawing inferences from other fields, the review proposed two possible explanations. One potential explanation is increased cognitive load resulting from complicated and interactive virtual environments and various presentation strategies (Makransky et al., 2019). Another possible explanation is that users prioritized spatial information rather than other factual information about the content (Parong et al., 2020). While more expansive and vivid virtual environments challenge marketers to direct consumers' attention to the correct information, future research could investigate why and what consumers pay attention to, which will shed insights into interface design and product placement strategies.

Finally, the review calls for more research on the presence and its behavioral outcomes, including time spent on the page, number of interactions, and the long versus short-term effect of presence. Technologies allow marketers to access consumers' mediated behavior via logged information, providing pieces of behavioral evidence in addition to their self-reports. Considering that users' self-reported data is only moderately correlated with their actual behavior (Parry et al., 2021), the authors encourage future research to combine consumers' self-report data with their actual media use data to generate a comprehensive understanding of consumers' marketing experience in an immersive environment.

5.3   Practical Implications

While the findings of this review are primarily conceptual, they shed light on practical designs, including system design, content design, and user experience design. Regarding system design, the current research suggests avoiding designs that break the experience of presence and pursuing those that highlight the hedonic value of the shopping experience and undermine the utilitarian value of the system to increase the adoption of the virtual environment. For instance, practitioners should be aware of system designs that break the presence and trigger motion sickness, such as sudden acceleration and stopping. These system-induced negative feelings disrupt consumers' immersive experience and reduce positive consequences of presence and negatively influence consumers' perceived usefulness of the system leading to higher negative attitudes toward the VR system and a decreased adoption rate (Alshaer et al., 2020; Nichols, 2000). In addition, previous research found that virtual environments increased users' system adoption when they generated feelings of presence and enjoyment but not when the utilitarian value of the environment was low, such as when product information was not easily readable. This suggests that practitioners should seek to design interactive marketing experiences to highlight the hedonic value of the experience and maximize the system's utilitarian value (Peukert et al., 2019).

While existing research from interactive marketing has investigated the amplifying effect of presence on positive affective outcomes (Klein, 2003; Shen et al., 2020; Tsai et al., 2020), additional evidence from other research fields has suggested practitioners consider the effect of presence on amplifying negative affective responses, such as psychological avoidance and persuasive message reactance, especially when message content may be negatively valenced (Kuo et al., 2016; Miyahira et al., 2010). Due to the experience of "presence," the technology allows consumers to experience things more as if they were real. Therefore, mediated content, such as violence and aggression, when presented in more immersive contexts, may also seem to be something consumers "experienced" rather than "viewed," potentially leading to increased fear and aggression (Gromer et al., 2018). On the other hand, researchers from the persuasion literature found an inconsistent influence of presence on negative affective responses, with some finding reduced counterarguments, but others finding it only works among low involvement participants (Breves, 2021; Chen & Yao, 2022; Oh & Jin, 2018). While researchers continue investigating the role of presence on users' negative affective responses, practitioners should avoid the potential risk of providing controversial media content and overly direct persuasive messages in the interactive and immersive marketing experience.

Finally, user experience design could pay more attention to consumers' avatars and subsequent influences on their self-perceptions. Feeling presence may be associated with changing consumers' self-perception, such as perceived efficacy and perceived control. Empowering consumers with more control and confirmation may turn immersive interactive marketing into a positive and rewarding experience.

5.4 *Limitations and Future Research*

The current research also bears several limitations. For instance, the current analysis of presence's conceptual development and empirical investigations only considers definitions cited and empirical tests conducted within the field of interactive marketing. While the findings objectively presented the current state of "presence" research in this field, future research could benefit from a broadened scope to include more literature further afield from that which traditionally considers interactive marketing experience. In addition, the scope of the current review is limited to theoretical considerations within the domain of presence. Future work would likely benefit from more empirical investigations, such as a meta-analysis reviewing the relationships between presence and different affective, cognitive, memorial, and behavioral consequences, or natural language processing-based analyses summarizing and analyzing the literature itself.

6 CONCLUSION

Technologies such as VR and AR fuel the development of interactive marketing by allowing consumers and marketers to exchange and create value via immersive environments. It induces a sense of presence that provides consumers with marketing experiences that transcend the constraints associated with more traditional media, making this concept a central process in the immersive experience (Biocca, 1997; Steuer, 1992). This chapter systematically reviewed the literature on presence within the confines of interactive marketing, focusing on its conceptual development and empirical consequences. More specifically, the current review was guided by three central research questions: (1) how presence has been conceptualized within the interactive marketing literature; (2) what interactive marketing research has revealed about the nature of presence, and its antecedents, correlates, and outcomes; (3) which areas within the literature hold the most potential for future research.

In view of the first research question, the authors identified 20 different definitions of presence within the literature, suggesting that the conceptualization of presence within interactive marketing has been quite varied and heterogeneous and that many of the definitions for presence used in the literature are imported from other bodies of literature. For the second research question, the authors identified the technological antecedents, subdimensions, and cognitive processes of presence highlighted in the interactive marketing literature. Vividness and interactivity were especially salient antecedents of presence, whereas the subdimensions and cognitive processes involved in presence were shown to vary quite widely. In view of the third research question, this review pointed out a number of currently understudied areas, including the influence of cognitive processes, adverse affective and cognitive outcomes, and conflicting evidence regarding memory and behavioral consequences of presence. In doing so, this systematic review provides a comprehensive picture of the state of current research investigating presence in interactive marketing and provides both a firm foundation and direction for future research in this critical area.

References

Alshaer, A., O'Hare, D., Archambault, P., Shirley, M., & Regenbrecht, H. (2020). How to observe users' movements in virtual environments: Viewpoint control in a power wheelchair simulator. *Human Factors*, 62(4), 656–670. Scopus. https://doi.org/10.1177/0018720819853682

Ahn, S. J. (Grace), Le, A. M. T., & Bailenson, J. (2013). The effect of embodied experiences on self-other merging, attitude, and helping behavior. *Media Psychology*, 16(1), 7–38.

Bailey, J., Bailenson, J. N., & Won, A. S. (2012). Presence and memory: Immersive virtual reality effects on Cued Recall. *Proceedings of the International Society for Presence Research Annual Conference*, 24–26.

Banerjee, S., & Longstreet, P. (2016). Mind in eBay, body in Macy's: Dual consciousness of virtuo-physical consumers and implications for marketers. *Journal of Research in Interactive Marketing*, 10(4), 288–304. https://doi.org/10.1108/JRIM-05-2015-0036

Baños, R. M., Botella, C., Alcañiz, M., Liaño, V., Guerrero, B., & Rey, B. (2004). Immersion and emotion: Their impact on the sense of presence. *CyberPsychology & Behavior*, 7(6), 734–741. https://doi.org/10.1089/cpb.2004.7.734

Bao, Z., & Wang, D. (2021). Examining consumer participation on brand microblogs in China: Perspectives from elaboration likelihood model, commitment–trust theory and social presence. *Journal of Research in Interactive Marketing*, 15(1), 10–29. https://doi.org/10.1108/JRIM-02-2019-0027

Barbot, B., & Kaufman, J. C. (2020). What makes immersive virtual reality the ultimate empathy machine? Discerning the underlying mechanisms of change.

Computers in Human Behavior, 111. Scopus. https://doi.org/10.1016/j.chb.2020.106431

Barreda-Ángeles, M., Aleix-Guillaume, S., & Pereda-Baños, A. (2020). Virtual reality storytelling as a double-edged sword: Immersive presentation of nonfiction 360°-video is associated with impaired cognitive information processing. *Communication Monographs*. Scopus. https://doi.org/10.1080/03637751.2020.1803496

Barreda-Ángeles, M., Aleix-Guillaume, S., & Pereda-Baños, A. (2021). Virtual reality storytelling as a double-edged sword: Immersive presentation of nonfiction 360°-video is associated with impaired cognitive information processing. *Communication Monographs, 88*(2), 154–173. https://doi.org/10.1080/03637751.2020.1803496

Besharat, A., Kumar, A., Lax, J. R., & Rydzik, E. J. (2013). Leveraging virtual attribute experience in video games to improve brand recall and learning. *Journal of Advertising, 42*(2–3), 170–182. https://doi.org/10.1080/00913367.2013.774593

Biocca, F. (1997). The cyborg's dilemma: Embodiment in virtual environments. *Proceedings Second International Conference on Cognitive Technology Humanizing the Information Age, 12–26,*. https://doi.org/10.1109/CT.1997.617676

Breves, P. (2021). Biased by being there: The persuasive impact of spatial presence on cognitive processing. *Computers in Human Behavior, 119*, 106723. https://doi.org/10.1016/j.chb.2021.106723

Breves, P., & Dodel, N. (2021). The influence of cybersickness and the media devices' mobility on the persuasive effects of 360° commercials. *Multimedia Tools and Applications, 80*(18), 27299–27322. https://doi.org/10.1007/s11042-021-11057-x

Bulu, S. T. (2012). Place presence, social presence, co-presence, and satisfaction in virtual worlds. *Computers and Education, 58*(1), 154–161. Scopus. https://doi.org/10.1016/j.compedu.2011.08.024

Chen, C., Hu, X., & Fisher, J. (2022). "What is "being there"? An ontology of the immersive experience. Paper to be presented in the 107th annual meeting of the *National Communication Association (NCA)*.

Chen, C., & Yao, M. Z. (2022). Strategic use of immersive media and narrative message in virtual marketing: Understanding the roles of telepresence and transportation. *Psychology & Marketing, 39*(3), 524–542. https://doi.org/10.1002/mar.21630

Cheng, K.-H., & Tsai, C.-C. (2019). A case study of immersive virtual field trips in an elementary classroom: Students' learning experience and teacher-student interaction behaviors. *Computers and Education, 140*. Scopus. https://doi.org/10.1016/j.compedu.2019.103600

Choi, Y. K., Miracle, G. E., & Biocca, F. (2001). The effects of anthropomorphic agents on advertising effectiveness and the mediating role of presence. *Journal of Interactive Advertising, 2*(1), 19–32. https://doi.org/10.1080/15252019.2001.10722055

Chowdhury, T. I., Costa, R., & Quarles, J. (2017). Information recall in VR disability simulation. *2017 IEEE Symposium on 3D User Interfaces (3DUI)*, 219–220. https://doi.org/10.1109/3DUI.2017.7893350

Cioppi, M., Curina, I., Forlani, F., & Pencarelli, T. (2019). Online presence, visibility and reputation: A systematic literature review in management studies. *Journal of Research in Interactive Marketing, 13*(4), 547–577. https://doi.org/10.1108/jrim-11-2018-0139

Cowan, K., & Ketron, S. (2019). Prioritizing marketing research in virtual reality: Development of an immersion/fantasy typology. *European Journal of Marketing*, 53(8), 1585–1611. https://doi.org/10.1108/EJM-10-2017-0733

Coyle, J. R., & Thorson, E. (2001). The effects of progressive levels of interactivity and vividness in web marketing sites. *Journal of Advertising*, 30(3), 65–77. https://doi.org/10.1080/00913367.2001.10673646

Cummings, J. J., & Bailenson, J. N. (2016). How immersive is enough? A meta-analysis of the effect of immersive technology on user presence. *Media Psychology*, 19(2), 272–309. https://doi.org/10.1080/15213269.2015.1015740

Daugherty, T., Li, H., & Biocca, F. (2008). Consumer learning and the effects of virtual experience relative to indirect and direct product experience. *Psychology & Marketing*, 25(7), 568–586. https://doi.org/10.1002/mar.20225

DeAndrea, D. C., & Holbert, R. L. (2017). Increasing clarity where it is needed most: Articulating and evaluating theoretical contributions. *Annals of the International Communication Association*, 41(2), 168–180. https://doi.org/10.1080/23808985.2017.1304163

Deng, S., Jiang, Y., Li, H., & Liu, Y. (2020). Who contributes what? Scrutinizing the activity data of 4.2 million Zhihu users via immersion scores. *Information Processing and Management*, 57(5). Scopus. https://doi.org/10.1016/j.ipm.2020.102274

Feng, Y. (2018). Facilitator or inhibitor? The use of 360-degree videos for immersive brand storytelling. *Journal of Interactive Advertising*, 18(1), 28–42. Scopus. https://doi.org/10.1080/15252019.2018.1446199

Feng, Y., Xie, Q., & Lou, C. (2019). The key to 360-degree video advertising: An examination of the degree of narrative structure. *Journal of Advertising*, 48(2), 137–152. https://doi.org/10.1080/00913367.2019.1585305

Fiore, A. M., Kim, J., & Lee, H.-H. (2005). Effect of image interactivity technology on consumer responses toward the online retailer. *Journal of Interactive Marketing*, 19(3), 38–53. https://doi.org/10.1002/dir.20042

Fitzsimons, G. J., & Lehmann, D. R. (2004). Reactance to recommendations: When unsolicited advice yields contrary responses. *Marketing Science*, 23(1), 82–94. https://doi.org/10.1287/mksc.1030.0033

Flanagin, A. J. (2020). The conduct and consequence of research on digital communication. *Journal of Computer-Mediated Communication*, 25(1), 23–31. https://doi.org/10.1093/jcmc/zmz019

Flavián, C., Ibáñez-Sánchez, S., & Orús, C. (2019). The impact of virtual, augmented and mixed reality technologies on the customer experience. *Journal of Business Research*, 100, 547–560. https://doi.org/10.1016/j.jbusres.2018.10.050

Georgiou, Y., Ioannou, A., & Ioannou, M. (2019). Investigating immersion and learning in a low-embodied versus high-embodied digital educational game: Lessons learned from an implementation in an authentic school classroom. *Multimodal Technologies and Interaction*, 3(4). Scopus. https://doi.org/10.3390/mti3040068

Gibson, J. J. (1979). The ecological approach to visual perception. In *The ecological approach to visual perception*. Houghton Mifflin.

Grinberg, A. M., Careaga, J. S., Mehl, M. R., & O'Connor, M.-F. (2014). Social engagement and user immersion in a socially based virtual world. *Computers in Human Behavior*, 36, 479–486. Scopus. https://doi.org/10.1016/j.chb.2014.04.008

Gromer, D., Madeira, O., Gast, P., Nehfischer, M., Jost, M., Müller, M., Mühlberger, A., & Pauli, P. (2018). Height simulation in a virtual reality cave system: Validity of fear responses and effects of an immersion manipulation. *Frontiers in Human Neuroscience, 12*. Scopus. https://doi.org/10.3389/fnhum.2018.00372

Hartmann, T., Wirth, W., Schramm, H., Klimmt, C., Vorderer, P., Gysbers, A., Böcking, S., Ravaja, N., Laarni, J., Saari, T., Gouveia, F., & Maria Sacau, A. (2016). The Spatial Presence Experience Scale (SPES): A short self-report measure for diverse media settings. *Journal of Media Psychology, 28*(1), 1–15. https://doi.org/10.1027/1864-1105/a000137

Heeter, C. (1992). Being there: The subjective experience of presence. *Presence: Teleoperators and Virtual Environments, 1*(2), 262–271. https://doi.org/10.1162/pres.1992.1.2.262

Jang, J. Y., Hur, H. J., & Choo, H. J. (2019). How to evoke consumer approach intention toward VR stores? Sequential mediation through telepresence and experiential value. *Fashion and Textiles, 6*(1). Scopus. https://doi.org/10.1186/s40691-018-0166-9

Jeandrain, A.-C. (2001). Consumer reactions in a realistic virtual shop: Influence on buying style. *Journal of Interactive Advertising, 2*(1), 2–9. https://doi.org/10.1080/15252019.2001.10722053

Keng, C.-J., & Lin, H.-Y. (2006). Impact of telepresence levels on internet advertising effects. *CyberPsychology & Behavior, 9*(1), 82–94. https://doi.org/10.1089/cpb.2006.9.82

Kilteni, K., Bergstrom, I., & Slater, M. (2013). Drumming in immersive virtual reality: The body shapes the way we play. *IEEE Transactions on Visualization and Computer Graphics, 19*(4), 597–605. https://doi.org/10.1109/TVCG.2013.29

Kilteni, K., Groten, R., & Slater, M. (2012). The sense of embodiment in virtual reality. *Presence, 21*(4), 373–387. https://doi.org/10.1162/PRES_a_00124

Kim, J. (Jay), Shinaprayoon, T., & Ahn, S. J. (Grace). (2022). Virtual tours encourage intentions to travel and willingness to pay via spatial presence, enjoyment, and destination image. *Journal of Current Issues & Research in Advertising, 43*(1), 90–105.https://doi.org/10.1080/10641734.2021.1962441

Kim, J.-H., Kim, M., Park, M., & Yoo, J. (2021). How interactivity and vividness influence consumer virtual reality shopping experience: The mediating role of telepresence. *Journal of Research in Interactive Marketing, 15*(3), 502–525. https://doi.org/10.1108/JRIM-07-2020-0148

Kim, S.-Y., Park, H., Jung, M., & Kim, K. (2020). Impact of body size match to an avatar on the body ownership illusion and user's subjective experience. *Cyberpsychology, Behavior, and Social Networking, 23*(4), 234–241. Scopus. https://doi.org/10.1089/cyber.2019.0136

Kim, T., & Biocca, F. (1997). Telepresence via television: Two dimensions of telepresence may have different connections to memory and persuasion. *Journal of Computer-Mediated Communication, 3*(2). https://doi.org/10.1111/j.1083-6101.1997.tb00073.x

Klein, L. R. (2003). Creating virtual product experiences: The role of telepresence. *Journal of Interactive Marketing, 17*(1), 41–55. https://doi.org/10.1002/dir.10046

Kuo, A., Lutz, R. J., & Hiler, J. L. (2016). Brave new World of Warcraft: A conceptual framework for active escapism. *Journal of Consumer Marketing, 33*(7), 498–506. https://doi.org/10.1108/JCM-04-2016-1775

Lee, K. M. (2004). Presence, explicated. *Communication Theory, 14*(1), 27–50. https://doi.org/10.1111/j.1468-2885.2004.tb00302.x

Lessiter, J., Freeman, J., Keogh, E., & Davidoff, J. (2001). A cross-media presence questionnaire: The ITC-Sense of Presence Inventory. *Presence: Teleoperators and Virtual Environments, 10*(3), 282–297. https://doi.org/10.1162/105474601300343612

Li, H., Daugherty, T., & Biocca, F. (2002). Impact of 3-D advertising on product knowledge, brand attitude, and purchase intention: The mediating role of presence. *Journal of Advertising, 31*(3), 43–57. https://doi.org/10.1080/00913367.2002.10673675

Lim, H., & Childs, M. (2020). Visual storytelling on Instagram: Branded photo narrative and the role of telepresence. *Journal of Research in Interactive Marketing, 14*(1), 33–50. https://doi.org/10.1108/JRIM-09-2018-0115

Ling, Y., Nefs, H. T., Brinkman, W.-P., Qu, C., & Heynderickx, I. (2013). The relationship between individual characteristics and experienced presence. *Computers in Human Behavior, 29*(4), 1519–1530. Scopus. https://doi.org/10.1016/j.chb.2012.12.010

Lombard, M., & Ditton, T. (1997). At the heart of it all: The concept of presence. *Journal of Computer-Mediated Communication, 3*(2). https://doi.org/10.1111/j.1083-6101.1997.tb00072.x

Lombard, M., Ditton, T. B., Crane, D., Davis, B., Gil-Egui, G., Horvath, K., & Rossman, J. (2000). *Measuring Presence: A Literature-Based Approach to the Development of a Standardized Paper-and-Pencil Instrument, 240*, 2–4.

Lombard, M., & Snyder-Duch, J. (2001). Interactive advertising and presence: A framework. *Journal of Interactive Advertising, 1*(2), 56–65. https://doi.org/10.1080/15252019.2001.10722051

Makransky, G., Terkildsen, T. S., & Mayer, R. E. (2019). Adding immersive virtual reality to a science lab simulation causes more presence but less learning. *Learning and Instruction, 60*, 225–236. Scopus. https://doi.org/10.1016/j.learninstruc.2017.12.007

Mania, K., & Chalmers, A. (2001). The effects of levels of immersion on memory and presence in virtual environments: A reality centered approach. *CyberPsychology & Behavior, 4*(2), 247–264. https://doi.org/10.1089/109493101300117938

Minsky, M. (1980, June). Telepresence. *OMNI Magazine.* https://web.media.mit.edu/~minsky/papers/Telepresence.html

Miyahira, S. D., Folen, R. A., Stetz, M., Rizzo, A., & Kawasaki, M. M. (2010). Use of immersive virtual reality for treating anger. *Annual Review of CyberTherapy and Telemedicine, 8*(1), 65–68. Scopus.

Moher, D., Liberati, A., Tetzlaff, J., Altman, D. G., & Group, T. P. (2009). Preferred reporting items for systematic reviews and meta-analyses: The PRISMA statement. *PLOS Medicine, 6*(7), e1000097. https://doi.org/10.1136/bmj.b2535

Murray, C. D., Fox, J., & Pettifer, S. (2007). Absorption, dissociation, locus of control, and presence in virtual reality. *Computers in Human Behavior, 23*(3), 1347–1354. Scopus. https://doi.org/10.1016/j.chb.2004.12.010

Naul, E., & Liu, M. (2020). Why story matters: A review of narrative in serious games. *Journal of Educational Computing Research, 58*(3), 687–707. Scopus. https://doi.org/10.1177/0735633119859904

Nelson, M. R., Yaros, R. A., & Keum, H. (2006). Examining the influence of telepresence on spectator and player processing of real and fictitious brands in a computer game. *Journal of Advertising, 35*(4), 87–99. https://doi.org/10.2753/JOA0091-3367350406

Nichols, S. (2000). *Individual characteristics and experiences of virtual reality induced symptoms and effects (VRISE)*, 538–541. Scopus. https://doi.org/10.1177/154193120004400514

Nicovich, S. G. (2005). The effect of involvement on Ad judgment in a video game environment: The mediating role of presence. *Journal of Interactive Advertising*, 6(1), 29–39. https://doi.org/10.1080/15252019.2005.10722105

Oh, C. S., Bailenson, J. N., & Welch, G. F. (2018). A systematic review of social presence: Definition, antecedents, and implications. *Frontiers in Robotics and AI*, 5, 114. https://doi.org/10.3389/frobt.2018.00114

Oh, J., & Jin, E. (2018). Interactivity benefits low self-efficacy smokers more: The combinatory effects of interactivity and self-efficacy on defensive response and quitting intention. *Journal of Interactive Advertising*, 18(2), 110–124. https://doi.org/10.1080/15252019.2018.1491812

Oh, J., Kang, H., Sudarshan, S., & Lee, J. A. (2020). Can liking, commenting, and sharing enhance persuasion? The interaction effect between modality interactivity and agency affordances on smokers' quitting intentions. *Health Communication*, 35(13), 1593–1604. https://doi.org/10.1080/10410236.2019.1654172

Page, M. J., Moher, D., Bossuyt, P. M., Boutron, I., Hoffmann, T. C., Mulrow, C. D., Shamseer, L., Tetzlaff, J. M., Akl, E. A., Brennan, S. E., Chou, R., Glanville, J., Grimshaw, J. M., Hróbjartsson, A., Lalu, M. M., Li, T., Loder, E. W., Mayo-Wilson, E., McDonald, S., … McKenzie, J. E. (2021). PRISMA 2020 explanation and elaboration: Updated guidance and exemplars for reporting systematic reviews. *BMJ*, 372, n160. https://doi.org/10.1136/bmj.n160

Papagiannidis, S., Pantano, E., See-To, E. W. K., Dennis, C., & Bourlakis, M. (2017). To immerse or not? Experimenting with two virtual retail environments. *Information Technology and People*, 30(1), 163–188. Scopus. https://doi.org/10.1108/ITP-03-2015-0069

Parong, J., Pollard, K. A., Files, B. T., Oiknine, A. H., Sinatra, A. M., Moss, J. D., Passaro, A., & Khooshabeh, P. (2020). The mediating role of presence differs across types of spatial learning in immersive technologies. *Computers in Human Behavior*, 107. Scopus. https://doi.org/10.1016/j.chb.2020.106290

Parry, D. A., Davidson, B. I., Sewall, C., Fisher, J. T., Mieczkowski, H., & Quintana, D. (2021). A systematic review and meta-analysis of discrepancies between self-reported and logged media use. *Nature Human Behaviour*. https://doi.org/10.1038/s41562-021-01117-5

Peat, J. K., Mellis, C., Williams, K., & Xuan, W. (2020). Health science research: A handbook of quantitative methods. *Routledge*. https://doi.org/10.4324/9781003115922

Peukert, C., Pfeiffer, J., Meißner, M., Pfeiffer, T., & Weinhardt, C. (2019). Shopping in virtual reality stores: The influence of immersion on system adoption. *Journal of Management Information Systems*, 36(3), 755–788. https://doi.org/10.1080/07421222.2019.1628889

Reinhard, R., Shah, K. G., Faust-Christmann, C. A., & Lachmann, T. (2020). Acting your avatar's age: Effects of virtual reality avatar embodiment on real-life walking speed. *Media Psychology*, 23(2), 293–315. Scopus. https://doi.org/10.1080/15213269.2019.1598435

Renaud, P., Rouleau, J. L., Granger, L., Barsetti, I., & Bouchard, S. (2002). Measuring sexual preferences in virtual reality: A pilot study. *Cyberpsychology and Behavior*, 5(1), 1–9. Scopus. https://doi.org/10.1089/109493102753685836

Rodgers, S., & Thorson, E. (2000). The interactive advertising model: How users perceive and process online ads. *Journal of Interactive Advertising, 1*(1), 41–60. https://doi.org/10.1080/15252019.2000.10722043

Rupp, M. A., Kozachuk, J., Michaelis, J. R., Odette, K. L., Smither, J. A., & McConnell, D. S. (2016). The effects of immersiveness and future VR expectations on subjective experiences during an educational 360° video. *Proceedings of the Human Factors and Ergonomics Society Annual Meeting, 60*(1), 2108–2112. https://doi.org/10.1177/1541931213601477

Sas, C., & O'Hare, G. M. P. (2003). Presence equation: An investigation into cognitive factors underlying presence. *Presence: Teleoperators and Virtual Environments, 12*(5), 523–537. https://doi.org/10.1162/105474603322761315

Schrader, C., & Bastiaens, T. J. (2012). The influence of virtual presence: Effects on experienced cognitive load and learning outcomes in educational computer games. *Computers in Human Behavior, 28*(2), 648–658. Scopus. https://doi.org/10.1016/j.chb.2011.11.011

Schubert, T., Friedmann, F., & Regenbrecht, H. (2001). The experience of presence: Factor analytic insights. *Presence: Teleoperators and Virtual Environments, 10*(3), 266–281. https://doi.org/10.1162/105474601300343603

Schubert, T. W. (2009). A new conception of spatial presence: Once again, with feeling. *Communication Theory, 19*(2), 161–187. https://doi.org/10.1111/j.1468-2885.2009.01340.x

Shafer, D. M., Carbonara, C. P., & Popova, L. (2011). Spatial presence and perceived reality as predictors of motion-based video game enjoyment. *Presence, 20*(6), 591–619. https://doi.org/10.1162/PRES_a_00084

Shen, J., Wang, Y., Chen, C., Nelson, M. R., & Yao, M. Z. (2020). Using virtual reality to promote the university brand: When do telepresence and system immersion matter? *Journal of Marketing Communications, 26*(4), 362–393. https://doi.org/10.1080/13527266.2019.1671480

Sheridan, T. B. (1992). Musings on telepresence and virtual presence. *Presence: Teleoperators and Virtual Environments, 1*(1), 120–126. https://doi.org/10.1162/pres.1992.1.1.120

Shin, D., & Biocca, F. (2018). Exploring immersive experience in journalism. *New Media and Society, 20*(8), 2800–2823. Scopus. https://doi.org/10.1177/1461444817733133

Shin, D.-H. (2017). The role of affordance in the experience of virtual reality learning: Technological and affective affordances in virtual reality. *Telematics & Informatics, 34*(8), 1826–1836. https://doi.org/10.1016/j.tele.2017.05.013

Slater, M. (1999). Measuring presence: A response to the witmer and singer presence questionnaire. *Presence: Teleoperators and Virtual Environments, 8*(5), 560–565.

Slater, M. (2009). Place illusion and plausibility can lead to realistic behaviour in immersive virtual environments. *Philosophical Transactions of the Royal Society b: Biological Sciences, 364*(1535), 3549–3557. https://doi.org/10.1098/rstb.2009.0138

Slater, M., & Steed, A. (2000). A virtual presence counter. *Presence, 9*(5), 413–434. https://doi.org/10.1162/105474600566925

Slater, M., Usoh, M., & Steed, A. (1994). Depth of presence in virtual environments. *Presence: Teleoperators and Virtual Environments, 3*(2), 130–144. https://doi.org/10.1162/pres.1994.3.2.130

Slater, M., & Wilbur, S. (1997). A Framework for Immersive Virtual Environments (FIVE): Speculations on the role of presence in virtual environments. *Presence: Teleoperators and Virtual Environments, 6*(6), 603–616. https://doi.org/10.1162/pres.1997.6.6.603

Song, J. H., & Zinkhan, G. M. (2008). Determinants of perceived web site interactivity. *Journal of Marketing, 72*(2), 99–113. https://doi.org/10.1509/jmkg.72.2.99

Steuer, J. (1992). Defining virtual reality: Dimensions determining telepresence. *Journal of Communication, 42*(4), 73–93. https://doi.org/10.1111/j.1460-2466.1992.tb00812.x

Suh, K.-S., & Chang, S. (2006). User interfaces and consumer perceptions of online stores: The role of telepresence. *Behaviour & Information Technology, 25*(2), 99–113. https://doi.org/10.1080/01449290500330398

Tsai, W.-H.S., Liu, Y., & Chuan, C.-H. (2021). How chatbots' social presence communication enhances consumer engagement: The mediating role of parasocial interaction and dialogue. *Journal of Research in Interactive Marketing, 15*(3), 460–482. https://doi.org/10.1108/JRIM-12-2019-0200

Tsai, W.-H. S., Tian, S. C., Chuan, C.-H., & Li, C. (2020). Inspection or play? A study of how augmented reality technology can be utilized in advertising. *Journal of Interactive Advertising, 20*(3), 244–257. https://doi.org/10.1080/15252019.2020.1738292

van Gelder, J.-L., de Vries, R. E., Demetriou, A., van Sintemaartensdijk, I., & Donker, T. (2019). The virtual reality scenario method: Moving from imagination to immersion in criminal decision-making research. *Journal of Research in Crime and Delinquency, 56*(3), 451–480. Scopus. https://doi.org/10.1177/0022427818819696

Wang, C. L. (2021). New frontiers and future directions in interactive marketing: Inaugural Editorial. *Journal of Research in Interactive Marketing, 15*(1), 1–9. https://doi.org/10.1108/JRIM-03-2021-270

Wang, Y., & Yao, M. Z. (2020). Did you notice the ads? examining the influence of telepresence and user control on the effectiveness of embedded billboard ads in a VR Racing Game. *Journal of Interactive Advertising, 20*(3), 258–272. https://doi.org/10.1080/15252019.2020.1846642

Weibel, D., & Wissmath, B. (2011). Immersion in computer games: The role of spatial presence and flow. *International Journal of Computer Games Technology, 2011*, 1–14. https://doi.org/10.1155/2011/282345

Whitbred, R., Skalski, P., Bracken, C., & Lieberman, E. (2010). When richer is poorer: Understanding the influence of channel richness and presence on the introduction of a mission statement. *PsychNology Journal, 8*(1), 115–139. Scopus.

Wirth, W., Hartmann, T., Böcking, S., Vorderer, P., Klimmt, C., Schramm, H., Saari, T., Laarni, J., Ravaja, N., Gouveia, F. R., Biocca, F., Sacau, A., Jäncke, L., Baumgartner, T., & Jäncke, P. (2007). A process model of the formation of spatial presence experiences. *Media Psychology, 9*(3), 493–525. https://doi.org/10.1080/15213260701283079

Witmer, B. G., & Singer, M. J. (1998). Measuring presence in virtual environments: A presence questionnaire. *PRESENCE: Teleoperators & Virtual Environments, 7*(3), 225–240. https://doi.org/10.1162/105474698565686

Wu, D.-Y., & Lin, J.-H. T. (2018). Ways of seeing matter: The impact of a naturally mapped perceptual system on the persuasive effects of immersive virtual reality advertising. *Communication Research Reports, 35*(5), 434–444. Scopus. https://doi.org/10.1080/08824096.2018.1525349

Wu, L., & Stilwell, M. A. (2018). Exploring the marketing potential of location-based mobile games. *Journal of Research in Interactive Marketing, 12*(1), 22–44. https://doi.org/10.1108/JRIM-06-2017-0041

Yung, R., Khoo-Lattimore, C., & Potter, L. E. (2020). Virtual reality and tourism marketing: Conceptualizing a framework on presence, emotion, and intention. *Current Issues in Tourism.* Scopus. https://doi.org/10.1080/13683500.2020.1820454

PART IV

Platform Revolution and Customer Participation

CHAPTER 19

The Platform Revolution in Interactive Marketing: Increasing Customer-Brand Engagement on Social Media Platforms

Zheng Shen

1 Introduction

Interactive marketing can be seen as a marketing process of two-way value creation and influence through active customer connection, engagement, and interaction (Wang, 2021). In this regard, customer-brand engagement is considered to be an important perspective in interactive marketing. Engagement is a tangible process between customers and products or brands that leads to behavioral affinity (Hollebeek et al., 2014; Vazquez, 2020). It involves enhancing the interaction between customers and brands, and the pertinent literature often links different concepts of engagement, such as customer engagement, brand engagement, and digital engagement (Kim et al., 2021; Wang et al., 2022; Zimand-Sheiner et al., 2021). Existing literature has shown that customer-brand engagement has a significant impact on customer perception of positive brand advertising, brand loyalty, purchase intention, and willingness to share (France et al., 2016; Graham & Wilder, 2020; Izogo & Mpinganjira, 2020). After the emergence of social media, brands have gradually become more active in incorporating social media into their interactive marketing strategy by creating brand pages, developing content, and promoting it. Prior studies indicate that social media allows brands to build network-based online communities that stimulate customer engagement by enabling customers to develop their social identities and satisfy social

Z. Shen (✉)
Zhejiang Sci-Tech University, Hangzhou, China
e-mail: janeshen@zstu.edu.cn

needs (Christodoulides, 2009; Tajfel, 1979; Vernuccio et al., 2016). As such, encouraging customer-brand engagement has become a focal point for brands looking to succeed in interactive marketing on social media.

As social media evolves, different social media platforms make brands difficult to track and coordinate their efforts (Devereux et al., 2020). During the golden age of social media, Facebook mostly dominated the market, gaining the largest market share, followed by the popularity of microblogs on Twitter, but in recent years, Instagram has surpassed Facebook as a platform that continues to grow rapidly (Perrin & Anderson, 2019). The platform revolution is shaping a new business ecosystem for customer connectivity and interactivity (Parker et al., 2016; Wang, 2021). Scholars argue that the pertinent literature is limited in the following aspects: (1) most of the studies limited content types (e.g., informational or entertaining content), and employed a singular social media platform to test social media engagement (e.g., Facebook or Instagram); (2) few studies considered the role of content format (e.g., picture, video, etc.), and the relationship with the choice of social media platform on predicting users' engagement behavior; and (3) most studies used survey methods to collect primary data (Shahbaznezhad et al., 2021). Unnava and Aravindakshan (2021) further posit that there has been limited analysis of social media platforms as a determinant of customer-brand engagement. Given the wide variety of social media platforms currently in use, our understanding of customer-brand engagement would benefit from further exploration of the different and new social media platforms.

With respect to the above, this chapter is motivated by prior studies calling for the investigation of customer behaviors and interactions in social media networks and different platforms in the context of future research directions in interactive marketing (Hamzah et al., 2021; Wang, 2021), and posed the following research questions: (1) What are the differences in customer-brand engagement on social media platforms? (2) How can customer-brand engagement be increased on multiple social media platforms? To clarify the answer, this chapter examined the effectiveness of customer-brand engagement on three popular social media platforms, Twitter, Instagram, and TikTok. Data were collected from 10 brands in different sectors and analyzed by data mining techniques. The findings reveal that social media platforms make a difference in customer-brand engagement on social media, and show that TikTok, an emerging social media platform, has higher customer-brand engagement than Twitter and Instagram, despite the latter being larger platforms and widely used by brands. Surprisingly, the findings indicate that customer-brand engagement on social media platforms can be increased by the choice of social media platform and brand content format, rather than brand content differentiation on social media platforms.

This chapter provides both theoretical and managerial implications. On a theoretical level, it extends the literature on customer-brand engagement in interactive marketing on social media. According to Pelletier et al. (2020), understanding customer engagement in the social media context is high on the academic research agenda. For this reason, this chapter extends the limited analysis of customer-brand engagement on social media platforms. Compared with previous studies, this chapter further fills a gap in the relevant literature on customer-brand engagement by employing multiple social media platforms. In particular, it extends the current limited understanding of customer-brand engagement on TikTok, an emerging social media platform. Also, the findings indicate that customer-brand engagement on social media platforms can be increased by the choice of social media platform and brand content format rather than brand content differentiation, extending the limited analysis on the role of brand content types and formats in the effectiveness of customer-brand engagement. In practice, the findings provide managerial insights for brand and marketing practitioners who have difficulty coordinating their efforts on multiple social media platforms. They may consider using TikTok to increase customer-brand engagement on social media, which is not widely used by brands yet. Alternatively, they may consider using short videos in their interactive marketing on Twitter and Instagram, which have higher customer-brand engagement on social media.

2 Literature Review

2.1 Customer Engagement and Its Determinants

Strengthening customer engagement has increased theoretical and managerial importance in the marketing literature (Garcia-de-Frutos & Estrella-Ramon, 2021; Gligor & Bozkurt, 2021; Ji et al., 2022). Customer engagement refers to customers' psychological process arising from the combination of intrinsic motivations, psychological mind states, customer activities, and contributions to firms (Santini et al., 2020). The existing literature considers the importance of customer engagement in marketing because of its potential predictive power regarding customer behavior and brand performance (Pansari & Kumar, 2017; Santini et al., 2020). Pansari and Kumar (2017) posit customer engagement forms relationships as it occurs when customers form satisfying relationships based on trust, commitment, and emotional ties. According to Santini et al. (2020), customer engagement contributes directly to brand performance and indirectly as mediated by behavioral intention and WOM.

Based on the importance of the above, scholars are increasingly interested in exploring the determinants that drive customer engagement. Determinants found in the extant literature include product factors (Hu & Li, 2011; Purnawirawan et al., 2012), brand factors (Anderson & Simester, 2014; Borah & Tellis, 2016), customer factors (Azar et al., 2016; Shao & Ross, 2015), and content factors (Chahal & Rani, 2017; Swani et al., 2013). Regarding product factors, scholars highlight that product quality can affect customer engagement, which exists in reviews (Purnawirawan et al., 2012). Hu and Li (2011) argue that more customer reviews of products are more positive customer engagement behaviors. For brand factors, Borah and Tellis

(2016) explain that negative chatter about one brand increases negative chatter for another brand. Related to customer factors, Shao and Ross (2015) emphasize that the motivation dimensions of customers have differential effects on customer interactions with a Facebook brand page community. Finally, in terms of content factors, previous research supports that effective content can drive customer traffic and help brands convert customers (Hanlon, 2019). For instance, Chahal and Rani (2017) state that customer-brand engagement on social media is a bidimensional structure comprising both informational and personal interests.

The above studies reveal the following limitations of the existing literature. For one thing, previous studies focused on customer engagement, e.g., Hu and Li (2011), Purnawirawan et al. (2012), etc. These studies aimed to increase customer engagement in online communities through electronic word-of-mouth in product reviews. In contrast, analysis of customer engagement with brands on social media platforms is limited. As evidenced in Santini et al. (2020), previous studies discussed brand factors in customer engagement studies from the perspective of customer engagement contributions rather than from the perspective of customer-brand engagement. For another, the analysis of social media itself as a determinant of customer-brand engagement has been limited in previous studies. In particular, although previous studies (e.g.,Chahal & Rani, 2017; Shao & Ross, 2015, etc.) explored customer-brand engagement on social media, they focused on investigating engagement on a singular social media platform and failed to consider the relationship with the choice of social media platform on predicting customer engagement behavior (Shahbaznezhad et al., 2021; Unnava & Aravindakshan, 2021). Therefore, this chapter attempts to fill the limitations of the existing literature by examining customer-brand engagement on multiple social media platforms.

2.2 Customer-Brand Engagement and Social Media Platforms

Early customer engagement research failed to address recent technological innovations that continue to open up new possibilities for customer-brand interactions (Paruthi & Kaur, 2017). As the technology evolved, customers were increasingly exposed to social media platforms as a means of expressing opinions and interacting with brands, which led to brands using social media to identify and interact with highly engaged customers for specialized marketing efforts (Baldus et al., 2015). As such, Hollebeek et al. (2014), in their study of social media setting, defined customer-brand engagement as brand-related cognitive, emotional, and behavioral activities that are positively evaluated by customers during or in relation to customer or brand interactions. Kircova et al. (2018) further explain that customer-brand engagement on social media platforms includes how customers use, share, and talk about the content related to brands.

Extant literature finds a strong relationship between brands' portrayal on social media and customer perceptions about brands (Liu et al., 2020). Hajli et al. (2017) state that brand strategies can be developed through social media because social interactions between customers and brands in online communities improve relationship quality and brand loyalty. Kamboj et al. (2018) support that social media significantly influences customer participation, which in turn influences brand trust and loyalty, and ultimately leads to having a positive brand image and purchase intention. Social media platforms are a subfield of social media and are defined as a web-based communication platform in which participants have uniquely identifiable profiles, publicly express connections, and consume, produce, and interact with user-generated content (Ellison & Boyd, 2014). Examples of social media platforms are Facebook, Instagram, TikTok, and more (Parker et al., 2016).

The relevant studies have the following characteristics. First, most of the studies focus on a singular social media platform, as mentioned earlier. In the golden age of social media, Facebook mostly dominated the market, gaining the largest market share, followed by the popularity of microblogs on Twitter. Scholars were interested in understanding customer engagement on Facebook (Carlson et al., 2018) or Twitter (Read et al., 2019). Later, scholars are more interested in customer engagement on Instagram, which has surpassed Facebook as a platform that continues to grow rapidly (Perrin & Anderson, 2019). Recently, scholars have paid attention to studying customer engagement on TikTok (Vinerean & Opreana, 2021). However, these studies are mainly from the perspective of social media marketing and content marketing, and the relevant analysis of customer-brand engagement is still limited because it is an emerging social media platform. Also, investigations of multiple social media platforms are limited (Shahbaznezhad et al., 2021), and the existing literature focuses on the comparisons on Facebook, Twitter, and Instagram. Unnava and Aravindakshan (2021) indicate that recent studies (e.g., Shahbaznezhad et al., 2021; Voorveld et al., 2018) discussed customer engagement on multiple social media platforms in terms of social media engagement rather than customer-brand engagement. Moreover, their study still investigated customer-brand engagement on Facebook, Twitter, and Instagram. Thus, this chapter tries to fill the research gap by studying customer-brand engagement on Twitter, Instagram, and TikTok.

2.3 *Customer-Brand Engagement Measurement in Social Media*

Existing literature supports the use of likes and comments as key metrics for measuring customer-brand engagement in social media (Godes & Mayzlin, 2009; Unnava & Aravindakshan, 2021). Likes are interpreted as customers accepting the perception of posts and holding positive attitudes toward brand images (Antonopoulos et al., 2016). Comments can be considered as a communication tool that helps marketers to understand customers in advance, as customers need to speed more energy expressing their thoughts, attitudes, and feelings when commenting than simply clicking the liking button (Levon & Steinfeld, 2015). Previous studies have shown that user engagement on social media, in the form of likes and comments can influence offline customer behavior positively (Lee et al., 2018; Mochon et al., 2017). For this reason, gaining customer engagement, such as likes and comments, has become almost an obsession for many brand and marketing practitioners. They are considered important tools for customizing a brand's online message to communicate effectively with customers (Kim, 2016). Consistent with the existing literature mentioned above, this chapter identified them as key predictors of customer-brand engagement on social media platforms.

Besides, the existing literature indicates that relevant studies used survey methods to collect primary data (Shahbaznezhad et al., 2021). Please see Table 1 for more details. Since emerging techniques such as data mining and natural language process have opened up new dimensions for academic research (Verma & Yadav, 2021), this chapter differentiates the prior studies by analyzing customer-brand engagement on three social media platforms through data mining.

3 Methods

To create sample data, this chapter first identified the most popular brands on Twitter, Instagram, and TikTok based on the official lists of the most engaging brands, named Best of Tweets, Instagram Trend Reports, and Year on TikTok. As a criterion, all selected brands actively use all three social media platforms. Consequently, 10 brands from different sectors were chosen (See Table 2). In line with previous studies (Godes & Mayzlin, 2009; Unnava & Aravindakshan, 2021), this chapter collected the number of followers, likes, and comments for these brands from January to June 2021 to calculate customer engagement rates.

After collection, the data were analyzed by data mining techniques. Data mining is the process of extracting high-quality information from a collection of documents and identifying predictive patterns through a series of analytical tools (Feldman & Sanger, 2007). The existing literature highlights several main reasons for using data mining in research: (1) unknown and valuable information can be extracted from the data; (2) meaningful patterns can be discovered through classification; (3) time and effort for data collection and analysis can be reduced (Weiss et al., 2010). In addition, the Information Resources Management Association (2018) endorses the use of various data mining techniques to monitor social media content, which is an indispensable tool for research on social media. Therefore, this chapter used data mining techniques to analyze the collected data.

The coding process was carried out in the following manner. With the support of Salloum et al.'s methodological framework for data mining on social media (2017), data of these ten brands were extracted from Twitter, Instagram, and TikTok, respectively. Based on customer engagement rates, data from highly engaging posts by brand on each platform were further analyzed in terms of brand content types and formats (Shahbaznezhad et al.,

Table 1 Comparison with recent relevant studies

Study	Social Media Platforms	Methods	Key Findings
Carlson et al. (2018)	Facebook	Survey	A theoretical framework showing how design characteristics of online service in social media brand pages induce customer value perceptions
Voorveld et al. (2018)	Facebook, YouTube, LinkedIn, Twitter, Google +, Instagram, Pinterest, Snapchat	Survey	Engagement is highly context-specific; it comprises various types of experiences on each social media platform such that each is experienced in a unique way
Santini et al. (2020)	Facebook, Twitter	Meta-analysis	Customer engagement is driven by satisfaction, positive emotions, and trust, but not by commitment
Shahbaznezhad et al. (2021)	Facebook, Instagram	Empirical	The effectiveness of social media content on users' engagement is moderated by content context
Unnava and Aravindakshan (2021)	Facebook, Twitter, Instagram	Empirical	Differential carryover, spillover, and direct effects within and across social media
Vinerean and Opreana (2021)	Facebook	Survey	Customer engagement is a multidimensional construct that is important for predicting and fostering customer loyalty

2021). The brand content data were separated into a representation of each word named tokens, which is a process known as tokenization, and then labeled with relative frequencies. Finally, these data were classified into different content types and formats based on their relative frequencies for the discussion of customer-brand engagement. The above steps were performed by Natural Language Toolkit (NLTK). Due to the word limit here, how to install and run NLTK is not described here, as the official documentation written by Bird et al. (2009) can be consulted.

Table 2 Brand descriptions

No	Brands	Sectors	Followers		
			Twitter	Instagram	TikTok
1	Starbucks	Beverages	11,009,518	17,838,018	1,800,000
2	Nike	Apparel, Sport	8,980,670	88,831,221	2,000,000
3	Disney	Entertainment	8,407,817	32,757,118	2,500,000
4	Burberry	Apparel, Luxury	8,190,906	18,848,413	86,400
5	H&M	Apparel	8,039,379	38,010,068	130,300
6	Gucci	Apparel, Luxury	6,666,503	46,847,070	1,600,000
7	GoPro	Electronics	2,104,075	18,544,078	1,800,000
8	Ford	Cars	1,382,867	5,047,560	41,900
9	Zara	Apparel	1,364,815	48,448,195	1,100,000
10	Dove	Beauty	186,450	687,362	19,200

4 Findings

4.1 Customer-Brand Engagement on Social Media Platforms

A total of 9,330 brand posts on Twitter, Instagram, and TikTok were analyzed for understanding the effectiveness of customer-brand engagement on social media platforms. The findings show significant differences in customer-brand engagement on three social media platforms (see Table 3). Although Twitter and Instagram have larger follower bases than TikTok, brands' posts on TikTok have the highest engagement rates with customers on social media, while brands' posts on Twitter have the lowest engagement rates with customers on social media. Respectively, customers' liking engagement with brands on TikTok is higher than that on Twitter and Instagram, and customers' commenting engagement with most brands on TikTok is highest except for H&M. In addition, the difference in customer-brand engagement for brands on Twitter and Instagram is smaller than the difference on TikTok. Namely, the difference in customer-brand engagement rates on Twitter is between 0.007 and 0.075%, and the difference in customer-brand engagement rates on Instagram is between 0.078 and 1.294%, however, the difference in customer-brand engagement rates on TikTok is between 2.151 and 174.427%. The significant difference in customer-brand engagement rates on TikTok indicates that brand and marketing practitioners have not developed unified strategies for interactive marketing on TikTok over Twitter and Instagram. Overall, the findings reveal that customer-brand engagement on social media platforms can be increased by the choice of social media platform, and TikTok, an emerging social media platform, has higher customer-brand engagement than Twitter and Instagram, despite the latter being larger platforms and widely used by brands.

Table 3 Customer-brand engagement rates of brands

Brands	Twitter				
	Avg Likes	Like Rates (%)	Avg Comments	Comment Rates (%)	Engagement Rates (%)
Starbucks	1246	0.011	143	0.001	0.012
Nike	7212	0.066	483	0.004	0.070
Disney	3312	0.039	62	0.001	0.040
Burberry	2620	0.032	173	0.002	0.034
H&M	681	0.008	79	0.000	0.008
Gucci	3405	0.051	470	0.007	0.058
GoPro	153	0.007	2	0.000	0.007
Ford	439	0.032	58	0.004	0.036
Zara	146	0.011	38	0.003	0.014
Dove	133	0.071	7	0.004	0.075
Brands	Instagram				
	Avg Likes	Like Rates (%)	Avg Comments	Comment Rates (%)	Engagement Rates (%)
Starbucks	49,341	0.277	670	0.004	0.281
Nike	233,553	0.124	3265	0.002	0.126
Disney	115,918	0.354	467	0.001	0.355
Burberry	14,766	0.078	55	0.003	0.078
H&M	29,513	0.078	87	0.000	0.078
Gucci	163,716	0.349	552	0.001	0.350
GoPro	35,315	0.190	320	0.002	0.192
Ford	64,628	1.280	683	0.014	1.294
Zara	36,764	0.076	833	0.002	0.078
Dove	1425	0.207	49	0.007	0.214
Brands	TikTok				
	Avg Likes	Like Rates (%)	Avg Comments	Comment Rates (%)	Engagement Rates (%)
Starbucks	68,334	3.796	1078	0.060	3.856
Nike	79,335	3.970	393	0.020	3.990
Disney	53,370	2.135	411	0.016	2.151
Burberry	29,977	34.696	303	0.351	35.047
H&M	8341	6.401	0	0.000	6.401
Gucci	80,318	5.020	1298	0.081	5.101
GoPro	693,770	38.543	7933	0.441	38.984

(continued)

Table 3 (continued)

Brands	TikTok				
	Avg Likes	Like Rates (%)	Avg Comments	Comment Rates (%)	Engagement Rates (%)
Ford	6681	15.945	626	1.494	17.439
Zara	68,914	6.265	409	0.037	6.302
Dove	33,360	173.750	130	0.677	174.427

Regarding brands, there are no significant differences between brand sectors and between luxury and non-luxury brands in terms of customer-brand engagement. Moreover, the findings indicate that different brand content on social media platforms makes no significant differences in customer-brand engagement. Specifically, Nike and Burberry use different brand content on three social media platforms. H&M and Gucci use the same brand content on Twitter and Instagram, but they use different brand content on TikTok. Dove uses different brand content on Twitter and Instagram, but it uses the same brand content on Instagram and TikTok. The rest of the brands use the same brand content on three social media platforms. In this context, the findings show insignificant differences in their customer-brand engagement. Therefore, the findings indicate that customer-brand engagement on social media platforms can be increased by employing different social media platforms rather than brand content differentiation on social media platforms.

4.2 Interactional Content of Brands on Social Media Platforms

Based on customer-brand engagement, high engaging brand posts on three social media platforms were further analyzed. The findings show that the informational content of brands is highly engaged with customers on TikTok, however, they are low engaged on Twitter and Instagram. In the case of TikTok, interactional content of brands was categorized into four types based on frequencies of words and hashtags (See Fig. 1): (1) *Informational content of brands.* This type of brand content includes announcing brand activities and introducing brand products (especially new releases) by tagging brand names and using other keywords such as "campaign", "collection", "#IcedCoffee", and "#MagicBoots". (2) *Educational content.* This type of brand content comes to customers in the form of tips and advice. For example, Nike posted a short video of a handstand in Nike shoes with the caption words "Pro Tip: STRECH before following this @Sky Brown #BreakDown! Let's go!". (3) *Festival content.* This type of brand content is related to holiday and seasonal recommendations such as "#holidayTikTok", "#Happy Holidays", "#GucciGift", etc. (4) *Entertaining content.* This type of brand content contains fun short videos and words of wisdom designed to promote customer-brand relationships, e.g., "Words to live by: #DovePartner @lizzo #Dove #SelfLove #SelfCare".

The findings reveal that the four types mentioned above also appear in brand content on Twitter and Instagram. As such, regarding the interactional content of brands, there are no significant differences in content types across the three social media platforms. Moreover, the findings indicate that the informational content of brands on TikTok is highly interactive with customers while interacting with customers on Twitter and Instagram is low. In other words, from the perspective of customer-brand engagement, there are significant differences in content types on three social media platforms. In addition, it is shown that public events are highly interactive with customers on Twitter and Instagram. For example, Dove launched a self-esteem project, and its content related to "hair discrimination", "black history month", and "pass the crown" is highly interactive with customers. However, this type of brand content is limited on TikTok, where it mainly introduces brand products.

In terms of brand content format, the findings reveal that brands introduce their products to customers in vivid detail through short videos on TikTok, which is highly interactive with customers. For example, Gucci uploaded a short video that demonstrates how to match Gucci outfits by showing how to match different types and colors of Gucci clothes one by one in the video. With 146,000 likes and 5300 comments, this short video is one of the most engaging brand posts for customers. Similarly, Zara shows how to use their different beauty products to match a beautiful makeup look in a short video, which has high customer-brand engagement with 887,600 likes and 8100 comments. Also, brand content with short videos is highly interactive with customers on Twitter and Instagram. For instance, a Nike post with a short video can have 54,700 likes and 1077 comments, while its posts have an average of 7212 likes and 483 comments, and its post with photos has 734 likes and 61 comments. Hence, brand content in different formats makes significant differences in customer-brand engagement, and brand content with short videos is highly interactive with customers on social media platforms.

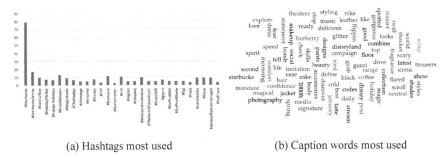

(a) Hashtags most used   (b) Caption words most used

Fig. 1 Hashtags and caption words most used

5 Discussion

5.1 Theoretical Implications

This chapter makes a three-fold contribution to the existing literature. First, this chapter extends the literature on customer-brand engagement in Interactive marketing on social media. Previous studies focused on customer engagement rather than customer-brand engagement on social media (Hu & Li, 2011; Purnawirawan et al., 2012; Santini et al., 2020). For this reason, there is limited analysis of customer-brand engagement on social media. Moreover, the analysis of social media itself as a determinant of customer-brand engagement has been limited in previous studies (Shahbaznezhad et al., 2021). As such, this chapter extends the existing literature by examining customer-brand engagement on different social media platforms. The findings are consistent with previous results that customer-brand engagement is highly context-specific and that it can be increased by the choice of social media platform (Shahbaznezhad et al., 2021; Unnava & Aravindakshan, 2021; Voorveld et al., 2018).

Second, this chapter fills a gap in the relevant literature on customer-brand engagement on multiple social media platforms, particularly the limited understanding of customer-brand engagement on TikTok. The pertinent literature is limited in its analysis of different social media platforms (Unnava & Aravindakshan, 2021). Most relevant studies have focused on a singular social media platform, especially Facebook, Twitter, or Instagram (Carlson et al., 2018; Shao & Ross, 2015; Vinerean & Opreana, 2021). As such, this chapter extends the above studies by examining customer-brand engagement on Twitter, Instagram, and TikTok. In particular, it extends the current limited understanding of customer-brand engagement on TikTok, an emerging social media platform. The findings support previous research that TikTok can affect customer engagement (Vinerean & Opreana, 2021). Based on Latane's Social Impact Theory (1981), as more users use TikTok, the platform becomes normalized, and building more immersive and engaging content can become more common (i.e., video sharing and music integration with content). Popular users help this impact grow even more as new users are attracted. Thus, this chapter shows that TikTok has higher customer-brand engagement than Twitter and Instagram, but is not yet widely used by brands.

Finally, this chapter extends the current limited understanding of customer-brand engagement on social media platforms in terms of brand content types and formats. Regarding brand content types, previously scholars argued one size does not fit all and emphasized the factors of social media content factors on customer engagement (Chahal & Rani, 2017; Pelletier et al., 2020; Swani et al., 2013). For this reason, brands adopt different content strategies for different social media platforms. For instance, GoPro uses Twitter primarily to post product information and communicate with customers, its Instagram to showcase the quality of its cameras and promote user-generated posts, and its TikTok to upload short videos showing tips and tutorials on how to use its products. The findings are inconsistent with previous studies that customer-brand engagement can be increased by different brand content across social media platforms. Instead, this chapter indicates that brand content differentiation on multiple social media platforms cannot significantly affect customer-brand engagement on social media platforms.

It is also evidenced by the findings in this chapter that informational content of brands such as announcements of brand activities and products have high levels of customer-brand engagement on TikTok. Earlier studies have also shown that social networking advertisements which are rich in terms of credible information content and thereby also entertaining in nature, which positively impacts the quality of life, usually generates a positive attitude toward the advertisement in the mind of the network user (Mukherjee & Banerjee, 2017; Taylor et al., 2011). The findings of the present chapter are in sync with earlier studies in this aspect, however, this chapter reveals that the engagement of informational content on Twitter and Instagram is low. This chapter argues that this is because of brand content formats. The findings show that customer-brand engagement on social media platforms can be increased by brand content formats, as evidenced by the high customer-brand engagement of brand content in short videos on Twitter, Instagram, and TikTok. Therefore, this chapter fills a gap in the limited analysis on the role of content formats in customer-brand engagement on social media (Shahbaznezhad et al., 2021), and highlights that customer-brand engagement on social media platforms can be increased by the choice of social media platforms and brand content formats, rather than brand content differentiation on different social media platforms.

5.2 Managerial Implications

From a practical perspective, this chapter also provides several insights for brand and marketing practitioners. Since TikTok has been shown to have high customer-brand engagement, brand and marketing practitioners are encouraged to use TikTok to increase customer-brand engagement on social media. When selecting the brands investigated in this chapter, it was found that TikTok is not widely used by brands yet. Many brands such as Sprout Social, Marlboro, and Costco do not have official TikTok accounts. For those brands already on TikTok, the number of followers is far less than on Twitter and Instagram and the difference in customer-brand engagement rates on TikTok is significant, suggesting that brands need to work on their TikTok brand pages to attract more followers and increase customer-brand engagement. Specifically, based on the findings in this chapter, it is recommended that brand and marketing practitioners use more informational content of brands to engage with customers on TikTok, which is highly interactive with customers on TikTok.

Furthermore, brand and marketing practitioners may consider using the same informational content of brands to engage with customers on Twitter,

Instagram, and TikTok. Currently, brand and marketing practitioners focus more on Twitter and Instagram than TikTok because they have larger follower bases, which can be traced by the frequency of brand posts, the number of brand posts and followers, and different brand content types. For this reason, brand and marketing practitioners have difficulty coordinating their efforts on three social media platforms. Considering customer-brand engagement on social media platforms cannot be increased by brand content differentiation on social media platforms, the use of the same informational content of brands can help brand practitioners save time and effort. Additionally, brand and marketing practitioners are advised to use the same informational content of brands together with short videos on Twitter and Instagram, as short videos are found to be highly interactive between brands and customers on both social media platforms. Finally, brand and marketing practitioners may consider using short videos together with other brand content types in their Interactive marketing on Twitter and Instagram in order to increase customer-brand engagement.

5.3 *Limitations and Future Research*

Naturally, this chapter has several limitations, which enlightens new directions for future research. For one thing, this chapter exemplified customer-brand engagement on social media platforms by brands of different sectors on Twitter, Instagram, and TikTok. Future research could consider exploring more brands from more sectors, a specific sector and different social media platforms (YouTube, Reddit, etc.) to test different effects of customer-brand engagement on social media. For instance, it would be interesting to further examine the effectiveness of social media platforms on customer-brand engagement for personal and organizational brands, as evidenced by Devereux et al. (2020) that small businesses with limited resources need to make important overall decisions about which platforms are best for marketing their business.

For another, this chapter finds that customer-brand engagement on social media is related to social media platforms and brand content formats, rather than brand content differentiation on social media platforms. In addition to these factors, other factors such as product factors (e.g., product types), customer factors (e.g., demographic groups), and influencers' effects (e.g., celebrities) have been proposed in the existing literature (Purnawirawan et al., 2012; Shao & Ross, 2015). These factors are not considered in this chapter because the focus of this chapter is on the brand factors of customer-brand engagement, and influencers are not frequently used by brands on TikTok. Therefore, future research could consider investigating these factors of customer-brand engagement on social media platforms such as customer motivation, perception, and trust.

REFERENCES

Anderson, E. T., & Simester, D. I. (2014). Reviews without a purchase: Low ratings, loyal customers, and deception. *Journal of Marketing Research, 51*(3), 249–269. https://doi.org/10.1509/jmr.13.0209

Antonopoulos, N., Giomelakis, D., Veglis, A., & Gardikiotis, A. (2016). Web third-person effect hypothesis: Do likes and shares affect users' perceptions? *Journalism Mass Communication, 6*(12), 711–729. https://doi.org/10.17265/2160-6579/2016.12.001

Azar, S. L., Machado, J. C., Vacas-de-Carvalho, L., & Mendes, A. (2016). Motivations to interact with brands on Facebook—Towards a typology of consumer-brand interactions. *Journal of Brand Management, 23*(2), 153–178. https://doi.org/10.1057/bm.2016.3

Baldus, B. J., Voorhees, C., & Calantone, R. (2015). Online brand community engagement: Scale development and validation. *Journal of Business Research, 68*(5), 978–985. https://doi.org/10.1016/j.busres.2014.09.035

Bird, S., Klein, E., & Loper, E. (2009). *Natural language processing with Python*. O'Reilly Media.

Borah, A., & Tellis, G. J. (2016). Halo (spillover) effects in social media: Do product recalls of one brand hurt or help rival brands? *Journal of Marketing Research, 53*(2), 143–160. https://doi.org/10.1509/jmr.13.0009

Carlson, J., Rahman, M. M., Voola, R., & Vries, N. J. (2018). Customer engagement behaviours in social media: Capturing innovation opportunities. *Journal of Services Marketing, 32*(1), 83–94. https://doi.org/10.1108/JSM-02-2017-0059

Chahal, H., & Rani, A. (2017). How trust moderates social media engagement and brand equity. *Journal of Research in Interactive Marketing, 11*(3), 312–335. https://doi.org/10.1108/JRIM-10-2016-0104

Christodoulides, G. (2009). Branding in the post-internet era. *Marketing Theory, 9*(1), 141–144. https://doi.org/10.1177/1470593108100071

Devereux, E., Grimmer, L., & Grimmer, M. (2020). Consumer engagement on social media: Evidence from small retailers. *Journal of Consumer Behaviour, 19*(2), 151–159. https://doi.org/10.1002/cb.1800

Ellison, N.B., & Boyd, D. (2014). Sociality through social network sites, Dutton. In W.H. (Ed.), *The Oxford handbook of internet studies*. Oxford University Press.

Feldman, R., & Sanger, J. (2007). *The text mining handbook: Advanced approaches in analyzing unstructured data*. Cambridge University Press.

France, C., Merrilees, B., & Miller, D. (2016). An integrated model of customer-brand engagement: Drivers and consequences. *Journal of Brand Management, 23*, 119–136. https://doi.org/10.1057/bm.2016.4

García-de-Frutos, N., & Estrella-Ramón, A. (2021). You absolutely (don't) need this! Examining differences on customer engagement components for (anti)haul Youtubers' videos. *Journal of Research in Interactive Marketing, 15*(1), 86–103. https://doi.org/10.1108/JRIM-11-2019-0181

Gligor, D., & Bozkurt, S. (2021). The role of perceived social media agility in customer engagement. *Journal of Research in Interactive Marketing, 15*(1), 125–146. https://doi.org/10.1108/JRIM-12-2019-0196

Godes, D., & Mayzlin, D. (2009). Firm-created word-of-mouth communication: Evidence from a field test. *Marketing Science, 28*(4), 721–739. https://doi.org/10.1287/mksc.1080.0444

Graham, K. W., & Wilder, K. M. (2020). Consumer-brand identity and online advertising message elaboration: Effect on attitudes, purchase intent and willingness to share. *Journal of Research in Interactive Marketing, 14*(1), 111–132. https://doi.org/10.1108/JRIM-01-2019-0011

Hajli, N., Shamugam, M., Papagiannidis, S., Zahay, D., & Richard, M. O. (2017). Branding co-creation with members of online brand communities. *Journal of Business Research, 70*, 136–144. https://doi.org/10.1016/j.busres.2016.08.026

Hamzah, Z. L., Wahab, H. A., & Waqas, M. (2021). Unveiling drivers and brand relationship implication of customer engagement with social media brand posts. *Journal of Research in Interactive Marketing, 15*(2), 336–358. https://doi.org/10.1108/JRIM-05-2020-0113

Hanlon, A. (2019). *Digital marketing: Strategic planning & integration*. Sage Publications Ltd.

Hollebeek, L. D., Glynn, M. S., & Brodie, R. J. (2014). Consumer brand engagement in social media: Conceptualization, scale development and validation. *Journal of Interactive Marketing, 28*(2), 149–165. https://doi.org/10.1016/j.intmar.2013.12.002

Hu, Y., & Li, X. (2011). Context-dependent product evaluations: An empirical analysis of Internet book reviews. *Journal of Interactive Marketing, 25*(3), 123–133. https://doi.org/10.1016/j.intmar.2010.10.001

Information Resources Management Association. (2018). *Fashion and textiles: Breakthroughs in research and practice*. IGI Global.

Izogo, E. E., & Mpinganjira, M. (2020). Behavioral consequences of customer inspiration: The role of social media inspirational content and cultural orientation. *Journal of Research in Interactive Marketing, 14*(4), 431–459. https://doi.org/10.1108/JRIM-09-2019-0145

Ji, C., Mieiro, S., & Huang, G. (2022). How social media advertising features influence consumption and sharing intentions: The mediation of customer engagement. *Journal of Research in Interactive Marketing, 16*(1), 137–153. https://doi.org/10.1108/JRIM-04-2020-0067

Kamboj, S., Sarmah, B., Gupta, S., & Dwivedi, Y. (2018). Examining branding co-creation in brand communities on social media: Applying the paradigm of stimulus-organism-response. *International Journal of Information Management, 39*, 169–185. https://doi.org/10.1016/j.ijinfomgt.2017.12.001

Kim, H. (2016). Who likes, shares, and comments on Facebook? A comparative study of Facebook use and engagement between U.S. and South Korean college students. *Asian Journal of Information and Communications, 8*(1), 69–83.

Kim, K. Y., Yim, M. Y.-C., Kim, E. (A.)., & Reeves, W. (2021). Exploring the optimized social advertising strategy that can generate consumer engagement with green messages on social media. *Journal of Research in Interactive Marketing, 15*(1), 30–48.https://doi.org/10.1108/JRIM-10-2019-0171

Kircova, I., Yaman, Y., & Kose, S. G. (2018). Instagram, Facebook or Twitter: Which engages best? A comparative study of consumer brand engagement and social commerce purchase intention. *European Journal of Economics and Business Studies, 4*(1), 268–278. https://doi.org/10.26417/ejes.v4i1.p268-278

Lee, D., Hosanagar, K., & Nair, H. (2018). Advertising content and consumer engagement on social media: Evidence from Facebook. *Management Science, 64*(11), 5105–5131. https://doi.org/10.1287/mnsc.2017.2902

Lev-On, A., & Steinfeld, N. (2015). Local engagement online: Municipal Facebook pages as hubs of interaction. *Government Information Quarterly, 32*(3), 299–307. https://doi.org/10.1016/j.giq.2015.05.007

Liu, L., Dzyabura, D., & Mizik, N. (2020). Visual listening in: Extracting brand image portrayed on social media. *Marketing Science, 39*(4), 669–686. https://doi.org/10.1287/mksc.2020.1226

Mochon, D., Johnson, K., Schwartz, J., & Ariely, D. (2017). What are likes worth? A Facebook page field experiment. *Journal of Marketing Research, 54*(2), 306–317. https://doi.org/10.1509/jmr.15.0409

Mukherjee, K., & Banerjee, N. (2017). Effect of social networking advertisements on shaping consumers' attitude. *Global Business Review, 18*(5), 1291–1306. https://doi.org/10.1177/0972150917710153

Pansari, A., & Kumar, V. (2017). Customer engagement: The construct, antecedents, and consequences. *Journal of the Academy of Marketing Science, 45*(3), 22–30. https://doi.org/10.1007/s11747-016-0485-6

Parker, G. G., Van Alstyne, M. W., & Choudary, S. P. (2016). *Platform revolution: How networked are transforming the economy-and how to make them work for you*. W.W. Norton & Company.

Paruthi, M., & Kaur, H. (2017). Scale development and validation for measuring online engagement. *Journal of Internet Commerce, 16*(2), 127–147. https://doi.org/10.1080/15332861.2017.1299497

Pelletier, M. J., Krallman, A., Adams, F. G., & Hancock, T. (2020). One size doesn't fit all: A uses and gratifications analysis of social media platforms. *Journal of Research in Interactive Marketing, 14*(2), 269–284. https://doi.org/10.1108/JRIM-10-2019-0159

Perrin, A., & Anderson, M. (2019, April 10). Share of U.S. adults using social media, including Facebook, is mostly unchanged since 2018. *Pew Research Center*. http://www.pewresearch.org/fact-tank/2019/04/10/share-of-u-s-adults-using-social-media-including-facebook-is-mostly-unchanged-since-2018. Accessed 15 December 2021.

Purnawirawan, N., De Pelsmacker, P., & Dens, N. (2012). Balance and sequence in online reviews: How perceived usefulness affects attitudes and intentions. *Journal of Interactive Marketing, 26*(4), 244–255. https://doi.org/10.1016/j.intmar.2012.04.002

Read, W., Robertson, N., McQuilken, L., & Ferdous, A. S. (2019). Consumer engagement on Twitter: Perceptions of the brand matter. *European Journal of Marketing, 53*(9), 1905–1933. https://doi.org/10.1108/EJM-10-2017-0772

Salloum, S. A., AI-Emran, M., & Shaalan, K. (2017). Mining social media text: Extracting knowledge from Facebook. *International Journal of Computing and Digital Systems, 6*(2), 73–81. https://doi.org/10.12785/ijcds/060203

Santini, F. O., Ladeira, W. J., Pinto, D. C., Herter, M. M., Sampaio, C. H., & Babin, B. J. (2020). Customer engagement in social media: A framework and meta-analysis. *Journal of the Academy of Marketing Science, 48*, 1211–1228. https://doi.org/10.1007/s11747-020-00731-5

Shahbaznezhad, H., Dolan, R., & Rashidirad, M. (2021). The role of social media content format and platform in users' engagement behavior. *Journal of Interactive Marketing, 53*(4), 47–65. https://doi.org/10.1016/j.intmar.2020.05.001

Shao, W., & Ross, M. (2015). Testing a conceptual model of Facebook brand page communities. *Journal of Research in Interactive Marketing, 9*(3), 239–258. https://doi.org/10.1108/JRIM-05-2014-0027

Swani, K., Milne, G., & Brown, B. P. (2013). Spreading the word through likes on Facebook: Evaluating the message strategy effectiveness of Fortune 500 companies. *Journal of Research in Interactive Marketing, 7*(4), 269–294. https://doi.org/10.1108/JRIM-05-2013-0026

Tajfel, H., & Turner, J. C. (1979). An integrative theory of intergroup conflict. In W. G. Austin & S. Worchel (Eds.), *The Social Pychology of Intergroup Relations* (pp. 33–48). Brooks/Cole.

Taylor, D. G., Lewin, J. E., & Strutton, D. (2011). Friends, fans, and followers: Do ads work on social networks? How gender and age shape receptivity. *Journal of Advertising Research, 51*(1), 258–275. https://doi.org/10.2501/JAR-51-1-258-275

Unnava, V., & Aravindakshan, A. (2021). How does consumer engagement evolve when brands post across multiple social media? *Journal of the Academy of Marketing Science, 49*, 864–881. https://doi.org/10.1007/s11747-021-00785-z

Vazquez, E. E. (2020). Effects of enduring involvement and perceived content vividness on digital engagement. *Journal of Research in Interactive Marketing, 14*(1), 1–16. https://doi.org/10.1108/JRIM-05-2018-0071

Verma, S., & Yadav, N. (2021). Past, present, and future of electronic word of mouth (EWOM). *Journal of Interactive Marketing, 53*(6), 111–128. https://doi.org/10.1016/j.intmar.2020.07.001

Vernuccio, M., Pagani, M., Barbarossa, C., & Pastore, A. (2016). The role of social-interactive engagement and social identity in the development of brand love through Facebook fan page. In M. Obal, N. Krey, & C. Bushardt (Eds.), Let's get engaged! Crossing the threshold of marketing's engagement era. *Developments in Marketing Science: Proceedings of the Academy of Marketing Science* (pp. 217–218). Springer. https://doi.org/10.1007/978-3-319-11815-4_69

Vinerean, S., & Opreana, A. (2021). Measuring customer engagement in social media marketing: A higher-order model. *Journal of Theoretical and Applied Electronic Commerce Research, 16*(7), 2633–2654. https://doi.org/10.3390/jtaer16070145

Voorveld, H. A. M., van Noort, G., Muntinga, D. G., & Bronner, F. (2018). Engagement with social media and social media advertising: The differentiating role of platform type. *Journal of Advertising, 47*(1), 38–54. https://doi.org/10.1080/00913367.2017.1405754

Wang, C. L. (2021). New frontiers and future directions in interactive marketing: Inaugural editorial. *Journal of Research in Interactive Marketing, 15*(1), 1–9. https://doi.org/10.1108/JRIM-03-2021-270

Wang, T., Limbu, Y. B., & Fang, X. (2022). Consumer brand engagement on social media in the COVID-19 pandemic: The roles of country-of-origin and consumer animosity. *Journal of Research in Interactive Marketing, 16*(1), 45–63. https://doi.org/10.1108/JRIM-03-2021-0065

Weiss, S. M., Indurkhya, N., Zhang, T., & Damerau, F. (2010). *Text mining: Predictive methods for analyzing unstructured information.* Springer Science & Business Media.

Zimand-Sheiner, D., Kol, O., & Levy, S. (2021). It makes a difference! Impact of social and personal message appeals on engagement with sponsored posts. *Journal of Research in Interactive Marketing, 15*(4), 641–660.

CHAPTER 20

When in Rome, Do as the Romans Do: Differences of Interactive Behaviors Across Social Media Networks

Qingjiang Yao

1 Introduction

Social media have grown into an instrumental marketing tool: in 2021, 42% of the world population, 93% of internet users, and 85% of mobile users spend a daily average of 2 h and 24 min on social media (40% of those users are for business purpose. Dean, 2021; Khoros, 2021); in the U.S., 72% of the population use social media (84% of 18–29, 81% of 30–49, 73% of 50–64; 66% of the males, 78% of the females; 69% of the Whites, 77% of the Blacks, and 80% of the Hispanics), who are more likely to have higher income, better education, and live in urban areas (Pelletier et al., 2020; Pew Research Center, 2021). More importantly, 51% of Americans and 40% of Canadians are now consuming news from social media (Walker & Matsa, 2021; Yao, 2021a), turning it into an indispensable source of information.

A survey of 4,300 marketers in the world (55% from the U.S.) shows that most of them use social media in campaigns (41% with full-time staff) to increase exposure (88%) or traffic to their websites (79%), generate leads (69%), develop loyal fans (61%), improve sales (60%), provide marketplace insights (56%), or grow business partnerships (50%. Stelzner, 2021). Social media advertising created 41.5 billion in revenue in 2020, raising by 16.3% from the previous year and accounting for 29.6% of all internet ad revenue

Q. Yao (✉)
Lamar University, Beaumont, TX, USA
e-mail: qyao@lamar.edu

(IAB, 2021). Social media have transformed marketing into a two-way, multi-sided value creation process (Wang, 2021) for marketers to connect, engage, coordinate, and collaborate with consumers.

Globally popular social media, based on visitor traffics, include YouTube, Tmall (a Chinese social shopping site), QQ (a Chinese social networking service, or SNS, site), Facebook, Taobao (a Chinese social shopping site), JD (a Chinese social shopping site), Amazon, Wikipedia, Weibo (a Chinese microblogging site), Zoom, Reddit, and Instagram. The U.S. top list of social media consists of YouTube, Amazon, Facebook, Zoom, Reddit, Wikipedia, eBay, Instagram, LinkedIn, Esty, Walmart, Twitter, and Twitch (https://www.alexa.com/topsites). Pew Research Center (2021) provides a similar U.S. ranking of social media based on percentage of U.S. adults as users: YouTube (81%), Facebook (69%), Instagram (40%), Pinterest (31%), LinkedIn (28%), Snapchat (25%), Twitter (23%), WhatsApp (23%), TikTok (21%), Reddit (18%), and Nextdoor (13%). Those different types of social media attract different segments of consumers, facilitate different uses and co-creation activities (Pelletier et al., 2020), and feature different functions for marketers to employ, who should "when in Rome, do as the Romans do" to build more effective interactive campaigns. This chapter categorizes social media into five types, provides category representatives, examines the demographics of their users, identifies their five major functions in interactive marketing, and discusses related measurement and ethical issues.

2 Categories, Representatives, and User Demographics of Social Media

Social media are widely defined as a group of online applications that are built on Web 2.0 and facilitate the creation and exchange of User Generated Content, which are usually categorized into six types: (1) collaborative projects/forums, (2) blogs and microblogs, (3) content communities, (4) social networking service (SNS) sites, (5) virtual game worlds, and (6) virtual social worlds (Kaplan & Haenlein, 2010; Li & Stacks, 2015). Researchers have also classified social media in other ways (e.g., Dewing, 2012; Moran, 2017; Quesenberry, 2019), and some categories are not included in the categorization above: ratings and reviews (Quesenberry, 2019) or consumer review networks (Moran, 2017), social shopping networks, and sharing economy networks (Moran, 2017). Meanwhile, some categories above (e.g., 2 and 3, 5 and 6) can be combined. This chapter regroups those classifications into five categories for parsimony and comprehensiveness, whose representatives' user profiles (suggesting specific marketing focuses and strategies) and marketing functions are discussed in the following section.

2.1 Social Networking

This is the most popular category of social media that enables users to connect with people and build or maintain personal, social, or professional relationships. SNS sites allow both parties in a relationship to see each other's activities equally. To ensure the quality of the relationships, limits of contacts or connections are usually installed. Representatives are Facebook (limited to 5,000 friends) and LinkedIn (limited to 30,000 connections); Snapchat also belongs to this category (limited to 6,000 friends. See Table 1). Point-to-point SNS media such as Facebook Messenger and WhatsApp are a special case in this category.

2.1.1 Facebook

Founded in 2004, Facebook has over 2.7 billion monthly active users globally (Rodriguez, 2021), with 86% of those aged 18–29, 77% 30–49, 54% females, and more than 81% of each income group, who in average spend 35 min per day, mostly from a mobile device (96%. Khoros, 2021). In the U.S., 70% of the users visit it at least once a day, 17% at least once a week, who are more likely to be women, those with a college degree or more, aged 18–29, or with an annual family income of $30 k–$49,999 (Pew Research Center, 2021). Because 47% of the U.S. adults get news from Facebook (64% of women vs. men, 35%; Whites, 60% vs. Hispanics, 20% and Blacks, 11%. Walker & Matsa, 2021), it has an immense influence on users and their Facebook friends or friends of friends (Bond et al., 2012). Most global marketers (93%) use Facebook, 54% think of it as the most important social platform for marketers, and 47% plan to increase their Facebook marketing in the next 12 months (Stelzner, 2021). Facebook marketing is particularly effective when consumers have low involvement or a stronger relationship with the brands, or physically live closer to the marketers (Xue, 2019); it does not focus on a specific usage intention or co-creation activity (Pelletier et al., 2020).

2.1.2 LinkedIn

Launched in 2003, LinkedIn is a professional SNS site and has almost 810 million members globally in more than 200 countries/territories (https://about.linkedin.com), with 57% being men, 60% aged 25–34, and over 77% outside of the U.S. (Newberry & Beveridge, 2022). In the U.S, it reaches 28% of the adults and is used more by men, the Whites or the Blacks, and those aged 30–49, 50–64, having a family income of more than $75 k (50%), with a college degree (50%), or living in suburban or urban areas (Pew Researcher Center, 2021). 27% of the users regularly consume news from it (Walker & Matsa, 2021). 61% of the global marketers (81% of the B2B marketers) use it; although only 15% report it as the most important social platform for marketers, more than half (54%) plan to increase LinkedIn marketing (Stelzner, 2021).

Table 1 User Demographics of the Representative Social Media

		SNS				Content Sharing				Social Knowledge	
		Facebook (%)	LinkedIn (%)	Snapchat (%)	YouTube (%)	Twitter (%)	Instagram (%)	TikTok (%)	Reddit (%)	Pinterest (%)
Gender	Men	61	31	22	82	25	36	17	23	16
	Women	77	26	28	80	22	44	24	12	46
Age	18–29	70	30	65	95	42	71	48	36	32
	30–49	77	36	24	91	27	48	22	22	34
	50–64	73	33	12	83	18	29	14	10	38
	65+	50	11	2	49	7	13	4	3	18
Ethnicity	White	67	29	23	79	22	35	18	17	34
	Black	74	27	26	84	29	49	30	17	35
	Hispanic	72	19	31	85	23	52	31	14	18
Family Income	< $30 K	70	12	25	75	12	35	22	10	21
	$30 K–$49,999	76	21	27	83	29	45	29	17	33
	$50 K–$74,999	61	21	29	79	22	39	20	20	29
	≥ $75 K	70	50	28	90	34	47	20	26	40
Education	≤ high school	64	10	21	70	14	30	21	9	22
	Some college	71	28	32	86	26	44	24	20	36
	College graduate	73	51	23	89	33	49	19	26	37
Living Area	Urban	70	30	28	84	27	45	24	18	30
	Suburban	70	33	25	81	23	41	20	21	32
	Rural	67	15	18	74	18	25	16	10	34

	SNS			Content Sharing					Social Knowledge	
	Facebook (%)	LinkedIn (%)	Snapchat (%)	YouTube (%)	Twitter (%)	Instagram (%)	TikTok (%)		Reddit (%)	Pinterest (%)
Total	69	28	25	81	23	40	21		18	31

Note Statistics are from the Pew Research Center (2021), which has no user info for the representatives of social media for shopping, rating, and reviewing media and virtual world. Entries are % of U.S. adults who say they ever use that social media

2.2 Content Sharing

This category of social media enables users to create and share textual, imagery, or audiovisual content to an audience, whose members are sometimes registered users and sometimes not. Content sharing platforms mainly facilitate a broadcasting model that allows the followers/subscribers to be updated by the content sharer. Examples are YouTube and Twitter; Instagram, TikTok, Twitch, and blogs or podcasts are also content-sharing social media.

2.2.1 YouTube

YouTube, a video-sharing platform launched in 2005 and acquired by Google in 2006, has 1.7 billion unique monthly users globally. Those users largely look for musical, gaming, and sports content, 54% male and 22% accessing via mobile, spending almost 24 h each month watching and visiting twice as many pages as desktop users; YouTube ads reach mostly males aged 25–34 or users from India or the U.S. (McLachlan, 2022). In the U.S., 54% of adults use YouTube daily and 29%, weekly, with 81% having used it. It is more popular among the younger generations of Americans (95% of 18–29 and 85% of 13–17), the Hispanics or Blacks, and those with a family income of more than $75 K (90%), with a college degree or some college education, or living in the urban or suburban areas (Pew Research Center, 2021). Americans use YouTube mainly for five purposes: to figure out how to do things they haven't done before (51%); to pass time (28%); to acquire info and decide whether to buy a product (19%); to understand things happening in the world (19%. Smith et al., 2018). 26% of American adults get news from it (Stocking et al., 2020) and 81% of the parents let children watch it (34% doing so regularly. Newberry, 2021a). More than half (55%) of global marketers use YouTube, although only 6% think of it as the most important social platform (Stelzner, 2021). A function of YouTube marketing is fulfilled by the YouTubers, influencers whose channels have thousands or more subscribers and can influence them in cognitive, affective, and behavioral aspects via self-connection, love, and trust (Correa et al., 2020). Ford, for instance, selected a group of YouTubers similar to their target consumers for Fiesta in the launching campaign and sent the new car to let them do fun things and post videos. That "Ford Fiesta Movement" campaign created 6.5 million views (Kodish, 2015).

2.2.2 Twitter

Launched in 2006, Twitter enables users to post messages up to 280 characters with photos or videos and has 211 million daily active users worldwide (Hutchinson, 2021), who are more likely 25–34 (38.5%) or 35–49 years old (20.7%. https://www.statista.com/statistics/283119/age-distribution-of-global-twitter-users/) and live outside of the U.S. (80%. Shel, 2020). Twitter content and ads are mostly consumed in the U.S., Japan (where Twitter is the most popular western social media), the UK, Saudi Arabia, and Brazil (Shel, 2020). In the U.S., it is used by 46% of the adults daily (27%, weekly) and preferred by men, Black people, and those aged 18–29 (42%), with some college education or above, with a family income of $75 K + , or live in urban or suburban areas (Pew Research Center, 2021). 55% of the users consume news regularly from it (Walker & Matsa, 2021) and 48% of the global marketers use it in 2021 (Stelzner, 2021). Twitter campaigns are more effective for informational and social purposes (Pelletier et al., 2020): for instance, realizing that 80% of women encountered negative chatters on social media, Dove countered back and created the #SpeakBeautiful Effect campaign on Twitter in 2016, gaining 800 million impressions (Harmeling et al., 2017).

2.3 Social Knowledge, News, and Bookmarking

These social media enable users to collectively build, share, or save news or knowledge. Examples are Wikipedia and Reddit; Pinterest is also in this category.

2.3.1 Wikipedia

Wikipedia is a social collaboration knowledge site founded in 2001. Available in 315 languages for more than 50 million registered users and with a daily average page view of 258 million, its top three languages are English, Cebuano, and Swedish, and its top three countries of editor feeders are the U.S., Germany, and Russia (Chang, 2022). Its most visited English pages cover the topics of ISIS, Google, Facebook, Bollywood movies, etc.; Japanese pages: world of comics, movies, etc.; Spanish pages: volleyball, WWI, etc.; Russian pages: VK, classmates, etc. (Anderson et al., 2016). It is used more by those aged 18–29, 62% v. 30–49, 52%; 50–64, 49%; 65 + , 33%. (https://www.statista.com/statistics/271189/us-wikipedia-users-by-age-group/); the Whites (55% v. Blacks, 43%; Hispanics, 40%), or people with some college education (52%) or above (69% v. high-school diploma holders, 41%; or below, 30%. Heimlich, 2011). Most of its English editors are male (84%) or from the U.S. (20%), who volunteer to edit to share knowledge (71%), make information free (69%), fulfill the fun of contribution (63%), or fulfill professional obligations (7%. Chang, 2022). Its content reliability has been recognized (Jerusalem Post Staff, 2022).

2.3.2 Reddit

Reddit, launched in 2005, is a social news and bookmarking forum that allows users to share and comment on news or issues and vote for their popularity. It has more than 2.5 million communities (subreddits) on different topics (top five: r/Askreddit, r/funny, r/todaylearned, r/Science, and r/pics) and 430 million monthly active users, mainly from the U.S. (46.8%), UK (6.4%), and Canada (5.3%. WebsiteBuilder, 2021). Reddit reaches 18% of the U.S. adults, used more by men, White or Black people, and those aged 18–29 (36%), with an annual family income of $50 K or above, or living in suburban or urban areas (Pew Research Center, 2021). Attractive posts should be under

120 characters and posted on the weekends or Mondays (Lin, 2021). 39% of its U.S. users regularly consume news from it (Walker & Matsa, 2021).

2.4 Social Shopping, Rating, and Reviewing

These social media allow users to find, shop, or review products/services on their platforms, in a business-to-business (B2B), business-to-consumer (B2C), or consumer-to-consumer (C2C) form. This category is often ignored by social media researchers but plays a significant role in interactive marketing. Representatives are Amazon and Yelp. Social media in other categories may also maintain such a function, such as Facebook's Marketplace.

2.4.1 Amazon

Created in 1994 as a small online bookstore, Amazon has evolved into a giant social shopping site with 300 million active users (197 million monthly active users), generating an annual revenue of more than $280 billion (Curry, 2022). Amazon enjoys about 50% of the U.S. e-commerce market and serves customers in more than 100 countries, who tend to be younger, wealthier, and more educated (Petrov, 2022). Amazon reviews, most extremely positive or negative, are found civil and helpful to users and written with the strategies of expressing disappointment or explicit complaints, expressing anger, drawing one's conclusion, or warning others; they improve customer perception of the usefulness and social presence of the social shopping site (Kilic & Karatepe, 2021). Amazon also has over 200 million prime customers worldwide, covering two-thirds of U.S. households (Petrov, 2022). It has 12.1% of the connected TV market, 55 million music users, 175 million prime video subscribers, and 67–85% of the e-book market (Curry, 2022).

2.4.2 Yelp

Yelp, founded in 2004, allows customers to evaluate and comment on local businesses and has 244 million reviews, which were mainly generated by customers with a college education or above (80%) or $100 K + annual household income (55%. https://www.yelp-press.com/company/fast-facts/default.aspx). Yelp users are also more likely to be female (53%), living in urban areas (50%), or relatively younger (25–34: 29%; 35–44: 28%), 78% of whom are active on social media daily. 12% of U.S. consumers use yelp, mostly discussing food and drinks (56%), movies and series (45%), vacation and travel (43%), music (42%), and even politics (25%). Users recommend the brands/products because they like the product (77%), brand (67%), customer service (54%), or discounts or giveaways (46%). 79% of them trust yelp reviews as much as recommendations from family or friends. 94% of the users are more likely to purchase if the reviews are positive, and 92% are less likely to buy when seeing negative reviews (Andre, 2022).

2.5 Virtual World

This category of social media enables users to enjoy social activities, interactions, or games in a computer-simulated, 360°, 3-D environment, whose essence is well caught in the concept "metaverse" (https://about.facebook.com/meta/), a term appearing in the sci-fi literature since 1992 and popularized lately by some tech giants such as Facebook's Mark Zuckerberg (Ravenscraft, 2021). Virtual world also tends to be ignored by social media researchers, but it represents the future of social media and interactive marketing because it can encompass all other categories of social media in one platform and is very promising with the quick development in big data, VR, AR, and artificial intelligence (Edelman, 2022). Representatives are Second Life or the Massively Multiplayer Online Role-Playing Games (MMORPGs) such as Roblox and World of Warcraft (WoW).

2.5.1 Second Life

Launched in 2003, Second Life, an immersive online social platform, enables its one million users (in their digital avatars) to live in a virtual world and work, build structures or communities, create arts, travel, involve in daily life or professional interactions, and buy or sell digital goods with digital currencies that can be converted into U.S. dollars (Edelman, 2022). Users tend to be in their 40–50s and creative, imaginative, or unconventional, some with physical or mental disabilities that hinder real-life interactions, some unsatisfied with their real-world identity or relationships, and some seeking fantasies with the magic powers of teleporting, flying, or changing the viewing angles (Buscemi, 2020; Jamison, 2017; Lee, 2017). Some users have integrated their virtual and real worlds and extended significant relationships in the former into the latter (Buscemi, 2020; Scarlette, 2022), creating a combination that is closer to the meaning of the buzzword "metaverse" (Ravenscraft, 2021). Many organizations, even universities, have bought lands and buildings in Second Life for branding or teaching (Rospiglios, 2022). The COVID-19 pandemic and the emergence of the metaverse concept reenergize Second Life, which will be further bolstered by its integration with VR and AR advancements (Edelman, 2022; Jamison, 2017).

2.5.2 MMORPGs

MMORPGs are video games played online with massive players simultaneously. Those virtual environments have pre-designed characters, settings, and storylines (themes) for players to choose and interact or compete with fellow players, trade digital commodities, and complete challenges to gain awards (Danka, 2020). Players are driven to the game mainly by status-seeking, flow, skills with the game, and social motivation (Dindar, 2018), or achievement, social interaction, and immersion (Kneer et al., 2019). Only about 41% of players are female, who lean more toward cooperative or self-identifiable games; males lean more toward competitive games, such as shooter or sports games, and are more likely to play obsessively (Kneer et al., 2019). The most popular MMORPGs include Roblox and World of Warcraft. Roblox, a free sandbox social gaming platform with over 150 million users, allows users to create or play games (Rospigliosi, 2022), many of which help users to learn real-life experiences in a virtual setting (Wardhana, 2021). WoW features a fantasy world in which gamers (approximately 1.2 million daily; https://mmostats.com) choose a character based on personalities, ideologies, or other factors, customize their avatars, and fight with or against other players (Morcos et al., 2021). VR and AR technologies are also popularizing the VR MMORPGs, such as Ilysia, Orbus VR, and VRKfraft. In 2016 Roblox also released its VR version (https://fictiontalk.com/2022/02/21/top-vr-mmo rpgs-to-play-in-2022/).

3   Main Interactive Marketing Functions of Social Media

Interactive marketing activities on social media can be very creative and mostly are executed in one or more of the following five forms.

3.1   Organic Contents

These are the texts, images, and videos created and posted through social media's natural function and are the major form of social media marketing. Fortune-500 companies are found heavy users of organic content. For them, on average, a Facebook post generates 960 likes, 88 comments, and 81 shares; a tweet generates 4 likes/favorites, 8 retweets, and less than 1 comment; a YouTube channel has 385 videos, 14,238 subscribers, and 9,314,198 video views, with each video about 3.5 min long and generating about 33,989 views, 87 likes, 9 dislikes, 13 comments, 40 shares (Li & Stacks, 2015). Research has shown that, when creating organic content, a video doubles the likes and shares, a photo increases the likes by 15% and shares by 11%, and an exclamation mark increases both the likes and shares by more than 50%; although recommended by some industry experts (e.g., Luttrell, 2019), a link/URL decreases the likes by 13%, comments by 16%, and shares by 20%, a tag/mention decreases the likes by 47%, and a hashtag decreases the comments by 19%. Some copy strategies are also proposed to increase audience interaction, such as writing snappy or short copies and asking questions (Yao, 2021a); using new titles, new images, quotes, and call to action; building a unique and related profile page; keeping the contents attractive, interactive, and fresh; adding badges, widgets, and apps; making the contents sharable; and honoring trust, respect, values, fluidity, tolerance, plain writing, sensibleness, friendliness, consistency, and clear consequences (Luttrell, 2019).

Organic posts can produce exciting results. For instance, Instagram is found the most preferred social media platform for entertainment and brand-involved co-creation activities (Pelletier et al., 2020), and in 2013, Mercedes Benz posted 150 stunning photo ads to its Instagram account in the "Take the Wheel" campaign, creating 87 million impressions and 2 million likes (Dua, 2014). The same year, when millions were watching the Super Bowl and a power outage happened, Oreo tweeted "you can still dunk in the dark," which was immediately retweeted 15,000 times and created a warm brand association (Nesamoney, 2015). Research by the Word-of-Mouth Marketing Association (WOMMA) finds that 78% of consumers are influenced by a brand's social media posts (Quesenberry, 2019).

3.2 Influencer Marketing and Social World-of-Mouth (WoM)

Social media influencers can be celebrities, successful athletes, or business executives, or other highly visible persons in the real world, whose social media usually have vast followers; but ordinary people effective in content creation on social media can also attract a substantial number of followers (Luttrell, 2019). For instance, with 192 K followers on TikTok, Viviane Audi is an "ordinary" influencer often working with Walmart and DSW (Newberry, 2021b). On Instagram, "ordinary" influencers Addison Rae (38.7 million followers), Huda Kattan (49 million followers), Khaby Lame (35.7 million followers), Kayla Itsines (13 million followers), and Zach King (24 million followers) can sometimes earn $1.6 million for each sponsored post (https://digitalmarketinginstitute.com/blog/9-of-the-biggest-social-media-influencers-on-instagram). The most popular Twitch streamers, "ordinary" influencers who are also active on Twitter and Instagram, can earn an hourly rate as high as $2398.62 (Miller, 2020). Compared to celebrity influencers, those "ordinary" influencers represent more of the future of interactive marketing with their closeness to consumers' lives and their active interaction with the consumers (Wang, 2021). Influencer marketing is more suitable with social media in the content-sharing and social news or knowledge categories, which have no follower limitation, although accounts with a small amount of followers/contacts (allowed on all social media) can still be useful in interactive B2B marketing (Harshita, Shetty, & Sairam, 2021).

Based on the size of followers, influencers are mostly classified into four types: mega, with followers of more than 1 million; macro, 100,000–1 million; micro, 1,000–100,000; nano, less than 1,000 (Ariestya et al., 2020; Harshita, Shetty, & Sairam, 2021). Some researchers also distinguish celebrity influencers from mega-influencers, because "they are famous independent of their social media activities" (Giuffredi et al., 2022, p. 20). Influencers need to maintain five main characteristics to accumulate fame and leadership on their platforms: (1) credibility, (2) storytelling and content quality, (3) actual and aspired image homophily, (4) consistency, and (5) fit with the platform (Al-Emadi & Yahia, 2020). To persuade, their posts should feature attractiveness, likability, parasocial relationship, entertainment, informational value, fairness of the social interaction, etc. (Rohde & Mau, 2021). While mega-influencers may increase followers' knowledge of the product/service, nano-influencers can ensure trustworthiness, and all influencers will be more effective if the sponsorship is disclosed (Giuffredi et al., 2022).

Some 18–24 years old (14%) and millennials (11%) have bought something in the past six months upon influencer recommendation, and 68% of U.S. marketers use influencers (93% on Instagram, 68% on Facebook and TikTok each, and 48% on YouTube), whom marketers use to generate relevance, reach, and resonance with their brand, in a way personalized to the consumers, and find with software such as Hootsuite, Right Relevance Pro, or Fourstarzz Influencer Recommendation Engine (Newberry, 2021b). When Buick promoted its 2013 luxury model Encore, it launched the "Pinboard to Dashboard" campaign, contracted 10 Pinterest influencers to demonstrate the interior and exterior designs of the car in their posts, and eventually attracted more than 17 million unique visitors from multiple social media platforms (Luttrell, 2019).

Influencer marketing often produces positive WoM on social media. WOMMA has officially announced its dedication to social media marketing, and its research finds that a typical U.S. consumer mentions a brand name about sixty times a week in online or offline conversations; Forrester Research estimates that consumers create about 500 billion social media impressions about products or services in a year; meanwhile, a Nielson study finds that 83% global consumers trust recommendations from people they know and 66% trusts consumer posts online (Quesenberry, 2019). Social media interaction and eWoM, together with trendiness, are key to enhancing consumer brand engagement, awareness, and knowledge (Cheung et al., 2019).

3.3 Social Advertising

Most social media have advertising functions, which can generate three forms of ads: search ads, display ads, and sponsored posts. Social advertising, a part of computational advertising, is fulfilled through social media's business account or ad management software, such as Amazon Ads (https://advertising.amazon.com. Riserbato, 2021), Meta Ads Manager (for Facebook and Instagram. https://www.facebook.com/business. Stec, 2021), and Google Ads (for YouTube. https://ads.google.com. Yao, 2021b). Social ads can reach users beyond followers of a brand or an influencer on the platforms or even the entire internet public.

Among the three forms of social ads, social search ads (on Amazon and Yelp. Riserbato, 2021) are created with keywords and triggered if consumers search with them. Those ads will then compete with other ads with similar keywords based on ad quality and bid price, and the winner will be deployed to the consumers' screens. Social display ads (on YouTube, Facebook, and blogs) are deployed in the social media platform's advertising areas based on the demographic, geographic, or lifestyle (interest) criteria set by the marketers and data collected from consumers' digital traces (Stec, 2021; Yao, 2021b). Those display ads are more effective in providing informative and engaging content, particularly when they are related to brand-personality attributes or user-generated content (UGC), geared toward more engaged consumers, and focused on personal relevance (Xue, 2019). Sponsored posts, a type of native advertising also called promoted or boosted posts, are embedded with the organic posts, only with "sponsored" (on Facebook, Twitter, etc.) or "promoted" (on LinkedIn, Reddit, etc.) marked. Sponsored posts congruent with the organic posts generate clear psychological engagement and affective responses, which indirectly stimulate behavioral engagement, but incongruent sponsored posts directly lead to behavioral engagement (Sheiner et al., 2021). All social ads can include texts, images, and videos, and marketers are mostly charged only when ads are clicked by interested consumers for further information or ordering (Riserbato, 2021; Stec, 2021; Yao, 2021b).

Social ads can also be deployed on one or more social media platforms, or even as a component of a bigger digital campaign that includes videos, websites, streaming, voice, TV, or digital outdoor platforms, through programmatic advertising platforms (Rogers, 2017). Those platforms deploy ads in multiple venues automatically based on preset audience criteria, budget, goals, and other campaign settings (Samuel et al., 2021), and they consist of demand-side platforms (DSP, such as Adobe Advertising Cloud and AdRoll), supply-side platforms (SSP, such as PubMatic, Google Ads, and Criteo), and ad-exchange/data-management platforms (DMP, such as Xandr and SmartyAds). Data are the key to the efficiency of programmatic advertising (Rogers, 2017).

3.4 Social Event Planning

Social media also allow marketers to organize events through some functions, such as Twitter live/streaming or chats, Reddit Ask Me Anything (AMA), and Snapchat filters and lenses. In a Reddit AMA, a person is interviewed by a vast community of users and answers their questions on live. Reddit AMAs can be used to generate brand exposure, enhance brand sentiment, collect consumer feedback, increase new users, interact with current customers, and get media coverage, as did by Nissan, *The Economist*, Audi, and SpaceX (https://www.semrush.com/blog/how-to-host-a-successful-reddit-ama/). On Snapchat, functions such as filters and lenses can be used to modify images or videos to make fun. In a 2016 campaign, Taco Bell invited consumers to use a Cinco de Mayo lens to turn themselves into a giant taco, which attracted more than 100 million users and generated 224 million views (Luttrell, 2019). Social media also provide features to help marketers organize offline events, such as countdowns, event pages, hashtags, influencers, scheduling, live streaming, giveaway contests, AR filters or lenses, social walls (displaying on the site), etc.

Shoppable live advertising/promotion, a type of live streaming promotional event on social media, has been bolstered by the COVID-19 pandemic (Plangger et al., 2021), in which influencers promote products/services to provoke instant purchases for their own businesses or their clients (e.g., https://advertising.amazon.com/solutions/products/amazon-live). Such live streaming needs to construct a sociable and interactive atmosphere to reduce purchasing friction (Plangger et al., 2021).

3.5 Social Listening and Social Care

Social media also provide a great channel to listen, understand, and audit consumer responses to the brand as well as competitors' activities and interactions with the consumers, which marketers call social listening. In social listening, marketers need to understand what the brand messages are, what consumers are saying and feeling about their brands, how the competitors communicate, and how consumers respond to competitor messages. Effective listening help brands to notice and solve crises early, find promotional opportunities, and provide customers post-purchase feedback (i.e., social care). For instance, when Barclays bank launched its person-to-person payment app, Pingit, it skipped the traditional long app-developing process and launched it quickly, and then used social listening and sentiment analysis to identify consumer thoughts and significantly improved the app immediately. When Fiat was designing its Fiat Mio, it conducted social listening through crowdsourcing, called on consumers for suggestions of improvement, and received thousands via Facebook and Twitter from people in 160 countries (Quesenberry, 2019).

4 SOCIAL MEDIA ANALYTICS, MEASUREMENT, AND ETHICAL ISSUES

When planning social media campaigns, social media analytics, measures, and ethical issues are also points of consideration to keep the campaigns effective and beneficial for both the businesses and the consumers in the long run.

4.1 Social Media Analytics and Measurement

Marketers always care about the effectiveness of their marketing activities, normally with a vast budget, and desire an ideal return on investment (ROI). Social media, albeit with their analytics, demand more effectiveness research because, as they are still emerging, their measures have not matured, and professionals disagree on what metrics measure the ROI more accurately: for instance, advertising professionals are more interested in brand awareness, PR professionals are more attracted to brand reputation, and management professionals are more attracted to financial outcomes such as sales or revenue (Chen, 2021; Li & Stacks, 2015).

Social media provide three types of analytics: descriptive analytics (insights into the past), predictive analytics (insights into the future), and prescriptive analytics (possible actions or outcomes). They answer questions such as who the influencers are, what the overall sentiment of conversation is, which platforms are driving the most engagement, and what keywords drive that engagement. A group of researchers, in their "Complete Social Media Measurement Standards," suggest measuring content and sourcing, reach and impressions, engagement and conversation, opinion and advocacy, influence, and impact and value (Luttrell, 2019).

Beyond basic analytics such as exposures/views, the number of followers/subscribers, or clicks, most social media are equipped with indicators such as liking (affective, and indicating consumption and agreement), commenting (cognitive, and indicating contribution), and sharing (conative, and indicating the action of distribution). Researchers have commonly agreed that liking signals the lightest version of audience participation, commenting reveals some self-association with the message and demands more thinking, and sharing constitutes more self-presentation or disclosure and requires even more assessment of the message's values, benefits, and risks (such as privacy concerns, informational control, and sensitivity). So, industry experts have roughly weighted the three forms of consumer engagement with seven likes equaling one comment and two comments equaling one share, resembling the traditional hierarchy of consumer responses but in an affection-conation-cognition order (Yao, 2021a). In social advertising, cost-per-click (CPC) is also considered a measure because the advertising budget is an important factor in campaign planning (Yao, 2021b). Researchers have also suggested using impressions and reach to measure awareness; using likes, comments, and shares to measure engagement; using volume and sentiment of social media conversations about the brand to measure share of voice (Chen, 2021). For social media influencers, a useful measure is authenticity, which has five dimensions: sincerity, truthful endorsement, visibility, expertise, and uniqueness (Lee & Eastin, 2021). With social listening and social care, response rate and time are useful metrics (Chen, 2021). Consumers' interaction with brands on social media is also found to directly and positively influence their knowledge of, affection for, and loyalty to those brands, which follow a cognition-affection-conation sequence (Zhang et al., 2021).

The ultimate measurement of effectiveness is ROI, which represents the stakeholders' expectations (ROE) and contains financial and non-financial indicators. Social media analytics are closely related to the nonfinancial indicators: the number of followers indicates the credibility of the company; the number of likes indicates its reputation; comments show consumers' relationship to it; shares reveal trust in the brand; the valence of comments represents consumers' confidence in the company. Those non-financial indicators contribute to some financial indicators such as stock return, total revenue, net income, or earnings per share (Li & Stacks, 2015). ROI can also be measured with referrals and conversions from your social media followers (Chen, 2021). With improved analytics and measurements, social media marketing can generate the most precise ROI (Nesamoney, 2015).

Social media analytics and measures, however, have room to improve, and conceptual differences between the KPIs on different social media platforms need further exploration. For example, only highly engaged consumers provide feedback that demands more mental effort such as commenting. Treating the commenting sample as the population of the consumers can bias the inference about consumer responses (Li & Stacks, 2015). Also, relationships between the basic metrics (such as the number of subscribers, posts, social shares, audience growth, and inbound links clicked) and intermediate metrics (such as impact and value, opinion and advocacy, influence, engagement and conversation, and time spent) should be explicated (Luttrell, 2019). Some new metrics (e.g., ad cost equivalency of viewing, cross-sharing) should also be established for more specific measurement (Nesamoney, 2015).

4.2 *Ethical Concerns About Social Media Interactive Marketing*

As interactive marketing is transforming from series of campaigns to consistent and seamless communication experiences (Wang, 2021), ethical decisions are increasingly important to maintain quality brand–consumer relationships, because unethical or inappropriate communications can reduce marketers' credibility and damage the marketing process (Quesenberry, 2019).

Social media have posed special challenges to marketing ethics. In addition to traditional ethical issues in marketing, such as intrusive ads, scams, spamming, misrepresentation, disclosing sensitive company or client information, and consumer privacy breach or invasion, which can all be presented in social media marketing (Facebook, for example, has been lately criticized for breaching consumer privacy and profiting on user data. Isaak & Hanna, 2018; Luttrell, 2019), social media have created their ethical issues. For instance, some accounts may have bought fake followers (Yao, 2021a); other accounts have been noticed for removing negative comments/reviews or paying for unauthentic positive ones; customers have been turned away by the obsessive use of social bots on brands' accounts; social media platforms have been found collecting and selling user data without permission (Quesenberry, 2019); some social media (e.g., TikTok) are considered too addictive to the young users and damaging to their brain, with an algorithm consistently recommending luring contents (Pierce, 2021); some social shopping sites have also been denounced for conducting obsessed marketing to stimulate impulsive buying (Hassan et al., 2020). Even for the just emerging virtual world, unethical or illegal conduct such as verbal/sexual harassment or virtual rapes has been reported (Shen, 2022), which can still ruin the marketing processes.

The best practices of ethical social media marketing, as identified by several trade organizations, are disclosing identify of the marketers and purposes/compensations for the marketing activities, complying with laws, regulations, and guides, and respecting the rules, contexts, and audiences of the social media platforms (Quesenberry, 2019). Honest and transparent policies on data collection and user privacy can also reduce users' privacy concerns and enhance their engagement (Jozani et al., 2020). Data surveillance (also called "dataveillance"), which amasses a huge volume of digital traces of individuals permanently without their self-knowledge to benefit target marketing, limits people's privacy and their possibility of self-invention (Schyff et al., 2020); it needs to be reduced to meet the minimum necessary standard and needs to be permission-based.

The ethics of social media marketing should always be checked and exalted as social media marketing advances with complex digital technologies. Related laws, ethics, and etiquettes need to continuously be a significant study topic (Quesenberry, 2019) and marketers' social media policies based on those studies must be established and constantly updated and honored (Luttrell, 2019).

5 GENERAL DISCUSSION

Social media have fundamentally revolutionized business operations, and no business can survive now without using social media to generate instant and positive interactions with customers (Li & Stacks, 2015; Pelletier et al., 2020). This chapter, based on a review of the literature, proposes a comprehensive and parsimonious categorization of social media: social networking (Facebook, LinkedIn, etc.); content sharing (YouTube, Twitter, etc.); social knowledge, news, and bookmarking (Wikipedia, Reddit, etc.); social shopping, rating, and reviewing (Amazon, Yelp, etc.); and virtual world (Second Life, MMORPGs, etc.). The chapter also identifies five main social media functions for interactive marketing: organic content; influencer marketing and social WoM; social advertising; social event planning, and social listening and social care. Social media analytics, measurement, and ethical issues related to interactive marketing are also examined.

Interactive marketing on social media can be even more promising with the maturing of VR, AR, big data, and artificial intelligence (Luttrell, 2019; Nesamoney, 2015; Wang, 2021). Consumer data have increasingly determined marketing success; so, more than 60% of marketers report collecting consumer demographic data, about 40% collecting consumer behavior data, online transaction data, and sales leads respectively, and over 30% collecting social metrics and campaign metrics respectively. Also, more than half of marketers report already using AI in campaign planning and executions (Quesenberry, 2019). The potential is tremendous, and ethical marketing needs to be exalted to build long-lasting and mutually beneficial social media campaigns (Luttrell, 2019; Quesenberry, 2019).

The changing landscape of marketing requires marketers to adopt a new consumer-driven mindset to build brands that will be personalized to consumers through smartphones, social media, and apps. Such personalization is highly based on consumer data and communication technology, and brand competitions will be "just an app or a tap away" (Nesamoney, 2015, p. 29). With the advancement of technology, platform revolution, and culture changes, social media marketing is transforming from person-to-person exchanges to multisided networks, from campaigns to consistent and seamless communication experiences, from promotion to gamification and synchronization of work, life, and entertainment; more consumer participation, interaction, life proximity, and convenience are expected (Wang, 2021). Marketers should study and participate in that transformation.

REFERENCES

Al-Emadi, F. A., & Yahia, I. B. (2020). Ordinary celebrities related criteria to harvest fame and influence on social media. *Journal of Research in Interactive Marketing*, 14(2), 195–213. https://doi.org/10.1108/JRIM-02-2018-0031

Anderson, M., Hitlin, P., & Atkinson, M. (2016, January 14). Wikipedia at 15: Millions of readers in scores of languages. Pew Research Center. https://www.pewresearch.org/fact-tank/2016/01/14/wikipedia-at-15/. Accessed 22 April 2022.

Andre, L. (2022). 78 Yelp statistics you must know: 2022 market share & user profile analysis. *FinancesOnline*. https://financesonline.com/yelp-statistics/. Accessed 22 April 2022.

Ariestya, A., Waluyo, L. S., & Faramita, A. (2020). Influencer size effecting climate change discourses: A study on Indonesian Twitter. *Journal of Content, Community, & Communication*, 11(6), 105–115. https://doi.org/10.31620/JCCC.06.20/08

Bond, R., Fariss, C., Jones, J., et al. (2012). A 61-million-person experiment in social influence and political mobilization. *Nature, 489*, 295–298. https://doi.org/10.1038/nature11421

Buscemi, J. (2020). Who's still on Second Life in 2020? *MIC*. https://www.mic.com/impact/second-life-still-has-dedicated-users-in-2020-heres-what-keeps-them-sticking-around-18693758. Accessed 22 April 2022.

Chang, J. (2022). 44 Essential Wikipedia statistics for 2022: Data on users, readers, & milestones. *FinancesOnline*. https://financesonline.com/wikipedia-statistics/. Accessed 22 April 2022.

Chen, J. (2021, March 26). The most important social media metrics to track. *Sproutsocial*. https://sproutsocial.com/insights/social-media-metrics/. Accessed 22 April 2022.

Cheung, M. L., Pires, G., & Rosenberger, P. J. (2019). The influence of perceived social media marketing elements on consumer-brand engagement and brand knowledge. *Asian Pacific Journal of Marketing and Logistics, 32*(3), 695–720. https://doi.org/10.1108/APJML-04-2019-0262

Correa, S. C. H., Soares, J. L., Christino, J. M. M., Gosling, M., & Goncalves, C. A. (2020). The influence of YouTubers on followers' use intention. *Journal of Research in Interactive Marketing, 14*(2), 173–194. https://doi.org/10.1108/JRIM-09-2019-0154

Curry, D. (2022, January 11). Amazon statistics (2022). *Business of Apps*. https://www.businessofapps.com/data/amazon-statistics/. Accessed 22 April 2022.

Danka, I. (2020). Motivation by gamification: Adapting motivational tools of massively multiplayer online role-playing games (MMORPGs) for peer-to-peer assessment in connectivist massive open online courses (cMOOCs). *International Review of Education, 66*, 75–92. https://doi.org/10.1007/s11159-020-09821-6

Dean, B. (2021, October 10). Social network usage & growth statistics: How many people use social media in 2022? *BackLinko*. https://backlinko.com/social-media-users. Accessed 22 April 2022.

Dewing, M. (2012) *Social media—An introduction*. Canada Parliamentary Information and Research Service. https://studylib.net/doc/8643666/social-media--an-introduction. Accessed 22 April 2022.

Dindar, M. (2018). Do people play MMORPGs for extrinsic or intrinsic rewards? *Telematics and Informatics, 35*(7), 1877–1886. https://doi.org/10.1016/j.tele.2018.06.001

Dua, T. (2014). Mercedes-Benz brings car configuring to Instagram. https://digiday.com/marketing/mercedes-benz-lets-users-build-custom-car-instagram/. Accessed 22 April 2022.

Edelman, G. (2022, January 27). How to build a better metaverse: Second Life creator Philip Rosedale wants to prevent the Facebook-ization of virtual reality. *WIRED*. https://www.wired.com/story/metaverse-philip-rosedale-second-life/. Accessed 22 April 2022.

Giuffredi, A., Petrova, A., & Malar, L. (2022). Sponsorship disclosure of influencers—A curse of blessing? *Journal of Interactive Marketing, 57*(1), 18–34. https://doi.org/10.1177/10949968221075686

Harmeling, C., Moffett, J., Arnold, M., & Carlson, B. (2017). Toward a theory of customer engagement marketing. *Journal of the Academy of Marketing Science, 45*, 312–335. https://doi.org/10.1007/s11747-016-0509-2

Harshita, S., Shetty, R., & Sairam, P. S. (2021). Social media marketing: B2B marketing via nano influencers. *Journal of University of Shanghai for Science and Technology, 23*(7), 1377–1387. https://jusst.org/wp-content/uploads/2021/07/Social-Media-Marketing-B2B-Marketing-via-Nano-Influencers.pdf. Accessed 22 April 2022.

Hassan, H., Hassan, J., Abdullah, S., & Abdullah, A. (2020). Social commerce in stimulating buying behavior intention, creating compulsive buying and inducing credit card debts among online users. *Journal of Physics: Conference Series, 1529*, 032012. https://doi.org/10.1088/1742-6596/1529/3/032012

Heimlich, R. (2011, January 13). Wikipedia users. Pew Research Center. https://www.pewresearch.org/fact-tank/2011/01/13/wikipedia-users/. Accessed 22 April 2022.

Hutchinson, A. (2021, October 26). Twitter rises to 211 million active users, though longer term growth targets looking harder to reach. *Social Media Today*. https://www.socialmediatoday.com/news/twitter-rises-to-211-million-active-users-though-longer-term-growth-target/608958/. Accessed 22 April 2022.

IAB. (2021, April 7). 2020/2021 IAB Internet advertising revenue report. Interactive Advertising Bureau. https://www.iab.com/insights/internet-advertising-revenue-report/. Accessed 22 April 2022.

Isaak, J., & Hanna, M. J. (2018). User data privacy: Facebook, Cambridge Analytica, and privacy protection. *Computer, 51*(8), 56–59. https://doi.org/10.1109/MC.2018.3191268

Jamison, L. (2017, December). The digital ruins of a forgotten future. *The Atlantic.* https://www.theatlantic.com/magazine/archive/2017/12/second-life-leslie-jamison/544149/. Accessed 22 April 2022.

Jerusalem Post Staff. (2022, January 8). Technion shares academic knowledge in Wikipedia entries. *The Jerusalem Post.* https://www.jpost.com/israel-news/article-695878. Accessed 22 April 2022.

Jozani, M., Ayaburi, E., Ko, M., & Choo, K.-K. (2020). Privacy concerns and benefits of engagement with social media-enabled apps: A privacy calculus perspective. *Computers in Human Behavior, 107,* 106260. https://doi.org/10.1016/j.chb.2020.106260

Kaplan, A., & Haenlein, M. (2010). Users of the world, unite! The challenges and opportunities of social media. *Business Horizons, 53,* 59–68. https://doi.org/10.1016/j.bushor.2009.09.003

Kilic, A. & Karatepe, C. (2021). Electronic complaints: An empirical study of negative reviews from Amazon.com users. *Advances in Language and literary Studies, 12*(5), 42–47. https://doi.org/10.7575/aiac.alls.v.12n.5.p.42

Khoros (2021). The 2021 social media demographics guide. https://khoros.com/resources/social-media-demographics-guide. Accessed 22 April 2022.

Kneer, J., Franken, S., & Reich, S. (2019). Not only for the (Tom) boys: Gender variables as predictors for playing motivations, passion, and addiction for MMORPGs. *Simulation & Gaming, 50*(1), 44–61. https://doi.org/10.1177/1046878118823033

Kodish, S. (2015). Cultivating relationships with customers: The social media challenge. *Journal of Leadership, Accountability, and Ethics, 12*(2), 81–91. http://t.www.na-businesspress.com/JLAE/KodishS_Web12_2_.pdf. Accessed 22 April 2022.

Lee, C. (2017, May 17). Who still hangs out on Second Life? More than half a million people. *The Globe and Mail.* https://www.theglobeandmail.com/life/relationships/who-still-hangs-out-on-second-life-more-than-half-a-million-people/article35019213/. Accessed 22 April 2022.

Lee, J. A., & Eastin, M. S. (2021). Perceived authenticity of social media influencers: Scale development and validation. *Journal of Research in Interactive Marketing, 15*(4), 822–841. https://doi.org/10.1108/JRIM-12-2020-0253

Li, C., & Stacks, D. (2015). *Measuring the impact of social media on business profit & success: A fortune 500 perspective.* Peter Lang.

Lin, Y. (2021, May 11). 10 Reddit statistics every marketer should know in 2021. *Oberlo.* https://www.oberlo.com/blog/reddit-statistics. Accessed 22 April 2022.

Luttrell, R. (2019). *Social media: How to engage, share, and connect* (3rd ed.). Rowman & Littlefield.

McLachlan, S. (2022, February 14). 23 YouTube stats that matter to marketers in 2022. *Hootsuite Blog.* https://blog.hootsuite.com/YouTube-stats-marketers/. Accessed 22 April 2022.

Miller, C (2020, February 10). Study reveals how much top Twitch streamers make per hour. *Game Rant.* https://gamerant.com/twitch-streamers-wages-per-hour/. Accessed 22 April 2022.

Morcos, M., Stavropoulos, V., Rennie, J. J., Clark, M., & Pontes, H. M. (2021). Internet gaming disorder: Compensating as a Draenei in World of Warcraft. *International Journal of Mental Health Addiction, 19,* 669–685. https://doi.org/10.1007/s11469-019-00098-x

Moran, M. (2017, June 19). 10 types of social media and how each can benefit your business. Published first on Hootsuite Social Media Management. https://medium.com/@UnifiedSocial/10-types-of-social-media-and-how-each-can-benefit-your-business- 344d1ae46def. Accessed 22 April 2022.

Nesamoney, D. (2015). *Personalized digital advertising: How data and technology are transforming how we market*. Person Education.

Newberry, C. (2021a, February 2). 25 YouTube statistics that may surprise you: 2021a Edition. *Hootsuite blog*. https://blog.hootsuite.com/YouTube-stats-marketers/. Accessed 22 April 2022.

Newberry, C. (2021b, August 10). Influencer marketing guide: How to work with influencers. *Hootsuite blog*. https://blog.hootsuite.com/influencer-marketing/. Accessed 22 April 2022.

Newberry, C., & Beveridge, C. (2022, April 6). 37 LinkedIn statistics you need to know in 2022. *Hootsuite Blog*. https://blog.hootsuite.com/linkedin-statistics-business/. Accessed 22 April 2022.

Pelletier, M. J., Krallman, A., Adams, F. G., & Hancock, T. (2020). One size doesn't fit all: A uses and gratifications analysis of social media platforms. *Journal of Research in Interactive Marketing, 14*(2), 269–284. https://doi.org/10.1108/JRIM-10-2019-0159

Petrov, C. (2022, February 6). 47 Amazon statistics to Bedazzle you in 2022. *techjury*. https://techjury.net/blog/amazon-statistics/#gref. Accessed 22 April 2022.

Pew Researcher Center. (2021, April 7). Social media fact sheet. Pew Research Center. https://www.pewresearch.org/internet/fact-sheet/social-media/. Accessed 22 April 2022.

Pierce, R. (2021, September 22). TikTok videos really get you hooked by tricking your brain: Sociologist. *Tech Times*. https://www.techtimes.com/articles/265687/20210922/tiktok-videos-really-get-you-hooked-by-tricking-your-brain-sociologist.htm. Accessed 22 April 2022.

Plangger, K., Cheng, Z. C., Hao, J., Wang, Y., Campbell, C., & Rosengren, S. (2021). Exploring the value of shoppable live advertising: Liveness and shoppability in advertising media and future research directions. *Journal of Advertising Research, 61*(2), 129–132. https://doi.org/10.2501/JAR-2021-008

Quesenberry, K. (2019). *Social media strategy: Marketing, advertising, and public relations in the consumer revolution* (2nd ed.). Rowman & Littlefield Publishers.

Ravenscraft, E. (2021, November 25). What is the metaverse, exactly? Everything you never wanted to know about the future of talking about the future. *WIRED*. https://www.wired.com/story/what-is-the-metaverse/. Accessed 22 April 2022.

Riserbato, R. (2021). The ultimate guide to Amazon advertising. *Hubspot Blog*. https://blog.hubspot.com/marketing/amazon-advertising. Accessed 22 April 2022.

Rodriguez, S. (2021, December 14). Instagram surpasses 2 billion monthly users while powering through a year of turmoil. *CNBC Tech Drives*. https://www.cnbc.com/2021/12/14/instagram-surpasses-2-billion-monthly-users.html. Accessed 22 April 2022.

Rogers, C. (2017, March 27). What is programmatic advertising? A beginner's guide. *Marketing Week*. https://www.marketingweek.com/programmatic-advertising/. Accessed 22 April 2022.

Rohde, P., & Mau, G. (2021). "It's selling like hotcakes": Deconstructing social media influencer marketing in long-form video content on YouTube via social influence heuristics. *European Journal of Marketing, 55*(10), 2700–2734. https://doi.org/10.1108/EJM-06-2019-0530

Rospigliosi, P. (2022). Metaverse or simulacra? Roblox, Minecraft, Meta and the turn to virtual reality for education, socialisation and work. *Interactive Learning Environments, 30*(1), 1–3. https://doi.org/10.1080/10494820.2022.2022899

Samuel, A., White, G. R. T., Thomas, R., & Jones, P. (2021). Programmatic advertising: An exegesis of consumer concerns. *Computers in Human Behavior, 116*, 106657. https://doi.org/10.1016/j.chb.2020.106657

Scarlette, S. (2022, February 21). I found true love in Second Life and met my boyfriend in person for the first time after a year. *Metro.* https://metro.co.uk/2022/02/21/i-fell-in-love-with-my-long-distance-boyfriend-on-second-life-16115065/. Accessed 22 April 2022.

Schyff, K., Flowerday, S., & Furnell, S. (2020). Duplicitous social media and data surveillance: An evaluation of privacy risk. *Computer & Security, 94*, 101822. https://doi.org/10.1016/j.cose.2020.101822

Sheiner, D. Z., Kol, O., & Levy, S. (2021). It makes a difference! Impact of social and personal message appeals on engagement with sponsored posts. *Journal of Research in Interactive Marketing, 15*(4), 641–660. https://doi.org/10.1108/JRIM-12-2019-0210

Shel, K. (2020, May 28). Top Twitter demographics that matter to social media marketers. *Hootsuite Blog.* https://blog.hootsuite.com/twitter-demographics/. Accessed 22 April 2022.

Shen, M. (2022, January 31). Sexual harassment in the metaverse? Women alleges rape in virtual world. *USA Today.* https://www.usatoday.com/story/tech/2022/01/31/woman-allegedly-groped-metaverse/9278578002/. Accessed 22 April 2022.

Smith, A., Toor, S., & van Kessel, P. (2018, November 7). Many turn to YouTube for children's content, news, how-to lessons. Pew Research Center. https://www.pewresearch.org/internet/2018/11/07/many-turn-to-YouTube-for-childrens-content-news-how-to-lessons/. Accessed 22 April 2022.

Stec, C. (2021). How to run Facebook ads: A step-by-step guide to advertising on Facebook. *Hubspot Blog.* https://blog.hubspot.com/marketing/facebook-paid-ad-checklist. Accessed 22 April 2022.

Stelzner, M. (2021, May 10). 2021 social media marketing industry report: How marketers are using social media to grow their businesses. *Social Media Examiner.* https://www.socialmediaexaminer.com/social-media-marketing-industry-report-2021/. Accessed 22 April 2022.

Stocking, G., van Kessel, P., Barthel, M., Matsa, K. E., & Khuzam, M. (2020, September 28). Many Americans get news on YouTube, Where news organizations and independent producers thrive side by side. Pew Research Center. https://www.pewresearch.org/journalism/2020/09/28/many-americans-get-news-on-YouTube-where-news-organizations-and-independent-producers-thrive-side-by-side/. Accessed 22 April 2022.

Walker, M., & Matsa, K. E. (2021, September 20). News consumption across social media in 2021: More than half of Twitter user get news on the site regularly. *Pew Research Center.* https://www.pewresearch.org/journalism/2021/09/20/news-consumption-across-social-media-in-2021/. Accessed 22 April 2022.

Wang, C. L. (2021). New frontiers and future directions in interactive marketing: Inaugural editorial. *Journal of Research in Interactive Marketing, 15*(1), 1–9. https://doi.org/10.1108/JRIM-03-2021-270

Wardhana, M. I. (2021). Learning through a social gaming platform. Proceedings of the *International Conference on Art, Design, Education and Cultural Studies (ICADECS), KnE Social Sciences*, 221–226. https://doi.org/10.18502/kss.v5i6.9199.
WebsiteBuilder. (2021, December 8). 109 Ridiculous Reddit statistics & facts to know in 2022. https://websitebuilder.org/blog/reddit-statistics/. Accessed 22 April 2022.
Xue, F. (2019). Facebook news feed ads: A Social impact theory perspective. *Journal of Research in Interactive Marketing, 13*(4), 529–546. https://doi.org/10.1108/JRIM-10-2018-0125
Yao, Q. J. (2021a). The news as international soft power: An analysis of the posting techniques of China's news media on Facebook and Twitter. In G. Yang & W. Wang (Eds.), *Engaging Social media in China: Platforms, publics, and production* (pp. 133–156). Michigan State University Press.
Yao, Q. J. (2021b). Informing, implying or directing? Testing the effects of message sidedness, conclusiveness and their interaction in national and local Google Ads campaigns. *Journal of Research in Interactive Marketing, 15*(4), 623–640. https://doi.org/10.1108/JRIM-09-2019-0141
Zhang, L., Zhao, H., & Cude, B. (2021). Luxury brands join hands: Building interactive alliances on social media. *Journal of Research in Interactive Marketing, 15*(4), 787–803. https://doi.org/10.1108/JRIM-02-2020-0041

CHAPTER 21

Enhancing Customer–Brand Interaction: Customer Engagement on Brand Pages of Social Networking Sites

Zalfa Laili Hamzah and Azean Johari

1 Introduction

The emergence of the digital era and social media, particularly social networking sites (SNSs), helped practitioners and academicians better understand how companies could enhance interactive customer experience on SNSs with a brand page to remain competitive in interactive marketing (Qin, 2020; Wang, 2021). Interactive marketing is featured as bi-directional value creation and mutual-influence marketing process through active customer connection, engagement, participation, and interaction (Wang, 2021). Interactive marketing has shifted beyond direct marketing as the market evolves into a platform for conversations and interaction among networked actors or participants through digital and mobile activities in platform ecosystems (Shankar & Malthouse, 2009; Lim et al., 2022). Therefore, understanding customer interaction and engagement is essential for successful interactive marketing (Shankar & Malthouse, 2009; Wang, 2021; Lim et al., 2022).

Previous research suggests that the interactive customer experience on SNSs has driven the creation of customer–brand relationships through its brand post characteristics, resulting in business profitability (Hamzah et al., 2021; Qin, 2020). Hamzah et al., (2021) found brand post characteristics that interactivity and novelty have a significant impact on consumer engagement with the brand post on social media. Interactivity in a brand post engages users

---

Z. L. Hamzah (✉) · A. Johari
Universiti Malaya, Kuala Lumpur, Malaysia
e-mail: zalfa@um.edu.my

by giving them a fast response, enabling organisations to get feedback from visitors, facilitating two-way connection, and most significantly, it is instantaneous. Even if the information on social media may be pleasant or harmful, these qualities motivate users to participate. Hamzah et al. (2021) also show that consumer interaction affects customer–brand relationship (i.e. brand love and customer brand identification). This finding implies that social media interactions and connections between customers and brands can result in deep bonds. This can be explained by the fact that customers' engagement with brands on social media results in the establishment of a close relationship with those brands. Because of the increasing importance of SNSs, managing the service interaction experience in these settings has become essential to marketers (Blasco-Arcas et al., 2016). Compared to traditional marketing, the interactive experience environment encouraged customers in spending considerable time online to perform various activities. Furthermore, in contrast to standard e-commerce sites built on user–machine interaction, SNSs platforms go beyond this type of interaction by encouraging social interactions between peers.

While there is no widespread consensus on the distinguishing qualities of SNSs, the platform focuses on developing customer–brand interactions and providing customers with better interaction opportunities (Blasco-Arcas et al., 2016). For example, customers can participate in the marketing, selling, comparing, curating, buying, and sharing of products and services due to these improved interaction opportunities. This encourages an active role of the customers in digital media. As a result, marketers invest in providing customers with seamless digital experiences and immediate customised solutions to engage them with their respective brands. Given this paradigm shift in the interactive environment, engaging customers on SNSs has become a strategic imperative for marketers to enhance customer trust and purchase intention (Islam & Rahman, 2016).

The popularity of SNSs has spurred an explosion of research into social media usage, particularly emphasising people's reasons for engaging SNSs (Hoffman & Novak, 2012). Among SNSs, it is reported that Facebook was the first social network to surpass one billion registered accounts and currently sits at more than 2.895 billion monthly active users. The company also owns four of the biggest social media platforms, with over one billion monthly active users: Facebook (core platform), WhatsApp, Facebook Messenger, and Instagram. In the third quarter of 2021, Facebook reported that over 3.58 billion people were using at least one of the company's core products (Facebook, WhatsApp, Instagram, or Messenger) each month, specifically YouTube with 2.291 billion, Whatsapp with 2.0 billion, Instagram with 1.393 billion, Wechat with 1.251 billion, and TikTok with 1.0 billion users (Statisca.com, 2022). Facebook brand pages have become a significant channel for consumers to interact with brands directly by engaging in brands' posts and messages (Tsai & Men, 2013). They engaged through liking, sharing, and commenting on the brand posts with other social media users. If one brand post receives various comments from Facebook users, users have high interaction with that brand page and other commenters, showing that customers have engaged with SNSs effectively.

Therefore, interactive experience and consumer engagement became a critical research priority in interactive marketing (Wang, 2021), per the Marketing Science Institute (MSI) for future research. However, Schratt-Bitter and Grabner-Kräuter (2014) reported a paucity of practical information on consumer engagement behaviour in SNSs. Thus, consumers' interactions with companies/brands on SNSs are the subject of this chapter, where the drivers of customer engagement on SNSs brand page and their impact on customer trust and purchase intention of fabric handicrafts are examined.

Previous studies have focussed more on the motivation of using social networking sites; however, the importance of consumer involvement, social benefits, and practical benefits to customer engagement and its impact on customer trust and purchase intention has been ignored (Jamid et al., 2017; Poorrezaei, 2016; Van Doorn et al., 2010; Vivek et al., 2012). Additionally, there is inconsistency in the research findings in examining the determinants of customer engagement: customer involvement (Alhidari et al., 2015; Kam et al., 2016; Vivek et al., 2012), practical benefits, and social benefits (Jahn & Kunz, 2012; Kang et al., 2014; Kujur & Singh, 2017). Understanding these relationships is essential as the knowledge will help marketers enhance the customers' interactive experience for customer engagement on SNSs. Kanankula, Jung, and Watchravesringkan (2015) found that practical and social benefits are essential to developing consumer trust in SNSs of general fashion industry. They suggest that future research should further investigate roles other than practical, social benefits, and customer engagement in influencing consumer trust in the context of other settings.

This chapter examines the antecedents and consequences of customer engagement with brand pages in fabric handicrafts through SNSs. SNSs have surpassed all other channels for businesses to communicate with their customers. An understanding of this customer engagement in the context of fabric handicraft brand page remains unclear (Chauhan & Pillai, 2013; Hajli, 2014; Jahn & Kunz, 2012; Jamid et al., 2017; Kam et al., 2016; Kang et al., 2014; Tafesse, 2016). This chapter elucidates the importance of understanding the enhancement of the interactive experience between brand–consumer, highlights ways in which practitioners can capitalise on customers' involvement, practical benefits, and social benefits, and the development of complementary strategies that will not only increase customers' engagement but also improve customers' trust and purchase intention.

This chapter begins with a literature review of concepts involved, previous studies on relationships between the concepts is discussed. Next, the methodology applied in this chapter is presented. Finally, the results, findings, discussions, implications, limitations, future studies direction, and conclusion are presented.

1.1 Literature Review

1.1.1 Social Networking Sites

Social networking sites (SNSs) are online spaces where users can establish profiles and form personal networks that link them to other users. It also refers to web-based services that allow customers to create a public or semi-public profile, communicate with others, and view and keep their list of connections within the system (Chang, 2013). The SNS has established a platform for interaction between marketers and customers, enhancing consumers' brand awareness and enabling them to obtain detailed information about a brand (Mukherjee & Banerjee, 2019). Nowadays, socialising and sharing are essential for social media users, as they will acquire a higher sense of belonging and engagement than they would by only browsing websites (Wang, 2021).

Therefore, the e-commerce sector has expanded to include SNSs where users share their interests and experiences through social selling and user-generated marketing. Hopkins (2012) stated that information shared on SNSs includes users' profiles, shared hobbies and interests, groups from previous schools and employers, favourite music, books and movies, photographs, and movie clips. This information is readily disclosed to as many people in the network as possible. The increasing popularity of SNSs changed the social platform for users and allowed them to interact and express their passion for their favourite brands with their friends, personal connections, and other acquaintances to freely join their favourite brand by providing positive comments on pictures and videos related to the brand or company, co-creation, social sharing, and the likes.

1.1.2 Nature of Social Networking Sites

Since social networking sites allow users to obtain information and express ideas, customers are no longer passive recipients of brand information. Instead, they are active creators and distributors of such information through social recommendations (Wang, 2021). As consumers, fans from brand communities function as catalysts for brand co-production, development, marketing, and distribution. The interactions and dialogues fan cultural groups and brand communities, draw new players and quicken market expansion (Humphrey et al., 2017). Therefore, customer engagement is essential, reflecting the customers' investment in brand-related interactions. Consumers engaged with SNSs brand pages and brand communities tend to exhibit higher trust, commitment, satisfaction, emotional bonding, and loyalty to the brand (Brodie et al., 2013). A highly involved consumer would be most likely invest their ideas, emotions, and actions in their favourite brands (Bowden, 2009). Consequently, social media involvement with fabric handicraft brands has become prevalent because social media enables easy-to-access possibilities to communicate and participate with companies and brand communities (Cabiddu et al., 2014).

The concept of SNSs has developed at a fast pace around the globe. Many internet users have created profiles on SNSs (e.g. Facebook, Twitter, or MySpace). Facebook is the most popular platform that offers the option to promote fan pages by encouraging the initial fans to follow pages, which, once the fan base is established, will become a personal relationship. The brand platforms enable customers to navigate their favourite shopping websites to discover the latest trends and get real-time recommendations. Users contribute to newsfeeds and share brand content by tagging friends on SNSs. Media sharing platforms enable marketers and consumers to share brand information through mobile marketing. Storytelling and ritualistic practice in virtual brand communities increase interactions between net celebrities and followers on Facebook and Baidu. Short video and live streaming services have resulted in faster selling via hosting and audience engagement (Wang, 2021).

Instagram followed this trend. It differs from other SNSs in that the activity is restricted by application use or the use of a downloaded application that can only be accessed on a mobile device such as a smartphone or tablet. As a result, Instagram has become an essential marketing component of brands and retailers, as customers respond better to visuals because they can recall 80% of what they see, 20% of what they read, and 10% of what they hear. Also, visual content on Instagram is processed 60,000 times faster in the brain compared to text, making Instagram an effective and robust platform for a business to establish excellent customer perception based on branded content.

Through the SNSs, customers will be able to respond to branded content, i.e. any pictures, videos, or any object posted by users and companies, by clicking the icons of 'like', 'follow' subsequent to writing comments and sharing information or experiences. These behaviours are called customer engagement. Customer engagement is defined as the readiness of the customer to participate and interact with a focal object actively, for instance, a brand, organisation, or community (Jamid et al., 2017). This engagement can vary positively or negatively, depending on the nature of the customers' interaction with various touch-points, physically or virtually. Customer engagement metrics are identified as like, add, view, share, comment, and follow, all of which influence online purchase behaviours.

1.1.3 Overview of Social Networking Sites Studies from the Interactive Marketing Perspective

SNSs provide an excellent platform for digital marketers to advertise their products and services in various formats, such as banner advertisements, brand fan pages, and video commercials, using free and paid social media marketing solutions. In addition, SNSs brand fan sites are technically versatile enough to accept various forms of media such as images, videos, and animations (Mukherjee & Banerjee, 2019).

Many social media academicians investigated several characteristics of these SNSs' marketing abilities and interactive marketing (Wang, 2021) and SNSs users' attitudes regarding advertisements placed on these sites (Akar & Topçu,

2011; Taylor et al., 2011). Taylor et al. (2011) examined many positive and negative advertisement qualities as predictors of SNSs attitude development, including self-brand congruity, peer influence, entertainment, information, quality of life, structure time, invasiveness, and privacy concern.

Mukherjee and Banerjee (2019) examined the impact of social media users' positive attitude towards the SNSs on the generation of a positive attitude towards social networking advertisements (SNA) of smartphone brands in India. The findings show that the perceived ease of use (PEOU) of the SNSs significantly and positively influenced the social networks' perceived usefulness (PU). Both PEOU and PU had a positive bearing on developing a positive attitude towards SNS use. A positive attitude towards SNSs use translates into a positive attitude towards the advertisements posted on the SNSs, while a positive attitude towards SNA positively affects brand attitude and purchase intention.

The influence of customer attitude towards the advertisement medium on attitude towards the advertisements delivered via that media was also explored. For example, attitude towards the website has previously been investigated in the context of web-based ads as a critical antecedent (Bruner & Kumar, 2000). In addition, previous research on media context and its impact on advertisement effectiveness of magazine advertisements indicated that a person's experience with a particular magazine might change their reaction to advertisements printed in the same magazine (Malthouse et al., 2007).

1.1.4 Customer Engagement

Customer engagement refers to the number of likes, comments, shares, and followers on SNSs (Zoha et al., 2017). A brand page is a dedicated and brand-moderated platform for brand communication and customer interaction on social media (Tafesse, 2015). The brand page affords greater interactive brand awareness, resulting in a richer social experience, which may drive customer engagement and build customer trust and purchase intention on SNSs. For instance, if a customer 'Likes', 'Comments,' or 'Shares' a brand, the brand will appear on their Facebook page and contribute to their profile. Thus, businesses should seize this opportunity to let potential customers become aware of the availability of their brands in the market.

Similarly, if a customer has bought a product and is tagged on SNSs, the brand's image may reflect their personality and support their self-expression. This is particularly important as service firms such as retailers increasingly incorporate customer engagement-related marketing activities such as maintaining a Facebook page to provide consumers with a platform for customer-brand and customer-to-customer interactions (Kam et al., 2016). Zoha et al. (2017) classified customer engagement metrics as liking, sharing, following, and commenting. 'Liking' on Facebook represents a form of a user to vote or an expression of appreciation of the content, while a 'dislike' shows their unwillingness to approve of some of the content. Therefore, liking the posts and sharing brand content such as videos, images, or links on SNSs, will provide content awareness to others in their user profile. The engagement activities could enhance communication and interactivity with a brand. Therefore, sharing Facebook brand content helps users simplify the purchase decision-making process.

Previous research found that positive SNSs interactions and involvement with a brand will affect customers. Consumers are more willing to buy from a brand, choose a brand over the competition, recommend a brand, increase spending, and develop a stronger customer bond. When customers actively interact on SNSs, they consider other customers' opinions and feedback to facilitate making purchase decisions. The higher the interaction experience on SNSs, the more the interaction with a brand page. Explicitly, this interaction could boost the customer engagement index rate, which increases overall brand visibility and help businesses increase brand awareness among potential customers.

1.2   Conceptual Framework Development

1.2.1   Stimulus–Organism–Response

The stimulus–organism–response (S-O-R) paradigm explains that atmospheric cues of a particular context influence consumer response through intervention effects of affective and cognitive states. Mehrabian and Russell (1974) suggested that the environmental stimuli (S) lead to an emotional reaction (O) that evokes behavioural responses (R) when the model has been applied in various retail settings to explain the consumer decision-making process (Chebat & Michon, 2003; Richard et al., 2009). As SNS emerged as the most rapidly growing form of a communication channel (Jung et al., 2013), researchers have begun focusing on various aspects of this new medium using the S-O-R framework. This chapter positions customer involvement, practical and social benefits as a stimulus, customer engagement as an organism, and customer trust and purchase intention as a response.

Although previous studies provided a framework for determining the factors that contribute to SNSs' success, the roles of customer involvement (Kam et al., 2016), practical benefits (Jahn & Kunz, 2012), social benefits (Kang et al., 2014), customer trust, and purchase intention as outcomes remain lacking. Customer trust is a significant belief that creates a positive attitude towards transaction behaviours. Trust can help minimise customers' risk perceptions when dealing with online stores by encouraging them to engage in trust-related behaviours such as sharing information and making purchases (McKnight et al., 2002).

1.2.2   Social Exchange Theory

The social exchange theory states that people make rational decisions to engage in a social exchange based on their evaluation of the costs and benefits of the transaction (Thibaut & Kelley, 1959). The theory refers to the transaction between two persons in a continuing relationship can be economic, social, or a combination of economic and social advantages and costs. For example, consumers who are involved with a social media brand, having made cognitive and/or affective effort in it, are more likely to continue engaging the brand to accrue further benefits, which result in reinforced brand self-connection and usage intent (Harrigan et al., 2018).

The social exchange theory is also a fundamental lens for understanding the interaction of customer engagement on SNSs due to its use in three crucial areas: interpersonal ties, relational exchange (brand-consumer relationships), and information exchange (content and information sharing) (Hayes et al., 2016). Interpersonal relationships are developed over a series of satisfactory interactions between customers wherein reciprocal gift-giving occurs, and participating parties equitably benefit (Hayes et al., 2016; Cook & Yamagishi, 1992). Relational exchanges occur between companies and customers (Morgan & Hunt, 1994). In these exchanges, trust is essential, which means that one side is expected to perform acts that will result in positive consequences. Finally, information exchange also occurs on SNSs where users may offer personal information by giving feedback in the form of 'Like', 'Comment', or 'Share' from shared posts or a feed of personal updates from others. Consumers compare the personal information and the effort they provide (inputs) with the outcomes they desire to determine their online informational responses (Mosteller & Poddar, 2017; Poddar et al., 2009). This chapter discusses the exchange of cognitive, emotional, social, economic, and physical resources between consumers and marketers in the context of SNSs of fabric handicraft brands.

1.3 Drivers of Customer Engagement on SNSs

1.3.1 Customer Involvement

Customer involvement refers to a person's perceived relevance to the object based on inherent needs, values, and interests (Zaichkowsky, 1985). Customer involvement is a cognitive, affective, or motivational construct indicating the state of mind or perceived personal relevance, but it is not regarded as a behaviour (Vivek et al., 2012). Alhidari et al. (2015) defined involvement as the level of importance, time, and effort an individual gives to SNS. Customer involvement is categorised into two: (1) High involvement refers to customers who are engaged in a more elaborate, extensive thought about a product/object, and (2) Low involvement states that customers are engaged in superficial processing, influenced by basic positive or negative cues.

Customer involvement is essential in the purchase decision-making process. When consumers are highly involved, they will engage SNSs by liking, sharing, following, and commenting on branded content or brand pages with other users. Researchers also highlighted involvement as one of the most critical subjects in determining customer engagement on SNSs (Kam et al., 2016). Customers' feelings, thoughts, and behaviours indicate greater involvement in SNSs. Thus, involvement is essential, as it can be regarded as one of the antecedents of customer engagement. Vivek et al. (2012) indicated that involvement and interaction were antecedents of customer engagement. Customers who are highly involved in SNSs, for instance, tend to spend more time, effort, and energy on the platforms. They are also more likely to engage and be persuaded to post on SNS, enhancing customer trust and purchase intention.

The level of involvement and interaction will influence customer engagement on the SNSs brand page. Activities related to engagement of SNSs include opinion-seeking and giving and sharing information, so it seems reasonable to assume that engagement would increase as people spend more time on SNSs. Additionally, users expose themselves to brand or marketing-related information on SNS.

1.3.2 Practical Benefits

Practical benefits are 'informational and instrumental benefits often achievable through companies' Facebook sites (Kananukul et al., 2015). The community can become a channel for customer feedback and questions, which leads to informational benefits' (Gummerus et al., 2012). The practical benefits are also called functional values (Jahn & Kunz, 2012). They found that functional value is one of the most critical drivers for attracting users to fan pages. This means fan pages must deliver exciting and innovative content to their fans. Posts that contain information act as the key motivational factors to create interaction and engagement with customers as they provide information about a brand or product (Kujur & Singh, 2017). Kujur and Singh (2017) found that information could influence consumers' online participation and engagement, while Kang et al. (2014) believed that functional benefits include ease and/or efficiency of commercial transactions and information exchange in online communities.

1.3.3 Social Benefits

Social benefits refer to the help and support members provide to each other (Kang et al., 2014) and consumers' opinions about the internet's contribution to society's well-being. Social benefits derive from the interaction between a company and the customer, referred to as recognition or friendship (Gummerus et al., 2012). Kang et al. (2014) also discussed social–psychological benefits, which are a combined concept of social and psychological benefits. Researchers suggested that social and psychological benefits can be combined as a single benefit factor in the context of online communities. Thus, it is suggested that the company actively interact with the customers to ensure that their brand page will succeed.

1.3.4 Customer Trust

Customer trust refers to the risk and uncertainty in an online environment (Hajli, 2014). Trust is conceptualised as the belief that a trusted party will fulfil the commitment despite the trusting party's dependency and vulnerability (Wang et al., 2016). Trust has been defined as a psychological trait formed from early childhood. A higher level of social presence, for instance, images or videos, signals the trustworthiness of an online vendor (Brengman & Karimov, 2012). Hence, it is essential to gain customer trust to mitigate negative perceptions and encourage online transactions. Brengman and Karimov (2012) highlighted one crucial factor that significantly influences forming new relationships: a person's general tendency to trust and distrust others. Hajli (2014) explained two main dimensions of trust; benevolence and credibility-based trust. Benevolence refers to a repeated seller-buyer relationship, while credibility-based trust believes that the other party in a transaction is reliable and relies on reputable information. Therefore, Hajli (2014) believes that trust has been shown in the context of online transactions through SNSs. In an online environment, trust can facilitate communication between individuals and encourage them to remain with the current network.

1.3.5   Purchase Intention
Purchase intention is an attitude that directly affects the intention (Tiruwa et al., 2016). When customers review the comments, they can judge the product's quality and build trust, increasing the tendency to buy. Taking part in online transactions requires buyers to deal with the opportunistic behaviours of sellers. Brengman and Karimov (2012) found that trust beliefs significantly impact customers' purchase intention, thus confirming the importance of trust in online environments' success. It also demonstrates that doubts regarding the integrity of the online seller can negatively affect purchase intentions. Therefore, when dealing with a company or brand webpage to enhance purchase intentions, it is crucial to portray a strong sense of justice, honesty, and objectivity to the online community (Brengman & Karimov, 2012). Hajli (2014) suggested that customer ratings and reviews on social networking sites would be an excellent approach to eliminating barriers. Communication between customers on social networking sites increases trust, and it is crucial to consider customers' intention to buy. They concluded that the higher the customer trust of the online seller is, the more likely their intention to buy the products will be.

1.3.6   Relationship Between Customer Involvement and Customer Engagement
Involvement refers to the degree of information processing and the importance a customer attaches to a product while purchasing it. Kam et al. (2016) studied enhancing customer relationships with retail service brands. Researchers conducted two separate studies and found that the concept of customer engagement plays a vital role in building customer–brand relationship quality and customer loyalty to the retail brand. Kam et al. (2016) tested the relationship between involvement and customer engagement. The

study was conducted to extend the effectiveness of building such a relationship in retail services. The results indicated that involvement significantly predicts customer engagement. Also, the link between customer involvement and customer engagement has been described consistently in previous studies (Vivek et al., 2012). Customer involvement is defined as an individual's importance, time, and effort to SNS (Alhidari et al., 2015). Customers who are highly involved in SNS tend to spend more time, effort, and energy and are more likely to engage with the posts, enhancing customer trust and purchase intention.

1.3.7 Relationship Between Practical Benefits and Customer Engagement

Practical benefits involve customers' recognition and relevant product or service information. The characteristics, uniqueness, and innovativeness of products or services are needed to guide customers to purchase. Therefore, practical benefits will be one of the antecedents of customer engagement on the fabric handicraft page. Customer engagement has been shaped based on their attitude(s) towards the content and the act of resharing or reposting the content (Kananukul et al., 2015). Thus, a positive attitude towards the product will lead to customers recommending it to others and indirectly persuading others to commit to the brand page. Therefore, businesses should provide accurate information or content on their brand page. Jahn and Kunz (2012) found that practical benefits significantly influence customer engagement.

1.3.8 Relationship Between Social Benefits and Customer Engagement

Social benefits refer to customers' participation in SNSs, such as brand communities on a particular brand page. Online brand communities communicate with a large audience and can facilitate social benefits. The more interactive information or content of products or services in SNSs, the richer the social benefits, which could drive customer engagement. Simon and Tossan (2018) and Kang et al. (2014) suggest that social benefits influenced customer engagement on the fabric handicraft page.

1.3.9 Relationship Between Customer Engagement and Customer Trust

Kananukul et al. (2015) indicated that users who trust SNSs are likelier to display trust in the brand. Customer trust is essential in building a relationship between customers and retailers. On SNSs, customers are likely to interact with a service provider who they trust. Thus, the customer must perceive trust in the SNSs and brands to develop loyalty and customer equity (Kananukul et al., 2015). In addition, Hajli (2014) reported that advancements on the internet and the emergence of Web 2.0 and social media had empowered customers to make a purchase decision efficiently ***Customer engagement has positively influenced customer trust.***

1.3.10 Relationship Between Customer Engagement and Purchase Intention

Jamid et al. (2017) studied the relationship between customer personality traits and customer engagement (CE) in the online brand community (OBC) context. Their findings also indicate a positive association between CE and purchase intention.

2 FABRIC HANDICRAFT

This chapter focuses on handicrafts made of fabric. Handicrafts are an artistic kind of commerce that are produced either entirely or partially by hand to symbolise the historical and cultural attractiveness of the country or region in which they were created. Malaysia is home to many different ethnic groups, which has resulted in the creation of a wide variety of handicrafts, each symbolising the cultural identity of a state in the country. The majority of handicrafts make use of natural resources that are ecologically safe.

Fabric handicrafts with its uniqueness add support to tourism industry in Malaysia. Most visitors seek handicrafts that can be exhibited and used as gifts. These goods are handcrafted, indirectly making handicrafts a labour-intensive business. It has been discovered that the handicrafts preferred by local visitors and tourists from other countries are pretty similar, which allowed handicraft manufacturers to standardise their handmade products. However, it should be pointed out that traditional handicrafts are less visible in the market due to a lack of significant support from the younger generation.

Although the fabric handicraft has high economic potential, few studies address ways to strengthen Malaysia's traditional handicraft industry, and although many studies have been conducted on entrepreneurship in Malaysia, few studies involved elucidating how entrepreneurs can help preserve and enhance the traditional handicraft sector by leveraging the power of social media to promote handicraft brands. Table 1 provides measurement items for measuring the constructs.

3 RESULTS, FINDINGS, AND DISCUSSION

This chapter analyses data and tests the relationships between the constructs using the partial least squares (PLS) structural equation model (SEM), SmartPLS 3.3.3. PLS is a variance-based structural equation method, making it the preferred method in studies where the primary objective is to predict and explain target constructs (Hair et al., 2013).

Discriminant validity, which determines whether the constructs are distinct, was confirmed when the Fornell-Larcker criterion was applied (see Tables 2 and 3) (Jarvis et al., 2003). With the Fornell-Larcker criterion being satisfied, each reflective construct's 'square root of the AVE' has to be greater than its correlation coefficients with other constructs. The shared variance with other latent variables is confirmed as larger than the indications. As a

Table 1 Measurement Items for All Constructs

Measurement Items

Customer involvement (CI)
This fabric handicraft is essential to me
This fabric handicraft means a lot to me
This fabric handicraft does matter to me
This fabric handicraft gives me a feeling of confidence
Practical Benefits (PB)
1.It is easy to find information about fabric handicraft
2.SNS usually make information about fabric handicraft immediately accessible
3.Most SNS provide timely information about fabric handicraft
4.Generally, SNSs are a good source of fabric handicraft
5.I visit SNSs just to look for information
Social benefits (SB)
I visit SNS because I want to provide information about fabric handicraft to other people
I visit SNS because I want to get help from other people
I visit SNS because I want to help other people
I visit SNS because I want to feel needed by other people
Customer engagement (CE)
1.I like posts that comprise photos
2.I like posts that comprise videos or links
3.I share posts that comprise photos which benefit others
4.I share posts that comprise videos or links which benefit others
5.I follow brand pages that I am interested in
6.I actively comment on posts that comprise photos
7.I actively comment on posts that comprise brand videos or links to brand videos
Customer Trust (CT)
1.I feel that SNS would act in the customer's best interests
2.I believe that SNS continues to be a good source of information about fabric handicraft over long term, thus enhancing my confidence
3.I feel confident that I can rely on SNS when I need information about fabric handicraft of this nature
4.I trust SNS in providing accurate information about fabric handicraft
5.I am comfortable making comments and/or sharing ideas with others about fabric handicraft on SNS
6.Based on my past and present experiences, I believe that this SNS deserves my trust
Purchase intention (PI)
In the near future, I would probably buy fabric handicraft
In the near future, I intend to buy fabric handicraft
In the near future, I would possibly buy fabric handicraft
In the near future, I would likely buy fabric handicraft
In the near future, I would definitely buy fabric handicraft

result, the discriminant validity (of the first-order components) is confirmed. Furthermore, the cross-loadings analysis confirmed the discriminant validity of the measurement items since each measurement item loaded the most on its assigned constructs in contrast to its cross-loadings on other constructs (Hair et al., 2016).

This chapter also employed a more rigorous test of discriminant validity suggested by Henseler et al. (2015). The heterotrait-monotrait ratio of correlations (HTMT) criteria based on a multitrait-multimethod matrix recommends proving discriminant validity, with the HTMT conservative threshold being less than 0.90. Except for two correlations, Table 4 demonstrates that

Table 2 Internal Consistency Reliability and Convergent Validity Test

Construct	Code items	Loadings	Cronbach Alpha	AVE	CR
Customer Engagement	CE1	0.766	0.856	0.887	0.529
	CE2	0.759			
	CE3	0.702			
	CE4	0.718			
	CE5	0.687			
	CE6	0.778			
	CE7	0.672			
Involvement	IV1	0.88	0.897	0.927	0.761
	IV2	0.909			
	IV3	0.858			
	IV4	0.841			
Practical Benefits	PB1	0.733	0.807	0.861	0.555
	PB2	0.859			
	PB3	0.746			
	PB4	0.695			
	PB5	0.677			
Purchase Intention	PI1	0.843	0.907	0.929	0.724
	PI2	0.862			
	PI3	0.873			
	PI4	0.819			
	PI5	0.858			
Social Benefits	SB1	0.668	0.762	0.846	0.58
	SB2	0.773			
	SB3	0.794			
	SB4	0.804			
Consumer Trust	TT1	0.694	0.826	0.873	0.534
	TT2	0.671			
	TT3	0.756			
	TT4	0.783			
	TT5	0.723			
	TT6	0.751			

Table 3 Discriminant Validity—Fornell and Larcker

	1	2	3	4	5	6
1. Consumer Trust	**0.731**					
2. Customer Engagement	0.538	**0.727**				
3. Involvement	0.352	0.303	**0.872**			
4. Practical Benefits	0.519	0.266	0.372	**0.745**		
5. Purchase Intention	0.599	0.37	0.357	0.305	**0.851**	
6. Social Benefits	0.529	0.435	0.435	0.467	0.384	**0.762**

Note Items in bold represent the Square Root of AVE

the correlation values corresponding to the relevant constructs did not violate HTMT.

Results from the structural model indicate the size and significance of the path coefficients and R2 values of customer trust and purchase intention CEB (see Fig. 1 and Table 5) (Hair et al., 2016). All paths presented in Fig. 1 were positive and significant (t > 1.96, p < 0.05) except for practical benefits and customer engagement. Furthermore, the model explains 53.8% of the variance in customer trust and 37% of the variance in purchase intentions.

Based on the analysis, the result displayed in Table 5 showed that customer involvement has a significant positive relationship with customer engagement ($\beta = 0.129$; t = 2.45; p = 0.007). This implies that consumers' interaction experience with the brand page through consumer involvement helps influence customer engagement in the fabric handicraft brand page context. Higher involvement with SNSs relates to higher levels of customer engagement. This result is supported by previous research (Bowden, 2009; Harrigan et al., 2018; Hollebeek, 2011), suggesting that highly involved consumers will likely direct their preferred brand's thoughts, emotions, and behaviours. The results also highlighted that customers engage in the fabric handicraft page when they actively comment on the page's information. When the fabric handicraft page is essential and is significant for them, they will engage themselves by leaving their comments and sharing information with other users.

Table 4 HTMT Discriminant Validity

	1	2	3	4	5	6
1. Consumer Trust						
2. Customer Engagement	0.605					
3. Involvement	0.412	0.311				
4. Practical Benefits	0.624	0.296	0.411			
5. Purchase Intention	0.681	0.366	0.411	0.365		
6. Social Benefits	0.665	0.484	0.533	0.613	0.447	

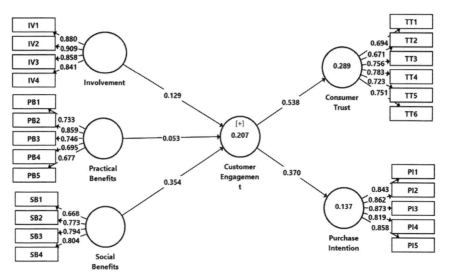

Fig. 1 Structural Model

Table 5 Results of Structural Model

	β Loading	Standard Deviation (STDEV)	T-values	P Values	LL 5.00%	UL 95.00%
Involvement > Customer Engagement	0.129	0.053	2.445	0.007	0.054	0.234
Practical Benefits > Customer Engagement	0.053	0.047	1.117	0.132	−0.041	0.117
Social Benefits > Customer Engagement	0.354	0.069	5.127	0.0001	0.215	0.448
Customer Engagement > Consumer Trust	0.538	0.035	15.157	0.0001	0.47	0.584
Customer Engagement > Purchase Intention	0.37	0.047	7.926	0.0001	0.28	0.439

Moreover, when customers share their comments, the fabric handicraft brand page attracts them.

Next, it was found practical benefits have no relationship with customer engagement in fabric handicraft brand pages (β = 0.053; t = 1.17; p = 0.132). This is inconsistent with previous studies reporting that practical benefits did not influence customer engagement (Jahn & Kunz, 2012). The possible reasons are that customers cannot easily find information, information is not accessible immediately, or there is not much information available about fabric handicrafts. On the other hand, SNSs are usually immediately accessible when searching for relevant information on fabric handicrafts.

Third, it was found that social benefits have significantly influenced customer engagement with fabric handicrafts posted on SNSs ($\beta = 0.354$; $t = 5.127$; $p = 0.0001$). The result is supported by Kang et al. (2014), stating that customers visit SNSs because they want to provide information or get help from others in the online community. In addition, the study also shows that customers are engaged because they want to be needed by others in the network.

Fourth, this chapter found that customer engagement has a significant positive influence on customer trust ($\beta = 0.538$; $t = 15.15$; $p = 0.0001$). This finding is supported by Hajli (2013) and shows that customers believe SNSs are good sources of information for a long-term period. Customers also rely on SNSs to find information about fabric handicrafts. It should also be pointed out that customers trust SNSs because they provide accurate information about fabric handicrafts. When customers engage with SNSs, they believe it continues to be a good source of information about fabric handicrafts over the long term, enhancing their confidence when the information provided is also accurate. Also, when highly engaged, they are comfortable commenting and/or sharing ideas with others about fabric handicrafts on SNS.

Finally, this chapter confirmed that customer engagement has a significant favourable influence on purchase intention ($\beta = 0.37$; $t = 7.926$; $p = 0.0001$). This finding is consistent with previous studies reporting significance in practical benefits (Hajli, 2013). Customer engagement with SNSs becomes a predictor of purchase intention of fabric handicrafts. The more they are engaged with the brand page, the higher the intention to purchase. However, when engagement is low, consumers have less interaction experience with the brand page, translating to a lowered intention to purchase.

4 Implications of the Study

This chapter theoretically contributes to SNSs by validating the role of customer involvement and social and practical benefits in influencing interaction in the model customer engagement in fabric handicraft brands.

4.1 Theoretical Implications

First, the S–O–R theory explains the model, which states that customer involvement, practical benefits, and social benefits serve as a stimulus that creates positive responses in users to increase purchase intention (Koo & Ju, 2010). In addition, customer involvement stimulates more attention to advertisements and understanding of product information (Kam et al., 2016). The significant relationship between customer involvement and customer engagement is consistent with Harrigan et al. (2018). Customer involvement influences the increasing interaction between customers and fabric handicraft brands by sharing content, video, and pictures, participating in community activities and exchanging ideas were also confirmed.

Second, the social exchange theory acknowledges practical and social benefits contributions to engaging with fabric handicraft brand pages. For example, it can be suggested that customers who are provided with helpful information tend to have a positive attitude towards informative advertisements on SNSs (Kujur & Singh, 2017). Exclusive content, online events, and contests are ways fan pages can use to achieve engagement (Jahn & Kunz, 2012). Perceived social benefits significantly impacted members' active participation on Facebook fan pages (Kang et al., 2014). A brand page requires regularly updating and delivery of value for the community members to ensure there is engagement. This can be seen through statistics of 'likes' or 'followers' remaining high (Jahn & Kunz, 2012).

4.2 Managerial Implications

Apart from the theoretical implications, the findings also provide managerial implications. First, this chapter provides insights for practitioners when utilising SNSs as a channel to enhance the interaction experience between customers and brands with their existing customers or initiate relationships with their potential customers. The chapter shows that customer engagement influences customer trust and purchase intention. Notably, a marketer should increase the feeling of the importance of a particular product and brand by emphasising that it is meaningful, matters, and builds confidence in customers. Marketers should quickly provide information about the fabric handicraft via multiple sources that are immediately accessible, timely information such as the product values, ingredients, and country of origin. They should also create awareness of social benefits from joining SNSs, (e.g. Facebook). This can be done by encouraging users to share and get help from others to find more information and recommendations. With higher customer involvement, consumers express their thoughts and feelings via liking or commenting on posts and generating new content on the sites by creating and distributing more information and materials about the targeted brand (e.g. sharing posts and/or uploading brand-related images), impacting their engagement with a brand page.

Second, managers could enhance the customer interaction experience by keeping track of which posts receive the most 'Likes' and 'Shares'. This will help a company determine what consumers are most engaged in, assuming postings about other brands have a consistently higher 'Likes' count than those about fabric handicrafts. In that case, companies may utilise that knowledge to develop a better and more socially responsible product messaging. Customers can be encouraged towards active engagement on SNSs by providing helpful information, promotions, and rapid responses. Practitioners must also create a harmonious online atmosphere where members may freely communicate and converse with other members using social media platforms.

Third, greater customer service should be provided via private messaging or direct communications to optimise speed. Customers who are highly involved will interact in greater engagement, for example, by asking questions, seeking assistance, or sharing their opinions. They can also help customers increase their confidence and trust by providing information which is reliable, includes its source, accurate and up-to-date.

Fourth, sharing tagged posts, tweets, or hashtags highlighting a product or service benefits companies in two significant ways. The first is that, it provides a chance to thank the consumer for their business and to acknowledge their positive experience. It also generates significant social proof that can be used to convert prospective consumers who are undecided making a purchase. If, for example, someone is unsure about how to behave in a social scenario that they have never experienced before, they might draw cues from the individuals around them. In the case of an online purchasing scenario, when individuals shop, they search for reviews, suggestions, and examples of how others have utilised a product before making their selection. This demonstrates the importance of obtaining customers' reviews based on their pleasant experiences.

5   Limitation and Future Studies

This chapter attempts to expand on previous research by developing a model to better explain better enhancing interaction experience for customer engagement on SNSs. However, this work had several limitations that affected the generalisation of the findings. Firstly, this work selected and tested a limited number of selected antecedents and consequences of customer engagement having interaction experiences on SNSs. Secondly, this work used Facebook and Instagram as the main platforms to distribute the questionnaires. Thirdly, this work did not consider the actual purchase and word-of-mouth behaviour. To increase the generalisability of the findings, we suggest that future research test other antecedents such as brand personality, social self-expression, customer participation, hedonic and utilitarian values, and consequences such as brand loyalty, brand commitment, and perceived quality in the fabric handicraft context. It would also be interesting to differentiate the meaning of customer engagement by investigating its dimensions. Additionally, compared to the millions of Facebook and Instagram users worldwide, this work is limited to a valid sample of users mainly from one country. It would be interesting to have samples from other countries and analyse users on other online social networking platforms.

6   Conclusion

This chapter has presented a research topic of enhancing customer–brand interaction of customer engagement on SNSs of fabric handicrafts. First, this chapter contributes to the existing literature on customer engagement and

SNSs. It explained the role of customer involvement and practical and social benefits as drivers and their impact on customer trust and purchase intention. Second, the relationship in the model can help practitioners understand the antecedents and consequences of customer engagement in effectively strategising and positioning their business. For example, suppose the relationships are confirmed that customer involvement, practical benefits and social benefits will lead to customer engagement. In that case, practitioners can focus on growing the fabric handicraft page with appropriate content and encouraging two-way communication and the pages' importance to customers. Additionally, if it is confirmed that customer engagement predicts customer trust and purchase intention, creating and managing the fabric handicraft page can achieve marketing objectives and contribute to its performance.

SNSs, through social media, became a new frontier for consumer brand engagement. Therefore, companies, brands, or marketers should anticipate and understand consumers' preferences to provide better interactive experiences to transform them into positive behaviour, particularly in fabric handicrafts. Thus, using appropriate strategies to enhance interactivity, such as increasing brand page content and visual content, improving consumer service, building communities, sharing reviews, and using hashtags, is essential in engaging customers, increasing customer trust and purchase intention.

The findings of this chaper enable the creation of practical insights for enhancing the interactivity experience for customer engagement with SNSs brand pages. Managers are continuously attempting to enhance customer engagement while also evaluating key performance metrics that lead to the generation of high engagement. Furthermore, given the importance of consumer involvement in the engagement process, businesses should strive to encourage active participation from current customers. User-generated content is essential for building customer trust than solely firm-generated content. Thus, the branded content on the SNSs, particularly on Facebook and Instagram, should be tailored to the customers' needs rather than the firm promoting it. Customers may be more likely to engage with a brand if online information and experiences excite their curiosity and are personally relevant.

REFERENCES

Akar, E., & Topçu, B. (2011). An examination of the factors influencing consumers' attitudes toward social media marketing. *Journal of Internet Commerce, 10*(1), 35–67.

Alhidari, A., Iyer, P., & Paswan, A. (2015). Personal level antecedents of eWOM and purchase intention, on social networking sites. *Journal of Customer Behaviour, 14*(2), 107–125.

Blasco-Arcas, L., Hernandez-Ortega, B. I., & Jimenez-Martinez, J. (2016). Engagement platforms: The role of emotions in fostering customer engagement and brand image in interactive media. *Journal of Service Theory and Practice, 26*(5), 559–589.

Bowden, J. L. H. (2009). The process of customer engagement: A conceptual framework. *Journal of Marketing Theory and Practice, 17*(1), 63–74.

Brengman, M., & Karimov, F. P. (2012). The effect of web communities on consumers' initial trust in B2C ecommerce websites. *Management Research Review, 35*(9), 791–817.

Brodie, R. J., Ilic, A., Juric, B., & Hollebeek, L. (2013). Consumer engagement in a virtual brand community: An exploratory analysis. *Journal of Business Research, 66*(1), 105–114.

Bruner, G. C., & Kumar, A. (2000). Web commercials and advertising hierarchy-of-effects. *Journal of Advertising Research, 40*(1–2), 35–42.

Cabiddu, F., De Carlo, M., & Piccoli, G. (2014). Social media affordances: Enabling customer engagement. *Annals of Tourism Research, 48*, 175–192.

Chang, C. C. (2013). Examining users' intention to continue using social network games: A flow experience perspective. *Telematics and Informatics, 30*(4), 311–321.

Chauhan, K., & Pillai, A. (2013). Role of content strategy in social media brand communities: A case of higher education institutes in India. *Journal of Product and Brand Management, 22*(1), 40–51.

Chebat, J. C., & Michon, R. (2003). Impact of ambient odors on mall shoppers' emotions, cognition, and spending: A test of competitive causal theories. *Journal of Business Research, 56*(7), 529–539.

Cook, K. S., & Yamagishi, T. (1992). Power in exchange networks: A power-dependence formulation. *Social networks, 14*(3–4), 245–265.

Gummerus, J., Liljander, V., Weman, E., & Pihlström, M. (2012). Customer engagement in a Facebook brand community. *Management Research Review, 35*(9), 857–877.

Hajli, M. N. (2014). A study of the impact of social media on consumers. *International Journal of Market Research, 56*(3), 387–404.

Hajli, M. (2013). A research framework for social commerce adoption. *Information Management and Computer Security, 21*(3), 144–154.

Hair, J. F., Ringle, C. M., & Sarstedt, M. (2013). Partial least squares structural equation modeling: Rigorous applications, better results and higher acceptance. *Long Range Planning, 46*(1–2), 1–12.

Hair Jr, J. F., Sarstedt, M., Matthews, L. M., & Ringle, C. M. (2016). Identifying and treating unobserved heterogeneity with FIMIX-PLS: Part I–method. *European Business Review, 28*(1), 63–76.

Hamzah, Z. L., Wahab, H. A., & Waqas, M. (2021). Unveiling drivers and brand relationship implications of consumer engagement with social media brand posts. *Journal of Research in Interactive Marketing, 15*(2), 336–358.

Harrigan, P., Evers, U., Miles, M. P., & Daly, T. (2018). Customer engagement and the relationship between involvement, engagement, self-brand connection and brand usage intent. *Journal of Business Research, 88,* 388–396.

Hayes, R. A., Carr, C. T., & Wohn, D. Y. (2016). One click, many meanings: Interpreting paralinguistic digital affordances in social media. *Journal of Broadcasting & Electronic Media, 60,* 171–187.

Henseler, J., Ringle, C. M., & Sarstedt, M. (2015). A new criterion for assessing discriminant validity in variancebased structural equation modeling. *Journal of the Academy of Marketing Science, 43*(1), 115–135.

Hoffman, D. L., & Novak, T. P. (2012). Toward a deeper understanding of social media. *Journal of Interactive Marketing, 26*(2), 69–70.

Hollebeek, L. (2011). Exploring customer brand engagement: Definition and themes. *Journal of Strategic Marketing, 19*(7), 555–573.

Hopkins, J. L. (2012). Can Facebook be an effective mechanism for generating growth and value in small businesses? *Journal of Systems and Information Technology, 14*(2), 131–141.

Humphrey Jr, W. F., Laverie, D. A., & Rinaldo, S. B. (2017). Brand choice via incidental social media exposure. *Journal of Research in Interactive Marketing, 11*(2), 110–130.

Jahn, B., & Kunz, W. (2012). How to transform consumers into fans of your brand. *Journal of Service Management, 23*(3), 344–361.

Jamid, U. I., Zillur, R., & Hollebeek, L. D. (2017). Personality factors as predictors of online consumer engagement: An empirical investigation. *Marketing Intelligence & Planning, 35*(4), 510–528.

Jarvis, C. B., MacKenzie, S. B., & Podsakoff, P. M. (2003). A critical review of construct indicators and measurement model misspecification in marketing and consumer research. *Journal of Consumer Research, 30*(2), 199–218.

Jung, T. H., Ineson, E. M., & Green, E. (2013). Online social networking: Relationship marketing in UK hotels. *Journal of Marketing Management, 29*(3–4), 393–420.

Kam, F. S., King, C., Sparks, B. A., & Wang, Y. (2016). Enhancing customer relationships with retail service brands: The role of customer engagement. *Journal of Service Management, 27*(2), 170–193.

Kananukul, C., Jung, S., & Watchravesringkan, K. (2015). Building customer equity through trust in social networking sites: A perspective from Thai consumers. *Journal of Research in Interactive Marketing, 9*(2), 148–166.

Kang, J., Tang, L., & Fiore, A. M. (2014). Enhancing consumer–brand relationships on restaurant Facebook fan pages: Maximizing consumer benefits and increasing active participation. *International Journal of Hospitality Management, 36,* 145–155.

Koo, D. M., & Ju, S. H. (2010). The interactional effects of atmospherics and perceptual curiosity on emotions and online shopping intention. *Computers in Human Behavior, 26*(3), 377–388.

Kujur, F., & Singh, S. (2017). Engaging customers through online participation in social networking sites. *Asia Pacific Management Review, 22*(1), 16–24.

Lim, W. M., Kumar, S., Pandey, N., Rasul, T., & Gaur, V. (2022). From direct marketing to interactive marketing: A retrospective review of the Journal of Research in Interactive Marketing. *Journal of Research in Interactive Marketing,* Vol. ahead-of-print No. ahead-of-print. https://doi.org/10.1108/JRIM-11-2021-0276

McKnight, D. H., Choudhury, V., & Kacmar, C. (2002). The impact of initial consumer trust on intentions to transact with a web site: A trust building model. *The Journal of Strategic Information Systems, 11*(3–4), 297–323.

Mehrabian, A., & Russell, J. A. (1974). The basic emotional impact of environments. *Perceptual and Motor Skills, 38*(1), 283–301.

Morgan, R. M., & Hunt, S. D. (1994). The commitment-trust theory of relationship marketing. *Journal of Marketing, 58*(3), 20–38.

Mosteller, J., & Poddar, A. (2017). To share and protect: Using regulatory focus theory to examine the privacy paradox of consumers' social media engagement and online privacy protection behaviors. *Journal of Interactive Marketing, 39*, 27–38.

Mukherjee, K., & Banerjee, N. (2019). Social networking sites and customers' attitude towards advertisements. *Journal of Research in Interactive Marketing, 13*(4), 477–491.

Poddar, A., Mosteller, J., & Ellen, P. S. (2009). Consumers' rules of engagement in online information exchanges. *Journal of Consumer Affairs, 43*(3), 419–448.

Poorrezaei, M. (2016). Customer engagement: Conceptualisation, measurement and validation (Order No. 28467703). Available from ProQuest Dissertations & Theses Global. (2572592783). https://doi.org/ezproxy.um.edu.my:2048/login?url=https://www.proquest.com/dissertations-theses/customer-engagement-conceptualisation-measurement/docview/2572592783/se-2?accountid=28930

Qin, Y. S. (2020). Fostering brand–consumer interactions in social media: The role of social media uses and gratifications. *Journal of Research in Interactive Marketing, 14*(3), 337–354.

Richard, P. J., Devinney, T. M., Yip, G. S., & Johnson, G. (2009). Measuring organizational performance: Towards methodological best practice. *Journal of Management, 35*(3), 718–804.

Schratt-Bitter, S., Grabner-Kräuter, S., & Breitenecker, R. (2014). Customer engagement behaviour in online social networks-the Facebook perspective. *International Journal of Networking and Virtual Organisations, 14*, 197–220.

Shankar, V., & Malthouse, E. C. (2009). A peek into the future of interactive marketing. *Journal of Interactive Marketing, 23*(1), 1–3.

Simon, F., & Tossan, V. (2018). Does brand-consumer social sharing matter? A relational framework of customer engagement to brand-hosted social media. *Journal of Business Research, 85*, 175–184.

Statisca.com. (2022). Facebook: Number of monthly active users worldwide 2008–2021. https://www.statista.com/statistics/264810/number-of-monthly-active-facebook-users-worldwide/. Accessed 2 February 2022.

Tafesse, W. (2015). Content strategies and audience response on Facebook brand pages. *Marketing Intelligence and Planning, 33*(6), 927–943.

Tafesse, W. (2016). An experiential model of consumer engagement in social media. *Journal of Product and Brand Management, 25*(5), 424–434.

Taylor, D. G., Lewin, J. E., & Strutton, D. (2011). Friends, fans, and followers: Do ads work on social networks? How gender and age shape receptivity. *Journal of Advertising Research, 51*(1), 258–275.

Thibaut, J. W., & Kelley, H. H. (1959). *The social psychology of groups*. Wiley.

Tiruwa, A., Yadav, R., & Suri, P. K. (2016). An exploration of online brand community (OBC) engagement and customer's intention to purchase. *Journal of Indian Business Research, 8*(4), 295–314.

Tsai, W. H. S., & Men, L. R. (2013). Motivations and antecedents of consumer engagement with brand pages on social networking sites. *Journal of Interactive Advertising*, *13*(2), 76–87.

Van Doorn, J., Lemon, K. N., Mittal, V., Nass, S., Pick, D., Pirner, P., & Verhoef, P. C. (2010). Customer engagement behavior: Theoretical foundations and research directions. *Journal of Service Research*, *13*(3), 253–266.

Vivek, S. D., Beatty, S. E., & Morgan, R. M. (2012). Customer engagement: Exploring customer relationships beyond purchase. *Journal of Marketing Theory and Practice*, *20*(2), 122–146.

Wang, C. L. (2021). New frontiers and future directions in interactive marketing: Inaugural Editorial. *Journal of Research in Interactive Marketing*, *15*(1), 1–9.

Wang, Y., Min, Q., & Han, S. (2016). Understanding the effects of trust and risk on individual behavior toward social media platforms: A meta-analysis of the empirical evidence. *Computers in Human Behavior*, *56*, 34–44.

Zaichkowsky, J. L. (1985). Measuring the involvement construct. *Journal of Consumer Research*, *12*(3), 341–352.

Zoha, R., Suberamanian, K., & Hasmah, Z. (2017). SM Analytics: Impact of SM engagement metrics on online purchase intention. *Journal of Engineering and Applied Sciences*, *12*(2), 283–289.

… CHAPTER 22

Live Streaming as an Interactive Marketing Media: Examining Douyin and Its Constructed Value and Cultural Preference of Consumption in E-commerce

Boris L. F. Pun and Anthony Y. H. Fung

"Please take a close look of this soup," said the live streaming host, holding a spoonful of soup in front of the camera, "the smell and taste are very similar to the soup I made in the last video, but this time it actually come from this instant soup pack."

1   INTRODUCTION: DOUYIN AND INTERACTIVE MARKETING

Having a sunny smile and blinking, Culinary Mr. Lee (the Douyin celebrity) continues to encourage the reviewers to ask their friends to join his e-commerce site and place an order, as they would receive a price discount if more than 300,000 orders have been placed.

This is a brief description of e-commerce that occurs every day on the Chinese online platform Douyin, which was never expected to be found on social media ten years ago. As a result of technological advancement and social media proliferation (Wang, 2021), social media no longer consists simply of social networking platforms, but has now developed into a virtual medium

B. L. F. Pun (✉) · A. Y. H. Fung
Chinese University of Hong Kong, Hong Kong, China
e-mail: borispun@cuhk.edu.hk

A. Y. H. Fung
e-mail: anthonyfung@cuhk.edu.hk

© The Author(s), under exclusive license to Springer Nature Switzerland AG 2023
C. L. Wang (ed.), *The Palgrave Handbook of Interactive Marketing*,
https://doi.org/10.1007/978-3-031-14961-0_22

for hosting business and sales negotiations between buyers and sellers. Understood as a significant outcome of interactive marketing due to its innovative bidirectional customer-and-seller interaction, e-commerce has become one of the most successful emergent global business models, and it has changed the value, preference, and culture of consumption. It now has an immense influence on the attitudes and decisions of consumers regarding their purchases, as shown in Graham and Wilder's study (2020), and it has also expanded the volume of purchases, particularly during the period of the COVID-19 pandemic, according to a study by Femenia-Serra et al. (2022). Such change has always varied with the innovation of different interactive social media applications, which has been well addressed by Masciantonio et al.'s study (2021) on the effect of social media during the COVID-19 pandemic. Many studies have specifically focused on Western social media tools such as Twitter and Instagram (i.e., Lee & Kim, 2020; Lee et al., 2022) due to its characteristically specific interface and marketing function, which leads to increased advertisement revenue and sponsorships as well as the emergence of online celebrities.

Douyin is comparatively different from Instagram in terms of its setting, function, and market, which also makes Douyin worth studying as one of the most suitable tools for live streaming and e-commerce with respect to interactive marketing. In terms of its setting and function, since the rise of short video uploading platforms (e.g., YouTube) and social networking platforms (e.g., Facebook) in the 2000s, public interest in short self-shot videos for quick social communication has grown rapidly. Unlike Instagram which was initially launched as a photo-sharing social networking application, Douyin features a short video sharing (around 15–60s) function, and it promotes the concept of friendly competition among youth on a collective site where they can record their actions in a video format and then share this with friends. Douyin was launched with great success in the Chinese market in August 2018 (Wang et. al., 2020). Douyin and its international version TikTok have captured almost 800 million active users worldwide and was ranked ninth in terms of social networking sites in 2020, covering over 150 countries and 75 languages in the world (Zeng et al., 2021). They also became the overall most popular app downloaded, particularly among young kids and youth (Geyser, 2021).

With respect to Douyin's role in the Chinese market, the high popularity of Douyin among youth in China allows the Douyin celebrities to gather a large audience pool, which can be converted into a commercial opportunity for e-commerce and live streaming sales, both of which are now highly popular in China. The study of Douyin in China also allows us to gain a comprehensive overview of the consumption and selling preferences in contemporary China, which have been influenced by President Xi's era of rapid modernization, characterized by a higher level of censorship but also freedom from control in the e-commerce consumption and selling activities hosted on social media platforms. This specific political condition has led to a unique version of e-commerce as conducted by Douyin in China compared with e-commerce in other countries, including the United States (Unni & Weinstein, 2021), India (Patel et al., 2020), Sri Lanka (Sachini & Mijetunga, 2019), Belgium (Cauberge et al., 2021), and the UK (Suárez-Álvarez & García-Jiménez, 2021). At the same time, there have only been a few studies conducted in China (Lee et al., 2020; Sha & Dong, 2021), and none of them have engaged in the discussion of interactive marketing and value and preference construction. Thus, a research gap exists in the study of e-commerce in China.

In this study of Douyin, Douyin celebrities, and their involvement in e-commerce and interactive marketing in China, the authors conducted a detailed literature review. The goal was to determine how Douyin exerts its influential manipulating power in the creative labor market (the pool of Douyin celebrities), information flow, and culture inside the community, and how it generates a sustainable and solid mechanism of interactive marketing under this specific format of Douyin. This chapter will provide examples of Douyin celebrities and their online e-commerce activities, and it will discuss the specific academic and economic implications of Douyin's mechanism of interactive marketing.

2 Literature Review

There has been extensive work published on the role of social media in interactive marketing, which has primarily highlighted the use of an interactive device to establish branding and influence consumers' attitudes and behaviors. For instance, the study of He et al. (2021) addressed the strong moderating effect of the brand content of brand-owned social media on consumers' attitudes toward brands. This finding has been supported by other studies, such as the research of Qin (2020) on branding and its strong effect on social media (Facebook) usage and the motives of consumers' interaction, or even on gambling behavior, as discussed in the study of Ji et al. (2022). The research of Al-Emadi and Yahia (2020) focused on the performance difference of users of various social media platforms like Instagram and Facebook, and the authors argued that a greater influence of social media could be observed in users of sites that offered a higher level of flexibility and participation. Synthesizing these current research findings can shed light on the current research gap, and to achieve this, a study of how influential Douyin is as a social media platform for interactive marketing would provide essential insights.

Compared with other interactive platforms such as Instagram and Facebook, the characteristics of the interactive function of Douyin have not been well addressed in existing literature. Many scholars have investigated the use of Douyin (or TikTok) in education (Escamilla-Fajardo et al., 2021; Khlaif & Salha, 2021), business (Mhalla et al., 2020), geopolitics (Gray, 2021), social movement (Hautea et al., 2021), promoting gender equality (Sachini & Mijetunga, 2019),[1] class struggle (Verma, 2020),[2] and socialization and identity construction (Wang & Omar, 2020). However, there has not been an effort to examine Douyin adequately as a research subject of interactive marketing to determine how it could achieve greater success in the Chinese market. Also, the existing literature on interactive marketing has not provided an appropriate lens through which this research gap can be viewed.

The goal of this chapter therefore is to propose a new perspective through which the authors can gain a better understanding of Douyin and its mechanisms that enhance the function of interactive marketing. In this section, the authors attempt to explore the relationships involved among Douyin, Douyin celebrities, and their involvement in e-commerce and interactive marketing through three existing perspectives: (1) Douyin recruits and fosters immaterial creative labor, (2) Douyin exerts influential manipulating power on both creators and users, and (3) Douyin and its function achieve a sense of community (SOC).

2.1 Douyin Recruits and Fosters Immaterial Creative Labor

The discussion of creative labor is often linked to Marxist concepts about labor being exploited by the production side. Fuchs (2014) interpreted the creativity and user-generated content as a symbol of exploitation and a form of work outsourcing to unpaid labor (the users). Hesmondhalgh and Baker (2013) added to the discussion the concept of self-exploitation as users are willing to obtain an emotional reward from their unpaid contribution (the so-called "affective labor" coined by Hardt [1999]). These studies addressed how an audience is influenced and blindly dedicates its time and effort in exchange for an immaterial return, under the value system constructed by production sectors (in this case, the social media platform Douyin).

The recent studies of Douyin also suggest a similar approach to understand the outcome of the Douyin usage, which is users producing their own value and reward through their creation. The active nature of users as labor in China has been widely discussed over the last ten years, for example, Zhang and Fung's (2014) study about consumers as creative labor in China's gaming industry. A report Digital content & Creative Media center of BNU. (2019) highlights the activeness of Douyin users, as they may not simply be victims of exploitation but may also be enjoying the specific mechanism of Douyin's work that introduces a global leisure-work condition for Chinese youth. This working condition may offer users what they really want, in terms of both

---

[1] Their research revealed that TikTok is the publicization of the girls' bedroom culture and is foregrounded in the issue of gender inequalities.

[2] The author explained how social media crosses over the social boundaries in the case of the Indian class hierarchy conflict.

material (income and sponsored products) and immaterial (reputation, pleasure, self-expression, autonomy, etc.) rewards. Such benefits are more than pure emotional rewards, and users most often originally aim for them. Duffy and Wissinger's study (2017) has also provided an insight into how some Douyin users establish a set of mythologies to create the image of glamour that helps them to "sublime" and transform themselves into Douyin celebrities (*wanghong* in Chinese). In other words, Douyin is treated as the "path of promotion," leading the users to gain more monetary revenue rather than being exploited by the merchants. In addition, Abidin (2018) explored the celebrity behaviors of Douyin and argued how the so-called "parasociality" is established intentionally by Douyin celebrities to highlight their "distinctiveness" from the masses, among whom they used to belong prior to the aid of Douyin.

Douyin is also becoming a social media tool for self-identity construction, to help an uploader to look more professional due to their video sharing on Douyin. There are many examples of this, such as non-lawyers promoting legal knowledge and rights on Douyin (Douvartzidis & Surman, 2020), or non-frontline doctors and nurses sharing some clinically oriented content, which they find on the internet, to engage "professionally" with the public (Lovett et al., 2021), especially at the time when COVID-19 and the implementation of lockdowns caused negative impacts on human beings (Byrne et al., 2021). In addition to these amateur undertakings, the authorities have also become involved in Douyin to promote official information to the masses. Health authorities in many countries have already integrated Douyin use with the current public health system during the pandemic outbreak for better health promotion and control (Eghtesadi & Florea, 2020). Following this trend, more and more Douyin celebrities have also moved their professional and occupational practices from other institutional domains to the platform for developing their business (Chen & Zhang, 2021). Moreover, Douyin celebrities sharing Douyin videos is about more than delivering professional knowledge: it is a conscious attempt to achieve the social recognition as distinctive "informative professionals" among the rest. It is an action purely driven by the pursuit immaterial credit, reputation, and image reconstruction.

From these few studies, they capture the overview of Douyin users' proactiveness in creating their own video outputs, so as to become happier, more distinctive, special, professional, and influential. Such positive outcomes allow Douyin to recruit and foster a large number of potential video uploaders (creative labor) and audience members (consumers and the labor-to-be). This large pool of users directly contributes commercial value for marketing purposes.

2.2 Douyin Exerts Influential Manipulating Power on Both Creators and Users

From a market perspective, it is not enough to know that a large number of Douyin users (Douyin celebrities and regular users) are exposed to its media content. It would be more important to know how the media content influences the Douyin users in their consumption activities. People can argue whether or not Douyin could exert such manipulating power on the consumption behavior of audience, as there are not many studies specifically discussing Douyin's users and the platform's marketing outcome. Thus, in this chapter, the authors contribute to answering this question by demonstrating how people have become much more susceptible to being easily influenced by social media. One of the most prominent examples is the change in human behavior caused by misinformation.

Misinformation from social media has been thoroughly addressed in academic research in recent years, ranging from the work of Stahl (2006) to the latest by Basch et al. (2021) and O'Brien and Alsmadi (2021). Regarding the influence of misinformation and how it affects behavior, Baumel et al. (2021) identified open access platforms such as Douyin as a major factor, since everyone can now gain access to the process of opinion exchange and information assimilation by means of social media tools, without causing the administrators and to suspect them of posting misinformation. This is a major issue for Douyin because of its high mobility of information interaction. Mujika et al. (2020) explained the virality of the contents of Douyin as being the result of greater audience interest in shorter, more immediate, instant, and highly visual content. This quality, coupled with the fact that some beliefs are easily reinforced within communities that already hold a certain ideological bias, especially political ones, reaffirms a reality constructed with unverified information that need not be based on factual evidence. The finding of Chang et al.'s study (2019) provided a very similar interpretation of audience behavior. Based on the idea of continued influence effect (CIE), the closer the receivers' habitus is to the misinformation, the stronger CIE the person will have. The consequence is that people might still rely on the misinformation and act upon it even after it is proven wrong and retracted. All such research has suggested that manipulating the information content can affect people's behavior when that information is circulated via social media tools.

The influence is not limited to physical outcomes, but it can also include mental ones. For example, Tasnim et al. (2020) found that during the global pandemic, misinformation spread faster on social media than it did by means of reliable sources, which led to a wider range of negative externalities, including virus infections, disordered supply and demand relationships, and civil disobedience to government policies. Such negative externalities, according to Abbas et. al. (2021), have resulted in mental health crises as people have become very alerted and sensitive to the influx of any kind of information, and have often become more vulnerable to so-called fake news. Spain, Portugal, Brazil, and the USA were reported to be some examples of countries being influenced by such disinformation on TikTok (Alonso-López et al., 2021). These examples reveal how an audience can blindly follow rumors and be directed by the influential power of social media, especially people with "knowledge-deficiency," thus affecting their attitudes and actions concerning social issues (Krishna, 2017).

The aforementioned research findings suggest that with respect to misinformation, recipients are highly vulnerable to being manipulated both physically and mentally when they access information content on social media platforms (Bautista et al., 2021; Kaye et al., 2021). It will be valid then to assume that Douyin can exert a similar influence for the purpose of marketing.

2.3 *Douyin and Its Function Achieve an SOC*

Under the same cultural habitus, the production and consumption of Douyin videos could connect the users and audience with visual and symbol interaction, especially between child's play and teenage pop culture (Leyn et al., 2021). This is specifically important during this period when social isolation has become more common in society due to the pandemic (for example, this has been found in the studies[3] of social isolation in UK due to lockdown). Unni and Weinstein (2021) surveyed Douyin content during the early stages of the pandemic, and they found a large body of content representing shared experiences that suggested that TikTok users may be in search for an SOC with humanity through shared experience. Traditionally, scholars have used the concept of an SOC to measure whether an environment satisfies an individual's social needs (Flaherty et al., 2014; Pretty et al., 1996; Sonn & Fisher, 1996). There are a handful of studies (Figueroa & Aguilera, 2020; Harwood, 2021; Udenze & Uzochukwu, 2021) that have observed how Douyin (TikTok) has been used to counter isolation and offer positive mental benefits to the users through connecting with each other via a virtual platform.

An understanding of the concept of SOC has been clearly established by studies of popular culture which have addressed the identity and bonding formation that occurs during in-group interaction and value exchange, for example, Booth's fandom study (2016) and Jenkins et al.'s study of participatory culture (2015). Roberta (2010) had already foreseen the importance of the SOC in fandom during the digital era, noting that more compatible platforms would provide an all-round experience (including entertainment, social networking, killing boredom, etc.) that individuals would come to heavily rely on. The platformization studies of Lin (2020) and Wang and Wu (2021) drew the same conclusion that Douyin can exert similar influence on the users in China by encouraging them to look for social relationships and connections on their platform.

---

[3] See Sai et al. (2021), Canady (2021), Waite et al. (2021), and Banks & Xu (2020).

This kind of connection allows the video creators to adopt and "inherit" a value system that dictates or includes such factors as taste and identity. Given that their gratification is directly linked to their use of social media (Whiting & William, 2013; Winter & Vaterlaus, 2021) for pursing happiness, youth and young adults are prone to bond their lives and socialization to this digital application. At the same time, Douyin video may influence its audience to think in the same way, so as to become a member of its community sharing a similar communal sense. In other words, the authors can conclude that, to a certain extent, Douyin cultivates its audience to adopt its constructed norms and tastes and take up the career of being Douyin celebrities that play to an audience.

2.4 Theoretical Suggestion: The Mechanism of Interactive Marketing on Douyin

Considering these three aspects in terms of Douyin, the authors can see how it operates and sustains itself as an interactive marketing mechanism. This mechanism indicates the importance of Douyin's platform which centralizes all the information, Douyin celebrities, and consumers (audience).

From the perspective of creative labor, Douyin provides a platform which participants can freely access, and it offers creative output (the Douyin video) that benefits the mutual parties (video creators and the platform organizer Douyin). Such mutual benefit fosters the growth of Douyin celebrities. The idea of creative labor also suggests that the video uploaders may not aim for material rewards, and that has proven to be crucial in the beginning stages of the platform's development as a large amount of free labor has been and will continue to be guaranteed.

From the perspective of the influential power of social media platforms, the creation of video enriches the resource and directs the flow of information inside the community, and at the same time, the Douyin platform provides users a full immersion into the specific information based on the program algorithm and the searching/browsing history of users. This practice allows the users to have a comprehensive media exposure to the information of products. Given the manipulating power of media, the authors believe that this setting helps to enhance the efficiency in interactive marketing output, literally, the sales of the products in live streaming e-commerce.

With respect to SOC, the Douyin celebrities can serve as the bridge connecting the merchants (companies) and the customers (Douyin users), facilitating the best opportunity for interactive marketing. Douyin users may adopt the idea of e-commerce as the culture of Douyin and thus easily accept the marketing activities presented on the social media platform.

As a result, this mechanism leads to an ultimate output of interactive marketing, requiring less input of resources needed for marketing. Compared with the original marketing approaches used in the past in which merchants have always relied on expensive and the professional commercial marketing sector, the mechanism of Douyin provides a more flexible and structured platform with a large number of experienced and low-paid laborers (Douyin celebrities). The cost for marketing spent by Douyin will be much less than that of the original approaches since there will be many potential freelancing laborers available in the labor market, and the heavy competition leads to lower costs and demands from competitors. In addition, the efficiency of marketing can be guaranteed based on the previous sales record of the Douyin celebrities, providing quantified and measured data for the marketing sectors, and observable and expectable outcomes they can foresee.

3 Main Body of the Chapter: Empirical Data of the Chinese Douyin Example to Support the Theoretical Framework

Having reviewed the mechanism, this chapter will move to the discussion of empirical data to support the proposed mechanism. To extract the data, the authors invited a large cohort of Douyin celebrities for in-depth interviews. On the one hand, this method allowed us to explore how the Douyin celebrities support interactive marketing and develop commercial selling/consumption activities. On the other hand, it provided us with data to help us to understand the value, preference, and culture revealed and constructed in these activities. The finding may offer an inspiring and valuable understanding of contemporary China, which would be distinctive because of the specific Chinese technique of coordinating online economic output with the promotion of digital nationalism under the Chinese cultural policy.

For the interviews, the authors designed a filtering procedure to exclude some of the non-job-related categories, and the authors arrived at five meaningful occupational clusters: fashion, beauty, health, education, and travel. Individual Douyin celebrities who had more than 10,000 followers were selected. A qualitative research approach was adopted, and 20 interviewees were chosen for face-to-face in-depth interviews. Their comments revealed important insights about the mechanism of interactive marketing on Douyin in the following aspects.

3.1 Findings Concerning the Douyin Celebrities Related to "Immaterial Creative Labor," "Sense of Community," and "Influence of Douyin"

Interviewees were asked to rank their agreement with the statements about engaging in e-commerce on Douyin, on a scale of 1 (the lowest level) to 5 (the greatest level). As shown in Table 1, 13 statements have been extracted from the complete set to illustrate the general comments of interviewees on the topics of "the immaterial value" (e.g., "I get a feeling of accomplishment from the job."), "the sense of community" (e.g., "I really care about the fate

Table 1 Users' satisfaction ratings for the Douyin platform

Items	Mean
I really care about the fate of the platform	4.56
I am extremely glad that I chose to create work here rather than on one of the other platforms I was considering at the time I joined	4.45
I speak highly of the platform to my friends	4.44
I find that my values and the platform's values are very similar	4.24
Morale on this platform is good	4.33
For me, Douyin is the best of all possible organizations for which to work	4.29
My platform inspires the best job performance from me	4.26
I get a feeling of accomplishment from the job	4.24
I would accept almost any type of production for promotion	3.11
I find benefit (like superiority) from "being somebody in the community Douyin"	4.49
I find benefit (like money) from creating work on Douyin	3.02

of the platform."), and "influence of Douyin" ("I find that my values and the platform's values are very similar."). All the items had a very high score of agreement (above 4 in the mean score) except "I would accept almost any type of production for promotion." and "I find benefit (like money) from creating work in Douyin," which only had an average score of 3.11 and 3.02, respectively.

Further elaboration was requested, and the interviewees shared their reasons for their choices. Respondents reported that they had a high level of engagement in their work with very high satisfaction with their "job." Their dream of being Douyin celebrities was encouraged after they watched thousands of Douyin videos shared by famous Douyin celebrities. Knowing that most of the Douyin celebrities were just simple Douyin users gave them confidence to dream of working in this Douyin celebrities' industry one day. They were all keen on being a creative laborer on the platform and assimilating the values of Douyin. Seldom did they raise complaints against their lifestyle and career pursuit on Douyin, and the strong sense of community and being highly influenced in Douyin appeared to be their primary reasons for wanting to be Douyin celebrities (by ranking specifically high in the statement "I really care about the fate of the platform."). This revealed their belief in the special advantage of the Douyin platform in terms of e-commerce.

The findings also suggest that the satisfaction derived is not purely about monetary reward but instead cultural values. Monetary reward was generally ranked as a relatively lower priority as only around 10% of Douyin celebrities earned a few thousand RMB a month, a mediocre salary, which is close to the median income in China (approximately 2,000 RMB as of 2018). The factor that keeps the creative labor and audience loyal to the platform could be the very strong SOC, and therefore they both share the desires for recognition as active and distinctive individuals. They all showed a very strong interest in the number of fans or followers on Douyin, stressing the value of cultural capital (pride, reputation, achievement, etc.) more than that of the economic capital (payment or the amount of commission and sponsorship). This was shown by the additional statements given during the interview session, where 17 out of 20 interviewees ranked the cultural capital higher than economic capital.

This case study based on interviewees may help us to better understand the thoughts of the Douyin celebrities about cultural capital. One anonymous Douyin celebrity the authors interviewed was a big-size fashion model, who uses the name X Size Charisma. Being bullied by the people surrounding her because of her body shape, she wanted to present how a big size girl could be confident. She took video of herself changing her dress to "self-designed" fashion, and she soon gained fame due to her optimistic viewpoint and sharing "positive energy." Suffice it to say, the audience on this big-size girl's webpage told her that she empowered them to be brave and respect themselves regardless of their appearance. The interviewee also explained that the platform also provided an opportunity for her to rebuild her confidence with many supporters. This cultural value may be even worth more than any economic gain she could get from working as a Douyin celebrity.

Another example of a Douyin celebrity expressing his aspiration to achieve altruistic values from doing work on Douyin is the man who goes by the pseudonym, Culinary Mr. Lee. On Douyin, Mr. Lee is a professional chef desiring to demonstrate his skill in cooking, so as to "help them [all online followers] without charging a single penny." With over 700,000 followers, Mr. Lee seldom asks for a big commission from the e-commerce he generates as he insists his Douyin work is for him building his reputation in the industry as well as enjoying being seen and praised by the audience.

3.2 General Discussion: The Application of Mechanism of Interactive Marketing in Douyin

The aforementioned data has provided us with insights into the mechanism of interactive marketing on Douyin, as it shows how Douyin provides a platform with which social media celebrities can construct an SOC, influence people's values, tastes, and preferences in social media, and support both video creators and users in their quest to become immaterial creative laborers.

Simultaneously, interactive marketing value is constructed as this mechanism provides an environment with many business opportunities for the merchants as Douyin celebrities have gathered an immense audience of prospective customers and a massive pool of relatively cheaper labor (Douyin celebrities). The potential benefits and growth of this e-commerce are significantly greater compared to that which is generated by the more traditional one-way directional promotion and sales. It achieves the goal of interactive marketing.

One interesting recurring point the authors noted in the 20 interview discussions concerned the actual practice of e-commerce on Douyin, as well as how the commercial sector connects with the audience through social media celebrities with the aid of platform. For example, according to X Size Charisma, her followers can purchase the dresses she wears in Taobao (the Chinese version of Amazon), to which the hyperlink is attached at the bottom of the video she displays. She stressed that she loves the convenient function of the platform as the number of views and link-clickings serve as proof of her "commercial value" in promoting products. These numbers are the key to finding potential merchants for future e-commerce, as they would also be directly proportional to the number of sales that specific Douyin celebrities can generate. This potential prosperity of Douyin live streaming e-commerce and interactive marketing has attracted thousands of laborers and merchants by means of millions of videos that have been constructed on the platform, and the mechanism successfully and continuously creates more income for users, merchants, and online celebrities (laborers).

There may have some questions about the sustainability of the mechanism of interactive marketing on Douyin. For example, if the laborization of Douyin users is as common as suggested in this chapter, the supply of laborers for Douyin will be saturated and affected negatively by fierce competition, which may result in the further exploitation of labor by the marketing commissioners. Indeed, some Douyin celebrities receive low incomes (with two-thirds of respondents earning less than 1,000 RMB monthly) that may not be attractive enough for them to remain in the industry. The reason why many laborers are nevertheless engaged probably goes back to the mechanism of the Douyin platform itself: people (laborers) are looking for non-monetary rewards as they are highly influenced by the culture inside the community that exists on Douyin.

The data demonstrate that the celebrities enjoy the working conditions and the opportunity for self-empowerment and the expression of alternative perspectives. The specific working conditions of creative labor have always been considered an important factor from a creative worker-centric perspective (Cunningham et al., 2019). In fact, the conclusion of David Lee's literature review (2013) stressed that precarity often pertains to creative labor's exploitation and self-exploitation in an unpaid or underpaid circumstance. The reason for such precarity, according to a study by Digital content & Creative Media center of BNU (2019), is that Douyin celebrities consider that the cultural factors of this cultural-cum-economic activity carry much more weight than wages.

This mechanism of interactive marketing has been addressed in different previous studies which discussed the economic function of social media platforms. Bucknell and Kottasz (2020) have explained how the youth who are seeking gratification from their usage of TikTok generate huge potential consumption power in the market. Lin and de Kloet (2019) and Craig and Cunningham (2021) investigated how Douyin celebrities create a system of digital cultural production (literally, entertainment) that constructs and then wastes the unexpected revenue. The consumption and production of a cultural commodity, according to Nieborg and Poell (2018), is the reason for digital creators to stay on the Douyin platform; it is also a typical attributor connecting the users to internet and thus forming a strong bond between them in their relationship formation (Mckenna et al., 2002).

Another interesting discussion point is the conversion of social capital of Douyin celebrity into e-commerce profit. In order to "survive" in this e-commerce industry, many Douyin celebrities are prone to listen closely to their audience, and forward their plea (normally the price negotiation, or even a half-price discount) to the merchants (who normally stay aside from the live stage of e-commerce). From a marketing perspective, the merchant is converting the Douyin celebrities' social capital (their social network and proximity to their followers) to money (the economic capital).

At the same time, Douyin celebrities who can reveal their followers' comment to the merchant, and negotiate better terms and profit for the users, would be more appreciated by their followers. Gifted by her followers with love, another celebrity known as Flower Jewelry realized that her popularity on Douyin may be attributed to her helping her followers to get a "good price" from the merchant. "Followers told me that there is a product looking good but the price is very high," she stated. Flower Jewelry shared her interaction with the audience during the interview. She explained that "Later on, I contact that merchant and seek for an opportunity of e-commerce.... I try my very best to 'fight' for a good price for my followers and urge them to 'boo' the price... it forces the merchants to lower the price." This story shows an interesting relationship of bargaining that takes place among the audience, merchants, and Douyin celebrities through Douyin's interactive marketing.

These findings may justify the emergence of interactive marketing on other online social platforms. With respect to the discussion of platformization, Douyin illustrates, as the best example, that digital technology creates a proactive engagement in capitalist activity. This is unlike in a consumerist society wherein professionals earn from their contribution and pay back on commodities for their identification. Douyin simply accelerates the process and presents the "illusion" to the user, thus skipping the concerns of economic capital and directly jumping to the pursuit of social capital. Through platformization, materializing cultural capital happens in a more compressed space and timeframe. That could be the reason why among the 20 interviewees, hardly anyone mentioned that they only needed money as a reward. The case of Culinary Mr. Lee described in this chapter demonstrates a practical example, showing how social recognition and reputation are more important to the doers. In this sense, because of gaining cultural and social capital, creative labors will remain in the market even if they are exploited for the gain of economic capital, and the sufficiency of labor in the pool ensures the further implementation of Douyin mechanism and interactive marketing.

4 Conclusion

Like Instagram, the China-made Douyin (or TikTok) significantly occupies the global market of social media, and by its nature, induces a social and cultural impact on society. The rise of Douyin celebrities and their video sharing enrich the labor and resource pool in the market, at the same time increasing information flow, potential audience, social awareness, and, of course, economic opportunity. With more and more merchants offering commissions to the Douyin celebrities, the authors may see the emergence of interactive marketing happening in new and even more dominant social media tools.

This chapter has examined the mechanism of the interactive marketing function in Douyin, and how the social media platform turns Douyin celebrities into immaterial creative labor influenced by its value and sense of community. The findings contribute a better understanding of emerging e-commerce businesses in China, and at the same time, provide insights into how the mechanism of interactive marketing can be constructed in order to ensure the sustainability of e-commerce on a social media platform like Douyin. The implications of this mechanism could apply to other Chinese social media platforms for interactive marketing in China such as Kuaishou and the like.

Acknowledgements This research project is funded by a grant from the Research Grant Council of HKSAR (Project no. GRF 14600618) and Key Fund of the National Social Science Foundation of China: Arts category (18ZD12).

References

Abbas, J., Wang, D., Su, Z., & Ziapour, A. (2021). The role of social media in the advent of COVID-19 pandemic: Crisis management, mental health challenges and implications. *Risk Management and Healthcare Policy, 14*, 1917.

Abidin, C. (2018). *Internet celebrity: Understanding fame online*. Emerald Publishing Company.

Al-Emadi, F. A., & Yahia, B. I. (2020). Ordinary celebrities related criteria to harvest fame and influence on social media. *Journal of Research in Interactive Marketing, 14*(2), 195–213.

Alonso-López, N., Bautista, P. S., & Giacomelli, F. (2021). Beyond challenges and viral dance moves: TikTok as a vehicle for disinformation and fact-checking in Spain, Portugal, Brazil, and the USA. *Anàlisi, 64*, 65–84.

Banks, J., & Xu, W. (2020). The mental health effects of the first two months of lockdown during the COVID-19 pandemic in the UK. *Fiscal Studies, Journal of Applied Public Economics, 41*(3), 685–708. https://doi.org/10.1111/1475-5890.12239

Basch, C. E., Jaime, C., Fera, J., Meleo-Erwin, Z., & Basch, C. H. (2021). A global pandemic in the time of viral memes: COVID-19 vaccine misinformation and disinformation on TikTok. *Human Vaccines & Immunotherapeutics, 17*(8), 2373–2377. https://doi.org/10.1080/21645515.2021.1894896

Baumel, N. M., Spatharakis, J. K., Karitsiotis, S. T., & Sellas, E. I. (2021). Dissemination of mask effectiveness misinformation using TikTok as a Medium. *Journal of Adolescent Health, 68*(5), 1021–1022. https://doi.org/10.1016/j.jadohealth.2021.01.029

Bautista, P. S., López, N. A., & Giacomelli, F. V. (2021). Fact-checking in TikTok. Communication and narrative forms to combat misinformation. *Revista Latina De Comunicación Social, 79*, 87–113. https://doi.org/10.4185/RLCS-2021-1522

Booth, P. (2016). *Digital Fandom 2.0. New media studies*. Peter Lang.

Bucknell, B. C., & Kottasz, R. (2020). Uses and gratifications sought by pre-adolescent and adolescent TikTok consumers. *Young Consumers, 21*(4), 463–478. https://doi.org/10.1108/YC-07-2020-1186

Byrne, A., Barber, R., & Lim, C. H. (2021). Impact of the COVID-19 pandemic—A mental health service perspective. *Progress in Neurology and Psychiatry., 25*(2), 27–33.

Canady, V. A. (2021). ED screening reveals most teens had suicidal thoughts during pandemic. *Mental Health Weekly, 31*(31), 1–7.

Cauberge, V., Van, W. I., De, J. S., Hudders, L., & Ponnet, K. (2021). How adolescents use social media to cope with feelings of loneliness and anxiety during COVID-19 lockdown. *Cyberpsychology, Behavior, and Social Networking, 24*(4), 250–257. https://doi.org/10.1089/cyber.2020.0478

Chang, E. P., Ecker, U. K., & Page, A. C. (2019). Not wallowing in misery—Retractions of negative misinformation are effective in depressive rumination. *Cognition and Emotion, 33*(5), 991–1005. https://doi.org/10.1080/02699931.2018.1533808

Chen, Z., & Zhang, Q. (2021). A survey study on successful marketing factors for Douyin (Tik-Tok). In F.F.-H. Nah & K. Siau (Eds.), *HCI in business, government and organizations* (pp. 22–42). Springer International Publishing.

Cunningham, S., Craig, D., & Lv, J. (2019). China's livestreaming industry: platforms, politics, and precarity. *International Journal of Cultural Studies, 22*(6), 719–736. https://doi.org/10.1177/1367877919834942

Craig, D., Lin, J., & Cunningham, S. (2021). *Wanghong as social media entertainment in China*. Springer International Publishing. https://doi.org/10.1007/978-3-030-65376-7_4

Digital content & Creative Media center of BNU. (2019). *Short video platform and creative labor*. https://www.sgpjbg.com/baogao/9572.html.

Douvartzidis, A., & Surman, C. (2020). Young lawyers: Flipping the switch: How to navigate the transition from young lawyer to TikTok star. *Bulletin (law Society of South Australia), 42*(5), 23–25.

Duffy, B., & Wissinger, E. (2017). Mythologies of creative work in the social media age: Fun, free, and "Just Being Me." *International Journal of Communication, 11*, 4652–4671.

Eghtesadi, M., & Florea, A. (2020). Facebook, Instagram, Reddit and TikTok: A proposal for health authorities to integrate popular social media platforms in contingency planning amid a global pandemic outbreak. *Canadian Journal of Public Health, 111*, 389–391. https://doi.org/10.17269/s41997-020-00343-0

Escamilla-Fajardo, P., Alguacil, M., & López-Carril, S. (2021). Incorporating TikTok in higher education: Pedagogical perspectives from a corporal expression sport sciences course. *Journal of Hospitality, Leisure, Sport & Tourism Education, 28*, 1–13. https://doi.org/10.1016/j.jhlste.2021.100302

Femenia-Serra, F., Gretzel, U., & Alzua-Sorzabal, A. (2022). Instagram travel influencers in #quarantine: Communicative practices and roles during COVID-19. *Tourism Management, 89*, 1044–1054.

Figueroa, C. A., & Aguilera, A. (2020). The need for a mental health technology revolution in the COVID-19 pandemic. *Frontiers in Psychiatry, 11*, 523. https://doi.org/10.3389/fpsyt.2020.00523

Flaherty, J., Zwick, R. R., & Bouchey, H. A. (2014). Revisiting the sense of community index: A confirmatory factor analysis and invariance test. *Journal of Community Psychology, 42*(8), 947–963. https://doi.org/10.1002/jcop.21664

Fuchs, C. (2014). *Social media: A critical introduction.* Sage.

Geyser, W. (2021, August 18). TikTok statistics—Revenue, users & engagement stats. Influencer Marketing Hub. https://influencermarketinghub.com/Tiktok-stats/

Graham, K. W., & Wilder, K. M. (2020). Consumer-brand identity and online advertising message elaboration: Effect on attitudes, purchase intent and willingness to share. *Journal of Research in Interactive Marketing, 14*(1), 111–132.

Gray, J. E. (2021). The geopolitics of 'platforms': The TikTok challenge. *Internet Policy Review, 10*(2). https://doi.org/10.14763/2021.2.1557

Harwood, E. (2021). TikTok, identity struggles and mental health issues: How are the youth of today coping? *Identity and Online Advocacy Conference.* http://networkconference.netstudies.org/2021/wp-content/uploads/2021/04/Tiktok-identity-struggles-and-mental-health-issues-How-are-the-youth-of-today-coping.pdf

Hardt, M. (1999). Affective labor. *Boundary, 26*(2), 89–100. http://www.jstor.org/stable/303793

Hautea, S., Parks, P., Takahashi, B., & Zeng, J. (2021). Showing they care (or don't): Affective publics and ambivalent climate activism on TikTok. *Social Media + Society.* https://doi.org/10.1177/20563051211012344

He, A. Z., Cai, Y., Cai, L., & Zhang, Y. (2021). Conversation, storytelling, or consumer interaction and participation? The impact of brand-owned social media content marketing on consumers' brand perceptions and attitudes. *Journal of Research in Interactive Marketing, 15*(3), 419–440.

Hesmondhalgh, D., & Baker, S. (2013). *Creative labor: Media works in three creative industries.* Routledge.

Jenkins H., Ito M., & Boyd, D. (2015). *Participatory culture in a networked era: A conversation on youth, learning, commerce, and politics.* Polity.

Ji, C., Mieiro, S., & Huang, G. (2022). How social media advertising features influence consumption and sharing intentions: The mediation of customer engagement. *Journal of Research in Interactive Marketing, 16*(1), 137–153.

Kaye, D. B. V., Rodriguez, A., Langton, K., & Wikström, P. (2021). You made this? I Made this: Practices of authorship and (mis)attribution on TikTok. *International Journal of Communication, 15*, 3195–3215.

Khlaif, Z., & Salha, S. (2021). Using TikTok in education: A form of micro-learning or nano-learning? *Interdisciplinary Journal of Virtual Learning in Medical Sciences, 12*(3), 2–7.

Krishna, A. (2017). Motivation with misinformation: Conceptualizing lacuna individuals and publics as knowledge-deficient, issue-negative activists. *Journal of Public Relations Research, 29*(4), 176–193. https://doi.org/10.1080/1062726X.2017.1363047

Lee, D. (2013). Creative labour in the cultural industries. *Sociopedia. isa,* https://doi.org/10.1177/205684601181

Lee, S., Chen, H., & Lee, Y. H. (2022). How endorser-product congruity and self-expressiveness affect Instagram micro-celebrities' native advertising effectiveness. *Journal of Product & Brand Management, 31*(1), 149–162.

Lee, S., & Kim, L. (2020). Influencer marketing on Instagram: How sponsorship disclosure, influencer credibility, and brand credibility impact the effectiveness of Instagram promotional post. *Journal of Global Fashion Marketing, 11*(3), 232–249.

Lee, Y., Yang, B. X., Liu, Q., Luo, D., Kang, L., Yang, F., & Lin, K. (2020). Synergistic effect of social media use and psychological distress on depression in China during the COVID-19 epidemic. *Psychiatry and Clinical Neurosciences.* https://doi.org/10.1111/pcn.13101

Leyn, T. E., Wolf, R. D., Abeele, A. V., & Marez, L. D. (2021). In-between child's play and teenage pop culture: Tweens TikTok & privacy. *Journal of Youth Studies.* https://doi.org/10.1080/13676261.2021.1939286

Lin, J. (2020). *One app, two versions: TikTok and the platformization from China* [Paper presentation]. AoIR 2020: The 21st Annual Conference of the Association of Internet Researchers. Virtual: AoIR. https://journals.uic.edu/ojs/index.php/spir/article/view/11357/9932

Lin, J., & de Kloet, J. (2019). Platformization of the unlikely creative class: Kuaishou and Chinese digital cultural production. *Society Media + Society, 5*(4). https://doi.org/10.1177/2056305119883430

Lovett, J. T., Munawar, K., Mohammed, S., & Prabhu, V. (2021). Radiology content on TikTok: Current use of a novel video-based social media platform and opportunities for radiology. *Current Problems in Diagnostic Radiology, 50*(2), 126–131. https://doi.org/10.1067/j.cpradiol.2020.10.004

Masciantonio, A., Bourguignon, D., Bouchat P., Balty, M., & Rime, B. (2021) Don't put all social network sites in one basket: Facebook, Instagram, Twitter, TikTok, and their relations with well-being during the COVID-19 pandemic. *PLoS ONE, 16*(3). https://doi.org/10.1371/journal.pone.0248384

McKenna, K. Y., Green, A. S., & Gleason, M. E. (2002). Relationship formation on the internet: What's the big attraction? *Journal of Social Issues, 58*(1), 9–31. https://spssi.onlinelibrary.wiley.com/doi/full/10.1111/1540-4560.00246

Mhalla, M., Jiang, Y., & Nasiri, A. (2020). Video-sharing apps business models: TikTok case study. *International Journal of Innovation and Technology Management, 17*(7), 2050050.

Mujika-Alberdi, A., Garcia-Arrizabalaga, I., & Gibaja-Martins, J. J. (2020). Media consumer behavior in the digital age. *Quaderns De Comunicació i Cultura, 31–46,*. https://doi.org/10.5565/rev/analisi.3227

Nieborg, D. B., & Poell, T. (2018). The platformization of cultural production: Theorizing the contingent cultural commodity. *New Media & Society, 20*(11), 4275–4292. https://doi.org/10.1177/1461444818769694

O'Brien, M. J., & Alsmadi, I. (2021, June 16). *Misinformation, disinformation and hoaxes: What's the difference?* The Conversation. https://theconversation.com/misinformation-disinformation-and-hoaxes-whats-the-difference-158491

Patel, M. P., Kute, V. B., Agarwal, S. K., & behalf of COVID, O. (2020). "Infodemic" COVID 19: More pandemic than the virus. *Indian Journal of Nephrology, 30*(3), 188.

Pretty, G. M., Conroy, C., Dugay, J., Fowler, K., & Williams, D. (1996). Sense of community and its relevance to adolescents of all ages. *Wiley Online Library,*

24(4), 365–379. https://onlinelibrary.wiley.com/doi/abs/10.1002/(SICI)1520-6629(199610)24:43.0.CO;2-T

Qin, Y. S. (2020). Fostering brand–consumer interactions in social media: The role of social media uses and gratifications. *Journal of Research in Interactive Marketing, 14*(3), 337–354.

Roberta, P. (2010). Fandom in the digital era. *Popular Communication, 8*(1), 84–95. https://doi.org/10.1080/15405700903502346

Sachini, P., & Mijetunga, M. (2019). How TikTok is a platform for performance and play for women in Sri Lanka. *GenderIT.org*. https://www.genderit.org/articles/how-Tiktok-platform-performance-and-play-women-sri-lanka

Sha, P., & Dong, X. (2021). Research on adolescents regarding the indirect effect of depression, anxiety, and stress between TikTok use disorder and memory loss. *International Journal of Environmental Research and Public Health, 18*(16), 88–120.

Sonn, C. C., & Fisher, A. T. (1996). Psychological sense of community in a politically constructed group. *Journal of Community Psychology, 24*(4), 417–430. https://doi.org/10.1002/(SICI)1520-6629(199610)24:4%3c417::AID-JCOP9%3e3.0.CO;2-Q

Stahl, B. C. (2006). On the difference or equality of information, misinformation, and disinformation: A critical research perspective. *Informing Science, 9*, 83–96. https://doi.org/10.28945/473

Suárez-Álvarez, R., & García-Jiménez, A. (2021). Centennials on TikTok: Type of video. Analysis and comparative Spain-Great Britain by gender, age, and nationality. *Revista Latina De Comunicación Social, 79*, 1–21.

Tasnim, S., Hossain, M. M., & Mazumder, H. (2020). Impact of rumors and misinformation on COVID-19 in social media. *Journal of Preventive Medicine and Public Health, 53*(3), 171–174. https://doi.org/10.3961/jpmph.20.094

Udenze, S., & Uzochukwu, C. E. (2021). Promoting mental wellbeing: Young adults' experience on TikTok during the COVID-19 pandemic lockdown in Nigeria. *Interações: Sociedade e as Novas Modernidades, 40*, 9–28.

Unni, Z., & Weinstein, E. (2021). Shelter in place, connect online: Trending TikTok content during the early days of the U.S. COVID-19 pandemic. *Journal of Adolescent Health, 68*(5), 863–868. https://doi.org/10.1016/j.jadohealth.2021.02.012

Verma, T. (2020). Cultural cringe: How caste and class affect the idea of culture in social media. *Feminist Media Studies, 21*(1), 159–161.

Waite, P., Pearcey, S., Shum, A., Raw, J., Patalay, P., & Creswell, C. (2021). How did the mental health of children and adolescents change during early lockdown during the COVID-19 pandemic in the UK? *JCPP, 1–10,*. https://doi.org/10.31234/osf.io/t8rfx

Wang, C. L. (2021). New frontiers and future directions in interactive marketing: Inaugural editorial. *Journal of Research in Interactive Marketing, 15*(1), 1–9.

Wang, W., & Wu, J. (2021). Short video platforms and local community building in China. *International Journal of Communication, 15*, 23.

Wang, Y. H., Gu, T. J., & Wang, S. Y. (2020). *Causes and characteristics of short video platform internet community taking the TikTok short video application as an example.* Proceedings of the 2019 IEEE International Conference on Consumer Electronics (pp. 1–2). https://doi/10.1109/ICCE-TW46550.2019.8992021.

Wang, D., & Omar, B. (2020). Watch, share or create: The influence of personality traits and user motivation on TikTok mobile video usage. *International Journal of Interactive Mobile Technologies, 14*(4), 121–137. https://doi.org/10.3991/ijim.v14 i04.12429

Whiting, A., & Williams, D. (2013). Why people use social media: A uses and gratifications approach. *Qualitative Market Research: an International Journal, 16*(4), 362–369. https://doi.org/10.1108/qmr-06-2013-0041

Winter, M., & Vaterlaus, J. M. (2021). TikTok: An exploratory study of young adults' uses and gratifications. *The Social Science Journal.* https://doi.org/10.1080/036 23319.2021.1969882

Zeng, J., Abidin, C., & Schäfer, M. S. (2021). Research perspectives on TikTok and its legacy apps—Introduction. *International Journal of Communication, 15*, 12.

Zhang, L., & Fung, A. (2014). Working as playing? consumer labor and the guild of online gaming in China. *New Media and Society, 16*(1), 38–54. https://doi.org/10.1177/1461444813477077

CHAPTER 23

Interactive Experience of Collaborative Online Shopping: Real-Time Interaction and Communication

Mohammad Rahim Esfidani and Behnam Izadi

1 INTRODUCTION

According to statistics, 90% of customers like to have a human connection during transactions (Gutzman, 2000), and 70% prefer to purchase with shopping pals (Chebat et al., 2014). The significance of collaborative online shopping (COS) has made it the subject of some studies (Cheng et al., 2013; Goswami et al., n.d.; Huang et al., 2011; Kim et al., 2013; Seedorf et al., 2014; Siau et al., 2013; Wei et al., 2017; Yue et al., 2014; Yue & Jiang, 2013; Zhu et al., 2010). Most scholars referred to the COS definition proposed by Zhu et al. (2010), a shopping activity in which an individual purchases synchronously with one or more remotely placed shopping companions at an online retailer. In COS, with an additional person joining in shopping, the shopping process becomes dynamic due to social interactions between individuals (Izadi et al., 2021). What draws attention to COS is its interactivity. Thus, different forms of interactions during the joint customer journey affect the customer experience.

Customer interactions with a high degree of quality are the key to identifying novel competitive advantage sources that allow individuals to create collaboratively different experiences. According to Prahalad and Ramaswamy

M. R. Esfidani (✉) · B. Izadi
University of Tehran, Tehran, Iran
e-mail: esfidani@ut.ac.ir

B. Izadi
e-mail: behnam_izadi@ut.ac.ir

(2002), customers define value as experiences in a market setting and force businesses to view value similarly. Marketing literature has a long history of discussing the creation of value jointly and the experience of value creation. Ramirez (1999) reviewed jointly created value, and Prahalad and Ramaswamy (2004) highlighted individuals' roles in creating value and the interactive aspect of value. Experience value of consumers, including emotional, utilitarian, and social value, is positively impacted by interactivity (Lucia-Palacios & Pérez-López, 2021). A significant transition happened, as the creation of value by the businesses changed to the co-creation of experiences via the interaction of businesses and individuals, mostly guided by individuals' competencies and needs (Akaka et al., 2015). Co-creation of value is described as a collaborative and concurrent peer-like activity that entails the development of new material and symbolic value (Nangpiire et al., 2021). Creating value is quickly evolving away from a product-orientation and corporation-orientation focus toward a more customized and interactive experience for customers. Brand platforms enable direct customer–brand connection by allowing customers to browse their preferred shopping web pages in order to find the freshest trends and get personalized recommendations in real time (Wang, 2021).

Customers try to understand the meaning of their experiences in a social setting through interpersonal interactions. The customer experiences can be communicated directly to other individuals or shared via social networking sites. Not all evaluations of experiences are pleasant, and hence unfavorable experiences may result in negative value creation (Helkkula et al., 2012). Interactive marketing, according to Wang (2021), is the process of creating two-way value and reciprocal influence by connecting, involving, and interacting with customers actively. This description highlights interactive marketing in three ways: first, it is bidirectional communication with reciprocal effects on social and corporate environments; second, it emphasizes customer responsiveness and frequently proactive behavior in the generation and exchange of value; and third, its interactivity entails individual involvement in real-time environmental control and adjustment. This description highlights the dialogue-oriented communication process with shared consequences in social and commercial domains, as well as the individuals' active involvement in defining the character of interactions (Nangpiire et al., 2021).

This chapter sheds insights on understanding COS through the lens of interactive marketing and discusses how individuals interact with each other and with the collaborative online shopping platform (COSP). The joint customer journey of shoppers during COS creates experiences for them through specific touchpoints. COS is distinguished from solo online shopping in two ways: first, the COSP acts as a brand-owned touchpoint (These touchpoints are consumer contacts that occur within the company's experience, which is developed and managed by the company and is under its control), and second, the COS provides a social touchpoint (These touchpoints recognize the essential roles of other individuals in the customer experience) by enabling individuals to communicate in real time (Lemon & Verhoef, 2016).

The customers' experience in COS is rooted in the interaction between shoppers and their companions and the interaction with COSP. The features of a COSP affect how individuals interact since shopping is often a social activity wherein relatives or friends join the shopper (Zhu et al., 2010). The interaction between shoppers and their companions is regarded as a social context (Helkkula et al., 2012). As a result, social context elements, such as social standards, regulations, criteria, norms, or values, influence consumer experience assessments. In the same way, social norms related to specific groups of individuals affect consumption decisions and interactions (Akaka et al., 2015).

COSP is an online social platform through which consumers co-navigate, communicate, and interact jointly. COSPs come in many different forms, which are completely considered in the following sections. Co-browsing, which the Samesurf and the Surfly provide, can be considered an example of COSP. Co-shoppers' interaction on COSPs results in value creation. According to Moon and Nass (1996), customers respond to computer-mediated communication (including the COSP) similar to the manner they react to human contact. While some argue that the brain interprets digital interaction similarly to human interaction, others argue that distinctions between how we perceive one another online and in person are rising (Jimenez & Morreale, 2015). However, the interaction of shoppers and their experience with COSPs is understudied. Researchers are trying to understand better social platform interactions' existing and future implications from both good and negative perspectives.

While COS has grown in popularity as a result of the widespread use of social media websites, not many researchers studied how to improve this form of the shopping experience (Kim et al., 2013). Interpersonal interactions during COS and individuals' interactions with the COSPs create an interactive experience. The main aim of this chapter is to provide a better comprehension of shoppers' interactive experience with shopping companions on COSP via a review of related literature. Hence, interactions with various types of COSPs (as the touchpoints) and the interaction of people with their companions (as the other touchpoints) have been discussed.

The chapter is organized as follows. First, customer experience and touchpoints are reviewed, so that interactions with customers take place through them. Then, the concept of interactivity is discussed. Afterward, interactivity through touchpoints of COS is put forward. During the next part, a literature review on consumers' interactive experience with COSP and the interactive experience of customers with shopping companions on the COSP is presented. The following section considers the different forms of interactivity during the interaction with COSP. Following that, various elements that can impact the shopping companion's interaction are proposed. Finally, the aforementioned content is reviewed and discussed, and conclusions are drawn from our discussion.

2 LITERATURE REVIEW

This section is divided into four sections: (1) the customer experience and touchpoints, (2) the definition of interactivity, (3) the literature on interactivity through touchpoints of COS, and (4) the literature on the interactive experience of customers with shopping companion on the COSP.

2.1 Customer Experience and Touchpoints

Prior research suggests that information about consumer experiences in online shopping contexts is still in its early stages (Yang et al., 2019). Interactions and touchpoints from the customer journey viewpoint have been examined in marketing literature recently (Kuehnl et al., 2019). Customers' subjective and internal reaction to any interaction with a firm is generally described as customer experience (Kuehnl et al., 2019; Stein & Ramaseshan, 2016). Customer experience and a customer journey map are commonly used to acquire a better understanding of how customers interact with a business (Richardson, 2010). It is important to note what individuals truly are interested in are meaningful experiences rather than products (Lemon & Verhoef, 2016). Marketing studies demonstrate that, when people look for some items, purchase these items, get service for them, and use these products in these situations, experiences happen. Customers gain experience whenever they interact with any aspect of a good, service, brand, or corporation, across numerous channels and at various times (Stein & Ramaseshan, 2016).

Experiences can also be generated through customers' use and consumption of products. Consumption-related experiences include hedonic aspects such as enjoyment and feelings. When customers look for brands, purchase them, and finally consume brands, brand experiences arise. Hence, brand experiences are subjective responses of individuals elicited by certain associated experiential elements in such a situation (Brakus et al., 2009). Leclerc and Schmitt (1999) take a multidimensional approach, identifying five distinct kinds of experiences: sensory (experiences via smell, taste, touch, sound, and sight), affective (how to elicit emotion during the consumption experience), cognitive (rational evaluation of the company and products), physical (experiences gained through engaging with other individuals), socio-identity (extends beyond a person's inner emotions, ideas, cognitions, and activities by connecting a person's self to a brand's broader social and cultural setting) experiences (Leclerc & Schmitt, 1999; Lemon & Verhoef, 2016).

There are numerous definitions of customer experience in the literature. A customer journey through sequential engagements/contacts between a customer and a firm covers all service delivery actions. This definition emphasizes the importance of touchpoints as the fundamental components of customer journeys (Cambra-Fierro et al., 2021). Touchpoints are widely thought of as encounters (i.e., print advertising, the website, and COSPs) with various components of a business. Every encounter results in a customer experience and explains what occurred from the individual's viewpoint. The term "encounter" refers to any type of interaction, communication, or customer engagement and is used to describe the fundamental units of customer journeys. The customer journey occurs in a context comprised of offline channels, including physical retail stores and brokers, and online channels, including search engines, e-commerce, and social media websites, all of which are permeated by a ubiquitous connection (Kannan & Kulkarni, 2022). The term "customer touchpoints" refers to "episodes of direct or indirect contact with a brand or a firm" (Hallikainen et al., 2019, p. 1). Marketers may utilize omnichannel touchpoints to provide a unified message and engage consumers on their preferred channels (Swan et al., 2019).

Keyser et al. (2020) claim that touchpoints differ in terms of control, nature, and stage of the consumer experience. Thus, (1) touchpoints can be controlled by firms or not, (2) touchpoints can be physical, human, digital, and a mix of these, and (3) touchpoints can be in the pre-purchase, purchase, and post-purchase stages. Also, touchpoints can be interactive and non-interactive. Digital touchpoints can be simplex (one-way communication) or complex (two-way communication) in terms of interactivity. Since all social touchpoints enable two-way communication, individuals can post comments and reply to them in real time; these touchpoints have a great degree of interactivity (Straker et al., 2015). *In the following section, the experience of interactivity is discussed.*

2.2   What is Interactivity?

Before discussing the interactive aspect of COS, it is necessary to define the concept of interactivity and its characteristics in this section. Interactivity is described as the capability of a technology to allow people to engage with and interact with material more readily. Interactivity in a virtual environment refers to the degree to which individuals may alter the content and appearance of an environment in real time (Kim et al., 2021). Interactivity is widely accepted as a natural component of face-to-face communication. It has been suggested, however, that it also occurs in contexts of mediated communication (Rafaeli, 1988). Interaction can be seen as a process of exchange in which people communicate info and sentiments in order to enhance relationship development (Wilson, 1976). Perceived interactivity is a psychological trait that is determined by the efficacy and scope of the audience. The scope of the audience is reflected in the communication's content. For example, real interpersonal communication is established on an individual's understanding of the source, whereas communication aimed at a larger audience is grounded on sociological or cultural assumptions about the target group (Newhagen et al., 1995).

Interpersonal customer interactions and interactions between the firm employees and customers, according to Kuuru and Närvänen (2019), are key drivers for experience in the retailing industry. The quality of interpersonal customer interaction, which relates to how customers evaluate their interactions, is a vital component of delivering a good customer experience (Kim & Choi, 2016). With the introduction of interactive marketing, the effect of one-way advertising and communication has decreased. Through digital/mobile activities in platform ecosystems, the market is becoming a venue for dialogues and interactions among linked individuals. Modern interactive marketing has also expanded beyond the domain of direct marketing (Wang, 2021). Thus, one of the components of interactive marketing is an interactive experience.

The interactive experience has a long history in the studies related to art, teaching, and museum visits. Dierking and Falk (1992) describe the interactive experience as activities in which the visitor is engaged while visiting the museum environment. Customers communicate a variety of different forms of information in order to generate distinct values. Given the fundamental role of interactions in value creation, it is reasonable to conceive the categories of interactive experience through the value paradigm: the most common types of customers' interpersonal interactions are (1) functional, (2) affective, and (3) expressive/symbolic. Functional interactions include sharing goods/services related-info to maximize practical advantages. The cognitive customer experience stresses how effectively products and services may be obtained (Lin et al., 2020). This part of the customer experience is connected to functionality, including the price and quality of goods/services, that assists individuals in evaluating goods/services and making purchasing decisions. The affective customer experience is concerned with the pleasure and entertainment that shopping provides (Gao et al., 2021). Affective interactions emphasize exchanges that bring emotional benefits to individuals, such as pleasure and enjoyment. The exchange of data that demonstrates a customer's beliefs/values, as well as projecting their self-concept, is referred to expressive/symbolic interaction (Lin et al., 2020).

In this chapter, the interactive experience is characterized as a customer's functional, affective, and expressive engagement with other people and objects. Reciprocity, speed of response, personalization, and nonverbal communication are all important aspects of interactivity of experience (Johnson et al., 2006; Merrilees, 2016; Song & Zinkhan, 2008).

- Reciprocity: Describe how participants switch roles, alternating between sending and receiving messages. This distinguishes interactive communication (in which senders alternate sending messages) from transactive communication (where senders transmit messages concurrently).
- Personalization: It is the degree to which one party's answer is contingent upon the other party's response. A response that is directly related to and pertinent to the query is conditional on this.
- Speed of response: It describes whether exchanging messages takes place in real time or not.

- Nonverbal communication: Refers to the extent to which many communication channels are employed. In a situation where a greater number of channels are used, the feedback becomes richer. Researchers have questioned the conventional approach to communication research, which neglects nonverbal components. Instead of that, they have recommended a greater emphasis on nonverbal parts of communication to foster a more extensive understanding of communication.

In the following section, the interactive touchpoints of COS are discussed, which are digital non-firm-controlled touchpoints used at the pre-purchase and purchase stage of COS.

2.3 Interactivity Through Touchpoints of COS

Supporting technologies for COS have gained quite a considerable interest. Prior studies have found that a COSP can be developed with a variety of supporting technological features. The supporting features make it easier for co-shoppers or the shopper and salesperson to interact and communicate. Zhu et al. (2010) *examine different forms of technological support, navigation, and communication support in COS*. Yue et al. (2014) indicated that present COSPs offer different co-navigation, communication, and information annotation supports. Goswami et al. (n.d.) identify the communication and decision support features as the website features for COS.

Businesses have also incorporated the different types of COS to enable co-shoppers to co-navigate and shop together. The Plurchase sidebar for Amazon.com and Zappos lets customers review the corresponding URLs to the goods that their partner is now viewing, go to that website with a click of a button, or engage in text chatting at a preferred moment. ShopTogether also offers comparable features. This capability is the location cue feature that enables shopping companions to navigate the internet independently using their own web browsers while keeping track of their partner's online activities or as navigation support, which enables shoppers to navigate to the same website being surfed by their partner through clicking the location cue indicator. BuddyShopping also incorporated split-screen navigation, which splits the browser into two displays of equal size. A shopper can operate his or her own screen and surf the website freely while remaining aware of how his or her shopping companion navigates the shared screen's web page. BevyUp created a platform that enables simultaneous interaction between numerous shoppers on the shared website via various tools. Since this function can connect shoppers on the same single browser, BevyUp's navigation support feature is known as the shared view. They are both surfing the internet at the same time at the same pace. Additionally, they will share the same view of a website page instantly (Yue et al., 2014). The shared co-navigation technology allows two or more users to visit the same pages concurrently using their own personal Web browsers (Twidale, 1995).

Navigation and communication, in general, are two types of supporting features that have been extensively examined in COSP studies and are presented in a variety of techniques in these studies. Text chat, voice chat, and video calls are the communication support features for COS in several studies (Goswami et al., n.d.; Siau et al., 2013; Yue et al., 2014; Zhu et al., 2010). Navigation support features can influence how co-shoppers move to the products of their interests collaboratively. Several techniques of navigation support have been investigated, including (1) separate navigation with location cue, (2) split-screen navigation, and (3) shared navigation (Cheng et al., 2013; Yue & Jiang, 2013; Yue et al., 2014; Zhu et al., 2010) (see Figs. 1, 2, and 3). COS technology combines co-navigation and communication supporting features to offer a platform for individuals' interactions. Also, other auxiliary features can support co-navigation, including live annotation[1] and switching control[2] of mouse navigation between participants.

According to the following examples, the supporting features of COS enhance the interactive experience of individuals during co-shopping:

- Switching control of the mouse navigation and two-way communication between participants in COS demonstrate reciprocity.
- Personalization is evident in the one-on-one communication between shoppers and their companions during the COS, as shoppers receive tailored feedback, suggestions, and comments. Also, individuals can use the live annotation feature of COSPs to give customized feedback and notices to their companions.
- The real-time communication and instant switching control of navigation between individuals highlight the speed of response in COS.
- Employing various medium bundles (including video calling, voice chatting, and text chatting) for communication during COS enables individuals for nonverbal communication. The live annotation feature is the other functional affordance that can facilitate nonverbal communication between individuals.

Previously, scholars considered interactivity as interpersonal conversations (Sundar et al., 2015). Rafaeli (1988) distinguished three aspects of interactivity: non-interactive, quasi-interactive, and completely interactive. According to this definition, when two individuals transmit messages without considering each other's messages, the exchange is termed non-interactive. It is reactive when one directly replies to the other's input. The message exchange

---

[1] Live annotation is a feature that enables users to write notes, draw, and highlight words while co-shopping. The live annotation tool enables co-shoppers to draw or type on the browser page for both users to see (Topaloglu, 2013).

[2] The capability of the end-user to manage the co-shopping session and navigate the mouse movement (Topaloglu, 2013).

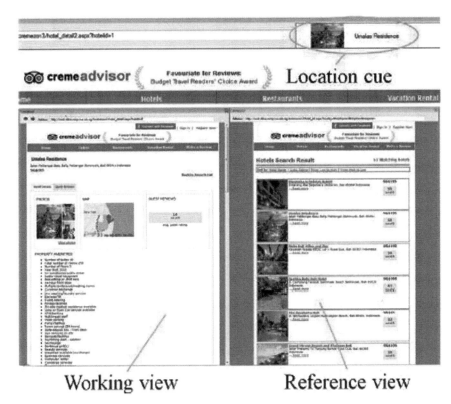

Fig. 1 Separate navigation with location cue (Yue et al., 2014)

is deemed fully interactive when the latter interactant reacts back, acknowledging the latest and all previous messages. Due to all the aforementioned supporting features of COSP, it is considered fully interactive.

2.4 Interactive Experience of COS Technology

The customer experience is shaped by the diversity of interactions between individuals and objects (Hoffman & Novak, 2018). The consequence of a series of interactions between a person and a corporation/product/service is the customer experience. This definition, however, appears to overlook the influence of other customers (Lin et al., 2020; Srivastava & Kaul, 2014) and collaborative shopping platforms. The interactive experience of COS is rooted in the interaction with COSPs and the shopping companion (see Fig. 4). As a result, the COS interactive experience corresponds to the following:

Interactive experience of COS = Interaction with COSP * Interaction with shopping companion

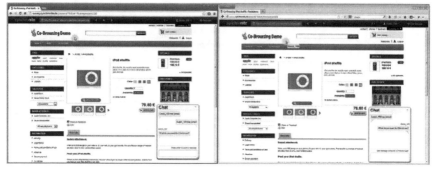

Fig. 1. Example of Co-shopping.

Fig. 2. Example of Social Co-browsing.

Fig. 2 Shared navigation (Wei et al., 2017)

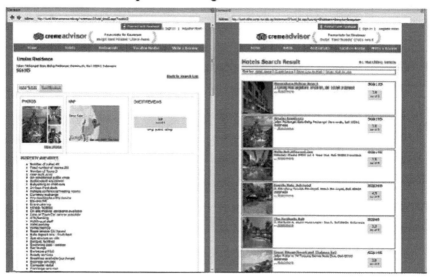

Fig. 3 Split screen navigation (Yue, 2014)

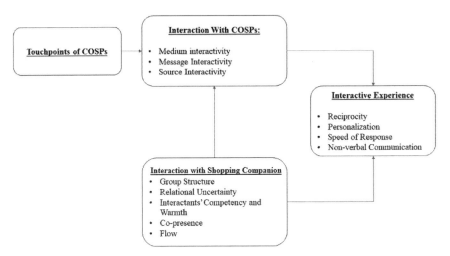

Fig. 4 Interactive experience of collaborative online shopping (*Source* Proposed by the authors)

2.4.1 Interactive Experience with COSPs

According to a rising number of studies, the computer is considered a social actor instead of just a medium by individuals in human–computer interactions. This idea is based on social response theory, which claims that if computers display features similar to humans or social cues, individuals will answer them by using social rules. Even in situations, humans completely know that they are dealing with devices, they regard computers as social agents (Wang et al., 2007).

Since people engage and interact with computers the same way they interact with humans, the interactivity effects model (Sundar et al., 2015) is used to understand the interactivity of COSPs. According to this model, COSP involves three distinct types of interaction: platform-level, message-level, and source-level.

- COSP interactivity: The term "medium (or modality) interactivity" refers to the numerous ways in which an interface can be interacted with, including clicking, hovering, dragging, and scrolling. All the abovementioned options have unique action possibilities, regulating how individuals can access, encode, and display the info given by the interface. It is, for example, argued that modality interactivity serves as a highlighting mechanism. Modality interactivity provides individuals the capability to control visual items and imitate their motions in numerous manners. These actions can help improve the speed, variety, and clarity with which one mentally represents the information displayed on the interface. This kind of interactivity is more related to the COSP interface's functional elements, and different tools are available for customers to access content

(Sundar et al., 2015). Thus, the live annotation feature of the COSP is related to medium interactivity.
- Message interactivity: Message interactivity is concerned with the nature of the user-system exchanges (or with other users) (Sundar et al., 2015). Since people respond to each other contingently during COS, real-time communication between individuals is an instance of message interactivity.
- Source interactivity: The extent to which the interface enables the person to act as the source of communication is known as source interactivity. Previously, the term "source interactivity" was used synonymously with the concept of customization—the higher the degree of customization, the more source interaction an interface provides (Sundar et al., 2015). Since the switching control of mouse navigation during COS between individuals enables them to find and customize information based on their companion needs and priorities, it can be an example of source interactivity. Thus, switching control can enhance individuals' self-expression. Enabling individuals to choose their desired media to communicate during COS is another instance of source interactivity.

The COSP can improve the interactive experience by enhancing the experience's interactivity and effective communication. Effective communication has a number of benefits, one of which is boosting the brand experience (Drennan et al., 2015) and assisting in the co-creation of value (Grissemann & Stokburger-Sauer, 2012). Comfort and trustworthiness in interaction emerge from effective communication (Kharouf et al., 2019).

2.4.2 Interactive Experience with Shopping Companion

Customers rarely journey alone from the point of need to the end of the purchase and beyond. The concept of the social customer journey is developed by Hamilton et al. (2021), which expands previous viewpoints on the path to purchase by highlighting the important role other individuals play during the customer journey. During one or more phases of the journey, co-shoppers interact with each other explicitly or implicitly. Shopping companions may impact the decision-maker and the shopping journey. The joint journey is a state of social journey wherein two or more consumers journey together. Therefore, co-shoppers' journey during COS is a joint journey. The influence of shopping partners on the consumer journey has been substantially enhanced by technology and other societal factors.

Customer experience is dependent on interaction with shopping companions. According to some studies, computer-mediated interaction, such as COSPs, has a detrimental influence on interpersonal effect and group solidarity (Walther, 1996). As a result, shopping may become task-oriented (rather than socio-emotional) when the COSP is being used. Kim and Choi (2016) argue that interaction with a friend (as opposed to audience interaction) improves the quality of the customer experience. Also, interactions with those with whom they have a high degree of social intimacy are more social–emotional in nature (Izadi et al., 2021). Thus, interaction with shopping companions on COSPs is influenced by interpersonal elements such as group structure, relationship uncertainty, perceived competency of the shopping companion, and co-presence.

Collaborative Shoppers Experience and Group Structure

One of the primary reasons for shopping is contacting individuals with similar interests to share viewpoints related to the specific product, receive their comments, and enjoy their shopping time together (Tauber, 1972). Yet, shopping together might be challenging because of the physical separation, as when two friends live in different areas. Fortunately, this constraint may be overcome through COS, as individuals do not necessarily have to be physically together (Zhu et al., 2010).

Several studies examined the influence of the shopping group structure (the status composition on COS) (Cheng et al., 2013; Yue et al., 2014). Stewart and Barrick (2000) described group structure as an indicator of how group members' roles are combined. Consumers' decision-making responsibilities and commitment levels with various statuses within a co-shopping group vary. Generally, there are three types of group structure in COS:

> (1) "co-buyers" structure, in which both shoppers are in charge of making decisions (e.g., shoppers purchase a birthday present for a mutual buddy), the two shoppers have equal commitment and hence equal decision-making authority (Yue & Jiang, 2013; Yue et al., 2014).
>
> (2) "buyer/advisor" structure, in which just one of the shoppers (the buyer) is in charge of making purchase decisions, while other shoppers (advisors) only make suggestions or comments on the buyer's shopping activity (e.g., a person wants to buy clothes and asks friends to accompany him/her and make comments) (Yue & Jiang, 2013; Yue et al., 2014).
>
> (3) "Buyer-Store Companion" structure, in this form of co-shoppers' status, a salesperson accompanied a customer during the shopping process. In this scenario, the store companion serves as an advisor to the customer during the shopping decision-making process (Izadi et al., 2021), but as Qiu and Benbasat (2005) noted, the nature of friends' relationship is distinct from the one between shoppers and salespeople. Generally, shoppers communicate with salespeople to seek advice. Shoppers are typically cautious and guarded with their suggestions, as their comments may be inaccurate and biased toward a commission or gain for the retailer (Zhu et al., 2010).

Yue et al. (2014) and Yue and Jiang (2013) discuss shopping decisions and the responsibilities that follow them in COSPs. In a status-heterogeneous group, higher status individuals can contribute more info for conversation, and their opinions and comments are more persuasive in the final choice. Shopping groups with varying status compositions interact differently in COS activities.

Shopping partners with varying levels of status share varying degrees of information. Additionally, those with higher status are more likely to exert control over shared space in a heterogeneous group. But there is a greater struggle for navigation control in a status homogeneous shopping group, and navigation control will be more handed and taken over compared to the shopping dyads with different statuses (Yue et al., 2014).

Relational Uncertainty Effect
Uncertainty is a natural result of individuals' efforts to establish interpersonal understanding in various circumstances. In more formal terms, uncertainty refers to the inability to predict and explain behavior. To put it another way, uncertainty is the absence of assurance about the outcome of interpersonal interactions. Accordingly, relational uncertainty in interpersonal relationships is regarded as people's level of confidence in their perceptions of engagement (Knobloch & Solomon, 2005).

When shoppers interact with a buyer-store companion, their key interest is reducing uncertainty or improving predictability regarding their own and other participants' behavior during the interaction (Berger & Calabrese, 1974). Thus, by lowering uncertainty, relational knowledge can contribute to improving the relationship. Individuals employ related data to the relationship between them and their communication partners to generate and analyze messages exchanged; this data is called relational knowledge (Simon & Tossan, 2018).

Consumers acquire information about the shopping companion through passive (passive strategies include no interaction between information seekers and their objectives. These strategies focus on unobtrusive target observation), active (encompass actions that gather information indirectly but do not involve direct interaction among information seekers and targets), and interactive strategies (are those that are used when people interact), most notably during initial interactions with strangers (Berger, 2002).

Uncertainty about relationships can also complicate interactions. Individuals with unclear relationship statuses are more prone to suffer from the lack of well-defined behavioral expectations and, as a result, should find communication comparatively demanding, convoluted, and tedious. Thus, relationship uncertainty will exacerbate the difficulty of interaction (Knobloch & Solomon, 2005). For instance, relational uncertainty may contribute to a sense of social exclusion on COSP. Individuals dislike social exclusion (de Waal-Andrews & Van Beest, 2012), resulting in a poor interaction experience.

Interactants' Competency and Warmth
The stereotype content model is based on two distinct traits: competence (intellectual, skillful, and practical) and warmth (reflects sociability, communion, and relationships) (Fiske et al., 1999; Zheng et al., 2021). According to the stereotype content model, proposed by Fiske et al. (1999), when customers contact a shopping companion for the first time on the COSPs

(for example, in buyer-store companion status), they are primarily interested in two things:

a. determining the intent of others, i.e., whether others have positive or negative attitudes toward them (warmth);
b. determining the effectiveness with which others can carry out their plans is determining the capability of others to benefit them (competence) (Halkias & Diamantopoulos, 2020).

Warmth is associated with hedonic values and results in a distinct experience of (exciting vs. boring) in products, brand personality (Stokburger-Sauer et al., 2012), and interactions. A memorable experience is derived from the hedonic value (of interaction) (Hwang et al., 2021) arising from Warmth. *Competence* is described as an individual's capacity or capability and is developed via performance (Waseem et al., 2018). Operational and role competencies have been studied by Sirdeshmukh et al. (2002).

Role competence is defined by Smith and Barclay (1997) as the extent to which partners consider one another to possess the necessary skills, abilities, and knowledge to complete a task effectively. On COSPs, the perceived role competency of the shopping companion contributes to the trustworthiness and enhances the quality of the interactive experience. Shopping companions' product recommendations and product knowledge, for example, influence the perceived role competency of them by shoppers. In a number of business interaction scenarios, the expectancy of a constantly competent partner's functioning has been highlighted as a prelude to creating trust (Sirdeshmukh et al., 2002). The relational dimension implies that an individual's competency is socially intersubjective, requiring knowledge of relational structures and their flexibility in specific circumstances. As actors' sense-making may be socially related to their interactions, such experiences are dynamic (Waseem et al., 2018). *Operational competence* is defined as the competent execution of visible behaviors as an indicator of "service in action" (e.g., accuracy and fluency of web moves and response speed of shopping companion) (Sirdeshmukh et al., 2002). Collaborative web moves of co-shoppers can be measured in terms of fluency and accuracy of web moves. The fluency of web moves is related to the efficiency of web moves, which is measured through uncoupling occurrence/resolution (i.e., an absence of coordination with someone's shopping companion) (Zhu et al., 2010) or gaze-conversation alignment and distraction by action (Yue et al., 2014). Any uncoupling or distraction incidents could impair the fluency of web moves. These are similar concepts that arise when co-shoppers do not refer to a certain product despite being on the same website or when one of the shoppers becomes confused by the other shopper's unexpected or sudden act, resulting in a lack of coordination (Zhu et al., 2010). The efficiency of web moves is determined by the accuracy of the web moves. In other words, the web moves are more accurate when they are more aligned with the shopping goal. If the web moves are precise, the number of unnecessary, redundant, and useless web moves is reduced. Additionally, the necessity for corrective web moves to rectify errors and inaccuracies will be decreased. To enhance operational competence, the web moves of co-shoppers must be fluent and accurate.

Co-Presence

Historically, the concept that other actors' presence impacts social interaction has been focused on physical proximity, with co-presence assumed to be a given, objective condition. Co-presence refers to the perception of actors' mutual entrainment, defined as the joint synchronization of the following factors: attention, emotion, and behavior (Campos-Castillo & Hitlin, 2013). In other words, co-presence is the extent to which users are aware of one another's presence; social presence or co-presence encompasses psychological and behavioral engagement (Kim et al., 2013).

According to Buttolo et al. (1997), shared interaction can be classified into three forms. (1) Users cannot adjust the environment in a *static virtual environment*. (2) In a *collaborative virtual environment*, only one person at a time is able to modify the same virtual item at the same time. (3) Individuals are able to edit the same virtual item simultaneously in a *cooperative virtual environment*. Directly or indirectly, individuals can view and touch one another via a shared object. By incorporating feedback and allowing participants to interact, a new degree of fun and a sense of co-presence or social presence is added (Nam et al., 2008).

According to Wang et al. (2007), socialness perception refers to the degree to which customers identify social presence on a retail Web site as a result of the usage of social cues. Consumers' shopping experiences are influenced by their social perceptions. The literature indicates that the shopping experience is influenced by the store's social environment and interactions between store personnel and customers at various points along the customer journey. Interaction with a shopping companion is critical for developing an interactive experience during COS. Interpersonal interactions that occur during COS can also have an impact on the customer experience (Srivastava & Kaul, 2014).

On COSPs, for example, individuals viewing the same screen contents concurrently creates a visible common ground. This experience, in which a shopper can observe the partner's mouse movement navigation process and be aware of the product/web page that the shopping partner views, enhances their awareness of their shared situation. This scenario is analogous to an in-store shopping experience in which two consumers collaboratively evaluate an item. Thus, both shoppers will have a sense of community, which will result in a social presence. Additionally, prior research has discovered that the richness of media has an impact on the amount of social presence perceived by communicators (Poole et al., 1999; Zmud et al., 1990). It is argued that face-to-face conversation is optimal since it provides verbal and nonverbal info, including facial expression, tone, and gesture, all of which can be critical, if not necessary, in establishing a communicative stance. Likewise, as voice can convey a variety of nonverbal clues that cannot be conveyed through text, including inflection, pitch, tone, and pauses, voice chat enables customers to maintain their language style and behavior. Therefore, voice chatting is more natural and brings co-shoppers closer socially than text chatting (Zhu et al., 2010). During COS, utilizing a variety of media bundles such as video calling, voice chatting, and text chatting can facilitate social presence.

Previous studies have focused on the concept of social presence in order to examine the absence of human warmth online (Shen, 2012). Psychological involvement is the customer's comprehension of the shopping companion's intention or reasoning via the lens of the customer's emotional state. Behavioral engagement is the extent to which the co-shopper partner perceives their interdependence, connection, and responsiveness to the customer's behaviors. When co-presence can be established during COS, the shopping experience will be social and relational to some extent. Thus, when technology features of COSP enable an individual to be completely aware of the shopping companion's presence, the COSP may be successful at creating co-presence and enhancing the relational and social aspects of the shopping experience (Kim et al., 2013).

Flow

Flow experience is used to highlight important elements that impact the experiences and activities of consumers in various circumstances (Cuevas et al., 2020). The concept of flow is important for discussing human–computer interactions. The flow theory, proposed by Csikszentmihalyi (1977), refers to a state in which individuals are highly immersed in a particular task/activity that looks as though nothing else matters. According to this theory, a flow state occurs when a person feels that the environment includes sufficient chances for action that are proportionate to the individual's capacity for action (Rodríguez-Torrico et al., 2021). While surfing the Net, an individual may encounter the following distinct factors of flow: (1) control, (2) focused attention, and (3) a strong sense of enjoyment. The control element is related to individuals' feeling in control of their computer interactions. Computer technologies provide this sense of control by adapting to individual feedback in ways that more static technologies cannot. Attention focus refers to a person's attention being focused on a limited stimulus field, thereby removing irrelevant attitudes and perceptions (Nusair & Parsa, 2011; Webster et al., 1993).

Co-shoppers may have difficulties if they are not viewing the same product, piece of information, or subject throughout their COS activity. Live annotation is used to take notes, draw, and highlight specific phrases during COS (Topaloglu, 2013). Yet, this chapter emphasizes the ability to draw something (such as a line, circle, or arrow). Because live annotation and the use of mouse pointing enable consumers to point to specific areas of the screen, it can increase shoppers' awareness of their environment and their web moves on the screen, resulting in a more accurate gaze-conversation alignment criterion established by Yue et al. (2014). As demonstrated by Zhu et al. (2010) and Yue et al. (2014), live annotation can successfully prevent/resolve possible uncoupling/distraction by action occurrences. Thus, live annotation and mouse pointing use by collaborative shoppers can enhance their control over the computer interactions to coordinate the product search and navigation objectives.

Different levels of common ground between participants through different forms of navigation, including separate navigation with location cue, split-screen navigation, and shared navigation (Cheng et al., 2013; Yue & Jiang, 2013; Yue et al., 2014; Zhu et al., 2010), can lead to different levels of attention focus during COS. Also, communication between co-shoppers can assist them in resolving the distractions, leading to increased attention focus.

Self-directed navigation via an interactive setting, according to Childers et al. (2001), contributes to the enjoyment of the shopping experience. Thus, co-navigation during COS can result in an enhanced sense of enjoyment. By the use of interactive COSPs features, co-shoppers are exposed to a continuous sequence of interactions, so a flow state is experienced in which their perceptions of time and the real world are becoming contorted, and self-control is reduced. As a result, the ease of online shopping and decreasing the costs related to search and transaction can develop the flow state (Nusair & Parsa, 2011).

3 General Discussions

Enhancing the interactive experiences of individuals during COS toward creating customer value can be an objective of marketers that can be fulfilled by improving both the interactive touchpoints of COSPs and the interpersonal interactions between shoppers and their companions. Previously, academics preferred to consider interactivity as the conversation between individuals. Today's media and communication technologies rely heavily on interactivity as an affordance. Digital media has fundamentally transformed our understanding of media by enabling interaction. Rather than only being channels through which people communicate, media are now seen as tools that allow us to control our interactions. These interactions may take place both with the media/other individuals. They cover a variety of activities, such as surfing an online store, speaking with friends who are physically separated, switching up the presentation style, etc. (Sundar et al., 2015).

Employing novel technologies into online shopping enables online shoppers to feel the same as what they experience in a retail environment; shopping online with friends or acquaintances. COS technologies allow individuals to journey jointly through web moves. During COS, customers engage and interact at certain touchpoints in the joint customer journey. Co-shoppers' joint customer journey during COS involves their interactions with one another and with the COSPs. Thus, COS can create interactive experiences for individuals through interpersonal interactions and interaction with the shopping platform.

The interactivity effects model of Sundar et al. (2015) is used to understand the interactivity of COSP. The interactivity of the COSP can be considered in three aspects, including message, source, and medium. Individuals can respond to each other contingently during COS, so real-time communication between individuals is an instance of message interactivity in COSP. The live annotation feature of the COSP is related to medium interactivity as it can improve the speed, variety, and clarity with which one mentally represents the information displayed on the COSP. The switching control of mouse navigation of COSP between individuals enables them to find and customize information based on their companion needs and priorities so that it can be an example of source interactivity. Also, enabling individuals to choose their desired media to communicate is another instance of source interactivity in COSP.

Businesses need to enhance the interactive experience of shoppers during COS in two ways. First, by improving the interactive touchpoints of COSPs via using the functional affordances, which are the features of COSPs, including switching control of mouse navigation, live annotation, and communication. Thus, the reciprocity of the COS interactive experience can be facilitated through switching control of mouse navigation between individuals and two-way communication between participants. The personalization of the COS interactive experience can be improved through one-on-one communication and the use of live annotation. The speed of response in the interactive experience of COS can be enhanced by real-time communication and instant switching control of mouse navigation between individuals. The nonverbal communication of interactive experience in COS can be improved via employing various medium bundles and the live annotation feature. Also, these features can be incorporated to facilitate common grounding and situational awareness in COS to make a situation for better interaction between individuals during the joint customer journey, as these are essential elements in group activities (Cheng et al., 2013; Zhu et al., 2010).

Second, businesses need to enhance the interactive experience during COS by improving the interpersonal interactions between shoppers and their companions by increasing the social presence and flow, decreasing the relational uncertainty, selecting a competent companion, and considering the appropriate shopping group structure (e.g., co-buyer, buyer-advisor, and buyer-store companion) for different shopping scenarios.

In a status homogeneous shopping group (i.e., co-buyer), there is a greater struggle for control of mouse navigation. Thus, navigation control will be more handed and taken over compared to the shopping group with different statuses (i.e., buyer-advisor or buyer-store companion). To decrease the occurrence of distraction due to the switching control of navigation, shoppers with a status homogeneous group structure need to use the live annotation more than the shopping group with different statuses.

The more shoppers perceive their companion as competent and warm, the more they will trust this shopping interaction, leading to a more positive interactive experience between online co-shoppers. Also, the familiarity of shopping companions with how to use the features of the COSPs enhances the shoppers' perception of the companions' competence, increases shopper trust with the companion, and consequently creates a positive interactive experience of COS. Thus, choosing a competent companion for COS is recommended to individuals, which can improve the fluency and accuracy of web moves and improve the interactive experience of shoppers.

The shared feelings and attention that communicate between the shoppers and their companions increase the feeling of social presence of individuals in COS. Also, marketers can direct shoppers to select a suitable media for communication during COS, which can be the best fit/option for the certain shopping task, to enhance the social presence. The social presence of other people in the COS process also improves the interactive experience of customers and makes the shopping process more enjoyable and fun.

Businesses need to encourage shoppers to socialize before starting the process of COS officially to decrease the relational uncertainty (i.e., by finding common interests between buyer and store companion). Utilizing the shared browser as the navigation technique for COS can create a common ground to increase the flow for a better interactive experience. Also, live annotation use can reduce distraction incidents and facilitates flow for an enhanced interactive experience.

This chapter attempted to study the effect of two factors related to interactivity (interaction with COSPs and interaction with shopping companions) from a technical (platform features) and social (interactant characteristics) perspective. Given the novelty of COS and the unknown complex psychological and social dimensions of shopping on the COSPs, studying the various social, psychological, and cultural aspects of this type of online shopping can provide new avenues for future studies to understand the complexities of COS.

Scholars can focus future research on proposing and developing new navigation features to improve the fluency and accuracy of collaborative web moves in subsequent studies, similar to the suggestion presented by Zhu et al. (2010) regarding the fluency issues. The shopping partner can influence numerous parts of the COS experience. In this chapter, some of the companion's characteristics are studied. However, the shopping experience may vary according to the kind of product that needs to be purchased (Chebat et al., 2014). Thus, future research might examine the effect of product categories on COS experiences. Additionally, given the variety of shopping motives, purchasing versus socializing (Goswami et al., n.d.), the optimal shopping companion will vary, and scholars should examine the shopping motives when determining who can be a better shopping partner.

The social network structure of shoppers and their positions within this network might provide insight into their co-shopping behavior (Gentina & Fosse-Gomez, 2011). Individuals who are well linked to other members of their networks receive a greater amount and quality of relevant information and ideas from those in their network, making them more receptive to peer influence (Lee et al., 2010). Gentina and Bonsu (2013) argue that adolescents' social statuses within a peer network affect the frequency of their shopping behavior with friends. Scholars might approach the companion qualities from a broader viewpoint than what is done in this chapter, the social network perspective. They can perform social network analysis on both shoppers and their companions to determine the centrality, proximity, and clustering coefficient (Wasserman & Faust, 1994) of shoppers as nodes in a social network. Stephen and Toubia (2010) conducted a similar study in social commerce, examining the relationship between sellers. As a result, they can better study the impact of a shopper's social network position on COS activities, identify the optimal shopping partner based on a shopper's social network, and subsequently improve the interactive shopping experience.

References

Akaka, M. A., Vargo, S. L., & Schau, H. J. (2015). The context of experience. *Journal of Service Management, 26*(2), 206–223.

Berger, C. R. (2002). Strategic and nonstrategic information acquisition. *Human Communication Research, 28*(2), 287–297.

Berger, C. R., & Calabrese, R. J. (1974). Some Explorations in initial interaction and beyond: Toward a developmental theory of interpersonal communication. *Human Communication Research, 1*(2), 99–112.

Brakus, J. J., Schmitt, B. H., & Zarantonello, L. (2009). Brand experience: What is it? how is it measured? Does it affect loyalty? *Journal of Marketing, 73*(3), 52–68.

Buttolo, P., Oboe, R., & Hannaford, B. (1997). Architectures for shared haptic virtual environments. *Computers & Graphics, 21*(4), 421–429.

Cambra-Fierro, J., Polo-Redondo, Y., & Trifu, A. (2021). Short-term and long-term effects of touchpoints on customer perceptions. *Journal of Retailing and Consumer Services, 61*, 102520.

Campos-Castillo, C., & Hitlin, S. (2013). Copresence: Revisiting a building block for social interaction theories. *Sociological Theory, 31*(2), 168–192.

Chebat, J.-C., Haj-Salem, N., & Oliveira, S. (2014). Why shopping pals make malls different? *Journal of Retailing and Consumer Services, 21*(2), 77–85.

Cheng, Y., Yue, Y., Jiang, Z., & Kim, H. J. (2013). The effects of navigation support and group structure on collaborative online shopping. *Lecture Notes in Computer Science (including subseries Lecture Notes in Artificial Intelligence and Lecture Notes in Bioinformatics), 8029 LNCS*, 250–259.

Childers, T. L., Carr, C. L., Peck, J., & Carson, S. (2001). Hedonic and utilitarian motivations for online retail shopping behavior. *Journal of Retailing, 77*(4), 511–535.

Csikszentmihalyi, M. (1977). *Beyond boredom and anxiety: The experience of play in work and games. The Jossey-Bass Behavioral Science Series*. Jossey-Bass.

Cuevas, L., Lyu, J., & Lim, H. (2020). Flow matters: Antecedents and outcomes of flow experience in social search on Instagram. *Journal of Research in Interactive Marketing, 15*(1), 49–67.

De Keyser, A., Verleye, K., Lemon, K. N., Keiningham, T. L., & Klaus, P. (2020). Moving the customer experience field forward: Introducing the touchpoints, context, qualities (TCQ) nomenclature. *Journal of Service Research, 23*(4), 433–455.

de Waal-Andrews, W., & Van Beest, I. (2012). When you don't quite get what you want: Psychological and interpersonal consequences of claiming inclusion. *Personality and Social Psychology Bulletin, 38*(10), 1367–1377.

Dierking, L. D., & Falk, J. H. (1992). Redefining the Museum experience: The interactive experience model. *Visitor Studies, 4*(1), 173–176.

Drennan, J., Bianchi, C., Cacho-Elizondo, S., Louriero, S., Guibert, N., & Proud, W. (2015). Examining the role of wine brand love on brand loyalty: A multi-country comparison. *International Journal of Hospitality Management, 49*, 47–55.

Fiske, S. T., Xu, J., Cuddy, A. C., & Glick, P. (1999). (Dis) respecting versus (Dis) liking: Status and interdependence predict ambivalent stereotypes of competence and warmth. *Journal of Social Issues, 55*(3), 473–489.

Gao, W., Fan, H., Li, W., & Wang, H. (2021). Crafting the customer experience in omnichannel contexts: The role of channel integration. *Journal of Business Research, 126*, 12–22.

Gentina, E., & Bonsu, S. K. (2013). Peer network position and shopping behavior among adolescents. *Journal of Retailing and Consumer Services, 20*(1), 87–93.

Gentina, E., & Fosse-Gomez, M.-H. (2011). Identifying adolescent peer group structure. *ACR European Advances*.

Goswami, S., Tan, C. H., & Teo, H. H. (n.d.). Exploring the website features that can support online collaborative shopping? *PACIS 2007—11th Pacific Asia Conference on Information Systems: Managing Diversity in Digital Enterprises*, July 4–July 6 Auckland, New Zealand. AIS, 32–45.

Grissemann, U. S., & Stokburger-Sauer, N. E. (2012). Customer co-creation of travel services: The role of company support and customer satisfaction with the co-creation performance. *Tourism Management, 33*(6), 1483–1492.

Gutzman, A. (2000). Real time chat: What are you waiting for. *Ecommerce Guide*. http://www.ecommerce-guide.com/solutions/%0Atechnology/article.php/322551

Halkias, G., & Diamantopoulos, A. (2020). Universal dimensions of individuals' perception: Revisiting the operationalization of warmth and competence with a mixed-method approach. *International Journal of Research in Marketing, 37*(4), 714–736.

Hallikainen, H., Alamäki, A., & Laukkanen, T. (2019). Individual preferences of digital touchpoints: A latent class analysis. *Journal of Retailing and Consumer Services, 50*, 386–393.

Hamilton, R., Ferraro, R., Haws, K. L., & Mukhopadhyay, A. (2021). Traveling with companions: The social customer journey. *Journal of Marketing, 85*(1), 68–92.

Helkkula, A., Kelleher, C., & Pihlström, M. (2012). Characterizing value as an experience: Implications for service researchers and managers. *Journal of Service Research, 15*(1), 59–75.

Hoffman, D. L., & Novak, T. P. (2018). Consumer and object experience in the internet of things: An assemblage theory approach. *Journal of Consumer Research, 44*(6), 1178–1204.

Huang, S., Benbasat, I., & Burton-Jones, A. (2011). The role of product recommendation agents in collaborative online shopping. *International Conference on Information Systems 2011, ICIS 2011, 2*, 1699–1708.

Hwang, J., Choe, J. Y. (Jacey), Kim, H. M., & Kim, J. J. (2021). The antecedents and consequences of memorable brand experience: Human baristas versus robot baristas. *Journal of Hospitality and Tourism Management, 48*, 561–571.

Izadi, B., Dong, L., & Esfidani, M. R. (2021). Stay home and shop together. *Journal of Electronic Commerce Research, 22*(1), 59–75.

Jimenez, Y., & Morreale, P. (2015). Social media use and impact on interpersonal communication. In *International Conference on Human-Computer Interaction* (pp. 91–96). Springer.

Johnson, G. J., Bruner, G. C., II., & Kumar, A. (2006). Interactivity and its facets revisited: Theory and empirical test. *Journal of Advertising, 35*(4), 35–52.

Kannan, P. K., & Kulkarni, G. (2022). The impact of covid-19 on customer journeys: Implications for interactive marketing. *Journal of Research in Interactive Marketing, 16*(1), 22–36.

Kharouf, H., Sekhon, H., Fazal-e-Hasan, S. M., Hickman, E., & Mortimer, G. (2019). The role of effective communication and trustworthiness in determining guests' loyalty. *Journal of Hospitality Marketing & Management, 28*(2), 240–262.

Kim, H. S., & Choi, B. (2016). The effects of three customer-to-customer interaction quality types on customer experience quality and citizenship behavior in mass service settings. *Journal of Services Marketing, 30*(4), 384–397.

Kim, H., Suh, K. S., & Lee, U. K. (2013). Effects of collaborative online shopping on shopping experience through social and relational perspectives. *Information & Management, 50*(4), 169–180.

Kim, J. H., Kim, M., Park, M., & Yoo, J. (2021). How interactivity and vividness influence consumer virtual reality shopping experience: The mediating role of telepresence. *Journal of Research in Interactive Marketing, 15*(3), 502–525.

Knobloch, L. K., & Solomon, D. H. (2005). Relational uncertainty and relational information processing: Questions without answers? *Communication Research, 32*(3), 349–388.

Kuehnl, C., Jozic, D., & Homburg, C. (2019). Effective customer journey design: Consumers' conception, measurement, and consequences. *Journal of the Academy of Marketing Science, 47*(3), 551–568.

Kuuru, T. K., & Närvänen, E. (2019). Embodied interaction in customer experience: A phenomenological study of group fitness. *Journal of Marketing Management, 35*(13–14), 1241–1266.

Leclerc, F., & Schmitt, B. H. (1999). The value of time in the context of waiting and delays. *Consumer Value*, (Routledge), 44–58.

Lee, S. H. M., Cotte, J., & Noseworthy, T. J. (2010). The role of network centrality in the flow of consumer influence. *Journal of Consumer Psychology, 20*(1), 66–77.

Lemon, K. N., & Verhoef, P. C. (2016). Understanding customer experience throughout the customer journey. *Journal of Marketing, 80*(6), 69–96.

Lin, H., Gursoy, D., & Zhang, M. (2020). Impact of customer-to-customer interactions on overall service experience: A social servicescape perspective. *International Journal of Hospitality Management, 87*, 102376.

Lucia-Palacios, L., & Pérez-López, R. (2021). How can autonomy improve consumer experience when interacting with smart products? *Journal of Research in Interactive Marketing*, Vol. ahead-of-print.

Merrilees, B. (2016). Interactive brand experience pathways to customer-brand engagement and value co-creation. *Journal of Product & Brand Management, 25*(5), 402–408.

Moon, Y., & Nass, C. (1996). How "real" are computer personalities? Psychological responses to personality types in human-computer interaction. *Communication Research, 23*(6), 651–674.

Nam, C. S., Shu, J., & Chung, D. (2008). The roles of sensory modalities in Collaborative Virtual Environments (CVEs). *Computers in Human Behavior, 24*(4), 1404–1417.

Nangpiire, C., Silva, J., & Alves, H. (2021). Customer engagement and value co-creation/destruction: The internal fostering and hindering factors and actors in the tourist/hotel experience. *Journal of Research in Interactive Marketing*, 16, 173–188.

Newhagen, J. E., Cordes, J. W., & Levy, M. R. (1995). Nightly@ nbc. com: Audience scope and the perception of interactivity in viewer mail on the internet. *Journal of communication, 45*(3), 164–175.

Nusair, K., & Parsa, H. G. (2011). Introducing flow theory to explain the interactive online shopping experience in a travel context. *International Journal of Hospitality & Tourism Administration, 12*(1), 1–20.

Poole, M. S., Gouran, D. S., & Frey, L. R. (1999). *The handbook of group communication theory and research*. Sage.

Prahalad, C. K., & Ramaswamy, V. (2002). The co-creation connection. *Strategy and business*, 50–61.

Prahalad, C. K., & Ramaswamy, V. (2004). Co-creation experiences: The next practice in value creation. *Journal of Interactive Marketing, 18*(3), 5–14.

Qiu, L., & Benbasat, I. (2005). An investigation into the effects of text-to-speech voice and 3D avatars on the perception of presence and flow of live help in electronic commerce. *ACM Transactions on Computer-Human Interaction (TOCHI), 12*(4), 329–355.

Rafaeli, S. (1988). From new media to communication. *Sage Annual Review of Communication Research: Advancing Communication Science*, 16, 110–134.

Ramirez, R. (1999). Value co-production: Intellectual origins and implications for practice and research. *Strategic Management Journal, 20*(1), 49–65.

Richardson, A. (2010). Touchpoints bring the customer experience to life. *Harvard Business Review*, 91, 12–30.

Rodríguez-Torrico, P., San José Cabezudo, R., San-Martín, S., & Trabold Apadula, L. (2021). Let it flow: The role of seamlessness and the optimal experience on consumer word of mouth in omnichannel marketing. *Journal of Research in Interactive Marketing*, Vol. ahead-of-print.

Seedorf, S., Thum, C., Schulze, T., & Pfrogner, L. (2014). Social co-browsing in online shopping: The impact of real-time collaboration on user engagement. *ECIS 2014 Proceedings—22nd European Conference on Information Systems*, 0–15.

Shen, J. (2012). Social Comparison, Social Presence, and Enjoyment in the Acceptance of Social Shopping Websites. *Journal of Electronic Commerce Research, 13*(3), 198.

Siau, K. L., Nah, F. F. H., & Sha, H. (2013). Efficacy of communication support in collaborative online shopping: The moderating effect of task types. *19th Americas Conference on Information Systems, AMCIS 2013—Hyperconnected World: Anything, Anywhere, Anytime*, 2(2010), 1301–1306.

Simon, F., & Tossan, V. (2018). Does brand-consumer social sharing matter? A relational framework of customer engagement to brand-hosted social media. *Journal of Business Research*, 85, 175–184.

Sirdeshmukh, D., Singh, J., & Sabol, B. (2002). Consumer trust, value, and loyalty in relational exchanges. *Journal of Marketing, 66*(1), 15–37.

Smith, J. B., & Barclay, D. W. (1997). The effects of organizational differences and trust on the effectiveness of selling partner relationships. *Journal of Marketing, 61*(1), 3–21.

Song, J. H., & Zinkhan, G. M. (2008). Determinants of perceived web site interactivity. *Journal of Marketing, 72*(2), 99–113.

Srivastava, M., & Kaul, D. (2014). Social interaction, convenience and customer satisfaction: The mediating effect of customer experience. *Journal of Retailing and Consumer Services, 21*(6), 1028–1037.

Stein, A., & Ramaseshan, B. (2016). Towards the identification of customer experience touch point elements. *Journal of Retailing and Consumer Services, 30*, 8–19.

Stephen, A. T., & Toubia, O. (2010). Deriving value from social commerce networks. *Journal of Marketing Research, 47*(2), 215–228.

Stewart, G. L., & Barrick, M. R. (2000). Team structure and performance: Assessing the mediating role of intrateam process and the moderating role of task type. *Academy of Management Journal, 43*(2), 135–148.

Stokburger-Sauer, N., Ratneshwar, S., & Sen, S. (2012). Drivers of consumer-brand identification. *International Journal of Research in Marketing, 29*(4), 406–418.

Straker, K., Wrigley, C., & Rosemann, M. (2015). Typologies and touchpoints: Designing multi-channel digital strategies. *Journal of Research in Interactive Marketing, 9*(2), 110–128.

Sundar, S. S., Jia, H., Waddell, T. F., & Huang, Y. (2015). Toward a Theory of Interactive Media Effects (TIME): Four models for explaining how interface features affect user psychology. In *The handbook of the psychology of communication technology* (pp. 47–86).

Swan, E. L., Dahl, A. J., & Peltier, J. W. (2019). Health-care marketing in an omni-channel environment: Exploring telemedicine and other digital touchpoints. *Journal of Research in Interactive Marketing, 13*(4), 602–618.

Tauber, E. M. (1972). Marketing notes and communications: Why do people shop? *Journal of Marketing, 36*(4), 46–49.

Topaloglu, C. (2013). *Shopping alone online Vs. co-browsing: A physiological and perceptual comparison*. Missouri University of Science and Technology, Rolla, MO.

Twidale, M. (1995). How to study and design for collaborative browsing in the digital library. In *How we do user-centered design and evaluation of digital libraries: Methodological forum* (Monticello, IL: Thirty-Seventh Allerton Institute, Allerton Park, University of Illinois, October 1995).

Walther, J. B. (1996). Computer-mediated communication: Impersonal, interpersonal, and hyperpersonal interaction. *Communication Research, 23*(1), 3–43.

Wang. (2021). New frontiers and future directions in interactive marketing: Inaugural editorial. *Journal of Research in Interactive Marketing, 15*(1), 1–9.

Wang, L. C., Baker, J., Wagner, J. A., & Wakefield, K. (2007). Can a retail web site be social? *Journal of Marketing, 71*(3), 143–157.

Waseem, D., Biggemann, S., & Garry, T. (2018). Value co-creation: The role of actor competence. *Industrial Marketing Management, 70*, 5–12.

Wasserman, S., & Faust, K. (1994). *Social network analysis: Methods and applications* (Vol. 8). Cambridge university press.

Webster, J., Trevino, L. K., & Ryan, L. (1993). The dimensionality and correlates of flow in human-computer interactions. *Computers in Human Behavior, 9*(4), 411–426.
Wei, J., Seedorf, S., Lowry, P. B., Thum, C., & Schulze, T. (2017). How increased social presence through co-browsing influences user engagement in collaborative online shopping. *Electronic Commerce Research and Applications, 24*, 84–99.
Wilson, D. T. (1976). Dyadic interaction: An exchange process. *ACR North American Advances, 2*, 394–397.
Yang, Y., Sun, X., & Wang, J. (2019). The value of reputation in electronic marketplaces: A moderating role of customer experience. *Journal of Research in Interactive Marketing, 13*(4), 578–601.
Yue, Y. (2014). *Two essays on interface design in collaborative and social e-commerce* (Unpublished doctoral dissertation). National University of Singapore, Singapore.
Yue, Y., & Jiang, Z. J. (2013). Enhancing shared understanding in collaborative online shopping. *International Conference on Information Systems (ICIS 2013): Reshaping Society Through Information Systems Design, 2*, 1441–1457.
Yue, Y., Ma, X., & Jiang, Z. (2014). Share your view: Impact of co-navigation support and status composition in collaborative online shopping. *Conference on Human Factors in Computing Systems—Proceedings*, 3299–3308.
Zheng, X., Xu, J., & Shen, H. (2021). To be respected or liked: The influence of social comparisons on consumer preference for competence—Versus warmth-oriented products. *International Journal of Research in Marketing, 39*(1), 170–189.
Zhu, L., Benbasat, I., & Jiang, Z. (2010). Let's shop online together: An empirical investigation of collaborative online shopping support. *Information Systems Research, 21*(4), 872–891.
Zmud, R. W., Lind, M. R., & Young, F. W. (1990). An attribute space for organizational communication channels. *Information Systems Research, 1*(4), 440–457.

1